Beginning Visual Basic® 2005

Thearon Willis and Bryan Newsome

WILEY

Wiley Publishing, Inc.

Beginning Visual Basic® 2005

Published by
Wiley Publishing, Inc.
10475 Crosspoint Boulevard
Indianapolis, IN 46256
www.wiley.com

Copyright © 2006 by Wiley Publishing, Inc., Indianapolis, Indiana

Published simultaneously in Canada

ISBN-10: 0-7645-7401-9

ISBN-13: 978-0-7645-7401-6

Manufactured in the United States of America

10 9 8 7 6 5 4 3

1MA/TR/QY/QW/IN

Library of Congress Cataloging-in-Publication Data

Willis, Thearon.
  Beginning Visual Basic 2005 / Thearon Willis and Bryan Newsome.
    p. cm.
  Includes bibliographical references and index.
  ISBN-13: 978-0-7645-7401-6 (paper/website)
  ISBN-10: 0-7645-7401-9 (paper/website)
  1. Microsoft Visual BASIC. 2. BASIC (Computer program language) I. Newsome, Bryan, 1971- II. Title.
  QA76.73.B3W5573 2005
  005.2'768--dc22
                                2005010385

For general information on our other products and services please contact our Customer Care Department within the United States at (800) 762-2974, outside the United States at (317) 572-3993 or fax (317) 572-4002.

Trademarks: Wiley, the Wiley logo, Wrox, the Wrox logo, Programmer to Programmer, and related trade dress are trade-marks or registered trademarks of John Wiley & Sons, Inc. and/or its affiliates, in the United States and other countries, and may not be used without written permission. Visual Basic is a registered trademark of Microsoft Corporation in the United States and/or other countries. All other trademarks are the property of their respective owners. Wiley Publishing, Inc., is not associated with any product or vendor mentioned in this book.

Wiley also publishes its books in a variety of electronic formats. Some content that appears in print may not be available in electronic books.

About the Authors

Thearon Willis is a Senior Consultant with over 20 years of programming experience. He started writing applications using the BASIC language in 1980 and later moved on to Visual Basic and finally to Visual Basic .NET.

Thearon began working with databases in 1987 and has been hooked on writing database applications every since. He has experience with SQL Server, Oracle, and DB2 but works with SQL Server on a daily basis. Thearon has programmed in several other languages, some of which include C++, assembly language, Pascal, and COBOL. However, he enjoys Visual Basic .NET the best because it provides the features needed to quickly build Windows and Web applications, as well as components and Web Services.

Thearon currently develops intranet applications, Web Services, and server-side and client-side utilities using Visual Basic .NET. Most of these applications and utilities are database-driven and make use of XML and XSL. Thearon lives with his wife Margie and daughter Stephanie in the Raleigh, North Carolina, area.

Bryan Newsome works in Charlotte, North Carolina, as a custom software project manager specializing in Microsoft solutions. He leads a team of developers focused on meeting the needs of each client and project using the latest technologies. Each day, he helps provide clients with solutions and mentoring on leading-edge Microsoft technologies. Bryan is a Microsoft Certified Application Developer for .NET.

Credits

Acquisitions Editor
Katie Mohr

Development Editor
Sydney Jones

Technical Editor
Todd Meister

Production Editor
William A. Barton

Copy Editor
Publication Services, Inc.

Editorial Manager
Mary Beth Wakefield

Vice President & Executive Group Publisher
Richard Swadley

Vice President and Publisher
Joseph B. Wikert

Project Coordinator
Ryan Steffen

Graphics and Production Specialists
Andrea Dahl
Lauren Goddard
Lynsey Osborn
Alicia South
Julie Trippetti

Quality Control Technicians
Leeann Harney
Carl William Pierce

Media Development Specialists
Angela Denny
Kit Malone
Travis Silvers

Proofreading and Indexing
TECHBOOKS Production Services

As always, I want to thank my wife Margie and my daughter Stephanie for the patience they have shown while I write another book. Without their love and support, none of this would be possible.

—*Thearon Willis*

To all of the friends and family that make my life special in the past, present, and future: Jennifer (love you, honey), Katelyn, Mom (I miss you), Dad, Ashley and Leslie, Judy and Tony, Jennifer S. and Steven. All my love and happiness to each of you.

—*Bryan Newsome*

Contents

Contents

Contents

Contents

Contents

Contents

Contents

Contents

Contents

Contents

Contents

Contents

Acknowledgments

This project was made possible by a number of people. First, thanks go out to Thearon for helping me get involved in a project like this. Thanks buddy. Next is everyone at Wiley Publishing, especially Sydney Jones, Katie Mohr, and Todd Meister. Without the help from you three, I would have been so lost and this book would not have been possible. Also, thanks to Annette Cloninger for helping me. And finally, thanks to my beautiful wife, Jennifer, for putting up with me while I put my life on hold for so many months to get this done (and some pretty late nights too).

—*Bryan Newsome*

Introduction

Visual Basic 2005 is Microsoft's latest version of the highly popular Visual Basic .NET programming language, one of the many languages supported in Visual Studio 2005. Visual Basic 2005's strength lies in its ease of use and the speed at which you can create Windows applications, Web applications, mobile device applications, and Web Services.

In this book, we will introduce you to programming with Visual Basic 2005 and show you how to create the types of applications and services mentioned above. Along the way you'll also learn about object-oriented techniques and learn how to create your own business objects and Windows controls.

Microsoft's .NET Framework provides Visual Basic 2005 programmers with the ability to create full object oriented programs, just like the ones created using C# or C++. The .NET Framework provides a set of base classes that are common to all programming languages in Visual Studio 2005, which provides you with the same ability to create object-oriented programs as a programmer using C# or C++.

This book will give you a thorough grounding in the basics of programming using Visual Basic 2005; from there the world is your oyster.

Who Is This Book For?

This book is designed to teach you how to write useful programs in Visual Basic 2005 as quickly and easily as possible.

There are two kinds of beginners for whom this book is ideal:

❑ You're a beginner to programming and you've chosen Visual Basic 2005 as the place to start. That's a great choice! Visual Basic 2005 is not only easy to learn; it's also fun to use and very powerful.

❑ You can program in another language but you're a beginner to .NET programming. Again, you've made a great choice! Whether you've come from Fortran or Visual Basic 6, you'll find that this book quickly gets you up to speed on what you need to know to get the most from Visual Basic 2005.

What Does This Book Cover?

Visual Basic 2005 offers a great deal of functionality in both tools and language. No one book could ever cover Visual Basic 2005 in its entirety—you would need a library of books. What this book aims to do is to get you started as quickly and easily as possible. It shows you the roadmap, so to speak, of what there is and where to go. Once we've taught you the basics of creating working applications (creating the windows and controls, how your code should handle unexpected events, what object-oriented programming is, how to use it in your applications, and so on) we'll show you some of the areas you might want to try your hand at next:

❑ Chapters 1 through 8 provide an introduction to Visual Studio 2005 and Windows programming.

❑ Chapter 9 provides an introduction to application debugging and error handling.

❑ Chapters 10 through 12 provide an introduction to object-oriented programming and building objects.

❑ Chapters 13 and 14 provide an introduction to graphics in Windows applications.

❑ Chapters 15 and 16 provide an introduction to programming with databases and covers Access, SQL Server, and ADO.NET.

❑ Chapter 17 provides an introduction to ASP.NET and shows you how to write applications for the Web.

❑ Chapter 19 provides a brief introduction to XML; a powerful tool for integrating your applications with others—regardless of the language they were written in.

❑ Chapter 20 introduces you to Web Services; a technology whereby functionality offered on the Internet can be accessed by your applications and seamlessly integrated into them.

❑ Chapter 21 introduces you to building applications for mobile devices using the Compact Framework classes.

What Do I Need to Run Visual Basic 2005?

Apart from a willingness to learn, all you'll need for the first 14 chapters are a PC running Windows 2000, Windows XP (Home or Professional Edition), or Windows Server 2003; Internet Explorer; and of course:

❑ Microsoft Visual Basic 2005 Express Edition

or

❑ Microsoft Visual Basic 2005 Standard Edition

or

❑ Microsoft Visual Basic 2005 Professional Edition

or

❑ Microsoft Visual Basic 2005 Team System

As the later chapters cover more advanced subject areas, you will need other software to get the most out of them. Also, Visual Basic 2005 Express does not support creating Web applications, mobile applications, and deployment projects:

❑ Chapter 15 requires Microsoft Access 2000.

❑ For Chapter 16, you will need to have access to SQL Server 2000, SQL Server 2005, or SQL Server 2005 Express.

Don't worry if you don't have these products already and want to wait a while before you purchase them. You should still find that you get a lot out of this book.

Conventions

We've used a number of different styles of text and layout in this book to help differentiate between the different kinds of information. Here are examples of the styles we use and an explanation of what they mean.

Try It Out   How Do They Work?

1. Each step has a number.

2. Follow the steps through.

3. Then read the subsequent "How It Works" to find out what's going on.

Background information, asides, and references appear in text like this.

❑ Bullets appear indented, with each new bullet marked like this.

Code has several styles. If it's a word that we're talking about in the text—for example, when discussing a `For...Next` loop, it's in `this font`. If it's a block of code that can be typed as a program and run, it's also in a gray box:

```
Private Sub btnAdd_Click(ByVal sender As System.Object, _
            ByVal e As System.EventArgs) Handles btnAdd.Click
   Dim n As Integer
   n = 27
   MessageBox.Show(n)
End Sub
```

Sometimes you'll see code in a mixture of styles, like this:

```
Private Sub btnAdd_Click(ByVal sender As System.Object, _
            ByVal e As System.EventArgs) Handles btnAdd.Click
   Dim n As Integer
   n = 27
   n = n + 2
   MessageBox.Show(n)
End Sub
```

In cases like this, the code with a white background is code that Visual Studio 2005 has automatically generated (in a Try It Out) or code you are already familiar with (in a How It Works); the lines highlighted in gray is a new addition to the code.

Customer Support

We always value hearing from our readers, and we want to know what you think about this book: what you liked, what you didn't like, and what you think we can do better next time. You can send us your comments by e-mail to feedback@wrox.com. Please be sure to mention the book title in your message.

How to Download the Sample Code for the Book

When you visit the Wrox site, www.wrox.com/, simply locate the title through our Search facility or by using one of the title lists. Click Download in the Code column or Download Code on the book's detail page.

The files that are available for download from our site have been archived using WinZip. When you have saved the attachments to a folder on your hard drive, you need to extract the files using a decompression program such as WinZip, PKUnzip, or UltimateZip. When you extract the files, the code is usually extracted into chapter folders. When you start the extraction process, ensure that your decompression software is set to use folder names.

Errata

We've made every effort to make sure that there are no errors in the text or in the code. However, no one is perfect, and mistakes do occur. If you find an error in one of our books, like a spelling mistake or a faulty piece of code, we would be very grateful to have your feedback. By sending in errata, you may save another reader from hours of frustration, and of course, you will be helping us provide even higher quality information. Simply e-mail the information to support@wrox.com; your information will be checked and, if correct, posted to the errata page for that title or used in subsequent editions of the book.

To find errata on the Web site, go to www.wrox.com/, and simply locate the title through our Advanced Search or title list. Click the Book Errata link, which is below the cover graphic on the book's detail page.

If you wish to query a problem in the book directly with an expert who knows the book in detail, then e-mail support@wrox.com, with the title of the book and the last four numbers of the ISBN in the subject field of the e-mail. A typical e-mail should include the following things:

❑ The title of the book, last four digits of the ISBN (4019), and page number of the problem in the Subject field

❑ Your name, contact information, and the problem in the body of the message

We won't send you junk mail. We need the details to save your time and ours. When you send an e-mail message, it will go through the following chain of support:

❑ **Customer Support**—Your message is delivered to our customer support staff, who are the first people to read it. They have files on most frequently asked questions and will answer anything general about the book or the Web site immediately.

❑ **Editorial**—Deeper queries are forwarded to the technical editors responsible for that book. They have experience with the programming language or particular product and are able to answer detailed technical questions on the subject.

❑ **The authors**—Finally, in the unlikely event that the editor cannot answer your problem, they will forward the request to the author. We do try to protect the author from any distractions to their writing; however, we are quite happy to forward specific requests to them. All Wrox authors help with the support on their books. They will e-mail the customer and the editor with their response, and again all readers should benefit.

The Wrox Support process can offer support only to issues that are directly pertinent to the content of our published title. Support for questions that fall outside the scope of normal book support is provided via the community lists at http://p2p.wrox.com/forum.

p2p.wrox.com

For author and peer discussions, join the P2P mailing lists. Our unique system provides programmer-to-programmer contact on mailing lists, forums, and newsgroups, all in addition to our one-to-one e-mail support system. If you post a query to P2P, you can be confident that it is being examined by many Wrox authors and other industry experts who are present on our mailing lists. At p2p.wrox.com you will find a number of different lists that will help you, not only while you read this book, but also as you develop your own applications. Particularly appropriate to this book are the beginning_vb and vb_dotnet lists.

To subscribe to a mailing list just follow these steps:

1. Go to http://p2p.wrox.com/.

2. Choose the appropriate category from the left menu bar.

3. Click the mailing list you wish to join.

4. Follow the instructions to subscribe and fill in your e-mail address and password.

5. Reply to the confirmation e-mail you receive.

6. Use the subscription manager to join more lists and set your e-mail preferences.

Why This System Offers the Best Support

You can choose to join the mailing lists, or you can receive them as a weekly digest. If you don't have the time, or facility, to receive the mailing list, you can search our online archives. Junk mails and spam are deleted, and your own e-mail address is protected by the unique Lyris system. Queries about joining or leaving lists, and any other general queries about lists, should be sent to listsupport@p2p.wrox.com.

Welcome to Visual Basic 2005

The goal of this book is to help you come up to speed with the Visual Basic 2005 language even if you have never programmed before. You will start slowly and build on what you learn. So take a deep breath, let it out slowly, and tell yourself you can do this. No sweat! No kidding!

Programming a computer is a lot like teaching a child to tie his shoes. Until you find the correct way of giving the instructions, not much gets accomplished. Visual Basic 2005 is a language in which you can tell your computer how to do things. But, like a child, the computer will understand only if you explain things very clearly. If you have never programmed before, this sounds like an arduous task, and sometimes it is. However, Visual Basic 2005 gives you a simple language to explain some complex things. Although it never hurts to have an understanding of what is happening at the lowest levels, Visual Basic 2005 frees the programmer from having to deal with the mundane complexities of writing Windows programs. You are free to concentrate on solving problems.

Visual Basic 2005 helps you create solutions that run on the Microsoft Windows operating system. If you are looking at this book, you might have already felt the need or the desire to create such programs. Even if you have never written a computer program before, as you progress through the Try It Out exercises in this book, you will become familiar with the various aspects of the Visual Basic 2005 language, as well as its foundation in Microsoft's .NET Framework. You will find that it is not nearly as difficult as you have been imagining. Before you know it, you will be feeling quite comfortable creating a variety of different types of programs with Visual Basic 2005. Also (as the name .NET implies) Visual Basic 2005 can be used to create applications for use over the Internet. You can also create mobile applications for Pocket PCs and SmartPhones. However, when learning any new technology, you have to walk before you can run, so in this book you will begin by focusing on Windows applications before extending your boundaries to other platforms.

In this chapter, we will cover the following subjects:

❑   The installation of Visual Basic 2005

❑   A tour of the Visual Basic 2005 Integrated Development Environment (IDE)

❑   How to create a simple Windows program

❑   How to use and leverage the integrated help system

Windows Versus DOS Programming

A Windows program is quite different from its ancient relative, the MS-DOS program. A DOS program follows a relatively strict path from beginning to end. Although this does not necessarily limit the functionality of the program, it does limit the road the user has to take to get to it. A DOS program is like walking down a hallway; to get to the end you have to walk down the hallway, passing any obstacles that you may encounter. A DOS program would only let you open certain doors along your stroll.

Windows, on the other hand, opened up the world of *event-driven programming. Events* in this context include, for example, clicking a button, resizing a window, or changing an entry in a text box. The code that you write responds to these events. To go back to the hallway analogy: In a Windows program, to get to the end of the hall, you just click on the end of the hall. The hallway can be ignored. If you get to the end and realize that is not where you wanted to be, you can just set off for the new destination without returning to your starting point. The program reacts to your movements and takes the necessary actions to complete your desired tasks (Visual Basic 2005).

Another big advantage in a Windows program is the *abstraction of the hardware;* which means that Windows takes care of communicating with the hardware for you. You do not need to know the inner workings of every laser printer on the market just to create output. You do not need to study the schematics for graphics cards to write your game. Windows wraps up this functionality by providing generic routines that communicate with the drivers written by hardware manufacturers. This is probably the main reason that Windows has been so successful. The generic routines are referred to as the Windows *Application Programming Interface* (API).

Before Visual Basic 1.0 was introduced to the world in 1991, developers had to be well versed in C and C++ programming, as well as the building blocks of the Windows system itself, the Windows API. This complexity meant that only dedicated and properly trained individuals were capable of turning out software that could run on Windows. Visual Basic changed all of that, and it has been estimated that there are now as many lines of production code written in Visual Basic as in any other language.

Visual Basic changed the face of Windows programming by removing the complex burden of writing code for the user interface (UI). By allowing programmers to *draw* their own UI, it freed them to concentrate on the business problems they were trying to solve. Once the UI is drawn, the programmer can then add the code to react to events.

Visual Basic has also been *extensible* from the very beginning. Third-party vendors quickly saw the market for reusable modules to aid developers. These modules, or *controls*, were originally referred to as VBXs (named after their file extension). Prior to Visual Basic 5.0, if you did not like the way a button behaved, you could either buy or create your own, but those controls had to be written in C or C++. Database access utilities were some of the first controls available. Version 5 of Visual Basic introduced the concept of *ActiveX*, which allowed developers to create their own *ActiveX controls*.

When Microsoft introduced Visual Basic 3.0, the programming world changed again. Now you could build database applications directly accessible to users (so-called *front-end applications*) completely with

Visual Basic. There was no need to rely on third-party controls. Microsoft accomplished this task with the introduction of *Data Access Objects* (DAO), which allowed programmers to manipulate data with the same ease as manipulating the user interface.

Versions 4.0 and 5.0 extended the capabilities of Version 3.0 to allow developers to target the new Windows 95 platform. Crucially they also made it easier for developers to write code, which could then be manipulated to make it usable to other language developers. Version 6.0 provided a new way to access databases with the integration of *ActiveX Data Objects* (ADO). The ADO feature was developed by Microsoft to aid Web developers using Active Server Pages to access databases. All of the improvements to Visual Basic over the years have ensured its dominant place in the programming world. It helps developers write robust and maintainable applications in record time.

With the release of Visual Basic .NET in February 2002, most of the restrictions that used to exist have been obliterated. In the past, Visual Basic has been criticized and maligned as a "toy" language, as it did not provide all of the features of more sophisticated languages such as C++ and Java. Now, Microsoft has removed these restrictions and made Visual Basic .NET a very powerful development tool. This trend continues with Visual Basic 2005. Although not as drastic a change as from Visual Basic 6 to Visual Basic .NET, there are enough improvements in the language and integrated development environment that Visual Basic 2005 is a welcome upgrade and is a great choice for programmers of all levels.

Installing Visual Basic 2005

You may own Visual Basic 2005 in either of the following forms:

❑   As part of Visual Studio 2005, a suite of tools and languages that also includes C# (pronounced "C-sharp"), J# (pronounced "J-sharp"), and Visual C++. The Visual Studio 2005 product line includes Visual Studio Standard Edition, Visual Studio Professional Edition, Visual Studio Tools for Office, and Visual Studio Team System. All of these versions come with progressively more tools for building and managing the development of larger, enterprise-wide applications.

❑   As the Express Edition, which includes a reduced set of the tools and features that are available with Visual Studio 2005.

Both enable you to create your own applications for the Windows platform. The installation procedure is straightforward. In fact, the Visual Studio Installer is smart enough to figure out exactly what your computer requires to make it work.

The descriptions in the Try It Out exercise that follows are based on installing Visual Studio 2005 Architect Edition. Most of the installation processes are very straightforward, and you can accept the default installation options for most environments. So, regardless of which edition you are installing, the installation process should be smooth when accepting the default installation options.

Try It Out   **Installing Visual Basic 2005**

1.   The Visual Studio 2005 CD has an auto-run feature, but if the Setup screen does not appear after inserting the CD, you have to run `setup.exe` from the root directory of the CD. To do this, go to your Windows Start menu (usually found right at the bottom of your screen) and select Run. Then type *d*:\ **setup.exe** into the Open box, where *d* is the drive letter of your CD drive. After the setup program initializes, you will see the screen as shown in Figure 1-1.

2. This dialog box shows the order in which the installation takes place. To function properly, Visual Basic 2005 requires that several updates be installed on your machine, such as Service Pack 1 for Windows XP. The setup program will inform you if these updates are not installed. You should then install any required updates before proceeding with the installation of Visual Studio 2005. Step 1 installs Visual Studio 2005, so click the Install Visual Studio link.

Figure 1-1

3. After agreeing to the End User License agreement, click Continue to proceed to the next step.

4. As with most installations, you will be presented with an option list of components to install (see Figure 1-2). You can choose to install only the features that you need. For example, if your drive space is limited and you have no immediate need for Visual C++ 2005, you can exclude it from the installation. You will also be given the chance to select the location of items (although the defaults should suffice unless your particular machine has special requirements). Any option that is not chosen at the initial setup can always be added later as your needs or interests change. However, if you plan on developing database applications such as those discussed in Chapter 16, you should choose to install SQL Server 2005 Express, which is the last option in the list.

Three sections of information are given for each feature:

❑ The Feature description box gives you an outline of each feature and its function.

❑ The Feature Install path section outlines where the required files will be installed.

❑ Finally, the Space Allocation section illustrates how the space on your hard drive will be affected by the installation as a whole.

When you are running Visual Basic 2005, a lot of information is swapped from the disk to memory and back again. Therefore, it is important to have some free space on your disk. There is no exact rule for determining how much free space you will need, but if you use your machine for development as well as other tasks, anything less than 100MB free space should be considered a full disk.

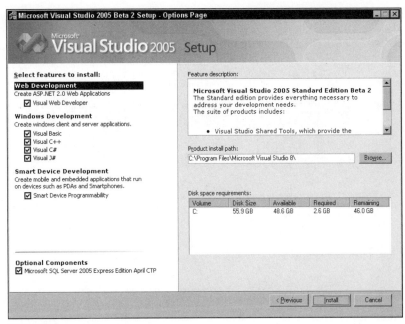

Figure 1-2

5. After you have chosen all the features you want, click Install. Installation will begin and you can sit back and relax for a bit. The setup time varies depending on how many features you chose to install. As a reference, the installation process took around 20 minutes on a 2.4-GHz computer with 512 MB RAM running Windows XP Professional.

6. When installation is completed, you will see a dialog informing you that the installation has completed.

Here you will see any problems that setup encountered along the way. You are also given the chance to look at the installation log. This log provides a list of all actions taken during the installation process. Unless your installation reported errors, the installation log can safely be ignored. The Visual Studio 2005 setup is nearly complete. Click Done to move on to installing the documentation.

7. The MSDN Library installation is simple and straightforward, and this section covers the high-lights. The first screen that you will see is the initial welcome screen. Click Next to proceed.

8. You will be allowed to select the amount of the documentation you want to install, as shown in Figure 1-3. Click Next to start the installation process.

If you have the spare hard drive space, it is a very good idea to install the full documentation. That way you have access to the full library, which will be important if you choose a limited set of options during the install and later add more features.

9. After the MSDN documentation has been installed, you are returned to the initial setup screen again, and the Service Releases option is available.

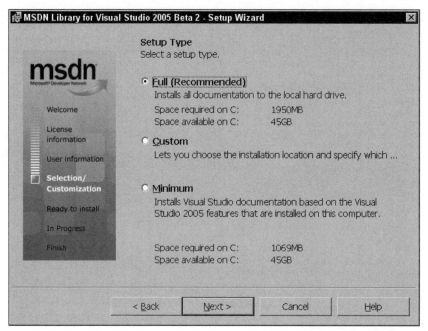

Figure 1-3

It is a good idea to select Service Releases to check for updates. Microsoft has done a good job of making software updates available through the Internet. These updates can include anything from additional documentation to bug fixes. You will be given the choice to install any updates via a Service Pack CD or the Internet. Obviously, the Internet option requires an active connection. Since updates can be quite large, a fast connection is highly recommended.

Once you have performed the update process, Visual Studio 2005 is ready to use. Now the real fun can begin! So get comfortable, relax, and let us enter the world of Visual Basic 2005.

The Visual Basic 2005 IDE

You don't actually need the Visual Basic 2005 product to write applications in the Visual Basic 2005 language. The actual ability to run Visual Basic 2005 code is included with the .NET Framework. You could actually just write all of your Visual Basic 2005 using a text editor such as Notepad. You could also hammer nails using your shoe as a hammer, but that slick pneumatic nailer sitting there is probably a lot more efficient. In the same way, by far the easiest way to write in Visual Basic 2005 is by using the Visual Studio 2005 Integrated Development Environment, also known as the IDE. This is what you actually see when working with Visual Basic 2005 — the windows, boxes, and so on. The IDE provides a wealth of features unavailable in ordinary text editors — such as code checking, visual representations of the finished application, and an explorer that displays all of the files that make up your project.

The Profile Setup Page

An IDE is a way of bringing together a suite of tools that makes developing software a lot easier. Fire up Visual Studio 2005 and see what you've got. If you used the default installation, go to your Windows Start menu and then Programs (All Programs on Windows XP and Windows Server 2003) ⇨ Microsoft Visual Studio 2005 ⇨ Microsoft Visual Studio 2005. A splash screen will briefly appear, and then you should find yourself presented with the Choose Default Environment Settings dialog box. Select the Visual Basic Development Settings option and then click Start Visual Studio. The Microsoft Development Environment will appear, as shown in Figure 1-4.

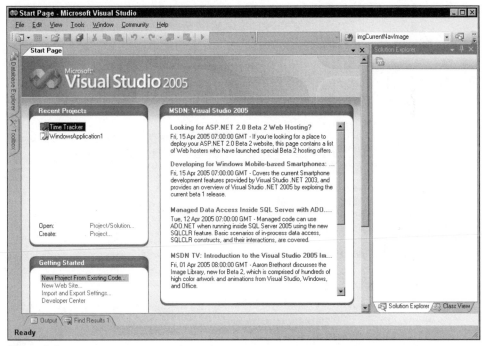

Figure 1-4

The Menu

By now, you may be a bit eager to start writing some code. But first, begin your exploration of the IDE by looking at the toolbar and menu, which, as you will learn are not really all that different from the toolbars and menus you have seen in other Microsoft software such as Word, Excel, and PowerPoint.

Visual Studio 2005's menu is *dynamic*, meaning that items will be added or removed depending on what you are trying to do. While you are looking at the blank IDE, the menu bar will consist only of the File, Edit, View, Data, Tools, Window, Community, and Help menus. When you start working on a project, however, the full Visual Studio 2005 menu appears as shown in Figure 1-5.

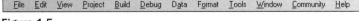

Figure 1-5

7

At this point, there is no need to cover each menu topic in great detail. You will become familiar with each of them as you progress through the book. Here is a quick rundown of what activities each menu item pertains to:

- ❑ **File:** It seems every Windows program has a File menu. It has become the standard where you should find, if nothing else, a way to exit the application. In this case, you can also find ways of opening and closing single files and whole projects.

- ❑ **Edit:** The Edit menu provides access to the items you would expect: Undo, Redo, Cut, Copy, Paste, and Delete.

- ❑ **View:** The View menu provides quick access to the windows that exist in the IDE, such as the Solution Explorer, Properties window, Output window, Toolbox, and so on.

- ❑ **Project:** The Project menu allows you to add various files to your application such as forms and classes.

- ❑ **Build:** The Build menu becomes important when you have completed your application and want to run it without the use of the Visual Basic 2005 environment (perhaps running it directly from your Windows Start menu, as you would any other application such as Word or Access).

- ❑ **Debug:** The Debug menu allows you to start and stop running your application within the Visual Basic 2005 IDE. It also gives you access to the Visual Studio 2005 debugger. The debugger allows you to step through your code while it is running to see how it is behaving.

- ❑ **Data**: The Data menu helps you to use information that comes from a database. It appears only when you are working with the visual part of your application (the [Design] tab will be the active one in the main window), not when you are writing code. Chapters 15 and 16 will introduce you to working with databases.

- ❑ **Format**: The Format menu also appears only when you are working with the visual part of your application. Items on the Format menu allow you to manipulate how the controls you create will appear on your forms.

- ❑ **Tools:** The Tools menu has commands to configure the Visual Studio 2005 IDE, as well as links to other external tools that may have been installed.

- ❑ **Window:** The Window menu has become standard for any application that allows more than one window to be open at a time, such as Word or Excel. The commands on this menu allow you to switch between the windows in the IDE.

- ❑ **Community:** The Community menu provides access to developer resources, where you can ask questions, search for code snippets, and send product feedback.

- ❑ **Help**: The Help menu provides access to the Visual Studio 2005 documentation. There are many different ways to access this information (for example, via the help contents, an index, or a search). The Help menu also has options that connect to the Microsoft Web site to obtain updates or report problems.

The Toolbars

Many toolbars are available within the IDE, including Formatting, Image Editor, and Text Editor, which you can add to and remove from the IDE via the View ⇨ Toolbars menu option. Each one provides quick access to often-used commands, preventing you from having to navigate through a series of menu options. For example, the leftmost icon (New Project) on the default toolbar (called the Standard toolbar), shown in Figure 1-6, is available from the menu by navigating to File ➪ New ➪ Project.

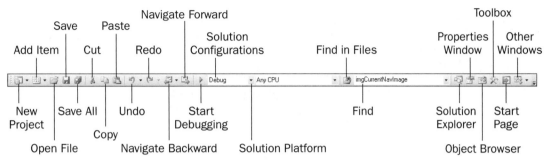

Figure 1-6

The toolbar is segmented into groups of related options, which are separated by a vertical bar. The first five icons provide access to the commonly used project and file manipulation options available through the File and Project menus, such as opening and saving files.

The next group of icons is for editing (Cut, Copy, and Paste). The third group of icons is for undoing and redoing edits and for navigating through your code.

The fourth group of icons provides the ability to start your application running (via the green triangle). You can also choose a configuration for your solution and target specific platforms.

The next section allows you to find text in your code throughout the entire document, project, or solution.

The final group of icons provides quick links back to the Solution Explorer, Properties window, Toolbox, Object Browser, Start Page, and other windows. If any of these windows is closed, clicking the appropriate icon will bring it back into view.

> *If you forget what a particular icon does, you can hover your mouse pointer over it so that a ToolTip appears displaying the name of the toolbar option.*

You could continue to look at each of the windows by clicking on the View menu and choosing the appropriate window. But, as you can see, they are all empty at this stage and therefore not too revealing. The best way to look at the capabilities of the IDE is to use it while writing some code.

Creating a Simple Application

To finish your exploration of the IDE, you need to create a project, so that the windows shown earlier in Figure 1-4 actually have some interesting content for you to look at. In the following Try It Out, you are going to create a very simple application called HelloUser that will allow you to enter a person's name and display a greeting to that person in a message box.

Try It Out   **Creating a HelloUser Project**

1.   Click the New Project button on the toolbar.

2.   The New Project dialog box will open. Make sure you have Visual Basic selected in the Project Types tree-view box to the left. Next, select Windows Application in the Templates box on the right. Finally, type **Hello User** in the Name text box and click OK. Your New Project dialog box should look like Figure 1-7.

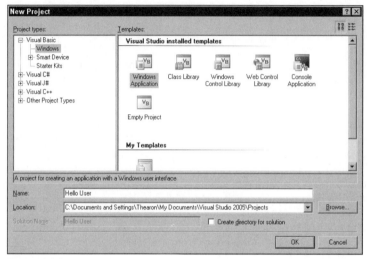

Figure 1-7

3.   The IDE will then create an empty Windows application for you. So far, your Hello User program consists of one blank window, called a Windows Form (or sometimes just a form), with the default name of Form1.vb, as shown in Figure 1-8.

Whenever Visual Studio 2005 creates a new file, either as part of the project creation process or when you create a new file, it will use a name that describes what it is (in this case, a form) followed by a number.

Windows in the Visual Studio 2005 IDE

At this point, you can see that the various windows in the IDE are beginning to show their purposes, and you should take a brief look at them now before you come back to the Try It Out. Note that if any of these windows are not visible on your screen, you can use the View menu to select and show them. Also, if you do not like the location of any particular window, you can move it by clicking on its title bar (the blue bar at the top) and dragging it to a new location. The windows in the IDE can *float* (stand out on their own) or be *docked* (as they appear in Figure 1-8). The following list introduces the most common windows:

❑   **Database Explorer:** The Database Explorer provides access to your defined database connections. Here you can create new database connections and view existing database connections. In Figure 1-8, the Database Explorer is a tab at the bottom of the Toolbox window.

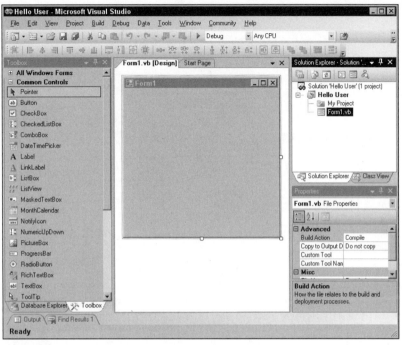

Figure 1-8

❑ **Toolbox:** The Toolbox contains reusable controls and components that can be added to your application. These can range from buttons to data connectors to customized controls that you have either purchased or developed.

❑ **Design window:** The Design window is where a lot of the action takes place. This is where you will draw your user interface on your forms. This window is sometimes referred to as the Designer.

❑ **Solution Explorer:** The Solution Explorer window contains a hierarchical view of your solution. A *solution* can contain many projects, whereas a *project* contains forms, classes, modules, and components that solve a particular problem.

❑ **Properties:** The Properties window shows what *properties* the selected object makes available. Although you can set these properties in your code, sometimes it is much easier to set them while you are designing your application (for example, drawing the controls on your form). You will notice that the File Name property has the value Form1.vb. This is the physical file name for the form's code and layout information.

Try It Out   Creating a HelloUser Project (cont.)

1. Change the name of your form to something more indicative of what your application is. Click on Form1.vb in the Solution Explorer window. Then, in the Properties window, change the File Name property from Form1.vb to **HelloUser.vb** and press Enter, as shown in Figure 1-9. When changing properties you must either press Enter or click off the property for it to take effect.

Figure 1-9

2. Notice that the form's filename has also been updated in the Solution Explorer to read `HelloUser.vb`.

3. Now click the form displayed in the Design window. The Properties window will change to display the form's Form properties (instead of the File properties, which you have just been looking at). You will notice that the Properties window is dramatically different. The difference is the result of two different views of the same file. When the form name is highlighted in the Solution Explorer window, the physical file properties of the form are displayed. When the form in the Design window is highlighted, the visual properties and logical properties of the form are displayed.

   The Properties window allows you to set a control's properties easily. Properties are a particular object's set of internal data; they usually describe appearance or behavior. In Figure 1-10 you can see that properties are grouped together in categories — Accessibility (not shown), Appearance (header is not shown), Behavior, Data, Design, Focus (not shown), Layout (not shown), Misc (not shown), and Window Style (not shown).

   You can see that under the Appearance category (header not shown), even though we changed the file name of the form to `HelloUser.vb`, *the text or caption of the form is still* `Form1`.

4. Right now, the title (Text property) of your form (displayed in the bar at the top) is `Form1`. This is not very descriptive, so change it to reflect the purpose of this application. Locate the Text property in the Appearance section of the Properties window. Change the Text property's value to **Hello from Visual Basic 2005** and press Enter. Notice that the form's title has been updated to reflect the change.

   If you have trouble finding properties, click the little AZ button on the toolbar toward the top of the Properties window. This changes the property listing from being ordered by category to being ordered by name.

5. You are now finished with the procedure. Click the Start button on the Visual Studio 2005 toolbar (the green triangle) to run the application. As you work through the book, whenever we say "run the project" or "start the project," just click the Start button. An empty window with the title Hello from Visual Basic 2005 is displayed.

Figure 1-10

That was simple, but your little application isn't doing much at the moment. Let us make it a little more interactive. To do this, you are going to add some controls—a label, a text box, and two buttons to the form. This will let you see how the Toolbox makes adding functionality quite simple. You may be wondering at this point when you will actually look at some code. Soon! The great thing about Visual Basic 2005 is that you can develop a fair amount of your application *without* writing any code. Sure, the code is still there, behind the scenes, but, as you will see, Visual Basic 2005 writes a lot of it for you.

The Toolbox

The Toolbox is accessed via the View ➪ Toolbox menu option, the Toolbox icon on the Standard menu bar, or by pressing Ctrl+Alt+X. Alternatively, the Toolbox tab is displayed on the left of the IDE; hovering your mouse over this tab will cause the Toolbox window to fly out, partially covering your form.

The Toolbox contains a Node type view of the various controls and components that can be placed onto your form. Controls such as text boxes, buttons, radio buttons, and combo boxes can be selected and then *drawn* onto your form. For the HelloUser application, you will be using only the controls in the Common Controls node. In Figure 1-11, you can see a listing of common controls for Windows Forms.

Controls can be added to your forms in any order, so it does not matter if you add the label control after the text box or the buttons before the label. In the next Try It Out, you start adding controls.

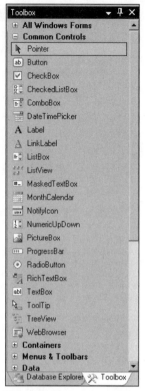

Figure 1-11

Adding Controls to the HelloUser Application

1. Stop the project if it is still running, because you now want to add some controls to your form. The simplest way to stop your project is to click the X button in the top-right corner of the form. Alternatively, you can click the blue square in the IDE (which displays a ToolTip that says "Stop Debugging" if you hover over it with your mouse pointer).

2. Add a Label control to the form. Click Label in the Toolbox and drag it over the form's Designer and drop it in the desired location. (You can also place controls on your form by double-clicking on the required control in the Toolbox or clicking on the control in the Toolbox and then drawing it on the form.)

3. If the Label control you have just drawn is not in the desired location, it really isn't a problem. Once the control is on the form, you can resize it or move it around. Figure 1-12 shows what the control looks like after you place it on the form. To move it, click the dotted border and drag it to the desired location. The label will automatically resize itself to fit the text that you enter in the Text property.

4. After drawing a control on the form, you should at least configure its name and the text that it will display. You will see that the Properties window to the right of the Designer has changed to `Label1`, telling you that you are currently examining the properties for it. In the Properties window, set your new label's Text property to **Enter Your Name**. Notice that, once you press enter or click off of the property, the label on the form has automatically resized itself to fit the Text property. Now set the Name property to **lblName**.

Figure 1-12

5. Now, directly beneath the label, you want to add a text box, so that you can enter a name. You are going to repeat the procedure you followed for adding the label, but this time make sure you select the TextBox control from the toolbar. After you have dragged-and-dropped (or double-clicked) the control into the appropriate position as shown in Figure 1-13, use the Properties window to set its Name property to **txtName**.

Notice the sizing handles on the left and right side of the control. You can use these handles to resize the text box horizontally.

Figure 1-13

6. In the bottom left corner of the form, add a Button control in exactly the same manner as you added the label and text box. Set its Name property to **btnOK** and its Text property to **&OK**. Your form should now look similar to the one shown in Figure 1-14.

The ampersand (&) is used in the Text property of buttons is to create a keyboard shortcut (known as a hot key). The letter with the & sign placed in front of it will become underlined (as shown in Figure 1-14) to signal users that they can select that button by pressing the Alt+letter key combination, instead of using the mouse (on some configurations the underline doesn't appear until the user presses Alt). In this particular instance, pressing Alt+O would be the same as clicking directly on the OK button. There is no need to write code to accomplish this.

Figure 1-14

7. Now add a second Button control to the bottom right corner of the form by dragging the Button control from the Toolbox onto your form. You'll notice that, as you get close to the bottom right of the form, a blue snap line will appear, as shown in Figure 1-15. This snap line will allow you to align this new Button control with the existing Button control on the form. The snap lines assist you in aligning controls to the left, right, top, or bottom of each other, depending on where you are trying to position the new control. The light blue line provides you with a consistent margin between the edge of your control and the edge of the form. Set the Name property to **btnExit** and the Text property to **E&xit**. Your form should look similar to Figure 1-16.

Figure 1-15

Figure 1-16

Now before you finish your sample application, let us briefly discuss some coding practices that you should be using.

Modified Hungarian Notation

You may have noticed that the names given to the controls look a little funny. Each name is prefixed with a shorthand identifier describing the type of control it is. This makes it much easier to understand what type of control you are working with when you are looking through the code. For example, say you had a control called simply Name, without a prefix of `lbl` or `txt`. You would not know whether you were working with a text box that accepted a name or with a label that displayed a name. Imagine if, in the previous Try It Out, you had named your label Name1 and your text box Name2 — you would very quickly become confused. What if you left your application for a month or two and then came back to it to make some changes?

When working with other developers, it is very important to keep the coding style consistent. One of the most commonly used styles for control names within application development in many languages was brought forth by Dr. Charles Simonyi, who worked for the Xerox Palo Alto Research Center (XPARC) before joining Microsoft. He came up with short prefix mnemonics that allowed programmers to easily identify the type of information a variable might contain. Since Simonyi is from Hungary, and the prefixes make the names look a little foreign, the name "Hungarian Notation" came into use for this system. Because the original notation was used in C/C++ development, the notation for Visual Basic 2005 is termed Modified. The following table shows some of the commonly used prefixes that you shall be using in this book.

Hungarian Notation can be a real time-saver when you are looking at code someone else wrote or at code that you wrote months earlier. However, by far the most important thing is to be consistent in your naming. When you start coding, pick a convention for your naming. It is recommended that you use the de facto standard Modified-Hungarian for Visual Basic 2005, but it is not required. Once you pick a convention, stick to it. When modifying others' code, use theirs. A standard naming convention followed throughout a project will save countless hours when the application is maintained. Now let's get back to the application. It's now time to write some actual code.

Control	Prefix
Button	btn
ComboBox	cbo
CheckBox	chk
Label	lbl
ListBox	lst
MainMenu	mnu
RadioButton	rdb
PictureBox	pic
TextBox	txt

The Code Editor

Now that you have the HelloUser form defined, you have to add some code to make it actually do something interesting. You have already seen how easy it is to add controls to a form. Providing the functionality behind those on-screen elements is no more difficult. To add the code for a control, you just double-click the control in question. This will open the code editor in the main window, shown in Figure 1-17.

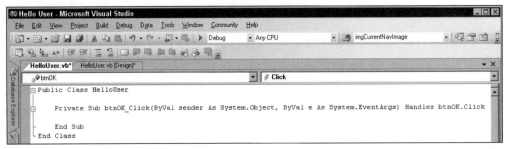

Figure 1-17

Notice that an additional tab has been created in the main window. Now you have the Design tab and the Code tab. You draw the controls on your form in the Design tab, and you write code for your form in the Code tab. One thing to note here is that Visual Studio 2005 has created a separate file for the code. The visual definition and the code behind exist in separate files: `HelloUser.Designer.vb` and `Hello User.vb`. This is actually the reason why building applications with Visual Basic 2005 is so slick and easy. Using the Design view you can visually lay out your application, and then, using Code view, you add just the bits of code to implement your desired functionality.

You will also notice that there are two combo boxes at the top of the window. These provide shortcuts to the various parts of your code. Hover your mouse on the combo box on the left, and you'll see a ToolTip appear, telling you that it is the Class Name combo box. If you expand this combo box, you will see a list of all the objects within your application. If you hover your mouse on the combo box on the right, you'll see a ToolTip telling you that this is the Method Name combo box. If you expand this combo box, you will see a list of all defined functions and subroutines for the object selected in the Class Name combo box. If this particular form had a lot of code behind it, these combo boxes would make navigating to the desired area very quick — jumping to the selected area in your code. However, since all of the code fits in the window, there are not a lot of places to get lost.

Try It Out   **Adding Code to the HelloUser Project**

1.   To begin adding the necessary code, click the Design tab to show the form again. Then double-click the OK button. The code window will open with the following code. This is the shell of the button's Click event and is the place where you enter the code that you want to run when you click the button. This code is known as an *event handler* and sometimes is also referred to as an *event procedure*:

```
Private Sub btnOK_Click(ByVal sender As System.Object, _
    ByVal e As System.EventArgs) Handles btnOK.Click

    End Sub
```

As a result of the typographic constraints in publishing, it is not possible to put the Sub declaration on one line. Visual Basic 2005 allows you to break up lines of code by using the underscore character (_) to signify a line continuation. The space before the underscore is required. Any whitespace preceding the code on the following line is ignored.

Sub is an example of a *keyword*. In programming terms, a keyword is a special word that is used to tell Visual Basic 2005 to do something special. In this case, it tells Visual Basic 2005 that this is a *subroutine,* a procedure that does not return a value. Anything that you type between the lines Private Sub and End Sub will make up the event procedure for the OK button.

2.   Now add the highlighted code into the procedure:

```
Private Sub btnOK_Click(ByVal sender As System.Object, _
    ByVal e As System.EventArgs) Handles btnOK.Click

        'Display a message box greeting the user
        MessageBox.Show("Hello," & txtName.Text & _
          "! Welcome to Visual Basic 2005.", _
          "Hello User Message")
    End Sub
```

Throughout this book, you will be presented with code that you should enter into your program if you are following along. Usually, we will make it pretty obvious where you put the code, but as we go, we will explain anything that looks out of the ordinary. The code with the gray background is code that you should enter.

3.   After you have added the preceding code, go back to the Design tab, and double-click the Exit button. Add the highlighted code to the btnExit_Click event procedure.

```
Private Sub btnExit_Click(ByVal sender As System.Object, _
    ByVal e As System.EventArgs) Handles btnExit.Click

        'End the program and close the form
        Me.Close()
    End Sub
```

19

You may be wondering what Me is. Me is a keyword that refers to the form. Just like the pronoun *me*, it is just shorthand for referring to one's self.

4. Now that the code is finished, the moment of truth has arrived and you can see your creation. First though, save your work by using File ➪ Save HelloUser.vb from the menu or by clicking the Save button on the toolbar.

5. Now click the Start button on the toolbar. You will notice a lot of activity in the Output window at the bottom of your screen. Provided you have not made any mistakes in entering the code, this information just lets you know which files are being loaded to run your application.

    It is at this point that Visual Studio 2005 will *compile* the code. Compiling is the activity of taking the Visual Basic 2005 source code that you have written and translating it into a form that the computer understands. After the compilation is complete, Visual Studio 2005 runs (also known as *executes*) the program, and you'll be able to see the results.

If Visual Basic 2005 encounters any errors, they will be displayed as tasks in the Task List window. Double-clicking a task transports you to the offending line of code. We will learn more about how to debug the errors in our code in Chapter 9.

6. When the application loads, you see the main form. Enter a name and click OK (or press the Alt+O key combination) (see Figure 1-18).

Figure 1-18

7. A window known as a message box appears, welcoming the person whose name was entered in the text box on the form — in this case Stephanie (see Figure 1-19).

Figure 1-19

8. After you close the message box by clicking the OK button, click the Exit button on your form. The application closes and you will be returned to the Visual Basic 2005 IDE.

How It Works

The code that you added to the Click event for the OK button will take the name that was entered in the text box and use it as part of the message that was displayed in Figure 1-19.

The first line of text entered in this procedure is actually a *comment*, text that is meant to be read by the human programmer who is writing or maintaining the code, not by the computer. Comments in Visual Basic 2005 begin with a single quote ('), and everything following on that line is considered a comment and ignored by the compiler. Comments will be discussed in detail in Chapter 3.

The MessageBox.Show method displays a message box that accepts various parameters. As used in your code, you have passed the string text to be displayed in the message box. This is accomplished through the *concatenation* of string constants defined by text enclosed in quotes. Concatenation of strings into one long string is performed through the use of the ampersand (&) character.

The code that follows concatenates a string constant of "Hello," followed by the value contained in the Text property of the txtName text box control followed by a string constant of "! Welcome to Visual Basic 2005." The second parameter being passed to the MessageBox.Show method is the caption to be used in the title bar of the Message Box dialog box.

Finally, the underscore (_) character used at the end of the lines in the following code enables you to split your code onto separate lines. This tells the compiler that the rest of the code for the parameter is continued on the next line. This is really useful when building long strings, because it allows you to view the entire code fragment in the Code Editor without having to scroll the Code Editor window to the right to view the entire line of code.

```
Private Sub btnOK_Click(ByVal sender As System.Object, _
    ByVal e As System.EventArgs) Handles btnOK.Click

    'Display a message box greeting the user
    MessageBox.Show("Hello," & txtName.Text & _
      "! Welcome to Visual Basic 2005.", _
      "Hello User Message")
End Sub
```

The next procedure that you added code for was the Exit button's Click event. Here you simply enter the code: Me.Close(). As explained earlier, the Me keyword refers to the form itself. The Close method of the form closes the form and releases all resources associated with it, thus ending the program.

```
Private Sub btnExit_Click(ByVal sender As System.Object, _
    ByVal e As System.EventArgs) Handles btnExit.Click

    'End the program and close the form
    Me.Close()
End Sub
```

Using the Help System

The Help system included in Visual Basic 2005 is an improvement over Help systems in previous versions. As you begin to learn Visual Basic 2005, you will probably become very familiar with the Help system. However, it is worthwhile to give you an overview, just to help speed your searches for information.

The Help menu contains the menu items shown in Figure 1-20:

Figure 1-20

As you can see, this menu contains a few more entries than the typical Windows application. The main reason for this is the vastness of the documentation. Few people could keep it all in their heads — but luckily, that is not a problem, because you can always quickly and easily refer to the Help system. Think of it as a safety net for your brain.

One really fantastic feature is Dynamic Help. When you select the Dynamic Help menu item from the Help menu, the Dynamic Help window is displayed with a list of relevant topics for whatever you may be working on. The Dynamic Help window can be displayed by clicking Help ➪ Dynamic Help on the menu bar. The Dynamic Help window is then displayed as a tab behind the Properties window.

Let us say, for example, that you are working with a text box (perhaps the text box in the HelloUser application) and want to find out some information; you just select the text box on our form or in the code window and you can see all the help topics that pertain to text boxes, as shown in Figure 1-21

The other help commands in the Help menu (Search, Contents, and Index), function just as they would in any other Windows application. The How Do I menu item displays the Visual Studio Help collection with a list of common tasks that are categorized. This makes finding help on common tasks fast and efficient.

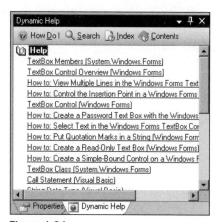

Figure 1-21

Summary

Hopefully, you are beginning to see that developing basic applications with Visual Basic 2005 is not that difficult. You have taken a look at the IDE and saw how it can help you put together software very quickly. The Toolbox enables you to add controls to your form and design a user interface very quickly and easily. The Properties window makes configuring those controls a snap, while the Solution Explorer gives you a bird's eye view of the files that make up your project. You even wrote a little code.

In the coming chapters, you will go into even more detail and get comfortable writing code. Before you go too far into Visual Basic 2005 itself, the next chapter will give you an introduction to the Microsoft .NET Framework. This Framework is what gives all of the .NET languages their ease of use, ease of interoperability, and simplicity in learning.

To summarize, you should now be familiar with:

- ❑ The Integrated Development Environment (IDE)
- ❑ Adding controls to your form in the Designer
- ❑ Setting the properties of your controls
- ❑ Adding code to your form in the code window

Exercise

Create a Windows Application with a Textbox and Button control that will display whatever is typed in the text box when the user clicks on the button.

The answers for this exercise and those at the end of all the other chapters can be found in Appendix D.

The Microsoft .NET Framework

The .NET Framework provides an unprecedented platform for building Windows, Web, and mobile applications with one or more languages. It is a definitive guide, encompassing and encapsulating where we have come from as a development community and, of course, where we are going.

Today, .NET has been a real success in many respects. Within the .NET Framework, new languages (C# and J#) have been born, and the well-established Visual Basic language has been reborn. The .NET Framework even supports legacy languages such as C++.

The .NET Framework provides the base for all development with Visual Studio 2005. It provides base classes, available to all Visual Studio 2005 languages. for such functions as accessing databases, parsing XML, displaying and processing Windows and Web forms, and providing security for your applications. All languages in Visual Studio 2005 share and use the same base classes, making your choice of a programming language in Visual Studio 2005 a matter of personal preference and syntax style.

In this chapter, you will examine the following topics:

❑ What the .NET Framework is

❑ The .NET vision

❑ Why Microsoft dared to spend $2 billion on a single development project

Microsoft's Reliance on Windows

In terms of the great corporations of the world, Microsoft is still a new kid on the block. It is a fabulously rich and successful one. Nonetheless, the company has grown from nothing to a corporate superpower in a very short time.

What is perhaps more interesting is that although the origin of Microsoft can be traced to the mid-1970s, it is really the Windows family of operating systems that has brought the company great success. Based on Presentation Manager for OS/2, Windows has seen many incarnations from Windows/286 to Windows XP, but the essential way that you use Windows and Windows applications has not changed in all that time. (Granted, there have been advances in the user interface and the hardware, but you still use the version of Excel included with Office XP in roughly the same way that you used the first version.)

The scary thing to Microsoft and its investors is that the pace of technological change means that they cannot be sure that Windows is going to be as relevant in 2011 as it is today. All it takes is one change in the way that people want to use computers, and the Windows platform's current incarnation may become obsolete.

It is unfair to say that Microsoft has been extremely lucky over the past several years in the way that it has reacted to the new opportunities offered by the Internet. Yes, luck was involved, but do not underestimate the number of smart people working for that company! Once they discovered that companies like Netscape were making money with the Internet and identified the risk, they turned a large corporation on a dime and went after an unexplored market with teeth bared. Their gamble has paid off, and with the invention of the .NET Framework, corporations and users can leverage the power of the Internet in new ways.

Luckily for Microsoft, the applications that drove the adoption of the Internet worked well on a desktop operating system. Microsoft managed to adapt the Windows platform to provide the two killer Internet applications (e-mail and the Web browser) to the end user with a minimum of hassle, securing the Windows platform for another few years. It also delivered several powerful tools for developers, such as Active Server Pages (ASP) and Internet Information Server (IIS), and improved existing tools such as Visual Basic and SQL, all of which made it easier for developers to build advanced Internet applications.

MSN 1.0

When the Internet started to become popular, Microsoft was trying to push the original incarnation of MSN. Rather than the successful portal that it is today, MSN was originally a proprietary dial-up service much like CompuServe. In the beginning, MSN did not provide access to the rich world of the Internet as we know today; it was a closed system. Let us call the original MSN "MSN 1.0."

MSN 1.0 provided an opportunity for innovative companies to steal a march on Microsoft, which was already seen as an unshakable behemoth thanks to the combination of Windows and Office.

Imagine an alternative 1995 in which Microsoft stuck to its guns with MSN 1.0, rather than plotting the course that brings it where it is today. Imagine that a large computer manufacturer, such as Dell, identified this burgeoning community of forward-thinking business leaders and geeks called the Internet. Also suppose Dell predicted that Microsoft's strategy was to usurp this community with MSN 1.0 — in other words, rather than cooperating with this community, Microsoft decided to crush it at all costs.

Now Dell needs to find a way to build this community. It predicts that home users and small businesses will love the Internet and so puts together a very low-cost PC. They need software to run on it and, luckily, predict that the Web and e-mail will be the killer applications of this new community. They find Linus Torvalds, who has been working on this thing called Linux since 1991, and they find Sun, which is keen to start pushing Java as a programming language to anyone who will listen. Another business partner builds a competent, usable suite of productivity applications for the platform using Java. Another business partner builds easy-to-use connectivity solutions that allow the computers to connect to the Internet and other computers in the LAN, easily and cheaply.

Dell, Sun, and their selected business partners start pushing this new computer to anyone and everyone. The concept is a success and, for the first time since 1981, the dominance of the IBM-compatible PC is reduced, and sales of Microsoft products plummet. This is all because Microsoft did not move on a critical opportunity.

We all know that this did not happen, but there is nothing outlandish or crazy about this idea. It could have happened, and that is what scared Microsoft. It came very close to losing everything, and .NET is its insurance against this happening again.

The .NET Vision

To understand .NET, you have to ignore the marketing hype from Microsoft and really think about what it is doing. With the first version of the framework and indeed even now, Microsoft appears to be pushing .NET as a platform for building Web Services and large-scale enterprise systems. Although we cover Web Services in Chapter 19, it is a tiny, tiny part of what .NET is about. In simple terms, .NET splits an operating systems platform (be it Windows, Linux, MacOS, whatever) into two layers: a programming layer and an execution layer.

All computer platforms are trying to achieve roughly the same effect: to provide applications to the user. If you wanted to write a book, you would have the choice of using the word processor in Star Office under Linux or Word under Windows. However, you would be using the computer in the same way; in other words, the application remains the same irrespective of the platform.

It is a common understanding that software support is a large part of any platform's success. Typically, the more high quality the available software is for a given platform, the larger the consumer adoption of that platform will be. The PC is the dominant platform because, back in the early 1980s, that is what the predominant target for software writers was. That trend has continued today, and people are writing applications that run on Windows targets for the Intel x86 type processors. The x86 processor harks back to the introduction of the Intel 8086 processor in 1979 and today includes the Intel Pentium 4 processor and competitors like AMD's Athlon and Duron.

So without .NET, developers are still reliant on Windows, and Windows is still reliant on Intel. Although the relationship between Microsoft and Intel is thought to be fairly symbiotic, it is reasonable to assume that the strategists at Microsoft, who are feeling (rightly) paranoid about the future, might want to lessen the dependence on a single family of chips too.

The Windows/Intel combination (sometimes known as Wintel) is what is known as the *execution layer*. This layer takes the code and runs it — simple as that.

Although .NET targeted the Windows platform, there is no reason why later versions of .NET cannot be directed at other platforms. Already, there are open-source projects trying to recreate .NET for other platforms. What this means is that a program written by a .NET developer on Windows could run unchanged on Linux. In fact, the Mono project (`.mono-project.com/`) has already released its first version of its product. This project has developed an open-source version of a C# compiler, a runtime for the Common Language Infrastructure (CLI, also known as the Common Intermediate Language — CIL), a subset of the .NET classes, and other .NET goodies independent of Microsoft's involvement.

.NET is a *programming layer*. It is totally owned and controlled by Microsoft. By turning all developers into .NET programmers rather than Windows programmers, software is written as .NET software, not Windows software.

To see the significance of this, imagine that a new platform is launched and starts eating up market share like crazy. Imagine that, like the Internet, this new platform offers a revolutionary way of working and living that offers real advantages. With the .NET vision in place, all Microsoft has to do to gain a foothold on this platform is develop a version of .NET that works on it. All of the .NET software now runs on the new platform, lessening the chance that the new platform will usurp Microsoft's market share.

This Sounds like Java

Some of this does sound a lot like Java. In fact, Java's mantra of "write once, run anywhere" fits nicely into the .NET doctrine. However, .NET is not a Java clone. Microsoft has a different approach.

To write in Java, developers were expected to learn a new language. This language was based on C++, and while C++ is a popular language, it is not the most popular language. In fact, the most popular language in terms of number of developers is Visual Basic, and, obviously, Microsoft owns it. Some estimates put the number of Visual Basic developers at approximately 3 million worldwide, but bear in mind that this number includes both Visual Basic professionals and people who tinker with macros in the various Office products.

Whereas Java is "one language, many platforms," .NET is "many languages, one platform, for now." Microsoft wants to remove the barrier to entry for .NET by making it accessible to anyone who has used pretty much any language. The three primary languages for .NET are Visual Basic 2005, C#, and J#. Visual Studio 2005 comes supplied with all of these. Although C# is not C++, the developers of C++ should be able to migrate to C# with about the same amount of relearning that a Visual Basic 6 developer will have to do in order to move to Visual Basic 2005. Of course the .NET Framework supports developers using C++ and allows them to write C++ applications using the .NET Framework.

With Java, Sun attempted to build from the ground-up something so abstracted from the operating system that when you compare an application written natively in something like Visual C++ with a Java equivalent, it becomes fairly obvious that the Java version will run slower and not look as good in terms of user interface. Sun tried to take too big a bite out of the problem by attempting to support everything, so in the end it did not support one single thing completely.

Microsoft's .NET strategy is more like a military campaign. First, it will use its understanding of the Windows platform to build .NET into something that will stand against a native C++ application. It will also try to bolster the lackluster uptake of Pocket PC with the Compact Framework. After it wins over the voters on Windows, it may invade another platform, most likely Linux. This second stage will prove the concept that .NET applications can be ported from one platform to the next. After invading and conquering Linux, it will move to another platform. Microsoft has been attempting to shake Solaris from the top spot in the server market for a long time, so it's likely that it'll go there next.

Where Now?

Microsoft has bet its future on .NET. With developers writing software for the programming layer rather than an execution layer, it really does not matter whether Windows is the dominant platform in 2011 or Linux is, or whether something totally off the radar will be. The remainder of this chapter drills into the mechanics of .NET and takes a detailed look at how the whole thing works.

Writing Software for Windows

To understand how .NET works, you need to look at how developers used to write software for Windows. The general principle was the same in both cases, only they had to do things in different ways to work with different technologies — the Component Object Model (COM), ActiveX Data Objects (ADO), and so forth.

Any software that you write has to interact with various parts of the operating system to do its job. If the software needs a block of memory to store data in, it interacts with the memory manager. To read a file from disk, you use the disk subsystem. To request a file from the network, you use the network subsystem. To draw a window on the screen, you use the graphics subsystem, and so on.

This *subsystems* approach breaks down, as far as .NET is concerned, because there is no commonality between the ways you use the subsystems on different platforms, despite the fact that platforms tend to have things in common. For example, even if you are writing an application for Linux, you may still need to use the network, disk, and screen subsystems. However, because different organizations developed these platforms, the way you open a file using the Linux platform may be different from the way you do it on Windows. If you want to move code that depends on one platform to another, you will probably have to rewrite portions of the code. You will also have to test the code to ensure it still works as intended.

Windows software communicates with the operating system and various subsystems using something called the Windows 32-bit Application Programming Interface (Win32 API). Although object-orientation in programming was around at the time, this API was designed to be an evolution of the original Windows API, which predates the massive adoption of object-oriented techniques that are discussed in Chapter 10.

It is not easy to port the Win32 API to other platforms, which is why there is no version of the Win32 API for Linux even though Linux has been around for a decade. There is a cut-down version of the Win32 API for the Mac, but this has never received much of an industry following.

The Win32 API provides all basic functionality, but now and again, Microsoft extends the capabilities of Windows with a new API. A classic example is the Windows Internet API, also known as the WinInet API. This API allows an application to download resources from a Web server, upload files to an FTP server, discover proxy settings, and so on. Again, it is not object oriented, but it does work.

A large factor in the success of early versions of Visual Basic is that it took the tricky-to-understand Win32 API calls and packaged them in a way that could be easily understood. Using the native Win32 API, it takes about a hundred lines of code to draw a window on the screen. The same effect can be achieved in Visual Basic with a few gestures of the mouse. Visual Basic represents an abstraction layer on top of the Win32 API that makes it easier for developers to use.

A long-time frustration for C++ developers was that a lot of the things that were very easy to do in Visual Basic remained not so much hard as laborious in C++. Developers like C++ because it gives them an amazing amount of control over how a program works, but their programs take longer to write. Microsoft introduced the Microsoft Foundation Classes (MFC) because of this overhead, which, along with the IDE of Visual Studio, brought the ease of Visual C++ development closer to that of Visual Basic.

The .NET Framework Classes

Unlike the Win32 API, .NET is totally object-oriented. Anything you want to do in .NET, you are going to be doing with an object. If you want to open a file, you create an object that knows how to do this. If you want to draw a window on the screen, you create an object that knows how to do this. When you get to Chapter 10, you will discover that this is called *encapsulation*; the functionality is encapsulated in an object, and you don't really care how it's done behind the scenes.

Although there is still the concept of subsystems in .NET, these subsystems are never accessed directly — instead they are abstracted away by the Framework classes. Either way, your .NET application never has to talk directly to the subsystem (although you can do so if you really need or want to). Rather, you talk to objects, which then talk to the subsystem. In Figure 2-1, the box marked `System.IO.File` is a class defined in the .NET Framework.

If you are talking to objects that talk to subsystems, do you really care what the subsystem looks like? Thankfully the answer is "no," and this is how Microsoft removes your reliance on Windows. If you know the name of a file, you use the same objects to open it whether you are running on a Windows XP machine, a Pocket PC, or even, using the Mono Project version of the .NET Framework, Linux. Likewise, if you need to display a window on the screen, you do not care whether it is on a Windows operating system or on a Mac.

The .NET Framework is actually a set of classes called *base classes*. The base classes in the .NET Framework are rather extensive and provide the functionality for just about anything that you need to do in a Windows or Web environment, from working with files to working with data to working with forms and controls.

The class library itself is vast, containing several thousand objects available to developers, although in your day-to-day development you will only need to understand a handful of these to create powerful applications.

Another really nice thing about the base classes in the .NET Framework is that they are the same irrespective of the language used. So, if you are writing a Visual Basic 2005 application, you use the same object as you would from within a C# or J# application. That object will have the same methods, properties, and events, meaning that there is very little difference in capabilities between the languages, since they all rely on the framework.

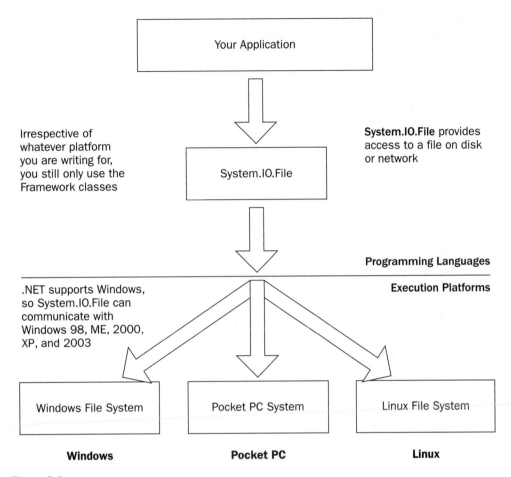

Figure 2-1

Executing Code

The base class library is only half the equation. After you have written the code that interacts with the classes, you still need to run it. This poses a tricky problem; to remove the reliance on the platform is to remove the reliance on the processor.

Whenever you write software for Windows, you are guaranteed that this code will run on an Intel x86 chip. With .NET, Microsoft does not want to make this guarantee. It might be that the dominant chip in 2008 is a Transmeta chip, or something you have never even seen. What needs to be done is to abstract .NET away from the processor, in a similar fashion to the way .NET is abstracted from the underlying subsystem implementations.

Programming languages are somewhere in between the languages that people speak every day and the language that the computer itself understands. The language that a computer uses is the *machine code* (sometimes called *machine instructions* or *machine language*) and consists entirely of zeros and ones, each corresponding to electrical current flowing or not flowing through this or that part of the chip. When you are using a PC with an Intel or competing processor, this language is more specifically known as x86 machine instructions.

If you wrote an application with Visual Basic 6, you had to *compile* it into a set of x86 machine instructions before you could deploy it. This machine code would then be installed and executed on any machine that supported x86 instructions and was also running Windows.

If you write an application with Visual Basic 2005, you still have to compile the code. However, you do not compile the Visual Basic 2005 code directly into x86 machine instructions, because that would mean that the resulting program would run only on processors that support this language — in other words, the program would run only on Intel chips and their compatible competitors. Instead, compilation creates something called *Microsoft Intermediate Language* (MSIL). This language is not dependent on any processor. It is a layer above the traditional machine code.

MSIL code will not just run on any processor, because processors do not understand MSIL. To run the code, it has to be further compiled, as shown in Figure 2-2, from MSIL code into the native code that the processor understands.

However, this approach also provides the industry with a subtle problem. In a world where .NET is extremely popular (some might say dominant), who is responsible for developing an MSIL-to-native compiler when a new processor is released? Is the new processor at the mercy of Microsoft's willingness to port .NET to the chip? Time, as they say, will tell!

Take a look at the thing that makes .NET work: the Common Language Runtime.

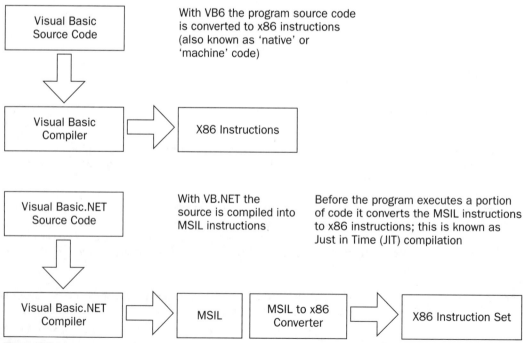

Figure 2-2

Common Language Runtime

The Common Language Runtime, also known as the CLR, is the heart of .NET. The Common Language Runtime takes your .NET application, compiles it into native processor code, and runs it. It provides an extensive range of functionalities for helping the applications run properly, so look at each one in turn.

- ❏   Code loading and execution
- ❏   Application isolation
- ❏   Memory management
- ❏   Security
- ❏   Exception handling
- ❏   Interoperation

Do not worry if you do not understand what all these are — the following sections discuss all of them except for memory management. Memory management is quite a complex subject and is discussed in Chapter 11.

Code Loading and Execution

This part of the Common Language Runtime deals with reading the MSIL code from the disk and running it. It compiles the code from MSIL into the native language (machine code) that the processor understands.

> *Java also has a concept similar to MSIL, known as byte code.*

Application Isolation

One important premise of modern operating systems like Windows and Linux is that applications are isolated from one another. This is critically important from both security and stability standpoints.

Imagine that you have a badly written program and it crashes the PC. Should this happen? No, you want only the badly behaved program to crash, as you do not want other applications or the operating system itself to be affected by a program running on it. For example, if your e-mail program crashes, you do not want to lose any unsaved changes in your word processor. With proper application isolation, one application crashing should not cause others to crash.

In some instances, even under Windows XP, a badly behaved program can do something so horrendous that the entire machine crashes. This is commonly known as a Blue Screen of Death, or BSOD, so called because your attractive Windows desktop is replaced with a stark blue screen with a smattering of white text "explaining" the problem. This problem should be alleviated in .NET, but it is unlikely to be completely solved.

The other aspect to application isolation is one of security. Imagine that you are writing a personal and sensitive e-mail. You do not want other applications running on your computer to be able to grab, or even stumble across, the contents of the e-mail and pass it on to someone else. Applications running in an isolated model cannot just take what they want. Instead, they have to ask whether they can have something, and they are given it only if the operating system permits it.

This level of application isolation is already available in Windows. .NET extends and enhances this functionality by further improving it.

Security

.NET has powerful support for the concept of code security. This was designed to give system administrators, users, and software developers a fine level of control over what a program can and cannot do.

Imagine that you have a program that scans your computer's hard disk looking for Word documents. You might think this is a useful program if it is the one that you run yourself to find documents that are missing. Now imagine that this program is delivered through e-mail and it automatically runs and e-mails copies of any "interesting" documents to someone else. You are less likely to find that useful.

This is the situation you find yourself in today with old-school Windows development. To all intents and purposes, Windows applications have unrestricted access over your computer and can do pretty much anything they want. That is why the Melissa and I Love You-type viruses are possible—Windows does not understand the difference between a benign script file you write yourself that, say, looks through your address book and sends e-mails to everyone, and those written by someone else and delivered as viruses.

With .NET this situation changes because of the security features built into the Common Language Runtime. Under the CLR, code requires *evidence* to run. This evidence can be policies set by you and your system administrator, as well as the origin of the code (for example, whether it came off your local machine, off a machine on your office network, or over the Internet).

Security is a very involved topic and is not covered in this book. However, you can find more information in . *NET Security Programming* (ISBN 0-471-22285-2), written by Donis Marshall and published by Wiley.

Interoperation

Interoperation in the .NET Framework is achieved on various levels not covered here. However, we must point out some of the types of interoperation that it provides. One kind of interoperation is at the core of the framework, where data types are shared by all managed languages. This is known as the Common Type System (CTS). This is a great improvement for language interoperability (see the section "The Common Type System and Common Language Specification" later in this chapter).

The other type of interoperation is that of communicating with existing Component Object Model (COM) interfaces. Because a large application software base is written in COM, it was inevitable that .NET should be able to communicate with existing COM libraries. This is also known as *COM interop*.

Exception Handling

Exception handling is the concept of dealing with "exceptional happenings" when you are running the code. Imagine that you have written a program that opens a file on disk. What if that file is not there?

Well, the fact that the file is not there is exceptional, and you need to deal with it in some way. It could be that you crash, or you could display a window asking the user to supply a new filename. Either way, you have a fine level of control over what happens when an error does occur.

.NET provides a powerful exception handler that can "catch" exceptions when they occur and give your programs the opportunity to react and deal with the problem in some way. Chapter 9 talks about exception handling in more detail, but for now, think of exception handling as something provided by the Common Language Runtime to all applications.

The Common Type System and Common Language Specification

One of the most important aspects of .NET that Microsoft had to get right is interlanguage operation. Remember, Microsoft's motivation was to get any developer using any language using .NET, and for this to happen, all languages had to be treated equally. Likewise, applications created in one language have to be understood by other languages. For example, if you create a class in Visual Basic 2005, a C# developer should be able to use and extend that class. Alternatively, you may need to define a string in C#, pass that string to an object built in Visual Basic 2005, and make that object understand and manipulate the string successfully.

The Common Type System (CTS) allows software written in different languages to work together. Before .NET, Visual Basic and C++ handled strings in completely differently ways, and you had to go through a conversion process each time you went from one to the other. With the Common Type System in place, Visual Basic 2005, C#, and other .NET languages use strings, integers, and so on, in the same way, and therefore no conversion needs to take place.

In addition, the Common Language Specification (CLS) was introduced by Microsoft to make it easier for language developers to adapt their languages to make them compatible with .NET.

> *The Common Type System and Common Language Specification are the foundation for this interoperation, but detailed discussion is, unfortunately, beyond the scope of this book.*

When talking to other .NET developers, it is likely that you will hear the term *managed code*. This simply describes code that runs inside the Common Language Runtime. In other words, you get all of the advantages of the Common Language Runtime, such as the memory management and all of the language interoperability features previously mentioned.

Code written in Visual Basic 2005, C#, and J# is automatically created as managed code. C++ code is not automatically created as managed code, because C++ does not fit well into the memory management scheme implemented by the Common Language Runtime. You can, if you are interested, turn on an option to create managed code from within C++, in which case you use the term *managed C++*.

Hand-in-hand with managed code is *managed data*. As you can probably guess, this is data managed by the Common Language Runtime, although in nearly all cases this data actually consists of objects. Objects managed by the Common Language Runtime can easily be passed between languages.

Summary

This chapter introduced the Microsoft .NET Framework and why Microsoft had to choose to radically change the way programs were written for Windows. You also saw that part of Microsoft's motivation for this was to move the dependence of developers from the execution platform (Windows, Linux, whatever) over to a new programming platform that it would always own.

After learning about why Microsoft developed .NET, you saw how writing for it is not much different from writing for Windows. You still have a layer that you program against; it is just that now, rather than being flat like the Win32 API, it is a rich set of classes that allows you to write true object-oriented programs. This chapter also discussed how these classes could be ported to other platforms and how our applications could transfer across.

Finally, you looked at some of the more technical aspects of the .NET Framework, specifically the Common Language Runtime.

To summarize, you should now understand:

- ❑ Microsoft's new business venture
- ❑ The goals of the .NET Framework
- ❑ The abstractions that the .NET Framework provides
- ❑ An introduction to the core of the .NET Framework

Writing Software

Now that you have gotten Visual Basic 2005 up and running and even written a simple but working program, you're going to look at the fundamentals behind the process of writing software and start putting together some exciting programs of your own.

In this chapter, you will:

❑ Learn about algorithms

❑ Learn to use variables

❑ Explore different data types including integers, floating-point numbers, strings, and dates

❑ Study scope

❑ Learn about debugging applications

❑ Learn more about how computers store data in memory

Information and Data

Information describes facts and can be presented or found in any format, whether that format is optimized for humans or for computers. For example, if you send four people out to different intersections to survey traffic, at the end of the process you will end up with four handwritten tallies of the number of cars that went past (say, a tally for each hour).

The term *data* is used to describe information that has been collated, ordered, and formatted in such a way that it can be directly used by a piece of computer software. The information you have (several notebooks full of handwritten scribbles) cannot be directly used by a piece of software. Rather, someone has to work with it to convert it into data. For example, the scribbles can be transferred to an Excel spreadsheet that can be directly used by a piece of software designed to analyze the results.

Chapter 3

Algorithms

The computer industry is commonly regarded as one that changes at an incredible speed. Most professionals find themselves constantly retraining and re-educating to keep their skills sharp and up to date. However, some aspects of computing haven't really changed since they were first invented and perhaps won't change within our lifetimes. The process and discipline of software development is a good example of an aspect of computer technology whose essential nature hasn't changed since the beginning.

For software to work, you need to have some data to work with. The software then takes this data and manipulates it into another form. For example, software may take your customer database stored as ones and zeros on your computer's disk and make it available for you to read on your computer's monitor. The on-board computer in your car constantly examines environmental and performance information and continually adjusts the fuel mix to make the car run more efficiently. Your telephone service provider records the calls you make and generates bills based on this information.

The base underpinning all software is the *algorithm*. Before you can write software to solve a problem, you have to break it down into a step-by-step description of how the problem is going to be solved. An algorithm is independent of the programming language, so, if you like, you can describe it to yourself either as a spoken language, with diagrams, or with whatever helps you visualize the problem.

Imagine that you work for a telephone company and need to produce bills based on calls that your customers make. Here's an algorithm that describes a possible solution:

1. On the first day of the month, you need to produce a bill for each customer you have.
2. For each customer, you have a list of calls that the customer has made in the previous month.
3. You know the duration of each call, and the time of day when the call was made. Based on this information, you can determine the cost of each call.
4. For each bill, you total up the cost of each call.
5. If a customer spends more than a preset limit, you give that customer a 10% discount.
6. You apply sales tax to each bill.
7. After you have the final bill, you need to print it.

Those seven points describe, fairly completely, an algorithm for a piece of software that generates bills for a telephone company. At the end of the day, it doesn't matter whether you build this solution in C++, Visual Basic 2005, C#, J#, Java, or whatever — the basic algorithms of the software never change. (However, it's important to realize that each of those seven parts of the algorithm may well be made up of smaller, more detailed algorithms.)

The good news for a newcomer to programming is that algorithms are usually easy to construct. There shouldn't be anything in the preceding algorithm that you don't understand. Algorithms always follow common-sense reasoning, although you may find yourself in a position in which you have to code algorithms that contain complex mathematical or scientific reasoning. It may not seem like common sense to you, but it will to someone else! The bad news is that the process of turning the algorithm into code can be arduous. As a programmer, learning how to construct algorithms is the most important skill you will ever obtain.

All good programmers respect the fact that the preferred language of the programmer is largely irrelevant. Different languages are good at doing different things. C++ gives the developer a lot of control over the way a program works; however, it's harder to write software in C++ than it is in Visual Basic 2005. Likewise, building the user interface for desktop applications is far easier to do in Visual Basic 2005 than it is in C++. (Some of these problems do go away when you use managed C++ with .NET, so this statement is less true today than it was years ago.) What you need to learn to do as a programmer is to adapt different languages to achieve solutions to a problem in the best possible way. Although when you begin programming you'll be "hooked" on one language, remember that different languages are focused toward developing different kinds of solutions. At some point, you may have to take your basic skills as an algorithm designer and coder to a new language.

What Is a Programming Language?

In one way, you can regard a programming language as anything capable of making a decision. Computers are very good at making decisions, but they have to be fairly basic, for example: "Is this number greater than three?" or "Is this car blue?"

If you have a complicated decision to make, the process of making that decision has to be broken down into simple parts that the computer can understand. You use algorithms to determine how to break down a complicated decision into simpler ones.

A good example of a problem that's hard for a computer to solve is recognizing peoples' faces. You can't just say to a computer, "Is this a picture of Dave?" Instead, you have to break the question down into a series of simpler questions that the computer can understand.

The decisions that you ask computers to make will have one of two possible answers: yes and no. These possibilities are also referred to as true and false and also as 1 and 0. In software terms, you cannot make a decision based on the question, "How much bigger is 10 compared to 4?" Instead, you have to make a decision based on the question, "Is 10 bigger than 4?" The difference is subtle, yet important — the first question does not yield an answer of yes or no, whereas the second question does. Of course, a computer is more than capable of answering the first question, but this is actually done through an operation; in other words, you have to actually subtract 4 from 10 to use the result in some other part of your algorithm.

You might be looking at the requirement for yes/no answers as a limitation, but it isn't really. Even in our everyday lives the decisions we make are of the same kind. Whenever you decide something, you accept (yes, true, 1) something and reject (no, false, 0) something else.

You are using Visual Basic 2005 for a language, but the important aspects of programming are largely language independent. Understanding that any software, no matter how flashy it is, or which language it is written in, is made up of *methods* (functions and subroutines: the lines of code that actually implement the algorithm) and *variables* (place holders for the data the methods manipulate) is key.

Variables

A variable is something that you store a value in as you work through your algorithm. You can then make a decision based on that value (for example, "Is it equal to 7?", "Is it more than 4?"), or you can perform operations on that value to change it into something else (for example, "Add 2 to the value", "Multiply it by 6", and so on).

Working with Variables

Before you get bogged down in code for a moment, look at another algorithm:

1. Create a variable called n and store in it the value 27.

2. Add 1 to the value of the variable called n and store that value in the variable called n.

3. Display the value of the variable called n to the user.

In this algorithm, you're creating a variable called n and storing in it the value 27. What this means is that there's a part of the computer's memory that is being used by the program to store the value 27. That piece of memory keeps storing that value until you change it or tell the program that you don't need it any more.

In the second step, you're performing an add operation. You're taking n and adding 1 to its value. After you've performed this operation, the piece of memory given over to storing n contains the value 28.

In the final point, you want to tell the user what the value of n is. So you read the current value from memory and write it out to the screen.

Again, there's nothing about the algorithm there that you can't understand. It's just common sense! However, the Visual Basic 2005 code looks a little more cryptic. In the following Try It Out, you learn more about working with variables first hand.

Try It Out   **Working with Variables**

1. Create a new project in Visual Studio 2005 by selecting File ➪ New ➪ Project from the menu bar. In the New Project dialog box, select Windows Application from the right-hand pane and enter the project name as **Variables** and click OK. (See Figure 3-1.)

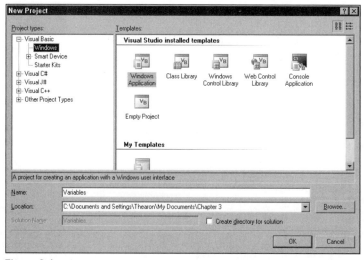

Figure 3-1

2. Make Form1 a little smaller and add a Button control from the Toolbox to it. Set the button's Text property to **Add 1 to intNumber** and its Name property to **btnAdd**. Your form should look like Figure 3-2.

Figure 3-2

3. Double-click the button to open the `btnAdd_Click` event handler. Add the following high-lighted code to it:

```
Private Sub btnAdd_Click(ByVal sender As System.Object, _
    ByVal e As System.EventArgs) Handles btnAdd.Click

    Dim intNumber As Integer
    intNumber = 27
    intNumber = intNumber + 1
    MessageBox.Show("Value of intNumber + 1 = " & intNumber, "Variables")
End Sub
```

4. Run the project, click the Add 1 to intNumber button, and you'll see a message box like the one in Figure 3-3.

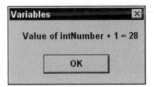

Figure 3-3

How It Works

The program starts at the top and works its way down, one line at a time, to the bottom. The first line defines a new variable, called `intNumber`:

```
Dim intNumber As Integer
```

`Dim` is a keyword. As stated in Chapter 1, a keyword has a special meaning in Visual Basic 2005 and is used for things such as commands. `Dim` tells Visual Basic 2005 that what follows is a variable definition.

Its curious name harks back to the original versions of the BASIC language. BASIC has always needed to know how much space to reserve for an array (discussed in Chapter 5), so it had a command to tell it the "dimensions" of the array — Dim for short. Visual Basic extends that command to all other kinds of variables as well to mean "make some space for" in general.

The variable name comes next and is `intNumber`. Notice that the variable name uses the Modified Hungarian notation discussed in Chapter 1. In this case the prefix `int` is short for Integer, which represents the data type for this variable, as described in the following paragraph. Then a name was chosen for this variable; in this case the name is `Number`. Whenever you see this variable throughout your code, you know that this variable will represent a number that is of the Integer data type.

`As Integer` tells Visual Basic 2005 what kind of value you want to store in the variable. This is known as the *data type*. For now, all you need to know is that this is used to tell Visual Basic 2005 that you expect to store an integer (whole number) value in the variable.

The next line sets the value of `intNumber`:

```
intNumber = 27
```

In other words, it stores the value `27` in the variable `intNumber`.

The next statement simply adds `1` to the variable `intNumber`:

```
intNumber = intNumber + 1
```

What this line actually means is "Keep the current value of `intNumber` and add `1` to it."

The final line displays a message box dialog box with the text `Value of intNumber + 1 =` and the current value of `intNumber`. You've also set the title of the message box dialog box to `Variables` to match the project name:

```
MessageBox.Show("Value of intNumber + 1 = " & intNumber, "Variables")
```

Comments and Whitespace

When writing software code, you must be constantly aware that you or someone else may have to change that code in the future. Therefore, you should try to make it as easy to understand as possible.

Comments

Comments are parts of a program that are ignored by the Visual Basic 2005 compiler, which means you can write whatever you like in them, be it English, C#, Perl, FORTRAN, Chinese, whatever. What they're supposed to do is help the human developer reading the code understand what each part of the code is supposed to be doing.

> All languages support comments, not just Visual Basic 2005. If you're looking at C# code, for example, you'll find that comments start with a double forward slash (//).

What's a good way of knowing when you need a comment? Well, it's different for different situations, but a good rule of thumb is to think about the algorithm. The program in the previous Try It Out had this algorithm:

1. Define a value for `intNumber`.

2. Add `1` to the value of `intNumber`.

3. Display the new value of `intNumber` to the user.

You can add comments to the code from that example to match the steps in the algorithm:

```
'Define a variable for intNumber
Dim intNumber As Integer
'Set the initial value
intNumber = 27
'Add 1 to the value of intNumber
intNumber = intNumber + 1
'Display the new value of intNumber
MessageBox.Show("Value of intNumber + 1 = " & intNumber, "Variables")
```

In Visual Basic 2005, you begin your comments with an apostrophe ('). Anything on the same line following that apostrophe is your comment. You can also add comments onto a line that already has code, like this:

```
intNumber = intNumber + 1 'Add 1 to the value of intNumber
```

This works just as well, because only comments (not code) follow the apostrophe. Notice that the comments in the preceding code, more or less, match the algorithm. A good technique for adding comments is to write a few words explaining the stage of the algorithm that's being expressed as software code.

You can also use the built-in XML Document Comment feature of Visual Studio 2005 to create comment blocks for your methods. To use this feature, place your cursor on the blank line preceding your method definition and type three consecutive apostrophes. The comment block will automatically be inserted as shown in the highlighted code here.

```
''' <summary>
'''
''' </summary>
''' <param name="sender"></param>
''' <param name="e"></param>
''' <remarks></remarks>
Private Sub btnAdd_Click(ByVal sender As System.Object, _
    ByVal e As System.EventArgs) Handles btnAdd.Click
```

What's really cool about this feature is that Visual Studio 2005 will automatically fill in the name values of the parameters in the comment block based on the parameters defined in your method. If your method does not have any parameters, the `<param>` element will not be inserted into the comment block.

Once a comment block has been inserted, you can provide a summary of what the method does and any special remarks that may need to be noted before this method is called or any other special requirements of the method. If the method returns a value, then a `<returns>` element will also be inserted, and you can insert the return value and description.

Comments are primarily used to make the code easier to understand, either to a new developer who's never seen your code before or to you when you haven't reviewed your code for a while. The purpose of a comment is to point out something that might not be immediately obvious or to summarize code to enable the developer to understand what's going on without having to ponder each and every line.

You'll find that programmers have their own guidelines about how to write comments. If you work for a larger software company, or your manager/mentor is hot on coding standards, they'll dictate which formats your comments should take and where you should and should not add comments to the code.

White Space

Another important aspect of writing readable code is to leave lots of *white space*. White space (space on the screen or page not occupied by characters) makes code easier to read, just as spaces do in English. In the last example, there is a blank line before each comment. This implies to anyone reading the code that each block is a unit of work, which it is.

You'll be coming back to the idea of white space in the next chapter when we discuss controlling the flow through your programs using special code blocks, but you'll find that the use of whitespace varies between developers. For now, remember not to be afraid to space out your code — it'll greatly improve the readability of your programs, especially as you write long chunks of code.

> *The compiler ignores white space and comments, so there are no performance differences between code with lots of white space and comments and code with none.*

Data Types

When you use variables, it's a good idea to know ahead of time the things that you want to store in them. So far in this chapter, you've seen a variable that holds an integer number.

When you define a variable, you must tell Visual Basic 2005 the type of data that should be stored in it. As you might have guessed, this is known as the *data type*, and all meaningful programming languages have a vast array of different data types to choose from. The data type of a variable has a great impact on how the computer will run your code. In this section, you'll take a deeper look at how variables work and how their types affect the performance of your program.

Working with Numbers

When you work with numbers in Visual Basic 2005, you'll be working with two kinds of numbers: *integers* and *floating-point numbers*. Both have very specific uses. Integers are usually not much use for calculations of quantities, for example, calculating how much money you have left on your mortgage or calculating how long it would take to fill a swimming pool with water. For these kinds of calculations, you're more likely to use floating-point variables because they can be used to represent numbers with fractional parts, whereas integer variables can hold only whole numbers.

On the other hand, oddly, you'll find that in your day-to-day activities you're far more likely to use integer variables than floating-point variables. Most of the software that you write will use numbers to keep track of what is going on by counting, rather than to calculate quantities.

For example, suppose you are writing a program that displays customer details on the screen. Let's also suppose you have 100 customers in your database. When the program starts, you'll display the first customer on the screen. You also need to keep track of which customer is being displayed, so that when the user says, "Next, please," you'll actually know which one is next.

Because a computer is more comfortable working with numbers than with anything else, you'll usually find that each customer has been given a unique number. This unique number will, in virtually all cases, be an integer. What this means is that each of your customers will have a unique integer number between 1 and 100 assigned to them. In your program, you'll also have a variable that stores the ID of the customer that you're currently looking at. When the user asks to see the next customer, you add one to that ID ("increment by one") and display the new customer.

You'll see how this kind of thing works as you move on to more advanced topics, but for now, rest assured that you're more likely to use integers than floating-point numbers. Take a look now at some common operations.

Common Integer Math Operations

In this section, you create a new project for your math operations.

Try It Out   Common Integer Math

1. Create a new project in Visual Studio 2005 by selecting File ➪ New ➪ Project from the menu. In the New Project dialog box, select Windows Application from the right pane (refer to Figure 3-1), and enter the project name as **IntegerMath** and click OK.

2. Using the Toolbox, add a new Button control to Form1 as before. Set its Name property to **btnIntMath** and its Text property to **Math Test**. Double-click it and add the following highlighted code to the new Click event handler that will be created:

```
Private Sub btnIntMath_Click(ByVal sender As System.Object, _
    ByVal e As System.EventArgs) Handles btnIntMath.Click
```

```
        'Declare variable
        Dim intNumber As Integer

        'Set number, add numbers, and display results
        intNumber = 16
        intNumber = intNumber + 8
        MessageBox.Show("Addition test... " & intNumber, "Integer Math")

        'Set number, subtract numbers, and display results
        intNumber = 24
        intNumber = intNumber - 2
        MessageBox.Show("Subtraction test... " & intNumber, "Integer Math")

        'Set number, multiply numbers, and display results
        intNumber = 6
        intNumber = intNumber * 10
        MessageBox.Show("Multiplication test... " & intNumber, "Integer Math")

        'Set number, divide numbers, and display results
```

```
        intNumber = 12
        intNumber = intNumber / 6
        MessageBox.Show("Division test... " & intNumber, "Integer Math")
    End Sub
```

3. Run the project and click the Math Test button. You'll be able to click through four message box dialog boxes, as shown in Figure 3-4.

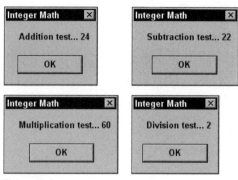

Figure 3-4

How It Works

Hopefully, none of the code you've seen should be too baffling. You've already seen the addition operator before. Here it is again:

```
'Set number, add numbers, and display results
intNumber = 16
intNumber = intNumber + 8
MessageBox.Show("Addition test... " & intNumber, "Integer Math")
```

So, all you're saying is this:

1. Let intNumber be equal to the value 16.

2. Then, let intNumber be equal to the current value of intNumber (which is 16) plus 8.

As you can see from the message dialog box shown in Figure 3-4, you get a result of 24, which is correct.

The subtraction operator is a minus (–) sign. Here it is in action:

```
'Set number, subtract numbers, and display results
intNumber = 24
intNumber = intNumber - 2
MessageBox.Show("Subtraction test... " & intNumber, "Integer Math")
```

Again, same deal as before:

1. Let intNumber be equal to the value 24.

2.   Let `intNumber` be equal to the current value of `intNumber` (which is 24) minus 2.

The multiplication operator is an asterisk (*). Here it is in action:

```
'Set number, multiply numbers, and display results
intNumber = 6
intNumber = intNumber * 10
MessageBox.Show("Multiplication test... " & intNumber, "Integer Math")
```

Here your algorithm states:

1.   Let `intNumber` be equal to the value 6.

2.   Let `intNumber` be equal to the current value of `intNumber` (which is 6) times 10.

Finally, the division operator is a forward slash (/). Here it is in action:

```
'Set number, divide numbers, and display results
intNumber = 12
intNumber = intNumber / 6
MessageBox.Show("Division test... " & intNumber, "Integer Math")
```

Again, all you're saying is:

1.   Let `intNumber` be equal to the value 12.

2.   Let `intNumber` be equal to the current value of `intNumber` (which is 12) divided by 6.

Integer Math Shorthand

In the next Try It Out, you'll see how can perform the same operations without having to write as much code by using *shorthand operators* (assignment operators). Although they look a little less logical than their more verbose counterparts, you'll soon learn to love them.

Try It Out   Using Shorthand Operators

1.   Go back to Visual Studio 2005 and open the code for `Form1.vb` again. Change the highlighted lines:

```
Private Sub btnIntMath_Click(ByVal sender As System.Object, _
    ByVal e As System.EventArgs) Handles btnIntMath.Click

    'Declare variable
    Dim intNumber As Integer

    'Set number, add numbers, and display results
    intNumber = 16
    intNumber += 8
    MessageBox.Show("Addition test... " & intNumber, "Integer Math")

    'Set number, subtract numbers, and display results
    intNumber = 24
    intNumber -= 2
    MessageBox.Show("Subtraction test... " & intNumber, "Integer Math")
```

```
        'Set number, multiply numbers, and display results
        intNumber = 6
        intNumber *= 10
        MessageBox.Show("Multiplication test... " & intNumber, "Integer Math")

        'Set number, divide numbers, and display results
        intNumber = 12
        intNumber /= 6
        MessageBox.Show("Division test... " & intNumber, "Integer Math")
    End Sub
```

2. Run the project and click the Math Test button. You'll get the same results as in the previous Try It Out.

How It Works

To use the shorthand version you just drop the last `intNumber` variable and move the operator to the left of the equals sign. Here is the old version:

```
intNumber = intNumber + 8
```

. . . and here's the new version:

```
intNumber += 8
```

The Problem with Integer Math

The main problem with integer math is that you can't do anything that involves a number with a fractional part. For example, you can't do this:

```
        'Try multiplying numbers...
        intNumber = 6
        intNumber = intNumber * 10.23
```

Or, rather, you can actually run that code, but you won't get the result you were expecting. Because `intNumber` has been defined as a variable designed to accept an integer only; the result is rounded up or down to the nearest integer. In this case, although the actual answer is 61.38, `intNumber` will be set to the value 61. If the answer were 61.73, `intNumber` would be set to 62.

A similar problem occurs with division. Here's another piece of code:

```
        'Try dividing numbers...
        intNumber = 12
        intNumber = intNumber / 7
```

This time the answer is 1.71. However, because the result has to be rounded up in order for it to be stored in `intNumber`, you end up with `intNumber` being set equal to 2. As you can imagine, if you were trying to write programs that actually calculated some form of value, you'd be in big trouble, as every step in the calculation would be subject to rounding errors.

In the next section, you'll look at how you can do these kinds of operations with floating-point numbers.

Floating-Point Math

So, you know that integers are not good for most mathematical calculations because most calculations of these types involve a fractional component of some quantity. Later in this chapter, you'll see how to use floating-point numbers to calculate the area of a circle, but in the next Try It Out, We'll just introduce the concepts.

Try It Out   Floating Point Math

1. Create a new Windows Application project in Visual Studio 2005 called **Floating-Pt Math**. As before, place a button on the form, setting its name to **btnFloatMath** and its Text to **Double Test**.

2. Double-click btnFloatMath and add the following highlighted code:

```
Private Sub btnFloatMath_Click(ByVal sender As System.Object, _
    ByVal e As System.EventArgs) Handles btnFloatMath.Click

    'Declare variable
    Dim dblNumber As Double

    'Set number, multiply numbers, and display results
    dblNumber = 45.34
    dblNumber *= 4.333
    MessageBox.Show("Multiplication test... " & dblNumber, "Floating Points")

    'Set number, divide numbers, and display results
    dblNumber = 12
    dblNumber /= 7
    MessageBox.Show("Division test... " & dblNumber, "Floating Points")
End Sub
```

3. Run the project and you'll see the results shown in Figure 3-5.

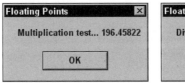
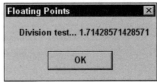

Figure 3-5

How It Works

Perhaps the most important change in this code is the way you're defining your variable:

```
'Declare variable
Dim dblNumber As Double
```

Rather than saying As Integer at the end, you're saying As Double. This tells Visual Basic 2005 that you want to create a variable that holds a double-precision floating-point number, rather than an integer number. This means that any operation performed on dblNumber will be a floating-point operation, rather than an integer operation. Also notice that you have used a different Modified Hungarian notation prefix to signify that this variable contains a number that is of the Double data type.

However, there's no difference in the way either of these operations is performed. Here, you set dblNumber to be a decimal number and then multiply it by another decimal number:

```
'Set number, multiply numbers, and display results
dblNumber = 45.34
dblNumber *= 4.333
MessageBox.Show("Multiplication test... " & dblNumber, "Floating Points")
```

When you run this, you get a result of 196.45822, which, as you can see, has a decimal component, and therefore you can use this in calculations.

Of course, floating-point numbers don't have to have an explicit decimal component:

```
'Set number, divide numbers, and display results
dblNumber = 12
dblNumber /= 7
MessageBox.Show("Division test... " & dblNumber, "Floating Points")
```

This result still yields a floating-point result, because dblNumber has been set up to hold such a result. You can see this by your result of 1.71428571428571, which is the same result you were looking for when you were examining integer math.

A floating-point number gets its name because it is stored like a number written in scientific notation on paper. In scientific notation, the number is given as a power of ten and a number between 1 and 10 that is multiplied by that power of ten to get the original number. For example, 10,001 is written $1.0001 \_ 10^4$, and 0.0010001 is written $1.0001 \_ 10^{-3}$. The decimal point "floats" to the position after the first digit in both cases. The advantage is that large numbers and small numbers are represented with the same degree of precision (in this example, one part in 10,000). A floating-point variable is stored in the same way inside the computer, but in base two instead of base ten (see "Storing Variables," later in this section).

Other States

Floating-point variables can hold a few other values besides decimal numbers. Specifically, these are:

❑   NaN — which means "not a number"

❑   Positive infinity

❑   Negative infinity

We won't show how to get all of the results here, but the mathematicians among you will recognize that .NET will cater to their advanced math needs.

Single-Precision Floating-Point Numbers

We've been saying "double-precision floating-point." In .NET, there are two main ways to represent floating-point numbers, depending on your needs. In certain cases the decimal fractional components of numbers can zoom off to infinity (pi being a particularly obvious example), but the computer does not have an infinite amount of space to hold digits, so there has to be some limit at which the computer stops keeping track of the digits to the right of the decimal point. The limit is related to the size of the variable, which is a subject discussed in much more detail toward the end of this chapter. There are also limits on how large the component to the left of the decimal point can be.

A double-precision floating-point number can hold any value between -1.7 (10^{308} and $+1.7$ (10^{308} to a great level of accuracy (one penny in 45 trillion dollars). A single-precision floating-point number can only hold between -3.4 (10^{38} and $+3.4$ (10^{38}. Again, this is still a pretty huge number, but it holds decimal components to a lesser degree of accuracy (one penny in only \$330,000)—the benefit being that single-precision floating-point numbers require less memory and calculations involving them are faster on some computers.

You should avoid using double-precision numbers unless you actually require more accuracy than the single-precision type allows. This is especially important in very large applications, where using double-precision numbers for variables that only require single-precision numbers could slow up your program significantly.

The calculations you're trying to perform will dictate which type of floating-point number you should use. If you want to use a single-precision number, use `As Single` rather than `As Double`, like this:

```
Dim sngNumber As Single
```

Working with Strings

A *string* is a sequence of characters, and you use double quotes to mark its beginning and end. You've seen how to use strings to display the results of simple programs on the screen. Strings are commonly used for exactly this function—telling the user what happened and what needs to happen next. Another common use is storing a piece of text for later use in an algorithm. You'll see lots of strings throughout the rest of the book. So far, you've used strings like this:

```
MessageBox.Show("Multiplication test... " & dblNumber, "Floating Points")
```

`"Multiplication test..."` and `"Floating Points"` are strings; you can tell because of the double quotes (`"`). However, what about `dblNumber`? The value contained within `dblNumber` is being converted to a string value that can be displayed on the screen. (This is a pretty advanced topic that's covered later in the chapter, but for now, concentrate on the fact that a conversion is taking place.) For example, if `dblNumber` represents the value `27`, to display it on the screen it has to be converted into a string two characters in length. In the next Try It Out, you look at some of the things you can do with strings.

Try It Out **Using Strings**

1. Create a new Windows application using the File ⇨ New ⇨ Project menu option. Call it **Strings**.

2. Using the Toolbox, draw a button with the Name property **btnStrings** on the form and set its Text property to **Using Strings**. Double-click it and then add the highlighted code:

```
Private Sub btnStrings_Click(ByVal sender As System.Object, _
    ByVal e As System.EventArgs) Handles btnStrings.Click
```

```
        'Declare variable
        Dim strData As String

        'Set the string value
        strData = "Hello, world!"

        'Display the results
        MessageBox.Show(strData, "Strings")
    End Sub
```

3. Run the project and click the Using Strings button. You'll see a message like the one in Figure 3-6.

Figure 3-6

How It Works

You can define a variable that holds a string using a similar notation to that used with the number variables, but this time using As String:

```
        'Declare variable
        Dim strData As String
```

You can also set that string to have a value, again as before:

```
        'Set the string value
        strData = "Hello, world!"
```

You need to use double quotes around the string value to *delimit* the string, meaning to mark where the string begins and where the string ends. This is an important point, because these double quotes tell the Visual Basic 2005 compiler not to try to compile the text that is contained within the string. If you don't include the quotes, Visual Basic 2005 treats the value stored in the variable as part of the program's code, tries to compile it, and can't, causing the whole program to fail to compile.

With the value Hello, world! stored in a string variable called strData, you can pass that variable to the message box whose job it is to then extract the value from the variable and display it. So, you can see that strings can be defined and used in the same way as the numeric values you saw before. Now look at how to perform operations on strings.

Concatenation

Concatenation means linking something together in a chain or series. If you have two strings that you join together, one after the other, you say they are concatenated. You can think of concatenation as addition for strings. In the next Try It Out, you work with concatenation.

Try It Out   Concatenation

1. View the Designer for `Form1` and add a new button. Set its Name property to **btnConcatenation** and its Text property to **Concatenation**. Double-click the button and add the following high-lighted code:

```
Private Sub btnConcatenation_Click(ByVal sender As System.Object, _
    ByVal e As System.EventArgs) Handles btnConcatenation.Click

        'Declare variables
        Dim strOne As String
        Dim strTwo As String
        Dim strResults As String

        'Set the string values
        strOne = "Hello"
        strTwo = ", world!"

        'Concatenate the strings
        strResults = strOne & strTwo

        'Display the results
        MessageBox.Show(strResults, "Strings")
End Sub
```

2. Run the project and click the Concatenation button. You'll see the same results that were shown in Figure 3-6.

How It Works

In this Try It Out, you start by declaring three variables that are String data types:

```
        'Declare variables
        Dim strOne As String
        Dim strTwo As String
        Dim strResults As String
```

Then you set the values of the first two strings.

```
        'Set the string values
        strOne = "Hello"
        strTwo = ", world!"
```

After you've set the values of the first two strings, you use the & operator to concatenate the two previous strings, setting the results of the concatenation in a new string variable called `strResults`:

```
        'Concatenate the strings
        strResults = strOne & strTwo
```

What you're saying here is "let `strResults` be equal to the current value of `strOne` followed by the current value of `strTwo`". By the time you call `MessageBox.Show`, `strResults` will be equal to `"Hello, world!"`, so you get the same value as before.

```
'Display the results
MessageBox.Show(strResults, "Strings")
```

Using the Concatenation Operator Inline

You don't have to define variables to use the concatenation operator. You can use it on the fly, as demonstrated in the next *Try It Out*.

Try It Out   Using Inline Concatenation

1. View the Designer for Form1 once again and add a new button. Set its Name property to **btnInlineConcatenation** and set its Text property to **Inline Concatenation**. Double-click the button and add the following highlighted code:

```
Private Sub btnInlineConcatenation_Click( _
    ByVal sender As System.Object, ByVal e As System.EventArgs) _
    Handles btnInlineConcatenation.Click

        'Declare variable
        Dim intNumber As Integer

        'Set the value
        intNumber = 26

        'Display the results
        MessageBox.Show("The value of intNumber is: " & intNumber, "Strings")
End Sub
```

2. Run the code and click the Inline Concatenation button. You'll see the results as shown in Figure 3-7.

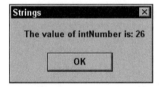

Figure 3-7

How It Works

You've already seen the concatenation operator being used like this in previous examples. What this is actually doing is converting the value stored in intNumber to a string so that it can be displayed on the screen. Look at this code:

```
'Display the results
MessageBox.Show("The value of intNumber is: " & intNumber, "Strings")
```

The portion that reads, "The value of intNumber is:" is actually a string, but you don't have to define it as a string variable. Visual Basic 2005 calls this a *string literal*, meaning that it's exactly as shown in the code and doesn't change. When you use the concatenation operator on this string together with `int Number`, `intNumber` is converted into a string and tacked onto the end of `"The value of intNumber is:"`. The result is one string, passed to `MessageBox.Show`, that contains both the base text and the current value of `intNumber`.

More String Operations

You can do plenty more with strings! Take a look at some of them in the next Try It Out. The first thing you'll do is look at a property of the string that can be used to return its length.

Try It Out   **Returning the Length of a String**

1. Using the Designer for Form1, add a TextBox control to the form and set its Name property to **txtString**. Add another Button control and set its Name property to **btnLength** and its Text property to **Length**. Rearrange the controls so that they look like Figure 3-8.

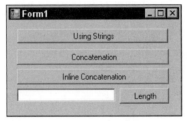

Figure 3-8

2. Double-click the Length button to open its Click event handler. Add the following highlighted code:

```
Private Sub btnLength_Click(ByVal sender As System.Object, _
    ByVal e As System.EventArgs) Handles btnLength.Click

        'Declare variable
        Dim strData As String

        'Get the text from the TextBox
        strData = txtString.Text

        'Display the length of the string
        MessageBox.Show(strData.Length & " character(s)", "Strings")
End Sub
```

3. Run the project and enter some text into the text box.

4. Click the Length button and you'll see results similar to those shown in Figure 3-9.

Figure 3-9

How It Works

The first thing that you do is declare a variable to contain string data. Then you extract the text from the text box and store it in your string variable called `strData`:

```
'Declare variable
Dim strData As String

'Get the text from the TextBox
strData = txtString.Text
```

Once you have the string, you can use the `Length` property to get an integer value that represents the number of characters in it. Remember, as far as a computer is concerned, characters include things like spaces and other punctuation marks:

```
'Display the length of the string
MessageBox.Show(strData.Length & " character(s)", "Strings")
```

Substrings

Common ways to manipulate strings in a program include using a set of characters that appears at the start, a set that appears at the end, or a set that appears somewhere in between. These are known as *substrings*.

In this Try It Out, you build on your previous application and get it to display the first three, middle three, and last three characters.

Try It Out   Working with Substrings

1. If the Strings program is running, close it.

2. Add another Button control to Form1 and set its Name property to **btnSplit** and its Text property to **Split**. Double-click the button and add code as highlighted here:

```
Private Sub btnSplit_Click(ByVal sender As System.Object, _
    ByVal e As System.EventArgs) Handles btnSplit.Click

    'Declare variable
    Dim strData As String

    'Get the text from the TextBox
    strData = txtString.Text

    'Display the first three characters
```

```
            MessageBox.Show(strData.Substring(0, 3), "Strings")

            'Display the middle three characters
            MessageBox.Show(strData.Substring(3, 3), "Strings")

            'Display the last three characters
            MessageBox.Show(strData.Substring(strData.Length - 3), "Strings")
    End Sub
```

3. Run the project. Enter the word **Cranberry** in the text box.

4. Click the Split button and you'll see three message boxes one after another as shown in Figure 3-10.

Figure 3-10

How It Works

The `Substring` method lets you grab a set of characters from any position in the string. The method can be used in one of two ways. The first way is to give it a starting point and a number of characters to grab. In the first instance, you're telling it to start at character position 0 — the beginning of the string — and grab three characters:

```
            'Display the first three characters
            MessageBox.Show(strData.Substring(0, 3), "Strings")
```

In the next instance, you to start three characters in from the start and grab three characters:

```
            'Display the middle three characters
            MessageBox.Show(strData.Substring(3, 3), "Strings")
```

In the final instance, you're providing only one parameter. This tells the `Substring` method to start at the given position and grab everything right up to the end. In this case, you're using the `Substring` method in combination with the `Length` method, so you're saying, "Grab everything from three characters in from the right of the string to the end."

```
            'Display the last three characters
            MessageBox.Show(strData.Substring(strData.Length - 3), "Strings")
```

Formatting Strings

Often when working with numbers, you'll need to alter the way they are displayed as a string. Figure 3-5 showed how a division operator works. In this case, you don't really need to see 14 decimal places — two or three would be fine! What you need to do is format the string so that you see everything to the left of the decimal point, but only three digits to the right, which is what you do in the next Try It Out.

| Try It Out | Formatting Strings |

1. Open the Floating-Pt Math project that you created previously in this chapter.

2. Open the Code Editor for `Form1` and make the following changes:

```
'Set number, divide numbers, and display results
dblNumber = 12
dblNumber /= 7

'Display the results without formatting
MessageBox.Show("Without formatting: " & dblNumber, "Floating Points")

'Display the results with formatting
MessageBox.Show("With formatting: " & String.Format("{0:n3}", dblNumber), _
    "Floating Points")
End Sub
```

3. Run the project. After the message box dialog box for the multiplication test is displayed, the next message box dialog box will display a result of `1.71428571428571`.

4. When you click OK, the next message box will display a result of `1.714`.

How It Works

The magic here is in the call to `String.Format`. This powerful method allows the formatting of numbers. The key is all in the first parameter, as this defines the format the final string will take:

```
MessageBox.Show("With formatting: " & String.Format("{0:n3}", dblNumber), _
    "Floating Points")
```

You passed `String.Format` two parameters. The first parameter, `"{0:n3}"`, is the format that you want. The second parameter, `dblNumber`, is the value that you want to format.

The `0` in the format tells `String.Format` to work with the zeroth data parameter, which is just a cute way of saying "the second parameter", or `dblNumber`. What follows the colon is how you want `dblNumber` to be formatted. You said n3, which means "floating-point number, three decimal places." You could have said n2 for "floating-point number, two decimal places."

Localized Formatting

When building .NET applications, it's important to realize that the user may be familiar with cultural conventions that are uncommon to you. For example, if you live in the United States, you're used to seeing the decimal separator as a period (.). However, if you live in France, the decimal separator is actually a comma (,).

Windows can deal with such problems for you based on the locale settings of the computer. If you use the .NET Framework in the correct way, by and large you'll never need to worry about this problem.

Here's an example — if you use a formatting string of n3 again, you are telling .NET that you want to format the number with thousands separators and also that you want the number displayed to three decimal places (1,714.286).

The equation changed from 12 / 7 to 12000 / 7 to allow the display of the thousands separator (,).

Now, if you tell your computer that you want to use the French locale settings, and you run the *same code* (you make no changes whatsoever to the application itself), you'll see 1 714,286.

You can change your language options by going to the Control Panel and clicking the Regional and Language Options icon and changing the language to French.

In France, the thousands separator is a space, not a comma, while the decimal separator is a comma, not a period. By using String.Format appropriately, you can write one application that works properly regardless of how the user has configured the locale settings on the computer.

Replacing Substrings

Another common string manipulation replaces occurrences of one string with another. To demonstrate this, in the next Try It Out you'll modify your Strings application to replaces the string "Hello" with the string "Goodbye".

Try It Out   Replacing Substrings

1.   Open the Strings program you were working with before.

2.   In Form1, add another Button control and set its Name property to **btnReplace** and set its Text property to **Replace.** Double-click the button and add the following highlighted code to its Click event handler:

```
Private Sub btnReplace_Click(ByVal sender As System.Object, _
    ByVal e As System.EventArgs) Handles btnReplace.Click

        'Declare variables
        Dim strData As String
        Dim strNewData As String

        'Get the text from the TextBox
        strData = txtString.Text

        'Replace the string occurance
        strNewData = strData.Replace("Hello", "Goodbye")

        'Display the new string
        MessageBox.Show(strNewData, "Strings")
    End Sub
```

3.   Run the project and enter **Hello world!** into the text box in this exact case.

4.   Click the Replace button. You should see a message box that says Goodbye world!

How It Works

`Replace` works by taking the substring to look for as the first parameter and the new substring to replace it with as the second parameter. After the replacement is made, a new string is returned that you can display in the usual way.

```
'Replace the string occurance
strNewData = strData.Replace("Hello", "Goodbye")
```

You're not limited to a single search and replace within this code. If you enter **Hello** twice into the text box and click the button, you'll notice two `Goodbyes`. However, the case is important — if you enter **hello**, it will not be replaced.

Using Dates

Another really common data type that you'll often use is `Date`. This data type holds, not surprisingly, a date value. You will learn to display the current date in the next Try It Out.

Try It Out   **Displaying the Current Date**

1. Create a new Windows Application project called **Date Demo**.

2. In the usual way, use the Toolbox to draw a new button control on the form. Call it **btnDate** and set its Text property to **Show Date**.

3. Double-click the button to bring up its Click event handler and add this code:

```
Private Sub btnDate_Click(ByVal sender As System.Object, _
    ByVal e As System.EventArgs) Handles btnDate.Click

        'Declare variable
        Dim dteData As Date

        'Get the current date and time
        dteData = Now

        'Display the results
        MessageBox.Show(dteData, "Date Demo")
    End Sub
```

4. Run the project and click the button. You should see something like Figure 3-11 depending on the locale settings on your machine.

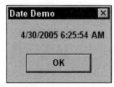

Figure 3-11

How It Works

The `Date` data type can be used to hold a value that represents any date and time. After creating the variable, you initialized it to the current date and time using `Now`:

```
'Declare variable
Dim dteData As Date

'Get the current date and time
dteData = Now
```

Date data types aren't any different from other data types, although you can do more with them. In the next couple of sections, you'll see ways to manipulate dates and control how they are displayed on the screen.

Formatting Date Strings

You've already seen one way in which dates can be formatted. By default, if you pass a `Date` variable to `MessageBox.Show`, the date and time are displayed as shown in Figure 3-11.

Because this machine is in the United States, the date is shown in m/d/yyyy format and the time is shown using the 12-hour clock. This is another example of how the computer's locale setting affects the formatting of different data types. For example, if you set your computer to the United Kingdom locale, the date is in dd/mm/yyyy format and the time is displayed using the 24-hour clock, for example, 07/08/2004 07:02:47.

Although you can control the date format to the nth degree, it's best to rely on .NET to ascertain how the user wants strings to look and automatically display them in their preferred format. In the next Try It Out, you'll look at four useful methods that enable you to format dates.

Try It Out   Formatting Dates

1. If the Date Demo program is running, close it.

2. Using the Code Editor for Form1, find the Click event handler for the button, and add the following code:

```
'Display the results
MessageBox.Show(dteData, "Date Demo")

'Display dates
MessageBox.Show(dteData.ToLongDateString, "Date Demo")
MessageBox.Show(dteData.ToShortDateString, "Date Demo")

'Display times
MessageBox.Show(dteData.ToLongTimeString, "Date Demo")
MessageBox.Show(dteData.ToShortTimeString, "Date Demo")
End Sub
```

3. Run the project. You'll be able to click through five message boxes. You have already seen the first message box dialog box; it displays the date and time according to your computers locale settings. The next message box dialog box will display the long date, and the next message box dialog box will display the short date. The fourth message box will display the long time, while the last message box will display the short time.

How It Works

You're seeing the four basic ways that you can display date and time in Windows applications, namely long date, short date, long time, and short time. The names of the formats are self-explanatory!

```
'Display dates
MessageBox.Show(dteData.ToLongDateString, "Date Demo")
MessageBox.Show(dteData.ToShortDateString, "Date Demo")

'Display times
MessageBox.Show(dteData.ToLongTimeString, "Date Demo")
MessageBox.Show(dteData.ToShortTimeString, "Date Demo")
```

Extracting Date Properties

When you have a variable of type Date, there are several properties that you can call to learn more about the date; let's look at them.

Try It Out   Extracting Date Properties

1. If the Date Demo project is running, close it.

2. Add another Button control to Form1 and set its Name property to **btnDateProperties** and its Text property to **Date Properties**. Double-click the button and add the following highlighted code to the Click event:

```
Private Sub btnDateProperties_Click(ByVal sender As System.Object, _
    ByVal e As System.EventArgs) Handles btnDateProperties.Click

    'Declare variable
    Dim dteData As Date

    'Get the current date and time
    dteData = Now

    'Display the various properties
    MessageBox.Show("Month: " & dteData.Month, "Date Demo")
    MessageBox.Show("Day: " & dteData.Day, "Date Demo")
    MessageBox.Show("Year: " & dteData.Year, "Date Demo")
    MessageBox.Show("Hour: " & dteData.Hour, "Date Demo")
    MessageBox.Show("Minute: " & dteData.Minute, "Date Demo")
    MessageBox.Show("Second: " & dteData.Second, "Date Demo")
    MessageBox.Show("Day of week: " & dteData.DayOfWeek, "Date Demo")
    MessageBox.Show("Day of year: " & dteData.DayOfYear, "Date Demo")
End Sub
```

3. Run the project. If you click the button, you'll see a set of fairly self-explanatory message boxes.

How It Works

Again, there's nothing here that's rocket science. If you want to know the hour, use the Hour property. To get at the year, use Year, and so on.

Date Constants

In the preceding Try It Out, you'll notice that when you called DayOfWeek, you were actually given an integer value, as shown in Figure 3-12.

Figure 3-12

The date that we're working with, April 30, 2005, is a Saturday, and, although it's not immediately obvious, Saturday is 6. As the first day of the week is Sunday in the United States, you start counting from Sunday, with Sunday being 0. However, there is a possibility that you're working on a computer whose locale setting starts the calendar on a Monday, in which case DayOfWeek would return 5. Complicated? Perhaps, but just remember that you can't guarantee that what you think is "Day 1" is always going to be Monday. Likewise, what's Wednesday in English is Mittwoch in German.

If you need to know the name of the day or the month in your application, a better approach is to get .NET to get the name for you, again from the particular locale settings of the computer, as you do in the next Try It Out.

Try It Out   **Getting the Names of the Weekday and the Month**

1.   If the Date Demo project is running, close it.

2.   In the Form Designer, add a new Button control and set its Name property to **btnDateNames** and its Text property to **Date Names**. Double-click the button and add the following highlighted code to the Click event handler:

```
Private Sub btnDateNames_Click(ByVal sender As System.Object, _
    ByVal e As System.EventArgs) Handles btnDateNames.Click

        'Declare variable
        Dim dteData As Date

        'Get the current date and time
        dteData = Now

        'Display the various properties
        MessageBox.Show("Weekday name: " & dteData.ToString("dddd"), "Date Demo")
        MessageBox.Show("Month name: " & dteData.ToString("MMMM"), "Date Demo")
    End Sub
```

3.   Run the project and click the button. You will see a message box that tells you the weekday name is Saturday and a second one that tells you that the month is April.

How It Works

When you used your `ToLongDateString` method and its siblings, you were basically allowing .NET to go look in the locale settings for the computer for the date format the user preferred. In this example, you're using the `ToString` method but supplying your own format string.

```
'Display the various properties
MessageBox.Show("Weekday name: " & dteData.ToString("dddd"), "Date Demo")
MessageBox.Show("Month name: " & dteData.ToString("MMMM"), "Date Demo")
```

Usually, it's best practice not to use `ToString` to format dates, because you should rely on the built-in formats, but here you're using the `"dddd"` string to get the weekday name and `"MMMM"` to get the month name. (The case is important here — `"mmmm"` won't work.)

To show this works, if the computer is set to use Italian locale settings, you get one message box telling you the weekday name is `Sabato` and another telling you the month name is `Agosto`.

Defining Date Literals

You know that if you want to use a string literal in your code, you can do this:

```
Dim strData As String
strData = "Woobie"
```

Date literals work in more or less the same way. However, you use pound signs (#) to delimit the start and end of the date. You learn to define date literals in the next Try It Out.

Try It Out   Defining Date Literals

1. If the Date Demo project is running, close it.

2. Add another Button control to the form and set its Name property to **btnDateLiterals** and its Text property to **Date Literals**. Double-click the button and add the following code to the Click event handler:

    ```
    Private Sub btnDateLiterals_Click(ByVal sender As System.Object, _
        ByVal e As System.EventArgs) Handles btnDateLiterals.Click

            'Declare variable
            Dim dteData As Date

            'Get the current date and time
            dteData = #5/5/1967 6:41:00 AM#

            'Display the date and time
            MessageBox.Show(dteData.ToLongDateString & " " & _
                dteData.ToLongTimeString, "Date Demo")
    End Sub
    ```

3. Run the project and click the button. You should see the message box shown in Figure 3-13.

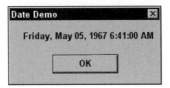

Figure 3-13

How It Works

When defining a date literal, it *must* be defined in mm/dd/yyyy format, regardless of the actual locale settings of the computer. You may or may not see an error if you try to define the date in the format dd/mm/yyyy. This is because you could put in a date in the format dd/mm/yyyy (for example, 06/07/2004) that is also a valid date in the required mm/dd/yyyy format. This requirement is to reduce ambiguity: Does 6/7/2004 mean July 6 or June 7?

In fact, this is a general truth of programming as a whole: There's no such thing as dialects when writing software. It's usually best to conform to North American standards. As you'll see through the rest of this book, this includes variables and method names, for example GetColor *rather than* GetColour.

It's also worth noting that you don't have to supply both a date *and* a time. You can supply one, the other, or both.

Manipulating Dates

One thing that's always been pretty tricky for programmers to do is manipulate dates. You all remember New Year's Eve 1999, waiting to see whether computers could deal with tipping into a new century. Also, dealing with leap years has always been a bit of a problem.

The next turn of the century that also features a leap year will be 2399 to 2400. In the next Try It Out, you'll take a look at how you can use some of the methods available on the Date data type to adjust the date around that particular leap year.

Try It Out   **Manipulating Dates**

1. If the Date Demo program is running, close it.

2. Add another Button control to the form and set its Name property to **btnDateManipulation** and its Text property **Date Manipulation**. Double-click the button and add the following code to the Click event handler:

```
Private Sub btnDateManipulation_Click(ByVal sender As System.Object, _
    ByVal e As System.EventArgs) Handles btnDateManipulation.Click

        'Declare variables
        Dim dteStartDate As Date
        Dim dteChangedDate As Date

        'Start off in 2400
        dteStartDate = #2/28/2400#
```

```
            'Add a day and display the results
            dteChangedDate = dteStartDate.AddDays(1)
            MessageBox.Show(dteChangedDate.ToLongDateString, "Date Demo")

            'Add some months and display the results
            dteChangedDate = dteStartDate.AddMonths(6)
            MessageBox.Show(dteChangedDate.ToLongDateString, "Date Demo")

            'Subtract a year and display the results
            dteChangedDate = dteStartDate.AddYears(-1)
            MessageBox.Show(dteChangedDate.ToLongDateString, "Date Demo")
    End Sub
```

3. Run the project and click the button. You'll see three message boxes, one after another. The first message box dialog box will display the long date for 2/29/2400, while the second message box dialog box will display the long date for 8/28/2400. Finally, the final message box dialog box will display the long date for 2/28/2399.

How It Works

`Date` supports several methods for manipulating dates. Here are three of them:

```
            'Add a day and display the results
            dteChangedDate = dteStartDate.AddDays(1)
            MessageBox.Show(dteChangedDate.ToLongDateString, "Date Demo")

            'Add some months and display the results
            dteChangedDate = dteStartDate.AddMonths(6)
            MessageBox.Show(dteChangedDate.ToLongDateString, "Date Demo")

            'Subtract a year and display the results
            dteChangedDate = dteStartDate.AddYears(-1)
            MessageBox.Show(dteChangedDate.ToLongDateString, "Date Demo")
```

It's worth noting that when you supply a negative number to the `Add` method when working with `Date` variables, the effect is subtraction (as you've seen by going from 2400 back to 2399). The other important `Add` methods are `AddHours`, `AddMinutes`, `AddSeconds`, and `AddMilliseconds`.

Boolean

So far, you've seen the `Integer`, `Double`, `Single`, `String`, and `Date` data types. The other one you need to look at is `Boolean`. Once you've done that, you've seen all of the simple data types that you're most likely to use in your programs.

A `Boolean` variable can be either `True` or `False`. It can never be anything else. `Boolean` values are really important when it's time for your programs to start making decisions, which is something you look at in much more detail in Chapter 4.

Storing Variables

The most limited resource on your computer is typically its memory. It is important that you try to get the most out of the available memory. Whenever you create a variable, you are using a piece of memory, so you must strive to use as few variables as possible and use the variables that you do have in the most efficient manner.

Today, absolute optimization of variables is not something you need to go into a deep level of detail about, for two reasons. First, computers have far more memory these days, so the days when programmers tried to cram payroll systems into 32KB of memory are long gone. Second, the compilers themselves have a great deal of intelligence built in these days, to help generate the most optimized code possible.

Binary

Computers use binary to represent everything. That means that whatever you store in a computer must be expressed as a binary pattern of ones and zeros. Take a simple integer, 27. In binary code, this number is actually 11011, each digit referring to a power of two. The diagram in Figure 3-14 shows how you represent 27 in the more familiar base-ten format, and then in binary.

10^7	10^6	10^5	10^4	10^3	10^2	10^1	10^0
10,000,000	1,000,000	100,000	10,000	1,000	100	10	1
0	0	0	0	0	0	2	7

2 x 10 + 7 x 1 = 27

In base-10, each digit represents a power of ten. To find what number the "pattern of base-10 digits" represents, you multiply the relevant number by the power of ten that the digit represents and add the results.

2^7	2^6	2^5	2^4	2^3	2^2	2^1	2^0
128	64	32	16	8	4	2	1
0	0	0	1	1	0	1	1

1 x 16 + 1 x 8 + 1 x 2 + 1 x 1 = 27

Figure 3-14

In base-2, or binary, each digit represents a power of two. To find what number the "pattern of binary digits" represents, you multiply the relevant number by the power of two that the digit represents and add the results.

Although this may appear to be a bit obscure, look what's happening. In base-10, the decimal system that you're familiar with; each digit fits into a "slot". This slot represents a power of ten—the first representing ten to the power zero, the second ten to the power one, and so on. If you want to know what number the pattern represents, you take each slot in turn, multiply it by the value it represents, and add the results.

The same applies to binary—it's just that you're not familiar with dealing with base twp. To convert the number back to base ten, you take the digit in each slot in turn and multiply that power of *two* by the number that the slot represents (zero or one). Add all of the results together and you get the number.

Bits and Bytes

In computer terms, a binary slot is called a *bit*. It is the smallest possible unit of information, the answer to a single yes/no question, represented by a part of the computer's circuitry that either has electricity flowing in it or not. The reason why there are eight slots/bits on the diagram in Figure 3-14 is that there are eight bits in a *byte*. A byte is the unit of measurement that you use when talking about computer memory.

A *kilobyte* or KB is 1,024 bytes. You use 1,024 rather than 1,000 because 1,024 is the 10th power of 2, so as far as the computer is concerned it's a "round number". Computers don't tend to think of things in terms of 10s like you do, so 1,024 is more natural to a computer than 1,000.

Likewise, a *megabyte* is 1,024 kilobytes, or 1,048,576 bytes. Again, that is another round number because this is the 20th power of 2. A *gigabyte* is 1,024 megabytes, or 1,073,741,824 bytes. (Again, think 2 to the power of 30 and you're on the right lines.) Finally, a *terabyte* is 2 to the 40th power, and a *petabyte* is 2 to the 50th power.

So what's the point of all this? Well, it's worth having an understanding of how computers store variables so that you can design your programs better. Suppose your computer has 256 MB of memory. That's 262,144 KB or 268,435,456 bytes or (multiply by 8) 2,147,483,648 bits. As you write your software, you have to make the best possible use of this available memory.

Representing Values

Most desktop computers in use today are 32-bit, which means that they're optimized for dealing with integer values that are 32 bits in length. The number you just saw in the example was an 8-bit number. With an 8-bit number, the largest value you can store is:

```
1x128 + 1x64 + 1x32 + 1x16 + 1x8 + 1x4 + 1x2 + 1x1 = 255
```

A 32-bit number can represent any value between -2,147,483,648 and 2,147,483,647. Now, you know that if you define a variable like this:

```
Dim intNumber As Integer
```

you want to store an integer number. In response to this, .NET will allocate a 32-bit block of memory in which you can store any number between 0 and 2,147,483,647. Also, remember you only have a finite amount of memory, and on your 256 MB computer; you can only store a maximum of 67,108,864 long numbers. Sounds like a lot, but remember that memory is for sharing. You shouldn't write software that deliberately tries to use as much memory as possible. Be frugal!

You also defined variables that were double-precision floating-point numbers, like this:

```
Dim dblNumber As Double
```

To represent a double-precision floating point number, you need 64 bits of memory. That means you can only store a maximum of 33,554,432 double-precision floating-point numbers.

Single-precision floating-point numbers take up 32 bits of memory — in other words half as much as a double-precision number and the same as an integer value.

If you do define an integer, whether you store 1, 3, 249, or 2,147,483,647, you're always using exactly the same amount of memory, 32 bits. The size of the number has no bearing on the amount of memory required to store it. This might seem incredibly wasteful, but the computer relies on numbers of the same type taking the same amount of storage. Without this, it would be unable to work at a decent speed.

Now look at how you define a string:

```
Dim strData As String
strData = "Hello, world!"
```

Unlike integers and doubles, strings do not have a fixed length. Each character in the string takes up two bytes, or 16 bits. So, to represent this 13-character string, you need 26 bytes, or 208 bits. That means that your computer is able to store only a little over two million strings of that length. Obviously, if the string is twice as long, you can hold half as many, and so on.

A common mistake that new programmers make is not taking into consideration the impact the data type has on storage. If you have a variable that's supposed to hold a string, and you try to hold a numeric value in it, like this:

```
Dim strData As String
strData = "65536"
```

you're using 10 bytes (or 80 bits) to store it. That's less efficient than storing the value in an integer type. To store this numerical value in a string, each character in the string has to be converted into a numerical representation. This is done according to something called *Unicode*, which is a standard way of defining the way computers store characters. Each character has a unique number between 0 and 65,535, and it's this value that is stored in each byte allocated to the string.

Here are the Unicode codes for each character in the string:

- ❑ "6": Unicode 54, binary 0000000000110110
- ❑ "5": Unicode 53, binary 0000000000110101
- ❑ "5": Unicode 53, binary 0000000000110101
- ❑ "3": Unicode 51, binary 0000000000110011
- ❑ "6": Unicode 54, binary 0000000000110110

Each character requires 16 bits, so to store a 5-digit number in a string requires 80 bits—five 16 bit numbers. What you should do is this:

```
Dim intNumber As Integer
intNumber = 65536
```

This stores the value as a single number binary pattern. An `Integer` uses 32 bits, so the binary representation will be 00000000000000010000000000000000, far smaller than the space needed to store it as a string.

Converting Values

Although strings seem natural to us, they're unnatural to a computer. A computer wants to take two numbers and perform some simple mathematical operation on them. However, a computer can perform such a vast number of these simple operations each second that you, as humans, get the results you want.

Let's imagine that a computer wants to add 1 to the value 27. You already know that you can represent 27 in binary as 11011. Figure 3-15 shows what happens.

As you can see, binary math is no different from decimal (base-10) math. If you try to add one to the first bit, it won't fit, so you revert it to zero and carry the one to the next bit. The same happens, and you carry the one to the third bit. At this point, you've finished, and if you add up the value you get 28, as intended.

2^7	2^6	2^5	2^4	2^3	2^2	2^1	2^0
128	64	32	16	8	4	2	1
0	0	0	1	1	0	1	1

1 x 16 + 1 x 8 + 1 x 2 + 1 x 1 = 27

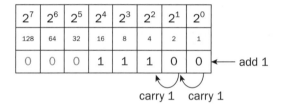

Just like the math you're familiar with, if we hit the "ceiling" value for the base (in this case "2"), we set the digit to "0" and carry "1".

1 x 16 + 1 x 8 + 1 x 4 = 28

Figure 3-15

Any value that you have in your program ultimately has to be converted to simple numbers for the computer to do anything with them. To make the program run more efficiently, you have to keep the number of conversions to a minimum. Here's an example:

```
Dim strData As String
strData = "27"
strData = strData + 1
MessageBox.Show(strData)
```

Let's look at what's happening:

1. You create a string variable called `strData`.

2. You assign the value `27` to that string. This uses 4 bytes of memory.

3. To add 1 to the value, the computer has to convert 27 to an internal, hidden integer variable that contains the value 27. This uses an additional 4 bytes of memory, taking the total to 8. However, more importantly, this conversion takes time!

4. When the string is converted to an integer, 1 is added to it.

5. The new value then has to be converted into a string.

6. The string containing the new value is displayed on the screen.

To write an efficient program, you don't want to be constantly converting variables between different types. You want to perform the conversion only when it's absolutely necessary.

Here's some more code that has the same effect:

```
Dim intNumber As Integer
intNumber = 27
intNumber = intNumber + 1
MessageBox.Show(intNumber)
```

1. You create an integer variable called intNumber.

2. You assign the value 27 to the variable.

3. You add 1 to the variable.

4. You convert the variable to a string and display it on the screen.

In this case, you have to do only one conversion, and it's a logical one. MessageBox.Show works in terms of strings and characters, so that's what it's most comfortable with.

What you have done is cut the conversions from two (string to integer, integer to string) down to one. This will make your program run more efficiently. Again, it's a small improvement, but imagine this improvement occurring hundreds of thousands of times each minute—you'll get an improvement in the performance of the system as a whole.

> It is absolutely vital that you work with the correct data type for your needs. In simple applications like the ones you've created in this chapter, a performance penalty is not really noticeable. However, when you write more complex, sophisticated applications, you'll really want to optimize your code by using the right data type.

Methods

A *method* is a self-contained block of code that "does something." Methods, also called *procedures*, are essential for two reasons. First, they break a program up and make it more understandable. Second, they promote code *reuse*—a topic you'll be spending most of your time on throughout the rest of this book.

As you know, when you write code you start with a high-level algorithm and keep refining the detail of that algorithm until you get the software code that expresses all of the algorithms up to and including the high-level one. A method describes a "line" in one of those algorithms, for example "open a file", "display text on screen", "print a document", and so on.

Knowing how to break a program up into methods is something that comes with experience. To add to the frustration, it's far easier to understand why you need to use methods when you're working on far more complex programs than the ones you've seen so far. In the rest of this section, we'll endeavor to show you how and why to use methods.

Why Use Methods?

In day-to-day use, you need to pass information to a method for it to produce the expected results. This might be a single integer value, a set of string values, or a combination of both. These are known as *input values*. However, some methods don't take input values, so having input values is not a requirement of a method. The method uses these input values and a combination of environmental information (for instance, facts about the current state of the program that the method knows about) to do something useful.

We say that when you give information to a method, you *pass* it data. You can also refer to that data as *parameters*. Finally, when you want to use a method, you *call* it.

> To summarize, you call a method, passing data in through parameters.

The reason for using methods is to promote this idea of code reuse. The principle behind using a method makes sense if you consider the program from a fairly high level. If you have an understanding of all the algorithms involved in a program, you can find commonality. If you need to do the same thing more than once, you should wrap it up into a method that you can reuse.

Imagine you have a program that comprises many algorithms. Some of those algorithms call for the area of a circle to be calculated. Because *some* of those algorithms need to know how to calculate the area of a circle, it's a good candidate for a method. You write code that knows how to find the area of a circle given its radius, *encapsulate* it ("wrap it up") into a method, which you can reuse it when you're coding the other algorithms. This means that you don't have to keep writing code that does the same thing — you do it once and reuse it as often as needed.

It might be the case that one algorithm needs to work out the area of a circle with 100 for its radius, and another needs to work out one with a radius of 200. By building the method in such a way that it takes the radius as a parameter, you can use the method from wherever you want.

> With Visual Basic 2005, you can define a method using the Sub *keyword or using the* Function *keyword.* Sub, *short for "subroutine," is used when the method doesn't return a value, as mentioned in Chapter 1.* Function *is used when the method returns a value.*

Methods You've Already Seen

The good news is that you've been using methods already. Consider this code that you wrote at the beginning of this chapter:

```
Private Sub btnAdd_Click(ByVal sender As System.Object, _
    ByVal e As System.EventArgs) Handles btnAdd.Click

        'Define a variable for intNumber
        Dim intNumber As Integer
```

```
        'Set the initial value
        intNumber = 27

        'Add 1 to the value of intNumber
        intNumber = intNumber + 1

        'Display the new value of intNumber
        MessageBox.Show("Value of intNumber + 1 = " & intNumber, "Variables")
    End Sub
```

That code is a method — it's a self-contained block of code that does something. In this case, it adds 1 to the value of intNumber and displays the result in a message box.

This method does not return a value (that is, it's a subroutine, so it starts with the Sub keyword and ends with the End Sub statement). Anything between these two statements is the code assigned to the method. Let's take a look at how the method is defined (this code was automatically created by Visual Basic 2005):

```
    Private Sub btnAdd_Click(ByVal sender As System.Object, _
        ByVal e As System.EventArgs) Handles btnAdd.Click
```

1. First of all, you have the word Private. The meaning of this keyword will be discussed in later chapters. For now, think of it as ensuring that this method cannot be called up by anything other than the user clicking the Add button.

2. Second, you have the keyword Sub to tell Visual Basic 2005 that you want to define a subroutine.

3. Third, you have btnAdd_Click. This is the name of the subroutine.

4. Fourth, you have ByVal sender As System.Object, ByVal e As System.EventArgs. This tells Visual Basic 2005 that the method takes two parameters — sender and e. We'll talk about this more later.

5. Finally, you have Handles btnAdd.Click. This tells Visual Basic 2005 that this method should be called whenever the Click event on the control btnAdd is fired.

In the next Try It Out, you take a look at how you can build a method that displays a message box and call the same method from three separate buttons.

Try It Out   Using Methods

1. Create a new Windows Application project called **Three Buttons**.

2. Use the Toolbox to draw three buttons on the form.

3. Double-click the first button (Button1) to create a new Click event handler. Add the highlighted code:

```
    Private Sub Button1_Click(ByVal sender As System.Object, _
        ByVal e As System.EventArgs) Handles Button1.Click
```

```
        'Call your method
        SayHello()
    End Sub



    Private Sub SayHello()
        'Display a message box
        MessageBox.Show("Hello, world!", "Three Buttons")
    End Sub
```

4. Run the project and you'll see the form with three buttons appear. Click the topmost button and you'll see Hello, world!

How It Works

As you know now, when you double-click a Button control in the Designer, a new method is automatically created:

```
    Private Sub Button1_Click(ByVal sender As System.Object, _
        ByVal e As System.EventArgs) Handles Button1.Click

    End Sub
```

The `Handles Button1.Click` statement at the end tells Visual Basic 2005 that this method should automatically be called when the Click event on the button is fired. As part of this, Visual Basic 2005 provides two parameters, which you don't have to worry about for now. Outside of this method, you've defined a new method:

```
    Private Sub SayHello()
        'Display a message box
        MessageBox.Show("Hello, world!", "Three Buttons")
    End Sub
```

The new method is called `SayHello`. Anything that appears between the two highlighted lines is part of the method and when that method is called, the code is executed. In this case, you've asked it to display a message box.

So you know that, when the button is clicked, Visual Basic 2005 will call the `Button1_Click` method. You then call the `SayHello` method. The upshot of all this is that when the button is clicked, the message box is displayed:

```
    Private Sub Button1_Click(ByVal sender As System.Object, _
        ByVal e As System.EventArgs) Handles Button1.Click

        'Call your method
        SayHello()
    End Sub
```

That should make the general premise behind methods a little clearer, but why did you need to break the code into a separate method to display the message box? You learn more about that in the next Try It Out.

Try It Out   Reusing the Method

1. If the project is running, close it.

2. Now double-click the second button. Add the highlighted code to the new event handler:

```
Private Sub Button2_Click(ByVal sender As System.Object, _
    ByVal e As System.EventArgs) Handles Button2.Click

        'Call your method
        SayHello()
End Sub
```

3. Flip back to Design view and double-click the third button. Add the highlighted code:

```
Private Sub Button3_Click(ByVal sender As System.Object, _
    ByVal e As System.EventArgs) Handles Button3.Click

        'Call your method
        SayHello()
End Sub
```

4. Now run the project. You'll notice that each of the buttons bring up the same message box when clicked.

5. Stop the project and find the SayHello method definition. Change the text to be displayed, like this:

```
Private Sub SayHello()
    'Display a message box

        MessageBox.Show("I have changed!", "Three Buttons")
End Sub
```

6. Run the project again and you'll notice that the text displayed on the message boxes has changed.

How It Works

Each of the event handlers calls the same SayHello() method:

```
Private Sub Button1_Click(ByVal sender As System.Object, _
    ByVal e As System.EventArgs) Handles Button1.Click

        'Call your method
        SayHello()
End Sub

Private Sub Button2_Click(ByVal sender As System.Object, _
    ByVal e As System.EventArgs) Handles Button2.Click

        'Call your method
        SayHello()
End Sub
```

```
Private Sub Button3_Click(ByVal sender As System.Object, _
    ByVal e As System.EventArgs) Handles Button3.Click

    'Call your method
    SayHello()
End Sub
```

You'll also notice that the `Handles` keyword on each of the methods ties the method to a different control — Button1, Button2, or Button3.

What's really important (and clever!) here is that when you change the way that `SayHello` works, the effect you see on each button is the same. This is a really important programming concept. You can centralize code in your application so that when you change it in once place, the effect is felt throughout the application. Likewise, this saves you from having to enter the same or very similar code repeatedly.

Building a Method

In the next Try It Out, you'll build a method that's capable of returning a value. Specifically, you'll build a method that can return the area of a circle if its radius is given. You can do this with the following algorithm:

1. Square the radius.

2. Multiply it by pi.

Try It Out   **Building a Method**

1. To try out this exercise, you can reuse the Three Buttons project you used before.

2. Add this code to define a new method (which will be a function, because it returns a value):

```
'CalculateAreaFromRadius - find the area of a circle
Private Function CalculateAreaFromRadius(ByVal radius As Double) As Double
    'Declare variables
    Dim dblRadiusSquared As Double
    Dim dblResult As Double

    'Square the radius
    dblRadiusSquared = radius * radius

    'Multiply it by pi
    dblResult = dblRadiusSquared * Math.PI

    'Return the result
    Return dblResult
End Function
```

3. Now delete the existing code from the `Button1_Click` event handler, and add this code:

```
Private Sub Button1_Click(ByVal sender As System.Object, _
    ByVal e As System.EventArgs) Handles Button1.Click
```

```
        'Declare variable
        Dim dblArea As Double

        'Calculate the area of a circle with radius 100
        dblArea = CalculateAreaFromRadius(100)

        'Print the results
        MessageBox.Show(dblArea, "Area")
    End Sub
```

4.   Run the project and click on Button1. You'll see results like the one shown Figure 3-16.

Figure 3-16

How It Works

First of all, you build a separate method called `CalculateAreaFromRadius`. You do this by using the `Private Function ... End Function` block.

```
    Private Function CalculateAreaFromRadius(ByVal radius As Double) As Double
    . . .
    End Function
```

Anything between `Private Function` and `End Function` is the *body* of the method and will be executed only when the method is called.

The `ByVal radius As Double` portion defines a parameter for the method. When a parameter is passed *by value*, as indicated here by the keyword `ByVal`, .NET in effect creates a new variable and stores the passed parameter information in it. Even if the method is called with a variable given for the parameter, the contents of that original variable are not modified by the method. In this case, you're telling .NET that you want to pass a parameter into the method called `radius`. In effect, this statement creates a variable called `radius`, just as if you had done this:

```
    Dim radius As Double
```

In fact, there's a little more. The variable will be automatically set to the value passed through as a parameter, so if you pass `200` through as the value of the parameter, what you're effectively doing is this:

```
    Dim radius As Double = 200
```

If you passed `999` as the value of the parameter, you'd have this:

```
    Dim radius As Double = 999
```

Another way of passing a parameter is by reference, using the keyword ByRef *instead of* ByVal. *When a parameter is passed by reference, the parameter name used within the method body effectively becomes another name for the variable specified when the method is called, so that anything the method does that modifies the parameter value modifies the original variable value as well.*

The As Double sitting at the end of the method declaration tells Visual Basic 2005 that this method will return a double-precision floating-point number back to whoever called it:

```
Private Function CalculateAreaFromRadius(ByVal radius As Double) As Double
```

Now you can look at the method properly. First off, you know that to find the area of a circle you have this algorithm:

1. Get a number that represents the radius of a circle.

2. Square the number.

3. Multiply it by pi (π).

And that's precisely what you've done:

```
'Declare variables
Dim dblRadiusSquared As Double
Dim dblResult As Double

'Square the radius
dblRadiusSquared = radius * radius

'Multiply it by pi
dblResult = dblRadiusSquared * Math.PI
```

The Math.PI in the previous code is a constant defined in Visual Basic 2005 that defines the value of pi (() for us. After the last line, you need to return the result to whatever code called the method. This is done with this statement:

```
'Return the result
Return dblResult
```

The code you added in Button1_Click calls the method and tells the user the results:

```
'Declare variable
Dim dblArea As Double

'Calculate the area of a circle with radius 100
dblArea = CalculateAreaFromRadius(100)

'Print the results
MessageBox.Show(dblArea, "Area")
```

The first thing to do is define a variable called dblArea that will contain the area of the circle. You set this variable to whatever value CalculateAreaFromRadius returns. Using parentheses at the end of a method name is how you send the parameters. In this case, you're passing just one parameter and you're passing the value 100.

After you call the method, you wait for the method to finish calculating the area. This area is returned from the method (the `Return` result line defined within `CalculateAreaFromRadius`) and stored in the variable `dblArea`. You can then display this on the screen in the usual way.

Choosing Method Names

The .NET Framework has a few standards for how things should be named. This helps developers move between languages — a topic discussed in Chapter 2. We recommend that whenever you create a method, you use *Pascal casing*. This is a practice in which the first letter in each word in the method is uppercase but nothing else is. This is merely a suggestion for best coding practices and is not a requirement of Visual Basic 2005. An example of this is as follows:

- ❑   `CalculateAreaFromRadius`
- ❑   `OpenXmlFile`
- ❑   `GetEnvironmentValue`

You'll notice that even when an abbreviation is used (in this case, XML), it *isn't* written in uppercase. This is to alleviate confusion for developers, who may or may not know how something should be capitalized.

We recommend that you always write parameter names in *camel casing*. (If you've ever seen Java code, you'll be familiar with this.) To get camel casing, you do the same as Pascal casing, but you don't capitalize the very first letter:

- ❑   `myAccount`
- ❑   `customerDetails`
- ❑   `updatedDnsRecord`

Again, abbreviations (such as DNS) are not treated as a special case, so they appear as a mix of upper and lowercase letters, just like in Pascal casing.

> *The name camel casing comes from the fact that the identifier has a hump in the middle, for example,* `camelCasing`*. Pascal casing comes from the fact that the convention was invented for use with the programming language Pascal.*

In Chapter 2, you saw that .NET isn't tied to a particular language. Because some languages are *case-sensitive* and others are not, it's important that you define standards to make life easier for programmers who may be coming from different programming language backgrounds.

The term "case sensitive" means that the positions of uppercase and lowercase letters are important. In a case-sensitive language, `MYACCOUNT` is not the same as `myAccount`. However, Visual Basic 2005 is *not* a case-sensitive language, meaning that for all intents and purposes you can do whatever you like with respect to capitalization, in other words `MYACCOUNT` would be the same as `mYacCounT`.

> *Note that languages such as Java, C#, C++, and J# are case-sensitive.*

Scope

When introducing the concept of methods, we described them as *self-contained*. This has an important effect on the way that variables are used and defined in methods. Imagine you have these two methods, both of which define a variable called `strName`:

```
Private Sub DisplaySebastiansName()
    'Declare variable and set value
    Dim strName As String
    strName = "Sebastian Blackwood"

    'Display results
    MessageBox.Show(strName, "Scope Demo")
End Sub

Private Sub DisplayBalthazarsName()
    'Declare variable and set value
    Dim strName As String
    strName = "Balthazar Keech"

    'Display results
    MessageBox.Show(strName, "Scope Demo")
End Sub
```

Even though both of these methods use a variable with the same name (`strName`), the "self-contained" feature of methods means that this is perfectly practicable and the variable names won't affect each other. Try it out next.

Try It Out   Scope

1. Create a new Windows Application project called **Scope Demo**.

2. Add a Button control to the form and set its Name property **btnScope** and its Text property to **Scope**. Double-click the button and add the following highlighted code to the Click event handler and the other two methods:

```
Private Sub btnScope_Click(ByVal sender As System.Object, _
    ByVal e As System.EventArgs) Handles btnScope.Click

    'Call a method
    DisplayBalthazarsName()
End Sub


Private Sub DisplaySebastiansName()
    'Declare variable and set value
    Dim strName As String
    strName = "Sebastian Blackwood"

    'Display results
    MessageBox.Show(strName, "Scope Demo")
End Sub
```

```
Private Sub DisplayBalthazarsName()
    'Declare variable and set value
    Dim strName As String
    strName = "Balthazar Keech"

    'Display results
    MessageBox.Show(strName, "Scope Demo")
End Sub
```

3. Run the project and you'll see the message box displaying the name Balthazar Keech when you click the button.

How It Works

What this exercise illustrates is that even though you've used the same variable name in two separate places, the program still works as intended:

```
Private Sub DisplaySebastiansName()
    'Declare variable and set value
    Dim strName As String
    strName = "Sebastian Blackwood"

    'Display results
    MessageBox.Show(strName, "Scope Demo")
End Sub

Private Sub DisplayBalthazarsName()
    'Declare variable and set value
    Dim strName As String
    strName = "Balthazar Keech"

    'Display results
    MessageBox.Show(strName, "Scope Demo")
End Sub
```

When a method starts running, the variables that are defined within that method (in other words, between Sub and End Sub, or between Function and End Function) are given *local scope*. The *scope* defines which parts of the program can see the variable, and *local* specifically means "within the current method".

The strName variable technically doesn't exist until the method starts running. At this point, .NET and Windows allocate memory to the variable so that it can be used in the code. First, you set the value and then you display the message box. Therefore, in this case as you're calling DisplayBalthazarsName, the variable is created the moment the method is called, you run the code in the method that alters the newly created version of strName, and when the method has finished, the variable is deleted.

You will see in the next chapter that scope can even be limited to loops within your subroutines and functions.

Summary

This chapter introduced the concept of writing software not just for Visual Basic 2005 but also for all programming languages. We started by introducing the concept of an algorithm — the underpinnings of all computer software. We then introduced the concept of variables, and you looked closely at the most commonly used data types: `Integer`, `Double`, `String`, `Date`, and `Boolean`. You saw how you could use these data types to perform operations such as mathematical operations, concatenating strings, returning the length of a string, splitting text into substrings, retrieving the current date, and extracting date properties. You then looked at how variables are stored in the computer.

After this, you looked at methods — what they are, why you need them, how to create them, and how the variables you declare within your methods have local scope within that method and do not apply outside of it. We also described the difference between a function and a subroutine.

To summarize, you should know:

❑   What an algorithm is and how it applies to software development

❑   How to declare and use the most common types of variables

❑   How to use the most common string functions when working with the `String` data type

❑   How to use the `Date` data type and display dates and times so that they are automatically localized to the user's computer settings

❑   How to create and use simple methods

Exercises

Exercise 1

Create a Windows application with two button controls. In the click event for the first button, declare two `Integer` variables and set their values to any number that you like. Perform any math operation on these variables and display the results in a message box.

In the click event for the second button, declare two `String` variables and set their values to anything that you like. Perform a string concatenation on these variables and display the results in a message box.

Exercise 2

Create a Windows application with a text box and a button control. In the button's click event, display three message boxes. The first message box should display the length of the string that was entered into the text box. The second message box should display the first half of the string, and the third message box should display the last half of the string.

Controlling the Flow

In Chapter 3, you learned about algorithms and their role in programming. In this chapter, you're going to look at how you can control the flow through your algorithms so that you can make decisions like, "If X is the case, go and do A; otherwise do B." This ability to make decisions is known as *branching*. You'll also see how you can repeat a section of code (a process known as *looping*) a specified number of times, or while a certain condition applies.

Specifically, you'll learn more about:

❑   The `If` statement

❑   `Select Case`

❑   `For` loops

❑   `Do` loops

Making Decisions

Algorithms often include decisions. In fact, it's this decision-making ability that makes computers do what they do so well. When you're writing code, you make two kinds of decisions. The first kind is used to find out what part of an algorithm you're currently working on or to cope with problems. For example, imagine you have a list of 10 people and need to write a piece of code to send an e-mail to each of them. To do this, after sending each e-mail, you ask, "Have I finished?" If so, you quit the algorithm; otherwise you get the next person in the list. As another example, you might need to open a file, so you ask, "Does the file exist?" You have to deal with both possible answers to that question.

The second kind of decision is used to perform a different part of the algorithm depending on one or more facts. Imagine you're going through your list of ten people so that you can send an e-mail to those who own a computer but telephone those who don't. As you look at each person, you use the fact that the person does or doesn't own a computer, to choose what you should do.

These decisions are all made in the same way, and it doesn't matter whether you have more of the first kind, more of the second kind, or whatever. Now, let's take a look at how to make a decision using the If statement.

The If Statement

The simplest way to make a decision in a Visual Basic 2005 program is to use the If . . . Then statement. You learn to use an If . . Then statement in the following Try It Out.

Try It Out   **A Simple If . . . Then Statement**

1. Create a Windows Application project called **Simple If**. Add a Button control, set its Name property to **btnIf**, and set its Text property to **If**. Double-click the button and add the following highlighted code:

```
Private Sub btnIf_Click(ByVal sender As System.Object, _
    ByVal e As System.EventArgs) Handles btnIf.Click

        'Declare and set a variable
        Dim intNumber As Integer = 27

        'Here's where you make a decision,
        'and tell the user what happened
        If intNumber = 27 Then
            MessageBox.Show("'intNumber' is, indeed, 27!", "Simple If")
        End If
    End Sub
```

2. Now run the project and click the If button. You'll see the message box dialog box shown in Figure 4-1.

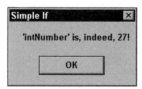

Figure 4-1

How It Works

First you declare an Integer variable called intNumber and set its value to 27, all in the same line of code, as shown here.

```
        'Declare and set a variable
        Dim intNumber As Integer = 27
```

Then you use an `If` ... `Then` statement to determine what you should do next. In this case, you say, "If `intNumber` is equal to 27...":

```
'Here's where you make a decision,
'and tell the user what happened
If intNumber = 27 Then
    MessageBox.Show("'intNumber' is, indeed, 27!", "Simple If")
End If
```

The code block that follows this will be executed only if `intNumber` equals 27. You end the code block with `End If`. Anything between `If` and `End If` is called only if the expression you're testing for is `True`.

So, as you walk through the code, you get to the `If` statement, and it's true. You drop into the code block that runs if the expression is true, and the text is displayed in a message box.

Notice that the code within the `If` ... `End If` block is automatically indented for you. This is to increase readability so that you can tell what code will run in the event of the condition being true. It's also good to add some white space before the `If` ... `Then` statement and after the `End If` statement to enhance readability further.

A simple `If` block like the previous one may also be written on one line, without an `End If` statement, for example:

```
If intNumber = 27 Then MessageBox.Show("'intNumber' is, indeed, 27!", "Simple If")
```

This works equally well — although you are limited to only one line of code within the `If` statement. So now you know what happens if your condition is true. But what happens if you fail the test and the result is false? You find out in the next Try It Out.

Try It Out   Failing the Test

1. Stop your Simple If program if it is still running. Add another Button control to the form and set its Name property to **btnAnotherIf** and its Text property to **Another If**. Double-click the button and add the following highlighted code:

```
Private Sub btnAnotherIf_Click(ByVal sender As System.Object, _
    ByVal e As System.EventArgs) Handles btnAnotherIf.Click

    'Declare and set a variable
    Dim intNumber As Integer = 27

    'Here's where you make a decision,
    'and tell the user what happened
    If intNumber = 1000 Then
        MessageBox.Show("'intNumber' is, indeed, 1000!", "Simple If")
    End If
End Sub
```

2. Run the code.

How It Works

In this case, the question "Is intNumber equal to 1000?" comes out false. The code block executes only if the statement is true, so it's skipped. If the statement were true, the line between the If and End If lines would have executed. However, in this instance the statement was false, so the next line to be executed was the first line directly following the End If line (which is End Sub). In effect, the "true" code block is skipped.

The Else Statement

If you want to run one piece of code if the condition is true and another piece if the condition is false, you use the Else statement. Expand on the previous Try It Out to see how it works.

Try It Out   The Else Statement

1. Change the code in the btnAnotherIf_Click procedure so that it looks like this:

```
Private Sub btnAnotherIf_Click(ByVal sender As System.Object, _
    ByVal e As System.EventArgs) Handles btnAnotherIf.Click

    'Declare and set a variable
    Dim intNumber As Integer = 27

    'Here's where you make a decision,
    'and tell the user what happened
    If intNumber = 1000 Then
        MessageBox.Show("'intNumber' is, indeed, 1000!", "Simple If")

    Else
        MessageBox.Show("'intNumber' is not 1000!", "Simple If")
    End If
End Sub
```

2. Run the code and you'll see the message box shown in Figure 4-2.

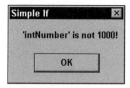

Figure 4-2

How It Works

The code following the Else statement runs if the condition in the If statement is not met. In this case, the value of intNumber is 27, but the condition being tested for is intNumber = 1000, so the code after the Else statement is run:

```
    Else
        MessageBox.Show("'intNumber' is not 1000!", "Simple If")
    End If
```

Allowing Multiple Alternatives with ElseIf

If you want to test for more than one condition, you need to make use of the ElseIf statement. Now take your Simple If program as an example to see how you can test for the value of intNumber being 27 and 1000.

The ElseIf Statement

1. Change the code in the btnAnotherIf_Click procedure so that it looks like this:

```
Private Sub btnAnotherIf_Click(ByVal sender As System.Object, _
    ByVal e As System.EventArgs) Handles btnAnotherIf.Click

    'Declare and set a variable
    Dim intNumber As Integer = 27

    'Here's where you make a decision,
    'and tell the user what happened
    If intNumber = 1000 Then
        MessageBox.Show("'intNumber' is, indeed, 1000!", "Simple If")

    ElseIf intNumber = 27 Then
        MessageBox.Show("'intNumber' is 27!", "Simple If")
    Else
        MessageBox.Show("'intNumber' is neither 1000 nor 27!", "Simple If")
    End If
End Sub
```

2. Run the code and you'll see the message box shown in Figure 4-3.

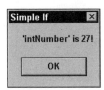

Figure 4-3

How It Works

This time the code in the ElseIf statement ran because intNumber met the condition intNumber = 27. Note that you can still include the Else statement at the end to catch instances where intNumber is neither 27 nor 1000, but something else entirely:

```
ElseIf intNumber = 27 Then
    MessageBox.Show("'intNumber' is 27!", "Simple If")
Else
    MessageBox.Show("'intNumber' is neither 1000 nor 27!", "Simple If")
End If
```

You can add as many ElseIf statements as you need to test for conditions. However, bear in mind that each ElseIf statement is executed as Visual Basic 2005 attempts to discover whether the condition is true. This slows your program if you have a lot of conditions to be tested. If this is the case, you should try to put the statements in the order they are most likely to be executed, with the most common one at the top. Alternatively, you should use a Select Case *block, which you will be looking at later in the chapter.*

Nested If Statements

It's possible to nest an If statement inside another:

```
If intX = 3 Then
    MessageBox.Show("intX = 3")

    If intY = 6 Then
        MessageBox.Show("intY = 6")
    End If

End If
```

There's no real limit to how far you can nest your If statements. However, the more levels of nesting you have, the harder it is to follow what's happening in your code. So try to keep the nesting of If statements to a minimum if you can.

Single-Line If Statement

The single-line form is typically used for short, simple tests, and it saves space in the text editor. However, it doesn't provide the structure and flexibility of the multiline form and is usually harder to read:

```
If intX = 3 Then MessageBox.Show("intX = 3") Else MessageBox.Show("intX is not 3")
```

You don't need an End If at the end of a single-line If . . . Then statement.

Multiple statements can also be executed within a single line If . . . Then statement. All statements must be on the same line and must be separated by colons, as in the following example:

```
If intX = 3 Then MessageBox.Show("intX = 3") : intX = intX + 1 : Total += intX
```

Comparison Operators

You know how to check whether a particular variable is equal to some value and execute code if this is the case. In fact, If is far more flexible than this. You can ask questions such as these, all of which have yes/no answers.

❑ Is intNumber greater than 49?

❑ Is intNumber less than 49?

❑ Is intNumber greater than or equal to 49?

❑ Is intNumber less than or equal to 49?

❑ Is strName not equal to Ben?

When working with string values, most of the time you'll use the Equal To or Not Equal To operators. When working with numeric values (both integer and floating-point), you can use all of these arithmetic operators discussed in the previous chapter.

Using Not Equal To

You have not used Not Equal To yet, so test the Not Equal To operator with strings.

Try It Out   **Using Not Equal To**

1. Create a new Windows Application project called **If Demo**.

2. When the Form Designer for Form1 appears, add a TextBox control and a Button control. Set the Name property for TextBox1 to **txtName** and the Text property to **Robbin**. Set the Name property for Button1 to **btnCheck** and the Text property to **Check**.

3. Double-click the Button control to create its Click event handler. Add the highlighted code:

```
Private Sub btnCheck_Click(ByVal sender As System.Object, _
    ByVal e As System.EventArgs) Handles btnCheck.Click

        'Declare a variable and get the name from the text box
        Dim strName As String
        strName = txtName.Text

        'Is the name Gretchen?
        If strName <> "Gretchen" Then
            MessageBox.Show("The name is *not* Gretchen.", "If Demo")
        End If
End Sub
```

4. Run the project and click the Check button. You will see a message box dialog box indicating that the name is not Gretchen.

How It Works

The Not Equal To operator looks like this: <>. When the button is clicked, the first thing you do is to retrieve the name from the text box by looking at its Text property:

```
        'Declare a variable and get the name from the text box
        Dim strName As String
        strName = txtName.Text
```

After you have the name, you use an If statement. This time, however, you use the Not Equal To operator rather than the Equal To operator. Also notice that you are comparing two string values.

```
        'Is the name Gretchen?
        If strName <> "Gretchen" Then
            MessageBox.Show("The name is *not* Gretchen.", "If Demo")
        End If
```

The code between Then and End If executes only if the answer to the question asked in the If statement is True. You'll probably find this a bit of a heady principle, because the question you're asking is, "Is strName not equal to Gretchen?" to which the answer is "Yes, the strName is *not* equal to

Gretchen." As the answer to this question is yes, or True, the code runs and the message box displays. However, if you enter Gretchen into the text box and click Check, nothing happens, because the answer to the question is "No, the strName *is* equal to Gretchen"; therefore you have a no, or False, answer.

If you try this, be sure to enter Gretchen *with an uppercase* G *and with the rest of the letters in lower-case; otherwise the application won't work properly. You'll see why later.*

An alternative way of checking that something does not equal something is to use the Not keyword. The condition in the If statement could have been written:

```
If Not strName = "Gretchen" Then
```

Using the Numeric Operators

In this section, you take a look at the four other comparison operators you can use. These are all fairly basic, so you'll go through this quite fast.

Try It Out   **Using Less Than**

1. If the project is running, close it. Open the Form Designer for Form1 and add another TextBox control and set its Name property to **txtValue**. Add another Button control and set its Name property to **btnCheckNumbers** and its Text property to **Check Numbers**.

2. Double-click the Check Numbers button and add the following highlighted code to its Click event handler:

```
Private Sub btnCheckNumbers_Click(ByVal sender As System.Object, _
    ByVal e As System.EventArgs) Handles btnCheckNumbers.Click

        'Declare variable
        Dim intNumber As Integer

        Try
            'Get the number from the text box
            intNumber = txtValue.Text
        Catch
        End Try

        'Is intNumber less than 27?
        If intNumber < 27 Then
            MessageBox.Show("Is 'intNumber' less than 27? Yes!", "If Demo")
        Else
            MessageBox.Show("Is 'intNumber' less than 27? No!", "If Demo")
        End If
    End Sub
```

3. Run the project. Enter a number into the text box and click the Check Numbers button. You'll be told whether the number entered is less than or greater than 27 as shown in Figure 4-4.

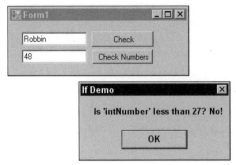

Figure 4-4

How It Works

First, you get the value back from the text box. However, there is a slight wrinkle. Because this is a text box, the end users are free to enter anything they like into it, and if a series of characters that cannot be converted into an integer is entered, the program will crash. Therefore, you add an *exception handler* to make sure that you always get a value back. If the user enters something invalid, intNumber remains 0 (the default value), otherwise it will be whatever is entered:

```
'Declare variable
Dim intNumber As Integer

Try
     'Get the number from the text box
     intNumber = txtValue.Text
Catch
End Try
```

You'll be introduced to exception handling properly in Chapter 9. For now, you can safely ignore it!

The Less Than operator looks like this: <. Here, you test to see whether the number entered was less than 27, and if it is, you say so in a message box; otherwise you say No:

```
'Is intNumber less than 27?
If intNumber < 27 Then
    MessageBox.Show("Is 'intNumber' less than 27? Yes!", "If Demo")
Else
    MessageBox.Show("Is 'intNumber' less than 27? No!", "If Demo")
End If
```

Here's something interesting though. If you actually enter 27 into the text box and click the button, you'll see a message box that tells you intNumber is not less than 27. The If statement said No, and it's right; intNumber is actually equal to 27 and the cutoff point for this operator is anything up to *but not including* the value itself. You can get around this problem with a different operator, as you'll see in the next Try It Out.

Try It Out   Using the Less Than Or Equal To Operator

1. Change the `If` statement in the `btnCheckNumbers_Click` event handler as shown here:

```
Try
    'Get the number from the text box
    intNumber = txtValue.Text
Catch
End Try
```

```
    'Is intNumber less than or equal to 27?
    If intNumber <= 27 Then
        MessageBox.Show("Is 'intNumber' less than or equal to 27? Yes!", _
            "If Demo")
    Else

        MessageBox.Show("Is 'intNumber' less than or equal to 27? No!", _
            "If Demo")
    End If
```

2. Now run the project and enter **27** into the text box. Click the Check Numbers button and you should see the results shown in Figure 4-5.

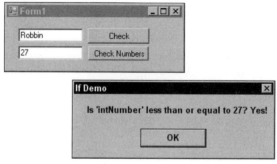

Figure 4-5

How It Works

The Less Than Or Equal To operator looks like this: <=. In this situation, you're extending the possible range of values up to and including the value you're checking. So, in this case when you enter 27, you get the answer, Yes, n is less than or equal to 27. This type of operator is known as an *inclusive operator*.

The final two operators look really similar to this, so let's look at them now.

Try It Out   Using Greater Than and Greater Than Or Equal To

1. Open the `Click` event handler and add these two additional `If` statements:

```
    'Is intNumber less than or equal to 27?
    If intNumber <= 27 Then
```

```
            MessageBox.Show("Is 'intNumber' less than or equal to 27? Yes!", _
                "If Demo")
        Else
            MessageBox.Show("Is 'intNumber' less than or equal to 27? No!", _
                "If Demo")
        End If
```

```
        'Is intNumber greater than 27?
        If intNumber > 27 Then
            MessageBox.Show("Is 'intNumber' greater than 27? Yes!", _
                "If Demo")
        Else
            MessageBox.Show("Is 'intNumber' greater than 27? No!", _
                            "If Demo")
        End If

        'Is intNumber greater than or equal to 27?
        If intNumber >= 27 Then
            MessageBox.Show("Is 'intNumber' greater than or equal to 27? Yes!", _
                "If Demo")
        Else
            MessageBox.Show("Is 'intNumber' greater than or equal to 27? No!", _
                "If Demo")
        End If
```
```
    End Sub
```

2. Run the program. This time enter a value of **99** and click the Check Numbers button. You'll see three message boxes one after the other. The first message box will indicate that `intNumber` is not less than or equal to 27, while the second message box will indicate that `intNumber` is greater than 27. The final message box will indicate that `intNumber` is greater than or equal to 27.

How It Works

The Greater Than and Greater Than Or Equal To operators are basically the opposite of their Less Than counterparts. This time, you're asking, "Is `intNumber` greater than 27?" and, "Is `intNumber` greater than or equal to 27?" The results speak for themselves.

The And and Or Operators

What happens when you need your `If` statement to test more than one condition? For example, if you want to make sure that "`intNumber` is less than 27 *and* greater than 10"? Or, how about checking that `strName` is "Sydney" or "Stephanie"? You can combine operators used with an `If` statement with the `And` and `Or` operators, as you do in the next Try It Out.

Try It Out Using the Or Operator

1. Create a new Windows application called **And Or Demo**.

2. In the Form Designer for Form1, add two TextBox controls and a Button control. Set the Name properties of the text boxes to **txtName1** and **txtName2** and the Name property of the button to **btnOrCheck**.

3. Set the Text property for txtName1 to **Sydney** and the Text property for txtName2 to **Stephanie**. Finally, set the Text property for btnOrCheck to **Or Check**. Your completed form should look similar to the one shown in Figure 4-6.

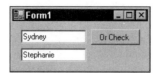

Figure 4-6

4. Double-click the button and add the following code to its `Click` event handler:

```
Private Sub btnOrCheck_Click(ByVal sender As System.Object, _
    ByVal e As System.EventArgs) Handles btnOrCheck.Click
```

```
    'Declare variables
    Dim strName1 As String, strName2 As String

    'Get the names
    strName1 = txtName1.Text
    strName2 = txtName2.Text

    'Is one of the names Sydney?
    If strName1 = "Sydney" Or strName2 = "Sydney" Then
        MessageBox.Show("One of the names is Sydney.", _
            "And Or Demo")
    Else
        MessageBox.Show("Neither of the names is Sydney.", _
            "And Or Demo")
    End If
End Sub
```

5. Run the project and click the button. You should see the results as shown in Figure 4-7.

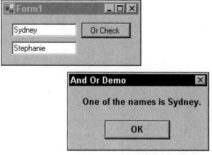

Figure 4-7

6. Click OK to dismiss the message box dialog box and flip the names around so that the top one (txtName1) is **Stephanie** and the bottom one (txtName2) is **Sydney**. Click the button again and you'll see a message box indicating that one of the names is Sydney.

7. Now, click OK to dismiss the message box again and this time change the names so that neither of them is Sydney. Click the button and you should see a message box indicating that neither of the names is Sydney.

How It Works

The Or operator is a great way of building If statements that compare two different values in a single hit. In your Click event handler, the first thing you do is declare your variables and then retrieve both names and store them in variables strName1 and strName2:

```
'Declare variables
Dim strName1 As String, strName2 As String

'Get the names
strName1 = txtName1.Text
strName2 = txtName2.Text
```

You'll notice that you've defined two variables on the same line. This is perfectly legitimate coding practice, although it can sometimes make the code look congested. The variables are separated with commas; notice that it's still important to use the As keyword to tell Visual Basic 2005 what data type each of the variables is.

Once you have both names, you use the Or operator to combine two separate If statements. The question you're asking here is, "Is strName1 equal to Sydney or is strName2 equal to Sydney?" The answer to this question (providing that one of the text boxes contains the name Sydney) is, "Yes, either strName1 is equal to Sydney or strName2 is equal to Sydney." Again, it's a yes/no or true/ false answer, even though the question is seemingly more complex:

```
'Is one of the names Sydney?
If strName1 = "Sydney" Or strName2 = "Sydney" Then
    MessageBox.Show("One of the names is Sydney.", _
        "And Or Demo")
Else
    MessageBox.Show("Neither of the names is Sydney.", _
        "And Or Demo")
End If
```

Using the And Operator

The And operator is conceptually similar to Or, except that both parts of the condition need to be satisfied, as you will see in the next Try It Out.

Try It Out   **Using the And Operator**

1. Add another Button control to the form and set its Name property to **btnAndCheck** and its Text property to **And Check**. Double-click the button and add the following highlighted code to its Click event handler:

```
Private Sub btnAndCheck_Click(ByVal sender As System.Object, _
    ByVal e As System.EventArgs) Handles btnAndCheck.Click

    'Declare variables
    Dim strName1 As String, strName2 As String

    'Get the names
    strName1 = txtName1.Text
    strName2 = txtName2.Text

    'Are both names Sydney?
    If strName1 = "Sydney" And strName2 = "Sydney" Then
        MessageBox.Show("Both names are Sydney.", _
            "And Or Demo")
    Else
        MessageBox.Show("One of the names is not Sydney.", _
            "And Or Demo")
    End If
End Sub
```

2. Run the program. Click the And Check button, and a message box tells you that one of the names is not Sydney.

3. However, if you change both names so that they are both Sydney and click the button, you'll see the results shown in Figure 4-8.

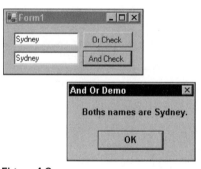

Figure 4-8

How It Works

After you've retrieved both names from the text boxes, you compare them. In this case, you're asking the question, "Is strName1 equal to Sydney *and* is strName2 equal to Sydney?" In this case, both parts of the If statement must be satisfied in order for the "Both names are Sydney" message box to be displayed:

```
'Are both names Sydney?
If strName1 = "Sydney" And strName2 = "Sydney" Then
    MessageBox.Show("Both names are Sydney.", _

        "And Or Demo")
```

```
        Else
            MessageBox.Show("One of the names is not Sydney.", _
                "And Or Demo")
        End If
```

More on And and Or

You've only seen And and Or used with strings. But they can be used with numeric values, like this:

```
If intX = 2 And intY = 2.3 Then
    MessageBox.Show("Hello, the conditions has been satisfied!")
End If
```

or

```
If intX = 2 Or intY = 2.3 Then
    MessageBox.Show("Hello, the conditions have been satisfied!")
End If
```

Also, in Visual Basic, there's no realistic limit to the number of And operators or Or operators that you can include in a statement. It's perfectly possible to do this:

```
If intA = 1 And intB = 2 And intC = 3 And intD = 4 And intE = 5 And _
    intF = 6 And intG = 7 And intH = 1 And intI = 2 And intJ = 3 And _
    intK = 4 And intL = 5 And intM = 6 And intN = 7 And intO = 1 And _
    intP = 2 And intQ = 3 And intR = 4 And intS = 5 And intT = 6 And _
    intU = 7 And intV = 1 And intW = 2 And intX = 3 And intY = 4 And _
    intZ = 5 Then
    MessageBox.Show("That's quite an If statement!")
End If
```

. . . although quite why you'd want to do so is beyond us!

Finally, it's possible to use parentheses to group operators and look for a value within a range. For example, say you want to determine whether the value of intX is between 12 and 20 exclusive or between 22 and 25 exclusive. You can use the following If . . . Then statement:

```
If (intX > 12 And intX < 20) Or (intX > 22 And intX < 25) Then
```

There are many other combinations of operators, far more than we have room to go into here. Rest assured that if you want to check for a condition, there is a combination to suit your needs.

String Comparison

When working with strings and If statements, you often run into the problem of uppercase and lower-case letters. A computer treats the characters "A" and "a" as separate entities, even though people consider them to be similar. This is known as *case sensitivity* — meaning that the case of the letters does matter when comparing strings. For example, if you run the following code, the message box would *not* be displayed.

```
Dim strName As String
strName = "Winston"
If strName = "WINSTON" Then
    MessageBox.Show("Aha! You are Winston.")
End If
```

Because WINSTON is not strictly speaking the same as Winston, because the case is different, this If statement will not return a message. However, in many cases you don't actually care about the case, so you have to find a way of comparing strings and ignoring the case of the characters. In the next Try It Out, you work with case-insensitive strings.

Using Case-Insensitive String Comparisons

1. Open the Form Designer for Form1 and add another Button control. Set the Name property to **btnStringCompare** and the Text property to **String Compare**.

2. Double-click the button to open its Click event handler and add the highlighted code:

```
Private Sub btnStringCompare_Click(ByVal sender As System.Object, _
    ByVal e As System.EventArgs) Handles btnStringCompare.Click

    'Declare variable
    Dim strName As String

    'Get the name
    strName = txtName2.Text

    'Compare the name
    If String.Compare(strName, "STEPHANIE", True) = 0 Then
        MessageBox.Show("Hello, Stephanie!", "And Or Demo")
    End If
End Sub
```

3. Run the project and click the button. You should see results like the ones shown in Figure 4-9.

Figure 4-9

4. Now, dismiss the message box and enter the name in the second text box as **StEpHaNiE**, or some other combination of upper- and lowercase letters, and click the button. You should still see a message box that says "Hello, Stephanie!"

5. However, if you enter a name that isn't Stephanie, the message box will not be displayed when you click the button.

How It Works

After you get the name back from the text box, you have to use a function to compare the two values rather than use the basic Equal To operator. In this instance, you're using the `Compare` method on `System.String` and giving it the two strings you want to compare. The first string is the value stored in `strName` (which is the value entered into the text box), with the second string being `"STEPHANIE"`. The last parameter that you supply is `True`, which tells `Compare` to perform a case-insensitive match; in other words, it should ignore the differences in case. If you had supplied `False` for this parameter, the comparison would have been case sensitive, in which case you would have been no better off than using the vanilla Equal To operator:

```
'Compare the name
If String.Compare(strName, "STEPHANIE", True) = 0 Then
    MessageBox.Show("Hello, Stephanie!", "And Or Demo")
End If
```

`String.Compare` returns a fairly curious result. It actually returns an integer, rather than a `True` or `False` value. This is because `String.Compare` can be used to determine *how* two strings are different rather than just a straightforward, "Yes, they are" or, "No, they're not." If the method returns `0`, the strings match. If the method returns a value that is not `0`, the strings do not match.

> `String.Compare` *returns an indication of how different two strings are in order to help you build sorting algorithms.*

Select Case

On occasion, you need to make a set of similar decisions like this:

❑   Is the customer called Bryan? If so, do this.

❑   Is the customer called Stephanie? If so, do this.

❑   Is the customer called Cathy? If so, do this.

❑   Is the customer called Betty? If so, do this.

❑   Is the customer called Edward? If so, do this.

You can obviously do this with a set of `If . . . Then` statements. In fact, it would look a little like this:

```
If Customer.Name = "Bryan" Then
    (do something)
ElseIf Customer.Name = "Stephanie" Then
    (do something)
```

```
ElseIf Customer.Name = "Cathy" Then
        (do something)
ElseIf Customer.Name = "Betty" Then
        (do something)
ElseIf Customer.Name = "Edward" Then
        (do something)
End If
```

Using Select Case

What happens if you decide you want to check `Customer.FirstName` instead of `Customer.Name`? You'd have to change every `If` statement, which is a pain. Also, if `Customer.Name` turns out to be `"Edward"`, you still have to go through the other four `If` statements, which is very inefficient. In the next Try It Out, you learn a better way!

Try It Out   **Using Select Case**

1. Create a new Windows Application project. Call it **Select Demo**. Set the Text property of the form to **Select Case**.

2. From the Toolbox, add a ListBox control to the form and set its Name property to **lstData**, its Dock property to **Fill**, and set its IntegralHeight property to False.

3. With the lstData selected in the Form Designer, look at the Properties window and select the Items property. Click the ellipsis dots button to the right of the property, and in the String Collection Editor that appears, add the five names on separate lines as shown in Figure 4-10.

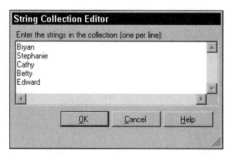

Figure 4-10

4. Click OK to save the changes, and the names are added to your list box. Now double-click lstData to create a new `SelectedIndexChanged` event handler and add the highlighted code:

```
Private Sub lstData_SelectedIndexChanged(ByVal sender As System.Object, _
    ByVal e As System.EventArgs) Handles lstData.SelectedIndexChanged

        'Declare variables
        Dim strName As String
        Dim strFavoriteColor As String

        'Get the selected name
        strName = lstData.Items(lstData.SelectedIndex)
```

```
'Use a Select Case to get the favorite color
'of the selected name
Select Case strName
    Case "Bryan"
        strFavoriteColor = "Madras Yellow"

    Case "Stephanie"
        strFavoriteColor = "Sea Blue"

    Case "Cathy"
        strFavoriteColor = "Morning Mist"

    Case "Betty"
        strFavoriteColor = "Passionate Purple"

    Case "Edward"
        strFavoriteColor = "Battleship Gray"
End Select

'Display the favorite color of the selected name
MessageBox.Show(strName & "'s favorite color is " & strFavoriteColor, _
            "Select Demo")
End Sub
```

5. Run the project. Whenever you click one of the names, a message box will appear as shown in Figure 4-11.

Figure 4-11

How It Works

The first thing you need to do in the `SelectedIndexChanged` handler is declare your variables and work out which name was selected. You do this by finding the item in the list that matches the current value of the `SelectedIndex` property:

```
'Declare variables
Dim strName As String
Dim strFavoriteColor As String

'Get the selected name
strName = lstData.Items(lstData.SelectedIndex)
```

Once you have that, you start a `Select Case` . . . `End Select` block. To do this, you need to supply the variable that you're matching against; in this case, you're using the name that was selected in the list.

Inside the `Select Case` . . . `End Select` block, you define separate `Case` statements for each condition to be checked against. In this example, you have five, and each one is set to respond to a different name. If a match can be found, Visual Basic 2005 executes the code immediately following the relevant `Case` statement.

For example, if you clicked Betty, the message box would display Passionate Purple as her favorite color, because Visual Basic 2005 would execute the line, `strFavoriteColor = "Passionate Purple"`. If you clicked Stephanie, the message box would display Sea Blue as her favorite color, because Visual Basic 2005 would execute `strFavoriteColor = "Sea Blue"`.

```
'Use a Select Case to get the favorite color
'of the selected name
Select Case strName
    Case "Bryan"
        strFavoriteColor = "Madras Yellow"

    Case "Stephanie"
        strFavoriteColor = "Sea Blue"

    Case "Cathy"
        strFavoriteColor = "Morning Mist"

    Case "Betty"
        strFavoriteColor = "Passionate Purple"

    Case "Edward"
        strFavoriteColor = "Battleship Gray"
End Select
```

After the `Select Case` . . . `End Select` block, you display a message box:

```
'Display the favorite color of the selected name
MessageBox.Show(strName & "'s favorite color is " & strFavoriteColor, _
            "Select Demo")
```

So how do you get out of a `Select Case` . . . `End Select` block? Well, as you're processing code that's beneath a `Case` statement, if you meet another `Case` statement, Visual Basic 2005 jumps out of the block and down to the line immediately following the block. Here's an illustration:

1. The user clicks Betty. The `SelectedIndexChanged` event is activated, and you store `"Betty"` in `strName`.

2. You reach the `Select Case` statement. This is set to compare the value in `strName` with one of the five supplied names.

3. Visual Basic 2005 finds a `Case` statement that satisfies the request and immediately moves to `strFavoriteColor = "Passionate Purple"`.

4. Visual Basic 2005 moves to the next line. This is another `Case` statement, and, seeing that you're already in one, you move to the first line after the `Select Case ... End Select` block and display the message box.

`Select Case` is a powerful and easy-to-use technique for making a choice from several options. However, you must leave the block as soon as another `Case` statement is reached.

Case-Insensitive Select Case

Just like `If`, `Select Case` is case sensitive; prove it to yourself in the next Try It Out.

Try It Out   Using Case-Sensitive Select Case

1. Open the Form Designer for Form1. Locate the Items property for the list box and open the String Collection Editor again.

2. Change all the names so that they appear in all uppercase letters as shown in Figure 4-12.

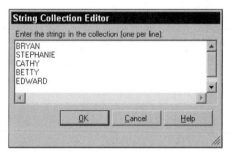

Figure 4-12

3. Click OK to save your changes and run the project. You'll notice that whenever you click a name, the message box doesn't specify a favorite color as shown in Figure 4-13.

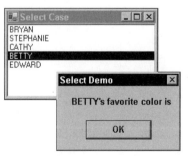

Figure 4-13

How It Works

Select Case performs a case-sensitive match, just like If. This means that if you provide the name CATHY or BETTY to the statement, there won't be a corresponding Case statement because you're trying to say:

```
If "CATHY" = "Cathy"
```

or

```
If "BETTY" = "Betty"
```

Earlier in this chapter, you took a look at how you can use the String.Compare method to perform case-insensitive comparisons with If statements. With Select Case, you can't use this method, so if you want to be insensitive towards case, you need to employ a different technique — the one you learn in the next Try It Out.

Try It Out   Case-Insensitive Select Case

1. Open the Code Editor for Form1 and make these changes to the event handler for SelectedIndexChanged. Pay special attention to the Case statements — the name that you're trying to match *must* be supplied in all lowercase letters:

```
Private Sub lstData_SelectedIndexChanged(ByVal sender As System.Object, _
    ByVal e As System.EventArgs) Handles lstData.SelectedIndexChanged

        'Declare variables
        Dim strName As String
        Dim strFavoriteColor As String

        'Get the selected name
        strName = lstData.Items(lstData.SelectedIndex)

        'Use a Select Case to get the favorite color
        'of the selected name

        Select Case strName.ToLower
            Case "bryan"
                strFavoriteColor = "Madras Yellow"

            Case "stephanie"
                strFavoriteColor = "Sea Blue"

            Case "cathy"
                strFavoriteColor = "Morning Mist"

            Case "betty"
                strFavoriteColor = "Passionate Purple"

            Case "edward"
                strFavoriteColor = "Battleship Gray"
        End Select
```

```
              'Display the favorite color of the selected name
              MessageBox.Show(strName & "'s favorite color is " & strFavoriteColor, _
                          "Select Demo")
      End Sub
```

2. Run the project and try again. This time you will see that the message box includes the favorite color of the person you click as shown in Figure 4-14.

Figure 4-14

How It Works

To make the selection case insensitive, you have to convert the strName variable into all lowercase letters. This is done using the ToLower method:

```
      Select Case strName.ToLower
```

This means that whatever string you're given (whether it's "BETTY" or "Betty") you always convert it to all lowercase ("betty"). However, when you do this, you have to make sure that you're comparing apples to apples (and not to Apples), which is why you had to convert the values you're checking against in the Case statements to all lowercase too. Therefore, if you are given "BETTY", you convert this to "betty", and then try to find the Case that matches "betty":

```
          Case "bryan"
              strFavoriteColor = "Madras Yellow"

          Case "stephanie"
              strFavoriteColor = "Sea Blue"

          Case "cathy"
              strFavoriteColor = "Morning Mist"

          Case "betty"
              strFavoriteColor = "Passionate Purple"

          Case "edward"
              strFavoriteColor = "Battleship Gray"
      End Select
```

Finally, once you have the favorite color, you display a message box as usual.

> *You could have done the opposite of this and converted all the names to uppercase and used* `strName.ToUpper` *instead of* `strName.ToLower`.

Multiple Selections

You're not limited to matching one value inside a `Select Case...End Select` block. You can also match multiple items. In the next Try It Out, you'll change the application so that you report the sex of whoever you click on.

Try It Out   Multiple Selections

1. Open the Code Editor for Form1 and change the code in the `SelectedIndexChanged` handler as highlighted here:

```
Private Sub lstData_SelectedIndexChanged(ByVal sender As System.Object, _
    ByVal e As System.EventArgs) Handles lstData.SelectedIndexChanged

    'Declare variables
    Dim strName As String
    Dim strFavoriteColor As String

    'Get the selected name
    strName = lstData.Items(lstData.SelectedIndex)

    'Use a Select Case to display a person's gender
    Select Case strName.ToLower
        Case "bryan", "edward"
            MessageBox.Show("Male", "Select Demo")
        Case "stephanie", "cathy", "betty"
            MessageBox.Show("Female", "Select Demo")
    End Select
End Sub
```

2. Run the project and click one of the female names. You will see results as shown in Figure 4-15.

Figure 4-15

How It Works

The code you use to get back the name and initialize the Select Case block remains the same. However, in each Case statement you can provide a list of possible values separated with commas. In the first one, you look for bryan *or* edward. If either of these matches, you run the code under the Case statement:

```
Case "bryan", "edward"
    MessageBox.Show("Male", "Select Demo")
```

In the second one, you look for stephanie *or* cathy *or* betty. If any of these three matches, you again run the code under the Case statement:

```
Case "stephanie", "cathy", "betty"
    MessageBox.Show("Female", "Select Demo")
```

It's important to realize that these are all *or* matches. You're saying "one *or* the other," not "one *and* the other."

The Case Else Statement

So what happens if none of the Case statements that you've included is matched? You saw this before when demonstrating the case-sensitive nature of Select Case. In the next Try It Out, you see it with the Case Else statement.

Using Case Else

1. Open the Form Designer for Form1. Locate the Items property for the list box and open the String Collection Editor again. Add another name to the collection and then click the OK button.

2. In the lstData_SelectedIndexChanged event handler, add the highlighted code:

```
'Use a Select Case to display a person's gender
Select Case strName.ToLower
    Case "bryan", "edward"
        MessageBox.Show("Male", "Select Demo")
    Case "stephanie", "cathy", "betty"
        MessageBox.Show("Female", "Select Demo")

    Case Else
        MessageBox.Show("I don't know this person's gender.", _
                        "Select Demo")
End Select
```

3. Run the project and click the last name that you just added, and you will see results similar to those shown in Figure 4-16.

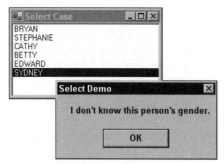

Figure 4-16

How It Works

The `Case Else` statement is used if none of the other supplied `Case` statements match what you're looking for. There isn't a `Case "sydney"` defined within the block, so you default to using whatever is underneath the `Case Else` statement. In this instance, you display a message box indicating that you do not know the gender of the person who's been selected.

Different Data Types with Select Case

In this chapter, you used `Select Case` with variables of type `String`. However, you can use `Select Case` with all basic data types in Visual Basic 2005, such as `Integer`, `Double`, and `Boolean`.

In day-to-day work, the most common types of `Select Case` are based on `String` and `Integer` data types. However, as a general rule, if a data type can be used in an `If` statement with the Equals (=) operator, it will work with `Select Case`.

Loops

When writing computer software, you often need to perform the same task several times to get the effect you want. For example, you might need to create a telephone bill for *all* customers, or read in 10 files from your computer's disk.

To accomplish this, you use a *loop*, and in this section, you'll take a look at the two main types of loops available in Visual Basic 2005:

❑   **For loops** — These loops occur a certain number of times (for example, exactly 10 times).

❑   **Do loops** — These loops keep running until a certain condition is reached (for example, until all of the data is processed).

The For . . . Next Loop

The simplest loop to understand is the For . . . Next loop, which you learn to build in the next Try It Out.

Building a For . . . Next Loop

1. Create a new Windows Application project called **Loops**.

2. Add a ListBox and a Button control to the form that appears.

3. Change the Name property of the list box to **lstData** and its IntegralHeight property to False.

4. Change the Name property of the button to **btnForNextLoop**. Also, set its Text property to **For Next Loop**. Your form should now look similar to the one shown in Figure 4-17.

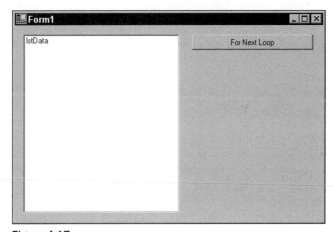

Figure 4-17

5. Double-click the button to create its Click event handler and add the highlighted code:

```
Private Sub btnForNextLoop_Click(ByVal sender As System.Object, _
    ByVal e As System.EventArgs) Handles btnForNextLoop.Click

        'Declare variable
        Dim intCount As Integer

        'Perform a loop
        For intCount = 1 To 5
            'Add the item to the list
            lstData.Items.Add("I'm item " & intCount & " in the list!")
        Next
    End Sub
```

6. Run the project and click the button. You should see results like those in Figure 4-18.

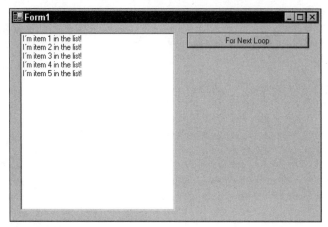

Figure 4-18

How It Works

First, inside the `Click` event handler, you define a variable:

```
'Declare variable
Dim intCount As Integer
```

Then you start the loop by using the `For` keyword. This tells Visual Basic 2005 that you want to create a loop. Everything that follows the `For` keyword is used to define how the loop should act. In this case, you're giving it the variable you just created and then telling it to count *from* 1 *to* 5:

```
'Perform a loop
For intCount = 1 To 5
```

The variable that you give the loop (in this case, `intCount`) is known as the *control variable*. When you first enter the loop, Visual Basic 2005 sets the control variable to the initial count value—in this case, 1. After the loop starts, Visual Basic 2005 moves to the first line within the `For` loop—in this case, the line that adds a string to the list box:

```
'Add the item to the list
lstData.Items.Add("I'm item " & intCount & " in the list!")
```

This time, this line of code adds `I'm item 1 in the list!` to the list box. Visual Basic 2005 then hits the `Next` statement, and that's where things start to get interesting:

```
Next
```

When the `Next` statement is executed, Visual Basic 2005 increments the control variable by one. The first time `Next` is executed, 1 changes to 2. Providing that the value of the control variable is less than or equal to the "stop" value (in this case, 5), Visual Basic 2005 moves back to the first line after the `For` statement, in this case:

```
'Add the item to the list
lstData.Items.Add("I'm item " & intCount & " in the list!")
```

This time, this line of code adds I'm item 2 in the list! to the list box. Again, after this line is executed, you run the Next statement. The value of intCount is now incremented from 2 to 3 and, because 3 is less than or equal to 5, you move back to the line that adds the item to the list. This happens until intCount is incremented from 5 to 6. As 6 is greater than the stop value for the loop, the loop stops.

When you're talking about loops, you tend to use the term iteration. One iteration includes one movement from the For statement to the Next statement. Your loop has five iterations.

Step

You don't have to start your loop at 1 — you can pick any value you like. You also don't have to increment the control value by 1 on each iteration — again, you can increment by any value you like. In the next Try It Out, you learn about the flexibility of Step.

Try It Out **Using Step**

1. Stop your project if it is still running. Add another Button control to your form and set its Name property to **btnForNextLoopWithStep** and its Text property to **For Next Loop w/Step**.

2. Double-click the button and add the following highlighted code in the Click event handler:

```
Private Sub btnForNextLoopWithStep_Click(ByVal sender As System.Object, _
    ByVal e As System.EventArgs) Handles btnForNextLoopWithStep.Click

        'Perform a loop
        For intCount As Integer = 4 To 62 Step 7
            'Add the item to the list
            lstData.Items.Add(intCount)
        Next
    End Sub
```

3. Run the project and click the button. You will see results like those in Figure 4-19.

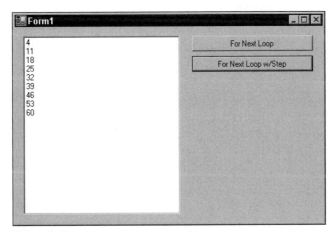

Figure 4-19

111

How It Works

The magic in this example all happens with this statement:

```
'Perform a loop
For intCount As Integer = 4 To 62 Step 7
```

First, notice that you didn't declare the `intCount` variable using a `Dim` statement. This has been done as part of the `For` statement and makes this variable local to this loop. Using the `As` keyword and the data type for the variable (in this case `Integer`), you have effectively declared an inline variable. Next, instead of using `1` as the start value, you're using `4`. This means that on the first iteration of the loop, `intCount` is set to `4`, and you can see this by the fact that the first item added to the list is indeed `4`. Also, you've used the `Step` keyword to tell the loop to increment the control value by `7` on each iteration rather than by the default of `1`. This is why, by the time you start running the second iteration of the loop, `intCount` is set to `11` and not `5`.

Although you gave `For` a stop value of `62`, the loop has actually stopped at `60` because the stop value is a *maximum*. After the ninth iteration, `intCount` is actually `67`, which is more than `62`, and so the loop stops.

Looping Backwards

By using a `Step` value that's less than `0` (or a negative number), you can make the loop go backwards rather than forward, as you see in the next Try It Out.

Try It Out   Looping Backwards

1. Stop your project if it is still running. Add another Button control to your form and set its Name property to **btnBackwardsForNextLoop** and its Text property to **Backwards For Next Loop**.

2. Double-click the button and add the following highlighted code in the `Click` event handler:

```
Private Sub btnBackwardsForNextLoop_Click(ByVal sender As System.Object, _
    ByVal e As System.EventArgs) Handles btnBackwardsForNextLoop.Click

        'Perform a loop
        For intCount As Integer = 10 To 1 Step -1
            'Add the item to the list
            lstData.Items.Add(intCount)
        Next
End Sub
```

3. Run the project and click the button. You should see results like those shown in Figure 4-20.

How It Works

If you use a negative number, like `-1`, `For` tries to add `-1` to the current control value. Adding a negative number has the effect of subtracting the number, so `intCount` goes from its start value of `10` to its new value of `9` and so on until the stop value is reached.

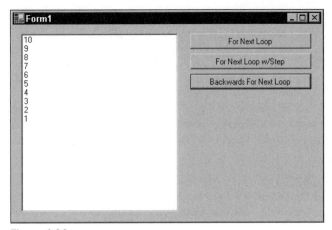

Figure 4-20

The For Each . . . Next Loop

In practical, day-to-day work, it's unlikely that you'll use For . . . Next loops as illustrated here. Because of way the .NET Framework typically works, you'll usually use a derivative of the For . . . Next loop called the For Each . . . Next loop.

In the algorithms you design, whenever a loop is necessary, you'll have a set of things to work through, and usually this set is expressed as an *array*. For example, you might want to look through all of the files in a folder, looking for ones that are over a particular size. When you ask the .NET Framework for a list of files, you are returned an array of objects, each object in that array describing a single file. In the next Try It Out, you'll modify your Loops application so that it returns a list of folders contained at the root of your C drive.

Try It Out   **For Each Loop**

1. Add another Button control to your form and set its Name property to **btnForEachLoop** and its Text property to **For Each Loop**.

2. Double-click the button and add the following highlighted code to the Click event handler:

```
Private Sub btnForEachLoop_Click(ByVal sender As System.Object, _
    ByVal e As System.EventArgs) Handles btnForEachLoop.Click

        'List each folder at the root of your C drive
        For Each strFolder As String In _
            My.Computer.FileSystem.GetDirectories("C:\")
            'Add the item to the list
            lstData.Items.Add(strFolder)
        Next
End Sub
```

3. Run the project and click the button. You should see a list of folders that are at the root of your C drive.

How It Works

The `My` namespace in the .NET Framework exposes several classes that make it easy for you to find the information that you'll use on a daily basis. In particular, the `Computer` class provides several other classes related to the computer that your program is running on. Since you want to find out about files and folders, you use the `FileSystem` class, which provides methods and properties for working with files and folders.

The `GetDirectories` method returns a *collection* of strings representing names of directories (or folders) on your computer. In this case, you use it to return a collection of names of folders in the root of the computer's C drive.

The principle with a `For Each . . . Next` loop is that for each iteration you'll be given the "thing" that you're supposed to be working with. You need to provide a source of things (in this case, a collection of strings representing folder names) and a control variable into which the current thing can be put. The `GetDirectories` method provides the collection, and the inline variable `strFolder` provides the control variable:

```
'List each folder at the root of your C drive
For Each strFolder As String In _
    My.Computer.FileSystem.GetDirectories("C:\")
Next
```

What this means is that on the first iteration, `strFolder` is equal to the first item in the string collection (in my case, `"C:\Documents and Settings"`). You then add that item to the list box:

```
'Add the item to the list
lstData.Items.Add(strFolder)
```

As with normal `For . . . Next` loops, for every iteration of the loop you're given a string containing a folder name, and you add that string to the list.

The Do . . . Loop Loops

The other kind of loop you can use is one that keeps happening until a certain condition is met. These are known as `Do . . . Loop` loops, and there are a number of variations.

The first one I'll introduce is the `Do Until . . . Loop`. This kind of loop keeps going until something happens. For this Try It Out, you're going to use the random number generator that's built into the .NET Framework and create a loop that will keep generating random numbers *until* it produces the number `10`. When you get the number `10`, you'll stop the loop.

Try It Out   Using the Do Until . . . Loop

1. In the Form Designer, add another Button control to your form and set its Name property to **btnDoUntilLoop** and its Text property to **Do Until Loop**.

2. Double-click the button and add the following highlighted code to its `Click` event handler:

```
Private Sub btnDoUntilLoop_Click(ByVal sender As System.Object, _
    ByVal e As System.EventArgs) Handles btnDoUntilLoop.Click
```

```
'Declare variables
Dim objRandom As New Random()
Dim intRandomNumber As Integer = 0

'Clear the list
lstData.Items.Clear()

'Process the loop until intRandomNumber = 10
Do Until intRandomNumber = 10
    'Get a random number between 0 and 24
    intRandomNumber = objRandom.Next(25)
    'Add the number to the list
    lstData.Items.Add(intRandomNumber)
Loop
End Sub
```

3. Run the project and click the button. You'll see results similar to the results shown in Figure 4-21. Keep clicking the button. You'll see that the number of elements in the list is different each time.

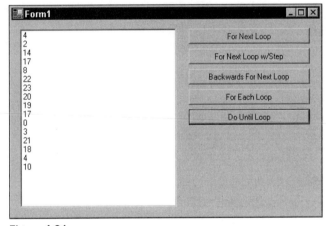

Figure 4-21

How It Works

A Do Until . . . Loop keeps running the loop until the given condition is met. When you use this type of loop, there isn't a control variable *per se*; rather, you have to keep track of the current position of the loop yourself—let's see how you do this. You begin by declaring a variable (also known as an object) for the Random class, which provides methods for generating random numbers. This object has been prefixed with obj to specify that this is an object derived from a class. The next variable that you declare is the intRandomNumber, and this variable will be used to receive the random number generated by your objRandom object:

```
'Declare variables
Dim objRandom As New Random()
Dim intRandomNumber As Integer = 0
```

Then you clear the list of any previous items that may have been added:

```
'Clear the list
lstData.Items.Clear()
```

Next, you set up the loop and tell it that you want to keep running the loop until intRandomNumber is equal to 10:

```
'Process the loop until intRandomNumber = 10
Do Until intRandomNumber = 10
```

With each iteration of the loop, you ask the random number generator for a new random number and store it in intRandomNumber. This is done by calling the Next method of objRandom to get a random number. In this case, you've passed 25 as a parameter to Next, meaning that any number returned should be between 0 and 24 inclusive — that is, the number you supply must be one larger than the biggest number you ever want to get. In other words, the bounds that you ask for are noninclusive. You then add the number that you got to the list:

```
'Get a random number between 0 and 24
intRandomNumber = objRandom.Next(25)
'Add the number to the list
lstData.Items.Add(intRandomNumber)
Loop
```

The magic happens when you get to the Loop statement. At this point, Visual Basic 2005 returns not to the first line within the loop, but instead to the Do Until line. When execution returns to Do Until, the expression is evaluated. Provided it returns False, the execution pointer moves to the first line within the loop. However, if intRandomNumber is 10, the expression returns True, and instead of moving to the first line within the loop, you continue at the first line immediately after Loop. In effect, the loop is stopped.

Do While . . . Loop

The conceptual opposite of a Do Until . . . Loop is a Do While . . . Loop. This kind of loop keeps iterating while a particular condition is True. Let's see it in action.

Try It Out   Using the Do While . . . Loop

1. Add another Button control to your form and set its Name property to **btnDoWhileLoop** and its Text property to **Do While Loop**.

2. Double-click the button and add the following highlighted code to the Click event handler:

```
Private Sub btnDoWhileLoop_Click(ByVal sender As System.Object, _
    ByVal e As System.EventArgs) Handles btnDoWhileLoop.Click

    'Declare variables
    Dim objRandom As New Random()
    Dim intRandomNumber As Integer = 0

    'Clear the list
    lstData.Items.Clear()
```

```
                'Process the loop while intRandomNumber < 15
                Do While intRandomNumber < 15
                    'Get a random number between 0 and 24
                    intRandomNumber = objRandom.Next(25)
                    'Add the number to the list
                    lstData.Items.Add(intRandomNumber)
                Loop
        End Sub
```

3. Run the project and click the button. You'll see something similar to the results shown in Figure 4-22.

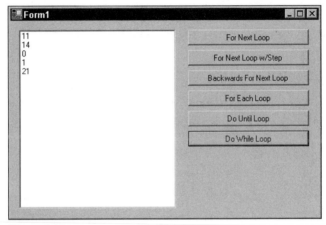

Figure 4-22

4. Every time you press the button, the loop executes until the random number generator produces a number greater than or equal to 15.

How It Works

A Do While...Loop keeps running so long as the given expression remains True. As soon as the expression becomes False, the loop quits. When you start the loop, you check to make sure that intRandomNumber is less than 15. If it is, the expression returns True, and you can run the code within the loop:

```
                'Process the loop while intRandomNumber < 15
                Do While intRandomNumber < 15
                    'Get a random number between 0 and 24
                    intRandomNumber = objRandom.Next(25)
                    'Add the number to the list
                    lstData.Items.Add(intRandomNumber)
                Loop
```

Again, when you get to the Loop statement, Visual Basic 2005 moves back up to the Do While statement. When it gets there, it evaluates the expression again. If it's True, you run the code inside the loop once more. If it's False (because intRandomNumber is greater than or equal to 15), you continue with the first line after Loop, effectively quitting the loop.

Acceptable Expressions for a Do . . . Loop

You might be wondering what kind of expressions you can use with the two variations of Do . . . Loop. If you can use it with an If statement, you can use it with a Do . . . Loop. For example, you can write this:

```
Do While intX > 10 And intX < 100
```

or

```
Do Until (intX > 10 And intX < 100) Or intY = True
```

or

```
Do While String.Compare(strA, strB) > 0
```

In short, it's a pretty powerful loop!

Other Versions of the Do . . . Loop

It's possible to put the Until or While statements after Loop rather than after Do. Consider these two loops:

```
Do While intX < 3
      intX += 1
Loop
```

and

```
Do
      intX += 1
Loop While intX < 3
```

At first glance, it looks like the While intX < 3 has just been moved around. You might think that these two loops are equivalent—but there's a subtle difference. Suppose the value of intX is greater than 3 (4 say) as these two Do loops start. The first loop will not run at all. However, the second loop will run *once*. When the Loop While intX < 3 line is executed, the loop will be exited. This happens despite the condition saying that intX must be less than 3.

Now consider these two Do Until loops:

```
Do Until intX = 3
      intX += 1
Loop
```

... and ...

```
Do
      intX += 1
Loop Until intX = 3
```

Again, although at first glance it looks like these two loops are equivalent, they're not and behave slightly differently. Let's say that intX is 3 this time. The first loop isn't going to run, as intX already meets the exit condition for this loop. However, the second loop will run *once*. Then when you execute Loop Until intX = 3 the first time, intX is now 4. So you go back to the start of the loop and increment intX to 5, and so on. In fact, this is a classic example of an infinite loop (something I'll discuss later in this chapter) and will not stop.

> *When you use* Loop While *or* Loop Until, *you are saying that, no matter what, you want the loop to execute at least once. In general, I find it's best to stick with* Do While *and* Do Until, *rather than use* Loop While *and* Loop Until.

You may also come across a variation of Do While . . . Loop called the While . . . End While. This convention is a throwback to previous versions of Visual Basic, but old-school developers may still use it with .NET code, so it's important that you can recognize it. These two are equivalent, but you should use the first one.

```
Do While intX < 3
    intX += 1
Loop
```

and

```
While intX < 3
    intX += 1
End While
```

Nested Loops

You might need to start a loop even though you're already working through another loop. This is known as *nesting*, and is similar in theory to the nesting that you saw when you looked at If statements. In this Try It Out, you'll see how you can create and run through a loop, even though you're already working through another one.

Try It Out   Using Nested Loops

1. In the Form Designer, add another Button control to your form and set its Name property to **btnNestedLoops** and its Text property to **Nested Loops**.

2. Double-click the button and add the following highlighted code to its Click event handler:

```
Private Sub btnNestedLoops_Click(ByVal sender As System.Object, _
    ByVal e As System.EventArgs) Handles btnNestedLoops.Click

        'Process an outer loop
        For intLoop1 As Integer = 1 To 2
            'Process a nested (inner) loop
            For intLoop2 As Integer = 1 To 3
                lstData.Items.Add(intLoop1 & ", " & intLoop2)
            Next
        Next
End Sub
```

3. Run the program and click the button. You should see results that look like those shown in Figure 4-23.

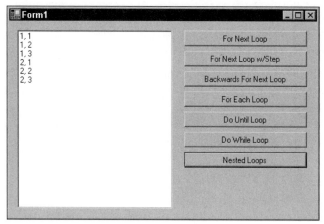

Figure 4-23

How It Works

This code is really quite simple. Your first loop (outer loop) iterates intLoop1 from 1 to 2, and the nested loop (inner loop) iterates intLoop2 from 1 to 3. Within the nested loop, you have a line of code to display the current values of intLoop1 and intLoop2:

```
'Process an outer loop
For intLoop1 As Integer = 1 To 2
    'Process a nested (inner) loop
    For intLoop2 As Integer = 1 To 3
        lstData.Items.Add(intLoop1 & ", " & intLoop2)
    Next
Next
```

Each For statement must be paired with a Next statement, and each Next statement that you reach always "belongs" to the last created For statement. In this case, the first Next statement you reach is for the 1 To 3 loop, which results in m being incremented. When the value of intLoop2 gets to be 4, you exit the inner loop.

After you've quit the inner loop, you hit another Next statement. This statement belongs to the first For statement, so intLoop1 is set to 2 and you move back to the first line within the first, outer loop — in this case, the other For statement. Once there, the loop starts once more. Although in this Try It Out you've seen two For . . . Next loops nested together, you can nest Do . . . While loops and even mix them, so you can have two Do . . . Loops nested inside a For loop and vice versa.

Quitting Early

Sometimes you don't want to see a loop through to its natural conclusion. For example, you might be looking through a list for something specific, and when you find it, there's no need to go through the remainder of the list.

In this Try It Out, you'll revise your program that looked through folders on the local drive, but this time, when you get to c:\Program Files, you'll display a message and quit.

Quitting a Loop Early

1. Add another Button control to your form and set its Name property to **btnQuittingAForLoop** and its Text property to **Quitting a For Loop**.

2. Double-click the button and add the following highlighted code to the Click event handler:

```
Private Sub btnQuittingAForLoop_Click(ByVal sender As System.Object, _
    ByVal e As System.EventArgs) Handles btnQuittingAForLoop.Click

        'List each folder at the root of your C drive
        For Each strFolder As String In _
            My.Computer.FileSystem.GetDirectories("C:\")

            'Add the item to the list
            lstData.Items.Add(strFolder)

            'Do you have the folder C:\Program Files?
            If String.Compare(strFolder, "c:\program files", True) = 0 Then

                'Tell the user
                MessageBox.Show("Found it, exiting the loop now.", "Loops")

                'Quit the loop early
                Exit For

            End If
        Next
    End Sub
```

3. Run the program and click the button. You'll see something similar to the results shown in Figure 4-24.

How It Works

This time, with each iteration, you use the String.Compare method that was discussed earlier to check the name of the folder to see whether it matches C:\Program Files:

```
        'Do you have the folder C:\Program Files?
        If String.Compare(strFolder, "c:\program files", True) = 0 Then
```

If it does, the first thing you do is display a message box:

```
            'Tell the user
            MessageBox.Show("Found it, exiting the loop now.", "Loops")
```

After the user has clicked OK to dismiss the message box, you use the Exit For statement to quit the loop. In this instance, the loop is short-circuited, and Visual Basic 2005 moves to the first line after the Next statement.

```
            'Quit the loop early
            Exit For
```

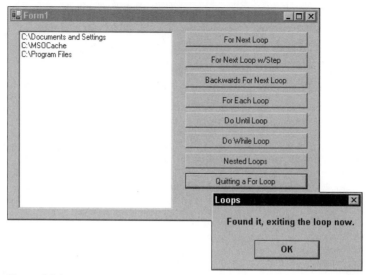

Figure 4-24

Of course, if the name of the folder doesn't match the one you're looking for, you keep looping. Using loops to find an item in a list is one of their most common uses. Once you've found the item you're looking for, using the Exit For statement to short-circuit the loop is a very easy way to improve the performance of your application.

Imagine you have a list of a thousand items to look through. You find the item you're looking for on the tenth iteration. If you don't quit the loop after you've found the item, you're effectively asking the computer to look through another 990 useless items. If, however, you do quit the loop early, you can move on and start running another part of the algorithm.

Quitting Do . . . Loops

As you might have guessed, you can quit a Do . . . Loop in more or less the same way, as you see in the next Try It Out.

Try It Out   Quitting a Do . . . Loop

1. Add another Button control to your form and set its Name property to **btnQuittingADoLoop** and its Text property to **Quitting a Do Loop**.

2. Double-click the button and add the following highlighted code to the Click event handler:

```
Private Sub btnQuittingADoLoop_Click(ByVal sender As System.Object, _
    ByVal e As System.EventArgs) Handles btnQuittingADoLoop.Click
```

```
        'Declare variable
        Dim intCount As Integer = 0

        'Process the loop
        Do While intCount < 10
```

```
            'Add the item to the list
            lstData.Items.Add(intCount)

            'Increment intCount by 1
            intCount += 1

            'Should you quit
            If intCount = 3 Then
                Exit Do
            End If

        Loop
End Sub
```

3. Run the project and click the button. You'll see a list containing the values 0, 1, and 2.

How It Works

In this case, because you're in a Do . . . Loop, you have to use Exit Do rather than Exit For. However, the principle is exactly the same. Exit Do will work with both the Do While . . . Loop and Do Until . . . Loop loops.

Infinite Loops

When building loops, you can create something called an *infinite loop*. What this means is a loop that, once started, will never finish. Consider this code:

```
Dim intX As Integer = 0
Do
    intX += 1
Loop Until intX = 0
```

This loop will start and run through the first iteration. Then when you execute Loop Until intX = 0 the first time, intX is 1. So you go back to the start of the loop again and increment intX to 2, and so on. What's important here is that it will never get to 0. The loop becomes infinite, and the program won't crash (at least not instantly), but it may well become unresponsive.

If you suspect a program has dropped into an infinite loop, you'll need to force the program to stop. With Windows XP, this is pretty easy. If you are running your program in Visual Studio 2005, flip over to it, and select Debug ➪ Stop Debugging from the menu. This will immediately stop the program. If you are running your compiled program, you'll need to use the Windows Task Manager. Press Ctrl+Alt+Del and select Task Manager. Your program should show as Not Responding. Select your program in the Task Manager and click End Task. Eventually this opens a dialog saying that the program is not responding (which you knew already) and asking whether you want to kill the program stone dead, so click End Task again.

In some extreme cases, the loop can take up so much processing power or other system resources that you won't be able to open Task Manager or flip over to Visual Studio. In these cases, you can persevere and try to use either of these methods; or you can reset your computer and chalk it up to experience.

Visual Studio 2005 does not automatically save your project before running the application, so you're likely to lose all of your program code if you have to reset. Therefore, it would be wise to save your project before you start running your code.

Summary

In this chapter, you took a detailed look at the various ways that programs can make decisions and loop through code. You first saw the alternative operators that can be used with If statements and examined how multiple operators could be combined by using the And and Or keywords. Additionally, you examined how case-insensitive string comparisons could be performed.

You then looked at Select Case, an efficient technique for choosing one outcome out of a group of possibilities. Next you examined the concept of looping within a program and were introduced to the two main types of loops: For loops and Do loops. For loops iterate a given number of times, and the derivative For Each loop can be used to loop automatically through a list of items in a collection. Do While loops iterate while a given condition remains True, whereas Do Until loops iterate until a given condition becomes True.

In summary, you should know how to use:

❑ If, ElseIf, and Else statements to test for multiple conditions

❑ Nested If statements

❑ Comparison operators and the String.Compare method

❑ The Select Case statement to perform multiple comparisons

❑ For . . . Next and For . . . Each loops

❑ Do . . . Loop and Do While . . . Loop statements

Exercises

Exercise 1

Create a Windows Application with a text box and a Button control. In the Click event of the Button, extract the number from the text box and use a Select Case statement with the numbers 1 through 5. In the Case statement for each number, display the number in a message box. Ensure that you provide code to handle numbers that are not in the range of 1 through 5.

Exercise 2

Create a Windows Application that contains a ListBox control and a Button control. In the Click event for the button, create a For . . . Next loop that will count from 1 to 10 and display the results in the list box. Then create another For . . . Next loop that will count backwards from 10 to 1 and also display those results in the list box.

Working with Data Structures

In the last couple of chapters, you worked with simple data types, naming `Integer` and `String` variables. While these data types are useful in their own rights, more complex programs call for working with *data structures*; that is, groups of data elements that are organized in a single unit. In this chapter, you learn about the various data structures available in Visual Basic 2005 and will see some ways in which you can work with complex sets of data. You will also learn how you can build powerful collection classes for working with, maintaining, and manipulating lists of complex data.

In this chapter, you will learn about:

❑ Arrays

❑ Enumerations

❑ Constants

❑ Structures

Understanding Arrays

A fairly common requirement in writing software is the ability to hold lists of similar or related data. You can provide this functionality by using an *array*. Arrays are just lists of data that have a single data type. For example, you might want to store a list of your friends' ages in an integer array or their names in a string array.

In this section, you take a look at how to define, populate, and use arrays in your applications.

Defining and Using Arrays

When you define an array, you're actually creating a variable that has more than one dimension. For example, if you define a variable as a string, as follows, you can only hold a single string value in it:

```
Dim strName As String
```

However, with an array you create a kind of multiplier effect with a variable, so you can hold more than one value in a single variable. An array is defined by entering the size of the array after the variable name. So, if you wanted to define a string array with 10 elements, you'd do this:

```
Dim strName(9) As String
```

The reason you use (9) *instead of* (10) *to get an array with 10 elements is explained in detail later. For now it is simply because numbering in an array starts at zero, so the first element is zero in an array, the second element is one in an array, and so on.*

Once you have an array, you can access individual elements in it by providing an index value between 0 and a maximum possible value — this maximum possible value happens to be one less than the total size of the array.

So, to set the element with index 2 in the array, you'd do this:

```
strName(2) = "Katie"
```

To get that same element back again, you'd do this:

```
MessageBox.Show(strName(2))
```

What's important is that other elements in the array are unaffected when you set their siblings. So, if you do this:

```
strName(3) = "Betty"
```

strName(2) remains set to "Katie".

Perhaps the easiest way to understand what an array looks like and how one works is to write some code that uses them.

Try It Out   **Defining and Using a Simple Array**

1. Using Visual Studio 2005, click the File menu and choose New ➪ Project. In the New Project dialog box, create a new Windows Application called **Array Demo**.

2. When the Designer for Form1 appears, add a ListBox control to the form. Using the Properties window set its Name property to **lstFriends** and its IntegralHeight property to False.

3. Now add a Button control to the form, set its Name property to **btnArrayElement**, and set its Text property to **Array Element**. Your form should now look something like Figure 5-1.

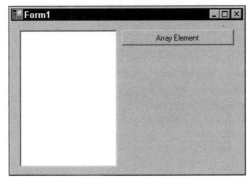

Figure 5-1

4. Double-click the button and add the following highlighted code to its `Click` event handler:

```
Private Sub btnArrayElement_Click(ByVal sender As System.Object, _
    ByVal e As System.EventArgs) Handles btnArrayElement.Click
```

```
        'Declare an array
        Dim strFriends(4) As String

        'Populate the array
        strFriends(0) = "Robbin"
        strFriends(1) = "Bryan"
        strFriends(2) = "Stephanie"
        strFriends(3) = "Sydney"
        strFriends(4) = "Katie"

        'Add the first array item to the list
        lstFriends.Items.Add(strFriends(0))
    End Sub
```

5. Run the project and click the button. The list box on your form will be *populated* with the name `Robbin`.

How It Works

When you define an array, you have to specify a data type and a size. In this case, you're specifying an array of type `String` and also defining an array size of `5`. The way the size is defined is a little quirky. You have to specify a number one less than the final size you want (you'll learn why shortly). So here, you have used the line:

```
        'Declare an array
        Dim strFriends(4) As String
```

In this way, you end up with an array of size 5. Another way of expressing this is to say that you have an array consisting of 5 *elements*.

Once done, you have your array, and you can access each item in the array by using an *index*. The index is given as a number in parentheses after the name of the array. Indexes start at zero and go up to one less than the number of items in the array. The following example sets all five possible items in the array to the names:

```
'Populate the array
strFriends(0) = "Robbin"
strFriends(1) = "Bryan"
strFriends(2) = "Stephanie"
strFriends(3) = "Sydney"
strFriends(4) = "Katie"
```

Just as you can use an index to set the items in an array, you can use an index to get items back out. In this case, you're asking for the item at position 0, which returns the first item in the array, namely Robbin:

```
'Add the first array item to the list
lstFriends.Items.Add(strFriends(0))
```

The reason the indexes and sizes seem skewed is because the indexes are zero-based, whereas humans tend to number things beginning at 1. When putting items into or retrieving items from an array, you have to adjust the position you want down by one to get the actual index; for example, the fifth item is actually at position 4, the first item is at position 0, and so on. When you define an array, you do not actually specify the size of the array but rather the upper *index bound* — that is, the highest possible value of the index that the array will support.

But why should the indexes be zero-based? Remember that to the computer, a variable represents the address of a location in the computer's memory. Given an array index, Visual Basic 2005 just multiplies the index by the size of one element and adds the product to the address of the array as a whole to get the address of the specified element. The starting address of the array as a whole is also the starting address of the first element in it. That is, the first element is zero times the size of an element away from the start of the whole array; the second element is 1 times the size of an element away from the start of the whole array; and so on.

Using For Each . . . Next

One common way to work with arrays is by using a For Each . . . Next loop. This loop was introduced in Chapter 4, when you used them with a string collection returned from the My.Computer.FileSystem.GetDirectories method. In the next Try It Out, you look at how you use For Each . . . Next with an array.

Try It Out   Using For Each . . . Next with an Array

1.   If the program is running, close it. Open the Code Editor for Form1 and add the following variable declaration at the top of your form class:

```
Public Class Form1
```

```
'Declare a form level array
Private strFriends(4) As String
```

2. In the Class Name combo box at the top left of your Code Editor, select (Form1 Events). In the Method Name combo box at the top right of your Code Editor, select the Load event. This causes the Form1_Load event handler to be inserted into your code. Add the following highlighted code to this procedure:

```
Private Sub Form1_Load(ByVal sender As Object, _
    ByVal e As System.EventArgs) Handles Me.Load

    'Populate the array
    strFriends(0) = "Robbin"
    strFriends(1) = "Bryan"
    strFriends(2) = "Stephanie"
    strFriends(3) = "Sydney"
    strFriends(4) = "Katie"
End Sub
```

3. Switch to the Form Designer and add another Button control. Set its Name property to **btnEnumerateArray** and its Text property to **Enumerate Array**.

4. Double-click this new button and add the following highlighted code to its Click event handler:

```
Private Sub btnEnumerateArray_Click(ByVal sender As System.Object, _
    ByVal e As System.EventArgs) Handles btnEnumerateArray.Click

    'Enumerate the array
    For Each strName As String In strFriends
        'Add the array item to the list
        lstFriends.Items.Add(strName)
    Next
End Sub
```

5. Run the project and click the button. You'll see results like those in Figure 5-2.

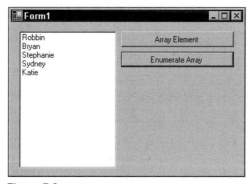

Figure 5-2

How It Works

You start this exercise by declaring an array variable that is local to the form, meaning that the variable is available to all procedures in the form class. Whenever variables are declared outside a method in the form class, they are available to all methods in the form.

```
'Declare a form-level array
Private strFriends(4) As String
```

Next you added the Load event handler for the form and then added code to populate the array. This procedure will be called whenever the form loads, ensuring that your array always gets populated.

```
Private Sub Form1_Load(ByVal sender As Object, _
    ByVal e As System.EventArgs) Handles Me.Load

    'Populate the array
    strFriends(0) = "Robbin"
    strFriends(1) = "Bryan"
    strFriends(2) = "Stephanie"
    strFriends(3) = "Sydney"
    strFriends(4) = "Katie"
End Sub
```

In Chapter 4, you saw the For Each . . . Next loop iterate through a string collection; in this example, it is used in an array. The principle is similar; you have to create a control variable that is of the same type as an element in the array and gives this to the loop when it starts. This has all been done in one line of code. The control variable, strName, is declared and used in the For Each statement by using the As String keyword.

The internals behind the loop move through the array starting at element 0 until it reaches the last element. For each iteration, you can examine the value of the control variable and do something with it; in this case, you add the name to the list.

```
'Enumerate the array
For Each strName As String In strFriends
    'Add the array item to the list
    lstFriends.Items.Add(strName)
Next
```

Also, notice that the items are added to the list in the same order that they appear in the array. That's because For Each . . . Next goes through from the first item to the last item as they are defined.

Passing Arrays as Parameters

It's extremely useful to be able to pass an array (which could be a list of values) to a function as a parameter. In the next Try It Out, you'll look at how to do this.

Try It Out   Passing Arrays as Parameters

1. Switch to the Form Designer and add another Button control. Set its Name property to **btnArraysAsParameters** and its Text property to **Arrays as Parameters**.

2. Double-click the button and add the following highlighted code to its `Click` event handler. You'll receive an error message that the `AddItemsToList` procedure is not defined. You can ignore this error because you'll be adding that procedure in the next step:

```
Private Sub btnArraysAsParameters_Click(ByVal sender As System.Object, _
    ByVal e As System.EventArgs) Handles btnArraysAsParameters.Click

        'List your friends
        AddItemsToList(strFriends)
End Sub
```

3. Now add the `AddItemsToList` procedure as follows:

```
Sub AddItemsToList(ByVal arrayList() As String)
        'Enumerate the array
        For Each strName As String In arrayList
            'Add the array item to the list
            lstFriends.Items.Add(strName)
        Next
End Sub
```

4. Run the project and click the button. You'll see the same results that were shown in Figure 5-2.

How It Works

The trick here is to tell the `AddItemsToList` function that the parameter it's expecting is an array of type `String`. You do this by using empty parentheses, like this:

```
Sub AddItemsToList(ByVal arrayList() As String)
```

If you specify an array but don't define a size (or upper bound value), you're telling Visual Basic 2005 that you don't know or care how big the array is. That means that you can pass an array of any size through to `AddItemsToList`. In the `btnArraysAsParameters_Click` procedure, you're sending your original array:

```
        'List your friends
        AddItemsToList(strFriends)
```

But what happens if you define another array of a different size? In the next Try It Out, you'll find out.

Try It Out   **Adding More Friends**

1. Stop your project if it is still running, and switch to the Form Designer. Add another Button control and set its Name property to **btnMoreArrayParameters** and its Text property to **More Array Parameters**.

2. Double-click the button and add the following highlighted code to its `Click` event handler:

```
Private Sub btnMoreArrayParameters_Click(ByVal sender As System.Object, _
    ByVal e As System.EventArgs) Handles btnMoreArrayParameters.Click
```

```
            'Declare an array
            Dim strMoreFriends(1) As String

            'Populate the array
            strMoreFriends(0) = "Matt"
            strMoreFriends(1) = "Margie"

            'List your friends
            AddItemsToList(strFriends)
            AddItemsToList(strMoreFriends)
    End Sub
```

3. Run the project and click the button. You will see the form shown in Figure 5-3.

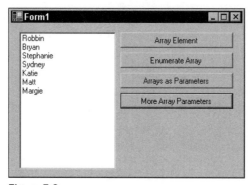

Figure 5-3

How It Works

What you have done here is proven that the array you pass as a parameter does not have to be of a fixed size. You created a new array of size 2 and passed it through to the same `AddItemsToList` function.

As you're writing code, you can tell whether a parameter is an array type by looking for empty parentheses in the IntelliSense pop-up box, as illustrated in Figure 5-4.

Figure 5-4

Not only are you informed that friends *is an array type, but you also see that the data type of the array is* String.

Sorting Arrays

It is sometimes useful to be able to take an array and sort it. In this Try It Out, you will see how you can take an array and sort it alphabetically.

Try It Out   **Sorting Arrays**

1. In the Form Designer, add another Button control and set its Name property to **btnSortingArrays** and its Text property to **Sorting Arrays.**

2. Double-click the button and add the following highlighted code to its `Click` event handler:

```
Private Sub btnSortingArrays_Click(ByVal sender As System.Object, _
     ByVal e As System.EventArgs) Handles btnSortingArrays.Click

        'Sort the array
        Array.Sort(strFriends)

        'List your friends
        AddItemsToList(strFriends)
End Sub
```

3. Run the project and click the button. You'll see the list box on your form populated with the names from your array sorted alphabetically.

How It Works

All arrays are internally implemented in a class called `System.Array`. In this case, you use a method on that class called `Sort`. The `Sort` method takes a single parameter — namely, the array you want to sort. The method then does as its name suggests and sorts it for you into an order appropriate to the data type of the array elements. In this case you are using a string array, so you get an alphanumeric sort. If you were to attempt to use this technique on an array containing integer or floating-point values, the array would be sorted in numeric order.

```
        'Sort the array
        Array.Sort(strFriends)
```

The ability to pass different parameter types in different calls to the same method name and to get behavior that is appropriate to the parameter types actually passed is called *method overloading*. We say that `Sort` is an overloaded method.

Going Backwards

`For Each ... Next` will go through an array in only one direction. It starts at position 0 and loops through to the end of the array. If you want to go through an array backwards (from the length -1 position to 0), you have two options.

First, you can step through the loop backwards by using a standard `For ... Next` loop to start at the upper index bound of the first dimension in the array and work your way to 0 using the `Step -1` keyword, as shown in the following example:

```
        For intIndex As Integer = strFriends.GetUpperBound(0) To 0 Step -1
            'Add the array item to the list
            lstFriends.Items.Add(strFriends(intIndex))
        Next
```

You can also call the `Reverse` method on the Array class to reverse the order of the array and then use your `For Each ... Next` loop, as shown in the next Try It Out.

Reversing An Array

1. Add another Button control in the Form Designer and set its Name property to **btnReversingAnArray** and its Text property to **Reversing an Array.**

2. Double-click the button and add the following highlighted code to its `Click` event handler:

```
Private Sub btnReversingAnArray_Click(ByVal sender As System.Object, _
    ByVal e As System.EventArgs) Handles btnReversingAnArray.Click

        'Reverse the order - elements will be in descending order
        Array.Reverse(strFriends)

        'List your friends
        AddItemsToList(strFriends)
End Sub
```

3. Run the project and click the button. You'll see the friends listed in reverse order as shown in Figure 5-5.

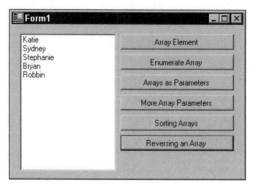

Figure 5-5

How It Works

The `Reverse` method reverses the order of elements in a one-dimensional array, which is what you are working with here. By passing the `strFriends` array to the `Reverse` method, you are asking the `Reverse` method to resequence the array from bottom to top:

```
        'Reverse the order - elements will be in descending order
        Array.Reverse(strFriends)
```

Once the items in your array have been reversed, you simply call the `AddItemsToList` procedure to have the items listed:

```
'List your friends
AddItemsToList(strFriends)
```

If you want to list your array in descending sorted order, you would call the `Sort` *method on the Array class to have the items sorted in ascending order and then call the* `Reverse` *method to have the sorted array reversed, putting it into descending order.*

Initializing Arrays with Values

It is possible to create an array in Visual Basic 2005 and populate it in one line of code, rather than having to write multiple lines of code to declare and populate the array as shown here:

```
'Declare an array
Dim strFriends(4) As String

'Populate the array
strFriends(0) = "Robbin"
strFriends(1) = "Bryan"
strFriends(2) = "Stephanie"
strFriends(3) = "Sydney"
strFriends(4) = "Katie"
```

You will learn more about initializing arrays with values in the next Try It Out.

Try It Out   **Initializing Arrays with Values**

1. Add another Button control in the Form Designer and set its Name property to **btnInitializingArraysWithValues** and its Text property to **Initializing Arrays with Values.**

2. Double-click the button and add the following highlighted code to its `Click` event handler:

```
Private Sub btnInitializingArraysWithValues_Click( _
    ByVal sender As System.Object, ByVal e As System.EventArgs) _
    Handles btnInitializingArraysWithValues.Click

    'Declare and populate an array
    Dim strMyFriends() As String = {"Robbin", "Bryan", "Stephanie", _
        "Sydney", "Katie"}

    'List your friends
    AddItemsToList(strMyFriends)
End Sub
```

3. Run the project and click the button. Your list box will be populated with the friends listed in this array.

How It Works

The pair of braces {} allows you to set the values that should be held in an array directly. In this instance, you have five values to enter into the array, separated with commas. Notice that when you do this, you don't specify an upper bound for the array; instead, you use empty parentheses. Visual Basic 2005 prefers to calculate the upper bound for you based on the values you supply.

```
'Declare and populate an array
Dim strMyFriends() As String = {"Robbin", "Bryan", "Stephanie", _
    "Sydney", "Katie"}
```

This technique can be quite awkward to use when populating large arrays. If your program relies on populating large arrays, you might want to use the method illustrated earlier: specifying the positions and the values.

Understanding Enumerations

So far, the variables you've seen had virtually no limitations on the kinds of data you can store in them. Technical limits notwithstanding, if you have a variable defined As Integer, you can put any number you like in it. The same holds true for String and Double. You have seen another variable type, however, that has only two possible values: Boolean variables can be either True or False and nothing else.

Often, when writing code, you want to limit the possible values that can be stored in a variable. For example, if you have a variable that stores the number of doors that a car has, do you really want to be able to store the value 163,234?

Using Enumerations

Enumerations allow you to build a new type of variable, based on one of these data types: Integer, Long, Short, or Byte. This variable can be set to one value of a set of possible values that you define, and ideally prevent someone from supplying invalid values. It is used to provide clarity in the code, as it can describe a particular value. In the following Try It Out, you'll look at how to build an application that looks at the time of day and, based on that, can record a DayAction of one of these possible values:

❑ Asleep

❑ Getting ready for work

❑ Traveling to work

❑ At work

❑ At lunch

❑ Traveling from work

❑ Relaxing with friends

❑ Getting ready for bed

Try It Out   **Using Enumerations**

1. Using Visual Studio 2005, create a new Windows Application project called **Enum Demo**.

2. Enumerations are typically defined as a member of the class that intends to use them (though this does not have to be the case). When the Designer for Form1 opens, open the Code Editor for the form and add the highlighted code to the top:

```
Public Class Form1
```

```
    'DayAction Enumeration
    Private Enum DayAction As Integer
        Asleep = 0
        GettingReadyForWork = 1
        TravelingToWork = 2
        AtWork = 3
        AtLunch = 4
        TravelingFromWork = 5
        RelaxingWithFriends = 6
        GettingReadyForBed = 7
    End Enum
```

3. With an enumeration defined, you can create new member variables that use the enumeration as their data type. Add this member:

```
    'Declare variable
    Private CurrentState As DayAction
```

4. Flip back to the Designer for Form1. Change the Text property of Form1 to **What's Matt Doing?**.

5. Now add a DateTimePicker control and set the following properties.

    ❑   Set Name to **dtpHour**.

    ❑   Set Format to Time.

    ❑   Set ShowUpDown to True.

    ❑   Set Value to **00:00 AM**.

    ❑   Set Size to **91, 20**.

6. Add a Label control to the form, set its Name property to **lblState**, and set its Text property to **State Not Initialized**. Resize your form so it looks similar to Figure 5-6.

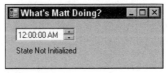

Figure 5-6

7. Double-click the background of the form to create a new Load event handler. Add the following highlighted code. You'll receive an error message that `Hour` is not defined; you can ignore this error, because in the next step you'll be defining `Hour` as a new *property* of the form:

```
Private Sub Form1_Load(ByVal sender As System.Object, _
    ByVal e As System.EventArgs) Handles MyBase.Load

    'Set the Hour property to the current hour
    Me.Hour = Now.Hour
End Sub
```

8. Now, add following code below the code you added in step 3 in the Code Editor for the form:

```
'Hour property
Private Property Hour() As Integer
    Get
        'Return the current hour displayed
        Return dtpHour.Value.Hour
    End Get
    Set(ByVal value As Integer)
        'Set the date using the hour passed to this property
        dtpHour.Value = _
            New Date(Now.Year, Now.Month, Now.Day, value, 0, 0)
        'Set the display text
        lblState.Text = "At " & value & ":00, Matt is "
    End Set
End Property
```

9. In the Class Name combo box at the top of the Code Editor, select dtpHour, and in the Method Name combo box, select the ValueChanged event. Add the following highlighted code to the event handler:

```
Private Sub dtpHour_ValueChanged(ByVal sender As Object, _
    ByVal e As System.EventArgs) Handles dtpHour.ValueChanged

    'Update the Hour property
    Me.Hour = dtpHour.Value.Hour
End Sub
```

10. Run the project. You will be able to click the up and down arrows in the date and time picker control and see the text updated to reflect the hour selected as shown in Figure 5-7.

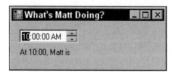

Figure 5-7

How It Works

In this application, the user will be able to use the date-time picker to choose the hour. You then look at the hour and determine which one of the eight states Matt is in at the given time. To achieve this, you have to keep the hour around somehow. To store the hour, you have created a property for the form in addition to the properties it already has, such as Name. The new property is called Hour, and it is used to set the current hour in the DateTimePicker control and the label control. The property is defined with a Property ... End Property statement:

```
Private Property Hour() As Integer
    Get
        . . .
        Return dtpHour.Value.Hour
    End Get
    Set(ByVal value As Integer)
        . . .
    End Set
End Property
```

Notice the Get ... End Get and Set ... End Set blocks inside the Property ... End Property statement. The Get block contains a Return statement and is called automatically to return the property value when the property name appears in an expression. The data type to be returned is not specified in the Get statement, because it was already declared As Integer in the Property statement. The Set block is called automatically when the value is set, such as by putting the property name to the left of an equals sign.

When the application starts, you set the Hour property to the current hour on your computer. You get this information from Now, a Date variable containing the current date and time:

```
Private Sub Form1_Load(ByVal sender As System.Object, _
    ByVal e As System.EventArgs) Handles MyBase.Load

    'Set the Hour property to the current hour
    Me.Hour = Now.Hour
End Sub
```

You also set the Hour property when the Value property changes in the DateTimePicker control:

```
Private Sub dtpHour_ValueChanged(ByVal sender As Object, _
    ByVal e As System.EventArgs) Handles dtpHour.ValueChanged

    'Update the Hour property
    Me.Hour = dtpHour.Value.Hour
End Sub
```

When the Hour property is set, you have to update the value of the DateTimePicker control to show the new hour value, and you have to update the label on the form as well. The code to perform these actions is put inside the Set block for the Hour property.

The first update that you perform is to update the Value property of the DateTimePicker control. The Value property of the date-time picker is a Date data type; thus, you cannot simply set the hour in this control, although you can retrieve just the hour from this property. In order to update this property, you must pass it a Date data type.

You do this by calling New (see Chapter 10) for the Date class, passing it the different date and time parts as shown in the code: year, month, day, hour, minute, second. You get the year, month, and day by extracting them from Now variable. The hour is passed using the value that was passed to this Hour property, and the minutes and seconds are passed as 0, since you do not want to update the specific minutes or seconds.

```
'Set the date using the hour passed to this property
dtpHour.Value = _
    New Date(Now.Year, Now.Month, Now.Day, value, 0, 0)
```

The second update performed by this Hour property is to update the label on the form using some static text and the hour that is being set in this property.

```
'Set the display text
lblState.Text = "At " & value & ":00, Matt is "
```

You have not evaluated the Hour property to determine the state, but you will do that next:

Determining the State

In the next Try It Out, you look at determining the state when the Hour property is set. You can take the hour returned by the DateTimePicker control and use it to determine which value in your enumeration it matches. This section demonstrates this and displays the value on your form.

Try It Out   Determining State

1.   Open the Code Editor for Form1 and modify the Hour property as follows:

```
Set(ByVal value As Integer)
    'Set the date using the hour passed to this property
    dtpHour.Value = _
        New Date(Now.Year, Now.Month, Now.Day, value, 0, 0)

    'Determine the state
    If value >= 6 And value < 7 Then
        CurrentState = DayAction.GettingReadyForWork
    ElseIf value >= 7 And value < 8 Then
        CurrentState = DayAction.TravelingToWork
    ElseIf value >= 8 And value < 13 Then
        CurrentState = DayAction.AtWork
    ElseIf value >= 13 And value < 14 Then
        CurrentState = DayAction.AtLunch
    ElseIf value >= 14 And value < 17 Then
        CurrentState = DayAction.AtWork
    ElseIf value >= 17 And value < 18 Then
        CurrentState = DayAction.TravelingFromWork
    ElseIf value >= 18 And value < 22 Then
        CurrentState = DayAction.RelaxingWithFriends
    ElseIf value >= 22 And value < 23 Then
        CurrentState = DayAction.GettingReadyForBed
    Else
```

```
                    CurrentState = DayAction.Asleep
             End If

        'Set the display text

             lblState.Text = "At " & value & ":00, Matt is " & CurrentState
      End Set
```

2. Run the project. You'll see something like Figure 5-8.

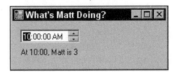

Figure 5-8

3. Here's the problem: The user doesn't know what 3 means. Close the project and find the following section of code at the end of the `Hour` property:

```
        'Set the display text
        lblState.Text = "At " & value & ":00, Matt is " & CurrentState
```

4. Change the last line to read as follows:

```
        'Set the display text
        lblState.Text = "At " & value & ":00, Matt is " & CurrentState.ToString
```

5. Now run the project and you'll see something like Figure 5-9.

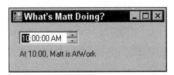

Figure 5-9

How It Works

As you typed the code, you might have noticed that whenever you tried to set a value against `CurrentState`, you were presented with an enumerated list of possibilities as shown in Figure 5-10.

Visual Studio 2005 knows that `CurrentState` is of type `DayAction`. It also knows that `DayAction` is an enumeration and that it defines eight possible values, each of which is displayed in the IntelliSense pop-up box. Clicking an item in the enumerated list causes a ToolTip to be displayed with the actual value of the item; for example, clicking `DayAction.RelaxingWithFriends` will display a ToolTip with a value of 6.

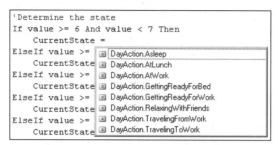

```
'Determine the state
If value >= 6 And value < 7 Then
    CurrentState =
ElseIf value >=    ▣ DayAction.Asleep
    CurrentState   ▣ DayAction.AtLunch
ElseIf value >=    ▣ DayAction.AtWork
    CurrentState   ▣ DayAction.GettingReadyForBed
ElseIf value >=    ▣ DayAction.GettingReadyForWork
    CurrentState   ▣ DayAction.RelaxingWithFriends
ElseIf value >=    ▣ DayAction.TravelingFromWork
    CurrentState   ▣ DayAction.TravelingToWork
```

Figure 5-10

Fundamentally though, because `DayAction` is based on an integer, `CurrentState` is an integer value. That's why, the first time you ran the project with the state determination code in place, you saw an integer at the end of the status string. At 10 A.M., you know that Matt is at work, or rather `CurrentState` equals `DayAction.AtWork`. You defined this as 3, which is why 3 is displayed at the end of the string.

What you've done in this Try It Out is to tack a call to the `ToString` method onto the end of the `CurrentState` variable. This results in a string representation of `DayAction` being used, rather than the integer representation.

Enumerations are incredibly useful when you want to store one of a possible set of values in a variable. As you start to drill into more complex objects in the Framework, you'll find that they are used all over the place!

Setting Invalid Values

One of the limitations of enumerations is that it is possible to store a value that technically isn't one of the possible defined values of the enumeration. For example, if you change the `Hour` property so that rather than setting `CurrentState` to `Asleep`, you can set it to 999:

```
ElseIf value >= 22 And value < 23 Then
    CurrentState = DayAction.GettingReadyForBed
Else
    CurrentState = 999
End If
```

If you build the project, you'll notice that Visual Basic 2005 doesn't flag this as an error. Further, if you actually run the project, you'll see that the value for `CurrentState` is shown in the text box as 999.

So, you can see that you can set a variable that references an enumeration to a value that is not defined in that enumeration and the application will still "work" (as long as the value is of the same type as the enumeration). If you build classes that use enumerations, you have to rely on the consumer of that class being well behaved. One technique to solve this problem would be to disallow invalid values in any properties that used the enumeration as their data type.

Understanding Constants

Another good programming practice that you need to look at is the *constant*. Imagine you have these two methods, each of which does something with a given file on the computer's disk. (Obviously, we're omitting the code here that actually manipulates the file.)

```
Public Sub DoSomething()
    'What's the filename?
    Dim strFileName As String = "c:\Temp\Demo.txt"
    'Open the file
    . . .
End Sub
Public Sub DoSomethingElse()
    'What's the filename?
    Dim strFileName As String = "c:\Temp\Demo.txt"
    'Do something with the file
    . . .
End Sub
```

Using Constants

The code defining a string literal gives the name of a file twice. This is poor programming practice because if both methods are supposed to access the same file, and if that filename changes, this change has to be made in two separate places.

In this instance, both methods are next to each other and the program itself is small, but imagine that you have a massive program in which a separate string literal pointing to the file is defined in 10, 50, or even 1,000 places. If you need to change the filename, you'll have to change it many times. This is exactly the kind of thing that leads to serious problems for maintaining software code.

What you need to do instead is define the filename globally and then use that global symbol for the filename in the code, rather than using a string literal. This is what a constant is. It is, in effect, a special kind of "variable" that cannot actually be varied when the program is running. In the next Try It Out, you learn to use constants.

Try It Out   Using Constants

1. Using Visual Studio 2005, create a new Windows Application project and call it **Constants Demo**.

2. When the Designer for Form1 opens, add three buttons. Set the Name property of the first button to **btnOne**, the second to **btnTwo**, and the third to **btnThree**. Change the Text property of each to **One**, **Two**, and **Three**, respectively. Your form should look like Figure 5-11.

Figure 5-11

3.   View the Code Editor and at the top of the class definition, add the highlighted code:

```
Public Class Form1

'File name constant
Private Const strFileName As String = "C:\Temp\Hello.txt"
```

4.   In the Class Name combo box at the top of the editor, select btnOne, and in the Method Name combo box select the Click event. Add the following highlighted code to the Click event handler:

```
Private Sub btnOne_Click(ByVal sender As Object, _
    ByVal e As System.EventArgs) Handles btnOne.Click

    'Using a constant
    MessageBox.Show("1: " & strFileName, "Constants Demo")
End Sub
```

5.   Now select btnTwo in the Class Name combo box and select its Click event in the Method Name combo box. Add the highlighted code:

```
Private Sub btnTwo_Click(ByVal sender As Object, _
    ByVal e As System.EventArgs) Handles btnTwo.Click

    'Using the constant again
    MessageBox.Show("2: " & strFileName, "Constants Demo")
End Sub
```

6.   Finally, select btnThree in the Class Name combo box and the Click event in the Method Name combo box. Add this code to the Click event handler:

```
Private Sub btnThree_Click(ByVal sender As Object, _
    ByVal e As System.EventArgs) Handles btnThree.Click

    'Reusing the constant one more time
    MessageBox.Show("3: " & strFileName, "Constants Demo")
End Sub
```

7.   Now run the project and click button One. You'll see the message box shown in Figure 5-12.

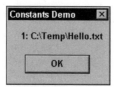

Figure 5-12

Likewise, you'll see the same filename if you click buttons Two or Three.

How It Works

A constant is actually a type of value that cannot be changed when the program is running. It is defined as a variable is, but you add `Const` to the definition.

```
'File name constant
Private Const strFileName As String = "C:\Temp\Hello.txt"
```

You'll notice that it has a data type, just like a variable, and you have to give it a value when it's defined — which makes sense, because you can't change it later.

When you want to use the constant, you refer to it just as you would refer to any variable:

```
Private Sub btnOne_Click(ByVal sender As Object, _
    ByVal e As System.EventArgs) Handles btnOne.Click

    'Using a constant
    MessageBox.Show("1: " & strFileName, "Constants Demo")
End Sub
```

As mentioned before, the appeal of a constant is that it allows you to change a value that's used throughout a piece of code by altering a single piece of code. However, be aware that you can change constants only at design time; you cannot change their values at run time. Look at how this works.

Different Constant Types

In this section, you've seen how to use a string constant, but you can use other types of variables as constants. There are some rules: Basically, a constant must not be able to change, so you should not store an object data type (which we will discuss in Chapter 10) in a constant.

Integers are very common types of constants. They can be defined like this:

```
Public Const intHoursAsleepPerDay As Integer = 8
```

Also, it's fairly common to see constants used with enumerations, like this:

```
Public Const intMattsTypicalState As DayAction = DayAction.AtWork
```

Structures

Applications very commonly need to store several pieces of information of different data types that all relate to one thing and must be kept together in a group, such as a customer's name and address (strings) and balance (a number). Usually, an object of a class is used to hold such a group of variables, as you'll discover in Chapter 10, but you can also use a *structure*. Structures are similar to class objects but are somewhat simpler, so they're discussed here.

Later on, as you design applications, you will need to be able to decide whether to use a structure or a class. As a rule of thumb, we suggest that if you end up putting a lot of methods on a structure, it should probably be a class. It's also relatively tricky to convert from a structure to a class later on, because structures and objects are created using different syntax rules, and sometimes the same syntax produces different results between structures and objects. So choose once and choose wisely!

Building Structures

Take a look at how you can build a structure.

Try It Out   Building a Structure

1. Using Visual Studio 2005, create a new Windows Application project. Call it **Structure Demo**.

2. When the project is created, right-click the project name in the Solution Explorer, choose the Add menu item from the context menu, and then choose the Class submenu item. In the Add New Item – Structure Demo dialog box, enter a name of **Customer** in the Name field and then click the Add button to have this item added to your project.

3. When the Code Editor appears, replace all existing code with the following code:

```
Public Structure Customer
    'Public members
    Public FirstName As String
    Public LastName As String
    Public Email As String
End Structure
```

Note that you must make sure to replace the Class *definition with the* Structure *definition!*

4. Open the Designer for Form1. Add four Label controls, four TextBox controls, and a Button control. Arrange your controls so that they look similar to Figure 5-13.

5. Set the Name properties as follows:

    ❑   Set Label1 to **lblName**.

    ❑   Set TextBox1 to **txtName**.

    ❑   Set Label2 to **lblFirstName**.

    ❑   Set TextBox2 to **txtFirstName**.

    ❑   Set Label3 to **lblLastName**.

    ❑   Set TextBox3 to **txtLastName**.

    ❑   Set Label4 to **lblEmail**.

    ❑   Set TextBox4 to **txtEmail**.

    ❑   Set Button1 to **btnTest**.

6. Set the Text properties of the following controls:

- ❏ Set lblName to **Name**.

- ❏ Set lblFirstName to **First Name**.

- ❏ Set lblLastName to **Last Name**.

- ❏ Set lblEmail to **E-mail**.

- ❏ Set btnTest to **Test**.

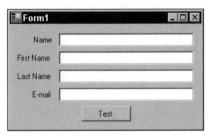

Figure 5-13

7. Double-click the button to create a new Click event handler. Add the following highlighted code. You'll receive an error message that `DisplayCustomer` is not defined; ignore this error, because you'll create the `DisplayCustomer` method in the next step:

```
Private Sub btnTest_Click(ByVal sender As System.Object, _
    ByVal e As System.EventArgs) Handles btnTest.Click
```

```
        'Create a new customer
        Dim objCustomer As Customer
        objCustomer.FirstName = "Michael"
        objCustomer.LastName = "Dell"
        objCustomer.Email = "mdell@somecompany.com"

        'Display the customer
        DisplayCustomer(objCustomer)
    End Sub
```

8. Next, add this procedure:

```
    Public Sub DisplayCustomer(ByVal customer As Customer)
        'Display the customer details on the form
        txtFirstName.Text = customer.FirstName
        txtLastName.Text = customer.LastName
        txtEmail.Text = customer.Email
    End Sub
```

9. Run your project and click the Test button, and you should see results similar to those shown in Figure 5-14.

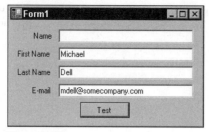

Figure 5-14

How It Works

You define a structure using a `Structure...End Structure` statement. Inside this block, the variables that make up the structure are declared by name and type: These variables are called *members* of the structure.

```
Public Structure Customer
    'Public members
    Public FirstName As String
    Public LastName As String
    Public Email As String
End Structure
```

Notice the keyword `Public` in front of each variable declaration as well as in front of the `Structure` statement. You have frequently seen `Private` used in similar positions. The `Public` keyword means that you can refer to the member (such as `FirstName`) outside of the definition of the `Customer` structure itself.

In the `btnTest_Click` procedure, you define a variable of type `Customer` using the `Dim` statement. (If `Customer` were a class, you would also have to initialize the variable by setting `objCustomer` equal to `New Customer`, as will be discussed in Chapter 10.)

```
Private Sub btnTest_Click(ByVal sender As System.Object, _
    ByVal e As System.EventArgs) Handles btnTest.Click

    'Create a new customer
    Dim objCustomer As Customer
```

Then you can access each of the member variables inside the `Customer` structure `objCustomer` by giving the name of the structure variable, followed by a dot, followed by the name of the member:

```
    objCustomer.FirstName = "Michael"
    objCustomer.LastName = "Dell"
    objCustomer.Email = "mdell@somecompany.com"

    'Display the customer
    DisplayCustomer(objCustomer)
End Sub
```

The `DisplayCustomer` procedure simply accepts a `Customer` structure as its input parameter and then accesses the members of the structure to set the `Text` properties of the text boxes on the form:

```
Public Sub DisplayCustomer(ByVal customer As Customer)
    'Display the customer details on the form
    txtFirstName.Text = customer.FirstName
    txtLastName.Text = customer.LastName
    txtEmail.Text = customer.Email
End Sub
```

Adding Properties to Structures

You can add properties to a structure, just as you did to the form in the Enum Demo project earlier in the chapter. You learn how in the next Try It Out.

Try It Out   **Adding a Name Property**

1.   Open the code editor for `Customer` and add this highlighted code to create a read-only property `Name`:

```
'Public members
Public FirstName As String
Public LastName As String
Public Email As String

'Name property
Public ReadOnly Property Name() As String
    Get
        Return FirstName & " " & LastName
    End Get
End Property
```

2.   Now, open the code editor for Form1. Modify the `DisplayCustomer` method with the highlighted code:

```
Public Sub DisplayCustomer(ByVal customer As Customer)
    'Display the customer details on the form

    txtName.Text = customer.Name
    txtFirstName.Text = customer.FirstName
    txtLastName.Text = customer.LastName
    txtEmail.Text = customer.Email
End Sub
```

3.   Run the project and click the Test button. You'll see that the Name text box, which was empty in Figure 5-14, is now populated with the customer's first and last name.

Working with ArrayLists

Suppose you need to store a set of `Customer` structures. You could use an array, but in some cases the array might not be so easy to use.

❏   If you need to add a new `Customer` to the array, you need to change the size of the array and insert the new item in the new last position in the array. (You'll learn how to change the size of an array later in this chapter.)

❏   If you need to remove a `Customer` from the array, you need to look at each item in the array in turn. When you find the one you want, you have to create another version of the array one element smaller than the original array and copy every item except the one you want to delete into the new array.

❏   If you need to replace a `Customer` in the array with another customer, you need to look at each item in turn until you find the one you want and then replace it manually.

The `ArrayList` provides a way to create an array that can be easily manipulated as you run your program.

Using an ArrayList

Look at using an `ArrayList` in this next Try It Out.

Try It Out   **Using an ArrayList**

1.   Switch to the Form Designer and rearrange the controls on the form and add a new ListBox control as shown in Figure 5-15. Set the Name property of the list box to **lstCustomers** and its IntegralHeight property to False.

You can click the form and press Ctrl+A to select all of the controls and then drag them to their new location.

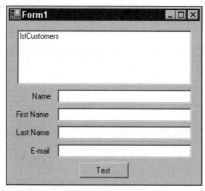

Figure 5-15

2.   Open the Code Editor for Form1 and add the member highlighted here to the top of the class definition:

```
Public Class Form1
```

```
    'Form level members
    Private objCustomers As New ArrayList
```

3. Now, add this method to Form1 to create a new customer:

```
Public Sub CreateCustomer(ByVal firstName As String, _
    ByVal lastName As String, ByVal email As String)

    'Declare a Customer object
    Dim objNewCustomer As Customer

    'Create the new customer
    objNewCustomer.FirstName = firstName
    objNewCustomer.LastName = lastName
    objNewCustomer.Email = email

    'Add the new customer to the list
    objCustomers.Add(objNewCustomer)

    'Add the new customer to the ListBox control
    lstCustomers.Items.Add(objNewCustomer)
End Sub
```

4. Modify the `btnTest_Click` method next, making these code changes:

```
Private Sub btnTest_Click(ByVal sender As System.Object, _
    ByVal e As System.EventArgs) Handles btnTest.Click

    'Create some customers
    CreateCustomer("Darrel", "Hilton", "dhilton@somecompany.com")
    CreateCustomer("Frank", "Peoples", "fpeoples@somecompany.com")
    CreateCustomer("Bill", "Scott", "bscott@somecompany.com")
End Sub
```

5. Run the project and click the Test button. You'll see results like those shown in Figure 5-16.

Figure 5-16

You are adding `Customer` structures to the list, but they are being displayed by the list as `Structure_Demo.Customer`; this is the full name of the structure. The ListBox control accepts string values, so, by specifying that you wanted to add the `Customer` structure to the list box, Visual Basic 2005 called the

ToString method of the Customer structure. By default, the ToString method for a structure returns the structure name, not the contents that you wanted to see. So what you want to do is tweak Customer so that it can display something more meaningful. Once you do that in the next Try It Out, you'll see how the ArrayList works.

Try It Out   **Overriding ToString**

1. Open the Code Editor for Customer and add this method to the structure, ensuring that it is below the member declarations. Remember from Chapter 3 that to insert an XML Document Comment block, you type three apostrophes above the method name:

```
''' <summary>
''' Overrides the default ToString method
''' </summary>
''' <returns>String</returns>
''' <remarks>Returns the customer name and email address</remarks>
Public Overrides Function ToString() As String
    Return Name & " (" & Email & ")"
End Function
```

2. Run the project and click the Test button. You'll see the same results as shown in Figure 5-17.

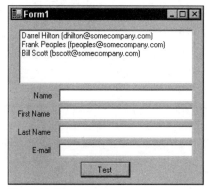

Figure 5-17

How It Works

Whenever a Customer structure is added to the list, the list box calls the ToString method on the structure to get a string representation of that structure. With this code, you *override* the default functionality of ToString so that, rather than returning just the name of the structure, you get some useful text:

```
''' <summary>
''' Overrides the default ToString method
''' </summary>
''' <returns>String</returns>
''' <remarks>Returns the customer name and email address</remarks>
Public Overrides Function ToString() As String
    Return Name & " (" & Email & ")"
End Function
```

An `ArrayList` can be used to store a list of objects/structures of any type (in contrast to a regular array). In fact, you can mix the types within an `ArrayList` — a topic we'll be talking about in a little while. In this example, you created a method called `CreateCustomer` that initializes a new `Customer` structure based on parameters that were passed to the method:

```
Public Sub CreateCustomer(ByVal firstName As String, _
    ByVal lastName As String, ByVal email As String)

    'Declare a Customer object
    Dim objNewCustomer As Customer

    'Create the new customer
    objNewCustomer.FirstName = firstName
    objNewCustomer.LastName = lastName
    objNewCustomer.Email = email
```

Once the structure has been initialized, you add it to the `ArrayList` stored in `objCustomers`:

```
    'Add the new customer to the list
    objCustomers.Add(objNewCustomer)
```

You also add it to the list box itself, like this:

```
    'Add the new customer to the ListBox control
    lstCustomers.Items.Add(objNewCustomer)
```

With `CreateCustomer` defined, you can just call it to add new members to the `ArrayList` and to the list box control when the user clicks the Test button:

```
Private Sub btnTest_Click(ByVal sender As System.Object, _
    ByVal e As System.EventArgs) Handles btnTest.Click

    'Create some customers
    CreateCustomer("Darrel", "Hilton", "dhilton@somecompany.com")
    CreateCustomer("Frank", "Peoples", "fpeoples@somecompany.com")
    CreateCustomer("Bill", "Scott", "bscott@somecompany.com")
End Sub
```

Deleting from an ArrayList

OK, so now you know the principle behind an `ArrayList`. You use it to do something that's traditionally hard to do with arrays but is pretty easy to do with an `ArrayList`, such as dynamically adding new values. Now let's look at how easy it is to delete items from an `ArrayList`.

Try It Out   **Deleting Customers**

1.   Using the Forms Designer, add a new Button control to the bottom of the form and set its Name property to **btnDelete** and its Text property to **Delete**.

2. Double-click the button and add the highlighted code. You'll receive an error message that `SelectedCustomer` is not defined; ignore this error, because you'll add the `SelectedCustomer` function in the next step:

```
Private Sub btnDelete_Click(ByVal sender As System.Object, _
    ByVal e As System.EventArgs) Handles btnDelete.Click

        'If no customer is selected in the ListBox then...
        If lstCustomers.SelectedIndex = -1 Then

            'Display a message
            MessageBox.Show("You must select a customer to delete.", _
                "Structure Demo")

            'Exit this method
            Exit Sub
        End If

        'Prompt the user to delete the selected customer
        If MessageBox.Show("Are you sure you want to delete " & _
            SelectedCustomer.Name & "?", "Structure Demo", _
            MessageBoxButtons.YesNo, MessageBoxIcon.Question) = _
            DialogResult.Yes Then

            'Get the customer to be deleted
            Dim objCustomerToDelete As Customer = SelectedCustomer

            'Remove the customer from the ArrayList
            objCustomers.Remove(objCustomerToDelete)

            'Remove the customer from the ListBox
            lstCustomers.Items.Remove(objCustomerToDelete)
        End If
End Sub
```

3. Next, add the `SelectedCustomer` property to the form as follows:

```
Public ReadOnly Property SelectedCustomer() As Customer
    Get
        If lstCustomers.SelectedIndex <> -1 Then
            'Return the selected customer
            Return lstCustomers.Items(lstCustomers.SelectedIndex)
        End If
    End Get
End Property
```

4. Run the project and click the Test button. *Do not* select a customer in the list box and then click the Delete button. You'll see a message box indicating that you must select a customer.

5. Now select a customer and click Delete. You'll see a confirmation dialog box similar to the one shown in Figure 5-18.

6. Click Yes, and the person you selected will be removed from the list.

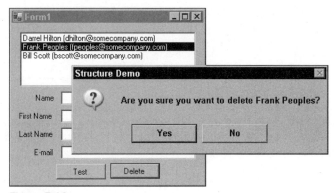

Figure 5-18

How It Works

The trick here is to build a read-only property that will return the Customer structure that's selected in the list box back to the caller on demand. The SelectedIndex property of the list box will return a value of -1 if no selection has been made. Otherwise it will return the zero-based index of the selected customer.

```
Public ReadOnly Property SelectedCustomer() As Customer
    Get
        If lstCustomers.SelectedIndex <> -1 Then
            'Return the selected customer
            Return lstCustomers.Items(lstCustomers.SelectedIndex)
        End If
    End Get
End Property
```

Like the Name property that you added to the Customer structure, this property is identified as read-only by the keyword ReadOnly. It contains a Get block but no Set block. The reason for making it read-only is that it constructs the value it returns from other information (the contents of the Customer structures in the list) that can be set and changed by other means.

Inside the Click event handler for the Delete button, you first test to see whether a customer has been selected in the list box. If no customer has been selected, you display a message box indicating that a customer must be selected. Then you exit the method allowing the user to select a customer and try again:

```
'If no customer is selected in the ListBox then...
If lstCustomers.SelectedIndex = -1 Then

    'Display a message
    MessageBox.Show("You must select a customer to delete.", _
        "Structure Demo")

    'Exit this method
    Exit Sub
End If
```

If a customer has been selected, you prompt the user to confirm the deletion:

```
'Prompt the user to delete the selected customer
If MessageBox.Show("Are you sure you want to delete " & _
    SelectedCustomer.Name & "?", "Structure Demo", _
    MessageBoxButtons.YesNo, MessageBoxIcon.Question) = _
    DialogResult.Yes Then
```

If the user does want to delete the customer, you get a return value from `MessageBox.Show` equal to `DialogResult.Yes`. Then you declare a customer structure to save the customer to be deleted and populate that structure with the selected customer:

```
'Get the customer to be deleted
Dim objCustomerToDelete As Customer = SelectedCustomer
```

The `Remove` method of the `ArrayList` can then be used to remove the selected customer:

```
'Remove the customer from the ArrayList
objCustomers.Remove(objCustomerToDelete)
```

You also use a similar technique to remove the customer from the list box as well:

```
'Remove the customer from the ListBox
lstCustomers.Items.Remove(objCustomerToDelete)
```

Showing Items in the ArrayList

For completeness, you'll want to add one more piece of functionality to enhance the user interface of your application. In the next Try It Out, you'll add code in the `SelectedIndexChanged` event for the Customers list box. Every time you select a new customer, the customer's details will be displayed in the text boxes on the form.

Try It Out   Showing Details of the Selected Item

1. Using the Forms Designer, double-click the list box. This will create a new `SelectedIndexChanged` event handler. Add the highlighted code:

    ```
    Private Sub lstCustomers_SelectedIndexChanged( _
        ByVal sender As System.Object, ByVal e As System.EventArgs) _
        Handles lstCustomers.SelectedIndexChanged

        'Display the customer details
        DisplayCustomer(SelectedCustomer)
    End Sub
    ```

2. Run the project and click the Test button to populate the list box. Now when you select a customer in the list box, that customer's information will appear in the fields at the bottom of the form, as shown in Figure 5-19.

Figure 5-19

Working with Collections

The `ArrayList` is a kind of *collection*, which the .NET Framework uses extensively. A collection is a way of easily creating ad hoc groups of similar or related items. If you take a look back at your Structure Demo code and peek into the `CreateCustomer` method, you'll notice that when adding items to the `ArrayList` and to the list box, you use a method called `Add`:

```
'Add the new customer to the list
objCustomers.Add(objNewCustomer)

'Add the new customer to the ListBox control
lstCustomers.Items.Add(objNewCustomer)
```

The code that deletes a customer uses a method called `Remove` on both objects:

```
'Remove the customer from the ArrayList
objCustomers.Remove(objCustomerToDelete)

'Remove the customer from the ListBox
lstCustomers.Items.Remove(objCustomerToDelete)
```

Microsoft is very keen to see developers use the collection paradigm whenever they need to work with a list of items. They also keen to see collections work in the same way, irrespective of what they actually hold — which is why you use `Add` to add an item and `Remove` to remove an item, even though you're using a `System.Collections.ArrayList` object in one case and a `System.Windows.Forms.List Box.ObjectCollection` object in another. Microsoft has taken a great deal of care with this feature when building the .NET Framework.

Consistency is good — it allows developers to map an understanding of one thing and use that same understanding with a similar thing. When designing data structures for use in your application, you should take steps to follow the conventions that Microsoft has laid down. For example, if you have a collection class and want to create a method that removes an item, call it `Remove`, not `Delete`. Developers using your class will have an intuitive understanding of what `Remove` does because they're familiar with

157

it. On the other hand, developers would do a double-take on seeing `Delete`, because that term has a different connotation.

One of the problems with using an `ArrayList` is that the developer who has an array list cannot guarantee that every item in the list is of the same type. For this reason, each time an item is extracted from the `ArrayList`, the type should be checked to avoid causing an error.

The solution is to create a *strongly typed* collection, which contains only elements of a particular type. Strongly typed collections are very easy to create. According to .NET best programming practices as defined by Microsoft, the best way to create one is to derive a new class from `System.Collections.CollectionBase` (discussed in the How It Works for the next Try It Out) and add two methods (`Add` and `Remove`) and one property (`Item`):

- ❑ `Add` adds a new item to the collection.

- ❑ `Remove` removes an item from the collection.

- ❑ `Item` returns the item at the given index in the collection.

Creating CustomerCollection

In this Try It Out, you create a `CustomerCollection` designed to hold a collection of `Customer` structures.

Try It Out   Creating CustomerCollection

1. In the Solution Explorer, right-click the project and choose Add from the context menu and then choose the Class submenu item. In the Add New Item – Structure Demo dialog box, enter **CustomerCollection** in the Name field and then click the Add button to have the class added to your project.

2. Add the following highlighted line in the Code Editor:

```
Public Class CustomerCollection

    Inherits Collections.CollectionBase
End Class
```

3. You'll need to add an `Add` method to add a customer to the collection. Add the following code:

```
'Add a customer to the collection
Public Sub Add(ByVal newCustomer As Customer)
    Me.List.Add(newCustomer)
End Sub
```

4. You need to add a `Remove` method to remove a customer from the collection, so add this method:

```
'Remove a customer from the collection
Public Sub Remove(ByVal oldCustomer As Customer)
    Me.List.Remove(oldCustomer)
End Sub
```

5. Open the Code Editor for the form and find the definition for the `objCustomers` member. Change its type from `ArrayList` to `CustomerCollection` as highlighted here:

```
Public Class Form1

    'Form level members

    Private objCustomers As New CustomerCollection
```

6. Finally, run the project. You'll notice that the application works as before.

How It Works

Your `CustomerCollection` is the first occasion for you to create a *class* explicitly (although you have been using them implicitly from the beginning). Classes and objects are discussed in Chapter 10 and thereafter. For now, note that, like a structure, a class represents a data type that groups one or more members that can be of different data types, and it can have properties and methods associated with it. Unlike a structure, a class can be *derived* from another class, in which case it *inherits* the members, properties, and methods of that other class (which is known as the *base class*) and can have further members, properties, and methods of its own.

Your `CustomerCollection` class inherits from the `Collections.CollectionBase` class, which contains a basic implementation of a collection that can hold any object. In that respect it's very similar to an `ArrayList`. The advantage comes when you add your own methods to this class.

Since you provided a version of the `Add` method that has a parameter type of `Customer`, it can accept and add only a `Customer` structure. Therefore, it's impossible to put anything into the collection that isn't a `Customer`. You can see there that IntelliSense is telling you that the only thing you can pass through to `Add` is a `Structure_Demo.Customer` structure.

Internally, `CollectionBase` provides you with a property called `List`, which in turn has `Add` and `Remove` methods that you can use to store items. That's precisely what you use when you need to add or remove items from the list:

```
        'Add a customer to the collection
        Public Sub Add(ByVal newCustomer As Customer)
            Me.List.Add(newCustomer)
        End Sub

        'Remove a customer from the collection
        Public Sub Remove(ByVal oldCustomer As Customer)
            Me.List.Remove(oldCustomer)
        End Sub
```

Building collections this way is a .NET best practice. As a newcomer to .NET programming, you may not appreciate just how useful this is, but trust us — it is! Whenever you need to use a collection of classes, this technique is the right way to go and one that you'll be familiar with.

Adding an Item Property

At the beginning of this section, you read that you were supposed to add two methods and one property. You've seen the methods but not the property, so take a look at it in the next Try It Out.

Adding an Item Property

1. Open the Code Editor for `CustomerCollection` and add this code:

```
'Item property to read or update a customer at a given position
'in the list
Default Public Property Item(ByVal index As Integer) As Customer
    Get
        Return Me.List.Item(index)
    End Get
    Set(ByVal value As Customer)
        Me.List.Item(index) = value
    End Set
End Property
```

2. To verify that this works, open the Code Editor for Form1. Modify the `SelectedCustomer` property with this code:

```
If lstCustomers.SelectedIndex <> -1 Then
    'Return the selected customer
    Return objCustomers(lstCustomers.SelectedIndex)
End If
```

3. Run the project. Click the Test button and notice that when you select items in the list, the details are shown in the fields as they were before.

How It Works

The `Item` property is actually very important; it gives the developer direct access to the data stored in the list but maintains the strongly typed nature of the collection.

If you look at the code again for `SelectedCustomer`, you'll notice that when you wanted to return the given item from within `objCustomers`, you didn't have to provide the property name of `Item`. Instead, `objCustomers` behaved as if it were an array:

```
If lstCustomers.SelectedIndex <> -1 Then
    'Return the selected customer
    Return objCustomers(lstCustomers.SelectedIndex)
End If
```

IntelliSense tells you to enter the index of the item that you require and that you should expect to get a `Customer` structure in return.

The reason you don't have to specify the property name of `Item` is that you marked the property as default by using the `Default` keyword:

```
'Item property to read or update a customer at a given position
'in the list
Default Public Property Item(ByVal index As Integer) As Customer
    Get
        Return Me.List.Item(index)
    End Get
```

```
        Set(ByVal value As Customer)
            Me.List.Item(index) = value
        End Set
    End Property
```

A given class can only have a single default property, and that property must take a parameter of some kind. This parameter must be an index or search term of some description. The one used here provides an index to an element in a collection list. You can have multiple overloaded versions of the same property so that, for example, you could provide an e-mail address rather than an index. This provides a great deal of flexibility to enhance your class further.

What you have at this point is the following:

❑ A way of storing a list of `Customer` structures, and just `Customer` structures

❑ A way of adding new items to the collection on demand

❑ A way of removing existing items from the collection on demand

❑ A way of accessing members in the collection as if it were an `ArrayList`

Building Lookup Tables with Hashtable

So far, whenever you want to find something in an array or in a collection, you have to provide an integer index representing the position of the item. It's quite common to end up needing a way of being able to look up an item in a collection when you have something other than an index. For example, you might want to find a customer when you provide an email address.

In this section you'll take a look at the `Hashtable`. This is a special kind of collection that works on a *key-value* principle.

Using Hashtables

A `Hashtable` is a collection in which each item is given a *key*. This key can be used at a later time to "unlock" the value. So, if you add Darrel's `Customer` structure to the `Hashtable`, you'll be given a key that matches his e-mail address of `dhilton@somecompany.com`. If at a later time you come along with that key, you'll be able to find his record quickly.

Whenever you add an object to the `Hashtable`, it calls a method `System.Object.GetHashCode`, which provides a unique integer value for that object that is the same every time it is called, and uses this integer ID as the key. Likewise, whenever you want to retrieve an object from the `Hashtable`, it calls `GetHashCode` on the object to get a lookup key and matches that key against the ones it has in the list. When it finds it, it will return the related value to you.

Lookups from a `Hashtable` are very, very fast. Irrespective of the object you pass in, you're only matching on a relatively small integer ID. You learn to use a `Hashtable` in the following Try It Out.

An integer ID takes up 4 bytes of memory, so if you pass in a 100-character string (which is 200-bytes long), the lookup code only needs to compare 4 bytes, which makes everything run really quickly.

Try It Out   Using a Hashtable

1. Open the Code Editor for the `CustomerCollection` class. Add the highlighted member to the top of the class definition:

```
Public Class CustomerCollection
    Inherits Collections.CollectionBase
```

```
    'Private member
    Private objEmailHashtable As New Hashtable
```

2. Next, add this read-only property to the class:

```
    'EmailHashtable property to return the Email Hashtable
    Public ReadOnly Property EmailHashtable() As Hashtable
        Get
            Return objEmailHashtable
        End Get
    End Property
```

3. Now, make this change to the `Add` method:

```
    'Add a customer to the collection
    Public Sub Add(ByVal newCustomer As Customer)
        Me.List.Add(newCustomer)
        'Add the email address to the Hashtable
        EmailHashtable.Add(newCustomer.Email, newCustomer)
    End Sub
```

4. Next, add this overloaded version of the `Item` property that allows you to find a customer by email address:

```
    'Overload Item property to find a customer by email address
    Default Public ReadOnly Property Item(ByVal email As String) As Customer
        Get
            Return EmailHashtable.Item(email)
        End Get
    End Property
```

5. Open the Form Designer for Form1, resize the Email text box smaller, and add a new Button control next to it as shown in Figure 5-20. Set the Name property of the button to **btnLookup** and the Text property to **Lookup**.

6. Double-click the Lookup button and add the following highlighted code to its `Click` event handler:

```
    Private Sub btnLookup_Click(ByVal sender As System.Object, _
        ByVal e As System.EventArgs) Handles btnLookup.Click
```

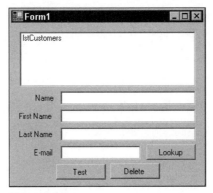

Figure 5-20

```
'Declare a customer object and set it to the customer
'with the email address to be found
Dim objFoundCustomer As Customer = objCustomers(txtEmail.Text)

If objFoundCustomer.Email IsNot Nothing Then
    'Display the customers name
    MessageBox.Show("The customers name is: " & objFoundCustomer.Name, _
                "Structure Demo")
Else
    'Display an error
    MessageBox.Show("There is no customer with the e-mail address " & _
        txtEmail.Text & ".", "Structure Demo")
End If
End Sub
```

7. Run the project and click the Test button to populate the list of customers. If you enter an email address that does not exist into the Email text box and click the Lookup button, you'll see a message box similar to the one shown in Figure 5-21.

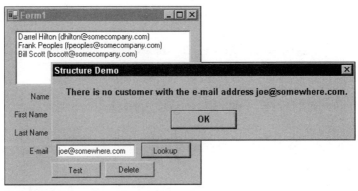

Figure 5-21

8. If you enter an email address that does exist, for example, `dhilton@somecompany.com`, the name of the customer will be shown in the message box.

How It Works

You've added a new member to the `CustomerCollection` class that can be used to hold a `Hashtable`:

```
'Private member
Private objEmailHashtable As New Hashtable
```

Whenever you add a new `Customer` to the collection, you also add it to the `Hashtable`:

```
'Add a customer to the collection
Public Sub Add(ByVal newCustomer As Customer)
    Me.List.Add(newCustomer)

    'Add the email address to the Hashtable
    EmailHashtable.Add(newCustomer.Email, newCustomer)
End Sub
```

However, unlike the kinds of `Add` methods that you saw earlier, the `EmailHashtable.Add` method takes two parameters. The first is the key, and you're using the email address as the key. The key can be any object you like, but it must be unique. You cannot supply the same key twice. (If you try to, an exception will be thrown.) The second parameter is the value that you want to link the key to, so whenever we give that key to the `Hashtable`, you get that object back.

The next trick is to create an overloaded version of the default `Item` property. This one, however, takes a string as its only parameter. IntelliSense will display the overloaded method as items 1 and 2 when you access it from your code.

This time you can provide either an index or an email address. If you use an email address, you end up using the overloaded version of the `Item` property, and this defers to the `Item` property of the `Hashtable` object. This takes a key and returns the related item, providing the key can be found:

```
'Overload Item property to find a customer by email address
Default Public ReadOnly Property Item(ByVal email As String) As Customer
    Get
        Return EmailHashtable.Item(email)
    End Get
End Property
```

So, at this point, you have a collection class that not only enables you to look up items by index but also allows you to look up customers by email address.

Cleaning Up: Remove, RemoveAt, and Clear

It isn't possible to use the same key twice in a `Hashtable`. Therefore, you have to take steps to ensure that what's in the `Hashtable` matches whatever is in the list itself.

Although you implemented the `Remove` method in your `CustomerCollection` class, the `Collection Base` class also provides the `RemoveAt` and `Clear` methods. Whereas `Remove` takes an object, `RemoveAt` takes an index. In the next Try It Out, you need to provide new implementations of these methods to adjust the `Hashtable`.

Try It Out   Cleaning Up the List

1. Open the Code Editor for Form1. Locate the `btnTest_Click` method and add the highlighted code to clear the two lists:

```
Private Sub btnTest_Click(ByVal sender As System.Object, _
    ByVal e As System.EventArgs) Handles btnTest.Click

        'Clear the lists
        objCustomers.Clear()
        lstCustomers.Items.Clear()

        'Create some customers
        CreateCustomer("Darrel", "Hilton", "dhilton@somecompany.com")
        CreateCustomer("Frank", "Peoples", "fpeoples@somecompany.com")
        CreateCustomer("Bill", "Scott", "bscott@somecompany.com")
End Sub
```

2. To demonstrate how a `Hashtable` cannot use the same key twice, run your project and click the Test button to have the customer list loaded. Now click the Test button again and you'll see the error message shown in Figure 5-22:

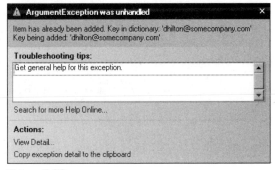

Figure 5-22

3. Click the Stop Debugging button on the toolbar in Visual Studio 2005 to stop the program.

4. Now add the following method to the `CustomerCollection` class:

```
'Provide a new implementation of the Clear method
Public Shadows Sub Clear()
    'Clear the CollectionBase
    MyBase.Clear()
    'Clear your hashtable
    EmailHashtable.Clear()
End Sub
```

5. Next, modify the `Remove` method as follows:

```
'Remove a customer from the collection
Public Sub Remove(ByVal oldCustomer As Customer)
    Me.List.Remove(oldCustomer)
    'Remove customer from the Hashtable
    EmailHashtable.Remove(oldCustomer.Email)
End Sub
```

6. Now add the `RemoveAt` method to override the default method defined in the
`CollectionBase` class:

```
'Provide a new implementation of the RemoveAt method
Public Shadows Sub RemoveAt(ByVal index As Integer)
    Remove(Item(index))
End Sub
```

7. Run the project and click the Test button to load the customers. Click the Test button again to
have the existing list of customers cleared before the customers are added again. Notice that this
time no exception has been thrown.

How It Works

The exception isn't thrown the second time around, because you are now making sure that the
`Hashtable` and the internal list maintained by `CollectionBase` are properly synchronized.
Specifically, whenever your `CustomerCollection` list is cleared using the `Clear` method, you make
sure that the `Hashtable` is also cleared.

To clear the internal list maintained by `CollectionBase`, you ask the base class to use its own `Clear`
implementation rather than trying to provide your own implementation. You do this by calling
`MyBase.Clear()`. Right after that, you call `Clear` on the `Hashtable`:

```
'Provide a new implementation of the Clear method
Public Shadows Sub Clear()
    'Clear the CollectionBase
    MyBase.Clear()
    'Clear your hashtable
    EmailHashtable.Clear()
End Sub
```

You'll also find that when you delete items from the collection by using `Remove`, the corresponding entry
is also removed from the `Hashtable`, because of this method that you added:

```
'Provide a new implementation of the RemoveAt method
Public Shadows Sub RemoveAt(ByVal index As Integer)
    Remove(Item(index))
End Sub
```

The `Shadows` keyword indicates that this `Clear` procedure should be used instead of the `Clear` in the
base class. The arguments and the return type do not have to match those in the base class procedure,
even though they do here.

You don't need to worry too much about the details of Shadows *and* Overrides *at this point, as they are discussed in detail in Chapter 10.*

Case Sensitivity

It's about this time that case sensitivity rears its ugly head again. If you run your project and click the Test button and then enter a valid email address in all uppercase letters, you'll see a message box indicating that there is no customer with that email address.

You need to get the collection to ignore case sensitivity on the key. In the next Try It Out, you do this by making sure that whenever you save a key, you transform the email address into all lowercase characters. Whenever you look up based on a key, you transform whatever you search for into lowercase characters too.

Try It Out   Case Sensitivity

1.   Open the Code Editor for the CustomerCollection class and make the highlighted change to the Add method:

```
'Add a customer to the collection
Public Sub Add(ByVal newCustomer As Customer)
    Me.List.Add(newCustomer)

    'Add the email address to the Hashtable

        EmailHashtable.Add(newCustomer.Email.ToLower, newCustomer)
End Sub
```

2.   Now, find the overloaded Item property that takes an e-mail address and modify this code:

```
'Overload Item property to find a customer by email address
Default Public ReadOnly Property Item(ByVal email As String) As Customer
    Get

            Return EmailHashtable.Item(email.ToLower)
    End Get
End Property
```

3.   Next, find the Remove method and modify this code:

```
'Remove a customer from the collection
Public Sub Remove(ByVal oldCustomer As Customer)
    Me.List.Remove(oldCustomer)

    'Remove customer from the Hashtable

        EmailHashtable.Remove(oldCustomer.Email.ToLower)
End Sub
```

4.   Run the project and click the Test button. Now if you enter a valid email address in all uppercase, the lookup will still work.

How It Works

Back in Chapter 4 you saw how you could do case-insensitive string comparisons using the `String.Compare` method. You can't use this technique here because the `Hashtable` is handling the comparison and, ideally, you don't want to produce your own version of the comparison code that the `Hashtable` uses just to do a case-insensitive match.

You can use the `ToLower` method available on strings. This creates a new string in which all of the characters are transformed into the lowercase equivalent, so whether you pass DHILTON@SOMECOMPANY.COM or DHilton@SomeCompany.com in, you always get dhilton@somecompany.com out.

When you add an item to the collection, you can get `ToLower` to convert the e-mail address stored in the `Customer` structure so that it is always in lowercase:

```
'Add the email address to the Hashtable
EmailHashtable.Add(newCustomer.Email.ToLower, newCustomer)
```

Likewise, when you actually do the lookup, you also turn whatever value is passed in as a parameter into all lowercase characters:

```
Return EmailHashtable.Item(email.ToLower)
```

Providing you're consistent with it, this action makes uppercase characters "go away" — in other words, you'll never end up with uppercase characters being stored in the key or being checked against the key.

This technique for removing the problem of uppercase characters can be used for normal string comparisons, but `String.Compare` *is more efficient.*

Advanced Array Manipulation

At the beginning of this chapter, the concept of arrays was introduced. I've left some of the more advanced discussions on arrays until later in the chapter, namely those involving adjusting the size of an array and multidimensional arrays.

Being able to manipulate the size of an array from code, and being able to store complex sets of data in an array is important, but with .NET it's far easier to achieve both of these using the collection functionality that the majority of this chapter has discussed. These next two sections are included for completeness and so that you can make the comparisons between the two for yourself.

Dynamic Arrays

When using an array, if you want to change its size in order to add items, or clean up space when you remove items, you need to use the `ReDim` keyword to make it a dynamic array. This is a short form of, not surprisingly, "redimension." In the next Try It Out, you'll reuse the Array Demo project you created at the start of the chapter and tweak it so that you can add new friends to the array after the initial array has been created.

Using ReDim

1. Find and open the Array Demo project. Open the Code Editor for `Form1` and modify the code in the `AddItemsToList` method so that it looks like this:

```
Sub AddItemsToList(ByVal arrayList() As String)
    'Enumerate the array
    For Each strName As String In arrayList
        'Add the array item to the list

        lstFriends.Items.Add("[" & strName & "]")
    Next
End Sub
```

2. Run the project and click the Initializing Arrays with Values button. Your form should look like Figure 5-23.

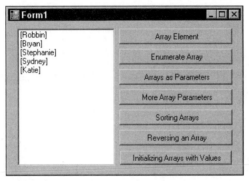

Figure 5-23

3. Now, stop the project and make the highlighted change to the `btnInitializingArraysWithValues_Click` method:

```
Private Sub btnInitializingArraysWithValues_Click( _
    ByVal sender As System.Object, ByVal e As System.EventArgs) _
    Handles btnInitializingArraysWithValues.Click

    'Declare and populate an array
    Dim strMyFriends() As String = {"Robbin", "Bryan", "Stephanie", _
        "Sydney", "Katie"}


    'Make the strMyFriends array larger
    ReDim strMyFriends(6)
    strMyFriends(5) = "Matt"
    strMyFriends(6) = "Jay"


    'List your friends
    AddItemsToList(strMyFriends)
End Sub
```

4. Run the project and click the Initializing Arrays with Values button. Your form should look like the one shown in Figure 5-24.

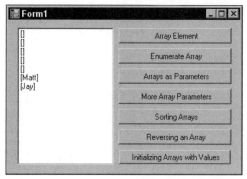

Figure 5-24

How It Works

After defining an array of 5 items, you use the `ReDim` keyword to re-dimension the array to have an upper boundary of 6, which, as you know, gives it a size of 7. After you do that, you have two new items in the array to play with—items 5 and 6:

```
'Make the strMyFriends array larger
ReDim strMyFriends(6)
strMyFriends(5) = "Matt"
strMyFriends(6) = "Jay"
```

Then, you can pass the resized array through to `AddItemsToList`:

```
'List your friends
AddItemsToList(strMyFriends)
```

But, as you can see from the results, the values for the first five items have been lost. (This is why you wrapped brackets around the results—if the name stored in the array is blank, you still see something appear in the list.) `ReDim` does indeed resize the array, but when an array is redimensioned, by default all of the values in the array are cleared, losing the values you defined when you initialized the array in the first place.

You can solve this problem by using the `Preserve` keyword.

Using Preserve

By including the `Preserve` keyword with the `ReDim` keyword, you can instruct Visual Basic 2005 to not clear the existing items. One thing to remember is that if you make an array smaller than it originally was, data will be lost from the eliminated elements even if you use `Preserve`. In the next Try It Out, you use `Preserve`.

Try It Out   Using Preserve

1. Open the Code Editor for Form1 and modify the
   `btnInitializingArraysWithValues_Click` method as follows:

   ```
   'Make the strMyFriends array larger
   ```

   ```
   ReDim Preserve strMyFriends(6)
   strMyFriends(5) = "Matt"
   strMyFriends(6) = "Jay"
   ```

2. Run the project again and click the Initializing Arrays with Values button. You should now find
   that the existing items in the array are preserved, as shown in Figure 5-25.

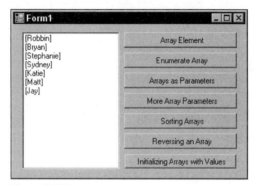

Figure 5-25

Summary

In this chapter, you saw some ways in which you could manage complex groups of data. You started by
looking at the concept of an array, or rather, defining a special type of variable that's configured to hold
a one-dimensional list of similar items rather than a single item.

You then looked at the concepts behind enumerations and constants. Both of these can be used to a great
effect in making more readable and manageable code. An enumeration lets you define human-readable,
common-sense titles to basic variable types. So rather than saying `"mode=3"`, you can say `"mode=My`
`Modes.Menu"`. Constants allow you to define literal values globally and use them elsewhere in your
code.

You then looked at structures. These are similar to classes and are well suited for storing groups of items
of information that all pertain to a particular thing or person. After looking at these, you moved on to
look at various types of collections, including the basic `ArrayList` and then saw how you could build
your own powerful collection classes inherited from `CollectionBase`. Finally, you looked at the
`Hashtable` class and covered some of the less-commonly used array functionality.

Chapter 5

To summarize, you should know how to:

❑ Define and redimension fixed and dynamic string arrays

❑ Enumerate through arrays and find their upper dimension

❑ Define an enumeration of values using the `Enum` class

❑ Create and use structures to manipulate sets of related data

❑ Use an `ArrayList` to hold any type of object

❑ Use collections to manage sets of related data

Exercises

Exercise 1

Create a Windows Application that contains three buttons. Add an enumeration of three names to your code. For the Click event for each button, display a message box containing a member name and value from the enumeration.

Exercise 2

Create a Windows Application that contains a TextBox control and a Button control. At the form level, create a names array initialized with a single name. In the Click event for the button control, add the code to redimension the array by one element preserving the existing data, add the new name from the text box to the array and to display the last name added to the array in a message box.

Hint: To determine the upper boundary of the array, use the `GetUpperBound(0)` method.

Building Windows Applications

When Microsoft first released Visual Basic 1.0, developers fell in love with it because it made building the user interface components of an application very simple. Instead of having to write thousands of lines of code to display windows — the very staple of a Windows application — developers could simply "draw" the window on the screen.

In Visual Basic (any version), a window is known as a *form*. With the .NET Framework, this form design capability has been brought to all of the managed languages as *Windows Forms*. You've been using these forms over the course of the previous five chapters, but you haven't really given that much thought to them — focusing instead on the code that you've written inside them.

In this chapter, you'll look in detail at Windows Forms and learn how you can use Visual Basic 2005 to put together fully featured Windows applications. In particular, you will look at:

❑   Adding more features using buttons, text boxes, and radio buttons

❑   Creating a simple toolbar and toolbar buttons to respond to events

❑   Creating additional forms in a Windows Forms application

Note that on occasion you'll hear developers refer to Windows Forms as Win Forms, which is a carry over from programming with Visual Basic 6.0 and earlier versions.

Responding to Events

Building a user interface using Windows Forms is all about responding to *events* (such as Click), so programming for Windows is commonly known as *event-driven programming*. To build a form, you paint controls onto a blank window called the Forms Designer using the mouse. Each of these controls is able to tell you when an event happens. For example, if you run your program and click a button that's been painted onto a form, that button will say, "Hey, I've been clicked!" and give you an opportunity to execute some code that you provide to respond to that event. You have already been using this feature.

Setting Up a Button Event

A good way to illustrate the event philosophy is to wire up a button to an event. An example would be the Click event, which is *fired* whenever the button is clicked. You have more events than just the Click event, although in day-to-day practice it's unlikely you'll use more than a handful of these. Even though you've already seen the Click event in action, this next Try It Out will go into some of the details of Code Editor and some more `Button` events that you have not seen up until this point.

Try It Out   **Using Button Events**

1. Start Visual Studio 2005 and select File ➪ New ➪ Project from the menu. In the New Project dialog box, select Visual Basic as the Project Type and Windows Application as the Templates type. Enter a project name of **Hello World 2** in the Name field and then click the OK button.

2. Click the form, and then, in the Properties window, change the Text property from Form1 to **Hello, world! 2.0**.

3. From the Toolbox, drag a Button control onto the form. Change its Text property to **Hello, world!** and its Name property to **btnSayHello**. Resize your button so that it looks similar to the one shown in Figure 6-1.

Figure 6-1

4. Double-click the button and add the following highlighted code to the Click event handler:

```
Private Sub btnSayHello_Click(ByVal sender As System.Object, _
    ByVal e As System.EventArgs) Handles btnSayHello.Click

        'Display a MessageBox
        MessageBox.Show("Hello, world!", Me.Text)
End Sub
```

5. Drop down the list in the Class Name combo box at the top of the code window. You'll see the options shown in Figure 6-2. Select Form1 in the Class Name combo box.

Figure 6-2

Notice that the last two items in the list are slightly indented. This tells you that (Form1 Events) and btnSayHello are all related to Form1. That is, the `btnSayHello` class is a member of `Form1`. As you add more members to the form, they will appear in this list.

6. Before you continue, take a quick look at the list in the Method Name combo box to the right of the Class Name combo box. Drop it down, and you'll see the options shown in Figure 6-3. These options are described in the list that follows the figure.

Figure 6-3

❑ The contents of the Method Name combo box change depending on the item selected in the Class Name combo box. This list lets you navigate through the methods related to the class you select in the Class Name combo box. In this case, its main job is to show you the methods and properties related to the class.

❑ The (Declarations) entry takes you to the top of the class where you can change the definition of the class and add member variables.

❑ The New method will create a new constructor for the class that you are working with. The constructor should contain any initialization code that needs to be executed for the class.

❑ The Finalize method will create a new method called `Finalize` and add it to the class and will be called when your program ends to release any unmanaged resources.

❑ The Dispose method takes you to the `Dispose` method for the class that you are working with and allows you to add any addition clean up code for your class.

❑ The InitializeComponent method takes you to the code that initializes the controls for the class that you are working with. You should not modify this method directly. Instead, you should use the Form Designer to modify the properties of the controls on your form.

❑ You'll notice that Visual Basic 2005 adds a small icon to the left of everything it displays in these lists. These can tell you what the item in the list actually is. A small purple box represents a method, a small blue box represents a member, four books stacked together represent a library, three squares joined together with lines represent a class, and a yellow lightning bolt represents an event.

Visual Studio may also decorate these icons with other icons to indicate the way they are defined. For example, next to Finalize you'll see a small key, which tells you the method is protected. The padlock icon tells us the item is private. It's not really important to memorize all of these now, but Visual Basic 2005 is fairly consistent with its representations, so if you do learn them over time, they will help you understand what's going on.

7. Select btnSayHello in the Class Name combo box. Now, drop down the Method Name combo box, as shown in Figure 6-4.

Figure 6-4

Since you selected btnSayHello in the Class Name combo box, the Method Name combo box now contains items that are exclusively rated to that control. In this case, you have a huge list of events. One of those events, Click, is shown in bold because you provided a definition for that event. If you select Click, you'll be taken to the method in Form1 that provides an event handler for this method.

8. Now add another event handler to the Button control. With btnSayHello still selected in the Class Name combo box, select the MouseEnter event in the Method Name combo box. A new event handler method will be created, and you need to add the following code to it as highlighted:

```
Private Sub btnSayHello_MouseEnter(ByVal sender As Object, _
    ByVal e As System.EventArgs) Handles btnSayHello.MouseEnter

        'Change the Button text
        btnSayHello.Text = "The mouse is here!"
End Sub
```

The MouseEnter event will be fired whenever the mouse pointer "enters" the control, in other words, crosses its boundary.

9. To complete this exercise, you need to add another event handler. Select btnSayHello in the Class Name combo box and select the MouseLeave event in the Method Name combo box. Again, a new event will be created, so add the highlighted code here:

```
Private Sub btnSayHello_MouseLeave(ByVal sender As Object, _
    ByVal e As System.EventArgs) Handles btnSayHello.MouseLeave

    'Change the Button text
    btnSayHello.Text = "The mouse has gone!"
End Sub
```

The MouseLeave event will be fired whenever the mouse pointer moves back outside of the control.

10. Run the project. Move the mouse over and away from the control, and you'll see the text change, as shown in Figure 6-5.

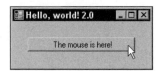

Figure 6-5

How It Works

Most of the controls that you use will have a dazzling array of events, although in day-to-day programming only a few of them will be consistently useful. For the Button control, the most useful is usually the Click event.

Visual Basic 2005 knows enough about the control to create the default event handlers for you automatically. This makes your life a lot easier and saves on typing!

When you created your MouseEnter event and added the highlighted code:

```
Private Sub btnSayHello_MouseEnter(ByVal sender As Object, _
    ByVal e As System.EventArgs) Handles btnSayHello.MouseEnter

    'Change the Button text
    btnSayHello.Text = "The mouse is here!"
End Sub
```

You'll notice that at the end of the method definition is the `Handles` keyword. This ties the method definition into the `btnSayHello.MouseEnter` event. When the button fires this event, your code will be executed.

Although previously you changed only the button's `Text` property at design time using the Properties window, here you can see that you can change it at run time too.

As a quick reminder here, design time is the term used to define the period of time that you actually writing the program, in other words, working with the Designer or adding code. Run time is the term used to define the period of time when the program is running.

Likewise, the MouseLeave event works in a very similar way:

```
Private Sub btnSayHello_MouseLeave(ByVal sender As Object, _
    ByVal e As System.EventArgs) Handles btnSayHello.MouseLeave

    'Change the Button text
    btnSayHello.Text = "The mouse has gone!"
End Sub
```

Building a Simple Application

Visual Studio 2005 comes with a comprehensive set of controls that you can use in your projects. For the most part, you'll be able to build all of your applications using just these controls, but in Chapter 13 you look at how you can create your own application.

Take a look at how you can use some of these controls to put together a basic application. In the following Try It Out, you build a basic Windows application that lets the user enter text into a form. The application will count the number of words and letters in the block of text that they enter.

Building the Form

The first job is to start a new project and build a form. This form will contain a multiline text box where you can enter text. It will also contain two radio buttons that will give you the option of counting either the words or the number of characters in the text box.

Try It Out   **Building the Form**

1.   Select File ➪ New ➪ Project from the Visual Studio 2005 menu and create a new Windows Application project. Enter a project name of **Word Counter** and click OK.

2.   Click on Form1 and, in the Properties window, set the Size property to **424, 312**, the StartPosition property to CenterScreen, and the Text property to **Word Counter**.

3.   Drag a TextBox control from the Toolbox and drop it on the form. Now change the properties of the text box as shown in the following list:

❑   Set Name to **txtWords**.

❑   Set Location to **8, 32**.

❑   Set Multiline to True.

❑   Set ScrollBars to Vertical.

❑   Set Size to **400, 217**.

4.   To tell the user what to do with the form, you add a label. Select the Label control from the Toolbox, drag and drop it just above the text box. Change the Text property to **Enter some text into this box**.

Strictly speaking, unless you're going to need to talk to the control from your code, you don't need to change its Name property. With the text box, you need to use its properties and methods to make the application work. However, the label is just there for esthetics, so you don't need to change the name for Label1. (This depends on how fussy you are—some developers give every control a specific name, whereas others name only specific controls that really need a name.)

It's worth noting that if you are going to refer to a control from Visual Basic 2005 code, it's a good coding practice to give the control a name. Developers should be able to determine what the control represents based on its name even if they've never seen your code before. Refer to the section on Modified Hungarian Notation in Chapter 1 for prefixes to use with your control names.

5. Your application is going to be capable of counting either the characters the user entered or the number of words. To allow the user to select the preferred count, you use two *radio buttons*. Draw two RadioButton controls onto the form next to each other below the text box. You need to refer to the radio buttons from your Visual Basic 2005 code, so change the properties as shown in the following lists:

   For the first radio button:

   ❑ Set Name to **radCountChars**.

   ❑ Set Checked to True.

   ❑ Set Text to **Chars**.

   For the second radio button:

   ❑ Set Name to **radCountWords**.

   ❑ Set Text to **Words**.

6. As the user types, you'll take the characters that the user enters and count up the words or characters as appropriate. You want to pass your results to the user, so add two new Label controls next to the RadioButton controls that you just added.

7. The first Label control (marked Label2) is just for esthetics, so change its Text property to **The results are:**. The second Label control will report the results, so you need to give it a name. Set the Name property as **lblResults** and clear the Text property.

8. You also need a Button control that will show a message box, so add a Button control to the form and align it to the bottom right of the text box. You don't strictly need this because the user can read the results on the form, but it will illustrate a couple of important points. Change the Name property to **btnShowMe** and the Text property to **Show Me!**. Your completed form should look similar to the one shown in Figure 6-6.

9. Now that you have the controls laid out on your form the way you want it, you can make sure you keep it that way. Make sure you select one of the controls and not the actual form, and then select Format ➪ Lock Controls from the menu. This sets the Locked property of each of the controls to True and prevents them from accidentally being moved, resized, or deleted.

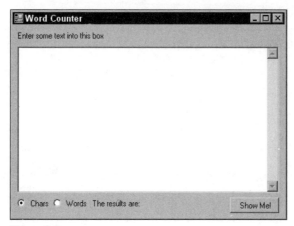

Figure 6-6

Counting Characters

With your form designed, you'll want to build some event handlers to count the number of characters in a block of text that the user types. Switch to the form's code view by right-clicking the form in the Solution Explorer and choosing View Code from the context menu or by right-clicking the form and choosing View Code from the context menu. Since your application will be able to count words and characters, you build separate functions for each. In this Try It Out, you write the code to count characters.

Try It Out   Counting Characters

1. Add this code to the Form1 class. Remember, to insert an XML Document Comment block, you need to type three apostrophes above the function:

```
''' <summary>
''' Count the characters in a block of text
''' </summary>
''' <param name="text">The string containing the text to count
''' characters in</param>
''' <returns>The number of characters in the string</returns>
''' <remarks></remarks>
Private Function CountCharacters(ByVal text As String) As Integer
    Return text.Length
End Function
```

2. Now you need to build an event handler for the text box. Select txtWords in the Class Name combo box and, in the Method Name combo box, select the TextChanged event. Add this high-lighted code to the event handler:

```
Private Sub txtWords_TextChanged(ByVal sender As Object, _
    ByVal e As System.EventArgs) Handles txtWords.TextChanged
```

```
          'Count the number of characters
          Dim intChars As Integer = CountCharacters(txtWords.Text)

          'Display the results
          lblResults.Text = intChars & " characters"
    End Sub
```

3. Run the project. Enter some text into the text box and you'll see a screen like the one in
        Figure 6-7.

Figure 6-7

How It Works

Notice that whenever you type a character into the text box, the label at the bottom of the form reports
the current number of characters. That's because the TextChanged event is fired whenever the user
changes the text in the box. This happens when new text is entered, when changes are made to existing
text, and when old text is deleted. You are "listening" for this event, and whenever you "hear" it (or
rather receive it), you call `CountCharacters` and pass in the block of text. As the user types text into the
txtWords text box, the Text property is updated to reflect the text that has been entered. You can get the
value for this property (in other words, the block of text) and pass it to `CountCharacters`:

```
          'Count the number of characters
          Dim intChars As Integer = CountCharacters(txtWords.Text)
```

The `CountCharacters` function in return counts the characters and passes back an integer representing
the number of characters that it has counted:

```
          Return text.Length
```

After you have the number of characters, you update the lblResults control:

```
          'Display the results
          lblResults.Text = intChars & " characters"
```

181

Counting Words

Although building a Visual Basic 2005 application is actually very easy, building an elegant solution to a problem requires a combination of thought and experience.

Take your application, for example. When the Words radio button is checked, you want to count the number of words, whereas when Chars is checked, you want to count the number of characters. This has three implications. First, when you respond to the `TextChanged` event, you need to call a different method that counts the words, rather than your existing method for counting characters. This isn't too difficult.

Second, whenever you select a different radio button, you need to change the text in the results from "characters" to "words" or back again. In a similar way, whenever the Show Me! button is clicked, you need to take the same result, but rather than displaying it in the Label control, you need to use a message box.

Now add some more event handlers to your code, and when you finish, examine the logic behind the techniques you used.

Try It Out   Counting Words

1. Stop your project if it is still running. The first thing you want to do is add another function that will count the number of words in a block of text. Add this code to create the `CountWords` function:

```
''' <summary>
''' Count the number of words in a block of text
''' </summary>
''' <param name="text">The string containing the text to count
''' words in</param>
''' <returns>The number of words in the string</returns>
''' <remarks></remarks>
Private Function CountWords(ByVal text As String) As Integer
    'Is the text box empty
    If txtWords.Text = String.Empty Then Return 0

    'Split the words
    Dim strWords() As String = text.Split(" ")

    'Return the number of words
    Return strWords.Length
End Function
```

2. The `UpdateDisplay` procedure deals with the hassle of getting the text from the text box and updating the display. It also understands whether it's supposed to find the number of words or number of characters by looking at the `Checked` property on the `radCountWords` radio button. Add this code to create the procedure:

```
Private Sub UpdateDisplay()
    'Do we want to count words?
    If radCountWords.Checked = True Then
```

```
            'Update the results
            lblResults.Text = CountWords(txtWords.Text) & " words"
        Else
            'Update the results
            lblResults.Text = CountCharacters(txtWords.Text) & " characters"
        End If
End Sub
```

3. Now, instead of calling `CountCharacters` from within your TextChanged handler, you want to call `UpdateDisplay`. Make the following change:

```
Private Sub txtWords_TextChanged(ByVal sender As Object, _
    ByVal e As System.EventArgs) Handles txtWords.TextChanged

        'Something changed so display the results
        UpdateDisplay()
End Sub
```

4. Finally, you want the display to alter when you change the radio button from Chars to Words and vice versa. To add the `CheckedChanged` event, select radCountWords in the Class Name combo box at the top of the code window and the CheckedChanged in the Method Name combo box. Add the following highlighted code to the event handler procedure:

```
Private Sub radCountWords_CheckedChanged(ByVal sender As Object, _
    ByVal e As System.EventArgs) Handles radCountWords.CheckedChanged

        'Something changed so display the results
        UpdateDisplay()
End Sub
```

5. Repeat the previous step for the `radCountChars` radio button:

```
Private Sub radCountChars_CheckedChanged(ByVal sender As Object, _
    ByVal e As System.EventArgs) Handles radCountChars.CheckedChanged

        'Something changed so display the results
        UpdateDisplay()
End Sub
```

6. Run the project. Enter some text in the box and check Words. Notice how the display changes as shown in Figure 6-8.

How It Works

Before you look at the technique that you used to put the form together, take a quick look at the `CountWords` function:

```
''' <summary>
''' Count the number of words in a block of text
''' </summary>
''' <param name="text">The string containing the text to count
''' words in</param>
''' <returns>The number of words in the string</returns>
''' <remarks></remarks>
```

```
Private Function CountWords(ByVal text As String) As Integer
    'Is the text box empty
    If txtWords.Text = String.Empty Then Return 0

    'Split the words
    Dim strWords() As String = text.Split(" ")

    'Return the number of words
    Return strWords.Length
End Function
```

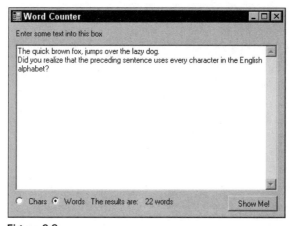

Figure 6-8

You start by checking to see whether the text box is empty by comparing the Text property of the text box to the Empty field of the String class. The Empty field of the String class is equivalent to a zero length string (" "); if no text has been entered, you immediately return from the function with a value of 0.

The Split method of the String class is used to take a string and turn it into an array of string objects. Here, the parameter you passed is equivalent to the "space" character, so you're effectively telling Split to break up the string based on a space. This means that Split returns an array containing each of the words in the string. You then return the length of this array, in other words, the number of words back to the caller.

> Note that because this code uses a single space character to split the text into words, you'll get unexpected behavior if you separate your words with more than one space character or use the Return key to start a new line.

One of the golden rules of programming is that you never write more code than you absolutely have to. In particular, when you find yourself in a position where you are going to write the same piece of code twice, try to find a workaround that requires that you write it only once. In this example, you have to change the value displayed in lblResults from two different places. The most sensible way to do this is to split the code that updates the label into a separate method; `UpdateDisplay`. You can then easily set up the TextChanged and CheckedChanged event handlers to call this method. The upshot of this is that you only have to write the tricky "get the text, find the results, and update them" routine once. This technique also creates code that is easier to change in the future and easier to debug when a problem is found.

```
Private Sub UpdateDisplay()
    'Do we want to count words?
    If radCountWords.Checked = True Then
        'Update the results
        lblResults.Text = CountWords(txtWords.Text) & " words"
    Else
        'Update the results
        lblResults.Text = CountCharacters(txtWords.Text) & " characters"
    End If
End Function
```

You'll find as you build applications that this technique of breaking out the code for an event handler is something you'll do quite often.

Creating the Show Me! Button Code

To finish this exercise, you need to write code for the Show Me! button. All you're going to do with this button is display a message box containing the same text that's displayed on lblResults.

Try It Out   **Coding the Show Me! Button**

1.   In the Code Editor, select btnShowMe from the Class Name combo box and then select the Click event in the Method Name combo box. Then add the highlighted code:

```
Private Sub btnShowMe_Click(ByVal sender As Object, _
    ByVal e As System.EventArgs) Handles btnShowMe.Click

        'Display the text contained in the Label control
        MessageBox.Show(lblResults.Text, "Word Counter")
    End Sub
```

2.   Run the project and type something into the text box. Then click the Show Me! button, and the same value will be displayed in the message box appears in the results Label control.

How It Works

When you click the button, the code in the Click event is using the `Text` property from the Label control as the `text` parameter (the message) for the `MessageBox.Show` method:

```
'Display the text contained in the Label control
MessageBox.Show(lblResults.Text, "Word Counter")
```

Creating More Complex Applications

Normal applications generally have a number of common elements. Among these are toolbars and status bars. Putting together an application that has these features is a fairly trivial task in Visual Basic 2005.

In the next section, you build an application that allows you to make changes to the text entered into a text box, such as changing its color and making it all uppercase or lowercase.

The Text Manipulation Project

In the next Try It Out you are going to build an application that allows you to manipulate the text in a text box. You'll be using a ToolBar control to change the color of the text in your text box and also to change the case of the text to either all uppercase letters or all lowercase letters.

The StatusBar control will also be used in your project to display the status of your actions as a result of clicking a button on the toolbar.

Your first step on the road to building your application is to create a new project.

Creating the Text Editor Project

1. Create a new Windows Application project and call it **Text Editor**.

2. Most of the time, Form1 isn't a very appropriate name for a form, as it's not very descriptive. Right-click the form in the Solution Explorer, select Rename, and change its name to **TextEditor.vb** as shown in Figure 6-9. Then press Enter to save the changes.

Figure 6-9

3. Now click on the form in the Forms Designer, and in the Properties window change the Text property to **Text Editor**.

4. In the screenshots, we're going to show the design window as quite small to save paper! You should explicitly set the size of the form by going to the Properties window of the form and setting the Size property to **600, 460**.

In the next section, you start building the user interface part of the application.

Creating the Toolbar

The toolbar contains a collection of buttons such as the toolbar in Visual Studio 2005. In the following Try It Out, you will create the toolbar and add the buttons to it.

Try It Out   **Adding the Toolbar**

1.   Select the ToolStrip control from the Toolbox and drag it and drop it on the form. It will auto-matically dock at the top of the form. Set the Stretch property to True to cause the toolbar to stretch across the entire form at run time.

2.   To add buttons to the toolbar you use a built-in editor. Find the Items property in the Properties window, select it, and left-click the ellipsis (...) to the right of (Collection).

3.   You're going to add six buttons to the toolbar: Clear, Red, Blue, Uppercase, Lowercase, and About.

4.   To add the first button, click the Add button in the Items Collection Editor. The Items Collection Editor displays a properties palette much like the one that you're used to using. For each button you need to change its name, display style, give it an icon, clear its text, and provide some explanatory tool tip text. Change the Name property to **tbrClear** as shown in Figure 6-10.

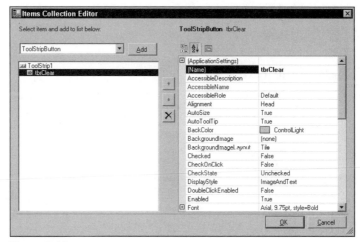

Figure 6-10

5.   Change the DisplayStyle property to Image.

6.   Locate the Image property and select it. Then click the ellipsis button for this property to invoke the Select Resource editor. In the Select Resource editor, click the Import button. In the Open dialog box, browse to the installation folder where Visual Studio 2005 was installed (the default installation path is shown here) and locate the following folder:

```
C:\Program Files\Microsoft Visual Studio 8\Common7\ VS2005ImageLibrary\
icons\WinXP
```

Select the `document.ico` file and then click the Open button to import the resource. Next, click the OK button in Select Resource editor and you'll be returned to the Items Collection Editor.

7.   Change the ImageScaling property to None, clear the Text property, and then set the ToolTipText property to **New**. This completes the steps necessary to create the first button.

8. You want to create a separator between the Clear button and the Red button. In the combo box in the Items Collection Editor, select Separator and then click the Add button. You can accept all default properties for this button.

9. Repeat steps 4 through 7 to create the Red button and use the following properties for this button. Before clicking the Add button, ensure you select Button in the combo box:

❑ Set Name to **tbrRed**.

❑ Set DisplayStyle to Image.

❑ Use `Common7\ VS2005ImageLibrary\icons\Misc\ servicestopped.ico` for the Image property.

❑ Set ImageScaling to None.

❑ Clear the Text property.

❑ Set the ToolTipText property to **Red**.

10. Repeat steps 4 through 7 to create the Blue button and use the following properties for this button:

❑ Set Name to **tbrBlue**.

❑ Set DisplayStyle to Image.

❑ Use `Common7\ VS2005ImageLibrary\icons\Misc\ services.ico` for the Image property.

❑ Set ImageScaling to None.

❑ Clear the Text property.

❑ Set the ToolTipText property to **Blue**.

11. You want to create a separator between the Blue button and the Uppercase button. In the combo box in the Items Collection Editor, select Separator and then click the Add button. You can accept all default properties for this button.

12. Repeat steps 4 through 7 to create the Uppercase button and use the following properties for this button. Before clicking the Add button, ensure you select Button in the combo box:

❑ Set Name to **tbrUpperCase**.

❑ Set DisplayStyle to Image.

❑ Use `Common7\VS2005ImageLibrary\icons\WinXP\fonfile.ico` for the Image property.

❑ Set ImageScaling to None.

❑ Clear the Text property.

❑ Set the ToolTipText property to **Upper Case**.

13. Repeat steps 4 through 7 to create the Lowercase button and use the following properties for this button:

❑ Set Name to **tbrLowerCase**.

❑ Set DisplayStyle to Image.

❑ Use `Common7\VS2005ImageLibrary\icons\WinXP\fonfont.ico` for the Image property.

❑ Set ImageScaling to None.

❑ Clear the Text property

❑ Set the ToolTipText property to **Lower Case**.

14. You want to create a separator between the Lowercase button and the Help button. In the combo box in the Items Collection Editor, select Separator and then click the Add button. You can accept all default properties for this button.

15. Repeat steps 4 through 7 to create the Help button and use the following properties for this button. Before clicking the Add button, ensure you select Button in the combo box:

❑ Set Name to **tbrHelpAbout**.

❑ Set DisplayStyle to Image.

❑ Use `Common7\VS2005ImageLibrary\icons\WinXP\help.ico` for the Image property.

❑ Set ImageScaling to None.

❑ Clear the Text property.

❑ Set the ToolTipText property to **About**.

16. Now click the OK button in the Items Collection Editor to close it.

17. Save your project by clicking the Save All button on the toolbar.

How It Works

The ToolStrip control docks to a particular position on the form. In this case, it docks itself to the top edge of the form.

The six buttons and three separators that you added to the toolbar actually appear as full members of the `TextEditor` class and have the usual events that you are accustomed to seeing. Later, you'll see how you can respond to the Click event for the various buttons.

A toolbar button can display text only, an image only, or both text and an image. However, most toolbars display only an image, so this is why you set the DisplayStyle property to Image. You did not want the image to scale smaller or larger automatically, so you set the ImageScaling property to None.

The ToolTipText property enables Visual Basic 2005 to display a ToolTip above the button whenever the user hovers the mouse over it. You don't need to worry about actually creating or showing a ToolTip; Visual Basic 2005 does this for you.

At this point, your toolbar should look similar to the one shown in Figure 6-11. Notice that the icons you used for the Red and Blue buttons look better than the bitmaps that you used for the other buttons. This is because the icons have a transparent background, and you'll typically find that icons look better on the toolbar buttons.

Figure 6-11

Creating the Status Bar

The status bar is a panel that sits at the bottom of an application window and tells the user what's going on. You create the status bar in the next Try It Out.

Adding a Status Bar

1. Drag a StatusStrip control from the Toolbox and drop it onto your form. You'll notice that it automatically glues itself to the bottom edge of the form and you'll only be able to change the height portion of its Size property if desired. Ensure the RenderMode property is set to System to make the status bar appear flat.

2. You need to add one StatusStripLabel to the Items collection of the StatusStrip so that you can display text on the status bar. Click the ellipsis button in the Items property to invoke the Items Collection Editor dialog box. In the Items Collection Editor dialog box, click the Add button to add a panel.

3. Set the following properties for the StatusStripLabel:

   ❏   Set Name to **sspStatus**.

   ❏   Set DisplayStyle to Text.

   ❏   Set Text to **Ready**.

4. Click the OK button to close the Items Collection Editor dialog box.

5. Open the Code Editor for the form and add the following code. You can quickly view the Code Editor by right clicking on the form and choosing View Code from the context menu:

```
'Get or set the text on the status bar
Public Property StatusText() As String
    Get
        Return sspStatus.Text
    End Get
    Set(ByVal value As String)
        sspStatus.Text = value
    End Set
End Property
```

There's no need to run the project at this point, so let's just talk about what you've done here.

How It Works

Visual Studio 2005 has some neat features for making form design easier. One thing that was always laborious in previous versions of Visual Basic and Visual C++ was to create a form that would automatically adjust itself when the user changed its size.

In Visual Studio 2005, controls have the capability to dock themselves to the edges of the form. By default, the StatusStrip control sets itself to dock to the bottom of the form, but you can change the docking location if so desired. So, when someone resizes the form, either at design time or at run time, the status bar (StatusStrip control) stays where you put it.

You may be wondering why you built a StatusText property to get and set the text on the status bar. Well, this comes back to abstraction. Ideally, you want to make sure that anyone using this class doesn't have to worry about how you've implemented the status bar. You might want to replace the .NET-supplied status bar with another control, and if you did, any users wanting to use your TextEditor class in their own applications (or developers wanting to add more functionality to this application later) would have to change their code to make sure it continued to work properly.

That's why you defined this property as Public. This means that others creating an instance of Text Editor to use its functionality in their own applications can change the status bar text if they want. If you don't want them to be able to change the text themselves, relying instead on other methods and properties on the form to change the text on their behalf, you would mark the property as Private.

As you work through this example, you'll see definitions of Public and Private. From this you'll be able to infer what functionality might be available to a developer using your TextEditor class.

Creating an Edit Box

The first thing you do in the next Try It Out is create a text box that can be used to edit the text entered. The text box has a MultiLine property, which by default is set to False. This property determines whether the text box should have only one line or can contain multiple lines. When you change this property to True, the text box control can be resized to any size that you want, and you can enter multiple lines of text in this control.

Try It Out   Creating an Edit Box

1. Open the Forms Designer for the TextEditor form, drag a TextBox control from the ToolBox, and drop it onto your form.

2. Change the following properties of the TextBox control:

    ❑   Set Name to **txtEdit**.

    ❑   Set Dock to Fill.

    ❑   Set MultiLine to True.

    ❑   Set ScrollBars to Vertical.

    Your form should now look like Figure 6-12.

Clearing the Edit Box

In the following Try It Out, you're going to create a property called EditText that will get or set the text you're going to edit. Then, clearing the edit box will simply be a matter of setting the EditText property to an empty string.

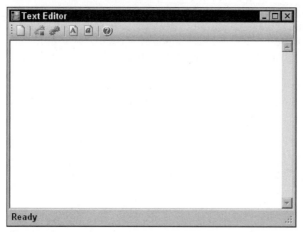

Figure 6-12

Clearing txtEdit

1. Add this code to `TextEditor`:

```
'Gets or sets the text that you're editing
Public Property EditText() As String
    Get
        Return txtEdit.Text
    End Get
    Set(ByVal value As String)
        txtEdit.Text = value
    End Set
End Property
```

As you have done earlier, when you created a property to abstract away the action of setting the status bar text, you created this property to give developers using the `TextEditor` form the ability to get or set the text of the document irrespective of how you actually implement the editor.

2. You can now build `ClearEditBox`, the method that actually clears your text box. Add the following code:

```
'Clears the txtEdit control
Public Sub ClearEditBox()
    'Set the EditText property
    EditText = String.Empty
    'Reset the font color
    txtEdit.ForeColor = Color.Black
    'Set the status bar text
    StatusText = "Text box cleared"
End Sub
```

3. Now select `txtEdit` in the Class Name combo box and the `TextChanged` event in the Method Name combo box at the top of the code editor. Add this code:

```
Private Sub txtEdit_TextChanged(ByVal sender As Object, _
    ByVal e As System.EventArgs) Handles txtEdit.TextChanged

    'Reset the status bar text
    StatusText = "Ready"
End Sub
```

How It Works

The first thing you want to do is clear your text box. In the next Try It Out, you see how you can call `ClearEditBox` from the toolbar.

All this procedure does is set the `EditText` property to an empty string by using the `Empty` field of the `String` class. Then it sets the `ForeColor` property of the text box (which is the color of the actual text) to black and places the text `Text box cleared` in the status bar.

```
'Clears the txtEdit control
Public Sub ClearEditBox()
    'Set the EditText property
    EditText = String.Empty
    'Reset the font color
    txtEdit.ForeColor = Color.Black
    'Set the status bar text
    StatusText = "Text box cleared"
End Sub
```

As mentioned, `EditText` abstracts the action of getting and setting the text in the box away from your actual implementation. This makes it easier for other developers down the line to use your `TextEditor` form class in their own applications:

```
'Gets or sets the text that you're editing
Public Property EditText() As String
    Get
        Return txtEdit.Text
    End Get
    Set(ByVal value As String)
        txtEdit.Text = value
    End Set
End Property
```

As you type, the `TextChanged` event handler will be repeatedly called:

```
Private Sub txtEdit_TextChanged(ByVal sender As Object, _
    ByVal e As System.EventArgs) Handles txtEdit.TextChanged

    'Reset the status bar text
    StatusText = "Ready"
End Sub
```

Changing the status bar text at this point resets any message that might have been set in the status bar. For example, if the user has to type a lot of text and looks down to see *Text box cleard*, he or she may be a little concerned. Setting it to "Ready" is a pretty standard way of informing the user that the computer is doing something or waiting. It does not mean anything specific.

Responding to Toolbar Buttons

In the next Try It Out, you'll start implementing the Click events for the various toolbar buttons on your toolbar. When you look at building application menus in Chapter 8, you'll notice that most menus provide the same functionality as your toolbar buttons, and you'll want to implement the code in your menu item Click events and have the corresponding toolbar buttons call the menu item Click events.

Try It Out   Responding to Toolbar Button Click Events

1. In the Code Editor, select tbrClear from the Class Name combo box, and in the Method Name combo box, select the Click event. Add the following highlighted code to the Click event handler:

```
Private Sub tbrClear_Click(ByVal sender As Object, _
    ByVal e As System.EventArgs) Handles tbrClear.Click

        'Clear the edit box
        ClearEditBox()
    End Sub
```

2. You need to create a procedure that will change the text in the edit box to red and update the status bar. Add the following code:

```
Public Sub RedText()
        'Make the text red
        txtEdit.ForeColor = Color.Red

        'Update the status bar text
        StatusText = "The text is red"
    End Sub
```

3. Next, select tbrRed in the Class Name combo box, select the Click event in the Method Name combo box, and add the following highlighted to the Click event handler:

```
Private Sub tbrRed_Click(ByVal sender As Object, _
    ByVal e As System.EventArgs) Handles tbrRed.Click

        'Make the text red
        RedText()
    End Sub
```

Run the project and enter some text. Click the Red button, and the text's color will change from black to red, as shown in Figure 6-13. Notice that if you continue typing in the edit box, the new text will also be red.

Figure 6-13

4. Click the Clear button to remove the text and revert the color of any new text to black.

5. Stop your project and return to the Code Editor. Add the following `BlueText` procedure to change the text in the edit box to blue:

```
Public Sub BlueText()
    'Make the text blue
    txtEdit.ForeColor = Color.Blue

    'Update the status bar text
    StatusText = "The text is blue"
End Sub
```

6. Now select tbrBlue in the Class Name combo box and the Click event in the Method Name combo box. Add the following highlighted code to the Click event handler:

```
Private Sub tbrBlue_Click(ByVal sender As Object, _
    ByVal e As System.EventArgs) Handles tbrBlue.Click

    'Make the text blue
    BlueText()
End Sub
```

7. You now need to create a procedure to change the text in the edit box to all uppercase. Add the following code to your project:

```
Public Sub UppercaseText()
    'Make the text uppercase
    EditText = EditText.ToUpper

    'Update the status bar text
    StatusText = "The text is all uppercase"
End Sub
```

8. Now select tbrUpperCase in the Class Name combo box and the Click event in the Method Name combo box. Add the following highlighted code to the Click event handler:

```
Private Sub tbrUpperCase_Click(ByVal sender As Object, _
    ByVal e As System.EventArgs) Handles tbrUpperCase.Click

    'Make the text uppercase
    UppercaseText()
End Sub
```

9. Now add the following procedure to change the text to all lowercase:

```
Public Sub LowercaseText()
    'Make the text lowercase
    EditText = EditText.ToLower

    'Update the status bar text
    StatusText = "The text is all lowercase"
End Sub
```

10. Now select tbrLowerCase in the Class Name combo box and the Click event in the Method Name combo box. Add the following code to the Click event handler:

```
Private Sub tbrLowerCase_Click(ByVal sender As Object, _
    ByVal e As System.EventArgs) Handles tbrLowerCase.Click

    'Make the text lowercase
    LowercaseText()
End Sub
```

11. Run the project and enter some text into the box in a mixture of lowercase and uppercase. Then click the Uppercase button to make the text all uppercase as shown in Figure 6-14. Clicking the Lowercase button will convert the text to all lowercase, and clicking on the Red or Blue buttons will cause the text to change color. Finally, clicking the Clear button will cause all text to be cleared and the color and case to be restored to the default.

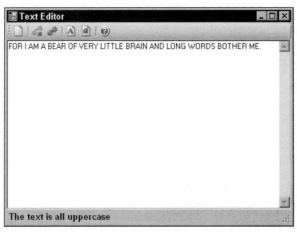

Figure 6-14

How It Works

This Try It Out was really quite simple. By this time, you are quite adept at creating the Click event handler for buttons on your form, and creating the Click event handler for a toolbar button is no different. The first thing that you did was to create the Click event handler for the Clear toolbar button and add the code to call the ClearEditBox procedure:

```
Private Sub tbrClear_Click(ByVal sender As Object, _
    ByVal e As System.EventArgs) Handles tbrClear.Click

    'Clear the edit box
    ClearEditBox()
End Sub
```

Next, you created the RedText procedure to change the text in the edit box to red and to update the status bar with the appropriate information. To change the color of the text in the edit box, you set the ForeColor property of the edit box using the Red constant from the Color enumeration. (The Color enumeration contains an extensive list of named colors.) The ForeColor property remains red until you set it to something else — so clicking the Clear button turns it back to black:

```
Public Sub RedText()
    'Make the text red
    txtEdit.ForeColor = Color.Red

    'Update the status bar text
    StatusText = "The text is red"
End Sub
```

You also change the text in the status bar using the StatusText property to display a message indicating the text color has changed. As soon as you start typing again, the message in the status bar is changed to "Ready", as set by the TextChanged event handler for the edit box.

In order to call the RedText procedure you added code to the Click event for the Red button on the toolbar:

```
'Make the text red
RedText()
```

The code for the Blue button on the toolbar works in the same manner. You created the BlueText procedure to set the ForeColor property of the edit box to Blue and then update the status bar with the appropriate message. You then call the BlueText procedure from the Click event of the Blue toolbar button.

If the user clicks on the Uppercase button on the toolbar, you call UppercaseText, which uses the ToUpper method to convert all the text held in EditText to uppercase text:

```
'Make the text uppercase
EditText = EditText.ToUpper
```

Likewise, if the user clicks on the Lowercase button, you call `LowercaseText`, which uses the `ToLower` method to convert all the text held in `EditText` to lowercase text:

```
'Make the text lowercase
EditText = EditText.ToLower
```

Each of these procedures is called from the Click event of the appropriate toolbar buttons, and these procedures also update the message in the status bar to reflect whether the text has been changed to red, blue, uppercase, or lowercase.

Understanding Focus

There's a problem with your Text Editor project. When you select another window and then switch back to the Text Editor window, the entire text in the box is highlighted. This happens because the *focus* has been set to the TextBox control. The control that has focus is the control that is currently selected, as shown in Figure 6-15. For example, if you have two buttons on a form, the code in the Click event handler for the button that has focus will be executed if you press Return.

Figure 6-15

If there are several text boxes on a form, any text you type will be entered into the text box that currently has the focus.

You can move focus between controls at run time by pressing the Tab key. For example, if the user of the form shown in Figure 6-15 pressed the Tab key, focus would jump to the "I do not" button. If the user pressed the Tab key again, focus would jump back to the "I have focus" button.

The order in which the focus moves between the controls on a form is not arbitrary. As you place controls on a form, they are assigned a value for their `TabIndex` property. The first control to be placed on the form has a `TabIndex` of 0, the second 1, the third 2, and so on. This is the same order in which the controls will have the focus as you tab through them. If you have placed all your controls on the form and are not happy with the resulting tab order, you can manually change it yourself by using the Properties window to set the `TabIndex` properties of the controls.

Note that, although labels have a `TabIndex` property, it is not possible to tab to them at run time. Instead, the focus moves to the next control that can receive it, such as a text box or button.

Visual Basic 2005 has a very handy feature for displaying the tab order of your controls. Select View ⇨ Tab Order, and your form will look something like Figure 6-16.

The tab order shown in the figure represents the order in which you placed your controls on the form. To remove the numbers, just select View ⇨ Tab Order once more.

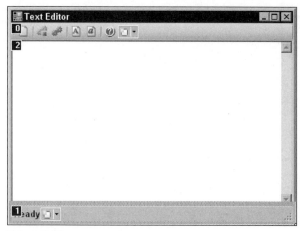

Figure 6-16

Using Multiple Forms

All Windows applications have two types of windows: normal windows and dialog boxes. A normal window provides the main user interface for an application. For example, if you use Word, you use a normal window for editing your documents.

On occasion, the application will display a dialog box when you want to access a special feature. This type of window "hijacks" the application and forces you to use just that window. For example, when you select the Print option in Word, a dialog box appears, and from that point on, until you close the dialog by clicking OK, Cancel, or the close box, you can't go back and change the document — the only thing you can use is the Print dialog box itself. Forms that do this are called *modal*. While they're up, you're in that mode.

Dialog boxes are discussed in more detail in Chapter 7. For now, you can focus on adding additional forms to your application. The form that you add in the next exercise is a simple modal form.

Help About

Most applications have an About dialog box that describes the application's name and copyright information. As you already have a toolbar button for this feature, you'll want to create this form now.

Try It Out   **Adding an About Box**

1. To add a new form to the project, you need to use the Solution Explorer. Right click the Text Editor project and select Add ⇨ Windows Form. In the Add New Item – Text Editor dialog box, shown in Figure 6-17, select the About Box in the Templates pane, enter **About.vb** in the Name field, and click the Add button to create the new form.

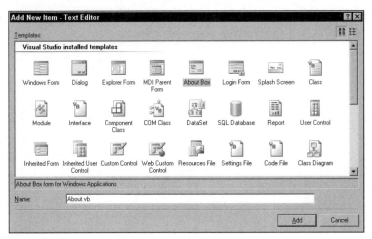

Figure 6-17

2. When the form's Designer appears, you'll notice that all of the normal details that are shown in an About dialog box are already on the form. This includes such items as the product name, version number, copyright information, etc.

3. Right-click the form and choose View Code from the context menu. You'll notice that the Load event for the form already contains a significant amount of code to populate the details on the About form. There is a TODO comment in the code that informs you that you need to update the assembly information for the application.

4. Right-click the project in the Solution Explorer and choose Properties from the context menu. Click the Assembly Information button in the Application pane of the Text Editor properties to display the Assembly Information dialog box. Edit the information in this dialog box as shown in Figure 6-18 and then click OK to close this dialog box.

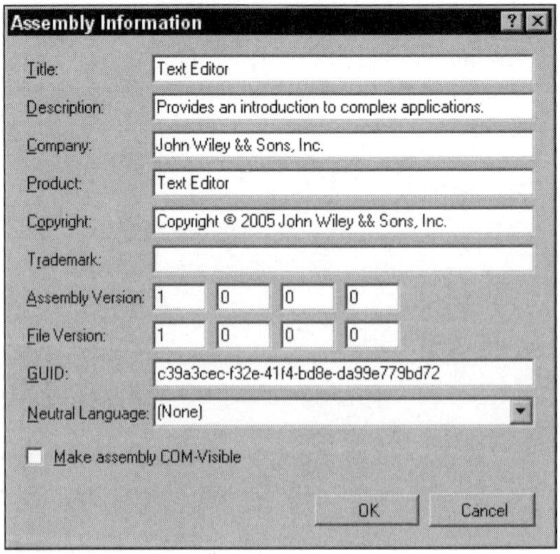

Figure 6-18

5. You need to write a procedure that will display the About dialog box, so add this code to the TextEditor form:

```
Public Sub ShowAboutBox()
    'Display the About dialog box
    Dim objAbout As New About
    objAbout.ShowDialog(Me)
End Sub
```

6. Finally, you need to call ShowAboutBox when the Help About button on the toolbar is clicked. In the Class Name combo box at the top of the Code Editor, select tbrHelpAbout and in the Method Name combo box, select the Click event. Add the following highlighted code to the Click event handler:

```
Private Sub tbrHelpAbout_Click(ByVal sender As Object, _
    ByVal e As System.EventArgs) Handles tbrHelpAbout.Click

    'Display the About dialog box
    ShowAboutBox()
End Sub
```

7. Run the project and click on the Help About button. You should see the dialog box shown in Figure 6-19.

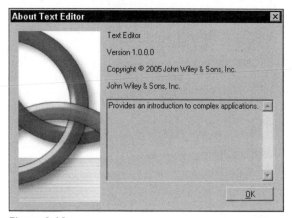

Figure 6-19

How It Works

There are a variety of prebuilt forms provided in Visual Studio 2005, as was shown in Figure 6-17. You choose to add the About Box form to your project to display an About dialog box from your application.

When the About form starts, it will fire the Load event, and this event already has the appropriate code written to load the fields on the form. You'll notice that this code makes efficient use of the My. Application.AssemblyInfo namespace to retrieve the appropriate information from your application's assembly for the About form:

```
Private Sub About_Load(ByVal sender As System.Object, _
    ByVal e As System.EventArgs) Handles MyBase.Load
    ' Set the title of the form.
    Dim ApplicationTitle As String
    If My.Application.AssemblyInfo.Title <> "" Then
        ApplicationTitle = My.Application.AssemblyInfo.Title
    Else
        ApplicationTitle = System.IO.Path.GetFileNameWithoutExtension( _
            My.Application.AssemblyInfo.Name)
    End If
    Me.Text = String.Format("About {0}", ApplicationTitle)
    ' Initialize all of the text displayed on the About Box.
    ' TODO: Customize the application's assembly information in the
    '     "Application" pane of the project
    '     properties dialog (under the "Project" menu).
    Me.LabelProductName.Text = My.Application.AssemblyInfo.ProductName
    Me.LabelVersion.Text = String.Format("Version {0}", _
        My.Application.AssemblyInfo.Version.ToString)
    Me.LabelCopyright.Text = My.Application.AssemblyInfo.LegalCopyright
    Me.LabelCompanyName.Text = My.Application.AssemblyInfo.CompanyName
    Me.TextBoxDescription.Text = My.Application.AssemblyInfo.Description
End Sub
```

The assembly information that you modified in the Assembly Information dialog box is used to populate the fields on your About form. If you added the text **John Wiley && Sons, Inc.** to the Company and Copyright fields in the Assembly Information dialog box as shown in Figure 6-18, you'll have noticed that two consecutive ampersands were used in John Wiley && Sons, Inc. The reason behind this is that the labels on your About form treat a single ampersand as the start of a code representing a special character. Two consecutive ampersands is then the code for the ampersand character itself.

To display another form, you have to create a new instance of it. That's exactly what you do in the ShowAboutBox procedure. Once you have created a new instance of the form, you use the ShowDialog method to show the About form modally. When you pass the Me keyword as a parameter to the ShowDialog method, you are specifying that the TextEditor form is the owner of the dialog being shown; in this case the About form:

```
Public Sub ShowAboutBox()
    'Display the About dialog box
    Dim objAbout As New About
    objAbout.ShowDialog(Me)
End Sub
```

To call the ShowAboutBox procedure, you had to add code to the Click event of the HelpAbout button on the toolbar:

```
Private Sub tbrHelpAbout_Click(ByVal sender As Object, _
    ByVal e As System.EventArgs) Handles tbrHelp.Click

    'Display the About dialog box
    ShowAboutBox()
End Sub
```

So, with very little effort and a minimal amount of code, you have added a lot of functionality to your Text Editor application. You can see firsthand how Visual Studio 2005 provides productivity and time-saving features such as prebuilt forms.

Summary

This chapter discussed some of the more advanced features of Windows forms and the commonly used controls. It discussed the event-driven nature of Windows and showed three events that can happen to a button (namely Click, MouseEnter, and MouseLeave).

You created a simple application that allowed you to enter some text and then choose between counting the number of characters or the number of words by using radio buttons.

You then turned your attention to building a more complex application that allowed you to edit text by changing its color or its case. This application showed how easy it was to build an application with toolbars and status bars. You even added an About dialog box to display basic information about your application such as the application title, description, version number, and copyright information.

To summarize, you should now know how to:

❑ Write code to respond to control events

❑ Set properties on controls to customize their look and behavior

❑ Use the ToolStrip and StatusStrip controls

❑ Display other forms in your application

Exercises

Exercise 1

Create a Windows application with two buttons. Add code to the MouseUp event for the first button to display a MessageBox with a message that the event has fired. Add code to the LostFocus event for the first button to also display a MessageBox with a message that the button has lost focus.

Exercise 2

Create a Windows application with a toolbar and status bar. At the bottom of the IDE, right-click the ToolStrip control and select the Insert Standard Items menu item to have the standard buttons added to the control. For the Click event for each of the ToolStripButton controls, display a message in the status bar indicating which button was clicked.

Displaying Dialog Boxes

Visual Basic 2005 provides several built-in dialog boxes that help you provide a rich user interface in your front-end applications. These dialog boxes provide the same common user interface that is found in most Windows applications. They also provide many properties and methods that allow you to customize these dialog boxes to suit your needs while still maintaining the standard look of Windows applications.

In this chapter, you will learn about the following:

- ❑ Creating a message box using different buttons and icons
- ❑ Creating an Open dialog box that enables you to open files
- ❑ Creating a Save dialog box that enables you to save files
- ❑ Creating a Font dialog box that enables you to apply the selected font to text
- ❑ Creating a Color dialog box that enables you to define and select custom colors
- ❑ Creating a Print dialog box that prints text from your application

This chapter explores these dialog boxes in depth and will show how you can use them in your Visual Basic 2005 applications to help you build a more professional looking application for your users.

The MessageBox Dialog Box

The MessageBox dialog box is one of those dialog boxes that you will use often as a developer. This dialog box enables you to display custom messages to your users and accept their input regarding the choice that they have made. This dialog box is very versatile; you can customize it by displaying a variety of icons with your messages and by choosing which buttons to display.

In the day-to-day operation of a computer, you have seen message boxes that display one of the icons shown in Figure 7-1. In this section, you learn how to create and display message boxes that use these icons.

Figure 7-1

The first icon in Figure 7-1 has three names: Error, Hand, and Stop. The second icon has only one name: Question. The third icon has two names: Exclamation and Warning. The final icon in Figure 7-1 has two names: Asterisk and Information.

When building a Windows application, at times you need to prompt the user for information or display a warning that something did not happen or something unexpected happened. For instance, suppose the user of your application modified some data and is trying to close the application without saving the data. You could display a message box that carries an information or warning icon and an appropriate message — that all unsaved data will be lost. You could also provide OK and Cancel buttons to allow the user to continue or cancel the operation.

This is where the MessageBox dialog box comes in: It enables you to quickly build custom dialog boxes that prompt the user for a decision while displaying your custom message, a choice of icons, and a choice of buttons. All of this functionality also allows you to display a message box to inform users of validation errors, and to display formatted system errors that are trapped by error handling.

Before you jump into some code, take a look at the `MessageBox` class. The `Show` method is called to display the MessageBox dialog box. The title, message, icons, and buttons displayed are determined by the parameters you pass to this method. This may seem complicated, but actually using MessageBox is very simple — as you have seen and will see in the following sections.

Available Icons for MessageBox

You saw the available icons in Figure 7-1. The following table outlines those four standard icons that you can display in a message box. The actual graphic displayed is a function of the operating system constants and (in the current implementations at least) there are four unique symbols with multiple field names assigned to them.

Member Name	Description
Asterisk	Specifies that the message box displays an information icon
Information	Specifies that the message box displays an information icon
Error	Specifies that the message box displays an error icon
Hand	Specifies that the message box displays an error icon
Stop	Specifies that the message box displays an error icon
Exclamation	Specifies that the message box displays an exclamation icon
Warning	Specifies that the message box displays an exclamation icon
Question	Specifies that the message box displays a question mark icon
None	Specifies the message box will not display any icon

Available Buttons for MessageBox

There are several combinations of buttons that you can display in a message box. The following table outlines them.

Member Name	Description
AbortRetryIgnore	Specifies that the message box displays Abort, Retry, and Ignore buttons
OK	Specifies that the message box displays an OK button
OKCancel	Specifies that the message box displays OK and Cancel buttons
RetryCancel	Specifies that the message box displays Retry and Cancel buttons
YesNo	Specifies that the message box displays Yes and No buttons
YesNoCancel	Specifies that the message box displays Yes, No, and Cancel buttons

Setting the Default Button

Along with displaying the appropriate buttons, you can instruct the message box to set a default button for you. This allows the user to read the message and press the Enter key to invoke the action for the default button without having to click the button itself with the mouse. The following table outlines the available default button options.

Member Name	Description
Button1	Specifies that the first button in the message box should be the default button
Button2	Specifies that the second button in the message box should be the default button
Button3	Specifies that the third button in the message box should be the default button

You set the default button relative to the MessageBox buttons, from left to right. Therefore, if you have the Yes, No, and Cancel buttons displayed and you choose the third button to be the default, Cancel will be the default button. Likewise, if you choose the third button to be the default and you have only OK and Cancel buttons, the first button becomes the default.

Miscellaneous Options

A couple of other options are available in the MessageBoxOptions enumeration and can be used with the message box and are shown in the following table.

Member Name	Description
Default DesktopOnly	Specifies that the message box be displayed on the active desktop
RightAlign	Specifies that the text in a message box will be right-aligned, as opposed to left-aligned, which is the default
RTLReading	Specifies that the text in a message box be displayed with the RTL (right-to-left) reading order; this applies only to languages that are read from right to left
Service Notification	Specifies that the message box be displayed on the active desktop. The caller is a Windows service notifying the user of an event.

The Show Method Syntax

You call the Show method to display the message box. The following code example displays the message box shown in Figure 7-2. Notice that the code specifies the text that is displayed in the message box as the first argument, followed by the text that is displayed in the title bar. Then you specify the buttons that should be displayed, followed by the type of icon that should be displayed beside the icon. Lastly, you specify the button that you want to set as the default button — in this case Button1.

If you want to run this code, start a new Windows Application project, double-click the form in the Designer to generate the Form1_Load event, and place the following code inside that procedure:

```
MessageBox.Show("My Text", "My Caption", MessageBoxButtons.OKCancel, _
MessageBoxIcon.Information, MessageBoxDefaultButton.Button1)
```

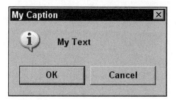

Figure 7-2

Now that you have seen the available icons, buttons, and default button fields, take a look at the Show method of the MessageBox class. You can specify the Show method in several ways; the more common syntaxes are shown in the following list:

❑ MessageBox.Show(*message text*)

❑ MessageBox.Show(*message text*, *caption*)

❑ MessageBox.Show(*message text*, *caption*, *buttons*)

❑ MessageBox.Show(*message text*, *caption*, *buttons*, *icon*)

❑ MessageBox.Show(*message text*, *caption*, *buttons*, *icon*, *default button*)

In the previous examples, *message text* represents the message that displays in the message box. This text can be static text (a literal string value) or supplied in the form of a string variable. The other parameters are optional:

❑ *Caption* represents either static text or a string variable that will be used to display text in the title bar of the message box. If this parameter is omitted, no text is displayed in the title bar.

❑ *Buttons* represents a value from the `MessageBoxButtons` enumeration. This parameter enables you to specify which of the available buttons to display in the MessageBox dialog box. If you omit this parameter, the OK button is displayed as the only button in the box.

❑ *Icon* represents a value from the `MessageBoxIcon` enumeration. This parameter enables you to specify which of the available icons displays in the MessageBox dialog box. If you omit this parameter, no icon is displayed.

❑ *Default Button* represents a value from the `MessageBoxDefaultButton` enumeration. This parameter enables you to specify which of the buttons is set as the default button in the MessageBox dialog box. If you omit this parameter, the first button displayed becomes the default button.

All the syntax examples shown in the previous section return a value from the `DialogResult` enumeration, which indicates which button in the MessageBox dialog box was chosen. The following table shows the available members in the `DialogResult` enumeration.

Member Name	Description
Abort	The return value is Abort and is the result of clicking the Abort button
Cancel	The return value is Cancel and is the result of clicking the Cancel button
Ignore	The return value is Ignore and is the result of clicking the Ignore button
No	The return value is No and is the result of clicking the No button
None	Nothing is returned, which means the dialog box continues running until a button is clicked
OK	The return value is OK and is the result of clicking the OK button
Retry	The return value is Retry and is the result of clicking the Retry button
Yes	The return value is Yes and is the result of clicking the Yes button

Example Message Boxes

Because multiple buttons can be displayed in a MessageBox dialog box, there are multiple ways to display a dialog box and check the results. Of course, if you were displaying only one button using the message box for notification, you would not have to check the results at all and could use a very simple syntax. This Try It Out demonstrates how to display two buttons in a message box and then check for the results from the message box to determine which button was clicked.

Try It Out   Creating a Two Button MessageBox

1. Start Visual Studio 2005 and select File ⇨ New ⇨ Project from the menu. In the New Project dialog box, select Windows Application in the Templates pane and enter a project name of **Simple MessageBox** in the Name field. Click OK to have this project created.

2. Click the form in the Forms Designer and then set its Text property to **Simple MessageBox**.

3. You want to add a Button control from the Toolbox to the form that will display a message box. Set its Name property to **btnShow** and its Text property to **Show**.

4. Next, you want to add a Label control to the form. This label will display results depending on which button in the message box a user clicks. Set the Name property to **lblResults** and the Text property to **Nothing Clicked**. Resize the form so your completed form looks similar to the one shown in Figure 7-3.

Figure 7-3

5. Double-click the Show button and add the highlighted code in the Click event handler:

```
Private Sub btnShow_Click(ByVal sender As System.Object, _
    ByVal e As System.EventArgs) Handles btnShow.Click

        If MessageBox.Show("Your Internet connection will be closed now.", _
            "Dial-Up Networking Notification", MessageBoxButtons.OKCancel, _
            Nothing, MessageBoxDefaultButton.Button1) =
                Windows.Forms.DialogResult.OK Then

            lblResults.Text = "OK Clicked"
            'Call some method here...
        Else
            lblResults.Text = "Cancel Clicked"
            'Call some method here...
        End If
End Sub
```

6. Run the project and then click the Show button. You should see a message box dialog box like the one shown in Figure 7-4.

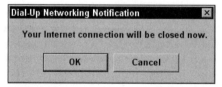

Figure 7-4

7. Click the OK or Cancel button and you'll see the results of the button clicked displayed on Form1.

How It Works

The code uses the `Show` method of the `MessageBox` class and uses an `If . . . End If` statement to see whether the user clicked the OK:

```
If MessageBox.Show("Your Internet connection will be closed now.", _
        "Dial-Up Networking Notification", MessageBoxButtons.OKCancel, _
        Nothing, MessageBoxDefaultButton.Button1) = DialogResult.OK Then
```

Notice that the code specifies that the OK and Cancel buttons are to be displayed in the dialog box and also that the OK button is to be the default button.

You have to specify something for the icon parameter, because this is required when you want to set the default button parameter. You did not want to display an icon, so you used the `Nothing` keyword.

Also notice that you check the results returned from MessageBox using `DialogResult.OK`. You could have just as easily have checked for `DialogResult.Cancel` and written the `If . . . End If` statement around that.

This is great if you want to test the results of only one or two buttons. But what happens when you want to test the results from a message box that contains three buttons?

Try It Out   **Testing a Three Button MessageBox**

1. Stop your project if it is still running and open the Forms Designer for Form1.

2. Add another Button control and set its Name property to **btn3Buttons** and its Text property to **3 Buttons**. Double-click the button and add the highlighted code to its Click event handler:

```
Private Sub btn3Buttons_Click(ByVal sender As System.Object, _
    ByVal e As System.EventArgs) Handles btn3Buttons.Click
```

```
'Declare a variable
Dim intResult As DialogResult

'Get the results of the button clicked
intResult = MessageBox.Show("The A drive is not ready." & _
    ControlChars.CrLf & ControlChars.CrLf & _
    "Please insert a diskette into the drive.", "Device Not Ready", _
    MessageBoxButtons.AbortRetryIgnore, MessageBoxIcon.Error, _
    MessageBoxDefaultButton.Button2)

'Process the results of the button clicked
Select Case intResult
    Case DialogResult.Abort
        'Do abort processing here...
        lblResults.Text = "Abort Clicked"
    Case DialogResult.Retry
        'Do retry processing here...
```

```
                lblResults.Text = "Retry Clicked"
            Case DialogResult.Ignore
                'Do ignore processing here...
                lblResults.Text = "Ignore Clicked"
        End Select
    End Sub
```

3. Run the project and click the 3 Buttons button. The message box dialog box shown in Figure 7-5 will be displayed and shows an icon and three buttons. Notice that the second button is the default this time around.

Figure 7-5

How It Works

The Show method returns a DialogResult, which is an Integer value. What you need to do in a case where there are three buttons is to capture the DialogResult in a variable and then test that variable.

In the following sample code, the first thing you do is declare a variable as a DialogResult to capture the DialogResult returned from the message box dialog box. Remember that the results returned from the dialog box are nothing more than an enumeration of Integer values. Next, you set the DialogResult in the variable.

```
'Declare a variable
Dim intResult As DialogResult

'Get the results of the button clicked
intResult = MessageBox.Show("The A drive is not ready." & _
    ControlChars.CrLf & ControlChars.CrLf & _
    "Please insert a diskette into the drive.", "Device Not Ready", _
    MessageBoxButtons.AbortRetryIgnore, MessageBoxIcon.Error, _
    MessageBoxDefaultButton.Button2)
```

Notice that the message in the Show method syntax is broken up into two sections separated with ControlChars.CrLf. This built-in constant provides a carriage-return-line-feed sequence, which allows you to break up your message and display it on separate lines.

Finally, you test the value of the intResult in a Select Case statement and act on it accordingly:

```
'Process the results of the button clicked
Select Case intResult
```

```
        Case DialogResult.Abort
            'Do abort processing here...
            lblResults.Text = "Abort Clicked"
        Case DialogResult.Retry
            'Do retry processing here...
            lblResults.Text = "Retry Clicked"
        Case DialogResult.Ignore
            'Do ignore processing here...
            lblResults.Text = "Ignore Clicked"
    End Select
```

In each of the `Case` statements, you write the name of the button selected in the label to indicate which button was clicked.

Now you have a general understanding of how the MessageBox dialog box works and you have a point of reference for the syntax. To familiarize yourself further with the MessageBox, try altering the values of the *caption*, *text*, *buttons*, *icon*, and *button* parameters in the previous examples.

Be careful not to overuse the MessageBox and display a message box for every little event. This can be a real annoyance to the user. You must use common sense and good judgment on when a message box is appropriate. You should display a MessageBox dialog box only when you absolutely need to inform the users that some type of error has occurred or when you need to warn the users that an action that they have requested is potentially damaging. An example of the latter is shutting down the application without saving their work. You would want to prompt the users to let them know that, if they continue, they will lose all unsaved work and give them an option to continue or cancel the action of shutting down the application.

The OpenDialog Control

A lot of Windows applications process data from files, so you need an interface to select files to open and save. The .NET Framework provides the `OpenFileDialog` and `SaveFileDialog` classes to do just that. In this section you'll take a look at the OpenFileDialog dialog control, and in the next section you'll look at the SaveFileDialog control.

When you use Windows applications, such as Microsoft Word or Paint, you see the same basic Open dialog box. This does not happen by accident. There is a standard set of application programming interfaces (API) available to every developer that allows you to provide this type of standard interface; however, using the API can be cumbersome and difficult for a beginner. Fortunately, all of this functionality is already built into the .NET Framework, so you can use it as you develop with Visual Basic 2005.

The OpenFileDialog Control

You can use OpenFileDialog as a .NET class by declaring a variable of that type in your code and modifying its properties in code, or as a control by dragging the control from the Toolbox onto the form at design time. In either case, the resulting objects will have the same methods, properties, and events.

You can find the OpenFileDialog control in the Toolbox under the Windows Forms tab, where you can drag and drop it onto your form. Then, all you need to do is set the properties and execute the appropriate method. To use `OpenFileDialog` as a class you declare your own objects of this type in order to use the dialog box. Then you have control over the scope of the dialog box and can declare an object for it when needed, use it, and then destroy it, thereby using fewer resources.

This section focuses on using OpenFileDialog as a control. Once you have a better understanding of this dialog box and feel comfortable using it, you can then expand your skills and use OpenFileDialog as a class by declaring your own objects for it. Using classes and objects is discussed in greater detail in Chapter 10.

You can use OpenFileDialog by simply invoking its ShowDialog method, producing results similar to that shown in Figure 7-6.

Figure 7-6

The Properties of OpenFileDialog

Although the dialog box shown in Figure 7-6 is the standard Open dialog in Windows, it provides no filtering. You see all file types listed in the window and are unable to specify a file type for filtering, because no filters exist. This is where the properties of OpenFileDialog come in. You can set some of the properties before the Open dialog box is displayed, thereby customizing the dialog box to your needs.

The following table lists some of the available properties for the OpenFileDialog control.

Property	Description
AddExtension	Indicates whether an extension is automatically added to a filename if the user omits the extension. This is mainly used in the SaveFileDialog, which you will see in the next section.
CheckFileExists	Indicates whether the dialog box displays a warning if the user specifies a filename that does not exist.
CheckPathExists	Indicates whether the dialog displays a warning if the user specifies a path that does not exist.
DefaultExt	Indicates the default filename extension.
DereferenceLinks	Used with shortcuts. Indicates whether the dialog box returns the location of the *file referenced by the shortcut* (True) or whether it returns only the location of the *shortcut itself* (False).
FileName	Indicates the filename of the selected file in the dialog box.
FileNames	Indicates the filenames of all selected files in the dialog box. This is a read-only property.
Filter	Indicates the current filename filter string, which determines the choices that appear in the Files of type: combo box in the dialog box.
FilterIndex	Indicates the index of the filter currently selected in the dialog box.
InitialDirectory	Indicates the initial directory displayed in the dialog box.
Multiselect	Indicates whether the dialog box allows multiple files to be selected.
ReadOnlyChecked	Indicates whether the read-only check box is selected.
RestoreDirectory	Indicates whether the dialog box restores the current directory before closing.
ShowHelp	Indicates whether the Help button is displayed in the dialog box.
ShowReadOnly	Indicates whether the dialog box contains a read-only check box.
Title	Indicates the title that is displayed in the title bar of the dialog box.
ValidateNames	Indicates whether the dialog box should only accept valid WIN32 file names.

The Methods of OpenFileDialog

Although many methods are available in the OpenFileDialog, you will be concentrating on the Show Dialog method in these examples. The following list contains some of the other available methods in OpenFileDialog:

❑ Dispose releases the resources used by the Open dialog box.

❑ OpenFile opens the file selected by the user with read-only permission. The file is specified by the FileName property.

215

❑ Reset resets all properties of the Open dialog box to their default values.

❑ ShowDialog shows the dialog box.

The ShowDialog method is straightforward, because it accepts either no parameters or the owner of the dialog box in the form of the Me keyword. So, before calling the ShowDialog method, you must set all the properties that you want to set. After the dialog box returns, you can query the properties to determine which file was selected, the directory, and the type of file selected. An example of the ShowDialog method is shown in the following code fragment:

```
OpenFileDialog1.ShowDialog()
```

The OpenFileDialog control returns a DialogResult of OK or Cancel, with OK corresponding to the Open button on the dialog box. This control does not actually open and read a file for you; it is merely a common interface that allows a user to locate and specify the file or files to be opened by the application. You need to query the OpenFileDialog properties that have been set by the control after the user clicks the Open button to determine which file or files should be opened.

Using the OpenFileDialog Control

Now that you have had a look at the OpenFileDialog control, you can put this knowledge to use by writing a program that uses this control.

The program in the next Try It Out uses the OpenFileDialog control to display the Open File dialog box. You use the dialog box to locate and select a text file, and then you'll read the contents of the file into a text box on your form using the My.Computer.FileSystem namespace.

Try It Out   Working with OpenFileDialog

1. Create a new Windows Application project called **Dialogs**.

2. To give your form a new name, in the Solution Explorer, right-click Form1.vb and choose Rename from the context menu. Then enter a new name of **Dialogs.vb**. Set the properties of the form as shown in the following list:

   ❑ Set Size to **456, 304**.

   ❑ Set StartPosition to **CenterScreen**.

   ❑ Set Text to **Dialogs**.

3. Since you are going to read the contents of a file into a text box, you want to add a text box to the form. You also want to add a button to the form so that you can invoke the Open File dialog box at will. Add these two controls to the form and set their properties according to the following list:

   ❑ Name the text box **txtFile** and set the following properties: Anchor = **Top,Bottom, Left,Right**; Location = **8, 8**; MultiLine = **True**; ScrollBars = **Vertical**; Size = **352, 264**.

   ❑ Name the Button control **btnOpen** and set the following properties: Anchor = **Top, Right**; Location = **367, 8**; Text = **Open**.

4. When you have finished placing the controls on your form and setting their properties, your form should look similar to Figure 7-7.

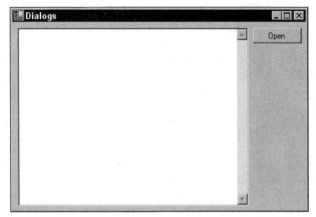

Figure 7-7

The reason you anchored your controls in this example is that, when you resize or maximize your form, the text box is resized appropriately to the size of the form, and the button stays in the upper right corner. You can test this at this point by running your project and resizing the form.

5. In the Toolbox, scroll down until you see the OpenFileDialog control and then drag it onto your form and drop it. The control will actually be added to the bottom on the workspace in the IDE.

At this point, you could click the control in the workspace and then set the various properties for this control in the Properties window. However, accept the default name and properties for this control as you'll set the various properties in code later.

6. Switch to the Code Editor for the form. Then declare a string variable that will contain a filename. You set this variable later in your code to the actual path and filename from the Open File dialog box:

```
Public Class Dialogs
    'Declare variable
    Private strFileName As String
```

7. Now you need to write some code in the Click event for the btnOpen button. In the Class Name combo box at the top of the Code Editor, select btnOpen, and in the Method Name combo select the Click event. Add the following highlighted code to the Click event handler:

```
Private Sub btnOpen_Click(ByVal sender As Object, _
    ByVal e As System.EventArgs) Handles btnOpen.Click

    'Set the Open dialog properties
    With OpenFileDialog1
        .Filter = "Text files (*.txt)|*.txt|All files (*.*)|*.*"
        .FilterIndex = 1
        .Title = "Demo Open File Dialog"
    End With
```

```
        'Show the Open dialog and if the user clicks the Open button,
        'load the file
        If OpenFileDialog1.ShowDialog = Windows.Forms.DialogResult.OK Then

        End If
    End Sub
```

8. Now it's time to use some of the prebuilt code snippets that come with Visual Studio 2005. Right click in the blank space between the `If` and `End If` statements and choose Insert Snippet from the context menu. In the drop-down menu that appears, double-click File System - Processing Drives, Folders, and Files and then scroll down the new list and double-click Read Text from a File. Your code should now look like this, and you'll notice that the filename `Test.txt` is highlighted, indicating that this code needs to be changed:

```
        If OpenFileDialog1.ShowDialog = Windows.Forms.DialogResult.OK
            Then
            Dim fileContents As String
            fileContents = My.Computer.FileSystem.ReadAllText("C:\Test.txt")
        End If
```

9. Modify the code in the `Try` block as shown here:

```
        Try
                'Save the file name
                strFileName = OpenFileDialog1.FileName
                'Read the contents of the file
                allText = My.Computer.FileSystem.ReadAllText(strFileName)
                'Display the file contents in the TextBox
                txtFile.Text = allText
        Catch fileException As Exception
```

10. Now run your project, and once your form is displayed, click the Open button to have the Open File dialog box displayed. Notice the custom caption in the title bar of the dialog box; you specified this in your code. If you click the Files of type: combo box, you will see two filters. Click the second filter to see all of the files in the current directory.

11. Now locate a text file on your computer and select it. Then click the Open button to have the file opened and the contents of that file placed in the text box on the form as shown in Figure 7-8.

12. For the final test, close your application and then start it again. Click the Open button on the form and notice that the Open File dialog box has opened in the last directory where you selected the last file from.

How It Works

Before displaying the Open File dialog box, you need to set some properties of `OpenFileDialog1` so that the dialog box is customized for your application. You can do this with a `With...End With` statement. The `With...End With` statement allows you to make repeated references to a single object without having to specify the object name over and over. You specify the object name once on the line with the `With` statement and then add all references to the properties of that object before the `End With` statement.

```
        With OpenFileDialog1
```

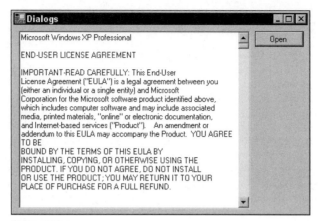

Figure 7-8

The first property that you set is the `Filter` property. This property enables you to define the filters that are displayed in the Files of type: combo box. When you define a file extension filter, you specify the filter description followed by a vertical bar (|) followed by the file extension. When you want the `Filter` property to contain multiple file extensions, as shown in the following code, you separate each file filter with a vertical bar as follows:

```
.Filter = "Text files (*.txt)|*.txt|All files (*.*)|*.*"
```

The next property that you set is the `FilterIndex` property. This property determines which filter is shown in the Files of type: combo box. The default value for this property is 1, which is the first filter:

```
.FilterIndex = 1
```

Finally, you set the `Title` property. This is the caption that is displayed in the title bar of the dialog box:

```
.Title = "Demo Open File Dialog"
```

To show the Open File dialog box, you use the `ShowDialog` method. Remember that the `ShowDialog` method returns a `DialogResult` value, there are only two possible results, and you can compare the results from the `ShowDialog` method to `Windows.Forms.DialogResult.OK` and `Windows.Forms.DialogResult.Cancel`. If the user clicks the Open button in the dialog box, the `ShowDialog` method returns a value of `OK`, and if the user clicks the Cancel button, the `ShowDialog` method returns `Cancel`:

```
If OpenFileDialog1.ShowDialog = Windows.Forms.DialogResult.OK Then
```

Next, you use the built-in code snippets provided by Visual Studio 2005 to simplify your programming tasks by using the Read Text from a File code snippet. This code snippet contains the necessary code to read the contents from a text file and to place those contents in a string variable.

You modified the code snippet to retrieve the path and filename that the user has chosen in the Open File dialog box and set it in your `strFileName` variable. The path and filename are contained in the `FileName` property of the OpenFileDialog control:

```
'Save the file name
strFileName = OpenFileDialog1.FileName
```

219

Next, you modify the code from the code snippet supplying the `strFileName` variable in the high-lighted section of code. This code will read the entire contents of the text file into the `allText` variable:

```
'Read the contents of the file
allText = My.Computer.FileSystem.ReadAllText(strFileName)
```

The final line of code that you wrote takes the contents of the `allText` variable and sets it in the Text property of the TextBox control, thereby populating the text box with the contents of your text file:

```
'Display the file contents in the TextBox
txtFile.Text = allText
```

There are many properties in the OpenFileDialog control that haven't been covered in this chapter, and you should feel free to experiment on your own to see all of the possibilities that this dialog box has to offer.

The SaveDialog Control

Now that you can open a file with the OpenFileDialog control, take a look at the SaveFileDialog control so that you can save a file. Again, the SaveFileDialog can be used as a control or a class. Once you have mastered the SaveFileDialog as a control, you will not have any problems using `SaveFileDialog` as a class.

After you open a file, you may need to make some modifications to it and then save it. The SaveFileDialog control provides the same functionality as the OpenFileDialog control, except in reverse. It allows you to choose the location and filename as you save a file. It is important to note that the SaveFileDialog control does not actually save your file; it merely provides a dialog box to allow the user to locate where the file should be saved and to provide a name for the file.

The Properties of SaveFileDialog

The following table lists some of the properties that are available in the SaveFileDialog control. As you can see, this control, or class if you will, contains a wealth of properties that can be used to customize how the dialog box will behave.

Property	Description
AddExtension	Indicates whether an extension is automatically added to a filename if the user omits the extension.
CheckFileExists	Indicates whether the dialog box displays a warning if the user specifies a file name that does not exist. This is useful when you want the user to save a file to an existing name.
CheckPathExists	Indicates whether the dialog box displays a warning if the user specifies a path that does not exist.
CreatePrompt	Indicates whether the dialog box prompts the user for permission to create a file if the user specifies a file that does not exist.

Property	Description
DefaultExt	Indicates the default file extension.
DereferenceLinks	Indicates whether the dialog box returns the location of the *file* referenced by the shortcut or whether it returns the location of the *shortcut itself*.
FileName	Indicates the filename of the selected file in the dialog box. This is a read-only property.
FileNames	Indicates the filenames of all selected files in the dialog box. This is a read-only property that is returned as a string array.
Filter	Indicates the current filename filter string, which determines the choices that appear in the Files of type combo box in the dialog box.
FilterIndex	Indicates the index of the filter currently selected in the dialog box.
InitialDirectory	Indicates the initial directory displayed in the dialog box.
OverwritePrompt	Indicates whether the dialog box displays a warning if the user specifies a filename that already exists.
RestoreDirectory	Indicates whether the dialog box restores the current directory before closing.
ShowHelp	Indicates whether the Help button is displayed in the dialog box.
Title	Indicates the title that is displayed in the title bar of the dialog box.
ValidateNames	Indicates whether the dialog box should accept only valid Win32 filenames.

The Methods of SaveFileDialog

The SaveFileDialog control exposes the same methods as the OpenFileDialog does. If you want to review these methods, go back to the section "The Methods of OpenFileDialog". All the examples will use the ShowDialog method to show the Save File dialog.

Using the SaveFileDialog Control

To see how to include the SaveFileDialog control in our project, you begin with the Dialogs project from the last Try It Out as a starting point and build upon it. In this exercise, you want to save the contents of the text box to a file.

You use the SaveFileDialog control to display a Save File dialog box that allows you to specify the location and name of the file. Then you write the contents of the text box on your form to the specified file, again using a built-in code snippet provided by Visual Studio 2005.

Try It Out: **Working with SaveFileDialog**

1. Open the Dialogs project from the last Try It Out.

2. On the form, add another button from the Toolbox and set its properties as follows:

    ❑   Set Name to **btnSave**.

    ❑   Set Anchor to **Top, Right**.

    ❑   Set Location to **367, 38**.

    ❑   Set Text to **Save**.

3. In the Toolbox, scroll down until you see the SaveFileDialog control and then drag and drop it onto your form. The control will be added to the bottom on the workspace in the IDE.

4. Double-click the Save button to bring up its Click event and add the highlighted code:

```
Private Sub btnSave_Click(ByVal sender As System.Object, _
    ByVal e As System.EventArgs) Handles btnSave.Click
```

```
        'Set the Save dialog properties
        With SaveFileDialog1
            .DefaultExt = "txt"
            .FileName = strFileName
            .Filter = "Text files (*.txt)|*.txt|All files (*.*)|*.*"
            .FilterIndex = 1
            .OverwritePrompt = True
            .Title = "Demo Save File Dialog"
        End With

        'Show the Save dialog and if the user clicks the Save button,
        'save the file
        If SaveFileDialog1.ShowDialog = Windows.Forms.DialogResult.OK Then

        End If
End Sub
```

5. Right click in the blank space between the `If` and `End If` statements and choose Insert Snippet... from the context menu. In the drop-down menu that appears, double-click File System - Processing Drives, Folders, and Files and then scroll down the new list and double-click Write New Text Files. Your code should now look like this and you'll notice that the filename `test.txt` is highlight as well as the string constant `"some text"`, indicating that this code needs to be changed:

```
        If SaveFileDialog1.ShowDialog = Windows.Forms.DialogResult.OK Then
            Try
                Dim filePath As String
                filePath = System.IO.Path.Combine( _
                    My.Computer.FileSystem.SpecialDirectories.MyDocuments, _
                    "test.txt")
                My.Computer.FileSystem.WriteAllText(filePath, "some text", True)
            Catch fileException As Exception
                Throw fileException
            End Try
        End If
```

6. Modify the code in the Try block as follows:

```
Try

    'Save the file name
    strFileName = SaveFileDialog1.FileName
    Dim filePath As String

    'Open or Create the file
    filePath = System.IO.Path.Combine( _
        My.Computer.FileSystem.SpecialDirectories.MyDocuments, _
        strFileName)
    'Replace the contents of the file
    My.Computer.FileSystem.WriteAllText(filePath, txtFile.Text, False)
Catch fileException As Exception
```

7. At this point, you are ready to test this code so run your project. Start with a simple test by opening an existing text file. Type some text into the text box on the form and then click the Save button. The Save dialog box will be displayed. Notice that the FileName combo box already has a filename in it. This is the filename that was set in the `strFileName` variable when you declared it in the previous Try It Out.

8. Enter a new filename, but do not put a file extension on it. Then click the Save button and the file will be saved. To verify this, click the Open button on the form to invoke the Open File dialog box. You will see your new file.

9. To test the `OverwritePrompt` property of the SaveFileDialog control, enter some more text in the text box on the form and then click the Save button. In the Save File dialog box, choose an existing filename and then click the Save button. You will be prompted to confirm replacement of the existing file as shown in Figure 7-9. If you choose Yes, the dialog box will return a `DialogResult` of `OK`, and the code inside your `If . . . End If` statement will be executed. If you choose No, you will be returned to the Save File dialog box so that you can enter another filename.

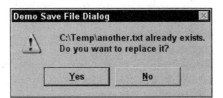

Figure 7-9

When the Open File or Save File dialog box is displayed, the context menu is fully functional and you can cut, copy, and paste files, as well as rename and delete them. There are other options in the context menu that vary depending on what software you have installed. For example, if you have WinZip installed, you will see the WinZip options on the context menu.

How It Works

Before displaying the Save File dialog box, you need to set some properties to customize the dialog box to your application. The first property you set is the `DefaultExt` property. This property automatically sets the file extension if one has not been specified. For example, if you specify a filename of `NewFile` with no extension, the dialog box will automatically add `.txt` to the filename when it returns, so that you end up with a filename of `NewFile.txt`.

```
.DefaultExt = "txt"
```

The `FileName` property is set to the same path and filename as was returned from the Open File dialog. This allows you to open a file, edit it, and then display the same filename when you show the Save File dialog box. Of course, you can override this filename in the application's Save File dialog box.

```
.FileName = strFileName
```

The next two properties are the same as in the OpenFileDialog control. They set the file extension filters to be displayed in the Save as type: combo box and set the initial filter:

```
.Filter = "Text files (*.txt)|*.txt|All files (*.*)|*.*"
.FilterIndex = 1
```

The `OverwritePrompt` property accepts a Boolean value of `True` or `False`. When set to `True`, this property prompts you with a MessageBox dialog box if you choose an existing filename. If you select Yes, the Save File dialog box returns a `DialogResult` of `OK`; if you select No, you are returned to the Save File dialog box to choose another filename. When the `OverwritePrompt` property is set to `False`, the Save File dialog box does not prompt you to overwrite an existing file, and your code will overwrite it without asking for the user's permission.

```
.OverwritePrompt = True
```

The `Title` property sets the caption in the title bar of the Save File dialog box:

```
.Title = "Demo Save File Dialog"
```

After you have the properties set, you want to show the dialog box. The `ShowDialog` method of the SaveFileDialog control also returns a `DialogResult`, so you can use the SaveFileDialog control in an `If . . . End If` statement to test the return value.

If the user clicks the Save button in the Save File dialog box, the dialog box returns a `DialogResult` of `OK`. If the user clicks the Cancel button in the dialog box, the dialog box returns a `DialogResult` of `Cancel`. The following code tests for `Windows.Forms.DialogResult.OK`:

```
If SaveFileDialog1.ShowDialog = Windows.Forms.DialogResult.OK Then
```

The first thing that you do here is save the path and filename chosen by the user in your `strFileName` variable. This is done in case the user has chosen a new filename in the dialog box:

```
Try
    'Save the file name
    strFileName = SaveFileDialog1.FileName
```

Then you modify the code snippet generated by Visual Studio 2005 by replacing the highlighted text with your variables. First you replace the text `"test.txt"` with your variable, `strFileName`. This line of code opens the file for output. Then you replace the text "some text" with the Text property of the text box on your form. This last line of code reads the contents of your text box and writes it to the file. The False parameter at the end of this line of code indicates whether text should be appended to the file. A value of False indicates that the contents of the file should be overwritten.

```
Dim filePath As String
'Open or Create the file
filePath = System.IO.Path.Combine( _
    My.Computer.FileSystem.SpecialDirectories.MyDocuments, _
    strFileName)
'Replace the contents of the file
My.Computer.FileSystem.WriteAllText(filePath, txtFile.Text, False)
```

The final bit of code in this If ... End If block merely wraps up the Try ... Catch block and the If ... End If statement.

```
        Catch fileException As Exception
        End Try
    End If
```

The FontDialog Control

Sometimes you may need to write an application that allows the user to choose the font in which they want their data to be displayed. Or perhaps you may want to see all available fonts installed on a particular system. This is where the FontDialog control comes in; it displays a list of all available fonts installed on your computer in a standard dialog that your users have become accustomed to.

Like the OpenFileDialog and SaveFileDialog controls, the FontDialog class can be used as a control by dragging it onto a form, or as a class by declaring it in code.

The FontDialog control is really easy to use; you just set some properties, show the dialog box, and then query the properties that you need.

The Properties of FontDialog

The following table lists some of its available properties.

Property	Description
AllowScriptChange	Indicates whether the user can change the character set specified in the Script drop-down box to display a character set other than the one currently displayed.
Color	Indicates the selected font color.
Font	Indicates the selected font.
FontMustExist	Indicates whether the dialog box specifies an error condition if the user attempts to enter a font or style that does not exist.

Property	Description
MaxSize	Indicates the maximum size (in points) a user can select.
MinSize	Indicates the minimum size (in points) a user can select.
ShowApply	Indicates whether the dialog box contains an Apply button.
ShowColor	Indicates whether the dialog box displays the color choice.
ShowEffects	Indicates whether the dialog box contains controls that allow the user to specify strikethrough, underline, and text color options.
ShowHelp	Indicates whether the dialog box displays a Help button.

The Methods of FontDialog

You will only be using one method (ShowDialog) of FontDialog in the forthcoming Try It Out. Other methods available include Reset, which allows you to reset all the properties to their default values.

Using the FontDialog Control

You can display the FontDialog control without setting any properties:

```
FontDialog1.ShowDialog()
```

The dialog box would then look like Figure 7-10.

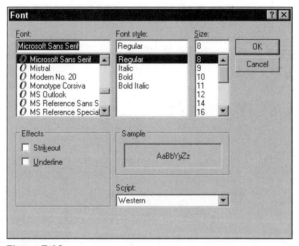

Figure 7-10

Notice that the Font dialog box contains an Effects section that enables you to check the options for Strikeout and Underline. However, color selection of the font is not provided by default. If you want this, you must set the `ShowColor` property before calling the `ShowDialog` method on the dialog box:

```
FontDialog1.ShowColor = True
FontDialog1.ShowDialog()
```

The `ShowDialog` method of this dialog box, like all of the ones that you have examined thus far, returns a `DialogResult`. This will be either `DialogResult.OK` or `DialogResult.Cancel`.

Once the dialog box returns, you can query for the Font and Color properties to see what font and color the user has chosen. You can then apply these properties to a control on your form or store them to a variable for later use.

Now that you know what the Font dialog looks like and how to call it, you can use it in a Try It Out. You need to use the program from the last two Try It Outs to open a file, and have the contents of the file read into the text box on the form. You then use the FontDialog control to display the Font dialog box, which allows you to select a font. Then you change the font in the text box to the font that you have chosen.

Try It Out   Working with FontDialog

1. Open the Dialogs project again.

2. On the form add another button from the Toolbox and set its properties according to the values shown in this list:

   ❑   Set Name to **btnFont**.

   ❑   Set Anchor to **Top, Right**.

   ❑   Set Location to **367, 68**.

   ❑   Set Text to **Font**.

3. You now need to add the FontDialog control to your project, so locate this control in the Toolbox and drag and drop it onto the form in the workspace below the form or on the form itself; the control will be automatically placed in the workspace below the form. Accept all default properties for this control.

4. You want to add code to the Click event of the Font button, so double-click it and add the following highlighted code:

```
Private Sub btnFont_Click(ByVal sender As System.Object, _
    ByVal e As System.EventArgs) Handles btnFont.Click

        'Set the FontDialog control properties
        FontDialog1.ShowColor = True

        'Show the Font dialog
        If FontDialog1.ShowDialog = Windows.Forms.DialogResult.OK Then
            'If the OK button was clicked set the font
            'in the text box on the form
```

```
                txtFile.Font = FontDialog1.Font
                'Set the color of the font in the text box on the form
                txtFile.ForeColor = FontDialog1.Color
            End If
        End Sub
```

5. Test your code by clicking the Start button on the toolbar. Once your form has been displayed, click the Font button to display the Font dialog box as shown in Figure 7-11. Choose a new font and color and then click OK.

6. Now add some text in the text box on your form. The text will appear with the new font and color that you have chosen.

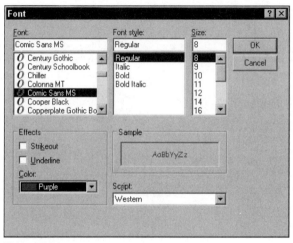

Figure 7-11

7. This same font and color will also be applied to the text that is loaded from a file. To demonstrate this, click the Open button on the form and open a text file. The text from the file is displayed in the same font and color that you chose in the Font dialog.

How It Works

You know that the Font dialog box does not show a Color box by default, so you begin by setting the ShowColor property of the FontDialog control to True so that the Color box is displayed:

```
        'Set the FontDialog control properties
        FontDialog1.ShowColor = True
```

Next, you actually show the Font dialog box. Remember the DialogResult returns a value of OK or Cancel, so that you can compare the return value from the FontDialog control to Windows.Forms. DialogResult.OK. If the button that the user clicked was OK, you execute the code within the If . . . End If statement:

```
        'Show the Font dialog
        If FontDialog1.ShowDialog = Windows.Forms.DialogResult.OK Then
```

```
            'If the OK button was clicked, set the font
            'in the text box on the form
            txtFile.Font = FontDialog1.Font
            'Set the color of the font in the text box on the form
            txtFile.ForeColor = FontDialog1.Color
        End If
```

You set the Font property of the text box (txtFile) equal to the Font property of the FontDialog control. This is the font that the user has chosen. Then you set the ForeColor property of the text box equal to the Color property of the FontDialog control, as this will be the color that the user has chosen. After these properties have been changed for the text box, the existing text in the text box is automatically updated to reflect the new font and color. If the text box does not contain any text, any new text that is typed or loaded into the text box will be of the new font and color.

The ColorDialog Control

Sometimes you may need to allow the user to customize the colors on their form. This may be the color of the form itself, a control, or of text in a text box. Visual Basic 2005 provides the ColorDialog control for all such requirements. Once again, the ColorDialog control can also be used as a class — declared in code without dragging a control onto the Form Designer.

The ColorDialog control, shown in Figure 7-12, allows the user to choose from 48 basic colors.

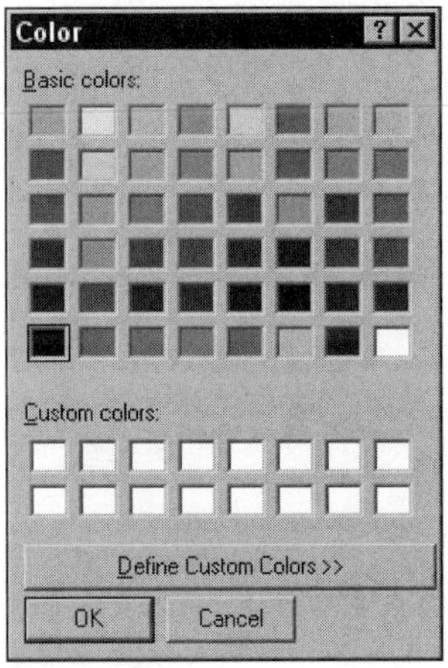

Figure 7-12

Notice that the users can also define their own custom colors, adding more flexibility to your applications. When the users click the Define Custom Colors button in the Color dialog box, they can adjust the color to suit their needs (see Figure 7-13).

Having this opportunity for customization and flexibility in your applications gives them a more professional appearance, plus your users are happy because they are allowed to customize the application to meet their own personal tastes.

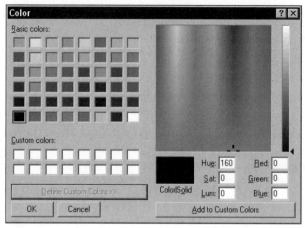

Figure 7-13

The Properties of ColorDialog

Before you dive into some code, take a look at some of the available properties for the ColorDialog control, shown in Table 7-9.

Property	Description
AllowFullOpen	Indicates whether the user can use the dialog box to define custom colors.
AnyColor	Indicates whether the dialog box displays all available colors in the set of basic colors.
Color	Indicates the color selected by the user.
CustomColors	Indicates the set of custom colors shown in the dialog box.
FullOpen	Indicates whether the controls used to create custom colors are visible when the dialog box is opened.
ShowHelp	Indicates whether a Help button appears in the dialog box.
SolidColorOnly	Indicates whether the dialog box will restrict users to selecting solid colors only.

There aren't many properties that you need to worry about for this dialog box, which makes it even simpler to use than the other dialog boxes that you have examined so far.

As with the other dialog box controls, ColorDialog contains a ShowDialog method. You have already seen this method in the previous examples, and since it is the same, it does not need to be discussed again.

Using the ColorDialog Control

All you need to do to display the Color Dialog box is to execute its ShowDialog method:

```
ColorDialog1.ShowDialog()
```

The ColorDialog control will return a DialogResult of OK or Cancel. Hence, you can use the previous statement in an If ... End If statement and test for a DialogResult of OK, as you have done in the previous examples that you have coded.

To retrieve the color that the user has chosen, you simply retrieve the value set in the Color property and assign it to a variable or any property of a control that supports colors, such as the ForeColor property of a text box:

```
txtFile.ForeColor = ColorDialog1.Color
```

In the next Try It Out, you continue using the same project and make the ColorDialog control display the Color dialog box. Then, if the dialog box returns a DialogResult of OK, you change the background color of the form.

Try It Out   Working with the ColorDialog Control

1. Switch to the Forms Designer in the Dialogs project.

2. On the form, add another Button control from the Toolbox and set its properties according to the values shown:

    ❑   Set Name to **btnColor**.

    ❑   Set Anchor to **Top, Right**.

    ❑   Set Location to **367, 98**.

    ❑   Set Text to **Color**.

3. Next, add a ColorDialog control to your project from the Toolbox. It will be added to the workspace below the form, and you will accept all default properties for this control.

4. Double-click the Color button to bring up its Click event handler and add the following high-lighted code:

```
Private Sub btnColor_Click(ByVal sender As System.Object, _
    ByVal e As System.EventArgs) Handles btnColor.Click

        'Show the Color dialog
        If ColorDialog1.ShowDialog = Windows.Forms.DialogResult.OK Then
            'Set the BackColor property of the form
            Me.BackColor = ColorDialog1.Color
        End If
    End Sub
```

5. That's all the code you need to add. To test your changes to this project, click the Start button.

6. Once the form is displayed, click the Color button to display the Color dialog box. Choose any color that you want, or create a custom color by clicking the Define Custom Colors button. Once you have chosen a color, click the OK button in the Color dialog box.

7. The background color of the form will be set to the color that you chose and the background color of the buttons will inherit the background color of the form.

8. As with the Font dialog box, you do not have to set the Color property of the ColorDialog control before displaying the Color dialog box again. It automatically remembers the color chosen, and this will be the color that is selected when the dialog box is displayed again. To test this, click the Color button again, and the color that you chose will be selected.

How It Works

This time you did not need to set any properties of the ColorDialog control, so you jumped right in and displayed it in an If . . . End If statement to check the DialogResult returned by the ShowDialog method of this dialog box:

```
'Show the Color dialog
If ColorDialog1.ShowDialog = Windows.Forms.DialogResult.OK Then
```

Within the If . . . End If statement, you added the code necessary to change the BackColor property of the form. Once the BackColor property was changed, each Button control on the form inherited the background color of the form; there was no code that you needed to write for this. The reason behind this is that the Button class is part of the System.Windows.Forms.Control namespace; thus, it automatically inherits the background color of the form:

```
'Set the BackColor property of the form
Me.BackColor = ColorDialog1.Color
```

The PrintDialog Control

Any application worth its salt will incorporate some kind of printing capabilities, whether it is basic printing or more sophisticated printing, such as allowing a user to print only selected text or a range of pages. In this next section of the chapter you explore basic printing. You take a look at several classes that help you to print text from a file.

Visual Basic 2005 provides the PrintDialog control. It does not actually do any printing but enables you to select the printer that you want to use and set the printer properties such as page orientation and print quality. It also enables you to specify the print range. You will not be using these features in this next example, but it is worth noting that this functionality is available in the PrintDialog control as shown in Figure 7-14.

Like the previous dialog boxes that you have examined, the Print dialog box provides OK and Cancel buttons; thus, its ShowDialog method returns a DialogResult of OK or Cancel. You can then use this result in an If . . . End If statement and test for the DialogResult.

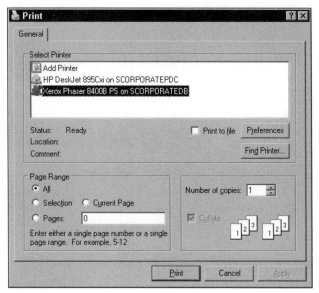

Figure 7-14

The Properties of PrintDialog

Take a quick look at some of the properties provided in PrintDialog shown in the following table.

Just like the other dialog boxes, PrintDialog exposes a `ShowDialog` method.

Property	Description
AllowPrintToFile	Indicates whether the Print to file check box is enabled.
AllowSelection	Indicates whether the Selection radio button is enabled.
AllowSomePages	Indicates whether the Pages radio button is enabled.
Document	Indicates the Print Document used to obtain the printer settings.
PrinterSettings	Indicates the printer settings that the dialog box will be modifying.
PrintToFile	Indicates whether the Print to file check box is checked.
ShowHelp	Indicates whether the Help button is displayed.
ShowNetwork	Indicates whether the Network button is displayed.

Using the PrintDialog Control

The only method that you will be using is the ShowDialog method, which will display the Print dialog box shown in Figure 7-14. As mentioned earlier, the PrintDialog control merely displays the Print dialog box; it does not actually do any printing. The following code fragment shows how you display the Print dialog box:

```
PrintDialog1.ShowDialog()
```

The PrintDocument Class

Before you can call the ShowDialog method of the PrintDialog control, you have to set the Document property of the PrintDialog class. This property accepts a PrintDocument class, which is used to obtain the printer settings and can send output to the printer. This class requires the System.Drawing.Printing namespace, so you must include this namespace before attempting to define an object that uses the PrintDocument class.

The Properties of the PrintDocument Class

Before you continue, take a look at some of the important properties of the PrintDocument class, listed in the following table.

Property	Description
DefaultPageSettings	Indicates the default page settings for the document.
DocumentName	Indicates the document name that is displayed while printing the document. This is also the name that appears in the Print Status dialog box and printer queue.
PrintController	Indicates the print controller that guides the printing process.
PrinterSettings	Indicates the printer that prints the document.

Printing a Document

The Print method of the PrintDocument class prints a document to the printer specified in the PrinterSettings property. When you call the Print method of the PrintDocument class, the PrintPage event is raised for each page as it prints. Therefore, you would need to create a procedure for that event and add an event handler for it. The procedure that you would create for the PrintPage event does the actual reading of your text file using the StreamReader object that you define.

Printing using the PrintDocument class requires a lot of coding and knowledge of how actual printing works. Fortunately, the .NET Framework provides the My.Computer.Printers namespace, which simplifies your job as a developer.

This namespace wraps up all the complexities of printing and provides you with methods and properties that allow you to print a text document with ease and just a few lines of code. You can use the DefaultPrinter method of this namespace to print to the default printer, or you can use the Item property to specify the printer that you want to print to. Using either one, you can print a text document with as little as two lines of code, as shown in this code snippet:

```
With My.Computer.Printers.DefaultPrinter
    .WriteLine(txtFile.Text)
    .Print()
End With
```

Now that you know a little bit about how printing works, look at how all this fits together in a Try It Out.

Try It Out   **Working with the PrintDialog Control**

1. Open the Dialogs project.

2. On the form, add another button from the Toolbox and set its properties according to the values shown:

   ❑   Set Name to **btnPrint**.

   ❑   Set Anchor to **Top, Right**.

   ❑   Set Location to **367, 128**.

   ❑   Set Text to **Print**.

3. Now add a PrintDialog control to the project, dragging and dropping it from the Toolbox onto the form. It will be added to the workspace below the form, and you will accept all default properties for this control.

4. Now switch to the Code Editor so that you can add the required namespaces for printing a file. Add these namespaces to the top of your class:

```
Imports System.IO
Imports System.Drawing.Printing

Public Class Dialogs
```

5. Now add the following variable declarations to the top of your class:

```
'Declare variable
Private strFileName As String

Private objStreamToPrint As StreamReader
Private objPrintFont As Font
```

6. Select btnPrint in the Class Name combo box and the Click event in the Method Name combo box. Add the following highlighted code to the btnPrint_Click event procedure:

```
Private Sub btnPrint_Click(ByVal sender As Object, _
    ByVal e As System.EventArgs) Handles btnPrint.Click

    'Declare an object for the PrintDocument class
    Dim objPrintDocument As PrintDocument = New PrintDocument()
```

235

```
                    'Set the DocumentName property
                    objPrintDocument.DocumentName = "Text File Print Demo"

                    'Set the PrintDialog properties
                    PrintDialog1.AllowPrintToFile = False
                    PrintDialog1.AllowSelection = False
                    PrintDialog1.AllowSomePages = False

                    'Set the Document property to the objPrintDocument object
                    PrintDialog1.Document = objPrintDocument

                    'Show the Print dialog
                    If PrintDialog1.ShowDialog() = Windows.Forms.DialogResult.OK Then
                        'If the user clicked on the OK button then set the StreamReader
                        'object to the file name in the strFileName variable
                        objStreamToPrint = New StreamReader(strFileName)

                        'Set the print font
                        objPrintFont = New Font("Arial", 10)

                        'Add an event handler for the PrintPage event of the
                        'objPrintDocument object
                        AddHandler objPrintDocument.PrintPage, _
                            AddressOf objPrintDocument_PrintPage

                        'Set the PrinterSettings property of the objPrintDocument
                        'object to the PrinterSettings property returned from the
                        'PrintDialog control
                        objPrintDocument.PrinterSettings = PrintDialog1.PrinterSettings

                        'Print the text file
                        objPrintDocument.Print()

                        'Clean up
                        objStreamToPrint.Close()
                        objStreamToPrint = Nothing
                    End If
                End Sub
```

7. Now add the following procedure to perform the actually printing:

```
    Private Sub objPrintDocument_PrintPage(ByVal sender As Object, _
        ByVal e As System.Drawing.Printing.PrintPageEventArgs)

        'Declare variables
        Dim sngLinesPerpage As Single = 0
        Dim sngVerticalPosition As Single = 0
        Dim intLineCount As Integer = 0
        Dim sngLeftMargin As Single = e.MarginBounds.Left
        Dim sngTopMargin As Single = e.MarginBounds.Top
        Dim strLine As String

        'Work out the number of lines per page.
```

```
'Use the MarginBounds on the event to do this
sngLinesPerpage = _
    e.MarginBounds.Height / objPrintFont.GetHeight(e.Graphics)

'Now iterate through the file printing out each line.
'This assumes that a single line is not wider than the page
'width. Check intLineCount first so that we don't read a line
'that we won't print
strLine = objStreamToPrint.ReadLine()

While (intLineCount < sngLinesPerpage And Not (strLine Is Nothing))

    'Calculate the vertical position on the page
    sngVerticalPosition = sngTopMargin + _
        (intLineCount * objPrintFont.GetHeight(e.Graphics))

    'Pass a StringFormat to DrawString for the
    'Print Preview control
    e.Graphics.DrawString(strLine, objPrintFont, Brushes.Black, _
        sngLeftMargin, sngVerticalPosition, New StringFormat())

    'Increment the line count
    intLineCount = intLineCount + 1

    'If the line count is less than the lines per page then
    'read another line of text
    If (intLineCount < sngLinesPerpage) Then
        strLine = objStreamToPrint.ReadLine()
    End If

End While

'If we have more lines then print another page
If (strLine <> Nothing) Then
    e.HasMorePages = True
Else
    e.HasMorePages = False
End If
End Sub
```

8. You are now ready to test your code, so run the project.

9. Click the Open button to open a file, and then click the Print button to display the Print dialog box shown in Figure 7-15.

Notice that the Print to file check box as well as the Selection and Pages radio buttons are disabled. This is because you set the `AllowPrintToFile`, `AllowSelection`, and `AllowSomePages` properties in the `PrintDialogno` control to `False`.

If you have more than one printer installed, as shown in Figure 7-15, you can choose the name of the printer that you want to use in the list.

10. Click the Print button in the Print dialog box to have your text printed.

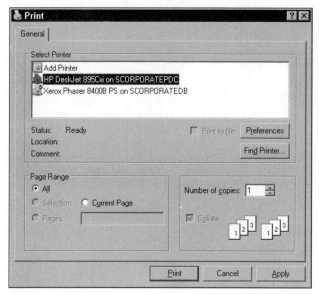

Figure 7-15

How It Works

You begin the `btnPrint` button's `Click` event procedure by declaring an object as a `PrintDocument`. You use this object to perform the actual printing:

```
Dim objPrintDocument As PrintDocument = New PrintDocument()
```

Next, you set the `DocumentName` property for the `PrintDocument` object. This will be the name that you see when the document is printing and also the name that is shown in the printer queue:

```
objPrintDocument.DocumentName = "Text File Print Demo"
```

You then set some properties of the `PrintDialog` control. This will control the options on the Print dialog box. Since you are only doing basic printing in this example, you want the Print to File check box to be disabled along with the Pages and Selection radio buttons. The next three lines of code do this by setting these properties to `False`:

```
PrintDialog1.AllowPrintToFile = False
PrintDialog1.AllowSelection = False
PrintDialog1.AllowSomePages = False
```

With the `PrintDialog` control's properties set, you set its `Document` property equal to the `PrintDocument` object:

```
PrintDialog1.Document = objPrintDocument
```

Then you show the Print dialog box, so you execute the `ShowDialog` method of the `PrintDialog` control in an `If` statement, as shown in the code next. Notice that you also are checking the `DialogResult` returned from the `PrintDialog` control:

```
If PrintDialog1.ShowDialog() = DialogResult.OK Then
```

If the user clicks the OK button in the Print dialog box, you actually want to execute the code for printing. The first thing that you do is to set the `objStreamToPrint` object to a new `StreamReader` class and pass it the `strFileName` variable:

```
objStreamToPrint = New StreamReader(strFileName)
```

Remember that this variable is set to the path and filename every time that you open or save a file. This will be the file that you print.

Next, you want to set the `objPrintFont` object to a valid font and font size. You have chosen an Arial font here and a font size of 10 points, but you could have put in any font and size that you wanted:

```
objPrintFont = New Font("Arial", 10)
```

You now want to add an event handler for the `PrintPage` event. Since the `objPrintDocument` object raises this event, you specify this object and the event. You then specify the address of the `objPrintDocument_PrintPage` procedure:

```
AddHandler objPrintDocument.PrintPage, _
        AddressOf objPrintDocument_PrintPage
```

Next, you set the `PrinterSettings` property of the `objPrintDocument` object equal to the `Printer Settings` property of the `PrintDialog` control. This specifies the printer used, page orientation, and print quality chosen by the user:

```
objPrintDocument.PrinterSettings = PrintDialog1.PrinterSettings
```

You then call the `Print` method of the `objPrintDocument` object. Calling this method will raise the `PrintPage` event and the code inside the `objPrintDocument_PrintPage` procedure will be executed:

```
objPrintDocument.Print()
```

In the `objPrintDocument_PrintPage` procedure, you need to add two parameters: the first of which is the `sender`. Like every other procedure defined in this project, this argument is an `object` that lets you know what object called this procedure. The second parameter that you need to add is the `Print PageEventArgs` object. The `PrintPage` event receives this argument and it contains data related to the `PrintPage` event, such as margin boundaries and page boundaries.

```
Private Sub objPrintDocument_PrintPage(ByVal sender As Object, _
        ByVal e As System.Drawing.Printing.PrintPageEventArgs)
```

The first thing that you want to do in this procedure is to declare some variables and set their default values. Notice that you are setting the values for the sngLeftMargin and sngTopMargin variables using the PrintPageEventArgs that were passed to this procedure:

```
Dim sngLinesPerpage As Single = 0
Dim sngVerticalPosition As Single = 0
Dim intLineCount As Integer = 0
Dim sngLeftMargin As Single = e.MarginBounds.Left
Dim sngTopMargin As Single = e.MarginBounds.Top
Dim strLine As String
```

Next, you want to determine the number of lines that will fit on one page. You do this using the MarginBounds.Height property of PrintPageEventArgs. This property was set when you set the PrinterSettings property of the objPrintDocument to the PrinterSettings property of the PrintDialog control. WYoue divide the MarginBounds.Height by the height of the font that was set in the objPrintFont:

```
sngLinesPerpage = _
            e.MarginBounds.Height / objPrintFont.GetHeight(e.Graphics)
```

Next, you read the first line from the text file and place the contents of that line in your strLine variable. Then you enter a loop to read and process all lines from the text file. You only want to process this loop while the intLineCount variable is less than the sngLinesPerPage variable and the strLine variable contains data to be printed:

```
strLine = objStreamToPrint.ReadLine()
While (intLineCount < sngLinesPerpage And Not (strLine Is Nothing))
```

Inside your While loop, you set the vertical position of the text to be printed. You calculate this position using the sngTopMargin variable and the intLineCount multiplied by the height of the printer font:

```
sngVerticalPosition = sngTopMargin + _
        (intLineCount * objPrintFont.GetHeight(e.Graphics))
```

Using the DrawString method of the Graphics class, you actually send a line of text to the printer. Here you pass the strLine variable (which contains a line of text to be printed), the font to be used when printing, the brush color to be used, the left margin, vertical position, and the format to be used:

```
e.Graphics.DrawString(strLine, objPrintFont, Brushes.Black, _
        sngLeftMargin, sngVerticalPosition, New StringFormat())
```

Next, you increment the line count on this page in the intLineCount variable:

```
intLineCount = intLineCount + 1
```

If the actual line count is less than the number of lines per page, you want to read another line from the text file to print. Then you go back to the beginning of your loop and process the next line of text:

```
If (intLineCount < sngLinesPerpage) Then
    strLine = objStreamToPrint.ReadLine()
```

```
        End If

    End While
```

Having completed your `While` loop, enter an `If` statement to test the value of `strLine`:

```
If (strLine <> Nothing) Then
    e.HasMorePages = True
Else
    e.HasMorePages = False
End If
```

If the `strLine` variable is not `Nothing`, then you have more printing to do so you set `HasMorePages` property to `True`, causing the `PrintPage` event to be fired again, and you will continue to read the text file and print another page.

If `strLine` is `Nothing`, you have no more printing to do so you set the `HasMorePages` property to `False`, causing the `Print` method of the `objPrintDocument` object to end processing and move to the next line of code within the `btnPrint_Click` event procedure.

Since the printing has completed, you clean up by closing the text file that was used for printing and freeing up the resources used by the `objStreamToPrint` object:

```
        objStreamToPrint.Close()
        objStreamToPrint = Nothing
```

The FolderBrowserDialog Control

Occasionally, you'll have a need to allow your users to select a folder instead of a file. Perhaps your application performs backups, or perhaps you need a folder to save temporary files. The FolderBrowserDialog control displays the Browse For Folder dialog box, which allows your users to select a folder. This dialog box does not display files — only folders, which provides an obvious way to allow your users to select a folder needed by your application.

Like the other dialog boxes that you have examined thus far, the FolderBrowserDialog control can also be used as a class declared in code. The Browse For Folder dialog box, shown in Figure 7-16 without any customization, allows the user to browse for and select a folder. Notice that there is also a Make New Folder button that allows a user to create and select a new folder.

Figure 7-16

The Properties of FolderBrowserDialog

Before you dive into some code, take a look at some of the available properties for the FolderBrowserDialog control, shown in the following table.

Property	Description
Description	Provides a descriptive message in the dialog box.
RootFolder	Indicates the root folder where the dialog box should start browsing from.
SelectedPath	Indicates the folder selected by the user.
ShowNewFolderButton	Indicates whether the Make New Folder button is shown in the dialog box.

This is one dialog control where you'll want to use all of the most common properties, as shown in Table 7-12, to customize the dialog box displayed.

As with the other dialog controls, the FolderBrowserDialog contains a ShowDialog method. You have already seen this method in the previous examples, and since it is the same, it does not need to be discussed again.

Using the FolderBrowserDialog Control

Before showing the Browse For Folder dialog box, you'll want to set some basic properties. The three main properties that you are most likely to set are shown in the following code snippet. The first of these properties is the Description property. This property allows you to provide a description or instructions for your users.

The next property is the `RootFolder` property and specifies the starting folder for the Browse For Folder dialog box. This property uses one of the constants from the `Environment.SpecialFolder` enumeration. Typically you would use the `MyComputer` constant to specify that browsing should start at the My Computer level or sometimes you may want to use to the `Personal` constant to start browsing at the My Documents level.

The final property shown in the code snippet is the `ShowNewFolderButton` property. This property has a default value of `True`, which indicates that the Make New Folder button should be displayed. However, if you do not want this button displayed, you need to specify this property and set it to a value of `False`:

```
FolderBrowserDialog1.Description = "Select a folder for your backups:"
FolderBrowserDialog1.RootFolder = Environment.SpecialFolder.MyComputer
FolderBrowserDialog1.ShowNewFolderButton = False
```

After you have set the necessary properties, you execute the `ShowDialog` method to display the dialog box:

```
FolderBrowserDialog1.ShowDialog()
```

The FolderBrowserDialog control will return a `DialogResult` of `OK` or `Cancel`. Hence, you can use the previous statement in an `If ... End If` statement and test for a `DialogResult` of `OK`, as you have done in the previous examples that you have coded.

To retrieve the folder that the user has chosen, you simply retrieve the value set in the `SelectedPath` property and assign it to a variable. The folder that is returned is a fully qualified path name. For example, if you chose a folder named `Temp` at the root of your C drive, the path returned would be `C:\Temp`:

```
strFolder = FolderBrowserDialog1.SelectedPath
```

In the next Try It Out, you continue using the same Dialogs project and have the FolderBrowserDialog control display the Browse For Folder dialog box. Then, if the dialog box returns a `DialogResult` of `OK`, you'll display the selected folder in the text box on your form.

Try It Out   Working with the FolderBrowserDialog Control

1. Switch to the Forms Designer in the Dialogs project.

2. On the form, add another Button control from the Toolbox and set its properties according to the values shown:

   ❑ Set Name to **btnBrowse**.

   ❑ Set Anchor to **Top, Right**.

   ❑ Set Location to **367, 158**.

   ❑ Set Text to **Browse**.

3. Next, add a FolderBrowserDialog control to your project from the Toolbox. It will be added to the workspace below the form. Accept all default properties for this control, because you'll set the necessary properties in your code.

4. Double-click the Browse button to bring up its Click event procedure, and add the following code:

```
Private Sub btnBrowse_Click(ByVal sender As System.Object, _
    ByVal e As System.EventArgs) Handles btnBrowse.Click

        'Set the FolderBrowserDialog control properties
        FolderBrowserDialog1.Description = "Select a folder for your backups:"
        FolderBrowserDialog1.RootFolder = Environment.SpecialFolder.MyComputer
        FolderBrowserDialog1.ShowNewFolderButton = False

        'Show the Browse For Folder dialog
        If FolderBrowserDialog1.ShowDialog = Windows.Forms.DialogResult.OK Then
            'Display the selected folder
            txtFile.Text = FolderBrowserDialog1.SelectedPath
        End If
End Sub
```

5. That's all the code you need to add. To test your changes to this project, click the Start button.

6. When your form displays, click the Browse button, and you'll see a Browse For Folder dialog similar to the one shown in Figure 7-17.

Figure 7-17

7. Now browse your computer and select a folder. When you click the OK button, the selected folder will be displayed in the text box on your form as shown in Figure 7-18. Notice that the folder returned contains a fully qualified path name.

How It Works

Before displaying the Browse For Folder dialog box, you needed to set some basic properties of the FolderBrowserDialog control to customize the look for this dialog box. You started by setting the Description property to provide some basic instructions for your user. Then you selected the root folder at which the Browse For Folder dialog box should start browsing. In this instance, you used the

MyComputer constant, which displayed all drives on your computer, as shown in Figure 7-17. Finally, you set the ShowNewFolderButton property to False so as not to display the Make New Folder button:

```
'Set the FolderBrowserDialog control properties
FolderBrowserDialog1.Description = "Select a folder for your backups:"
FolderBrowserDialog1.RootFolder = Environment.SpecialFolder.MyComputer
FolderBrowserDialog1.ShowNewFolderButton = False
```

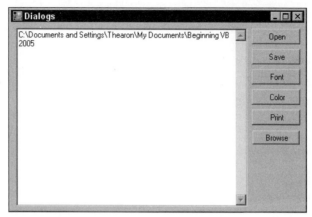

Figure 7-18

Then you displayed the dialog box in an If ... End If statement to check the DialogResult returned by the ShowDialog method of the FolderBrowserDialog control:

```
'Show the Browse For Folder dialog
If FolderBrowserDialog1.ShowDialog = Windows.Forms.DialogResult.OK Then
```

Within the If ... End If statement, you added the code necessary to display the folder selected in the text box on your form, using the SelectedPath property:

```
        'Display the selected folder
        txtFile.Text = FolderBrowserDialog1.SelectedPath
End If
```

Summary

This chapter has taken a look at some of the dialog boxes that are provided in Visual Basic 2005. You examined the MessageBox dialog box, and the OpenFileDialog, SaveFileDialog, FontDialog, ColorDialog, PrintDialog, and FolderBrowserDialog controls. Each of these dialog boxes will help you provide a common interface in your applications for their respective functions. They also hide a lot of the complexities required to perform their tasks, allowing you to concentrate on the logic needed to make your application functional and feature-rich.

Although you used the controls from the Toolbox for all of these dialog boxes, except the MessageBox dialog box, remember that these controls can also be used as normal classes. This means that the classes that these dialog boxes use expose the same properties and methods that you've seen, whether you are selecting a control visually or writing code using the class. You can define your own objects and set them to these classes, and then use the objects to perform the tasks that you performed using the controls. This provides better control over the scope of the objects. For example, you could define an object, set it to the OpenDialog class, use it, and then destroy it all in the same procedure. This method uses resources only in the procedure that defines and uses the OpenDialog class, and reduces the size of your executable.

To summarize, you should now know how to:

❑   Use the MessageBox dialog box to display messages

❑   Display icons and buttons in the MessageBox dialog box

❑   Use the OpenFileDialog control and read the contents of a file

❑   Use the SaveFileDialog control and save the contents of a text box to a file

❑   Use the FontDialog control to set the font and color of text in a text box

❑   Use the ColorDialog control to set the background color of your form

❑   Use the PrintDialog control to print text

❑   Use the FolderBrowserDialog control to get a selected folder

Exercises

Exercise 1

Create a simple Windows application with a TextBox control and two Button controls. Set the buttons to open a file and to save a file. Use the OpenFileDialog class (not the control) and the SaveFileDialog class to open and save your files.

Hint: To use the corresponding classes for the controls use the following statements:

```
Dim objOpenFileDialog As New OpenFileDialog
Dim objSaveFileDialog As New SaveFileDialog
```

Exercise 2

Create a simple Windows application with a Label control and a Button control. Set the button to display the Browse For Folder dialog box with the Make New Folder button displayed. Use My Documents as the root folder at which the dialog starts browsing. Use the FolderBrowserDialog class (not the control) and display the selected folder in the label on your form.

Creating Menus

Menus are a part of every good application and provide not only an easy way to navigate within an application but also useful tools for working with that application. Take, for example, Visual Studio 2005. It provides menus for navigating the various windows that it displays and useful tools for making the job of development easier through menus and context menus (also called pop-up menus) for cutting, copying, and pasting code. It also provides menu items for searching through code.

This chapter takes a look at creating menus in your Visual Basic 2005 applications. You explore how to create and manage menus and submenus and how to create context menus and override the default context menus. Visual Studio 2005 provides two menu controls in the Toolbox, and you will be exploring both of these.

In this chapter, you will:

- ❏ Create menus
- ❏ Create submenus
- ❏ Create context menus

Understanding Menu Features

The MenuStrip control in Visual Studio 2005 provides several key features. First and foremost, it provides a quick and easy way to add menus, menu items, and submenu items to your application. It also provides a built-in editor that allows you to add, edit, and delete menu items at the drop of a hat.

The menu items that you create may contain images, access keys, shortcut keys, and check marks as well as text labels.

Images

Everyone has seen images on the menus in their applications, such as Microsoft Word and even Visual Studio 2005 itself. Up until now, developers were unable to create menu items with images without some custom programming or purchasing a third-party control. Visual Studio 2005 now provides an Image property for a menu item that makes adding an image to your menu items a breeze.

Access Keys

An *access key* (also known as an *accelerator key*) enables you to navigate the menus using the Alt key and a letter that is underlined in the menu item. When the access key is pressed, the menu will appear on the screen, and the user can navigate through it using the arrow keys or the mouse.

Shortcut Keys

Shortcut keys enable you to invoke the menu item without displaying the menus at all. Shortcut keys usually consist of a control key and a letter, such as Ctrl+X to cut text.

Check Marks

A *check mark* symbol can be placed next to a menu item in lieu of an image, typically to indicate that the menu item is being used. For example, if you click the View menu in Visual Studio 2005 and then select the Toolbars menu item, you see a submenu that has many submenu items, some of which have check marks. The submenu items that have check marks indicate the toolbars that are currently displayed.

Figure 8-1 shows many of the available features that you can incorporate into your menus. As you can see, this sample menu provides all the features that were just mentioned plus a *separator*. A separator looks like a raised ridge and provides a logical separation between groups of menu items.

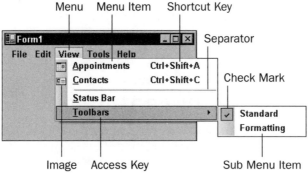

Figure 8-1

Figure 8-1 shows the menu the way it looks when the project is being run. Figure 8-2 shows how the menu looks in Design mode.

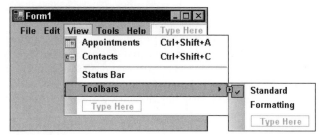

Figure 8-2

The first thing that you'll notice when using the MenuStrip control is that it provides a means to allow you to add another menu, menu item, or submenu item quickly. Each time you add one of these, another blank text area is added.

The second thing that you may notice is the absence of underlines indicating the access keys, since they are not displayed in Design mode.

The Properties Window

While you are creating or editing a menu, the Properties window displays the available properties that can be set for the menu being edited, as shown in Figure 8-3, which shows the properties for the Toolbars menu item.

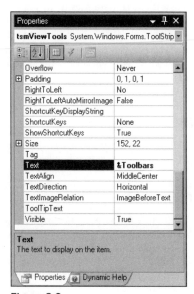

Figure 8-3

You can create as many menus, menu items, and submenu items as you need. You can even go as deep as you need to when creating submenu items by creating another submenu within a submenu.

Keep in mind, though, that if the menus are hard to navigate, or if it is hard to find the items your users are looking for, the users will rapidly lose faith in your application.

You should stick with the standard format for menus that you see in most Windows applications today. These are the menus that you see in Visual Studio 2005, Microsoft Word, or Microsoft Outlook. For example, you always have a File menu and an Exit menu item in the File menu to exit from the application. If your application provides cut, copy, and paste functionality, you would place these menu items in the Edit menu, and so on.

The MSDN library that was installed with Visual Studio 2005 contains a section on User Interface Design and Development. This section contains many topics that address the user interface and the Windows user interface. You can explore these topics for more details on Windows user-interface design-related topics.

The key is to make your menus look and feel like the menus in other Windows applications so that the users can feel comfortable using your application. This way they do not feel like they have to learn the basics of Windows all over again. Some menu items will be specific to your application but the key to incorporating them is to ensure that they fall into a general menu category that users are familiar with or to place them in your own menu category. You would then place this new menu in the appropriate place in the menu bar, generally in the middle.

Creating Menus

Now you move on and see how easy it is to create menus in your applications. In the following Try It Out, you are going to create a form that contains a menu bar, two toolbars, and two text boxes. The menu bar will contain five menus: File, Edit, View, Tools, and Help, and a few menu items and submenu items. This will enable you to fully exercise the features of the menu controls. Since there are several steps involved in building this application, this process will be broken down into several sections, the first of which is "Designing the Menus."

Designing the Menus

You will be implementing code behind the menu items to demonstrate the menu and how to add code to your menu items, so let's get started.

Try It Out   Creating Menus

1. Start Visual Studio 2005 and click File ➪ New ➪ Project. In the New Project dialog box, select Windows Application in the Templates pane and enter a project name of **Menus** in the Name field. Click the OK button to have the project created.

2. Click the form in the Forms Designer and set the following properties of the form:

   ❑ Size to **300, 168**.

   ❑ StartPosition to CenterScreen.

   ❑ Text to **Menu Demo**.

3. Drag a MenuStrip control from the Toolbox and drop it on your form. It will be automatically positioned at the top of your form. The control will also be added to the bottom of the development environment, just like the dialog box controls discussed in Chapter 7.

4. At the bottom of the IDE, right click on the MenuStrip1 control and select the Insert Standard Items context menu item to have the standard menu items automatically inserted.

5. Notice that there is a box to the right of the Help menu as shown in Figure 8-4. This is where you can type the next menu item. Or you can use the Items Collection Editor, which is what you will do now.

In the Properties window, click the ellipsis dots (...) button next to the Items property. In the Items Collection Editor dialog box, click the Add button to add a new menu item.

To be consistent with the current naming standard already in use with the other menu items, set the Name property for this new menu item to **viewToolStripMenuItem**.

Now set the Text property to **&View**. An ampersand (&) in the menu name provides an access key for the menu or menu item. The letter before which the ampersand appears will be the letter used to access this menu item in combination with the Alt key. So for this menu, you will be able to access and expand the View menu by pressing Alt+V. You'll see this when you run your project later.

You want to position this menu between the Edit and Tools menu so click the up arrow to the right of the menu items until the View menu is positioned between editToolStripMenuItem and toolsToolStripMenuItem in the list.

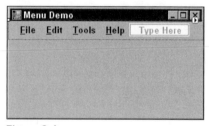

Figure 8-4

6. Now locate the DropDownItems property and click the ellipsis dots button next to it so that you can add menu items beneath the View menu. A second Items Collection Editor will appear, and its caption will read "Items Collection Editor (viewToolStripMenuItem.DropDownItems)".

There will only be one menu item under the View menu, and that will be Toolbars. Click the Add button in the Item Collections Editor to add a MenuItem.

Again, you want to be consistent with the naming standard already being used so set the Name property to **toolbarToolStripMenuItem**. Then set the Text property to **&Toolbars**.

7. You want to add two submenu items under the Toolbars menu item, so locate the DropDownItems property and click the ellipsis button next to it.

In the Item Collections Editor, click the Add button to add a new menu item. Set the Name property for this submenu item to **mainToolStripMenuItem** and the Text property to **&Main**.

When you add a toolbar to this project, it will be displayed by default, so this submenu item should be checked to indicate that the toolbar is displayed. Set the Checked property to True to cause this submenu item to be checked by default and the CheckOnClick property to True to allow the check mark next to this submenu item to be toggled on and off.

8. The next submenu item that you add is Formatting. Click the Add button to add a new menu item and set the Name property for this submenu item to **formattingToolStripMenuItem** and the Text property to **&Formatting**.

    Since this toolbar will not be shown by default, you need to leave the Checked property set to False. You do, however, need to set the CheckOnClick property to True so that the submenu item can toggle the check mark on and off.

    Keep clicking the OK button in the Items Collection Editors until all of the editors are closed.

9. If you run your project at this point and click the View menu and then the Toolbars menu item, you see the submenu items as shown in Figure 8-5. You can also click the other menus and see their menu items.

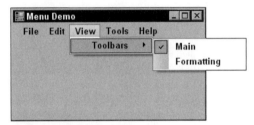

Figure 8-5

How It Works

Visual Studio 2005 takes care of a lot of the details for you by providing the Insert Standard Items context menu item in the MenuStrip control. By clicking this menu item, Visual Studio 2005 created the standard menus and menu items found in most common applications. This allows you to concentrate on only the menus and menu items that are custom to your application, which is what you did by adding the View menu, Toolbars menu item, and Main and Formatting submenu items.

Adding Toolbars and Controls

In this section, you add the toolbars and buttons for the toolbars that the application needs. The menus created in the previous section will control the displaying and hiding of these toolbars. You will also be adding a couple of TextBox controls that will be used in the application to cut, copy, and paste text using the toolbar buttons and menu items.

Try It Out   **Adding Toolbars and Controls**

1. You need to add two toolbars to the form, so locate the ToolStrip control in the Toolbox and drag and drop it on your form; it automatically aligns itself to the top of the form below the menu. Set the Name property to **tspFormatting** and its Visible property to False, because you don't want this toolbar to be shown by default.

2. You want to add four buttons to this toolbar, so click the ellipsis dots button next to the Items property in the Properties window.

In the Items Collection Editor dialog box, click the Add button to add the first button. Since you really won't be using these buttons, you can accept the default name and ToolTip text for these buttons. Ensure the DisplayStyle property is set to Image, and then click the ellipsis dots button next to the Image property.

In the Select Resource dialog box, click the Import button and browse to `C:\Program Files\ Microsoft Visual Studio 8\Common7\VS2005ImageLibrary\bitmaps\commands\high color` folder. This path assumes a default installation of Visual Studio 2005. In the Open dialog box, select `AlignTableCellMiddleLeftJustHS.bmp` and then click the Open button. Next, click the OK button in the Select Resource dialog box to close it.

3. In the Items Collection Editor dialog box, click the Add button again to add the second button. Ensure the DisplayStyle property is set to Image and then set Image property to the `Align TableCellMiddleCenter.bmp` file.

4. In the Items Collection Editor dialog box, click the Add button again to add the next button. Ensure the DisplayStyle property is set to Image and then set the Image property to the `AlignTableCellMiddleRight.bmp` file.

5. Now click the OK button in the Items Collection Editor dialog box to close it.

6. Next, add a second toolbar to the form in the same manner. It aligns itself above the first toolbar. Set its Name property to **tspMain**. The default toolbar buttons will be fine for this project, so right-click the tspMain control at the bottom of the IDE and select Insert Standard Items from the context menu to have the standard toolbar buttons added.

7. Now add a Panel control from the toolbox to your form and set its Dock property to Fill.

8. Add two TextBox controls to the Panel control and accept their default properties. Their location and size are not important, but they should be wide enough to enter text in. Your completed form should now look similar to the one shown in Figure 8-6. Notice that your second toolbar is not visible since you set its Visible property to False.

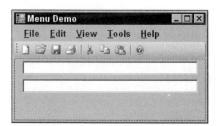

Figure 8-6

If you run your project at this point you will see the menus, the main toolbar, and two text boxes. The formatting toolbar is not visible at this point because the Visible property was set to False.

How It Works

You took a look at toolbars in Chapter 6, so review the Text Editor project for details on how the ToolStrip control works. The ToolStrip control, like the MenuStrip control, provides the Insert Standard Items context menu item, which does a lot of the grunt work for you by inserting the standard toolbar buttons, as was shown in Figure 8-6. This without a doubt provides the most efficient means of having the standard toolbar buttons added to the ToolStrip control. You can, of course, rearrange the buttons that have been added and even add new buttons and delete existing buttons.

Because you set the Visible property to False for the `tspFormatting` ToolStrip control, that control does not take up any space on your form at design time after the control loses focus.

Coding Menus

Now that you have finally added all of your controls to the form, it's time to start writing some code to make these controls work. First, you have to add functionality to make the menus work. After you have done that, add code to make some of the buttons on the main toolbar work.

Try It Out   Coding the File Menu

1. Start by switching to the Code Editor for the form. In the Class Name combo box at the top of the Code Editor, select newToolStripMenuItem and select the Click event in the Method Name combo box. Add the following highlighted code to the Click event handler:

```
Private Sub newToolStripMenuItem_Click(ByVal sender As Object, _
    ByVal e As System.EventArgs) Handles newToolStripMenuItem.Click

        'Clear the text boxes
        TextBox1.Text = String.Empty
        TextBox2.Text = String.Empty

        'Set focus to the first text box
        TextBox1.Focus()
End Sub
```

2. Now add the procedure for the New button on the toolbar by selecting newToolStripButton from the Class Name combo box and the Click event from the Method Name combo box. Add the following highlighted code to this procedure:

```
Private Sub newToolStripButton_Click(ByVal sender As Object, _
    ByVal e As System.EventArgs) Handles newToolStripButton.Click

        'Call the newToolStripMenuItem_Click procedure
        newToolStripMenuItem_Click(sender, e)
End Sub
```

3. Now select exitToolStripMenuItem from the Class Name combo box and the Click event from the Method Name combo box and add the following highlighted code to the procedure:

```
Private Sub exitToolStripMenuItem_Click(ByVal sender As Object, _
    ByVal e As System.EventArgs) Handles exitToolStripMenuItem.Click
```

```
        'Close the form and end
        Me.Close()
End Sub
```

How It Works

To clear the text boxes on the form in the `newToolStripMenuItem_Click` procedure, add the following code. All you are doing here is setting the `Text` property of the text boxes to an empty string. The next line of code sets focus to the first text box by calling the `Focus` method of that text box:

```
'Clear the text boxes
TextBox1.Text = String.Empty
TextBox2.Text = String.Empty

'Set focus to the first text box
TextBox1.Focus()
```

Now when you click the New menu item under the File menu, the text boxes on the form are cleared of all text, and TextBox1 will have the focus and will be ready to accept text.

The New button on the toolbar should perform the same function, but you don't want to write the same code twice. Here you could put the text in the previous procedure in a separate procedure and call that procedure from both the `newToolStripMenuItem_Click` and `newToolStripButton_Click` procedures. Instead, you have the code in the `newToolStripMenuItem_Click` procedure and simply call that procedure from within the `newToolStripButton_Click` procedure. Since both procedures accept the same parameters, you simply pass the parameters received in this procedure to the procedure you are calling:

```
'Call the newToolStripMenuItem_Click procedure
newToolStripMenuItem_Click(sender, e)
```

Now you can click the New button on the toolbar or click the New menu item on the File menu and have the same results, clearing the text boxes on your form.

When you click the Exit menu item, you want the program to end. In the `exitToolStripMenuItem_Click` procedure, you added the following code. The `Me` keyword refers to the class where the code is executing and, in this case, refers to the form class. The `Close` method closes the form, releases all resources, and ends the program:

```
'Close the form and end
Me.Close()
```

That takes care of the code for the File menu and its corresponding toolbar button, so you want to move on to the Edit menu and add the code for those menu items.

Try It Out   Coding the Edit Menu

1. The first menu item in the Edit menu is the Undo menu item. Select undoToolStripMenuItem in the Class Name combo box and select the Click event in the Method Name combo box. Add the following highlighted code to the Click event handler:

```
Private Sub undoToolStripMenuItem_Click(ByVal sender As Object, _
    ByVal e As System.EventArgs) Handles undoToolStripMenuItem.Click

    'Declare a TextBox object and set it to the ActiveControl
    Dim objTextBox As TextBox = Me.ActiveControl
    'Undo the last operation
    objTextBox.Undo()
End Sub
```

2. The next menu item that you want to add code for is the Cut menu item. Select cutToolStripMenuItem in the Class Name combo and the Click event in the Method Name combo box. Add the highlighted code here:

```
Private Sub cutToolStripMenuItem_Click(ByVal sender As Object, _
    ByVal e As System.EventArgs) Handles cutToolStripMenuItem.Click

    'Declare a TextBox object and set it to the ActiveControl
    Dim objTextBox As TextBox = Me.ActiveControl
    'Copy the text to the clipboard and clear the field
    objTextBox.Cut()
End Sub
```

3. You'll want the Cut button on the toolbar to call the code for the Cut menu item. Select cutToolStripButton in the Class Name combo and the Click event in the Method Name combo box. Add the following highlighted code:

```
Private Sub cutToolStripButton_Click(ByVal sender As Object, _
    ByVal e As System.EventArgs) Handles cutToolStripButton.Click

    'Call the cutToolStripMenuItem_Click procedure
    cutToolStripMenuItem_Click(sender, e)
End Sub
```

4. The next menu item that you need to code is the Copy menu item. Select copyToolStripMenuItem in the Class Name combo and the Click event in the Method Name combo box and then add the following highlighted code:

```
Private Sub copyToolStripMenuItem_Click(ByVal sender As Object, _
    ByVal e As System.EventArgs) Handles copyToolStripMenuItem.Click

    'Declare a TextBox object and set it to the ActiveControl
    Dim objTextBox As TextBox = Me.ActiveControl
    'Copy the text to the clipboard
    objTextBox.Copy()
End Sub
```

5. You want the Copy button on the toolbar to call the procedure you just added. Select copyToolStripButton in the Class Name combo and the Click event in the Method Name combo box and then add the following highlighted code:

```
Private Sub copyToolStripButton_Click(ByVal sender As Object, _
    ByVal e As System.EventArgs) Handles copyToolStripButton.Click
```

```
            'Call the copyToolStripMenuItem_Click procedure
            copyToolStripMenuItem_Click(sender, e)
      End Sub
```

6. The Paste menu item is next so select pasteToolStripMenuItem in the Class Name combo box and the Click event in the Method Name combo box. Add the following highlighted code to the Click event handler:

```
Private Sub pasteToolStripMenuItem_Click(ByVal sender As Object, _
      ByVal e As System.EventArgs) Handles pasteToolStripMenuItem.Click

            'Declare a TextBox object and set it to the ActiveControl
            Dim objTextBox As TextBox = Me.ActiveControl
            'Copy the data from the clipboard to the textbox
            objTextBox.Paste()
      End Sub
```

7. The Paste toolbar button should execute the code in the pasteToolStripMenuItem_Click procedure. Select pasteToolStripButton in the Class Name combo box and the Click event in the Method Name combo box and add the following highlighted code:

```
Private Sub pasteToolStripButton_Click(ByVal sender As Object, _
      ByVal e As System.EventArgs) Handles pasteToolStripButton.Click

            'Call the pasteToolStripMenuItem_Click procedure
            pasteToolStripMenuItem_Click(sender, e)
      End Sub
```

8. The last menu item under the Edit menu that you'll write code for is the Select All menu item. Select selectAllToolStripMenuItem in the Class Name combo box and the Click event in the Method Name combo box and add the following highlighted code:

```
Private Sub selectAllToolStripMenuItem_Click(ByVal sender As Object, _
      ByVal e As System.EventArgs) Handles selectAllToolStripMenuItem.Click

            'Declare a TextBox object and set it to the ActiveControl
            Dim objTextBox As TextBox = Me.ActiveControl
            'Select all text
            objTextBox.SelectAll()
      End Sub
```

How It Works

You added the code for the Edit menu starting with the Undo menu item. Since you have two text boxes on your form, you need a way to determine which text box you are dealing with or a generic way of handling an undo operation for both text boxes. In this example, you go with the latter option and provide a generic way to handle both text boxes.

You do this by declaring a variable as a TextBox control and setting it to the ActiveControl property of the form, which retrieves the active control on the form. This is the control that has focus:

```
            'Declare a TextBox object and set it to the ActiveControl
            Dim objTextBox As TextBox = Me.ActiveControl
```

Note that the menu and toolbar are never set as the active control. This allows you to use the menus and toolbar buttons and always reference the active control.

Now that you have a reference to the active control on the form, you can invoke the Undo method as shown in the last line of code here. The Undo method is a method of the TextBox class and will undo the last operation in that text box if it can be undone.

```
'Undo the last operation
objTextBox.Undo()
```

The ActiveControl *property works fine in this small example, because all you are dealing with is two text boxes. However, in a real-world application, you would need to test the active control to see whether it supports the method that you were using (for example,* Undo*).*

The next menu item under the Edit menu that you write code for is the Cut menu item. The first thing that you do in this procedure is to again get a reference to the active control on the form and set it to the TextBox object that you declared.

Then you invoke the Cut method. This is a method of the TextBox class and will copy the selected text to the Clipboard and then remove the selected text from the text box:

```
'Declare a TextBox object and set it to the ActiveControl
Dim objTextBox As TextBox = Me.ActiveControl
'Copy the text to the clipboard and clear the field
objTextBox.Cut()
```

Since you have a Cut button on the toolbar, you want that procedure to call the Cut menu item procedure, because you have already written the code for that:

```
Private Sub cutToolStripButton_Click(ByVal sender As Object, _
    ByVal e As System.EventArgs) Handles cutToolStripButton.Click

    'Call the cutToolStripMenuItem_Click procedure
    cutToolStripMenuItem_Click(sender, e)
End Sub
```

Next, you write code for the Copy menu item. Again, you declare a TextBox object and get a reference to the active control on the form for the Copy menu item. Then you invoke the Copy method to have the text in the active text box copied to the Clipboard:

```
'Declare a TextBox object and set it to the ActiveControl
Dim objTextBox As TextBox = Me.ActiveControl
'Copy the text to the clipboard
objTextBox.Copy()
```

You also have a Copy button on the toolbar and you want to call the procedure for the Copy menu item:

```
Private Sub copyToolStripButton_Click(ByVal sender As Object, _
    ByVal e As System.EventArgs) Handles copyToolStripButton.Click

    'Call the copyToolStripMenuItem_Click procedure
    copyToolStripMenuItem_Click(sender, e)
End Sub
```

For the Click event for the Paste menu item, the first thing that you do is to get a reference to the active control by setting it to your TextBox object that you have declared. Then you invoke the `Paste` method, which will paste the text contents of the Clipboard into your text box:

```
'Declare a TextBox object and set it to the ActiveControl
Dim objTextBox As TextBox = Me.ActiveControl
'Copy the data from the clipboard to the textbox
objTextBox.Paste()
```

Again you have the corresponding button on the toolbar, and you want the Paste button to call the procedure for the Paste menu item:

```
Private Sub pasteToolStripButton_Click(ByVal sender As Object, _
    ByVal e As System.EventArgs) Handles pasteToolStripButton.Click

    'Call the pasteToolStripMenuItem_Click procedure
    pasteToolStripMenuItem_Click(sender, e)
End Sub
```

Lastly, for the Select All menu item, you once again get a reference to the active control by setting it to the TextBox object that you declared. Then you invoke the `SelectAll` method, which will select all text in the text box that is active:

```
'Declare a TextBox object and set it to the ActiveControl
Dim objTextBox As TextBox = Me.ActiveControl
'Select all text
objTextBox.SelectAll()
```

Coding the View Menu and Toolbars

Now that you added the code to make the Edit menu items and the corresponding toolbar buttons functional, the next step is to make the menu items under the View menu functional.

Try It Out   Coding the View Menu

1. In the Class Name combo box, select mainToolStripMenuItem and in the Method Name combo box select the Click event. Add the following highlighted code to the Click event handler:

```
Private Sub mainToolStripMenuItem_Click(ByVal sender As Object, _
    ByVal e As System.EventArgs) Handles mainToolStripMenuItem.Click

    'Toggle the visibility of the Main toolbar
    'based on this menu item's Checked property
    If mainToolStripMenuItem.Checked Then
        tspMain.Visible = True
    Else
        tspMain.Visible = False
    End If
End Sub
```

2.   You need to add the same type of code that you just added to the Formatting submenu item. Select formattingToolStripMenuItem in the Class Name combo box and the Click event in the Method Name combo box and add the following highlighted code:

```
Private Sub formattingToolStripMenuItem_Click(ByVal sender As Object, _
    ByVal e As System.EventArgs) Handles formattingToolStripMenuItem.Click

        'Toggle the visibility of the Formatting toolbar
        'based on this menu item's Checked property
        If formattingToolStripMenuItem.Checked Then
            tspFormatting.Visible = True
        Else
            tspFormatting.Visible = False
        End If
    End Sub
```

How It Works

When the Main submenu item under the Tools menu item is clicked, the submenu item either displays a check mark or removes it based on the current state of the `Checked` property of the submenu item. You add code in the Click event of this submenu item to either hide or show the Main toolbar by setting its `Visible` property to `True` or `False`:

```
        'Toggle the visibility of the Main toolbar
        'based on this menu item's Checked property
        If mainToolStripMenuItem.Checked Then
            tspMain.Visible = True
        Else
            tspMain.Visible = False
        End If
```

The same principle works for the Formatting submenu item, and its code is very similar to that of the Main submenu item:

```
        'Toggle the visibility of the Formatting toolbar
        'based on this menu item's Checked property
        If formattingToolStripMenuItem.Checked Then
            tspFormatting.Visible = True
        Else
            tspFormatting.Visible = False
        End If
```

Testing Your Code

As your applications become more complex, testing your code becomes increasingly important. The more errors that you find and fix during your testing, the better able you will be to implement an application that is both stable and reliable for your users. This translates into satisfied users and earns a good reputation for you for delivering a quality product.

You need not only to test the functionality of your application but also to test various scenarios that a user might encounter or perform. For example, suppose you have a database application that gathers user input from a form and inserts it into a database. A good application will validate all user input before trying to insert the data into the database, and a good test plan will try to break the data validation code. This will ensure that your validation code handles all possible scenarios and functions properly.

Try It Out   **Testing Your Code**

1.   It's now time to test your code! Click the Run toolbar button. When your form loads, the only toolbar that you should see is the main toolbar, as shown in Figure 8-7.

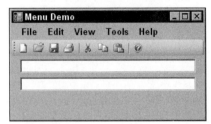

Figure 8-7

2.   Click the View menu and then click the Toolbars menu item. Notice that the Main submenu item is checked and the main toolbar is visible. Go ahead and click the Formatting submenu item. The Formatting toolbar is displayed along with the main toolbar.

Notice that the controls on your form shifted down when the Formatting toolbar was displayed. The reason that this happened was that you placed a Panel control on your form, set its Dock property to Fill, and then placed your TextBox controls on the Panel control. Doing this allows the controls on your form to be repositioned, either to take up the space when a toolbar is hidden or to make room for the toolbar when it is shown; much like the behavior in Microsoft Word or Visual Studio 2005.

3.   If you click the View menu again and then click the Toolbars menu item, you will see that both the Main and Formatting submenu items are checked. The checked submenu items indicate that the toolbar is visible, and an unchecked submenu item indicates that the toolbar is not visible.

4.   Now test the functionality of the Edit menu. Click in the first text box and type some text. Then click the Edit menu and select the Select All menu item. Once you select the Select All menu item, the text in the text box is highlighted.

5.   You now want to copy the text in the first text box while the text is highlighted. Hover your mouse over the Copy button on the toolbar to view the ToolTip. Now either click on the Copy button on the toolbar or select the Edit ⇨ Copy menu item.

Place your cursor in the second text box, and then either click the Paste button on the toolbar or select Edit ⇨ Paste. The text is pasted into the second text box, as shown in Figure 8-8.

6.   Click the first text box and then click Edit ⇨ Undo. Notice that the changes you made to the first text box have been undone. You might have expected that the text in the second text box would be removed, but Windows keeps track of the cut, copy, and paste operations for each control individually; so there's nothing you need to do.

7.   The last item on the Edit menu to test is the Cut menu item. Type some more text in the first text box, and then highlight the text in the first text box by clicking the Edit menu and selecting the Select All menu item. Then either click the Cut icon on the toolbar or select Edit ⇨ Cut. The text is copied to the Clipboard and is then removed from the text box.

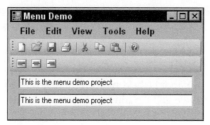

Figure 8-8

Place your cursor in the second text box at the end of the text there. Then paste the text in this text box using the Paste shortcut key Ctrl+V. The text has been placed at the end of the existing text in the text box. This is how Windows' cut, copy, and paste operations work, and, as you can see, there was very little code required to implement this functionality in your program.

8. Now click the File menu and choose the New menu item. The text in the text boxes is cleared. The only menu item left to test is the Exit menu item under the File menu.

9. Before testing the Exit menu item, take a quick look at context menus. Type some text in one of the text boxes. Now, right-click in that text box, and you will see a context menu pop up as shown in Figure 8-9. Notice that this context menu appeared automatically; there was no code that you needed to add to have this done. This is a feature of the Windows operating system, and Visual Studio 2005 provides a way to override the default context menus, as you will see in the next section.

Figure 8-9

10. To test the last bit of functionality of your program, select File ⇨ Exit, and your program will end.

Context Menus

Context menus are menus that pop up when a user clicks the right mouse button over a control or window. This provides the users with quick access to the most commonly used commands for the control that they are working with. As you just saw, the context menu that appeared provides you with a way to manage the text in a text box.

Context menus are customized for the control that you are working with, and in more complex applications, such as Visual Studio 2005 or Microsoft Word, they provide quick access to the commands for the task that is being performed.

You saw that Windows provides a default context menu for the TextBox control that you are working with, and you can override the default context menu if your application's needs dictate that you do so. For example, suppose that you have an application in which you want the user to be able to copy the text in a text box but not actually cut or paste text in that text box. This would be an ideal situation to provide your own context menu to allow only the operations that you want.

Visual Studio 2005 provides a ContextMenuStrip control that you can place on your form and customize, just as you did the MenuStrip control. However, the main difference between the MenuStrip control and the ContextMenuStrip control is that you can create only one top-level menu with the ContextMenuStrip control. You can still create submenu items with the ContextMenuStrip if you need to.

Most controls in the toolbox have a `ContextMenuStrip` property that can be set to the context menu that you define. When you right-click that control, the context menu that you defined is displayed instead of the default context menu.

Some controls, such as the ComboBox and ListBox controls, do not have a default context menu. This is because they contain a collection of items, not a single item like simple controls such as the TextBox. They do, however, have a `ContextMenuStrip` property that can be set to a context menu that you define.

The ComboBox control does not provide a context menu when its `DropDownStyle` *property is set to* `Drop DownList`, *but it does provide a context menu when its* `DropDownStyle` *property is set to* `Simple` *or* `DropDown`.

Creating Context Menus

Now that you know what context menus are, you are ready to learn how to create and use them in your Visual Basic 2005 applications. In the next Try It Out, you will be expanding the code in the previous Try It Out section by adding a context menu to work with your text boxes. You add one context menu and use it for both text boxes. You could just as easily create two context menus, one for each text box, and have the context menus perform different functions.

Try It Out   Creating Context Menus

1. View the form in the Forms Designer and then click the toolbox to locate the ContextMenuStrip control. Drag and drop it onto your form. It will be added at the bottom of the development environment just as the MenuStrip control was.

2. In the Properties window, click the ellipsis dots button next to the Items property. You'll be adding five menu items in your context menu in the next several steps.

3. Click the Add button in the Items Collection Editor dialog box to add the first menu item and set the Name property to **contextUndoToolStripMenuItem**. Click the ellipsis dots button next to the Image property and then click the Import button in the Select Resource dialog box. Locate an Undo bitmap or icon file on your computer and click the Open button. Click OK in the Select Resource dialog box to close it and to return to the Items Collection Editor. Locate the Text property and set it to **Undo**.

4. You want to add a separator between the Undo menu item and the next menu item. Select Separator in the List combo box in the Items Collection Editor dialog box and then click the Add button. You'll want to accept all default properties for the separator.

5. Now select MenuItem in the combo box and click the Add button again to add the next menu item and set the Name property to **contextCutToolStripMenuItem**. Click the ellipsis dots button next to the Image property and, in the Select Resource dialog box, locate a Cut bitmap or icon file. Finally, set the Text property to **Cut**.

6. Click the Add button again to add the next menu item and set the Name property to **context CopyToolStripMenuItem**. Click the ellipsis dots button next to the Image property and, in the Select Resource dialog box, locate a Copy bitmap or icon file. Finally, set the Text property to **Copy**.

7. Click the Add button once again to add the next menu item and set the Name property to **contextPasteToolStripMenuItem**. Click the ellipse button next to the Image property and in the Select Resource dialog box, import the PASTE.BMP file. Then set the Text property to **Paste**.

8. Now you want to add a separator between the Paste menu item and the next menu item. Select Separator in the combo box in the Items Collection Editor dialog box and then click the Add button. Again, you'll want to accept all default properties for the separator.

9. Now select MenuItem in the combo box and click the Add button to add the final menu item. Set the Name property to **contextSelectAllToolStripMenuItem** and the Text property to **Select All**. There is no image for this menu item. Finally, click OK in the Items Collection Editor dialog box to close it.

10. When you are done, click any part of the form, and the context menu will disappear. (You can always make it reappear by clicking the ContextMenuStrip1 control at the bottom of the development environment.)

11. Click the first text box on your form. In the Properties window, select ContextMenuStrip1 in the drop-down list for the ContextMenuStrip property. Repeat the same action for the second text box to assign a context menu in the ContextMenuStrip property.

12. Now test your context menu for look and feel. At this point, you haven't added any code to it, but you can ensure that it looks visually correct. Run the application; then right-click in the first text box, and you will see the context menu that you have just added, as shown in Figure 8-10. The same context menu will appear if you also right-click in the second text box.

13. Stop your program and switch to the Code Editor for your form so that you can add the code for the context menus. The first procedure that you want to add is that for the Undo context menu item. Select contextUndoToolStripMenuItem in the Class Name combo box and the Click event in the Method Name combo box and add the following highlighted code:

```
Private Sub contextUndoToolStripMenuItem_Click(ByVal sender As Object, _
    ByVal e As System.EventArgs) Handles contextUndoToolStripMenuItem.Click

        'Call the undoToolStripMenuItem_Click procedure
        undoToolStripMenuItem_Click(sender, e)
End Sub
```

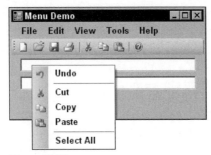

Figure 8-10

14. Select contextCutToolStripMenuItem in the Class Name combo box and the Click event in the Method Name combo box. Add the following highlighted code to the Click event handler:

```
Private Sub contextCutToolStripMenuItem_Click(ByVal sender As Object, _
    ByVal e As System.EventArgs) Handles contextCutToolStripMenuItem.Click

    'Call the cutToolStripMenuItem_Click procedure
    cutToolStripMenuItem_Click(sender, e)
End Sub
```

15. For the Copy context menu item, select contextCopyToolStripMenuItem in the Class Name combo box and the Click event in the Method Name combo box and then add the following highlighted code:

```
Private Sub contextCopyToolStripMenuItem_Click(ByVal sender As Object, _
    ByVal e As System.EventArgs) Handles contextCopyToolStripMenuItem.Click

    'Call the copyToolStripMenuItem_Click procedure
    copyToolStripMenuItem_Click(sender, e)
End Sub
```

16. Select contextPasteToolStripMenuItem in the Class Name combo box for the Paste context menu item and the Click event in the Method Name combo box. Then add the following highlighted code:

```
Private Sub contextPasteToolStripMenuItem_Click(ByVal sender As Object, _
    ByVal e As System.EventArgs) Handles contextPasteToolStripMenuItem.Click

    'Call the pasteToolStripMenuItem_Click procedure
    pasteToolStripMenuItem_Click(sender, e)
End Sub
```

17. The last procedure that you need to perform is for the Select All context menu item. Select contextSelectAllToolStripMenuItem in the Class Name combo box and the Click event in the Method Name combo box and then add the following highlighted code:

```
Private Sub contextSelectAllToolStripMenuItem_Click(ByVal sender As Object, _
    ByVal e As System.EventArgs) _
    Handles contextSelectAllToolStripMenuItem.Click
```

```
                'Call the selectAllToolStripMenuItem_Click procedure
                selectAllToolStripMenuItem_Click(sender, e)
        End Sub
```

18. That's all the code that you need to add to implement your own context menu. Pretty simple, huh? Now run your project to see your context menu in action and test it. You can test the context menu by clicking each of the context menu items shown. They will perform the same functions as their counterparts in the toolbar and Edit menu.

Do you see the difference in your context menu from the one shown in Figure 8-9? Your context menu has a cleaner look and shows the icons for the various menu items. There is one other subtle difference: Your menu items are all enabled when some of them shouldn't be. You'll rectify this in the next Try It Out.

How It Works

The ContextMenuStrip works in the same manner as the MenuStrip, and you should have been able to follow along and create a context menu with ease. You may have noticed that you use a prefix of `context` for your context menu names in this exercise. This will distinguish these menu items as context menu items and will also group these menu items together in the Class Name combo box in the Code Editor, as you probably already noticed.

The code you added here was a no-brainer, as you have already written the code to perform undo, cut, copy, and paste operations. In this exercise, you merely call the corresponding menu item procedures in your Click event handlers for the context menu items.

Enabling and Disabling Menu Items and Toolbar Buttons

Now that you have implemented a context menu and have it functioning, you are ready to write some code to complete the functionality in your application. In this next Try It Out, you will implement the necessary code to enable and disable menu items, context menu items, and toolbar buttons.

Try It Out   Creating Context Menus

1. You need to create a procedure that can be called to toggle all of the Edit menu items, toolbar buttons, and context menu items, enabling and disabling them as needed. They will be enabled and disabled based upon what should be available to the user. You should call this procedure `ToggleMenus`, so stop your program and add the following procedure at the end of your existing code.

```
Private Sub ToggleMenus()
    'Declare a TextBox object and set it to the ActiveControl
    Dim objTextBox As TextBox = Me.ActiveControl

    'Toggle the Undo menu items
    undoToolStripMenuItem.Enabled = objTextBox.CanUndo
    contextUndoToolStripMenuItem.Enabled = objTextBox.CanUndo

    'Toggle the Cut toolbar button and menu items
    cutToolStripButton.Enabled = objTextBox.SelectionLength
    cutToolStripMenuItem.Enabled = objTextBox.SelectionLength
    contextCutToolStripMenuItem.Enabled = objTextBox.SelectionLength
```

```
            'Toggle the Copy toolbar button and menu items
            copyToolStripButton.Enabled = objTextBox.SelectionLength
            copyToolStripMenuItem.Enabled = objTextBox.SelectionLength
            contextCopyToolStripMenuItem.Enabled = objTextBox.SelectionLength

            'Toggle the Paste toolbar button and menu items
            pasteToolStripButton.Enabled = My.Computer.Clipboard.ContainsText
            pasteToolStripMenuItem.Enabled = My.Computer.Clipboard.ContainsText
            contextPasteToolStripMenuItem.Enabled = _
                My.Computer.Clipboard.ContainsText

            'Toggle the Select All menu items
            selectAllToolStripMenuItem.Enabled = _
                objTextBox.SelectionLength < objTextBox.Text.Length
            contextSelectAllToolStripMenuItem.Enabled = _
                objTextBox.SelectionLength < objTextBox.Text.Length
        End Sub
```

That's it! All of that code will toggle the Edit menu items, the context menu items, and the toolbar buttons. Now all you need is to figure out when and where to call this procedure.

2. Since you are checking for only the two text boxes on your form, you can call the `ToggleMenu` procedure when the user moves the mouse into a text box. This way, you will toggle the Edit menu items and toolbar buttons when the user is in a text box, and the code will be applied against the text box that you are in. To do this, select TextBox1 in the Class Name combo box and the MouseMove event in the Method Name combo box. Add the following highlighted code to the `MouseMove` event handler:

```
Private Sub TextBox1_MouseMove(ByVal sender As Object, _
    ByVal e As System.Windows.Forms.MouseEventArgs) Handles TextBox1.MouseMove

        'Toggle the menu items and toolbar buttons
        ToggleMenus()
End Sub
```

3. Repeat this process for the second text box on the form and add the same code:

```
Private Sub TextBox2_MouseMove(ByVal sender As Object, _
    ByVal e As System.Windows.Forms.MouseEventArgs) Handles TextBox2.MouseMove

        'Toggle the menu items and toolbar buttons
        ToggleMenus()
End Sub
```

4. Now run your project again. Once the form has been displayed, click in the first text box and enter some text. Then, right-click in the text box to display your context menu. Now the context menu has the appropriate menu items enabled as shown in Figure 8-11.

Notice also that the appropriate toolbar buttons are also enabled and disabled. If you click the Edit menu, you will see that the appropriate menu items there are also enabled and disabled. If you click the Select All menu item or context menu item, you see the toolbar buttons change as well as the menu items under the Edit menu and context menu.

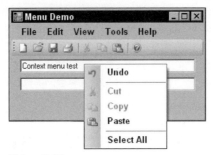

Figure 8-11

How It Works

The first thing that you do in the `ToggleMenus` procedure is to declare an object and set it equal to the active TextBox control. You saw this in the "Coding the Edit Menu" Try It Out exercise, and this object has all of the properties that the active text box has:

```
'Declare a TextBox object and set it to the ActiveControl
Dim objTextBox As TextBox = Me.ActiveControl
```

The first Edit menu item is Undo, so you start with that one. The `TextBox` class has a property called `CanUndo`, which returns a `True` or `False` value indicating whether or not the last operation performed in the text box can be undone.

You use the `CanUndo` property to set the `Enabled` property of the Edit menu item. The `Enabled` property is set using a `Boolean` value, which works out great, because the `CanUndo` property returns a `Boolean` value. The following code shows how you set the `Enabled` property of the Undo menu item and context menu item:

```
'Toggle the Undo menu items
undoToolStripMenuItem.Enabled = objTextBox.CanUndo
contextUndoToolStripMenuItem.Enabled = objTextBox.CanUndo
```

The next menu item in the Edit menu that you wrote code for is the Cut menu item. This time you use the `SelectionLength` property of your TextBox object. `SelectionLength` returns the number of characters selected in a text box. You can use this number to act as a `True` or `False` value because a value of `False` in Visual Basic 2005 is 0 and a value of `True` is 1. Since the value of `False` is always evaluated first, any number other than 0 evaluates to `True`.

Therefore, if no text is selected, the `SelectionLength` property will return 0, and you will disable the Cut toolbar button, Cut menu item, and Cut context menu item. If no text is selected, you don't want to allow the user to perform this operation:

```
'Toggle the Cut toolbar button and menu items
cutToolStripButton.Enabled = objTextBox.SelectionLength
cutToolStripMenuItem.Enabled = objTextBox.SelectionLength
contextCutToolStripMenuItem.Enabled = objTextBox.SelectionLength
```

The next menu item in the Edit menu is the Copy menu item. Again, you use the `SelectionLength` property to determine whether any text is selected in the text box and to set the `Enabled` property appropriately based on the value returned by the `SelectionLength` property:

```
'Toggle the Copy toolbar button and menu items
copyToolStripButton.Enabled = objTextBox.SelectionLength
copyToolStripMenuItem.Enabled = objTextBox.SelectionLength
contextCopyToolStripMenuItem.Enabled = objTextBox.SelectionLength
```

The next menu item in the Edit menu is the Paste menu item. Setting the `Enabled` property of this menu item requires a little more work.

You query the `ContainsText` property of the `My.Computer.Clipboard` object to receive a `Boolean` value indicating whether the Clipboard contains any text. Using this return value you can set the `Enabled` property of the Paste toolbar button, Paste menu item, and context menu item as shown in the following code:

```
'Toggle the Paste toolbar button and menu items
pasteToolStripButton.Enabled = My.Computer.Clipboard.ContainsText
pasteToolStripMenuItem.Enabled = My.Computer.Clipboard.ContainsText
contextPasteToolStripMenuItem.Enabled = _
    My.Computer.Clipboard.ContainsText
```

The last Edit menu item is the Select All menu item. Again, you use the `SelectionLength` property to determine whether any text has been selected. If all of the text has been selected, then you set the `Enabled` property to `False`, and set it to `True` at all other times. To do so, you compare the length of the selected text to the length of the text in the text box:

```
'Toggle the Select All menu items
selectAllToolStripMenuItem.Enabled = _
    objTextBox.SelectionLength < objTextBox.Text.Length
contextSelectAllToolStripMenuItem.Enabled = _
    objTextBox.SelectionLength < objTextBox.Text.Length
```

To enable and disable the menu items, context menu items and toolbar buttons, you have to call the `ToggleMenus` procedure. The best place to do this is in the `MouseMove` event of the text boxes. The `MouseMove` event is fired when the mouse is moved over the control, which typically indicates that the user is about to click in the text box and do something:

```
Private Sub TextBox1_MouseMove(ByVal sender As Object, _
    ByVal e As System.Windows.Forms.MouseEventArgs) Handles TextBox1.MouseMove

    'Toggle the menu items and toolbar buttons
    ToggleMenus()
End Sub
```

Summary

This chapter has looked at how to implement menus, menu items, and submenu items. You also saw how to implement multiple toolbars, although that was not the focus of the chapter. Through practical hands-on exercises you have seen how to create menus, menu items, and submenu items. You have also seen how to add access keys, shortcut keys, and images to these menu items.

Since you used the Edit menu in the Try It Outs, you have also seen how easy it is to implement basic editing techniques in your application by using the properties of the TextBox control and the Clipboard object. You can see how easy it is to provide this functionality to your users — something users have come to expect in every good Windows application.

You also explored how to create and implement context menus and to override the default context menus provided by Windows. Since you had already coded the procedure to implement undo, cut, copy, and paste operations, you simply reused that code in your context menus.

Now that you have completed work in this chapter, you should know how to:

❑   Add a MenuStrip control to your form and add menus, menu items, and submenu items.

❑   Customize the menu items with a check mark.

❑   Add access keys and shortcut keys to your menu items.

❑   Add a ContextMenuStrip control to your form and add menu items.

❑   Use the properties of the TextBox control to toggle the Enabled property of menu items.

Exercise

To give your Menus project the standard look of a typical Windows application, add a StatusStrip control to the form and add the necessary code to display a message when text is cut, copied, or pasted.

Debugging and Error Handling

Debugging is an essential part of any development project, as it helps you find errors in your code and in your logic. Visual Studio 2005 has a sophisticated debugger built right into the development environment. This debugger is the same for all languages that Visual Studio 2005 supports. So once you have mastered debugging in one language, you can debug in any language that you can write in Visual Studio 2005.

No matter how good your code is, there are always going to be some unexpected circumstances that will cause your code to fail. If you do not anticipate and handle errors, your users will see a default error message about an unhandled exception, which is provided by the common language run-time package. This is not a user-friendly message and usually does not clearly inform the user about what is going on or how to correct it.

This is where error handling comes in. Visual Studio 2005 also provides common structured error-handling functions that are used across all languages. These functions allow you to test a block of code and catch any errors that may occur. If an error does occur, you can write your own user-friendly message that informs the user of what happened and how to correct it, or you can simply handle the error and continue processing.

This chapter looks at some of the debugging features available in Visual Studio 2005 and provides a walk-through of debugging a program. You examine how to set breakpoints in your code to stop execution at any given point, how to watch the value of a variable change, and how to control the number of times a loop can execute before stopping. All of these can help you determine just what is going on inside your code. Finally, this chapter takes a look at the structured error-handling functions provided by Visual Studio 2005.

In this chapter, you will:

- ❑ Examine the major types of errors that you may encounter and how to correct them
- ❑ Examine and walk through debugging a program
- ❑ Examine and implement error handling in a program

Major Error Types

Error types can be broken down into three major categories: syntax, execution, and logic. This section will show you the important differences among these three types of errors and how to correct them.

Knowing what type of errors are possible and how to correct them will significantly speed up the development process. Of course, sometimes you just can't find the error on your own. Don't waste too much time trying to find errors in your code by yourself in these situations. Coming back to a nagging problem after a short coffee break can often help you crack it. Otherwise, ask a colleague to have a look at your code with you; two pairs of eyes are often better than one in these cases.

Syntax Errors

Syntax errors, the easiest type of errors to spot and fix, occur when the code you have written cannot be "understood" by the compiler because instructions are incomplete, supplied in unexpected order, or cannot be processed at all. An example of this would be declaring a variable of one name and misspelling this name in your code when you set or query the variable.

The development environment in Visual Studio 2005 has a really sophisticated syntax-checking mechanism, making it hard, but not impossible, to have syntax errors in your code. It provides instant syntax checking of variables and objects and will let you know immediately when you have a syntax error.

Suppose you try to declare a variable as `Private` in a procedure. Visual Studio 2005 will underline the declaration with a blue wavy line indicating that the declaration is in error. If the Integrated Development Environment (IDE) can automatically correct the syntax error, you'll see a little orange rectangular box at the end of the blue wavy line, as shown in Figure 9-1, indicating that AutoCorrect options are available for this syntax error. AutoCorrect is a feature of Visual Studio 2005 that provides error correction options that the IDE will suggest to correct the error.

Figure 9-1

When you hover your mouse over the code in error, you'll receive a ToolTip, telling you what the error is, and a small gray box with a red circle and a white exclamation point. If you then move your mouse into the gray box, a down arrow will appear, shown in Figure 9-2, to let you know that a dialog box is available with some suggested error correction options.

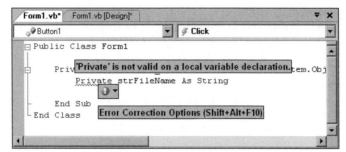

Figure 9-2

Clicking the down arrow or pressing Shift+Alt+F10 will cause the Error Correction Options dialog box to appear as shown in Figure 9-3. This dialog box presents one or more choices to you for correcting the error. In this instance, there is only one choice to correct the syntax error as shown in the dialog box in Figure 9-3.

Notice that the dialog box shows you how your code can be corrected: by replacing the `Private` keyword with the `Dim` keyword. The sample code displayed in the dialog box has your offending statement in strikethrough and the suggested correction preceding it. Above the code in the dialog box is a hyperlink that will replace the `Private` keyword with the `Dim` keyword. Click this link to apply the fix to your code.

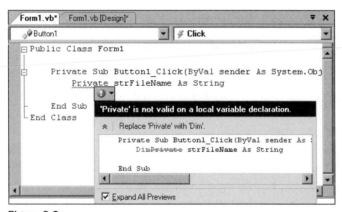

Figure 9-3

Another option available for reviewing all the errors in your code is the Error List window. This window displays a grid with all the errors' descriptions, the files they exist in, and the line numbers and column numbers of the error. If your solution contains multiple projects, it will also display the project that each error exists in.

The Error List can be accessed by clicking the Error List tab at the bottom of the IDE. Once the Error List window is displayed, you can double-click any error to be taken to that specific error in your code.

Sometimes you'll receive warnings, displayed with a green wavy line under the code in question. These are just warnings and your code will compile. However, you should heed these warnings and try to correct these errors if possible, because they may produce undesirable results at run time.

As an example, a warning would occur in the line of code shown in Figure 9-3 once the `Private` keyword was replaced with the `Dim` keyword. The IDE would give you a warning that the variable, `strFileName`, is unused in the procedure. Simply initializing the variable or referencing the variable in code would cause this warning to go away.

Keep in mind that you can hover your mouse over errors and warnings in your code to cause the appropriate ToolTip to be displayed informing you of the problem. As a reminder, if the IDE can provide the AutoCorrect feature for errors, the blue wavy line will contain an orange rectangular box at the end of the blue wavy line.

The IDE also provides IntelliSense to assist in preventing syntax errors. IntelliSense provides a host of features such as providing a drop-down list of members for classes, structures, and namespaces as shown in Figure 9-4. This enables you to choose the correct member for the class, structure, or namespace that you are working with. It also provides ToolTip information for the selected member or method, also shown in Figure 9-4.

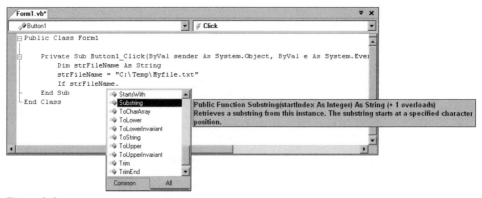

Figure 9-4

These IntelliSense features provide two major benefits. First, you do not have to remember all the available members for the class. You simply scroll through the list to find the member that you want to work with. To select the member in the list that you want to work with, you press the Tab or Enter key or double-click the member. Second, the features help to prevent syntax errors because you are less likely to misspell member names or try to use members that do not exist in the given class.

Another great feature of IntelliSense is that it provides a parameter list for the method that you are working with. IntelliSense will list the number, names, and types of the parameters required by the function, as shown in Figure 9-4. This is also a time saver, as you do not have to remember the required parameters for every class member that you work with, or indeed search the product documentation for what you need.

If the method is overloaded — that is, there are several methods with the same name but different parameters — the ToolTip will indicate this as shown in Figure 9-4 with the text "(+ 1 overloads)". Also, when you start to work with the member, a pop-up list enables you to scroll through the different overloaded methods, as shown in Figure 9-5 for the Substring method of the String class, by simply clicking the up and down arrows to view the different overloaded methods.

```
If strFileName.Substring(
  ▲1 of 2▼   Substring (startIndex As Integer) As String
startIndex:
     The starting character position of a substring in this instance.
```

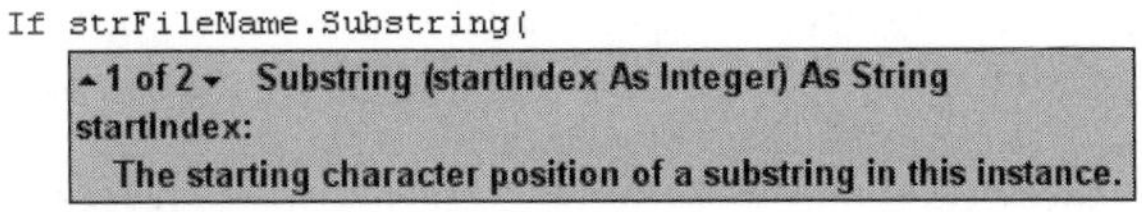

Figure 9-5

Plenty of built-in features in the development environment can help prevent syntax errors. All you need to do is to be aware of these features and take advantage of them to help prevent syntax errors in your code.

Execution Errors

Execution errors (or *run-time errors*) occur while your program is executing. These errors are often caused because something outside of the application, such as a user, database, or hard disk, does not behave as expected.

Developers need to anticipate the possibility of execution errors and build appropriate error-handling logic. Implementing the appropriate error handling will not prevent execution errors, but will allow you to handle them either by gracefully shutting down your application or bypassing the code that failed and giving the user the opportunity to perform that action again. Error handling is covered later in this chapter.

The best way to prevent execution errors is to try anticipating the error before it occurs and to use error handling to trap and handle the error. You must also thoroughly test your code before deploying it.

Most execution errors can be found while you are testing your code in the development environment. This allows you to handle the errors and debug your code at the same time. You can then see what type of errors may occur and implement the appropriate error-handling logic. Debugging, where you find and handle any execution errors that may crop up, is covered later in the "Debugging" section.

Logic Errors

Logic errors (or *semantic errors*) give unexpected or unwanted results because you did not fully understand what the code you were writing did. Probably the most common logic error is an infinite loop:

```
Private Sub PerformLoopExample()
    Dim intIndex As Integer
    Do While intIndex < 10
        'some logic here
    Loop
End Sub
```

If the code inside the loop does not set `intIndex` to `10` or above, this loop will just keep going forever. This is a very simple example, but even experienced developers find themselves writing and executing loops whose exit condition can never be satisfied.

Logic errors can be the most difficult to find and troubleshoot, because it is very difficult to be sure that your program is completely free from logic errors.

Another type of logic error occurs when a comparison fails to give the result you expect. Say you made a comparison between a string variable, set by your code from a database field or from the text in a file, and the text entered by the user. You do not want the comparison to be case sensitive, so you might write code like this:

```
If strFileName = txtInput.Text Then
    ...perform some logic
End If
```

However, if `strFileName` is set to `Index.HTML` and `txtInput.Text` is set to `index.html`, the comparison will fail. One way to prevent this logic error is to convert both fields being compared to either uppercase or lowercase. This way, the results of the comparison would be `True` if the user entered the same text as that contained in the variable, even if the case was different. The next code fragment shows how you can accomplish this:

```
If strFileName.ToUpper = txtInput.Text.ToUpper Then
    ...perform some logic
End If
```

The `ToUpper` method of the `String` class converts the characters in the string to all uppercase and returns the converted results. Since the `Text` property of a text box is also a string, you can use the same method to convert the text to all uppercase. This would make the comparison in the previous example equal.

An alternative to using either the `ToUpper` or `ToLower` methods of the `String` class is to use the `Compare` method of the `String` class, as shown in the next example. This allows you to compare the two strings ignoring the case of the strings. This was covered in the String Comparison section in Chapter 4.

```
If String.Compare(strFileName, txtInput.Text, True) Then
    . . . perform some logic
End If
```

Since logic errors are the hardest errors to troubleshoot and can cause applications to fail or give unexpected and unwanted results, you must check the logic carefully as you code and try to plan for all possible errors that may be encountered by a user. As you become more experienced you will encounter and learn from the common errors that you and your users make.

One of the best ways to identify and fix logic errors is to use the debugging features of Visual Studio 2005. Using these features, you can find loops that execute too many times or comparisons that do not give the expected result.

Debugging

Debugging code is a part of life — even experienced developers will make mistakes and need to debug their code. Knowing how to efficiently debug your code can make the difference between enjoying your job as a developer and hating it.

In the next few sections, you'll create a sample project and then debug that project while learning about the Exception Assistant, working with breakpoints, and learning how to step through your code and to use the Watch and Locals windows to examine variables and objects in your code.

Creating a Sample Project

In this section, you take a look at some of the built-in debugging features in the Visual Studio 2005 development environment through various Try It Out exercises. You will write a simple program and learn how to use the most common and useful debugging features available.

You begin this process by creating a program that will use three classes that you create. Classes and objects are covered in greater detail in the next chapter, but by creating and using these classes, you'll be able to learn about some of the other features in Visual Basic 2005 as well as learn how to debug your programs. These classes will be used to provide data that will be displayed in a list box on your form. These classes introduce two powerful concepts in particular: the generic class with type constraints and the interface. These concepts will be explained in the following How It Works.

Try It Out   **Creating a Sample Project to Debug**

1. Create a new Windows Application project called **Debugging**.

2. In the Solution Explorer window, rename the form to **Debug.vb** by right-clicking the form and choosing Rename from the context menu. Now click the form in the Forms Designer and then set the form's properties in the Properties window as shown:

    ❑   Set Size to **481, 336**.

    ❑   Set StartPosition to CenterScreen.

    ❑   Set Text to **Debug Demo**.

3. Next, you want to add some basic controls to the form and set their properties, as shown in the following list:

    ❑   Create a Button control named **btnStart** and set these properties: Location = **13, 13**; Text = **Start**.

    ❑   Create a ListBox control named **lstData**, and set these properties: Anchor = Top, Bottom, Left, Right; Integral Height = False; Location = **13, 43**; Size = **448, 254**.

4. Right click the Debugging project in the Solution Explorer, choose Add from the context menu, and then choose the Class sub menu item. In the Add New Item – Debugging dialog box, enter a class name of **Customer** in the Name field and then click the Add button.

5. Add the following highlighted code to the Customer class:

```
Public Class Customer
```

```
Private intCustomerID As Integer
Private strName As String

Public Sub New(ByVal customerID As Integer, ByVal name As String)
    intCustomerID = customerID
    strName = name
End Sub

Public ReadOnly Property CustomerID() As Integer
    Get
        Return intCustomerID
    End Get
End Property

Public Property CustomerName() As String
    Get
        Return strName
    End Get
    Set(ByVal value As String)
        strName = value
    End Set
End Property
End Class
```

6. Before moving on to create the next class, take a quick look at the AutoCorrect option in Visual
    Studio 2005 so that you can get first-hand experience with this feature. The `CustomerName`
    property that you just created should really be a `ReadOnly` property. Insert the `ReadOnly`
    keyword between `Public` and `Property` and then click the next line of code.

7. You'll notice that the `Set` statement in this property has a blue wavy line underneath it indicat-
    ing an error. If you hover your mouse over the line of code in error, you'll get a tool tip inform-
    ing you that a `ReadOnly` property cannot have a `Set` statement.

8. Click the small gray box with a red circle and white exclamation point to display the Error
    Correction Options dialog box, shown in Figure 9-6.

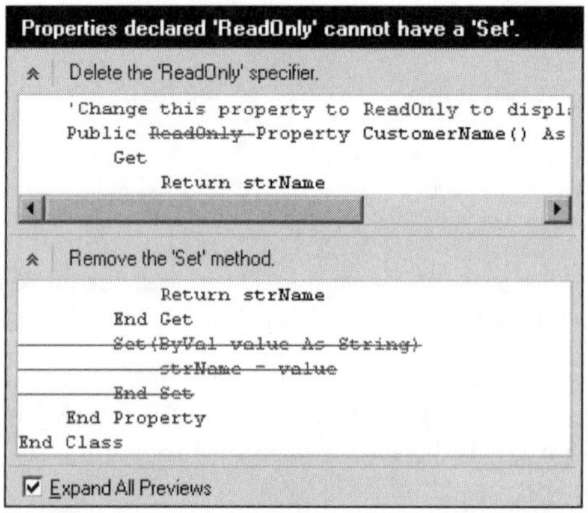

Figure 9-6

9. Notice that you have two options to choose from. The option that you want is the second one, which is to remove the `Set` method. Click the hyperlink to have the AutoCorrect feature remove the `Set` statement from this property.

10. Now add another class to the Debugging project, called **Generics**. Then modify the Class statement as highlighted here:

```
Public Class Generics(Of elementType)

End Class
```

11. Now add the following highlighted code to the `Generics` class:

```
Public Class Generics(Of elementType)

    'This class provides a demonstration of Generics
    'Declare Private variables
    Private strKey() As String
    Private elmValue() As elementType

    Public Sub Add(ByVal key As String, ByVal value As elementType)
        'Check to see if the objects have been initialized
        If strKey IsNot Nothing Then
            'Objects have been initialized
            ReDim Preserve strKey(strKey.GetUpperBound(0) + 1)
            ReDim Preserve elmValue(elmValue.GetUpperBound(0) + 1)
        Else
            'Initialize the objects
            ReDim strKey(0)
            ReDim elmValue(0)
        End If

        'Set the values
        strKey(strKey.GetUpperBound(0)) = key
        elmValue(elmValue.GetUpperBound(0)) = value
    End Sub

    Public ReadOnly Property Key(ByVal Index As Integer) As String
        Get
            Return strKey(Index)
        End Get
    End Property

    Public ReadOnly Property Value(ByVal Index As Integer) As elementType
        Get
            Return elmValue(Index)
        End Get
    End Property
End Class
```

12. Add one more class to the Debugging project, called **Computer**. This is an example of a class that *implements* the `IDisposable` *interface*, which will be explained in the How It Works. Enter the highlighted code below. Once you press the Enter key, Visual Studio 2005 will insert the remaining code listed here automatically.

```
Public Class Computer
```

279

```
    Implements IDisposable

    Private disposed As Boolean = False

    ' IDisposable
    Private Overloads Sub Dispose(ByVal disposing As Boolean)
        If Not Me.disposed Then
            If disposing Then
                ' TODO: put code to dispose managed resources
            End If

            ' TODO: put code to free unmanaged resources here
        End If
        Me.disposed = True
    End Sub

#Region " IDisposable Support "
    ' This code added by Visual Basic to correctly implement the disposable
pattern.
    Public Overloads Sub Dispose() Implements IDisposable.Dispose
        ' Do not change this code.  Put cleanup code in Dispose(ByVal disposing As
Boolean) above.
        Dispose(True)
        GC.SuppressFinalize(Me)
    End Sub

    Protected Overrides Sub Finalize()
        ' Do not change this code.  Put cleanup code in Dispose(ByVal disposing As
Boolean) above.
        Dispose(False)
        MyBase.Finalize()
    End Sub
#End Region

End Class
```

13. Add the following two properties to the end of the `Computer` class:

```
    Public ReadOnly Property FreeMemory() As String
        Get
            'Using the My namespace
            Return Format(( _
                My.Computer.Info.AvailablePhysicalMemory.ToString \ 1024), _
                "#,###,##0") & " K"
        End Get
    End Property

    Public ReadOnly Property TotalMemory() As String
        Get
            'Using the My namespace
            Return Format(( _
                My.Computer.Info.TotalPhysicalMemory.ToString \ 1024), _
                "#,###,##0") & " K"
        End Get
    End Property
```

14. Now switch to the code for the Debug form and add the following highlighted `Imports` statement:

```
Imports System.Collections.Generic

Public Class Debug
```

15. You need to add a few private variable declarations next. Add the following code:

```
Public Class Debug

    'Using the Generics class
    Private objStringValues As New Generics(Of String)
    Private objIntegerValues As New Generics(Of Integer)

    'Using the List<T> class
    Private objCustomerList As New List(Of Customer)
```

16. Add the following `ListCustomer` procedure to add customers to the list box on your form:

```
    Private Sub ListCustomer(ByVal customerToList As Customer)
        lstData.Items.Add(customerToList.CustomerID & _
            " - " & customerToList.CustomerName)
    End Sub
```

17. The rest of the code that will be added will be added to the Start button Click event handler. Select btnStart in the Class Name combo box at the top of the Code Editor and then select the Click event in the Method Name combo box. Add this highlighted code to the Click event handler:

```
    Private Sub btnStart_Click(ByVal sender As Object, _
        ByVal e As System.EventArgs) Handles btnStart.Click

        'Declare variables
        Dim strData As String

        lstData.Items.Add("String variable data:")
        If strData.Length > 0 Then
            lstData.Items.Add(strData)
        End If

        'Add an empty string to the ListBox
        lstData.Items.Add(String.Empty)

        'Demonstrates the use of the List<T> class
        lstData.Items.Add("Customers in the Customer Class:")
        objCustomerList.Add(New Customer(1001, "Henry For"))
        objCustomerList.Add(New Customer(1002, "Orville Wright"))
        For Each objCustomer As Customer In objCustomerList
            ListCustomer(objCustomer)
        Next

        'Add an empty string to the ListBox
        lstData.Items.Add(String.Empty)
```

```
'Demonstrates the use of Generics
lstData.Items.Add("Generics Class Key/Value Pairs using String Values:")
objStringValues.Add("1001", "Henry Ford")
lstData.Items.Add(objStringValues.Key(0) & " = " & _
    objStringValues.Value(0))

'Add an empty string to the ListBox
lstData.Items.Add(String.Empty)

'Demonstrates the use of Generics
lstData.Items.Add("Generics Class Key/Value Pairs using Integer Values:")
objIntegerValues.Add("Henry Ford", 1001)
lstData.Items.Add(objIntegerValues.Key(0) & " = " & _
    objIntegerValues.Value(0))

'Add an empty string to the ListBox
lstData.Items.Add(String.Empty)

'Demonstrates the use of the Using statement
'Allows acquisition, usage and disposal of the resource
lstData.Items.Add("Computer Class Properties:")
Using objMemory As New Computer
    lstData.Items.Add("FreeMemory = " & objMemory.FreeMemory)
    lstData.Items.Add("TotalMemory = " & objMemory.TotalMemory)
End Using

'Add an empty string to the ListBox
lstData.Items.Add(String.Empty)

'Demonstrates the use of the Continue statement
Dim strPassword As String = "POpPassword"
Dim strLowerCaseLetters As String = String.Empty
'Extract lowercase characters from string
For intIndex As Integer = 0 To strPassword.Length - 1
    'Demonstrates the use of the Continue statement
    'If no uppercase character is found, continue the loop
    If Not strPassword.Substring(intIndex, 1) Like "[a-z]" Then
        'No upper case character found, continue loop
        Continue For
    End If
    'Lowercase character found, save it
    strLowerCaseLetters &= strPassword.Substring(intIndex, 1)
Next

'Display lowercase characters
lstData.Items.Add("Password lower case characters:")
lstData.Items.Add(strLowerCaseLetters)
End Sub
```

18. Before examining how the code works, hover your mouse over the Error List tab at the bottom of the IDE so that the Error List window appears as shown in Figure 9-7. If the Error List tab is not visible, select View ⇨ Other Windows ⇨ Error List from the menu bar. Notice that you have one warning about a potential error in your code. The line in question will cause an error when you run your project; however, this is deliberate and is intended to demonstrate some of the debugging capabilities of Visual Studio 2005. You can ignore this warning for now, because you'll be correcting it shortly.

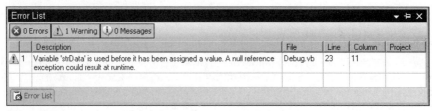

Figure 9-7

How It Works

After building the UI for the Debugging project, which is very straightforward, you add the `Customer` class. This class is also straightforward and contains two private variables, a constructor, and two properties.

The two variables in the `Customer` class are declared as `Private`, which means that these variables will be accessible only to the procedures in the class:

```
Public Class Customer
    Private intCustomerID As Integer
    Private strName As String
```

The *constructor* for this class — a method called whenever a new object of this class is to be created — is defined as a `Public` procedure with a procedure name of `New`. All constructors for classes in the .NET Framework must be declared with a procedure name of `New`.

This constructor accepts two input parameters: `customerID` and `name`. The parameters are used to set the values in the private variables defined for this class:

```
Public Sub New(ByVal customerID As Integer, ByVal name As String)
    intCustomerID = customerID
    strName = name
End Sub
```

Two properties are defined: `CustomerID` and `CustomerName`. These are read-only properties, meaning that the consumer of this class can use these properties only to read the Customer ID and customer name; consumers cannot change them:

```
Public ReadOnly Property CustomerID() As Integer
    Get
        Return intCustomerID
    End Get
End Property

Public Property CustomerName() As String
    Get
```

```
            Return strName
        End Get
    End Property
End Class
```

The next class that you add to the Debugging project is the `Generics` class. This class will be used to demonstrate the use of Generics in Visual Basic 2005.

The `Collections` class in the .NET Framework allows you to store data in the collection in a key/value pair. The key is always a string value that identifies the value, also known as an *item*. The item is defined as an object, which allows you to use the `Collection` class to store any data type that you want in the item. So, for instance, you can use the `Collection` class to store `Integer` values or you can use it to store `String` values. No type checking is performed. This lack of specificity can lead to performance problems as well as run-time problems.

Suppose you intend to use the `Collection` class to store `Integer` values. If (through poor coding practices) you allowed a `String` value to be added to the collection, you would not receive a run-time error when adding the item, but you could receive one when you tried to access the item.

The performance problems that you will encounter are the conversion of the data going into the collection and the data coming out of the collection. When you add an item to the collection, the data must be converted from its native data type to an `Object` data type, since that is how the `Item` property is defined. Likewise, when you retrieve an item from the collection, the item must be converted from an `Object` data type to the data type that you are using.

In Chapter 5, when working with `ArrayLists` (which are a kind of collection), you solved the problem of being able to store items of the wrong type by creating a strongly typed collection class. This did not solve the performance problem. Both problems are solved in Visual Basic 2005 through Generics and through the introduction of *type constraints*. A type constraint is specified on a class such as `Collection` by using the `Of` keyword followed by a list of type name placeholders that are replaced by actual type names when an object of the class is created. This provides type safety by not allowing you to add an item that is not of the same data type that was defined for the class. It also improves performance because the item does not have to be converted to and from the `Object` data type. The data type for the item will be defined using the data type that was defined for the class. You'll see how all of this works in more detail as you explore the rest of the code and as you go through the debugging process.

After adding the `Generics` class, you modify the class by adding a type constraint using the `Of` keyword and defining a type list, which in this case contains only one type. This type name is a placeholder that will be used throughout the class to represent the data type that this class will be working with. The actual data type is defined when an object of the class is created, as you'll see later in your code:

```
Public Class Generics(Of elementType)

End Class
```

You add two private variables to this class, with both of these variables being defined as an array. The first variable is a defined as a `String` data type, while the second variable is defined as a generic data type which will be set when an object of the class is created. Notice that you have used the type name `elementType`, which was defined at the class level. This type name will be replaced automatically by the data type that is used to create the `Generics` object.

```
Public Class Generics(Of elementType)
    'This class provides a demonstration of Generics

    'Declare Private variables
    Private strKey() As String
    Private elmValue() As elementType
```

The Add method allows you to add items to your collection. Notice that this method accepts two parameters; one for the key and the other for the value, making a key/value pair. The key parameter is always a string value, and the value parameter will be defined using the data type that is used when a Generics collection is created.

The first thing that you want to do in this procedure is to see whether the variable arrays have been initialized. You do this by using the IsNot operator and comparing the strKey array to a value of Nothing. If the array is not equal to a value of Nothing, the array has already been initialized, and you simply need to increment the array dimension by 1. This is done by first getting the current upper bounds of the array and then adding 1 to it.

If the variable arrays have not been initialized, you need to initialize them using the ReDim statement as shown in the Else statement in the code that follows.

Once the arrays have been expanded or initialized, you then add the key and value to the arrays:

```
Public Sub Add(ByVal key As String, ByVal value As elementType)
    'Check to see if the objects have been initialized
    If strKey IsNot Nothing Then
        'Objects have been initialized
        ReDim Preserve strKey(strKey.GetUpperBound(0) + 1)
        ReDim Preserve elmValue(elmValue.GetUpperBound(0) + 1)
    Else
        'Initialize the objects
        ReDim strKey(0)
        ReDim elmValue(0)
    End If

    'Set the values
    strKey(strKey.GetUpperBound(0)) = key
    elmValue(elmValue.GetUpperBound(0)) = value
End Sub
```

You add two read-only properties to this class to return the key and the value for a key/value pair. Notice that the Value property is defined to return the data type that will be used when a Generics object is created.

```
Public ReadOnly Property Key(ByVal Index As Integer) As String
    Get
        Return strKey(Index)
    End Get
End Property

Public ReadOnly Property Value(ByVal Index As Integer) As elementType
    Get
```

```
            Return elmValue(Index)
        End Get
    End Property
End Class
```

The final class that you added was the Computer class. This class implements the IDisposable interface. An interface in this sense is a set of methods and properties common to all classes that implement it. In this case, the IDisposable interface contains methods for releasing memory resources when an object of the class is disposed of. Methods that use this class should call the Dispose method when they are through with a Computer object.

To implement the interface, you add the Implements statement and specify the IDisposable interface. Once you press the Enter key, Visual Studio 2005 adds the code from the IDisposable interface to your class, as shown in the code that follows.

```
Public Class Computer
    Implements IDisposable

    Private disposed As Boolean = False

    ' IDisposable
    Private Overloads Sub Dispose(ByVal disposing As Boolean)
        If Not Me.disposed Then
            If disposing Then
                ' TODO: put code to dispose managed resources
            End If

            ' TODO: put code to free unmanaged resources here
        End If
        Me.disposed = True
    End Sub

#Region " IDisposable Support "
    ' This code added by Visual Basic to correctly implement the disposable
pattern.
    Public Overloads Sub Dispose() Implements IDisposable.Dispose
        ' Do not change this code.  Put cleanup code in Dispose(ByVal disposing As
Boolean) above.
        Dispose(True)
        GC.SuppressFinalize(Me)
    End Sub

    Protected Overrides Sub Finalize()
        ' Do not change this code.  Put cleanup code in Dispose(ByVal disposing As
Boolean) above.
        Dispose(False)
        MyBase.Finalize()
    End Sub
#End Region

End Class
```

You add two read-only properties to this class; FreeMemory and TotalMemory. These properties will return the available memory on your computer as well as the total amount of memory on your computer. These properties use the My.Computer.Info namespace to access the amount of available memory and the total amount of memory.

The AvailablePhysicalMemory and TotalPhysicalMemory properties of the My.Computer.Info namespace return the available and total memory in bytes. However, we as users are used to seeing these numbers in kilobytes. Therefore you convert the number of bytes into kilobytes and then have that number formatted using commas.

> Remember that there are 1024 bytes to a kilobyte, 1024 kilobytes to a megabyte, and so on. The number that you pass to the Format function will be in kilobytes after you divide the number of bytes by 1024.

You'll then add a space to the formatted number and then the letter K indicating that the available and total memory figures are in kilobytes:

```
Public ReadOnly Property FreeMemory() As String
    Get
        'Using the My namespace
        Return Format(( _
            My.Computer.Info.AvailablePhysicalMemory.ToString \ 1024), _
            "#,###,##0") & " K"
    End Get
End Property

Public ReadOnly Property TotalMemory() As String
    Get
        'Using the My namespace
        Return Format(( _
            My.Computer.Info.TotalPhysicalMemory.ToString \ 1024), _
            "#,###,##0") & " K"
    End Get
End Property
```

You add code to the Debug form class next. This class uses a class List<T>, which is a generic list class. You'll be using this class to hold a list of Customer objects created from your Customer class. The List<T> class uses a dynamically sized array to hold the objects of the type that you specify: You need to *import* the System.Collections.Generic namespace in order to access the List<T> class. You accomplish that requirement by using an Imports statement.

```
Imports System.Collections.Generic
```

Next you define three private objects at the class level; these objects will be available to all procedures in this class. The first two objects use your Generics class. Remember that the Generics class used the Of keyword to define a type list. In the declaration of your objects, you use similar Of clauses to specify that the Generics class should be using a String data type in the type list for the first object and an Integer data type for the second object. The data type specified here will be applied throughout the Generics class.

The last object that you define here is an object that will hold an array of `Customer` objects created from your `Customer` class:

```
'Using the Generics class
Private objStringValues As New Generics(Of String)
Private objIntegerValues As New Generics(Of Integer)

'Using the List<T> class
Private objCustomerList As New List(Of Customer)
```

The `ListCustomer` procedure will simply accept a `Customer` object as input and will add the `Customer ID` and `Customer Name` to the list box on your form:

```
Private Sub ListCustomer(ByVal customerToList As Customer)
    lstData.Items.Add(customerToList.CustomerID & _
        " - " & customerToList.CustomerName)
End Sub
```

The Click event handler for the Start button contains the rest of the code for your project. You start this procedure by declaring a local `String` variable that will be used to demonstrate checking to see whether a variable has been initialized.

The code following the variable declaration checks the length of the variable and then adds the contents of the variable to the list box on the form.

```
Private Sub btnStart_Click(ByVal sender As Object, _
    ByVal e As System.EventArgs) Handles btnStart.Click

    'Declare variables
    Dim strData As String

    lstData.Items.Add("String variable data:")
    If strData.Length > 0 Then
        lstData.Items.Add(strData)
    End If
```

Since you will be writing the various results of your processing to the list box on your form, you'll want to add a blank entry to the list box to separate your results for aesthetic reasons, which is what the next line of code does. Here you simply use the `Empty` method of the `String` class to return an empty string to be added to the list box.

```
'Add an empty string to the ListBox
lstData.Items.Add(String.Empty)
```

This next section of code demonstrates the use of the `List<T>` class, as the comment in the code indicates. You add two new `Customer` objects to the `objCustomerList` object and then display those customers in the list box. Using a `For Each ... Next` loop to iterate through the collection of `Customer` objects, you add each customer to the list box by calling the `ListCustomer` function passing that function the `Customer` object.

```
'Demonstrates the use of the List<T> class
lstData.Items.Add("Customers in the Customer Class:")
```

```
objCustomerList.Add(New Customer(1001, "Henry For"))
objCustomerList.Add(New Customer(1002, "Orville Wright"))
For Each objCustomer As Customer In objCustomerList
    ListCustomer(objCustomer)
Next
```

Again you add a blank entry to the list box and use the objects that were defined using your Generics class. The first object, objStringValues, uses the Generics class with a String data type, as the object name indicates. Remember that the Add method in this class accepts a key/value pair and that the key parameter is always a String value. The value parameter uses the data type that was used to initialize this class, which in this case is also a string.

Once you add a key/value pair to your objStringValues object, you want to display that data in the list box on your form. You do this by accessing the Key and Value properties in the Generics class from which this object was derived:

```
'Add an empty string to the ListBox
lstData.Items.Add(String.Empty)

'Demonstrates the use of Generics
lstData.Items.Add("Generics Class Key/Value Pairs using String Values:")
objStringValues.Add("1001", "Henry Ford")
lstData.Items.Add(objStringValues.Key(0) & " = " & _
    objStringValues.Value(0))
```

Again you add another blank line to the list box and then add a key/value pair that uses an Integer data type for the value parameter to the objIntegerValues object. Then you add that key/value pair to the list box.

```
'Add an empty string to the ListBox
lstData.Items.Add(String.Empty)

'Demonstrates the use of Generics
lstData.Items.Add("Generics Class Key/Value Pairs using Integer Values:")
objIntegerValues.Add("Henry Ford", 1001)
lstData.Items.Add(objIntegerValues.Key(0) & " = " & _
    objIntegerValues.Value(0))
```

After you add another blank line to the list box, you use a Using . . . End Using block to create a new object of the Computer class, add the free memory and total memory of your computer to the list box, and then dispose of the Computer class.

When you use a class, you typically instantiate it using the New keyword as you did with your Generics class, use the class and then dispose of the class by calling its Dispose method if it implements one. The problem with that scenario is that when an exception occurs, the resource may or may not be disposed of. Even if you implement the code using structure error handling, a topic I'll discuss later in this chapter, you are not always guaranteed to be able to dispose of the class.

The Using statement is an efficient means of acquiring a resource, using it, and then disposing of it, regardless of whether an exception occurs. There is one caveat to this: the class that you use in a Using . . . End Using block must implement the IDisposable interface. This is why you added this interface to your Computer class.

Notice in the following code that the object name, objMemory, has not been defined anywhere except in the Using statement. The Using statement takes care of declaring this object for you and sets it to a new instance of the class that you specify, which in this case is the Computer class. Keep in mind that the object, objMemory, will be local to the Using . . . End Using block and you can only reference it within this block.

When the End Using statement is reached, the CLR (Common Language Runtime) will automatically call the Dispose method on the Computer class, thereby releasing its reference to it, and the Computer class will execute any cleanup code that has been implemented in the Dispose method.

```
'Add an empty string to the ListBox
lstData.Items.Add(String.Empty)

'Demonstrates the use of the Using statement
'Allows acquisition, usage and disposal of the resource
lstData.Items.Add("Computer Class Properties:")
Using objMemory As New Computer
    lstData.Items.Add("FreeMemory = " & objMemory.FreeMemory)
    lstData.Items.Add("TotalMemory = " & objMemory.TotalMemory)
End Using
```

Once again you add another blank line to the list box, and then you get to the final bit of code in this procedure. In this section of code I wanted to demonstrate the use of the Continue statement. The Continue statement is an efficient means of immediately transferring control to the next iteration of a loop. Instead of coding a lot of If . . . Then statements in a loop, you can merely test to see whether a condition is what you want and if it is not, you can call the Continue statement to pass control to the next iteration of a Do, For, or While loop.

Take a look at the code that you have here. First you declare a couple of variables and set their values. The first variable, strPassword, is declared and set to a password that contains upper- and lowercase letters. The second variable, strLowerCaseLetters, is declared and set to an empty string so that the variable is initialized.

Next, you set up a For . . . Next loop to check each character in the strPassword variable. The If . . . Then statement uses the Like operator to compare a character in the password variable to a pattern of letters. If a match is found, the Like operator will return a value of True. However, you are using a negative comparison here, because you have included the Not keyword in the If . . . Then statement, so if the character in the password variable is not like one of the letters in the pattern, [a-z], you'll execute the next statement, which is the Continue statement.

If the character in the password variable is a lowercase letter, you concatenate the character to the strLowerCaseLetters variable, which is why you needed to initialize this variable to an empty string when you declared it.

Finally, after all lowercase letters have been extracted from the password variable, you display the results of the strLowerCaseLetters variable in the list box on your form.

```
'Add an empty string to the ListBox
lstData.Items.Add(String.Empty)

'Demonstrates the use of the Continue statement
```

```
Dim strPassword As String = "POpPassword"
Dim strLowerCaseLetters As String = String.Empty
'Extract lowercase characters from string
For intIndex As Integer = 0 To strPassword.Length - 1
    'Demonstrates the use of the Continue statement
    'If no uppercase character is found, continue the loop
    If Not strPassword.Substring(intIndex, 1) Like "[a-z]" Then
        'No uppercase character found, continue loop
        Continue For
    End If
    'Lowercase character found, save it
    strLowerCaseLetters &= strPassword.Substring(intIndex, 1)
Next

'Display lowercase characters
lstData.Items.Add("Password lower case characters:")
lstData.Items.Add(strLowerCaseLetters)
End Sub
```

At this point you are probably pretty eager to run your project and test your code. In this next Try It Out, you will examine the Exception Assistant in Visual Studio 2005. This useful assistant provides help when an unhandled exception occurs in your code.

Try It Out   Exception Assistant

1. Start your project by clicking the Start button on the toolbar or by clicking the Debug menu and choosing the Start menu item.

2. When your form is displayed, click the Start button on your form to have your code in the `Click` event handler for the Start button executed. You'll immediately see the Exception Assistant shown in Figure 9-8.

Notice that the Exception Assistant dialog box displays the type of exception that occurred in the title bar of the dialog box. It also provides links to some basic troubleshooting tips and also a link at the bottom that provides the details of the exception.

Figure 9-8

3. Click the View Detail link in Exception Assistant dialog box to view the View Detail dialog box shown in Figure 9-9. You are mainly interested in the exception message, and, as you can see, it informs you that the object reference has not been set to an instance of an object. Basically, you have not initialized the variable strData.

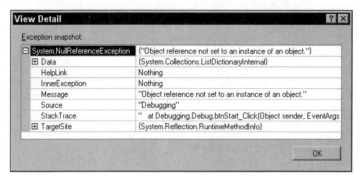

Figure 9-9

4. Click the OK button to close the View Detail dialog box and then click the X in the upper right-hand corner of the Exception Assistant dialog box to close it.

5. Now click the Stop Debugging button on the toolbar or click the Debug menu and select the Stop Debugging menu item.

6. Locate the following section of code at the beginning of the btnStart_Click procedure:

```
If strData.Length > 0 Then
    lstData.Items.Add(strData)
End If
```

7. Modify that code as shown here:

```
If strData IsNot Nothing Then
    If strData.Length > 0 Then
        lstData.Items.Add(strData)
    End If
Else
    strData = "String now initialized"
    lstData.Items.Add(strData)
End If
```

8. Now run your project and click the Start button on your form once it is displayed. All of your code should have executed, and the list box should be populated with the various results of the processing that took place in the btnStart_Click procedure.

How It Works

When an unhandled error occurs in your code while debugging, the Exception Assistant dialog box is displayed and provides troubleshooting tips for the exception as well as a link to view the details of the exception as was shown in Figure 9-8. Figure 9-9 displayed the View Detail dialog box which provides the detailed information about the exception which can also be an invaluable tool for determining the exact cause of the exception.

You modified the code that caused the error as shown here. Because the string variable strData was declared but never initialized, the variable is Nothing. This means that it has not been set to an instance of the String class and therefore the properties and methods of the variable cannot be referenced without causing a NullReferenceException as shown in Figure 9-8.

To rectify this problem, you first test the strData variable to see if it is not equal to Nothing by using the IsNot operator as shown in the first line of code here. If the variable has been initialized, then you can execute the code in the If statement. Otherwise, processing falls through to the Else statement and here you set the variable to a string constant and then display the contents of the variable in the list box.

```
If strData IsNot Nothing Then
    If strData.Length > 0 Then
        lstData.Items.Add(strData)
    End If
Else
    strData = "String now initialized"
    lstData.Items.Add(strData)
End If
```

An alternative to the previous code example would be to use a Try...Catch block to handle the exception. This technique will be demonstrated later in this chapter.

Setting Breakpoints

When trying to debug a large program, you may find that you want to debug only a section of code, that is, you want your code to run up to a certain point and then stop. This is where breakpoints come in handy; they cause execution of your code to stop anywhere a breakpoint is set. You can set breakpoints anywhere in your code and your code will run up to that point and stop.

> Note that execution of the code will stop before the line on which the breakpoint is set.

You can set breakpoints when you write your code, and you can also set them at run time by switching to your code and setting the breakpoint at the desired location. You cannot set a breakpoint while your program is actually executing a section of code such as the code in a loop, but you can when the program is idle and waiting for user input.

When the development environment encounters a breakpoint, execution of your code halts, and your program is considered to be in break mode. While your program is in break mode, a lot of debugging features are available. In fact, a lot of debugging features are available to you only while your program is in break mode.

You can set breakpoints by clicking the gray margin next to the line of code on which you want to set the breakpoint. When the breakpoint is set, you will see a solid red circle in the gray margin and the line will be highlighted in red. When you are done with a particular breakpoint you can remove it by clicking the solid red circle. You see more of this in the Try It Out exercise in this section.

Sometimes you'll want to debug code in a loop, such as one that reads data from a file. You know that the first x number of records are good, and it is time-consuming to step through all the code repetitively until you get to what you suspect is the bad record. A breakpoint can be set inside the loop and you can set a hit counter on it. The code inside the loop will execute the number of times that you specified in the hit counter and then stop and place you in break mode. This can be a real time saver, and you will be taking a look at breakpoint hit counts later in this section. You can also set a condition on a breakpoint, such as when a variable contains a certain value or when the value of a variable changes. You also take a look at this later in this section.

Before you begin, you should display the Debug toolbar in the development environment, because this will make it easier to quickly see and choose the debugging options that you want. You can do this in one of two ways. Either right-click an empty space on the current toolbar and choose Debug in the context menu or select View ➪ Toolbars ➪ Debug from the menu.

Try It Out   Working with Breakpoints

1. The first thing that you want to do is to set a breakpoint in your code. Using Figure 9-10 as a guide, set the breakpoint in your code by clicking the gray margin to the left of the line of code shown.

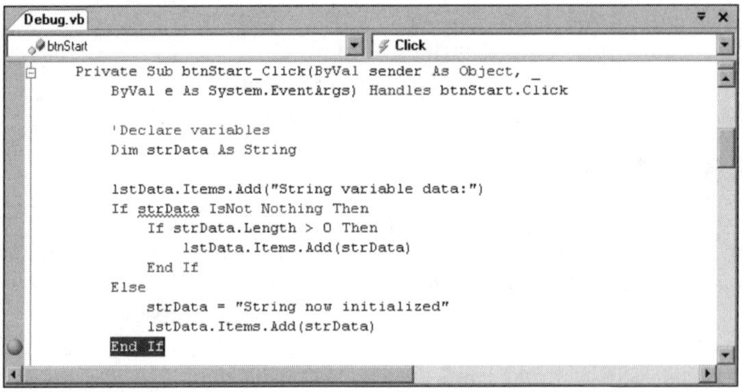

```
Debug.vb                                                        ▼ ✕
btnStart                              ▼    ⚡ Click                ▼
    Private Sub btnStart_Click(ByVal sender As Object, _
        ByVal e As System.EventArgs) Handles btnStart.Click

        'Declare variables
        Dim strData As String

        lstData.Items.Add("String variable data:")
        If strData IsNot Nothing Then
            If strData.Length > 0 Then
                lstData.Items.Add(strData)
            End If
        Else
            strData = "String now initialized"
            lstData.Items.Add(strData)
        End If
```

Figure 9-10

2. Now run the project.

3. To get to the code where the breakpoint is set, click the Start button on your form. The code executes up to the breakpoint, and the development environment window receives focus, making it the topmost window. The entire line should be highlighted in yellow and the breakpoint circle in the margin should now contain a yellow arrow in it pointing to the line of code where execution has been paused, which is the End If statement that was shown in Figure 9-10.

    Also notice that there are a few new windows at the bottom of the development environment. What you see will vary depending on which windows you have specified to be shown — you can choose different ones using the tabs at the bottom.

Take a pause in the Try It Out to learn about some of the features of the IDE in debug mode.

The Breakpoints Window

You can display the Breakpoints window, if the tab is not shown, in the bottom-right of the IDE by clicking the Breakpoints icon on the Debug toolbar or by selecting Debug ➪ Windows ➪ Breakpoints. The Breakpoints window shows what line of code the current breakpoint is at, any conditions it has, and the hit count if applicable, as shown in Figure 9-11.

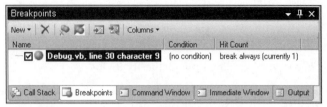

Figure 9-11

The Breakpoints window shows all the breakpoints you have set in your code. When a breakpoint is encountered, it is highlighted in the code and also highlighted in the Breakpoint window, as shown in Figure 9-11. In this window, you can set new breakpoints, delete existing breakpoints, and change the properties of the breakpoints. You will see more of this later in the chapter.

Useful Icons on the Debug Toolbar

In this Try It Out, you want to step through your code line by line. On the Debug toolbar there are three icons of particular interest to you as shown in Figure 9-12.

❑ The first icon is the Step Into icon. When you click this icon, you can step through your code line by line. This includes stepping into any function or procedure that the code calls and working through it line by line.

❑ The second icon is the Step Over icon. This works in a similar way to Step Into, but you pass straight over the procedures and functions — they still execute, but all in one go. You then move straight on to the next line in the block of code that called the procedure.

❑ Last is the Step Out icon. This icon allows you to jump to the end of the procedure or function that you are currently in and to move to the line of code *after* the line that called the procedure or function. This is handy when you step into a long procedure and want to get out of it. The rest of the code in the procedure still gets executed, but you do not step through it.

Figure 9-12

There is one more really useful button worth adding to the toolbar: Run To Cursor. The Run To Cursor icon enables you to place your cursor anywhere in the code following the current breakpoint where execution has been paused and then click this icon. The code between the current breakpoint and where the cursor is positioned will be executed, and execution will stop on the line of code where the cursor is located.

To add this button, you right-click any empty area of the toolbar and choose Customize from the context menu. In the Customize dialog, click the Commands tab, and then select Debug in the Categories list. In the Commands list, select Run To Cursor. After you select Run To Cursor, you drag its icon from the Commands list onto the debug toolbar, to form a group of icons as shown in Figure 9-13, and then click the Close button to close the Customize dialog box.

Figure 9-13

You are now ready to continue working through the Try It Out.

Try It Out   Working with Breakpoints (cont.)

1. You ended the last step of the Try It Out at the breakpoint. Before continuing, you want to examine the contents of the string variable, strData. Hover your mouse over the variable to view a Data Tip, as shown in Figure 9-14. Notice that the variable name is listed along with its contents, a magnifying glass, and a down arrow.

Clicking the contents of the variable in the Data Tip puts you in edit mode for the variable, and you can actually change the contents of that variable. Clicking the magnifying glass will cause the contents of the variable to be displayed automatically in the Text Visualizer dialog box, which is a useful tool for displaying the data for string variables that contain a significant amount of data. Clicking the down arrow provides you a drop-down list of options for viewing the contents of the variable and will contain an option for Text Visualizer, XML Visualizer, and HTML Visualizer.

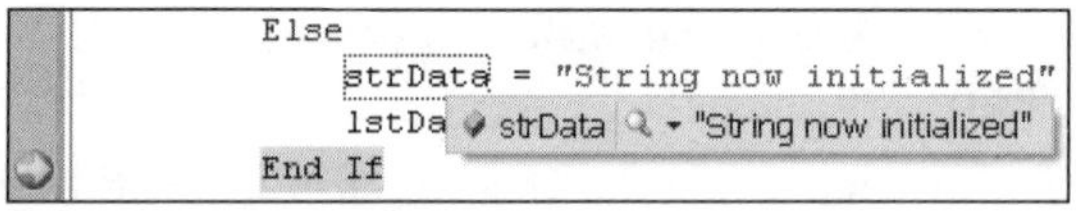

```
        Else
            strData = "String now initialized"
            lstDa ✓ strData 🔍 ▾ "String now initialized"
        End If
```

Figure 9-14

2. Now you'll want to test the debugging icons on the toolbar, starting with the Run To Cursor icon first. Place your cursor on the line of code that calls the ListCustomer procedure as shown in Figure 9-15.

Now click the Run To Cursor icon on the toolbar. The code between the breakpoint at the End If statement shown in Figure 9-14 and the line of code that calls the ListCustomer procedure, shown in Figure 9-15, will be executed. Your project will stop execution on the line of code on which you have your cursor.

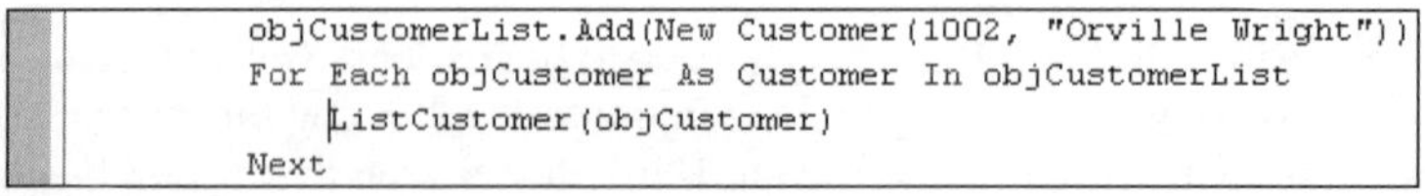

```
        objCustomerList.Add(New Customer(1002, "Orville Wright"))
        For Each objCustomer As Customer In objCustomerList
            ListCustomer(objCustomer)
        Next
```

Figure 9-15

3. Click the Step Into icon next, and you should now be at the beginning of the `ListCustomer` procedure. Data Tips can be displayed for objects that contain multiple values as well as variables that contain only a single value.

   Hover your mouse over the `customerToList` parameter for this procedure to display the Data Tip for this object. You'll see a plus sign next to the object name in the Data Tip. Click the plus sign, or simply hover your mouse over it, and the contents of the object will be displayed as shown in Figure 9-16.

   Notice that this Data Tip not only displays the properties in the `Customer` class, the class that the `customerToList` object is derived from, but also the private variables in that class. You also have the same options for viewing the contents of string variables, which is indicated by the presence of the magnifying glass and down arrow icons.

   Since the text, which is supposed to read `"Henry Ford"`, is misspelled, you'll want to correct it in the Data Tip. This can be done by editing either the property `CustomerName` or the `strName` variable in the Data Tip. Click on the text `"Henry For"` in the Data Tip to be put into edit mode. Correct the text by adding the letter `d` at the end of the text and then click the name or variable name in the Data Tip. Notice that the text for both the property and variable has been updated with your corrections.

   It should be noted that you can change the contents of `Integer` data types in the Data Tip as well.

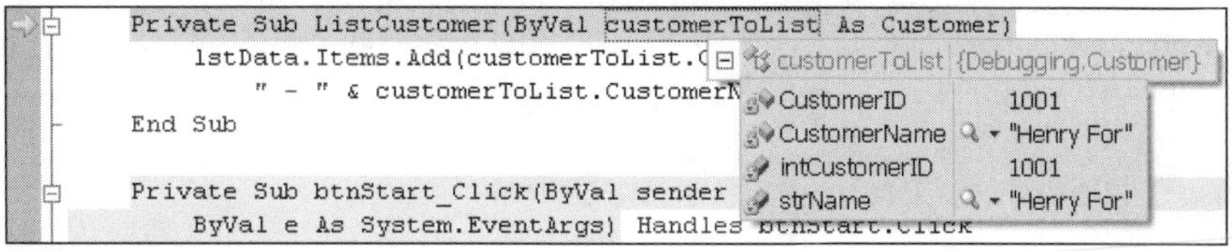

Figure 9-16

4. Click the Step Into icon once more and you should be at the first line of code in the `ListCustomer` procedure.

5. Since you do not want to see any of this code at this time, you are going to step out of this procedure. This places you back at the line of code that called this procedure. Click the Step Out icon. Notice that you are taken out of the `ListCustomer` procedure and back to where the call originated.

6. Now click the Step Into icon twice more so that you are back at the call to the `ListCustomer` procedure once again.

7. The final icon to be tested is the Step Over icon. Click this icon now and notice that you have totally stepped over the execution of the `ListCustomer` procedure. The procedure was actually executed. However, since you chose to step over it, the debugger does not show you that the procedure was executed.

8. Now you want to continue processing as normal and have the rest of the code execute without interruption. If you hover your mouse over the Start icon on the toolbar, you will notice that the ToolTip has been changed from Start to Continue. Click this icon to let the rest of the code run. You should now see your completed form as shown in Figure 9-17.

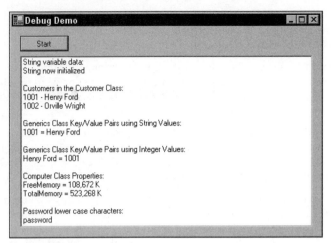

Figure 9-17

In the next Try It Out, you will be examining the Breakpoint Hit Count dialog box. The Breakpoint Hit Count dialog box allows you to define the number of executions of a loop should be performed before the IDE stops execution of your code and puts it into break mode. As we have already described, this is useful for processing loops, because you can specify how many iterations the loop should make before you encounter a breakpoint.

Try It Out   Using the Breakpoint's Hit Count

1. Stop your project and set a breakpoint in the For loop as shown in Figure 9-18. Remember that to set a breakpoint, you need to click in the gray margin on the line of code where the breakpoint should be.

    Now start your project again by clicking the Start icon on the toolbar.

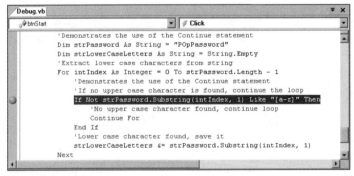

Figure 9-18

2. In the Breakpoints window, right-click the second breakpoint and choose Hit Count from the context menu to invoke the Breakpoint Hit Count dialog box.

3. The breakpoint that you currently have set will halt execution every time it is encountered. Change it to break only when the loop enters its third execution. You do this by selecting "break when the hit count is equal to" in the drop-down list and then entering the number **3** in the text box displayed next to it, as shown in Figure 9-19.

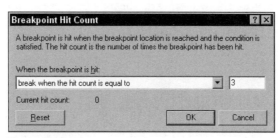

Breakpoint Hit Count

A breakpoint is hit when the breakpoint location is reached and the condition is satisfied. The hit count is the number of times the breakpoint has been hit.

When the breakpoint is hit:

`break when the hit count is equal to`   `3`

Current hit count: 0

Reset   OK   Cancel

Figure 9-19

Click the OK button to close this dialog box. Notice the Hit Count column in the Breakpoints window in the IDE. The second breakpoint now displays the Hit Count condition that you just defined.

4. At this point, click the Start button on the form. By clicking the Start button you are again stopped at your first breakpoint.

5. This breakpoint is highlighted in the Breakpoints window. You no longer need this breakpoint, so click it and then click the Delete icon in the Breakpoints window; the breakpoint will be deleted. Your code is still paused at this point, so click the Continue button on the Debug toolbar.

6. You are now stopped at your breakpoint in the `For` loop as it enters its third execution. Notice that the Breakpoints window shows the hit count criteria that you selected and also the current hit count.

As you can see, this is a handy way to have a loop execute a definite number of iterations before breaking at a defined breakpoint.

7. Now let your code continue executing by clicking the Continue button on the Debug toolbar.

8. Stop your project once the form has been displayed.

In this next Try It Out, you'll modify the properties of the only breakpoint that you have left.

Try It Out   Changing Breakpoint Properties

1. In the last Try It Out, you modified the breakpoint while the project was running. This time you'll modify the breakpoint while the project is stopped. To view the Breakpoints window, click the Debug menu, choose Windows, and then choose the Breakpoints sub menu item.

2. In the Breakpoints window right-click the breakpoint, and choose Hit Count from the context menu to display the Breakpoint Hit Count dialog box. Notice the Reset button. When you click this button, you reset the hit counter for the next execution, but this is not what you'll do at this point.

3. Here you'll change the hit count back to its original setting. Select "break always" in the drop-down box and then click the OK button to close this dialog box.

4. To set a specific condition for this breakpoint, right-click the breakpoint and choose Condition from the context menu to invoke Breakpoint Condition dialog box. Enter the condition as shown in Figure 9-20. This will cause this breakpoint to break only when the variable intIndex is equal to 3. Notice that you could also specify that the breakpoint would be activated when the value of a variable changes. Click the OK button to close the dialog box and then start your project.

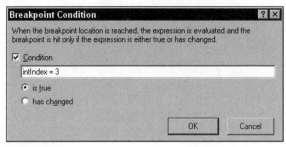

Figure 9-20

5. Now click the Start button on your form. Once the intIndex variable is equal to 3, the break-point will be activated, and the execution of the code will be paused at the line where the break-point is specified. Notice that this is actually your fourth time into the loop, as the For ... Next loop specifies a starting index of 0 for the variable intIndex.

6. Finally, go ahead and let your code finish executing by clicking the Continue button on the Debug toolbar. Once your form is displayed, go ahead and stop your project.

Debugging Using the Watch Window

The Watch window provides a method for you to watch variables and expressions easily while the code is executing — this can be invaluable when you are trying to debug unwanted results in a variable. You can even change the values of variables in the Watch window. You can also add as many variables and expressions as needed to debug your program. This provides a mechanism that allows you to watch the values of your variables change without any intervention on your part.

You can add and delete a variable or expression to the QuickWatch dialog box only when your program is in break mode. Therefore, before you run your program, you need to set a breakpoint before the vari-able or expression that you want to watch. Once the breakpoint has been reached, you can add as many Watch variables or expressions as needed.

In the following Try It Out, you add the intIndex variable to the Watch window and also add an expression using the intIndex variable. This enables you to observe this variable and expression as you step through your code.

Try It Out   **Using QuickWatch**

1.   Start your program again. When your form displays, switch to the IDE and clear the current breakpoint by deleting it in the Breakpoints window or by clicking it in the gray margin where it is set. Then set a new breakpoint as shown in Figure 9-21.

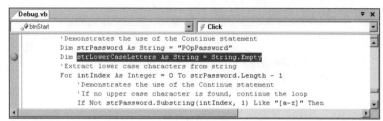

Figure 9-21

2.   You can only add a QuickWatch variable or expression while your program is paused. Click the Start button on the form so the breakpoint will be encountered and your program paused.

3.   Once the breakpoint has been encountered, right-click the variable, intIndex, in the For . . . Next loop and choose QuickWatch from the context menu to invoke the QuickWatch dialog box. Notice that this variable has not only been added to the Expression drop-down box but has also been placed in the Current value grid in the dialog, as shown in Figure 9-22. Click the Add Watch button to add this variable to the Watch window.

Since the variable is declared in the For . . . Next *loop, you see an error here. You can safely ignore this error, because once the loop has started processing, the variable will be declared.*

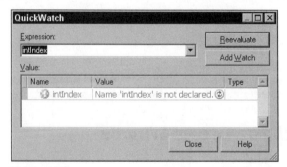

Figure 9-22

4.   While you have the QuickWatch dialog box open, set an expression to be evaluated. Add the expression **intIndex = 1** in the Expression drop-down box. Then click the Add Watch button to have this expression added to the Watch window. Now close the QuickWatch dialog box by clicking the Close button.

5.   If you do not see the Watch window at the bottom of the IDE, select Debug ⇨ Windows ⇨ Watch ⇨ Watch 1. You should now see a variable and an expression in the Watch window as shown in Figure 9-23.

The second watch expression that you added here will return a value of True when the intIndex variable equals 1, so Visual Studio 2005 will set the type to Boolean once you enter the For . . . Next loop.

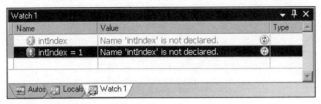

Figure 9-23

6. Step through your code line by line so that you can watch the value of the variable and expression change. Click the Step Into icon on the Debug toolbar to step to the next line of code. Keep clicking the Step Into icon to see the values of the variable and expression in the Watch window change.

As you step through the loop in your code, you will continue to see the value for the intIndex *variable change in the Watch window. When the value of the variable in the Watch window turns color, as shown in Figure 9-24, the value has just been changed. You can manually change the value anytime by entering a new value in the Value column in the Watch window.*

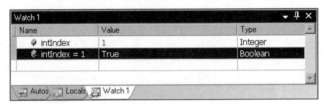

Figure 9-24

7. When you are done, click the Continue icon on the Debug toolbar to let your code finish executing. Then stop your project once the form has been displayed.

Debugging with the Locals Window

The Locals window is similar to the Watch window, except that it shows all variables and objects for the current function or procedure. The Locals window also lets you change the value of a variable or object, and the same rules that apply to the Watch window apply here (that is, the program must be paused before a value can be changed). The text for a value that has just changed also turns red, making it easy to spot the variable or object that has just changed.

The Locals window is great if you want a quick glance at everything that is going on in a function or procedure, but it is not very useful for watching the values of one or two variables or expressions. The reason for this is that the Locals window contains all variables and objects in a procedure or function. Therefore, if you have a lot of variables and objects, you will have to scroll through the window constantly to view the various variables and objects. This is where the Watch window comes in handy; it lets you watch just the variables that you need. In this Try It Out, you examine the contents of the Locals window in two different procedures. This will demonstrate how the contents of the Locals window change from one procedure to the next.

Try It Out   Using the Locals Window

1. To prepare for this exercise, you need to have the current breakpoint set and set a new breakpoint in the `ListCustomer` procedure. Locate the `ListCustomer` procedure and set a breakpoint on the one line of code in that procedure:

    ```
    lstData.Items.Add(customerToList.CustomerID & _
        " - " & customerToList.CustomerName)
    ```

2. Now start your program.

3. If you do not see the Locals window at the bottom of the IDE, select Debug ⇨ Windows ⇨ Locals. Notice that at this point the Locals window contains no variables or objects. This is because you have not entered a procedure or function. Click the Start button on the form, and your breakpoint in the `ListCustomer` procedure will be encountered first and execution will be paused.

4. Notice the various objects and their types listed in the Locals window. The first item in the list is `Me`, which is the form itself. If you expand this item, you will see all the objects and controls associated with your form. If you expand the `customerToList` object, you'll see the properties and variables defined in the `Customer` class from which this object is derived as shown in Figure 9-25.

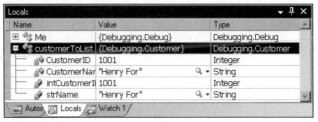

Figure 9-25

5. Now click the Continue icon on the Debug toolbar until you encounter your second breakpoint.

6. Now take a look at the Locals window, and you will see a different set of objects and variables. The one constant item in both procedures is `Me`, which is associated with the form.

7. If you step through a couple of lines of code in the loop where the breakpoint has paused your program, you will see the values in the Locals window change, and when a value changes it turns red. This is the same behavior that you saw in the Watch window. You can continue to step through your code, or you can click the Continue icon on the Debug toolbar to let your program run to completion.

After you change your build configuration from Debug to Release, debugging is no longer available; even if you have breakpoints set in your code, they will not be encountered.

8. To clear all breakpoints in your code, you can delete each breakpoint in the Breakpoints window, or you can click the Debug menu and choose Delete All Breakpoints. Once you are done, stop your project.

Error Handling

Error handling is an essential part of any good code. In Visual Basic 2005 the error mechanism is based on the concept of *exceptions* that can be *thrown* to raise an error and *caught* when the error is handled. If you do not provide any type of error handling and an error occurs, your user will receive a message about an unhandled exception, which is provided by the CLR, and then the program may terminate, depending on the type of error encountered. This is not a user-friendly message and does not inform the user about the true nature of the error or how to resolve it. The unhandled error could also cause users to lose the data that they were working with or leave the user and the data in an unknown state.

Visual Studio 2005 provides *structured error-handling* statements that are common across all languages. Structured error handling is a way to organize blocks of code in a structure that will handle errors. In this section you examine structured error handling and how it can be incorporated into your programs with very little effort.

Structured error handling in Visual Studio 2005 is incorporated with the `Try...Catch...Finally` block. You execute the code that might throw an exception in the `Try` block, and you handle anticipated errors in the `Catch` block. The `Finally` block, which is optional, is always executed, if present, and allows you to place any cleanup code there regardless of whether an error has occurred. If an error occurs that was not handled in the `Catch` block, the CLR will display its standard error message and terminate your program. Therefore, it is important to try to anticipate all possible errors for the code that is contained in the `Try` block.

Take a look at the syntax for the `Try...Catch...Finally` statement:

```
Try
    [try statements]
Catch exceptionvariable As exceptiontype
    [catch statements]
[Additional Catch blocks]
Finally
    [finallystatements]
End Try
```

❑ The try statements are the statements to be executed that may cause an error.

❑ The `exceptionvariable` can be any variable name. It will be set to contain the value of the error that is thrown.

❑ The `exceptiontype` specifies the exception class type type that the exception belongs to. If this type is not supplied, your `Catch` block will handle any exception defined in the `System.Exception` class. This argument allows you to specify the type of exception that you maybe looking for. An example of a specific exception is `IOException`, which is used when performing any type of IO (input/output) against a file.

❑   The catch statements are the statements that handle and process the error that has occurred.

❑   The finally statements are the statements to be executed after all other processing has occurred.

You can have multiple Catch blocks, meaning that you can test for multiple errors with different exception types within the same Try block. When an error occurs among the try statements, control is passed to the appropriate Catch block for processing.

When you define a Catch block, you can specify a variable name for the exception and define the type of exception you want to catch, as shown in the following code fragment. This code defines an exception variable with a name of IOExceptionErr, and the type of exception is an IOException. This example traps any type of IO exception that may occur when processing files and stores the error information in an object named IOExceptionErr:

```
Catch IOExceptionErr As IOException
   ...
   code to handle the exception goes here
   ...
```

When dealing with mathematical expressions, you can define and catch the various errors that you may encounter such as a divide-by-zero exception. You can also catch errors such as overflow errors, which may occur when multiplying two numbers and trying to place the result in a variable that is too small for the result. However, in cases such as these, it may be better to check for problems in advance — you should use exceptions only in exceptional circumstances.

Using Structured Error Handling

In the next Try It Out you add some structured error handling to the sample program with which you have been working. When you first ran the Debugging project you received the NullReferenceException that was shown in Figure 9-8, because you tried to access the properties of the strData string variable before it had been set. This code is a prime candidate for structured error handling. You temporarily bypassed the problem at that point by using an If . . . Then . . . Else statement to first see whether the variable had been initialized. A cleaner way to handle such a case is in a Try . . . Catch block.

Try It Out   Structured Error Handling

1.   Modify the code for the strData variable in the btnStart_Click procedure as shown:

```
lstData.Items.Add("String variable data:")
Try
    If strData.Length > 0 Then
        lstData.Items.Add(strData)
    End If
Catch NullReferenceExceptionErr As NullReferenceException
    strData = "String now initialized"
    lstData.Items.Add(strData)
End Try
```

How It Works

The code you entered contains a `Try` block and a `Catch` block. You have opted not to use the `Finally` block in this error-handling routine because the `Catch` block performs the necessary code to set the `strData` variable and have the contents of that variable added to the list box on your form:

```
Try
    If strData.Length > 0 Then
        lstData.Items.Add(strData)
    End If
Catch NullReferenceExceptionErr As NullReferenceException
    strData = "String now initialized"
    lstData.Items.Add(strData)
End Try
```

When you try to access the `Length` property of the `strData` variable in the `Try` block, a `Null ReferenceException` exception will be thrown because the variable has been declared but not set.

The error that you want to trap is a `NullReferenceException`, and that exception is specified in the `Catch` block. You defined the variable `NullReferenceExceptionErr` for the exception variable argument; as the standard practice among most developers is to use the exception name along with a suffix of `Err`. You then defined the type of exception that you want to test for and trap.

You place your error-handling code within the `Catch` block, as you have done here. When a `Null ReferenceException` occurs, you set the `strData` variable to a string constant and then add the contents of that variable to the list box on your form.

Try It Out   Testing Your Error Handler

1. Set a breakpoint on the `Try` statement and then run your project. Once the form is displayed, click the Start button.

2. Once the breakpoint is encountered, right-click the variable `strData` and choose Add Watch from the context menu. Click the Watch 1 window so that you can view the contents of the variable.

3. At this point, the `strData` variable has a value of `Nothing`. Click the Step Into icon on the toolbar, and you'll be taken to the first line of code in the `Try` block.

4. Now click the Step Into icon again. A `NullReferenceException` will be thrown, and you'll be taken to the `Catch` block.

5. Note the value of the variable in the Watch 1 window, click the Step Into icon once more, and note the value of the variable in the Watch 1 window, as shown in Figure 9-26.

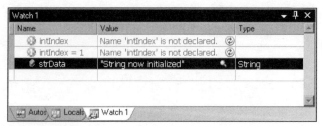

Figure 9-26

6. Click the Continue icon on the toolbar to allow the rest of your code to run.

As you become more familiar with the types of errors that can occur, you will be able to write more sophisticated structured error handlers. This comes only with experience and testing. You will discover more errors and will be able to handle them only by thoroughly testing your code. The online documentation for most methods that you use in Visual Studio 2005 will have Exceptions sections that list and explain the possible exceptions that could occur by using the method.

Summary

This chapter looked at some useful debugging tools that are built into the Visual Studio 2005 development environment. You saw how easy it is to debug your programs as you stepped through the various Try It Out sections.

Having thoroughly covered breakpoints, you saw how you can stop the execution of your program at any given point. As useful as this is, setting breakpoints with a hit counter in a loop is even more useful, because you are able to execute a loop several times before encountering a breakpoint in the loop.

You also examined some of the various windows available while debugging your program, such as the Locals window and the Watch window. These windows provide you with valuable information about the variables and expressions in your program. You are able to watch the values change and are able to change the values to control the execution of your code.

You should know what types of major errors you may encounter while developing and debugging your code. You should be able to recognize syntax and execution errors and possibly correct them. While debugging a program for logic errors may be difficult at first, it does become easier with time and experience.

This chapter also covered structured error handling, and you should incorporate this knowledge into your programs at every opportunity. Structured error handling provides you with the opportunity to handle and correct errors at runtime.

In summary, you should know the following:

- ❏ How to recognize and correct major types of errors
- ❏ How to successfully use breakpoints to debug your program
- ❏ How to use the Locals and Watch windows to see and change variables and expressions
- ❏ How to use structured error handling

Exercises

Exercise 1

Using your Debugging project, add a `Try . . . Catch` block to the `ListCustomer` procedure to handle an `Exception` error. In the `Catch` block, add code to display a message box with the error message.

Exercise 2

The `Try . . . Catch` block that you added in Exercise 1 should never throw an error. However, you can throw your own error so that you can test your code in the `Catch` block. Add a `Throw` statement as the first line of code in the `Try` block. Consult the online help for the syntax of the `Throw` statement.

Building Objects

You may have heard the term *object-oriented* a lot since you first started using computers. You may also have heard that it is a scary and tricky subject to understand. In its early years it was, but today's modern tools and languages make object orientation (OO) a wonderfully easy-to-understand concept that brings massive benefits to software developers. This is mainly because languages such as Visual Basic, C++, and of course Visual Basic 2005 and C# have matured to a point where they make creating objects and the software that uses them very easy indeed. With these development tools, you will have no problem understanding even the most advanced object-oriented concepts and will be able to use them to build exciting object-based applications.

You have been using objects and classes throughout this book, but in this chapter you'll look at object orientation in detail and build on the foundations of the previous chapters to start producing some cool applications using Visual Basic 2005.

In this chapter, you will:

❑ Build a reusable object with methods and properties

❑ Inherit the object that you build in another object

❑ Override methods and properties in your base object

❑ Create your own namespace

Understanding Objects

An object is almost anything you can think of. We work with physical objects all the time: televisions, cars, customers, reports, light bulbs — anything. In computer terms, an object is a representation of a thing that we want to manipulate in our application. Sometimes, the two definitions map exactly onto each other. So, if you have a physical car object sitting in your driveway and want to describe it in software terms, you build a software car object that sits in your computer.

Likewise, if you need to write a piece of software that generates a bill for a customer, you may well have a Bill object and a Customer object. The Customer object represents the customer and may be capable of having a name, address, and also have the capability to generate the bill. The Bill object would represent an instance of a bill for a customer and would be able to impart the details of the bill and may also have the capability to print itself.

What is important here is the concept that the object has the intelligence to produce actions related to it — the Customer object can generate the bill. In effect, if you have a Customer object representing a customer, you can simply say to it: "Produce a bill for me." The Customer object would then go away and do all the hard work related to creating the bill. Likewise, once you have a Bill object, you can say to it: "Print yourself." What you have here are two examples of object behavior.

Objects are unbelievably useful because they turn software engineering into something conceptually similar to wooden building blocks. You arrange the blocks (the objects) to build something greater than the sum of the parts. The power of objects comes from the fact that, as someone using objects, you don't need to understand how they work behind the scenes. You're familiar with this with real-world objects too. When you use a mobile phone, you don't need to understand how it works inside. Even if you do understand how a mobile phone works inside — even if you made it yourself — it's still much easier to use the mobile phone's simple interface. The interface can also prevent you from accidentally doing something that breaks the phone. The same is true with computer objects. Even if you build all the objects yourself, having the complicated workings hidden behind a simple interface can make your life much easier and safer.

Object orientation was first explained to me by using a television metaphor. Look at the television in your home. There are several things you know how to do with it:

- ❏ Watch the image on the screen
- ❏ Change channel
- ❏ Change volume
- ❏ Switch it on or off

What you don't have to do is understand how everything works to allow you to carry out these activities. If asked, I couldn't put together the components needed to make a modern television. I could, with a little research and patience, come up with something fairly basic, but nothing as complex as the one sitting in my home. However, I do understand how to use a television. I know how to change the channel, change the volume, switch it on and off, and so on.

Objects in software engineering work in basically the same way. Once you have an object, you can use it and ask it do things without having to understand how the internals of it actually work. This is phenomenally powerful, as you'll see soon.

Software objects typically have the following characteristics:

- ❏ **Identity** — *User:* "What are you?" *TV:* "I'm a TV."
- ❏ **State** — *User:* "What channel am I watching?" *TV:* "You're watching Channel 4."
- ❏ **Behavior** — *User:* "Please turn up the volume to 50%." Then, we can use the State again. *User:* "How loud is the volume?" *TV:* "50%."

Encapsulation

The core concept behind object-orientation is *encapsulation*. This is a big word, but it's very simple to understand. What this means is that the functionality is wrapped up in a self-contained manner and that you don't need to understand what it's actually doing when you ask it to do something.

If you remember in Chapter 3, you built a function that calculated the area of a circle. In that function, you encapsulated the logic of calculating the area in such a way that anyone using the function could find the area without having to know how to perform the operation. This is the same concept but taken to the next level.

> *Objects are often referred to as black boxes. If you imagine software objects as small plastic boxes with buttons on the top and connectors on the side, with a basic understanding of what the box does, together with a general understanding of how boxes generally plug together, you can build up a complex system with them without ever having to have the capability of building a box independently.*

Methods and Properties

You interact with objects through methods and properties. These can be defined as:

❑ *Methods* are ways of instructing an object to do something.

❑ *Properties* are things that describe features of an object.

A method was defined previously as a self-contained block of code that does something. This is true, but it is a rather simplistic definition. In fact the strict definition of a method applies only to OO and is a way to manipulate an object — a way to instruct it to perform certain behaviors. In previous chapters you created methods that instructed an object — in most cases a form — to do something. When you create a form in Visual Basic 2005, you are actually defining a new type of `Form` object.

So, if you need to turn on the TV, you need to find a method that does this, because a method is something you get the object to do. When you invoke the method, the object itself is supposed to understand what to do to satisfy the request. To drive the point home, you don't care what it actually does; you just say, "Switch on." It's up to the TV to switch on relays to deliver power, boot up the circuitry, warm up the electron gun, and all the other things that you don't need to understand!

> *Invoke means the same as call, but is more OO-friendly. It reminds us that we are invoking a method on something, rather than just calling a chunk of code.*

On the other hand, if you need to change the channel, you might set the channel property. If you want to tune into Channel 10, you set the channel property to the value 10. Again, the object is responsible for reacting to the request, and you don't care about the technical hoops it has to go through to do that.

Events

In Visual Basic 2005 you listen for events to determine when something has happened to a control on a form. You can consider an event as something that an object does. In effect, someone using an object can listen to events, like a Click event on a button or a PowerOn event on a TV. When the event is received, the developer can take some action. In OO terms, there is the SwitchOn method that gets invoked on the TV object; when the TV has warmed up (some old TVs take ages to warm up), it raises a PowerOn event. You could then respond to this event by adjusting the volume to the required level.

An event might also be used when the performer of an action is not the only entity interested in the action taking place. For example, when you have the TV on, you might go and get a drink during a commercial break. But while you're in the kitchen, you keep your ears open for when the program starts again. Effectively you are listening for a ProgramResume event. You do not cause the program to resume, but you do want to know when it does.

Visibility

To build decent objects you have to make them easy for other developers to use. For example, internally it might be really important for your TV object to know what frequency the tuner needs, but does the person using the TV care? More importantly, do you actually want the developer to be able to change this frequency directly? What you're trying to do is make the object more "abstract."

Some parts of your object will be private, whereas other parts will be public. The public interface is available for others to use. The private parts are what you expect the object itself to use internally. The logic for the object exists in the private parts and may include methods and properties that are important but won't get called from outside the object. For example, a TV object might have methods for ConnectPower, WarmUp, and so on. These would be private and would all be called from the public SwitchOn method. Similarly, while there is a public Channel property there will probably be a private Frequency property. The TV could not work without knowing the signal frequency it was receiving, but the users are only interested in the channel.

Now that you understand the basics of object orientation, take look at how you can use objects within an application.

You'll notice that some of the code samples you have seen in previous chapters included a line that looked similar to this:

```
lstData.Items.Add(strData)
```

That's a classic example of object orientation! lstData is, in fact, an object. Items is a property of the lstData object. The Items property is an object in its own right and has an Add method. The period (.) tells Visual Basic 2005 that the word to the right is a *member* of the word to the left. So, Items is a member of lstData and Add is a member of Items. Members are either properties or methods of an object.

lstData is an instance of a class called System.Windows.Forms.ListBox (or just ListBox). This class is part of the .NET Framework you learned about in Chapter 2.

The ListBox class can display a list of items on the form and let a user choose a particular one. Again, here's the concept of encapsulation. You as a user of ListBox don't need to know anything about technologies involved in displaying the list or listening for input. You may not have even heard of GDI+, stdin, keyboard drivers, display drivers, or anything else that goes into the complex action of displaying a list on a form, yet you still have the capability to do it.

The ListBox is an example of an object that you can see. Users can look at a program running and know that there is a ListBox involved. Most objects in OO programming are invisible and represent something in memory.

What Is a Class?

A *class* is the definition of a particular kind of object. The class is made up of the software code needed to store and retrieve the values of the properties, carry out the methods, and undergo the events pertaining to that kind of object. This is effectively the circuitry inside the black box. If you want to build a software object, you have to understand how the internals work. You express those internals with Visual Basic 2005 code. So, when the software developer using your object says "Turn up the volume," you have to know how to instruct the amplifier to increase the output. (As a side note, remember that the amplifier is just another object. You don't necessarily need to know how it works inside. In OO programming, you will often find that one object is made up of other objects with some code to link them — just as a TV is made of standard components and a bit of custom circuitry.)

Each object belonging to a class is an *instance* of the class. So, if you have 50 TV objects, you have 50 instances of the TV class. The action of creating an instance is called *instantiation*. From now on, we will say that you "create classes" but "instantiate objects." The difference is used to reduce ambiguity. Creating a class is done at design time when you're building your software and involves writing the actual code. Instantiating an object is done at run time, when your program is being used.

A classic analogy is the cookie cutter. You can go out to your workshop and shape a piece of metal in the shape of a Christmas tree. You do this once and put the cutter in a drawer in your kitchen. Whenever you need to create Christmas tree cookies, you roll some dough (the computer's memory) and stamp out however many you need. In effect you're instantiating cookies. You can reuse the cutter later to create more cookies, each the same shape as the ones before.

Once you've instantiated the objects, you can manipulate each object's properties defined for the class, and you can invoke the methods defined for the class on the object. For example, suppose you build a class once at design time that represents a television. You can instantiate the class twice to make two objects from that class — say, one to represent the TV in the living room and one to represent the TV in the bedroom. Because both instances of the object share the same class, both instances have the same properties and methods. To turn on either TV you invoke the `SwitchOn` method on it. To change the channel you set its `Channel` property, and so on.

Building Classes

You have already started building classes, particularly in Chapters 5 and 9. In general, when you design an algorithm, you will discover certain objects described. You need to abstract these real-world objects into a software representation. Here's an example:

1. Select a list of 10 customers from the database.
2. Go through each customer and prepare a bill for each.
3. When each bill has been prepared, print it on a printer.

For a pure object-oriented application (and with .NET you will end up using objects to represent everything) every real-world object will need a software object. For example:

❑ `Customer`: An object that represents a customer

❑ `Bill`: An object that represents a bill that is produced

❑ `Printer`: An object that represents a hardware printer that can be used to print the bill

313

When you write software in Visual Basic 2005, you are given a vast set of classes called the Microsoft .NET Framework Classes. These classes describe virtually everything about the computing environment that you're trying to write software for. Writing object-oriented software for .NET is simply an issue of using objects that fit your needs and creating new objects if required. Typically, while building an application, some of the classes you need will be included in the .NET Framework, whereas you will have to build others yourself.

For example, some objects in the .NET Framework provide printing functionality and database access functionality. As your algorithm calls for both kinds of functionality, you don't need to write your own. If you need to print something, you create an object that understands how to print, tell it what you want to print, and then tell it to print it. Again, this is encapsulation — you don't care how to turn your document into PostScript commands and send it down the wire to the printer; the object knows how to do this for itself. In this example, there are classes that deal with printing that you can use to print bills, although there's no specific `Printer` object.

In some cases, objects that you need to represent do not exist in the .NET Framework. In this example, you need a `Customer` object and a `Bill` object.

Reusability

Perhaps the hardest aspect of object-oriented programming is to understand how to divide up the responsibility for the work. One of the most beautiful aspects of object orientation is *code reuse*. Imagine that your company has a need for several different applications: one to display customer bills, one to register a new customer, and one to track customer complaints. In each of those applications, you need to have a `Customer` object.

To simplify the issue, those three projects are not going to be undertaken simultaneously. You start by doing the first; when finished, you move on to the second; when you've finished that, you move on to the third. Do you want to build a new `Customer` class for each project, or do you want to build the class once and reuse it in each of the other two projects?

Reuse is typically regarded as something that's universally good, although there is a tradeoff. Ideally, if you build a `Customer` class for one project, and another project you're working on calls for another `Customer` class, you should use the same one. However, it may well be the case that you can't just plug the class into another project for some reason. We say "for some reason" because there are no hard and fast rules when it comes to class design and reuse. It may also be the case that it's easier or more cost-effective to build simple classes for each project rather than try to create one complex object that does everything. This might sound like it requires a degree in clairvoyance, but luckily it comes with experience! As you develop more and more applications, you'll gain a better understanding of how to design great, reusable objects.

Each object should be responsible for activities involving itself and no more. We've discussed only two objects — `Bill` and `Customer` — so you'll look only at those.

The activity of printing a bill (say, for telephone charges) follows this algorithm:

❑ For a given customer, find the call details for the last period.

❑ Go through each call and calculate the price of each one.

- ❏ Aggregate the cost of each call into a total.

- ❏ Apply tax charges.

- ❏ Print out the bill, with the customer's name, address, and bill summary on the first page and then the bill details on subsequent pages.

You have only two places where you can code this algorithm: the `Bill` object or the `Customer` object. Which one do you choose?

The calls made are really a property of the `Customer`. Basically, you are using these details to create a bill. Most of the functionality would be placed in the `Bill` object. A `Customer` is responsible for representing a customer, not representing a bill. When you create a `Bill` object, you would associate it with a particular customer by using a `Cust` property, like this:

```
myBill.Cust = myCustomer
```

The `Bill` object would then know that it was a bill for a given customer (represented by the `myCustomer` object) and could use the customer's details when creating a bill. You might want to change some other properties of the `Bill`, such as where it will be mailed to, whether it should contain a warning because it is overdue, and so on. Finally, the `Bill` would have a `Print` method:

```
myBill.Print()
```

The `Bill` object would then *use* a `Printer` object in order to print the bill. The `Bill` object would be said to be the user or *consumer* of the `Printer` object. It would even be said to consume the `Printer` object, even though (at least you hope) the printer is not used up or destroyed in printing the bill.

Designing an Object

Contrary to what we've said so far, in this first project this chapter you're not going to define an algorithm and then build objects to support it. For this rather academic example, we're going to walk you through some of the features of a typical object — in this case, a car.

There are certain facts you might want to know about the object:

- ❏ *What it looks like:* A car includes things like make, model, color, number of doors, and so on. These aspects of the car will rarely change during the object's lifetime.

- ❏ *Its capabilities:* Horsepower, engine size, cylinder configuration, and so on.

- ❏ *What it's doing:* Whether it's stationary, moving forward or backwards, and its speed and direction.

- ❏ *Where it is:* The Global Positioning System (GPS) coordinates of its current position. This is effectively its position relative to another object (the planet Earth). Likewise, controls on forms have coordinates that describe their location relative to the form (say, in pixels to the right of and below the top left corner).

You might also want to be able to control the object, for example:

❑　Tell it to accelerate.

❑　Tell it to decelerate.

❑　Tell it to turn left.

❑　Tell it to turn right.

❑　Tell it to straighten out of a turn.

❑　Tell it to do a three-point-turn.

❑　Tell it to stop completely.

There are three concepts of an object that you need to be aware of: identity, state, and behavior. We'll assume that the identity aspect is covered because you know what the class is, so the state and behavior are of interest here.

State

State describes facts about the object now. For example, a car's location and speed are part of its state. When designing objects, you need to think about what aspects of state you need to handle. It might not be useful to know a customer's speed, for example, but you might well want to know that customer's current address.

State tends to be implemented as values inside an object. Some of these values will be publicly available through properties, and some will be private. Also, some aspects of state might be publicly readable but not changeable. For example, cars have a speedometer that is readable to anybody using the car. But you can't change the car's speed by playing with the speedometer — you need to alter the car's behavior by using the brake or accelerator.

Behavior

While a car might have a read-only Speed property, it would have methods to accelerate and decelerate. When you invoke an object's method, you are telling your object to do something — so behavior is usually associated with methods. Properties can also be associated with behavior. When you set a property to a particular value (such as by changing the setting of a control), you can trigger behavior.

Behavior is implemented as a set of Visual Basic 2005 statements that do something. This will usually involve one or both of the following:

❑　*Changing its own state:* When you invoke the `accelerate` method on a car, it should get faster if it is capable of doing so.

❑　*Somehow affecting the "world" outside the object:* This could be manipulating other objects in the application, displaying something to the user, saving something to a disk, or printing a document.

In this chapter, you won't build all of the properties and methods discussed. Instead, you'll build a handful of the more interesting ones. You begin in the following Try It Out by creating your new project and the Car class.

Creating a New Project and the Car Class

1. Start Visual Basic 2005 and select File ⇨ New ⇨ Project from the menu.

2. When the New Project dialog box appears, select the Console Application template and enter the name of the project as **Objects**. Click OK to create the project.

3. You now need to create a new class. This is done through the Solution Explorer, so right-click on the Objects project and select Add ⇨ Class. This will prompt you for a new class name, so enter **Car.vb** as the class name and click Add. The new class has been added to the Solution Explorer and the editor now shows the code listing for it, albeit empty.

Storing State

State describes what the object understands about itself, so if you give a car object some state, for example, "You are blue," you're giving the car object a fact: "The car I represent is blue."

So how do you actually manage state in your classes? Well, state is typically held in variables, and you define those variables within the class. You see how to do this in a moment.

Usually, the methods and properties you build will either affect or use the state in some way. Imagine you've built a property that changes the color of the car. When you set that property, the variable that's responsible for storing the state will be changed to reflect the new value that it has been given. When you retrieve (*get*) that property, the variable responsible for storing the state will be read, and the current value will be returned to the caller.

In a way, then, properties *are* behavior. Under the hood, a public property has two methods: a Get method and a Set method (defined by Get ... End Get and Set ... End Set blocks of code, as you have already encountered in Chapter 5). A simple Get method for the Color property will contain code to tell the caller what color the car is. A simple Set method for the Color property will set a value that represents the car's color. In a real application, though, Color would probably mean something more than just remembering a value. In a driving game, for example, the Set method of the Color property would need to make the screen display change the color in which the car is shown on the screen.

When a property has no behavior at all, you can cheat. In the next Try It Out, you create a Color "property" by declaring a Color variable and making it public. When a property is implemented like this, it is also called a *field*. Although this can be a useful and very fast technique for adding properties, declaring a field instead of the Property, Get, and Set blocks is not actually recommended, but for this small example it is just fine.

Creating an Object and Adding a Color Property

1. In the Car class, add this code:

```
Public Color As String
```

2. That's it! However, you do need a way of consuming the class so that you can see it working. Open Module1.vb and add this code:

```
Sub Main()
    'Create a new car object
```

```
        Dim objCar As New Car

        'Set the Color property to Red
        objCar.Color = "Red"

        'Show what the value of the property is
        Console.WriteLine("My car is this color:")
        Console.WriteLine(objCar.Color)

        'Wait for input from the user
        Console.ReadLine()
    End Sub
```

3. Now run the project. A new window will appear similar to Figure 10-1.

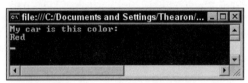

Figure 10-1

4. Press Enter to end the program.

How It Works

Defining the field is easy. The line of code

```
    Public Color As String
```

tells the class that you want to create a variable called `Color` and you want the field to hold a string of text characters. The use of the `Public` keyword when you declare the `Color` variable tells the class that the variable is accessible to developers using the `Car` class, not only from within the class itself.

> *Variables defined in the location between the* `Public Class` *and* `End Class` *lines, but outside of any functions, are known as member variables in the class itself and as fields to consumers of the class.*

Using the object is simple, and you do this from within `Module1.vb`. This process actually takes two steps. First, you have to declare a variable to refer to an object for the class; second, you instantiate the object. The following line of code creates an object variable called `objCar` and tells it that it's going to hold exclusively any objects created using the `Car` class:

```
    Dim objCar As Car
```

When you define the variable, it doesn't yet have an object instance associated with it; you are simply identifying the type of object. It's a bit like telling the computer to give you a hook that you can hang a `Car` object on, and call the hook `objCar`. You haven't hung anything on it yet—to do that you have to create an instance of the class. This is done using the `New` keyword:

```
    Set objCar = New Car
```

But Visual Basic 2005 allows you to combine both steps into one line of code:

```
'Create a new car object
Dim objCar As New Car
```

So, what you're saying here is: "let `objCar` refer to a newly created object instantiated from the class `Car`." In other words, "create a new car and hang it on the hook called `objCar`." You now have a `Car` object and can refer to it with the name `objCar`.

> *Note that in OO programming, the same object can be hanging on several different hooks at the same time and, therefore, have several different names. This might seem confusing, but in most cases it is a really intuitive way to work. Imagine how cool it would be if your keys could be on several hooks at the same time — they'd be so much easier to find!*

After you have an object instance, you can set its properties and call its methods. Here is how you set the `Color` property:

```
'Set the Color property to Red
objCar.Color = "Red"
```

Once the property has been set, it can be retrieved again as many times as you want or its value changed at a later point. Here, retrieval is illustrated by passing the `Color` property to the `WriteLine` method on the `Console` class:

```
'Show what the value of the property is
Console.WriteLine("My car is this color:")
Console.WriteLine(objCar.Color)
```

The `Console.ReadLine` line means that the program does not continue until you press Enter. Basically the console window is waiting for input from you.

```
'Wait for input from the user
Console.ReadLine()
```

> *Console applications are a good way to test in-memory objects because you don't need to worry about setting up a user interface. You can just display lines of text whenever you want. The objects you build will work just as well in a Windows application, though.*

Even though this is not really a property from the point of view of a developer using the class, it works just like one. In fact, "real" properties are methods that look like variables to users of the class. Whether you use a method or a property really depends on what the users of your class will find easier. You'll start to see this in the next section.

Real Properties

Now that you've seen how to cheat, let's see how to do things properly. The property you saw can be set to pretty much anything. As long as it's a string, it will be accepted. Also, setting the property doesn't do anything except change the object's internal state. Often you want to control what values a property can be set to; for example, you might have a list of valid colors that a car can be. You might also want to associate a change to a property with a particular action. For example, when you change a channel on the TV, you want it to do a bit more than just change its mind about what channel it's displaying. You want the TV to show a different picture! Just changing the value of a variable won't help here.

Another reason to use real properties is that you want to prevent the user of the class from directly changing the value. This is called a *read-only property*. The car's speed is a good example of how a class that models a real-world object should behave like that real-world object. If you are going 60 mph, you cannot simply change the speed to a value you prefer. You can read the speed of a car from the speedometer, but you cannot change (write) the speed of the car by physically moving the needle around the dial with your finger. You have to control the car in another fashion, which you do by stepping on the gas pedal to accelerate or on the brake pedal to decelerate. To model this feature in the Car class, you use methods (Accelerate, Decelerate) that affect the speed and keep a read-only property around called Speed that will report on the current speed of the vehicle.

You'll still need to keep the speed around in a member variable, but what you need is a member variable that can be seen or manipulated only by the class itself. You accomplish this by using the Private keyword:

```
Private _speed As Integer
```

The _speed variable is marked as Private and can, therefore, be accessed only by functions defined inside the class itself. Users of Car will not even be aware of its presence. In the style we use and recommend in this book, private members are camelCased rather than PascalCased, so that you can easily tell whether something is public or private when you use it. When a private variable maps directly to a public property, you prefix the variable name with an underscore (_).

Now you'll see how you can build a property that will give the user of the object read-only access to the car's speed.

Try It Out   Adding a Speed Property

1. To define a private variable, use the Private instead of the Public keyword. Add this statement to the Car class:

```
Public Color As String
```

```
Private _speed As Integer
```

2. To report the speed, you need to build a read-only property. Add this code to your Car class:

```
'Speed - read-only property to return the speed
Public ReadOnly Property Speed() As Integer
    Get
        Return _speed
    End Get
End Property
```

3. Now, you build a method called Accelerate that will adjust the speed of the car by however many miles-per-hour you give it. Add this code after the Speed property:

```
'Accelerate - add mph to the speed
Public Sub Accelerate(ByVal accelerateBy As Integer)
```

```
        'Adjust the speed
        _speed += accelerateBy
    End Sub
```

4. To test the object, you need to make some changes to the Main procedure in Module1. Open the
    file and modify the code as shown:

```
Sub Main()
    'Create a new car object
    Dim objCar As New Car

    'Report the speed
    Console.WriteLine("The car's speed is:")
    Console.WriteLine(objCar.Speed)

    'Accelerate
    objCar.Accelerate(5)

    'Report the new speed
    Console.WriteLine("The car's speed is now:")
    Console.WriteLine(objCar.Speed)

    'Wait for input from the user
    Console.ReadLine()
End Sub
```

5. Now run the project. A new window will appear similar to Figure 10-2.

Figure 10-2

How It Works

The first thing you do is define a private member variable called _speed in the Car class:

```
    Private _speed As Integer
```

By default, when the object is created, _speed will have a value of zero because this is the default value
for the Integer data type.

You then define a read-only property that returns the current speed:

```
    'Speed - readonly property to return the speed
    Public ReadOnly Property Speed() As Integer
        Get
            Return _speed
        End Get
    End Property
```

When you define properties, you can set them to be read-only (through the ReadOnly keyword), write-only (through the WriteOnly keyword), or both readable and writable by using neither. Reading a property is known as *getting* the value, whereas writing to a property is known as *setting* the value. The code between Get and End Get will be executed when the property is read. In this case, the only thing you're doing is returning the value currently stored in _speed.

You also created a method called Accelerate. This method doesn't have to return a value, so you use the Sub keyword:

```
'Accelerate - add mph to the speed
Public Sub Accelerate(ByVal accelerateBy As Integer)
    'Adjust the speed
    _speed += accelerateBy
End Sub
```

The method takes a single parameter called accelerateBy, which you use to tell the method how much to increase the speed by. You'll notice that the only action of the method is to adjust the internal member _speed. In real life, the pressure on the accelerator pedal, along with factors such as wind speed and road surface, will affect the speed. The speed will be an outcome of several factors—not something you can just change. You need some complex code to simulate this. Here you are just keeping things simple and incrementing the _speed variable with the value passed to the method.

Accelerating a car is another example of encapsulation. To accelerate the car in a real-world implementation you need an actuator of some kind to open the throttle further until the required speed is reached. As consumers of the object, you don't care how this is done. All you care about is how to tell the car to accelerate.

Consuming this new functionality is simple. First, you create the variable and instantiate the object as you did in the last exercise:

```
'Create a new car object
Dim objCar As New Car
```

Next, you write the current speed:

```
'Report the speed
Console.WriteLine("The car's speed is:")
Console.WriteLine(objCar.Speed)
```

Notice how you're using the read-only Speed property to get the current speed of the car. When the object is first created, the internal _speed member will be set at 0.

Now you call Accelerate and use it to increase the speed of the car:

```
'Accelerate
objCar.Accelerate(5)
```

Finally, you write out the new speed:

```
'Report the new speed
Console.WriteLine("The car's speed is now:")
Console.WriteLine(objCar.Speed)
```

Read/Write Properties

So, why would you need to use the `Property` keyword to define properties that are both readable and writable if you can achieve the same effect with a line like this?

```
Public Color As String
```

Well, if you build the property manually using the `Property` keyword, you can write code that is executed whenever the property is set or gotten. This is extremely powerful!

For example, the `Property` keyword allows you to provide validation for new values. Imagine you had a property called `NumberOfDoors`. You wouldn't want this to be set to nonsense values like 0 or 23453. Rather, you would have some possible range. For modern cars this is going to range from 2 to 5.

> *This is an important consideration for developers building objects. It's imperative that you make life as easy as possible for a developer to consume your object. Dealing with problems like making sure a car can't have 10 million doors is an important aspect of object design.*

Likewise, you might not have the information to return to the consumer of your object when you are asked to return the property; you might have to retrieve the value from somewhere, or otherwise calculate it. You might have a property that describes the total number of orders a customer has ever made or the total number of chew toys a dog has destroyed in his life. If you build this as a property, you can intercept the instruction to get the value and find the actual value you require on demand from some other data store, such as a database or a Web service. You'll see this covered in later chapters.

For now, let's deal with the number-of-doors problem.

Try It Out   Adding a NumberOfDoors Property

1. The first thing you need to do is build a private member that will hold the number of doors. You're going to define this member as having a default of 5. Add this code in the `Car` class as highlighted below:

    ```
    Public Color As String
    Private _speed As Integer

        Private _numberOfDoors As Integer = 5
    ```

2. Now you can build a property that will get and set the number of doors, provided the number of doors is always between 2 and 5. Add this code to your `Car` class directly beneath the `Accelerate` method:

    ```
    'NumberOfDoors - get/set the number of doors
    Public Property NumberOfDoors() As Integer
        'Called when the property is read
        Get
            Return _numberOfDoors
        End Get
        'Called when the property is set
        Set(ByVal value As Integer)
            'Is the new value between two and five
    ```

```
            If value >= 2 And value <= 5 Then
                _numberOfDoors = value
            End If
        End Set
    End Property
```

In this chapter, you're going to ignore the problem of telling the developer if the user has provided an invalid value for a property. Ideally, whenever this happens, you need to throw an exception. The developer will be able to detect this exception and behave accordingly. (For example, if the user typed the number of doors as 9999 into a text box, the program could display a message box telling the user that they have provided an invalid value for the number of doors, since no car has that many doors.) You learned about exception handling in Chapter 9.

3. To test the property, you need to change the `Main` procedure in Module1 by modifying the code as indicated here:

```
Sub Main()
    'Create a new car object
    Dim objCar As New Car

    'Report the number of doors
    Console.WriteLine("The number of doors is:")
    Console.WriteLine(objCar.NumberOfDoors)

    'Try changing the number of doors to 1000
    objCar.NumberOfDoors = 1000

    'Report the number of doors
    Console.WriteLine("The number of doors is:")
    Console.WriteLine(objCar.NumberOfDoors)

    'Now try changing the number of doors to 2
    objCar.NumberOfDoors = 2

    'Report the number of doors
    Console.WriteLine("The number of doors is:")
    Console.WriteLine(objCar.NumberOfDoors)

    'Wait for input from the user
    Console.ReadLine()
End Sub
```

Try running the project. You should see a screen like the one in Figure 10-3.

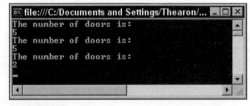

Figure 10-3

How It Works

First you define a private member variable called _numberOfDoors. You also assign the default value of 5 to this variable.

```
Private _numberOfDoors As Integer = 5
```

The motivation behind setting a value at this point is simple: You want _numberOfDoors to always be between 2 and 5. When the object is created, the _numberOfDoors will be assigned a value of 5. Without this assignment, _numberOfDoors would have a default value of 0. This would be inconsistent with the understanding that the number of doors must always be between 2 and 5, so you guard against it.

Next comes the property itself. The Get portion is simple — just return the value held in _numberOfDoors — but the Set portion involves a check to ensure that the new value is valid. The new value is passed in through a parameter called value:

```
'NumberOfDoors - get/set the number of doors
Public Property NumberOfDoors() As Integer
    'Called when the property is read
    Get
        Return _numberOfDoors
    End Get
    'Called when the property is set
    Set(ByVal value As Integer)
        'Is the new value between two and five
        If value >= 2 And value <= 5 Then
            _numberOfDoors = value
        End If
    End Set
End Property
```

The test code you add to Module1 is not very complex. You simply display the initial value of _number OfDoors and then try to change it to 1000. The validation code in the NumberOfDoors property won't change the _numberOfDoors member variable if an inconsistent number is used, so when you report the number of doors again, you find it hasn't changed from 5. Lastly, you try setting it to 2, which is a valid value, and this time, when you report the number of doors, you get an output of 2.

Even though read–write properties and public variables seem to work the same way, they are very different. When your Visual Basic 2005 code is compiled, the compiled code treats property calls as a call to a method. Always using properties instead of public variables makes your objects more flexible and extendable. Of course, using public variables is easier and quicker. You need to decide what is most important in each case.

The IsMoving Method

When building objects you should always have the following question in the back of your mind. "How can I make this object easier to use?" For example, if the consumer needs to know whether the car is moving, what would be the easiest way to determine this?

One way would be to look at the Speed property. If this is zero, it can be assumed that the car has stopped. (On most cars the speed is not reported when the car is moving in reverse. So assume, for now, that you have only forward gears!) However, relying on the developers using the object to understand this relies on their having an understanding of whatever is being modeled. Common sense tells us that an object with a speed of "zero mph" is stationary, but should you assume anyone consuming the object shares your idea of common sense?

Instead, it's good practice to create methods that deal with these eventualities. One way you can solve this problem is by creating an IsMoving method.

Try It Out   Adding an IsMoving Method

1. All the IsMoving method needs in order to work is a simple test to look at the speed of the car and make a True or False determination as to whether it's moving. Add this code to the Car class after the NumberOfDoors property:

```
'IsMoving - is the car moving?
Public Function IsMoving() As Boolean
    'Is the car's speed zero?
    If Speed = 0 Then
        Return False
    Else
        Return True
    End If
End Function
```

2. To test this method, make these changes to the Main procedure in Module1 with this new code as indicated:

```
Sub Main()
    'Create a new car object
    Dim objCar As New Car

    'Accelerate the car to 25mph
    objCar.Accelerate(25)

    'Report whether or not the car is moving
    If objCar.IsMoving = True Then
        Console.WriteLine("The car is moving.")
    Else
        Console.WriteLine("The car is stopped.")
    End If

    'Wait for input from the user
    Console.ReadLine()
End Sub
```

3. Now try running the project. A new window will appear similar to Figure 10-4.

Figure 10-4

How It Works

You created a simple method that examines the value of the Speed property and returns True if the speed is not zero, False if it is.

```
'IsMoving - is the car moving?
Public Function IsMoving() As Boolean
    'Is the car's speed zero?
    If Speed = 0 Then
        Return False
    Else
        Return True
    End If
End Function
```

Although this method is simple, it removes the conceptual leap required on the part of the consumer to understand whether the object is moving. There's no confusion as to whether the car is moving based on interpreting the value of one or more properties; one simple method returns a definitive answer.

Of course, before you go off building hundreds of methods for every eventuality, remember that ironically, the more methods and properties an object has, the harder it is to understand. Take care while designing the object and try to strike the right balance between too few and too many methods and properties.

You may be wondering why you used a method here when this is actually a property. All you are doing is reporting the object's state without affecting its behavior. There is no reason for not using a property here. However, using a method does remind users of the object that this value is calculated and is not a simple report of an internal variable. It also adds a bit of variety to your examples and reminds you how easy it is to add a method!

Constructors

One of the most important aspects of object design is the concept of a *constructor*. As mentioned in Chapter 9, this is a piece of initialization code that runs whenever an object is instantiated. It's extremely useful for occasions when you need the object to be set up in a particular way before you use it. For example, it can be used to set up default values, just as you did for the number of doors earlier.

Creating a Constructor

In this Try It Out, you take a look at a simple constructor.

Try It Out   Creating a Constructor

1.   For the sake of this discussion, you're going to remove the default value of 5 from the
_numberOfDoors member. Make this change to the Car class:

```
Public Color As String
Private _speed As Integer

Private _numberOfDoors As Integer
```

2.   Now, add this method, which will form the constructor. Any code within this method will be
executed whenever an object is created from the Car class:

```
'Constructor
Public Sub New()
    'Set the default values
    Color = "White"
    _speed = 0
    _numberOfDoors = 5
End Sub
```

Setting the _speed to 0 here is actually redundant, as it will have that value already (since all
Integer variables are set to 0 when they are declared), but it's included to make the example complete.

3.   To test the action of the constructor, you're going to create a separate procedure that displays the
car's details. Add the DisplayCarDetails procedure in Module1:

```
'DisplayCarDetails - procedure that displays a car's details
Sub DisplayCarDetails(ByVal theCar As Car)
    'Display the details of the car
    Console.WriteLine("Color: " & theCar.Color)
    Console.WriteLine("Number of doors: " & theCar.NumberOfDoors)
    Console.WriteLine("Current speed: " & theCar.Speed)
End Sub
```

4.   Now modify the Main procedure in Module1 to call the DisplayCarDetails procedure:

```
Sub Main()
    'Create a new car object
    Dim objCar As New Car

    'Display the details of the car
    DisplayCarDetails(objCar)

    'Wait for input from the user
    Console.ReadLine()
End Sub
```

5.   Now try running the project, and you should see an output similar to Figure 10-5.

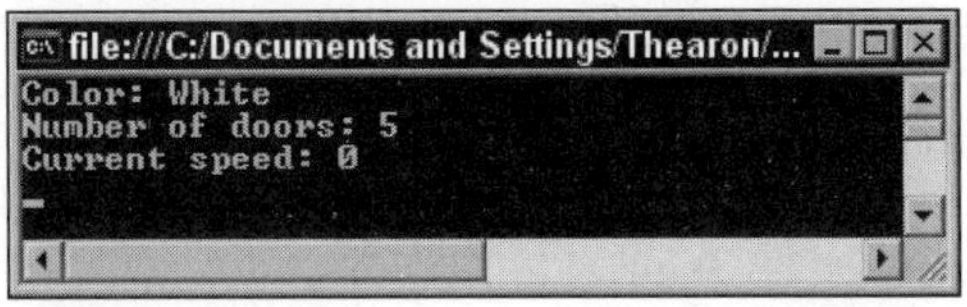

Figure 10-5

How It Works

The code in the constructor is called whenever an object is created. This is where you take an opportunity to set the values for the members:

```
'Constructor
Public Sub New()
    'Set the default values
    Color = "White"
    _speed = 0
    _numberOfDoors = 5
End Sub
```

You see the results of the changes made to the properties when you run the project and see the details of the car displayed in the window. A constructor must always be a subroutine (defined with the Sub keyword) and must always be called New. This provides consistency in the .NET Framework for all class constructors and the framework will always execute this procedure when a class is instantiated.

When you test the object, you use a separate function called DisplayCarDetails in Module1. This is useful when you need to see the details of more than one Car object or want to see the details of the Car object multiple times in your code.

Inheritance

Although the subject of *inheritance* is quite an advanced object-oriented programming topic, it is really useful. In fact, the .NET Framework itself makes heavy use of it, and you have already created classes that inherit from another class — every Windows form that you write is a new class inherited from a simple blank form (the starting point when you create a form).

Inheritance is used to create objects that have "everything another object has, but also some of their own bits and pieces." It's used to extend the functionality of objects, but it doesn't require you to have an understanding of how the internals of the object work. This is in line with your quest of building and using objects without having to understand how the original programmers put them together.

Inheritance enables you to, in effect, take another class and bolt on your own functionality, either by adding new methods and properties or by replacing existing methods and properties. For example, you can move from a general car class to more specific variations — for example, sports car, SUV, van, and so on.

So, if you wanted to model a sports car, it is likely that you would want to have a default number of doors as 2 instead of 5, and you might also like to have properties and methods that help you understand the performance of the car, such as `Weight` and `PowerToWeightRatio`, as shown in Figure 10-6.

One thing that you need to understand about inheritance is the way that access to public and private members is controlled. Any public member, such as `Color`, is accessible to inheriting classes. However, private members such as `_speed` are not. This means that if `SportsCar` has to change the speed of the car, it has to do so through the properties and methods provided in the `Car` class itself.

In other commonly encountered terminology, the inheriting class is called a derived class, and the class it inherits from is its base class. `Car` is the base class from which `SportsCar` is derived. The terms subclass and superclass are also used. `SportsCar` is a subclass of `Car`; `Car` is the superclass of `Sports Car`. The "sub" and "super" prefixes mean the same as they do in speaking of subsets and supersets in mathematics.

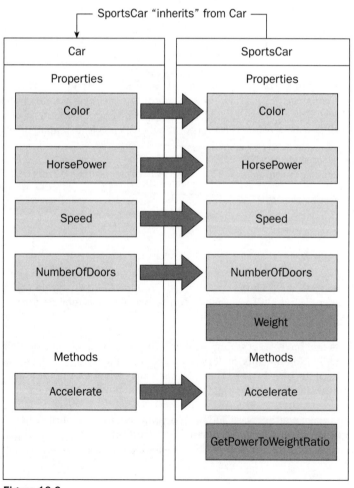

Figure 10-6

Adding New Methods and Properties

To illustrate inheritance, in the next Try It Out you create a new class called `SportsCar`, which inherits from `Car` and enables you to see the power-to-weight ratio of your sports car.

Inheriting from Car

1. For the purpose of this demonstration, you need to add an additional public variable to the `Car` class that represents the horsepower of the car. Of course, if you want to make it really robust, you would use a property and ensure a sensible range of values. But here, simplicity and speed win out. Open the `Car` class and add this line of code as indicated:

    ```
    Public Color As String
    ```

    ```
    Public HorsePower As Integer
    Private _speed As Integer
    Private _numberOfDoors As Integer
    ```

2. Now, create a new class in the usual way by right-clicking the Objects project in the Solution Explorer and selecting Add ⇨ Class. Enter the name of the class as **SportsCar.vb** and click Add.

3. To tell `SportsCar` that it inherits from `Car`, you need to use the `Inherits` keyword. Add this code to `SportsCar`:

    ```
    Public Class SportsCar
    ```

    ```
        Inherits Car
    End Class
    ```

4. At this point, `SportsCar` has all the methods and properties that `Car` has. What you want to do now is add a new public variable called `Weight` to the `SportsCar` class:

    ```
        Public Weight As Integer
    ```

5. To test the new class you need to add a new procedure to Module1. Add the following procedure:

    ```
    'DisplaySportsCarDetails - procedure that displays a sports car's details
    Sub DisplaySportsCarDetails(ByVal theCar As SportsCar)
        'Display the details of the sports car
        Console.WriteLine()
        Console.WriteLine("Sports Car Horsepower: " & theCar.HorsePower)
        Console.WriteLine("Sports Car Weight: " & theCar.Weight)
    End Sub
    ```

6. Now you need to modify the `Main` procedure in Module1. Pay close attention to the fact that you need to create a `SportsCar` object, not a `Car` object, in order to get at the `Weight` property. Add the new code as indicated:

    ```
    Sub Main()
    ```

    ```
        'Create a new sports car object
        Dim objCar As New SportsCar
    ```

```
        'Modify the number of doors
        objCar.NumberOfDoors = 2

        'Set the horsepower and weight(kg)
        objCar.HorsePower = 240
        objCar.Weight = 1085

        'Display the details of the car
        DisplayCarDetails(objCar)

        DisplaySportsCarDetails(objCar)

        'Wait for input from the user
        Console.ReadLine()
    End Sub
```

7. Try running the project and you'll see an output similar to that shown in Figure 10-7.

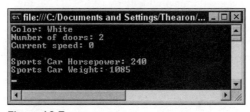

Figure 10-7

How It Works

The directive to make `SportsCar` inherit from `Car` is done with the `Inherits` keyword:

```
Public Class SportsCar
    Inherits Car
```

At this point, the new `SportsCar` class contains all the methods and properties in the `Car` class, but it cannot see or modify the private member variables. When you add your new property:

```
    Public Weight As Integer
```

you now have a new property that's available only when you create instances of `SportsCar` and not available to you if you are creating plain instances of `Car`. This is an important point to realize—if you don't create an instance of `SportsCar`, you'll get a compile error if you try to access the `Weight` property. `Weight` isn't, and never has been, a property of `Car` (see Figure 10-6 for a clarification of this situation).

The new `DisplaySportsCarDetails` procedure displays the `Horsepower` property from the `Car` class and the `Weight` property from the `SportsCar` class. Remember that, since the `SportsCar` class inherits from the `Car` class, it contains all of the methods and properties in the `Car` class:

```
        'DisplaySportsCarDetails - procedure that displays a sports car's details
        Sub DisplaySportsCarDetails(ByVal theCar As SportsCar)
```

```
      'Display the details of the sports car
      Console.WriteLine()
      Console.WriteLine("Sports Car Horsepower: " & theCar.HorsePower)
      Console.WriteLine("Sports Car Weight: " & theCar.Weight)
   End Sub
```

You instantiate a new `SportsCar` object in your `Main` procedure, and this allows you to get and set the value for the `Weight` property:

```
      'Create a new sports car object
      Dim objCar As New SportsCar
```

You are able to call the `DisplayCarDetails` procedure and pass it a `SportsCar` object, because `SportsCar` is a subclass of `Car` — that is, every `SportsCar` is also a `Car`. The `DisplayCarDetails` procedure does not access any of the properties of the `SportsCar` class, so call this procedure passing it the `SportsCar` object that you created. You then call the `DisplaySportsCarDetails` procedure to display the properties of both the `Car` class and the `SportsCar` class:

```
      'Display the details of the car
      DisplayCarDetails(objCar)
      DisplaySportsCarDetails(objCar)
```

Adding a GetPowerToWeightRatio Method

A `GetPowerToWeightRatio` method could be implemented as a read-only property (in which case you would probably call it `PowerToWeightRatio` instead), but for this discussion you'll add it as a method in the next Try It Out.

Try It Out   Adding a GetPowerToWeightRatio Method

1. For this method, all you need to do is divide the horsepower by the weight. Add this code to the `SportsCar` class:

```
'GetPowerToWeightRatio - work out the power to weight
Public Function GetPowerToWeightRatio() As Double
    'Calculate the horsepower
    Return CType(HorsePower, Double) / CType(Weight, Double)
End Function
```

2. To see the results, add the highlighted code to the `DisplaySportsCarDetails` procedure in Module1:

```
'DisplaySportsCarDetails - procedure that displays a sports car's details
Sub DisplaySportsCarDetails(ByVal theCar As SportsCar)
    'Display the details of the sports car
    Console.WriteLine()
    Console.WriteLine("Sports Car Horsepower: " & theCar.HorsePower)
    Console.WriteLine("Sports Car Weight: " & theCar.Weight)

    Console.WriteLine("Power to Weight Ratio: " & theCar.GetPowerToWeightRatio)
End Sub
```

Run the project and you'll see something similar to Figure 10-8.

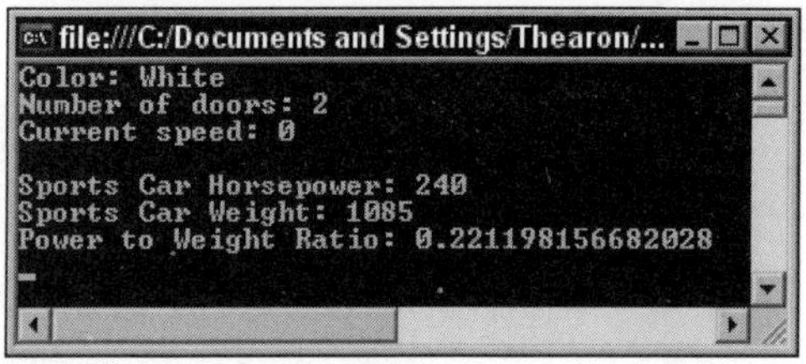

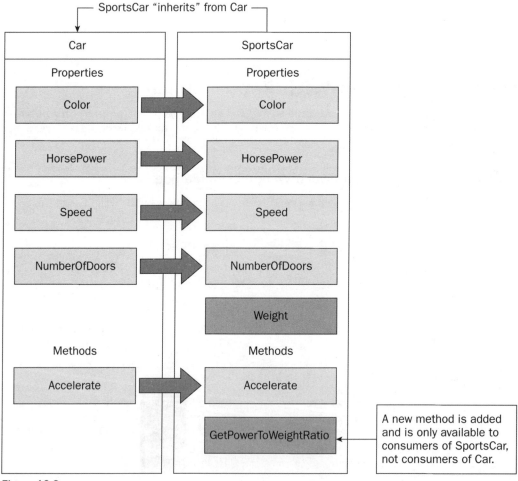

Figure 10-8

How It Works

Again, all you've done is add a new method to the new class called `GetPowerToWeightRatio`. This method then becomes available to anyone working with an instance of `SportsCar` as shown in Figure 10-9.

Figure 10-9

The only thing you have to be careful of is that if you divide an integer by an integer you get an integer result, but what you actually want here is a floating-point number. You have to convert the integer `HorsePower` and `Weight` properties to `Double` values in order to see the results:

```
'Calculate the horsepower
Return CType(HorsePower, Double) / CType(Weight, Double)
```

Changing Defaults

In addition to adding new properties and methods, you might want to change the way an existing method or property works from that of the base class. To do this, you need to create your own implementation of the method or property.

Think back to the discussion on constructors. These are methods that are called whenever the object is created and let you get the object into a state where it can be used by a developer. In this constructor you set the default _numberOfDoors value to be 5. However, in a sports car, this number should ideally be 2, which is what you set using the `NumberOfDoors` property. But wouldn't it be nice to have this automatically done in the constructor of the `SportsCar` class?

If you are creating a derived class want to replace a method or property existing in the base class with your own, the process is called *overriding*. In this next Try It Out, you learn how to override the base class's constructor.

Try It Out   Overriding a Constructor

1. To override the constructor in the base class, all you have to do is create your own constructor in the `SportsCar` class. Add this code to `SportsCar`:

```
'Constructor
Public Sub New()
    'Change the default values
    Color = "Green"
    NumberOfDoors = 2
End Sub
```

2. Remove the following code from the `Main` procedure in Module1.

```
'Modify the number of doors
objCar.NumberOfDoors = 2
```

3. Run your project to test your constructor in the `SportsCar` class. You should see output similar to Figure 10-10.

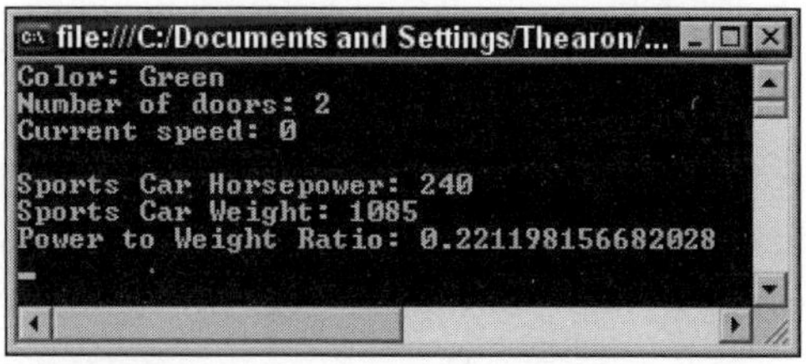

```
file:///C:/Documents and Settings/Thearon/...
Color: Green
Number of doors: 2
Current speed: 0

Sports Car Horsepower: 240
Sports Car Weight: 1085
Power to Weight Ratio: 0.221198156682028
```

Figure 10-10

How It Works

The new constructor that you added to SportsCar runs after the existing one in Car. .NET knows that it's supposed to run the code in the constructor of the base class before running the new constructor in the class that inherits from it, so in effect it runs this code first:

```
'Constructor
Public Sub New()
    'Set the default values
    Color = "White"
    _speed = 0
    _numberOfDoors = 5
End Sub
```

And then it runs this code:

```
'Constructor
Public Sub New()
    'Change the default values
    Color = "Green"
    NumberOfDoors = 2
End Sub
```

To summarize what happens:

1. The constructor on the base class Car is called.
2. Color is set to White.
3. _speed is set to 0.
4. _numberOfDoors is set to 5.
5. The constructor on the new class SportsCar is called.
6. Color is set to Green.
7. NumberOfDoors is set to 2.

Because you defined _numberOfDoors as a private member in Car, you cannot directly access it from inherited classes, just as you wouldn't be able to access it directly from a consumer of the class. Instead, you rely on being able to set an appropriate value through the NumberOfDoors property.

Polymorphism: Scary Word, Simple Concept

Another very common word mentioned when talking about object-oriented programming is *polymorphism*. This is, perhaps the scariest term, but one of the easiest to understand! In fact, you have already done it in the previous example.

Look again at the code for DisplayCarDetails:

```
'DisplayCarDetails - procedure that displays a car's details
Sub DisplayCarDetails(ByVal theCar As Car)
    'Display the details of the car
```

```
        Console.WriteLine("Color: " & theCar.Color)
        Console.WriteLine("Number of doors: " & theCar.NumberOfDoors)
        Console.WriteLine("Current speed: " & theCar.Speed)
    End Sub
```

The first line says that the parameter you want to accept is a `Car` object. But when you call the object, you're actually passing it a `SportsCar` object.

Look at how you create the object and call `DisplayCarDetails`:

```
        'Create a new sportscar object
        Dim objCar As New SportsCar

        'Display the details of the car
        DisplayCarDetails(objCar)
```

How can it be that if the function takes a `Car` object, you're allowed to pass it as a `SportsCar` object?

Well, *polymorphism* (which comes from the Greek for "many forms") means that an object can be treated as if it were a different kind of object, provided common sense prevails. In this case, you can treat a `SportsCar` object like a `Car` object because `SportsCar` inherits from `Car`. This act of inheritance dictates that what a `SportsCar` object can do must include everything that a `Car` object can do; therefore, you can treat the two objects in the same way. If you need to call a method on `Car`, `SportsCar` must also implement the method.

This does not hold true the other way round. Your `DisplaySportsCarDetails` function, defined like this:

```
    Sub DisplaySportsCarDetails(ByVal theCar As SportsCar)
```

cannot accept a `Car` object. `Car` is not guaranteed to be able to do everything a `SportsCar` can do, because the extra methods and properties you add to `SportsCar` won't exist on `Car`. `SportsCar` is a more specific type of `Car`.

So, to summarize, when people talk about polymorphism, this is the action they are referring to — the principle that an object can behave as if it were another object without the developer having to go through too many hoops to make it happen.

Overriding More Methods

Although you've overridden `Car`'s constructor, for completeness you should look at how to override a normal method.

To override a method you need to have the method in the base `Car` class. Because `Accelerate` shouldn't change depending on whether you have a sports car or a normal car, and `IsMoving` was added for ease of use — and hence doesn't really count in this instance as it isn't a behavior of the object — you need to add a new method called `CalculateAccelerationRate`. Assume that on a normal car this is a constant, and on a sports car you change it so that it takes the power-to-weight ratio into consideration. In the following Try It Out, you add another method to override.

Try It Out **Adding and Overriding Another Method**

1. Add this method to the `Car` class:

```
'CalculateAccelerationRate - assume a constant for a normal car
Public Function CalculateAccelerationRate() As Double
    'If we assume a normal car goes from 0-60 in 14 seconds,
    'that's an average rate of 4.2 mph/s
    Return 4.2
End Function
```

2. Now to test the method, change the `DisplayCarDetails` procedure in Module1 to read like this:

```
'DisplayCarDetails - procedure that displays a car's details
Sub DisplayCarDetails(ByVal theCar As Car)
    'Display the details of the car
    Console.WriteLine("Color: " & theCar.Color)
    Console.WriteLine("Number of doors: " & theCar.NumberOfDoors)
    Console.WriteLine("Current speed: " & theCar.Speed)

    Console.WriteLine("Acceleration rate: " & _
        theCar.CalculateAccelerationRate)
End Sub
```

3. Run the project and you'll get an output similar to Figure 10-11.

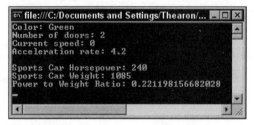

Figure 10-11

You've built a method on `Car` as normal. This method always returns a value of 4.2 mph/s for the acceleration rate.

Of course, our acceleration calculation algorithm is pure fantasy — no car is going to accelerate at the same rate irrespective of the gear, environment, current speed, and so on.

4. To override the method, you just have to provide a new implementation in `SportsCar`. However, there's one thing you need to do first. To override a method you have to mark it as `Overridable`. To do this, open the `Car` class again and add the `Overridable` keyword to the method:

```
Public Overridable Function CalculateAccelerationRate() As Double
```

5. Now, you can create a method with the same name in the SportsCar class. In order to override the method in the base class, you must add the Overrides keyword before the method type (Function or Procedure):

```
'CalculateAccelerationRate - take the power/weight into consideration
Public Overrides Function CalculateAccelerationRate() As Double
    'You'll assume the same 4.2 value, but you'll multiply it
    'by the power/weight ratio
    Return 4.2 * GetPowerToWeightRatio()
End Function
```

You didn't add the Overrides *keyword when you overrode the constructor; you didn't need to! Visual Basic 2005 handled this for you.*

6. Now if you run the project, you get an adjusted acceleration rate as shown in Figure 10-12.

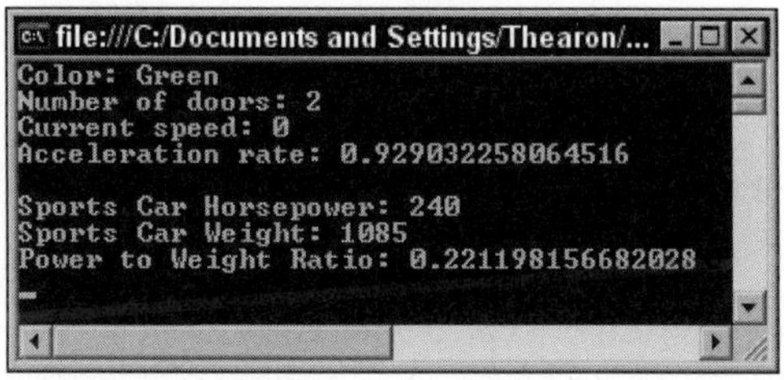

Figure 10-12

How It Works

Overriding the method lets you create your own implementation of an existing method on the object. Again, coming back to this concept of encapsulation, the object consumer doesn't have to know that anything is different about the object—they just call the method in the same way as they would for a normal Car object. This time, however, they get a different result rather than the constant value they always got on the normal Car object.

When you override a method, it's quite different from overriding a constructor. When you override a constructor, the original constructor still gets called first. When you override a method, the original method gets called only if you specifically call it from inside the new overriding method using MyBase.Method Name. *For example, you could invoke* MyBase.CalculateAccelerationRate *from* SportsCar *to return a value of* 4.2.

Inheriting from the Object Class

The final thing to look at, with respect to inheritance, is that if you create a class without using the Inherits clause, the class will automatically inherit from a class called Object. This object provides you with a few methods that you can guarantee will be supported by every object you ever have. Most of these methods are beyond the scope of this book. However, the two most useful methods at this level are:

❑   `ToString`: This method returns a string representation of the object. You can override this to provide a helpful string value for any object; for example, you might want a person object to return that person's name. If you do not override it, it will return the name of the class.

❑   `GetType`: This method returns a `Type` object that represents the data type of the object.

Remember, you do not have to inherit explicitly from `Object`. This happens automatically.

Objects and Structures

You created a structure in Chapter 5. Like a class, a structure provides a way to group several pieces of information together that all refer to one thing. A structure can even have methods and properties as well as member variables, just as a class can. Here are some of the differences between structures and classes.

In terms of semantics, structures are known as *value types* and classes are known as *reference types*. That is, a variable representing a structure means the actual chunk of computer memory that stores the contents of the structure itself, whereas a variable representing a class instance is actually, as you have seen, a "hook" on which the object hangs.

This explains the difference in instantiation—you don't need to use the `New` keyword to instantiate a structure before you use it, because it is a value type, just like an integer. You do have to use the `New` keyword with a form or other complex object because it is a class instance—a reference type.

You have seen that two different object variable "hooks" can be used to hang up the same object. If you set a property in the object using one of the hooks, its value will be as you set it if you get it using the other hook.

```
Dim objMyCar As New Car       'objMyCar.Color is "White"
Set objThisCar = objMyCar     'same object, different hooks
objThisCar.Color = "Beige"    'now objMyCar.Color is also "Beige"
```

Two different structure variables, on the other hand, always refer to different groups of pieces of information.

```
Dim structMyCustomer As Customer, structThisCustomer As Customer
structMyCustomer.FirstName = "Victor"
structThisCustomer = structMyCustomer  'different structures
structThisCustomer.FirstName = "Victoria"
'structMyCustomer.FirstName is still "Victor"
```

Also, you cannot inherit from a structure—another important consideration when choosing whether to use a class or a structure.

The Framework Classes

Although we discussed the .NET Framework in general in Chapter 2, take a look now at some aspects of the .NET Framework's construction that can help you when building objects. In particular, you want to take a look at namespaces and how you can create your own namespaces for use within your objects.

Namespaces

The .NET Framework is actually a vast collection of classes. There are around 3,500 classes in the .NET Framework all told, so how are you as a developer supposed to find the ones that you want?

The .NET Framework is divided into a broad set of namespaces that group similar classes together. This limits the number of classes that you have to hunt through if you're looking for a specific piece of functionality.

These namespaces are also hierarchical in nature, meaning that a namespace can contain other namespaces that further group classes together. Each class must belong to exactly one namespace — it can't belong to multiple namespaces.

Most of the .NET Framework classes are lumped together in a namespace called `System`, or namespaces that are also contained within `System`. For example:

❑   `System.Data` contains classes related to accessing data stored in a database.

❑   `System.Xml` contains classes used to read and write XML documents.

❑   `System.Windows.Forms` contains classes for drawing windows on the screen.

❑   `System.Net` contains classes for communicating over a network.

The fact that namespaces exist means that all of the objects you've been using actually have longer names than the one's used in your software code. Until this point, you've been using a shorthand notation to refer to classes.

In fact, earlier when we said that everything has to be derived from `Object`, we were stretching it a bit. Because `Object` is contained within the `System` namespace, its full name is `System.Object`. Likewise, `Console` is actually shorthand for `System.Console`, meaning that this line:

```
Console.ReadLine()
```

is actually the same as this line:

```
System.Console.ReadLine()
```

This can get a little silly, especially when you end up with object names like `System.Web.Services.Description.ServiceDescription`*!*

.NET automatically creates a shorthand version of all the classes within `System`, so you don't have to type `System` all the time. Later, you'll see how you can add shorthand references to other namespaces.

There is also the `My` namespace, which you've already seen in use in some of the earlier chapters. This namespace provides access to the most common classes that you're most likely to need in your everyday programming tasks.

Like the `System` namespace, the `My` namespace contains a collection of other classes, which in turn contain classes of their own. At the top level, there is the `My.Application` class, which provides a wealth of information related to the currently executing application such as the application's assembly name, the current path to the application's executable file, and so on. There is also the `My.Computer` class, which provides detailed information about the computer the application is executing on, such as the amount of free space on the hard drive and the amount of available memory.

The `My.Forms` class provides access to the various forms in the application and allows you to manipulate those forms easily; for example, you can show, hide, and close them. There is also the `My.Resources` class, which provides quick and easy access to an application's resource files if it contains them. You can place localized text strings and images in a resource file and use the `My.Resources` class to gain access to these resources for use in your application.

The `My.Settings` class provides access to an application's configuration file if it has one and allows you to quickly read the settings needed by your application such as startup settings or database connection information. It also allows you to create, persist, and save user settings for your application. Finally, there is the `My.User` class, which provides a wealth of information related to the current user of your application, such as login name and the domain name that the user is logged into.

Every class must be in exactly one namespace, but what about the classes we've made so far? Well, this project has a default namespace, and your new classes are placed into this namespace. In the next Try It Out, you discover a current namespace.

Try It Out Finding the Name of the Current Namespace

1. To see the namespace that you're using, right-click the Objects project in the Solution Explorer and select Properties.

2. The Root Namespace entry in the Objects Property Pages window gives the name of the namespace that will be used for new classes, as shown in Figure 10-13.

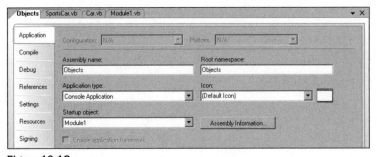

Figure 10-13

What this means is that your classes will have the text `Objects` prefixed to them, like this:

❑   The `Car` class is actually called `Objects.Car`.

❑   The `SportsCar` class is actually called `Objects.SportsCar`.

As you may have guessed, .NET automatically creates a shorthand version of your classes too, so you can refer to `SportsCar` instead of having to type `Objects.SportsCar`.

The motivation behind using namespaces is to make life easier for developers using your classes. Imagine that you give this project to another developer for use and they have already built their own class called Car. How do they tell the difference between their class and your class?

Well, yours will actually be called Objects.Car, whereas theirs will have a name like MyOwnProject.Car or YaddaYadda.Car. Namespaces remove the ambiguity of class names. (Of course, we didn't choose a very good namespace, because it doesn't really describe the classes that the namespace contains — we just chosen a namespace that illustrated the purpose of the chapter.)

The Imports Statement

Now you know you don't need to prefix your classes with Car or System because .NET automatically creates a shorthand version, but how do you do this yourself? The answer is the Imports statement!

If you go back to Chapter 9, you might remember this code from the top of the Debug form:

```
Imports System.Collections.Generic

Public Class Debug
```

You may recall this code as well:

```
'Using the List<T> class
Private objCustomerList As New List(Of Customer)
```

You used the Imports statement to import the System.Collections.Generic namespace into your project. You needed to do this to gain access to the List<T> class. The full name of this class is System.Collections.Generic.List(Of T), but because you had added a namespace import declaration, you could just write List(Of Customer) instead, substituting the Customer class in place of the T parameter.

All Imports statements must be written right at the top of the code file you want to use them in, before any other code including the Class declaration.

The only drawback happens if you import two namespaces that have an identically named class or child namespace and Visual Basic 2005 cannot tell what it is you are after (like Car.Car and MyOwnProject.Car). If this happens, you will be informed by Visual Basic 2005 that the name is ambiguous — in which case the quickest and easiest thing to do is to specify the full name that you're after.

Creating Your Own Namespace

Namespaces are defined by wrapping the Class ... End Class definition in a Namespace ... End Namespace definition. By default, classes created in Visual Basic 2005 are automatically assigned to a root namespace. Visual Studio 2005 automatically names this root namespace based on the project name. In the next Try It Out, you learn to create a namespace.

Try It Out   **Creating a Namespace**

1. Using the Solution Explorer, right-click the project and select Properties. The Root Namespace field tells you the name. In this case, the root namespace name is Objects.

2. It's often recommended that you build your namespaces such that the full names of the classes you develop are prefixed with the name of your company. So, if my company was called MyCodeWidgets, ideally I would want my `Car` class called `MyCodeWidgets.Car`. To do this, change the Root Namespace field from Objects to **MyCodeWidgets** (see Figure 10-14). Then click the Save button on the toolbar to have this change applied to your project.

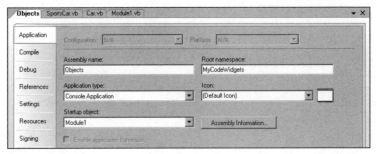

Figure 10-14

3. Visual Studio 2005's Object Browser is a useful tool that allows you to see what classes you have available in your project. You can find it by selecting View ⇨ Object Browser from the menu bar. When the Object Browser is displayed, the first item is usually the project. You can navigate down into it to find your `Car` class (see Figure 10-15).

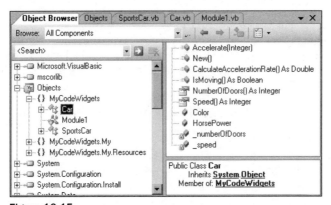

Figure 10-15

4. Note that you can also see the methods, properties, and member variables listed for the class. Pertinent to this discussion, however, is the namespace. This is immediately above the class and is indicated by the icon containing the open and closed brace symbols ({ }).

That's fine, but imagine now that you have two projects both containing a class called `Car`. You need to use namespaces to separate the `Car` class in one project from the `Car` class in another. Open the Code Editor for `Car` and add `Namespace CarPerformance` before the class definition and `End Namespace` after it. (I've omitted the code for brevity.)

```
Namespace CarPerformance
    Public Class Car
    . . .
    End Class
End Namespace
```

5. Now open the Object Browser again and you'll see a screen like the one in Figure 10-16.

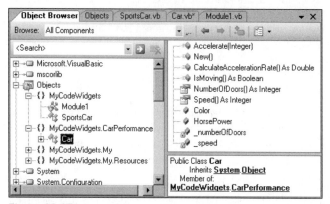

Figure 10-16

6. Since you have added the `CarPerformance` namespace to the `Car` class, any code that references the `Car` class will need to import that namespace in order to be able to access the shorthand methods of the `Car` class. Add this `Imports` statement to the very top of the `SportsCar` class and Module1 module.

```
Imports MyCodeWidgets.CarPerformance
```

How It Works

What you've done is put `Car` inside a namespace called `CarPerformance`. Because this namespace is contained within `MyCodeWidgets`, the full name of the class becomes `MyCodeWidgets.Car Performance.Car`. If you put the classes of the other (imaginary) project into `CarDiagnostics`, it would be called `MyCodeWidgets.CarDiagnostics.Car`. Notice how `Module1` still appears directly inside `MyCodeWidgets`. That's because you haven't wrapped the definition for `Module1` in a namespace as you did with `Car`. Running your project at this point will produce the same results as before.

Inheritance in the .NET Framework

Inheritance is quite an advanced object-oriented topic. However, it's really important to include this here because the .NET Framework makes heavy use of inheritance.

One thing to understand about inheritance in .NET is that no class can inherit directly from more than one class. As everything must inherit from `System.Object`, if a class does not specifically state that it inherits from another class, it inherits directly from `System.Object`. The upshot of this is that everything must inherit directly from exactly one class (everything, that is, except `System.Object` itself).

When we say that each class must inherit directly from exactly one class, we mean that each class can mention only one class in its `Inherits` statement. The class that it's inheriting from can also inherit from another class. So, for example, you could create a class called `Porsche` that is inherited from `SportsCar`. You could then say that it *indirectly* inherits from `Car`, but it *directly* inherits from only one class — `SportsCar`. In fact, many classes indirectly inherit from lots of classes — but there is always a direct ancestry, where each class has exactly one parent.

You may want to have some functionality in different classes that are not related to each other by inheritance. You can solve the problem by putting that functionality in an interface that both classes implement, like the `IDisposable` interface you encountered in Chapter 9.

Summary

In this chapter, you looked at how to start building your own objects. You kicked off by learning how to design an object in terms of the properties and methods that it should support and then built a class that represented a car. You then started adding properties and methods to that class and used it from within your application.

Before moving on to the subject of inheritance, you looked at how an object can be given a constructor — a block of code that's executed whenever an object is created. The discussion of inheritance demonstrated a number of key aspects of object-oriented design, including polymorphism and overriding.

To summarize, you should know how to:

❑ Create properties and methods in a class

❑ Provide a constructor for your class to initialize the state of your class

❑ Inherit another class

❑ Override properties and methods in the inheriting class

❑ Create your own namespace for a class

Exercises

Exercise 1

Modify your `Car` class to implement the `IDisposable` interface. In the `Main` procedure in Module1, add code to dispose of the `objCar` object after calling the `DisplaySportsCarDetails` procedure.

Exercise 2

Modify the code in the `Main` procedure in Module1 to encapsulate the declaration and usage of the `SportsCar` class in a `Using ... End Using` statement. Remember that the `Using ... End Using` statement automatically handles disposal of objects that implement the `IDisposable` interface.

Advanced Object-Oriented Techniques

In Chapter 10, you looked at how you can build your own objects. Prior to that, you had been mostly using objects that already existed in the .NET Framework to build your applications. In this chapter, you'll be taking a look at some more object-oriented software development techniques.

In the first half of this chapter, you create your own classes. You will create a single-tier application like the others we have discussed so far in this book. The idea of creating two-tier applications, as opposed to single-tier applications, will be introduced in Chapter 13. You will then learn about creating your own shared properties and methods. These are very useful when you want a method or property to apply to a class as a whole rather than a specific instance of that class. Finally, you look at memory management in Visual Studio 2005 and what you can do to clean up your objects properly.

In this chapter, you will:

❑   Create classes that can be used by multiple applications

❑   Learn about shared properties and methods

❑   Learn about memory management in the .NET Framework

Building a Favorites Viewer

In the first half of this chapter, you're going to build a simple application that displays all your Internet Explorer favorites and provides a button that you can click to open the URL in Internet Explorer. This application illustrates a key point regarding code reuse and some of the reasons why building code in an object-oriented fashion is so powerful.

Internet Shortcuts and Favorites

You're most likely familiar with the concepts of favorites in Internet Explorer. What you may not know is how Internet Explorer stores those favorites. In fact, the Favorites list is available to all other applications — provided you know where to look.

Windows applications have the option of storing data in separate user folders within a main folder called C:\Documents and Settings. In Figure 11-1 you can see that my computer has a couple of user folders: Margie and Thearon.

Administrator is the default administrator on your computer for users who are using a Windows 2000 operating system or Windows XP Professional. All Users contains items available to all users, irrespective of who they log in as. And Default User is a special folder that Windows uses whenever a new user logs onto the computer for the first time.

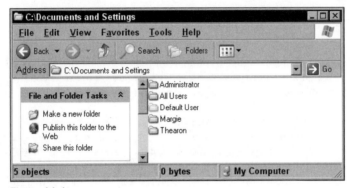

Figure 11-1

Depending on how the security of your computer is configured, you may not be able to access the C:\Documents and Settings folder. If you can, open the folder whose name matches the name that you supply when you log on. In the screenshots throughout this chapter, I've used Thearon. (If you cannot consistently open the folder, ask your system administrator to help you log in as a different user or give you the appropriate permissions.) If you open this folder, you'll find another group of folders. You'll see something like Figure 11-2 (though it may look different depending upon how your login is configured).

You'll notice that on my computer some of these folder icons appear as faint icons, whereas others appear as normal folder icons. My computer is configured to show all folders, so you may find that on your machine the faint folders do not appear because these are normally hidden. This doesn't matter, because the one you're specifically looking for — Favorites — will appear whatever your system settings are.

This folder (Thearon on my computer) is where Windows stores a lot of folders that are related to the operation of your computer for your login account, for example:

❑   Cookies stores the cookies that are placed on the computer by Web sites that you visit.

❑   Desktop stores the folders and links that appear on your desktop.

❑   Favorites stores a list of Internet Explorer favorites.

❑   My Documents stores the default location for storing Microsoft Office and other application data.

❑   Start Menu stores a list of folders and links that appear when you press the Start button.

❑   User Data stores specific user data related to the applications that you run.

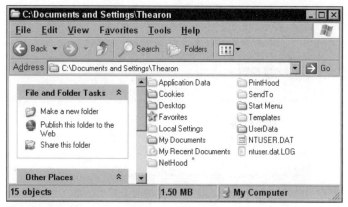

Figure 11-2

It's the Favorites folder that you're interested in here, so open it. You'll see something like Figure 11-3 (obviously, this list will be different on your computer, because you'll have different favorites).

Figure 11-3

You'll notice that the links inside this folder relate to the links that appear in the Favorites menu in your browser. If you double-click one of those links, you'll see that Internet Explorer opens and navigates to the URL that the favorite points to.

You can be fairly confident at this stage that, if you have a folder of links that appear to be favorites, you can create an application that opens this folder and can do something with the links — namely, iterate through all of them, add each of them to a list, find out what URL it belongs to, and provide a way to open that URL from your application. In the example that follows, you're going to ignore the folders and just deal with the favorites that appear in the root Favorites folder.

Your final application will look like Figure 11-4.

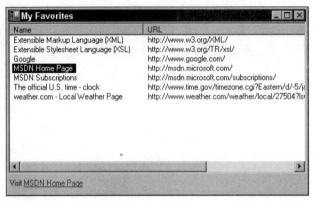

Figure 11-4

Using Classes

So far in this book, you've built basic applications that do something, but most functionality that they provide has been coded into the applications' forms. Here, you're about to build some functionality that can load a list of favorites from a user's computer and provide a way to open Internet Explorer to show the URL. However, you do it in a way that means you can use the *list of favorites* functionality elsewhere.

The best way to build this application is to create a set of classes that include the following classes:

❑ `WebFavorite`, which represents a single favorite and has member variables such as `Name` and `Url`

❑ `Favorites`, which can scan the favorites list on the user's computer, creating a new `Web Favorite` object for each favorite

❑ `WebFavoriteCollection`, which contains a collection of `WebFavorite` objects

These three classes provide the *back-end* functionality of the application — in other words, all classes that do something but do not present the user with an interface. This isolates the code in the classes and allows you to reuse the code from different parts of the application — *code reuse*. You also need a *front end* to this application, which, in this case, will be a Windows form with a couple of controls on it.

In the next few sections, you build your classes and Windows application and come up with the application shown in Figure 11-4. You start by building the Windows Application project in the following Try It Out.

Try It Out   **Creating Favorites Viewer**

1. Open Visual Studio 2005 and create a new Visual Basic Windows Application project called **Favorites Viewer**.

2. Modify Form1, setting these properties:

    ❑   Set Size to **464, 280**.

    ❑   Set StartPosition to CenterScreen.

    ❑   Set Text to **My Favorites**.

3. Add a ListView control to the form and size it to look similar to Figure 11-5 and set these properties:

    ❑   Set Name to **lstFavorites**.

    ❑   Set Anchor to Top, Bottom, Left, Right.

    ❑   Set View to Details.

4. Select the Columns property in the Properties window for the lstFavorites control. Click the ellipsis dots (...) button to display the ColumnHeader Collection Editor dialog box.

5. Click the Add button. Set these properties on the new column header:

    ❑   Set Name to **hdrName**.

    ❑   Set Text to **Name**.

    ❑   Set Width to **250**.

6. Click the Add button again to add a second column. Set these properties on the new column header:

    ❑   Set Name to **hdrUrl**.

    ❑   Set Text to **URL**.

    ❑   Set Width to **250**.

7. Click OK to close the editor.

8. Add a LinkLabel control to the bottom of the form and set these properties:

    ❑   Set Name to **lnkUrl**.

    ❑   Set Anchor to Bottom, Left, Right.

    ❑   Set TextAlign to MiddleLeft.

9. Your completed form should now look similar to the one shown in Figure 11-5.

How It Works

All that you've done here is to build the basic shell of the application, the form that will display the results of the processing. You started by modifying some basic properties of the form and then added two controls: a list view and a link label. The ListView control will be used to display the name and URL of each favorite in your Favorites folder. The LinkLabel control will be used to launch a browser with the selected favorite URL in the list.

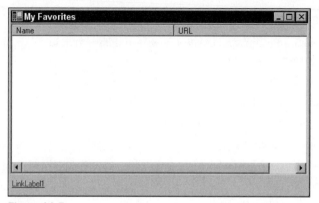

Figure 11-5

That's the basics of the form put together. In the next Try It Out, you look at how you can add the back-end classes. In previous chapters, you learned how to add classes to a Visual Studio 2005 project, so you will use this knowledge to create the back end of your application.

Try It Out   Building WebFavorite

1. Using the Solution Explorer, right-click Favorites Viewer. Select Add ⇨ Class from the menu to display the Add New Item – Favorites Viewer dialog box. Enter a name of **WebFavorite.vb** and then click the Add button.

2. Add this namespace import declaration to the top of the code listing:

```
Imports System.IO

Public Class WebFavorite
```

3. This class will need to implement the IDisposable interface, so add this Implements statement. When you press Enter, Visual Studio 2005 inserts the members and methods associated with the IDisposable interface:

```
Public Class WebFavorite

    Implements IDisposable
```

4. Now add these two members after the IDisposable interface code inserted by Visual Studio 2005:

```
#End Region

    'Public Members
    Public Name As String
    Public Url As String
```

5. Now add the Load method, which will load the member variables in this class:

```
    Public Sub Load(ByVal fileName As String)
        'Declare variables
```

```
        Dim strData As String
        Dim strLines() As String
        Dim strLine As String
        Dim objFileInfo As New FileInfo(fileName)

        'Set the Name member to the file name minus the extension
        Name = objFileInfo.Name.Substring(0, _
            objFileInfo.Name.Length - objFileInfo.Extension.Length)

        Try
            'Read the entire contents of the file
            strData = My.Computer.FileSystem.ReadAllText(fileName)

            'Split the lines of data in the file
            strLines = strData.Split(New String() {ControlChars.CrLf}, _
                StringSplitOptions.RemoveEmptyEntries)

            'Process each line looking for the URL
            For Each strLine In strLines
                'Does the line of data start with URL=
                If strLine.StartsWith("URL=") Then
                    'Yes, set the Url member to the actual URL
                    Url = strLine.Substring(4)
                    'Exit the For...Next loop
                    Exit For
                End If
            Next
        Catch IOExceptionErr As IOException
            'Return the exception to the caller
            Throw New Exception(IOExceptionErr.Message)
        End Try
    End Sub
```

How It Works

It will be useful to examine how the WebFavorite class populates itself when the Load method is invoked.

The first thing you do is declare the variables needed by this method. The strData variable will be used to receive the entire contents of the favorite's shortcut file. The strLines() variable will be used to create an array containing each individual line of data from the strData variable, and the strLine variable will be used to iterate through the array of lines. Finally, the objFileInfo object will be used to get the file information from the full path and filename passed to this method.

```
Public Sub Load(ByVal fileName As String)
    'Declare variables
    Dim strData As String
    Dim strLines() As String
    Dim strLine As String
    Dim objFileInfo As New FileInfo(fileName)
```

Next, the Name member is set to just the filename of the favorite's shortcut file; for example Extensible Markup Language (XML). This is the name of the favorite that shows up on the Favorites list in the browser. The fileName parameter that will be passed to this method will contain the complete path to the file, the filename, and the file extension (for example, `C:\Documents and Settings\Thearon\Favorites\Extensible Markup Language (XML).url`). What you have to do is extract only the filename from the complete path.

You do this by using the `objFileInfo` object, which has been initialized to an instance of the `FileInfo` class with the `fileName` variable passed to it. The `FileInfo` class provides several methods that return the various parts of the complete file path and name, such as only the filename and only the file extension.

You use the `Name` property of the `objFileInfo` object to get just the filename and extension of the file without the path, and you use the `Substring` method of the `Name` property to extract the filename minus the file extension. To supply the parameters to the `Substring` method, you also use the `Length` property of the `Name` property in the `objFileInfo` object to determine how long the filename is and the `Length` property of the `Extension` property to determine how long the file extension is.

So basically what you're saying here is, "Take a substring, starting at the first character, and continue for the complete length of the string minus the length of the `Extension` property." This, in effect, removes the `.url` from the end. Remember that the array of characters that make up a string is zero-based; thus you specify a starting position of `0` for the `SubString` method.

```
'Set the Name member to the file name minus the extension
Name = objFileInfo.Name.Substring(0, _
    objFileInfo.Name.Length - objFileInfo.Extension.Length)
```

You read the entire contents of the file next into the `strData`. Because you are reading from a file, you'll want to encapsulate the logic in a `Try...Catch` block to handle any IO exceptions that might occur.

The first thing that you do in this `Try...Catch` block is read the entire contents of the file into the `strData` variable. This is done using the `My.Computer` namespace and the `ReadAllText` method of the `FileSystem` class. This method will handle all the details of opening the file, reading the entire contents, closing the file, and releasing the resources used to perform these operations.

```
Try
    'Read the entire contents of the file
    strData = My.Computer.FileSystem.ReadAllText(fileName)
```

After the contents of the file have been read, the `strData` variable will contain something similar to the data shown here. This is the data from the `C:\Documents and Settings\Thearon\Favorites\Extensible Markup Language (XML).url` shortcut file.

```
[DEFAULT]
BASEURL=http://www.w3.org/XML/
[InternetShortcut]
URL=http://www.w3.org/XML/
Modified=B0C9EC877EB3C401E2
```

Now that you have the entire contents of the favorite's shortcut file in a single string variable, you want to split the contents of the `strData` variable into separate lines. This is done using the `Split` method of the `String` class, from which the `strData` variable is derived. The `Split` method is an overloaded method, and the version that you are using here accepts an array of strings that separate each line as the first parameter and the split options as the second parameter.

The data in the `strData` variable is separated with a carriage return and line feed character combination, and thus you provide a string array containing only one entry, `ControlChars.CrLf`, as the first parameter of the `Split` method. The split options parameter of the `Split` method is a value in the `StringSplitOptions` enumeration that let you specify how empty elements are handled. Here you specify the `RemoveEmptyEntries` constant of that enumeration, to remove any empty entries in the array that gets returned.

```
'Split the lines of data in the file
strLines = strData.Split(New String() {ControlChars.CrLf}, _
    StringSplitOptions.RemoveEmptyEntries)
```

Next you need to process each line of data in the `strLines` array using a For . . . Next loop. You are looking for the line of data that begins with `"URL="`. Using an If . . . Then statement, you check the `strLine` variable to see whether it begins with the specified text. The `StartsWith` method of the `String` class, the class from which the `strLine` variable is derived, returns a `Boolean` value of `True` if the string that is being tested contains the string that is passed to this method and a value of `False` if it does not.

If the line of data being tested starts with the text `"URL="`, then it is the actual URL that you want to save in the `Url` member of the class. This is done by using the `SubString` method to get the URL in the `strLine` variable minus the beginning text. In order to do this, you pass a starting position of 4 to the `SubString` method, telling it to start extracting data starting at position 4, because positions 0 – 3 contain the text `"URL="`. Once you find the data that you are looking for and set the `Url` member, there's no need to process the rest of the `strLines` array, so you exit the For . . . Next loop.

```
'Process each line looking for the URL
For Each strLine In strLines
    'Does the line of data start with URL=
    If strLine.StartsWith("URL=") Then
        'Yes, set the Url member to the actual URL
        Url = strLine.Substring(4)
        'Exit the For...Next loop
        Exit For
    End If
Next
```

The `Catch` block will handle any IO exception that might be thrown. Here you want to return the exception back to the caller of this method, so you throw a new `Exception` and pass it the `Message` property of the `IOExceptionErr` variable. This gracefully handles any IO exceptions in this class and returns the message of the exception to the caller.

```
Catch IOExceptionErr As IOException
    'Return the exception to the caller
    Throw New Exception(IOExceptionErr.Message)
End Try
End Sub
```

Scanning Favorites

So that you can scan the favorites, in the next Try It Out you add a couple of new classes to the project. The first, `WebFavoriteCollection`, will be used to hold a collection of `WebFavorite` objects. The second, `Favorites`, will physically scan the Favorites folder on the computer, create new `WebFavorite` objects, and add them to the collection.

Try It Out   Scanning Favorites

1. Using the Solution Explorer, create a new class called **WebFavoriteCollection**. This class will be instantiated to an object that can hold a number of WebFavorite objects.

2. Add the highlighted code in your class:

```
Public Class WebFavoriteCollection

    Inherits CollectionBase

    Public Sub Add(ByVal Favorite As WebFavorite)
        'Add item to the collection
        List.Add(Favorite)
    End Sub

    Public Sub Remove(ByVal Index As Integer)
        'Remove item from collection
        If Index >= 0 And Index < Count Then
            List.Remove(Index)
        End If
    End Sub

    Public ReadOnly Property Item(ByVal Index As Integer) As WebFavorite
        Get
            'Get an item from the collection by its index
            Return CType(List.Item(Index), WebFavorite)
        End Get
    End Property
End Class
```

3. Create another new class called **Favorites**. This will be used to scan the Favorites folder and return a WebFavoriteCollection containing a WebFavorite object for each favorite in the folder. Like the WebFavorite class, this class will implement the IDisposable interface. Enter the following highlighted code and press Enter to add the properties and methods of the IDisposable interface to your class:

```
Public Class Favorites

    Implements IDisposable
```

4. Next, add this member below the code for the IDisposable interface:

```
    'Public member
    Public FavoritesCollection As WebFavoriteCollection
```

5. You need a read-only property that can return the path to the user's Favorites folder. Add the following code to the Favorites class:

```
    Public ReadOnly Property FavoritesFolder() As String
        Get
            'Return the path to the user's Favorites folder
            Return Environment.GetFolderPath( _
```

```
                        Environment.SpecialFolder.Favorites)
        End Get
End Property
```

6. Finally, you need a method that's capable of scanning through the Favorites folder looking for files. When it finds one, it will create a `WebFavorite` object and add it to the Favorites collection. You provide two versions of this method — one that automatically determines the path of the favorites by using the `FavoritesFolder` property and one that scans through a given folder. To create this overloaded method, add the following code to the `Favorites` class:

```
Public Sub ScanFavorites()
    'Scan the Favorites folder
    ScanFavorites(FavoritesFolder)
End Sub

Public Sub ScanFavorites(ByVal folderName As String)
    'If the FavoritesCollection member has not been instantiated
    'then instaniate it
    If FavoritesCollection Is Nothing Then
        FavoritesCollection = New WebFavoriteCollection
    End If

    'Process each file in the Favorites folder
    For Each strFile As String In _
        My.Computer.FileSystem.GetFiles(folderName)

        'If the file has a url extension...
        If strFile.EndsWith(".url", True, Nothing) Then

            Try
                'Create and use a new instanace of the
                'WebFavorite class
                Using objWebFavorite As New WebFavorite
                    'Load the file information
                    objWebFavorite.Load(strFile)

                    'Add the object to the collection
                    FavoritesCollection.Add(objWebFavorite)
                End Using
            Catch ExceptionErr As Exception
                'Return the exception to the caller
                Throw New Exception(ExceptionErr.Message)
            End Try

        End If

    Next
End Sub
```

To make all of this work, you need to have the Favorites Viewer project create an instance of a `Favorites` object, scan the favorites, and add each one it finds to the list. This will be done in the next Try It Out.

How It Works

There's a lot to take in there, but a good starting point is the `WebFavoriteCollection` class. This illustrates an important best practice when working with lists of objects. As you saw in Chapter 5, you can hold lists of objects in one of two ways: in an array or in a collection.

When building classes that work with lists, the best practice is to use a collection. You should build collections that are also tied into using whatever types you're working with, so in this example you built a `WebFavoriteCollection` class that exclusively holds a collection of `WebFavorite` objects.

You derived `WebFavoriteCollection` from `CollectionBase`. This provides the basic list that the collection will use:

```
Public Class WebFavoriteCollection
    Inherits CollectionBase
```

To fit in with the .NET Framework's way of doing things, you need to define three methods on a collection that you build. The `Add` method adds an item to the collection:

```
Public Sub Add(ByVal Favorite As WebFavorite)
    'Add item to the collection
    List.Add(Favorite)
End Sub
```

The `List` property is a protected member of `CollectionBase` that only code within classes inheriting from `CollectionBase` can access. You access this property to add, remove, and find items in the list. You can see from the `Add` method here that you specified that the item must be a `WebFavorite` object. This is why you're supposed to build collections using this technique — because you can add objects only of type `WebFavorite`; anyone who has hold of a `WebFavoriteCollection` object knows that it will contain objects only of type `WebFavorite`. This makes life much easier for users, because they will not get nasty surprises when they discover it contains something else, and therefore reduces the chance of errors. The `Remove` method that you built removes an item from the list:

```
Public Sub Remove(ByVal Index As Integer)
    'Remove item from collection
    If Index >= 0 And Index < Count Then
        List.Remove(Index)
    End If
End Sub
```

The `Item` method lets you get an item from the list when given a specific index:

```
Public ReadOnly Property Item(ByVal Index As Integer) As WebFavorite
    Get
        'Get an item from the collection by its index
        Return CType(List.Item(Index), WebFavorite)
    End Get
End Property
```

So how do you populate this collection? Well, in the `Favorites` class you built an overloaded method called `ScanFavorites`. The second version of this method takes a folder and examines it for files that end in `.url`. But before you look at that, you need to look at the `FavoritesFolder` property.

Since the location of the Favorites folder can change depending on the currently logged-in user, you have to ask Windows where this folder actually is. To do this, you use the shared `GetFolderPath` method of the `System.Environment` class:

```
Public ReadOnly Property FavoritesFolder() As String
    Get
        'Return the path to the user's Favorites folder
        Return Environment.GetFolderPath( _
            Environment.SpecialFolder.Favorites)
    End Get
End Property
```

The `GetFolderPath` method uses one of the constants from the `Environment.SpecialFolder` enumeration. This enumeration provides constants for many different special folders that you are likely to need access to when writing applications.

When the application asks this class to load in the favorites from the Favorites folder, it calls `Scan Favorites`. The first version of this method accepts no parameters. It looks up the location of the user's Favorites folder and passes that to the second version of this overloaded method:

```
Public Sub ScanFavorites()
    'Scan the Favorites folder
    ScanFavorites(FavoritesFolder)
End Sub
```

The first thing that the second version of this overloaded method does is check to ensure that the `FavoritesCollection` member has been instantiated using the `WebFavoriteCollection` class. If it hasn't, it instantiates this member using that class.

```
Public Sub ScanFavorites(ByVal folderName As String)
    'If the FavoritesCollection member has not been instantiated
    'then instaniate it
    If FavoritesCollection Is Nothing Then
        FavoritesCollection = New WebFavoriteCollection
    End If
```

Now you want to get a list of files in the Favorites folder and process them. You do this by calling the `GetFiles` method in the `FileSystem` class and passing it the path and name of the Favorites folder. This class exists in the `My.Computer` namespace as indicated by the following code.

The `GetFiles` method returns an array of filenames, and you process this array using a `For Each...Next` loop. You declare the variable, `strFile`, in-line in the `For Each` loop, as indicated in the following code, and this variable will be set to a filename in the Favorites folder for each iteration of the loop.

```
'Process each file in the Favorites folder
For Each strFile As String In _
    My.Computer.FileSystem.GetFiles(folderName)
```

Within the loop, you first test the filename to see whether it is a Favorites file by checking to see whether it contains a `.url` file extension. The `strFile` variable is derived from the `String` class; thus you can use the `EndsWith` method to determine whether the filename ends with the `.url` file extension.

The EndsWith method is an overloaded method, and the version that you are using here accepts three parameters. The first parameter accepts the value to be compared to the end of the string, and here you supply the text .url. The next parameter accepts a Boolean value indicating whether the EndsWith method should ignore the case of the text when making the comparison. You do want to ignore the case when making the comparison, so you pass a value of True for this parameter. The final parameter accepts the culture information that will be used when making the comparison. Passing a value of Nothing here indicates that you want to use the current culture information defined on the user's computer.

```
'If the file has a url extension...
If strFile.EndsWith(".url", True, Nothing) Then
```

If the filename being processed does contain the .url file extension, then you want to load the file information and have it added to the Favorites collection. Since you are using the WebFavorite class and this class reads the file, the potential for an exception exists. Therefore, you need to encapsulate the next block of code in a Try . . . Catch block to handle any exceptions that might be thrown by the WebFavorite class.

The first thing that you do in the Try block is use a Using . . . End Using block to declare, instantiate, use, and destroy the WebFavorite class. Remember that you can use the Using statement only with a class that implements the IDisposable interface, which is why you added that interface to the Web Favorite class.

The first thing that you do in the Using . . . End Using block is call the Load method on the objWeb Favorite object, passing it the filename of the favorite's shortcut file. Then you add the objWeb Favorite to the Favorites collection.

```
Try
    'Create and use a new instanace of the
    'WebFavorite class
    Using objWebFavorite As New WebFavorite
        'Load the file information
        objWebFavorite.Load(strFile)

        'Add the object to the collection
        FavoritesCollection.Add(objWebFavorite)
    End Using
```

The Catch block contains the necessary code to handle an exception that might be thrown by the WebFavorite class and to return that exception to the caller of this method. This is done by throwing a new Exception, passing it the message received in the ExceptionErr variable.

```
    Catch ExceptionErr As Exception
        'Return the exception to the caller
        Throw New Exception(ExceptionErr.Message)
    End Try

        End If


    Next
End Sub
```

In this next Try It Out, you'll implement the functionality in your form to use the `Favorites` class to gather all of your Internet Favorites and the `WebFavorite` class to load those shortcuts in the list view control on your form.

Creating an Instance of a Favorites Object

1. In the form code, select (Form1 Events) in the Class Name combo box and select Load in the Method Name combo box. Add the highlighted code:

```
Private Sub Form1_Load(ByVal sender As Object, ByVal e As System.EventArgs) _
    Handles Me.Load

        Try
            'Create and use a new instanace of the Favorites class
            Using objFavorites As New Favorites

                'Scan the Favorites folder
                objFavorites.ScanFavorites()

                'Process each objWebFavorite object in the
                'favorites collection
                For Each objWebFavorite As WebFavorite In _
                    objFavorites.FavoritesCollection

                    'Declare a ListViewItem object
                    Dim objListViewItem As New ListViewItem
                    'Set the properties of the ListViewItem object
                    objListViewItem.Text = objWebFavorite.Name
                    objListViewItem.SubItems.Add(objWebFavorite.Url)
                    'Add the ListViewItem object to the ListView
                    lstFavorites.Items.Add(objListViewItem)
                Next

            End Using
        Catch ExceptionErr As Exception
            'Display the error
            MessageBox.Show(ExceptionErr.Message, "Favorites Viewer", _
                MessageBoxButtons.OK, MessageBoxIcon.Warning)
        End Try
End Sub
```

2. Run the project and you should see something like Figure 11-6.

How It Works

Since both the `Favorites` and `WebFavorite` classes can throw an exception, you must handle any exceptions that might be thrown. Therefore, all of your code is encapsulated in a `Try ... Catch` block. You use a `Using ... End Using` statement to declare, instantiate, and destroy the object created using the `Favorites` class. Regardless of whether this class throws an exception, the `Using` statement will destroy the `objFavorites` object that it declares.

```
Private Sub Form1_Load(ByVal sender As Object, ByVal e As System.EventArgs) _
    Handles Me.Load
```

```
Try
    'Create and use a new instanace of the Favorites class
    Using objFavorites As New Favorites
```

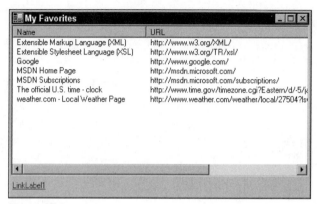

Figure 11-6

Inside the `Using ... End Using` block you have the `objFavorites` object scan the users Favorites folder by calling the `ScanFavorites` method. The effect here is that a new `WebFavoritesCollection` object will be created and filled and will be accessible through the `FavoritesCollection` property.

```
    'Scan the Favorites folder
    objFavorites.ScanFavorites()
```

After the `ScanFavorites` method has finished, you take each `WebFavorite` in the `Favorites Collection` and add it to the list view control on your form. You do this by first declaring a `ListView Item` and then setting the `Text` property to the Favorite name. Then you add the URL of the favorite to the `SubItems` collection, and finally you add the `objListViewItem` to the `Items` collection of the list view control.

```
    'Process each objWebFavorite object in the
    'favorites collection
    For Each objWebFavorite As WebFavorite In _
        objFavorites.FavoritesCollection

        'Declare a ListViewItem object
        Dim objListViewItem As New ListViewItem
        'Set the properties of the ListViewItem object
        objListViewItem.Text = objWebFavorite.Name
        objListViewItem.SubItems.Add(objWebFavorite.Url)
        'Add the ListViewItem object to the ListView
        lstFavorites.Items.Add(objListViewItem)
    Next

    End Using
```

You wrap up this code with the Catch block, which will handle any exceptions thrown and display the exception message in a message box dialog box.

```
Catch ExceptionErr As Exception
    'Display the error
    MessageBox.Show(ExceptionErr.Message, "Favorites Viewer", _
        MessageBoxButtons.OK, MessageBoxIcon.Warning)
    End Try
End Sub
```

That's it! Now you can display a list of the favorites installed on the user's machine. However, you can't actually view favorites, so let's look at that now.

Viewing Favorites

Now that all of your code is in place to retrieve and display a list of favorites, in the next Try It Out you'll to add some code to display the selected favorite in the LinkLabel control on your form and then add some code to the control to process the selected link in Internet Explorer.

Try It Out   Viewing Favorites

1.   In the Code Editor for Form1, click lstFavorites in the Class Name combo box and the Click event in the Method Name combo box. Add the following highlighted code to the Click event handler:

```
Private Sub lstFavorites_Click(ByVal sender As Object, _
    ByVal e As System.EventArgs) Handles lstFavorites.Click

    'Update the link label control Text property
    lnkUrl.Text = "Visit " & lstFavorites.SelectedItems.Item(0).Text

    'Clear the default hyperlink
    lnkUrl.Links.Clear()

    'Add the selected hyperlink to the LinkCollection
    lnkUrl.Links.Add(6, lstFavorites.SelectedItems.Item(0).Text.Length, _
        lstFavorites.SelectedItems.Item(0).SubItems(1).Text)
End Sub
```

2.   Next, click lnkUrl in the Class Name combo box and select the LinkClicked event in the Method Name combo box. Add the following highlighted code to the LinkClicked event:

```
Private Sub lnkUrl_LinkClicked(ByVal sender As Object, _
    ByVal e As System.Windows.Forms.LinkLabelLinkClickedEventArgs) _
    Handles lnkUrl.LinkClicked

    'Process the selected link
    Process.Start(e.Link.LinkData)
End Sub
```

3. Run the project. You should now see that when a URL is selected from the list, the LinkLabel control changes to reflect the name of the selected item. (Refer to Figure 11-4.) If you click the link, Internet Explorer will open the URL in the LinkLabel control's LinkCollection.

How It Works

When you click an item in the list view control, the Click event is fired for that control. You added code the Click event to load the link label control with the selected link. You start by first setting the `Text` property of the LinkLabel control. This is the text that will be displayed on the form as shown in Figure 11-4.

You set the `Text` property using the static text `"Visit` followed by the actual favorite name. The Favorite name is retrieved from the list view control's `Item` collection. Each row in the list view control is called an item and the first column contains the text of the item. Each column past the first column in a row is called a sub item and is a sub item of the item (the text in the first column). The text that gets displayed in the link label is taken from the `Text` property of the `Item` collection.

```
Private Sub lstFavorites_Click(ByVal sender As Object, _
    ByVal e As System.EventArgs) Handles lstFavorites.Click

    'Update the link label control Text property
    lnkUrl.Text = "Visit " & lstFavorites.SelectedItems.Item(0).Text
```

The `Links` property of the LinkLabel control contains a `LinkCollection` that contains a default hyperlink consisting of the text that is displayed in the LinkLabel control. You want to clear this collection and set it using the correct hyperlink for the selected Favorite. You do this by calling the `Clear` method on the `Links` property.

```
    'Clear the default hyperlink
    lnkUrl.Links.Clear()
```

Finally, you want to add your hyperlink using the subitem of the selected item in the ListView control. The `Add` method of the `Links` property is an overloaded method, and the method that you are using here expects three parameters: `start`, `length`, and `linkdata`. The `start` parameter specifies the starting position of the text in the `Text` property that you want as the hyperlink, and the `length` parameter specifies how long the hyperlink should be.

You do not want the word "Visit" to be part of the hyperlink, so you specify the starting position to be 6, which also accounts for the space after the word "Visit". Then you specify the `length` parameter using the `Length` property of the `Text` property of selected item in the list view control. Finally, you need to specify the `linkdata` parameter by specifying the selected subitem from the list view control. This sub item contains the actual URL for the favorite.

```
        'Add the selected hyperlink to the LinkCollection
        lnkUrl.Links.Add(6, lstFavorites.SelectedItems.Item(0).Text.Length, _
            lstFavorites.SelectedItems.Item(0).SubItems(1).Text)
    End Sub
```

When a hyperlink on the LinkLabel control is clicked, it fires the LinkClicked event, and this is where you have placed your code to process the hyperlink of the favorite being displayed in this control. The `LinkLabelLinkClickedEventArgs` class contains information about the link label and, in particular, the actual hyperlink in the `LinkCollection`.

To retrieve the hyperlink, you access the LinkData property of the Link property. Then you pass this data to the Start method of the Process class, which will cause a browser to be opened and to display the selected hyperlink.

```
Private Sub lnkUrl_LinkClicked(ByVal sender As Object, _
    ByVal e As System.Windows.Forms.LinkLabelLinkClickedEventArgs) _
    Handles lnkUrl.LinkClicked

    'Process the selected link
    Process.Start(e.Link.LinkData)
End Sub
```

An Alternative Favorite Viewer

You know that building separate classes promotes code reuse, but let's prove that. If code reuse is such a hot idea, you should be able to build another application that can use the functionality in the classes to find and open favorites without having to rewrite or change any of the code.

In this case, you might have given a colleague the Favorites, WebFavorite, and WebFavorite Collection classes, and that colleague should be able to build a new application that uses this functionality without having to understand the internals of how Internet shortcuts work or how Windows stores the user's favorites.

Building a Favorites Tray

In this section, you build an application that displays a small icon on the system tray. Clicking this icon will open a list of the user's favorites as a menu, as shown in Figure 11-7. Clicking a favorite automatically opens Internet Explorer to the URL.

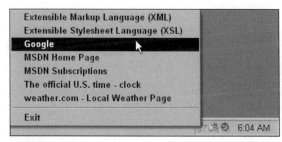

Figure 11-7

To demonstrate this principle of code reuse, you need to create a new Visual Basic 2005 project.

Try It Out   **Building a Favorites Tray**

1. Using Visual Studio, select File ➪ Add ➪ New Project from the menu and create a new Visual Basic 2005 Windows Application project called **Favorites Tray**.

2. When the Designer for Form1 appears, change the WindowState property to Minimized and change the ShowInTaskbar property to False. This will, effectively, prevent the form from being displayed.

3. Using the Toolbox, drag a NotifyIcon control onto the form. Set the Name property of the new control to **icnNotify** and set the Text property to **Right-click me to view Favorites**.

4. Next, open the Code Editor for Form1. In the Class Name combo box at the top of the Code Editor, select (Form1 Events), and in the Method Name combo box select VisibleChanged. Add this highlighted code to the event handler:

```
Private Sub Form1_VisibleChanged(ByVal sender As Object, _
    ByVal e As System.EventArgs) Handles Me.VisibleChanged

    'If the user can see us, hide us
    If Me.Visible = True Then Me.Visible = False
End Sub
```

5. You now need to design a new icon. If you don't do this, the icon won't be displayed on the task bar and your application won't do anything. Using the Solution Explorer, right-click the Favorites Tray project and select Add ➪ New Item. Scroll down the Templates list and select Icon File, as shown in Figure 11-8. Enter the filename as **Tray.ico** and click Add.

Figure 11-8

6. This displays Visual Studio 2005's Image Editor. You can use this to design new icons, new cursors, and new bitmap images for use in your applications. It's fairly intuitive to use, so I won't go through how you actually draw in much detail. In the toolbar you'll find a list of tools that you can use to design the icon, as shown in Figure 11-9.

Figure 11-9

7. From the menu, select Image ⇨ Show Colors Window to bring up the palette of colors shown in Figure 11-10, if they are not already displayed.

Figure 11-10

8. Before you start painting, you'll need to change the icon type. By default, Visual Studio 2005 will create a 32_32 pixel icon, which is too large to fit on the system tray. From the menu, select Image ⇨ New Image Type. Then in the New Icon Image Type dialog box, select 16x16, 256 colors and click OK.

9. This creates a new subicon within the image file, but you need to delete the main 32x32 icon, otherwise things will get confusing. From the menu again, select Image ⇨ Current Icon Image Types ⇨ 32x32, 16 colors. Then, immediately select Image ⇨ Delete Image Type from the menu. Repeat this process for the 16x16, 16 color image. When done, you should be left with only the 16x16, 256 color image.

10. If you're feeling creative, you can design your own icon for this application. On the other hand, you can do what we've done, which is to use a screen capture utility to take the favorites icon from Internet Explorer. Our preferred utility is SnagIt (www.techsmith.com/), but a number of graphics programs offer this functionality.

11. Save the icon by selecting File ⇨ Save Tray.ico from the menu.

12. Go back to the Form Designer and select the icnNotify control at the bottom of the IDE. Use the Icon property in the properties list to open the icon you just created in the NotifyIcon control.

13. Right-click the Favorites Tray project in the Solution Explorer and select Set As Startup Project. Now try running the project. You should discover that the tray icon is added to your system tray as shown in Figure 11-11, but no form window will appear. If you hover your mouse over the icon, you'll see the message that you set in the Text property of the Notify Icon control.

Figure 11-11

14. Also, you'll notice that there appears to be no way to stop the program! Flip back to Visual Studio and select Debug ⇨ Stop Debugging from the menu.

15. When you do this, although the program will stop, the icon will remain in the tray. To get rid of it, hover the mouse over it and it should disappear.

Windows redraws the icons in the system tray only when necessary (for example, when the mouse is passed over an icon).

How It Works

Setting a form to appear minimized (`WindowState = Minimized`) and telling it not to appear in the taskbar (`ShowInTaskbar = False`) has the effect of creating a window that's hidden. You need a form to support the tray icon, but you don't need the form for any other reason. However, this is only half the battle, because the form could appear in the Alt+ Tab application switching list, unless you add the following code, which you already did:

```
Private Sub Form1_VisibleChanged(ByVal sender As Object, _
    ByVal e As System.EventArgs) Handles Me.VisibleChanged

    'If the user can see us, hide us
    If Me.Visible = True Then Me.Visible = False
End Sub
```

This event handler has a brute force approach that says, "If the user can see me, hide me."

Displaying Favorites

In the next Try It Out, let's look at how to display the favorites. The first thing you need to do is include the classes built in `Favorites Viewer` in this Favorites Tray solution. You can then use the `Favorites` object to get a list of favorites back and build a menu.

Try It Out   Displaying Favorites

1. To display favorites, you need to get hold of the classes defined in the Favorites Viewer project. To do this you need to add the `Favorites`, `WebFavorite`, and `WebFavoriteCollection` classes to this solution.

Using the Solution Explorer, right-click the Favorites Tray project and select Add ⇨ Existing Item. Click the Browse button and find the `Favorites` class. This will be in the Favorites Viewer project folder. After clicking Add the class appears in the Solution Explorer for this project. You can select multiple files at once by holding down the Ctrl key.

2. Repeat this for the `WebFavorite` and `WebFavoriteCollection` classes.

3. Now, create a new class in Favorites Tray by clicking the project once more and selecting Add ⇨ Class. Call the new class **WebFavoriteMenuItem.vb** and then click the Add button to add this class to the project.

4. Set the new class to inherit from `System.Windows.Forms.MenuItem` by adding this code:

```
Public Class WebFavoriteMenuItem
    Inherits MenuItem
```

5. Add this member and method to the class:

```
'Public member
Public Favorite As WebFavorite

'Constructor
Public Sub New(ByVal newFavorite As WebFavorite)
    'Set the property
    Favorite = newFavorite
```

```
    'Update the text
    Text = Favorite.Name
End Sub
```

6. Unlike `ListViewItem`, `MenuItem` objects can react to themselves being clicked by overloading the Click method. In the Class Name combo box at the top of the Code Editor, select (WebFavoriteMenuItem Events) and then select the Click event in the Method Name combo box. Add the following highlighted code to the Click event handler:

```
Private Sub WebFavoriteMenuItem_Click(ByVal sender As Object, _
    ByVal e As System.EventArgs) Handles Me.Click
```

```
    'Open the favorite
    If Not Favorite Is Nothing Then
        Process.Start(Favorite.Url)
    End If
End Sub
```

7. You need to do a similar trick to add an Exit option to your pop-up menu. Using the Solution Explorer create a new class called **ExitMenuItem.vb** in the Favorites Tray project. Add the following highlighted code to this class:

```
Public Class ExitMenuItem
```

```
    Inherits MenuItem

    'Constructor
    Public Sub New()
        Text = "Exit"
    End Sub

    Private Sub ExitMenuItem_Click(ByVal sender As Object, _
        ByVal e As System.EventArgs) Handles Me.Click

        Application.Exit()
    End Sub
End Class
```

8. Finally, you're in a position where you can load the favorites and create a menu for use with the tray icon. Add these members to Form1:

```
Public Class Form1
    'Public member
    Public Favorites As New Favorites()

    'Private member
    Private _loadCalled As Boolean = False
```

9. In the Class Name combo select (Form1 Events) and, in the Method Name combo box, select the Load event. Now add the following highlighted code to this event handler:

```
Private Sub Form1_Load(ByVal sender As Object, _
    ByVal e As System.EventArgs) Handles Me.Load
```

```
              'Load the favorites
              Favorites.ScanFavorites()

              'Create a new context menu
              Dim objMenu As New ContextMenu()

              'Process each favorite
              For Each objWebFavorite As WebFavorite In Favorites.FavoritesCollection
                  'Create a menu item
                  Dim objItem As New WebFavoriteMenuItem(objWebFavorite)
                  'Add it to the menu
                  objMenu.MenuItems.Add(objItem)
              Next

              'Add a separator menu item
              objMenu.MenuItems.Add("-")

              'Now add the Exit menu item
              objMenu.MenuItems.Add(New ExitMenuItem())

              'Finally, tell the tray icon to use this menu
              icnNotify.ContextMenu = objMenu

              'Set the load flag and hide ourselves
              _loadCalled = True
              Me.Hide()
          End Sub
```

10. Modify the `Form1_VisibleChanged` procedure as follows:

```
      Private Sub Form1_VisibleChanged(ByVal sender As Object, _
          ByVal e As System.EventArgs) Handles Me.VisibleChanged

              'Don't set the Visible property until the Load event has
              'been processed
              If _loadCalled = False Then
                  Return
              End If

              'If the user can see us, hide us
              If Me.Visible = True Then Me.Visible = False
          End Sub
```

11. Run the project, and the icon will appear on the system tray. Right-click the icon, and you'll see a list of favorites as shown in Figure 11-12. Clicking one will open Internet Explorer, while clicking Exit will close the application.

How It Works

One thing to note is that, because of the order of events that are fired for your form, you have to create a variable in Form1 called `_loadCalled`. This variable makes sure that your favorites get loaded in the form's Load event.

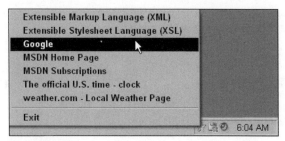

Figure 11-12

The `WebFavoriteMenuItem` class accepts a `WebFavorite` object in its constructor, and it configures itself as a menu item using the class. However, this class provides a Click method that you can overload. So, when the user selects the item from the menu, you can immediately open up the URL:

```
Private Sub WebFavoriteMenuItem_Click(ByVal sender As Object, _
    ByVal e As System.EventArgs) Handles Me.Click

    'Open the favorite
    If Not Favorite Is Nothing Then
        Process.Start(Favorite.Url)
    End If
End Sub
```

The `ExitMenuItem` class does a similar thing. When this item is clicked, you call the shared `Application.Exit` method to quit the program:

```
Private Sub ExitMenuItem_Click(ByVal sender As Object, _
    ByVal e As System.EventArgs) Handles Me.Click

    Application.Exit()
End Sub
```

The important thing here is not the construction of the application itself but rather the fact that you can reuse the functionality you built in a different project. This underlines the fundamental motive for reuse; it means you don't have to "reinvent the wheel" every time you want to do something.

The method of reuse described here was to add the existing classes to your new project, hence making a second copy of them. This isn't efficient, because it takes double the amount of storage needed for the classes; however, the classes are small, so the cost of memory is minimal. It did save you from having to create the classes from scratch, allowing you to reuse the existing code, and it was very easy to do.

An alternative way of reusing classes is to create them in a class library. This class library is a separate project that can be referenced by a number of different applications so that only one copy of the code is required. This is discussed in Chapter 12.

Using Shared Properties and Methods

On occasion, you might find it useful to be able to access methods and properties that are not tied to an instance of an object but are still associated with a class.

371

Imagine you have a class that stores the user name and password of a user for a computer program. You might have something that looks like this:

```
Public Class User
    'Public members
    Public Username As String

    'Private members
    Private _password As String
End Class
```

Now imagine that the password for a user has to be of a minimum length. You create a separate member to store the length and implement a property like this:

```
Public Class User
    'Public members
    Public Username As String
    Public MinPasswordLength As Integer = 6

    'Private members
    Private _password As String

    'Password property
    Public Property Password() As String
        Get
            Return _password
        End Get
        Set(ByVal value As String)
            If value.Length >= MinPasswordLength Then
                _password = value
            End If
        End Set
    End Property
End Class
```

That seems fairly straightforward. But now imagine that you have 5000 user objects in memory. Each `MinPasswordLength` variable takes up 4 bytes of memory, meaning that 20KB of memory is being used just to store the same value. Although 20KB of memory isn't a lot for modern computer systems, it's extremely inefficient, and there is a better way.

Using Shared Procedures

Ideally, you want to store the value for the minimum password length in memory against a specific class once and share that memory between all of the objects created from that class, as you'll do in the following Try It Out.

Try It Out   Using Shared Properties

1. Open Visual Studio 2005 and create a new Visual Basic Windows Application project. Call it **SharedDemo**.

2. When the Designer for Form1 appears, change the Text property of the form to **Shared Demo** and then drag a ListBox, a Label, and a NumericUpDown control from the Toolbox onto the form as shown in Figure 11-13.

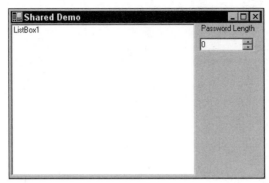

Figure 11-13

3. Set the Name property of the ListBox control to **lstUsers**.

4. Set the Name property of the NumericUpDown control to **nupMinPasswordLength**, set the Maximum property to **10**, and set the Value property to **6**.

5. Using the Solution Explorer, create a new class named **User**. Add the highlighted code to the class:

```
Public Class User

    'Public members
    Public Username As String
    Public Shared MinPasswordLength As Integer = 6

    'Private members
    Private _password As String

    'Password property
    Public Property Password() As String
        Get
            Return _password
        End Get
        Set(ByVal value As String)
            If value.Length >= MinPasswordLength Then
                _password = value
            End If
        End Set
    End Property
End Class
```

6. Switch to the Code Editor for Form1 and add this highlighted member:

```
Public Class Form1

    'Private member
    Private arrUserList As New ArrayList()
```

7. Next, add this method to the `Form1` class:

```
Private Sub UpdateDisplay()
    'Clear the list
    lstUsers.Items.Clear()

    'Add the users to the list box
    For Each objUser As User In arrUserList
        lstUsers.Items.Add(objUser.Username & ", " & objUser.Password & _
            " (" & User.MinPasswordLength & ")")
    Next
End Sub
```

8. Select (Form1 Events) in the Class Name combo box at the top of the Code Editor and the Load event in the Method Name combo box. Add the highlighted code to the Load event:

```
Private Sub Form1_Load(ByVal sender As Object, _
    ByVal e As System.EventArgs) Handles Me.Load

    'Load 100 users
    For intIndex As Integer = 1 To 100
        'Create a new user
        Dim objUser As New User
        objUser.Username = "Robbin" & intIndex
        objUser.Password = "password15"
        'Add the user to the array list
        arrUserList.Add(objUser)
    Next

    'Update the display
    UpdateDisplay()
End Sub
```

9. Select nupMinPasswordLength in the Class Name combo box at the top of the Code Editor and the ValueChanged event in the Method Name combo box. Add the highlighted code to the ValueChanged event:

```
Private Sub nupMinPasswordLength_ValueChanged(ByVal sender As Object, _
    ByVal e As System.EventArgs) Handles nupMinPasswordLength.ValueChanged

    'Set the minimum password length
    User.MinPasswordLength = nupMinPasswordLength.Value
    'Update the display
    UpdateDisplay()
End Sub
```

10. Run the project. You should see a screen like the one shown in Figure 11-14.

11. Scroll the NumericUpDown control up or down, and the list will update itself and the number in parentheses will change to correspond to the number shown in the NumericUpDown control.

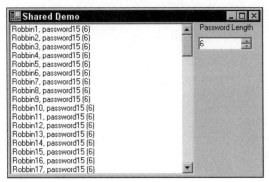

Figure 11-14

How It Works

To create a member variable, property, or method on an object that is shared, you use the Shared keyword.

```
Public Shared MinPasswordLength As Integer = 6
```

This tells Visual Basic 2005 that the item should be available to all instances of the class.

Shared members can be accessed from within nonshared properties and methods as well as from shared properties and methods. For example, here's the Password property, which can access the shared MinPasswordLength member:

```
'Password property
Public Property Password() As String
    Get
        Return _password
    End Get
    Set(ByVal value As String)
        If value.Length >= MinPasswordLength Then
            _password = value
        End If
    End Set
End Property
```

What's important to realize here is that although the Password property and _password member "belong" to the particular instance of the User class, MinPasswordLength does not, therefore, if it is changed the effect is felt throughout all the object instances built from the class in question.

In the form, UpdateDisplay is used to populate the list. You can gain access to MinPasswordLength as if it were a normal, nonshared public member of the User object:

```
Private Sub UpdateDisplay()
    'Clear the list
    lstUsers.Items.Clear()

    'Add the users to the list box
```

```
            For Each objUser As User In arrUserList
                lstUsers.Items.Add(objUser.Username & ", " & objUser.Password & _
                    " (" & User.MinPasswordLength & ")")
            Next
        End Sub
```

At this point, you have a listing of users that shows that the `MinPasswordLength` value of each is set to 6 (refer to Figure 11-15).

Things start to get interesting when you scroll the NumericUpDown control and change `MinPassword Length`. As this is a shared member, you don't specifically *need* an instance of the class. Instead, you can set the property just by using the *class* name:

```
    Private Sub nupMinPasswordLength_ValueChanged(ByVal sender As Object, _
        ByVal e As System.EventArgs) Handles nupMinPasswordLength.ValueChanged

        'Set the minimum password length
        User.MinPasswordLength = nupMinPasswordLength.Value
        'Update the display
        UpdateDisplay()
    End Sub
```

When building this method, you may have noticed that after you had typed `User.`, Visual Studio 2005's IntelliSense popped up a list of members, including the `MinPasswordLength` property, as shown in Figure 11-15.

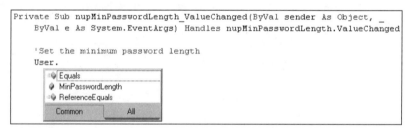

Figure 11-15

Shared members, properties, and methods can all be accessed through the class directly — you don't specifically need an instance of the class.

When you change this member with code in the `ValueChanged` event handler, you update the display, and this time you can see that the perceived value of `MinPasswordLength` has seemingly been changed for *all* instances of `User`, even though you changed it in only one place.

Using Shared Methods

Although you've seen how to make a public member variable shared, you haven't seen how to do this with a method. In the following Try It Out, you look at an example of how to build a shared method that can create new instances of `User`. The main limitation with a shared method is that you can access other shared methods and shared properties only in the class in which it is defined.

This is a fairly artificial example of using a shared method, as you could do the same job here with a customized constructor.

Try It Out   **Using a Shared Method**

1.   Open the Code Editor for `User`. Add this highlighted code to the `User` class:

```
Public Shared Function CreateUser(ByVal userName As String, _
    ByVal password As String) As User

    'Delcare a new User object
    Dim objUser As New User()

    'Set the User properties
    objUser.Username = userName
    objUser.Password = password

    'Return the new user
    Return objUser
End Function
```

2.   Open the Code Editor for Form1 and locate the Load event handler. Change the code so that it looks like this. You'll notice that as you type in the code, as soon as you type `User.`, IntelliSense offers `CreateUser` as an option:

```
Private Sub Form1_Load(ByVal sender As Object, _
    ByVal e As System.EventArgs) Handles Me.Load

    'Load 100 users
    For intIndex As Integer = 1 To 100
        'Create a new user
        Dim objUser As New User

        objUser = User.CreateUser("Robbin" & intIndex, "password15")
        'Add the user to the array list
        arrUserList.Add(objUser)
    Next

    'Update the display
    UpdateDisplay()
End Sub
```

3.   If you run the project, you'll get the same results as the previous example.

How It Works

The important thing to look at here is the fact that `CreateUser` appears in the IntelliSense list after you type the class name. This is because it is shared and you do not need a specific instance of a class to access it. You created the method as a shared method by using the `Shared` keyword:

```
Public Shared Function CreateUser(ByVal userName As String, _
    ByVal password As String) As User
```

One thing to consider with shared methods is that you can access only members of the class that are also shared. You cannot access nonshared methods, simply because you don't know what instance of the class you're actually running on. Likewise, you cannot access Me from within a shared method for the same reason.

Understanding Object-Oriented Programming and Memory Management

Object-orientation has an impact on how memory is used in an operating system. .NET is heavily object-oriented, so it makes sense that .NET would have to optimize the way it uses memory to best suit the way objects are used.

Whenever you create an object, you're using memory. Most of the objects you use have *state*, which describes what an object "knows." The methods and properties that an object has will either affect or work with that state. For example, an object that describes a file on disk will have state that describes its name, size, folder, and so on. Some of the state will be publicly accessible through properties. For example, a property called Size will return the size of the file. Some state will be private to the object and is used to keep track of what the object has done or what it needs to do.

Objects use memory in two ways. First, something needs to keep track of the objects that exist on the system in memory. This is usually a task shared between you as an application developer and .NET's Common Language Runtime (CLR). If you create an object, you'll have to hold a reference to it in your program's memory so that you know where it is when you need to use its methods and properties. The CLR also needs to keep track of the object to determine when you no longer need it. Secondly, the CLR needs to allocate memory to the object so that the object can store its state. The more state an object has, the more memory it will need to use it.

The most expensive resource on a computer is the memory. I mean *expense* here in terms of what you get for your money. For about $100, I can buy an 80GB hard drive, but for the same amount of money I can't buy 1GB of memory. Retrieving data from memory is thousands of times faster than retrieving it from disk so there's a tradeoff — if you need fast access, you have to store it in memory, but there isn't as much memory available as there is hard disk space.

When building an application, you want to use as little memory as possible, so there's an implication that you want to have as few objects as possible and that those objects should have as little state as possible. The upside is that, today, computers have a lot more memory than they used to have, so your programs can use more memory than their predecessors of 10 years ago. However, you still need to be cognizant of your application's memory usage.

The CLR manages memory in several distinct ways. First, it's responsible for creating objects at the request of the application. With a heavily object-oriented programming platform like .NET, this is going to happen all the time, so Microsoft has spent an enormous amount of time making sure that the CLR creates objects in the most efficient way. The CLR, for example, can create objects far faster than its Component Object Model (COM) predecessor could. Secondly, the CLR is responsible for cleaning up memory when it's no longer needed. In the developer community, the manner in which the CLR cleans up objects is one of the most controversial.

Imagine you're writing a routine that opens a file from disk and displays the contents on the screen. Well, with .NET you could use perhaps two .NET Framework objects to open the file and read its contents — namely `System.IO.FileStream` and `System.IO.StreamReader`. However, after the contents have been read, do you need these objects anymore? Probably not, so what you want to do is to remove your references to the objects and make the memory the objects were using available for creating more objects.

Imagine now that you don't remove your references to the objects. In this situation, the memory that the objects were using can't be used by anyone else. Now imagine that happening several thousand times. What happens is that the amount of memory that's being wasted keeps growing. In extreme circumstances, the computer will run out of memory, meaning that other applications wouldn't ever be able to create any objects. This is a pretty catastrophic state of affairs.

We describe an object that is no longer needed but that holds onto memory as a *leak*. Memory leaks are one of the biggest causes of reliability problems on Windows, because when a program is no longer able to obtain memory, it will crash.

With .NET this *should* never happen, or, at the very least, to leak memory you would have to go to some pretty extreme steps. This is because of a feature called *garbage collection*. When an object is no longer being used, the *Garbage Collector* (GC) automatically removes the object from memory and makes the memory it was using available to other programs.

Garbage Collection

The GC works by keeping track of how many parts of a program have a reference to an object. If it gets to the point where there are no open references to the object, it is deleted.

To understand this, think back to our discussion of scope in Chapter 3. Imagine you create a method and at the top of that method define a variable with local scope. That variable is used to store an object (it doesn't matter what kind of object is used for this discussion). At this point, one part of the program "knows" about the object's existence — that is, the variable is holding a reference to the object. When you return from the method, the variable will go out of scope, and therefore the variable will "forget" about the object's existence; in other words, the only reference to the object is lost. At this point, no one "knows" about the object, and so it can be safely deleted.

For an example, look at the following code:

```
Dim objObject As New MyObject
Console.WriteLine(objObject.GetType().FullName)
objObject = Nothing
```

This code snippet creates a new object from class `MyObject`, invokes a method on it, and then removes the reference to the object. In this case, when you create the object, the `objObject` variable is the only thing that holds a reference to it. In the last line, `objObject` is set to `Nothing`, hence removing the only reference to the object. The GC is then free to remove the reference to the object.

The GC does not run constantly. Instead, it runs periodically based on a complex algorithm that measures the amount of work the computer is doing and how many objects might need to be deleted. When the GC runs, it looks through the master list of all the objects the program has ever created and any that can be deleted at this point.

In old-school programming, programmers were responsible for deleting their own objects and had the freedom to say to an object, "You, now, clean yourself up and get out of memory." With .NET this ability is gone. Rather, an object will be deleted at some *indeterminate* time in the future.

Exactly when this happens is nondeterministic—in other words, as a developer you don't know when the GC is going to run. This means that there is no immediate connection between the removal of the last reference to an object and the physical removal of that object from memory. This is known as *non-deterministic finalization*.

Releasing Resources

In some cases, objects that you build may need access to certain system and network resources, such as files and database connections. Using these resources requires a certain discipline to ensure that you don't inadvertently cause problems.

Here's an example—if you create a new file, write some data to it, but forget to close it, no one else will be able to read data from that file. This is because you have an *exclusive lock* on the file; it doesn't make sense for someone to be able to read from a file when it's still being written to. You must take care to release system resources should you open them.

When an object has access to scarce system or network resources like this, it's important that the caller tells the object that it can release those resources as soon as they're no longer needed. For example, here's some code that creates a file:

```
'Open a file
Dim objFileStream As New FileStream("c:\myfile.txt", FileMode.Create)
'Do something with the file
...
'Close the file
objFileStream.Close()
'Release your reference to the object
objFileStream = Nothing
```

As soon as you finish working with the file, you call `Close`. This tells .NET that the consumer is finished with the file and Windows can make it available for other applications to use. This is known as *releasing the lock*. When you release the object reference by setting `objFileStream = Nothing` in the next line, this is an entirely separate action from calling `Close`.

The `FileStream` object releases the lock on the file when its `Finalize` method is called. However, as you've just learned, the time period between the instance of the `FileStream` object becoming a candidate for garbage collection (which happens when `objFileStream = Nothing`) and `Finalize` being called is nondeterministic. So, if you had not called `Close`, the file would have remained open for a period of time, which would have caused problems for anyone else who needed to use the file.

Another way to release resources within objects is to implement the `IDisposable` interface, which you did with the `WebFavorite` and `Favorites` classes. This interface provides a `Dispose` method for your objects, in which you can put code to clean up the resources used in that class.

Ideally, the consumer of these objects would call the `Dispose` methods on these objects when they are done using them, but if they do not, the `Finalize` method in these objects will when the GC runs.

Defragmentation and Compaction

As the last part in its bag of tricks, the Garbage Collector is able to defragment and compact memory. In much the same way that your computer's hard disk needs periodic defragmentation to make it run more efficiently, so does memory. Imagine you create 10 small objects in memory, each about 1KB in size. Imagine that .NET allocates them all on top of each other, so you end up taking up one 10KB piece of memory. (In reality, we don't usually care where objects exist in memory, so this discussion is a bit academic.)

Now imagine you want to create another object and this object is of medium size, say about 3KB. .NET will have to create this object at the end of the 10KB block. This means that you'll have allocated 13KB in total.

Now imagine that you delete every other small object, so now your 10KB block of memory has holes in it. Not much of a problem, but imagine you want to create another 3KB object. Although there's 5KB of space in the original block, you can't put it there because no gap is big enough. Instead, it has to go on the end, meaning your application is now taking up 16KB of memory.

What the GC can do is defragment memory, which means that it removes the gaps when objects have been removed, as shown in Figure 11-16. The upshot of this is that your application uses memory more efficiently, so applications take up less memory.

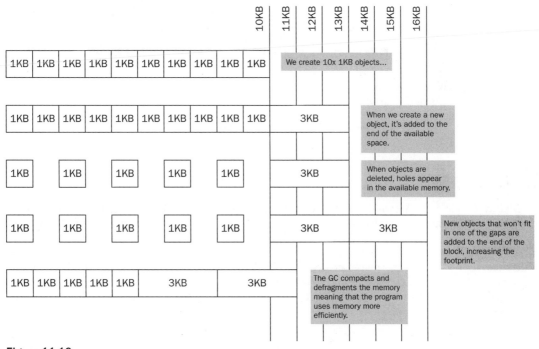

Figure 11-16

Although this may not seem like a big deal on a PC with 512MB of memory available, consider that .NET could potentially be running on much smaller devices where memory usage is a big deal, for example, a mobile device with 32MB of memory in total. Besides, imagine making 3,000 5KB savings in this example; then you've have saved over 15MB of memory! Chapter 22 will introduce you to writing applications for mobile devices and to topics that you need to be aware of when coding for these devices.

Summary

In this chapter, you took a look at some more valuable techniques that you are able to use to assist the building of object-oriented software. Initially, you examined the idea of reuse. Specifically, you looked at classes that would allow you to examine the Internet Explorer Favorites stored on the user's computer. You consumed these classes from two applications — one standard desktop application and also a mini-application that exists on the system tray.

You then examined the idea of shared members, properties, and methods. Sharing these kinds of items is a powerful way to make common functionality available to all classes in an application.

Finally, you examined how consumers of objects should ensure that scarce systems resources are freed whenever an object is deleted by the Garbage Collector using the `Dispose` and `Finalize` methods.

To summarize, you should know how to:

❑ Build a class that inherits from the `System.Collections.CollectionBase` namespace and add methods that allow you to add and remove objects from the collection and provide a property that allows an application to query for the number of items in the collection

❑ Use the collection class in your own application creating objects and adding them to the collection

❑ Use shared properties and methods in a class that can be shared among all instantiated instances of the class

❑ Properly dispose of resources to make efficient use of the Garbage Collector

Exercise

Modify the Favorites Viewer project to select the first favorite in the list view control automatically after it has been loaded so that the link label control will display the first item when the form is displayed.

You'll also need to modify the Load event in Form1, and you'll want to ensure that the list view control contains one or more items before proceeding. You'll do this by querying the `Count` property of the Items property of the list view control. Then you'll select the first item in the list view control using the `lstFavorites.Items(0).Selected` property and then call the Click event for the list box control to update the link label control.

Building Class Libraries

In this chapter, you're going to look at building libraries of classes. This will gather together many of the concepts you've learned in this book, so let's have a quick review. So far, you've learned a lot about developing Windows Applications by dragging controls onto forms, editing their properties, and adding code. When you edit a form in the Form Designer, you are actually designing a new class that inherits from the System.Windows.Forms.Form class.

When you make changes to the form in the designer, the designer works out what code needs to be added to the class. You can view this code by clicking the Show All Files icon in the Solution Explorer and then opening the designer-generated code for your form. When you run the program, an instance of this class is created — an object. Like most objects, the form has state and behavior — you can have variables and controls on the form (state) and you can perform actions when, for example, the user clicks a button on the form (behavior). In theory, you could write your forms without using the designer at all; very few programmers work this way while creating Windows forms.

Right from the start you've been creating classes. You've also looked at creating your own classes from scratch. Recall what you studied about building objects in Chapter 10, where you created a project called Objects, which contained the classes Car and SportsCar. These classes were used in a console application because it made the objects easier to test, but they would have worked just as well in a Windows application. You could even have used them in a Web application or Web Service. In fact, one of the key benefits of using classes is that once you've designed a good one, you can use it over and over again in different applications.

In this chapter, you will:

- ❑ Create your own class libraries and learn how to get information about existing libraries that are not part of the .NET Framework

- ❑ Learn to assign strong-name assemblies (compiled files) to ensure that all assemblies have a unique identity

- ❑ Register assemblies in a repository called the Global Assembly Cache (GAC) so that they can be shared between applications on the same computer

Understanding Class Libraries

In Chapter 11 you used the same classes in two different applications. You built a favorites viewer in your application and a task bar application using the same underlying classes. You did this by creating the class in one application and then adding a copy of that code to the second. This was a quick and easy way of reusing code, but there were some problems with it:

❑   To use the class you needed to have access to the source code file. One of the advantages of classes and objects is that they can be a "black box." Developers should not need to know what goes on inside the classes they use. It is often a good thing if they don't. Also, if you've developed a class, you might want to keep your source secret. You might be happy to let people use it, but not let them copy the way it works or "improve" it, or even claim it as their own work.

❑   Every time the program that uses the class is compiled, the class needs to be compiled too. This is not really a problem if the application uses a few simple classes, but if it's using a lot of complex classes, it will make compilation slower. It will also make the resulting program very big because one .exe file will include all of the classes.

❑   If you realize that there is a bug in the class or that there is a way to make it faster or more efficient, you need to make the change in lots of different places — in every application that uses the class.

The solution is class libraries. A *class library* is a collection of classes that compile to a file: a Windows Dynamic Link Library (DLL, or .dll file). You cannot run a class library by itself, but you can use the classes in it from your applications. You can use a class library without the source code; it does not need to be recompiled when the application is compiled, and if the library changes, the applications using it will automatically get the advantage of the improved code.

Creating a Class Library

These are instructions for creating a class library in Visual Studio 2005 Standard Edition or above.

Try It Out   **Creating a Class Library**

1.   In Visual Studio 2005 select File ➪ New Project.

2.   Select Visual Basic from the Project Types list and then choose the Class Library icon from the Templates list as shown in Figure 12-1. Enter the name **InternetFavorites**.

3.   Click OK. A new Class Library project will be created with a default class called Class1.vb. Right-click Class1.vb in the Solution Explorer and choose Delete.

How It Works

That was really easy. Let's just think about what Visual Studio 2005 is doing during these two steps. First, you choose a Class Library project. The template that you choose controls how Visual Studio 2005 sets up the project. The most obvious difference is that when you start a Windows application you get a blank form in the Forms Designer. The blank form is called Form1.vb. When you start a class library, you get no designer and a blank class called Class1.vb.

Figure 12-1

There are also more subtle differences. When you create a Windows application, Visual Studio 2005 knows that you will be compiling it into a program that can run. When you choose a Class Library, Visual Studio 2005 knows that the resulting library will not be run on its own — so the choices you make here affect what Visual Studio 2005 does when you build the project. Selecting a Class Library means that Visual Studio 2005 will build the project into a `.dll` file instead of an `.exe` file.

After clicking OK, you delete the blank class that Visual Studio 2005 generates. Having classes with the name `Class1` is not very helpful — it's much better to start from scratch with meaningful file and class names.

In the last chapter you created classes and used the same Visual Basic 2005 class in two projects: Favorites Viewer and Favorites Tray. In the following sections you see how to convert these applications so that both of them use a copy of the same compiled class library. Of course, this is a somewhat unrealistic situation. Usually, you would build a class library and application rather than create an application and then split it into a smaller application and a class library. However, this will give you a good idea of how you would create a class library from scratch, and it will be much faster. First of all, open the Favorites Viewer project using another instance of Visual Studio 2005. Remember that this project consists of the following files:

❑   `Favorites.vb` contains the `Favorites` class.

❑   `WebFavorite.vb` contains the `WebFavorite` class.

❑   `WebFavoriteCollection.vb` contains the `WebFavoriteCollection` class.

❑   `Form1.vb` contains the `Form1` class, which represents the application's main form.

Of these, the first three listed are also used in the Favorites Tray. The remaining file is specific to this particular application. You want to build a class library that contains `Favorites`, `WebFavorite`, and `WebFavoriteCollection`.

Building a Class Library for Favorites Viewer

When you're writing Visual Basic 2005 applications, a solution can contain multiple projects. At the moment you have one project in the solution: the Favorites Viewer application. In the next Try It Out, you add a Class Library project to this solution and then move the classes from the Windows Application project to the Class Library project.

Try It Out   Adding a Class Library Project to an Existing Solution

1. Switch to the InternetFavorites project.

2. Save the project and then close Visual Studio 2005.

3. Open the Favorites Viewer project.

4. Click the File menu and select Add ➪ Existing Project.

5. Navigate to the where you saved your InternetFavorites solution and then select the Internet Favorites.vbproj file. Click Open to add this project to the solution.

6. Right-click the Favorites Viewer project in the Solution Explorer and select Set As StartUp Project.

7. Now right-click the Favorites Tray project in the Solution Explorer and select Remove.

How It Works

Now you have two projects within your solution. You have a Windows application and a class library. Currently, the class library is empty; all the classes that you want to add to the class library are in the Windows application project.

You have already seen how to add a new class to a Windows application, and you can add new classes to a class library in exactly the same way. You just right-click the InternetFavorites project and select Add ➪ Class. You don't want to do that, though, because the classes already exist. The quickest way to move a class between two projects in the same solution is to drag and drop them, which is what you do in the next Try It Out.

Try It Out   Moving Classes Between Projects

1. Select the Favorites.vb file in the Solution Explorer, as shown in Figure 12-2, and drag it onto the InternetFavorites project. This causes a copy of the Favorites class to be added to the InternetFavorites project.

Figure 12-2

2. Follow the same procedure for `WebFavorite.vb` and `WebFavoriteCollection.vb`.

3. Now right-click the `Favorites.vb` file in the Favorites Viewer project and select Delete from the context menu to delete the file from that project.

4. Follow the same procedure for `WebFavorite.vb` and `WebFavoriteCollection.vb`.

You now have a Class Library project and a Windows Application project. However, even though they are both contained in the same solution, they cannot see each other. If you try running the application now, you will see an error that type `Favorites` is not defined.

These errors occur because the code in `Form1.vb` cannot see the classes in the class library. There are two stages to solving this problem:

❑ Add a reference to the Class Library project, so that the Windows application knows to look for the compiled `InternetFavorites.dll` file that contains the classes. Previously, all code was compiled into one file, so you didn't need to do this.

❑ Add an `Imports` statement to Form1, so that it can see the classes in the `InternetFavorites` namespace without giving a fully qualified name (that is, including the namespace as well as the class name). Previously, all classes were in the same namespace, so you didn't need to do this. As you saw in Chapter 4, classes are by default given their project name as their namespace.

If this doesn't seem very clear — don't worry! Both of these things are easy to do.

Try It Out   Adding a Reference and Imports Statement

1. Right-click the Favorites Viewer project in the Solution Explorer and select Add Reference.

2. Select the Projects tab in the Add Reference dialog box and you'll see that the InternetFavorites project is already populated in the list, as shown in Figure 12-3. Click OK to have this reference added to your Favorites Viewer project.

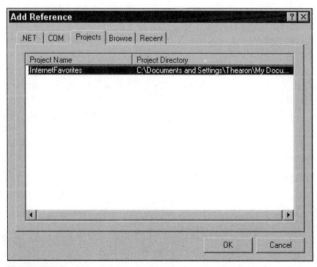

Figure 12-3

3. Right-click `Form1.vb` in the Solution Explorer and select View Code. Add the following line right at the very top of the code file:

```
Imports InternetFavorites
```

How It Works

By adding a reference in steps 1 and 2, you tell Visual Studio 2005 that the `Favorites Viewer.exe` file will require the `InternetFavorites.dll` file to run. Visual Studio 2005 can use the classes exposed from `InternetFavorites` to check the syntax of the code, so the automatic underlining of errors and so on will work correctly.

> *Whenever you want to use a class library you must add a reference to it. You can add references to projects within the solution or to compiled DLLs if you wish.*

However, if you tried to run the application before you perform step 3, you would still get errors, because the classes in the Favorites Viewer application would be trying to use classes in the `InternetFavorites` class library without giving a fully qualified name. Unless you specify otherwise, classes are given the name of the project they are in as their namespace name. This means that the classes you moved from Favorites Viewer to InternetFavorites changed namespace too.

The easiest way to cope with this problem is to add an `Imports` statement to the top of the classes that rely on this class library. This is what you did in step 3, but remember that you have two other choices:

❑ You can use fully qualified names every time you want to access a class in the class library from a class in the application. This would have required quite a few changes.

❑ You can change the namespace of either the classes in the application or the classes in the class library. If the namespace was the same for both projects, you would not need to use fully qualified names or have an `Imports` statement. However, because the two projects are quite different, it would not really be sensible to give both of them the same namespace.

The `Imports` statement means that any time there is a reference to a class that is not qualified with a namespace, the Visual Basic 2005 compiler will check the `InternetFavorites` namespace to see whether a matching class exists there. Therefore, the compiler will be able to resolve the class name when you insert the `Imports` statement.

That's it! You have converted your Windows application into a small client application and a class library. Run the application and it will work perfectly, and you'll see the same results you saw in the last chapter; the application will display a list of your Internet Favorites shortcuts.

Note that when you run this application, Visual Studio 2005 compiles the class library to a DLL, then compiles the application to an EXE, and then runs the EXE. It needs to compile the DLL first because the compiler depends upon it while compiling the EXE.

A Multitiered Application

In the previous demonstration, you split your application into two *tiers* or layers. The class library is a tier that handles the concept of a favorite and obtains a list of the user's favorites from their computer. The other tier presents the favorites to the user and enables the user to perform actions on them. Class libraries are really a powerful tool for creating tiered applications, because they enable you to completely separate the code that exists in different tiers. You may often hear the term *n-tier design*. What this means is that an application has at least three separate tiers. Usually, these three tiers are:

❑   A *data tier* is concerned with obtaining raw data from a data source such as a database, text file, or, in this case, your Favorites folder and then writing data back. It generally doesn't worry about what the data means. It just enables data read and write operations.

❑   A *business tier* is concerned with applying certain business rules to the data retrieved from the data source or ensuring that data that is being written to the data source obeys these rules. In this case, there may be certain sites that you would not want to list in your Favorites viewer, or you may want to ensure that URLs are valid before displaying them. The business tier may also contain code for manipulating or working with data — for example, the code needed to open a particular favorite.

❑   A *presentation tier* displays the data to the users and lets them interact with it in some way. In this case, you have a Windows Form that displays a list of favorites and a link button that lets users view them.

Your application is so small that there's no practical need to separate the data tier and the business tier. However, in a big application it can make the project far more manageable, even if it does mean spending a bit more time on design before the coding starts.

One of the great things about tiers is that you can mix and match them quite easily. For example, if a new browser becomes popular, then you could change the data tier to read a different data format but still use the same presentation tier and business tier. This would be much easier if the data tier and business tier were separate.

Soon, you are going to use your class library, which is really a combination of the business and data tiers, in conjunction with a different presentation tier, namely the Favorites Tray application.

> *In this chapter, you are working with existing projects so that you can concentrate specifically on class libraries rather than on writing code. In most cases you would develop the class library first and then develop applications to use that library. Of course, as you were building the application, you might decide to modify the library slightly. Using Visual Studio 2005 you can do this very easily. When working in Visual Studio 2005 you can make any changes you like to the code in the library, and the change will instantly be available in the application.*

Using Strong Names

Your complete solution now compiles to two files: a DLL and an EXE. You have written both files. Nobody else is writing applications that rely on the DLL, and nobody else is going to change the DLL. In real life, this is often not the case. Often you use off-the-shelf DLLs, or two separate developers are working on the DLL and the EXE.

For example, imagine that Matt is working on `InternetFavorites.dll` and Robbin is working on `Favorites Viewer.exe`. Matt decides that `ScanFavorites` is not a very good name for a method and changes it to `LoadFavorites`. Then he recompiles the DLL. Later, Robbin runs `Favorites Viewer.exe`. `Favorites Viewer.exe` tries to call `ScanFavorites` in the DLL, but the method no longer exists. This generates an error and the program doesn't work.

Of course, Matt shouldn't really have made the change to the DLL. He should have known that applications existed that required the ScanFavorites method. All too often, however, developers of libraries don't realize this. They make changes to DLLs that render existing software unusable.

Another possible scenario is that Jay is working on a system to manage favorites, and he creates a file called InternetFavorites that is different from the one that Matt developed. There is a danger that the two different DLLs will be confused, and once again Favorites Viewer will stop working.

These DLL management problems have been a nightmare for Windows developers, and it spawned the expression "DLL Hell." However, Visual Basic 2005 goes a long way toward solving the problem. The problem is connected with two things:

❑ There can be several versions of a DLL, and these can all work in different ways. It is not possible to tell the version from the filename alone.

❑ Different people can write DLLs with the same filename.

Strongly named assemblies store information about their version and their author within the assembly itself. Because of this, it would be possible to tell the difference between the DLL used (when Favorites Viewer compiled) and the changed version. It would also be possible to tell the difference between Matt's InternetFavorites.dll and Jay's InternetFavorites.dll. Strong naming can also store information about other properties that will help to uniquely identify an assembly (for example, the culture for which it was written), but you will concentrate on version and author.

Signing Assemblies

One way to certify who wrote an assembly is to sign it. To do this, you generate a key pair and sign the assembly with it. A key-pair is unique and, therefore, can identify the person or company who wrote an assembly. The principles behind assembly signing are quite advanced, but the actual practice is quite simple.

> *A strongly named assembly cannot reference a simply named assembly, because it would lose the versioning control that it enjoys.*

Two steps are involved in creating a strongly named or signed assembly:

❑ Create a key pair that you can use to sign your assembly, as you do in the next Try It Out.

❑ Apply this key pair to your assembly, so that it will be used to sign the assembly at the time of compilation.

Try It Out   Creating a Key Pair

1. First, you create a new key pair. From the Windows Start menu select All Programs ➪ Microsoft Visual Studio 2005 ➪ Visual Studio 2005 Tools ➪ Visual Studio 2005 Command Prompt.

2. Type the following into the command prompt that appears:

```
sn -k InternetFavoriteskey.snk
```

This will generate a key pair in the folder where the command is run (in this case, C:\Program Files\Microsoft Visual Studio 8\VC).

How It Works

Running the Visual Studio 2005 command prompt opens a DOS-style command window with the environment set up so that you can use the .NET command-line tools. You use this environment to run the Visual Studio 2005 strong naming command, `sn`. The `k` switch means that the command will generate a new key pair and write it to the specified file.

Now you have a key pair in the file `C:\Program Files\Microsoft Visual Studio 8\VC\Internet Favoriteskey.snk`. If you want, you can move this to a more convenient location, such as your project folder for the InternetFavorites project. After this, in the next Try It Out, you use it to sign your assembly.

Try It Out   Signing the FavoritesLib Assembly

1. In the Solution Explorer, double-click the My Project file in the InternetFavorites project.

2. Now click the Signing tab along the left side of the project file, as shown in Figure 12-4.

3. Check the "Sign the assembly" check box.

4. In the Choose a strong name key file combo box, select <Browse...> and then browse to the location of your key file and select it.

5. Build your project, and the DLL will then be strongly named.

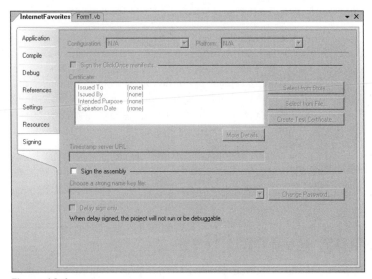

Figure 12-4

How It Works

When you compile an assembly with a key file, it adds a copy of your public key to the assembly. It also adds a hash of the whole assembly, encrypted using the private key.

With public–private key cryptography, a message encrypted with one key can be decrypted only with the other key. You can't use the same key to encrypt and decrypt. You can give a public key to a lot of people and they can encrypt messages with it. If you keep the private key secret, nobody else will be able to read the encrypted messages—even if they have a copy of the public key.

You can also make this work the other way around. If you encrypt a message with the private key, people can use the public key to decrypt it. If the decryption works and you haven't let somebody else get their hands on your private key, it proves that you wrote the message.

Part of the purpose of signing an assembly is to prove who wrote it and to prove that it has not been tampered with. This could be done by encrypting the whole assembly using the private key and then decrypting the whole assembly using the public key, when it needs to be used. However, this would be very slow. Instead, the Visual Basic 2005 compiler takes a hash of the assembly and encrypts that using the private key. If anybody tries to tamper with the assembly, the hash will cease to be valid.

Assembly Versions

Visual Basic 2005 automatically keeps track of versions for you. When you build an assembly, a number signifying the version is automatically updated. There are four elements of this number: major version, minor version, build, and revision. If you click the Application tab of the project file and then click the Assembly Information button, you see the assembly version near the bottom of the Assembly Information dialog box.

This means that when you compile this assembly, the major version will be 1, the minor version will be 0, and the build and revision number will be generated by Visual Studio 2005. Every time you recompile the assembly, Visual Basic 2005 will adjust these numbers to ensure that every compilation has a unique version number. You could choose to replace the build and revision numbers with your own hard-coded numbers and increment them yourself, but if you're happy with Visual Basic 2005's decision, then you can just leave it. If you are changing an assembly significantly, you may want to change the major or minor version—and, of course, you are free to do that.

It is recommended that you set the entire version number manually, especially when you are releasing the assembly formally, so that you have complete control. It will then be easier to manage different versions and bring in fewer unfortunate deployment problems.

Registering Assemblies

You've seen how an assembly can contain information to prove who wrote it (in the sense that a unique identifier is unique per publisher) and information to prove its own version. This is really useful, because it means that executables using these assemblies know what assembly author and version to look for in place of just a filename. However, this doesn't prevent Matt from overwriting an existing DLL with a new version—it just means that applications using the DLL will be able to tell that it's changed.

This is where the Global Assembly Cache (GAC) comes in. The GAC can ensure that several versions of the same assembly are always available. If your application requires the InternetFavorites assembly version 1 and Matt's application requires the assembly version 2, both can go in the GAC and both can be available. Moreover, assemblies with the same name but written by different people can go in the GAC. You can guarantee that your applications will use the same assembly while running as they did when they were compiled, provided the required assembly is in the GAC.

To register an assembly into the GAC, you simply need to drag the relevant `.dll` file into the GAC (located in the `c:\winnt\assembly` on Windows 2000 or `c:\windows\assembly` on Windows XP).

Gacutil Utility

`Gacutil.exe` is a utility provided with the .NET Framework for installing/uninstalling assemblies into the GAC via a command line.

From the Windows Start menu, select Programs ⇨ Microsoft Visual Studio 2005 ⇨ Visual Studio 2005 Tools ⇨ Visual Studio Command Prompt. Navigate to the bin folder for your InternetFavorites project and then enter the following command to install your assembly into the GAC:

```
Gacutil -i internetfavorites.dll
```

In the console window, you can use the `i` and `u` options to install and uninstall, respectively.

```
Gacutil -u internetfavorites
```

Why Is My Assembly Not Visible in the References Dialog Box?

It is important to understand that the GAC is not shown in the References dialog box within Visual Studio. For this reason, after you add your assembly to the GAC, you will not see it in the References dialog box and must browse for it.

Visual Studio does, however, look for assemblies to load into the References dialog box by checking keys in the Registry that map to physical paths on your drive. In the next Try It Out, you list your assembly in the References dialog box.

Try It Out   Getting Your Assembly Listed in the References Dialog Box

1. Click Start and Select Run.

2. Type **regedit** and press Enter.

3. In the Registry Editor locate the key `HKEY_LOCAL_MACHINE\SOFTWARE\Microsoft\.NET Framework\AssemblyFolders`.

4. Right-click AssemblyFolders and select New ⇨ Key.

5. Create the key with any name that you wish. We named ours **Developer Assemblies**.

6. Double-click (Default) value key in the pane and enter a path. We added **C:\Developer Assemblies**. (See Figure 12-5.)

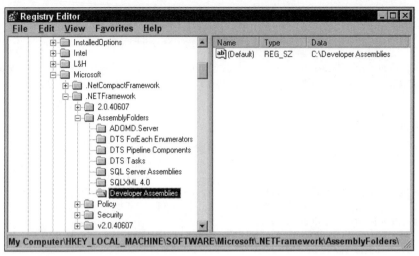

Figure 12-5

7. Open Windows Explorer and create the new directory that you specified in the previous step, if it doesn't exist, and then copy the InternetFavorites.dll into this directory

8. You may have to stop and start Visual Studio 2005 for this to take affect, but when you do, you will see the assembly listed in this directory from within the References Dialog Box as shown in Figure 12-6.

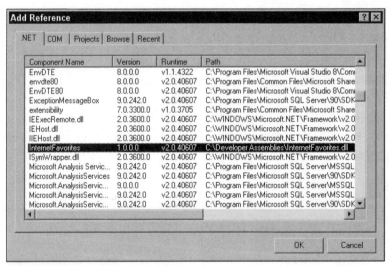

Figure 12-6

Designing Class Libraries

By now, you should be aware of how useful class libraries are, and you have an understanding of the nature of classes, objects, and class libraries.

When designing an application, it is best to understand what you are dealing with. Much like an architect designing a house, you need to understand how things work (the rules, the regulations, and the recommendations) in order to know how to draw the best plan.

When software architects plan, draw out, and generate template code for components and applications, they may use a drawing tool such as Microsoft Visio, which integrates with Visual Studio 2005. Visio contains various types of symbol libraries that can be used for creating schematics, flowcharts, and other diagrams. A very well-known set of descriptive symbols and diagram types is Unified Modeling Language (UML), which has its own symbols and rules for drawing software and architecture models. UML has various types of symbol libraries containing symbols that have different meaning and functions. These symbols have been derived from previous modeling symbols to form something of a fusion of styles. UML also has many types of diagrams. These diagrams range from deployment-type diagrams to component definition diagrams.

If you wish to learn more about UML, take a look at the UML Bible (Wiley, ISBN: 0-7645-2604-9).

If the questions "How many parameters and methods should an object expose?" and "Should an object have properties rather than methods?" are not answered correctly, your object would not be rendered completely useless, although it may be ineffective. There are, however, some things to consider.

Imagine a class library that contains over 40 methods and properties on each of its 20 or so classes. Also imagine that each class's methods contain at least 15 parameters. This component might be a little daunting — in fact, a component should never be designed this way.

Instead, when designing your objects, try to follow the golden rule: simplicity. Simplicity is probably the most crucial element that you can have in your classes. While creating an extremely large class library is not necessarily a bad thing, using a small number of related classes, aided by a few other class libraries, is by far a better solution.

When you're dealing with a large, complex set of business rules for a large system, the code within the library can be extremely complicated, often leading to debugging and maintenance nightmares. In many situations, getting around the fact that many objects need to be created is a difficult task, but the point that needs to come across is that there are many situations that lend themselves to reuse. The more reusable the classes are, the smaller the end-product will be and the easier it will be to create new applications that need the same functionality provided by the components.

Every developer who uses your class library should be able to do so successfully, without any major effort or a tremendous amount of reading. You can achieve this in the following ways:

❑ Try to keep your methods to five or six parameters *maximum,* unless completely necessary. This will make coding easier.

❑ Make sure that all of those parameters and your methods have meaningful names. Try to spell out the function rather than keeping it short. As an example, it is not easy to identify the meaning of StdNo as it is to identify the meaning of StudentNumber.

Chapter 12

❑ Do not overexert yourself by adding every conceivable method and functional enhancement that an object can have; rather think ahead but code later. You can easily complicate matters for your developers by granting them too many choices, and, at the same time, you may be adding functionality that will never be used.

❑ Try to keep classes within your library to a minimum, because better reuse comes from keeping your libraries smaller.

❑ Properties are extremely useful in a class, and they enable it to be used more easily.

Using Third-Party Class Libraries

A class library compiles to a .dll file. To use the class library you need only the DLL, you don't need the source code. This means that you can give your DLL to other people to use and you can use other people's DLLs in your own applications. To demonstrate how to use a DLL, you're going to use the `InternetFavorites.dll` file that you created in the next Try It Out.

Using InternetFavorites.dll

You've already seen how to create references to other projects in a solution. This is a really good way to develop and test class libraries and applications at the same time. In this example you're going to pretend that you didn't create `InternetFavorites.dll`. You're going to modify the Favorites Tray application so that it uses `InternetFavorites.dll`. This is a very quick way to demonstrate the use of DLLs, but remember that in real life you would add a reference to the DLL early on in developing the application and then write code to use the DLL.

Try It Out   Using FavoritesLib.dll in the Favorites Tray Application

1. Open the Favorites Tray project.

2. Delete the following files from the project: `Favorites.vb`, `WebFavorite.vb`, and `WebFavoriteCollection.vb`.

3. Now you need to add a reference to `InternetFavorites.dll`. Right-click the Favorites Tray project and select Add Reference. Scroll down the list of components in the .NET tab until you find `InternetFavorites`. Select it and then click the OK button to close the Add Reference dialog box.

4. Remember that the classes in the class library are in the `InternetFavorites` namespace, so you need to tell your code to look in that namespace for class names you use. Add the following Imports statement to the top of `Form1.vb` and `WebFavoriteMenuItem.vb`:

```
Imports InternetFavorites
```

You do not need to add it to `ExitMenuItem.vb` because this class does not use any of the classes in the library.

5. Run the program. It will work as normal, but will be using the class library now instead of classes within the application's .exe file.

How It Works

This process works more easily than adding a reference to another project does. You still use the classes in the class library in exactly the same way regardless of whether you reference the Class Library project or the compiled DLL. The main difference is that you cannot see or edit the class library's source code.

However, the Visual Studio 2005 environment can still tell a lot about the classes even without the source code. For example, IntelliSense still works. This is because Visual Studio 2005 can tell from the DLL itself what methods and properties are available on each class. You can investigate a class without using IntelliSense but using the Object Browser.

Viewing Classes with the Object Browser

To view classes that can be used within Visual Basic 2005, you can use a quick and easy tool known as the Object Browser. You can also use the Object Browser to view class names and method names on objects. The Object Browser window can be viewed inside Visual Studio 2005 by pressing F2. It is also available by clicking the View ⇨ Object Browser menu or by clicking the Object Browser icon on the toolbar.

The Object Browser is basically used for a quick reference to the classes you need to see. The Object Browser will show all assemblies that are used in the current Solution, including Visual Basic Projects and compiled DLLs.

The browser shows all members including methods, enumerations, and constants. Each member type is shown with a different icon. Figure 12-7 shows the `InternetFavorites.Favorites` class. You select this class by choosing the InternetFavorites assembly and then within that the InternetFavorites namespace and then within that the Favorites class.

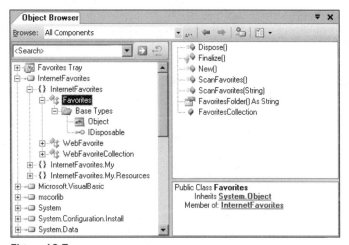

Figure 12-7

Remember that an assembly can contain several namespaces and that the same namespace can be spread across several assemblies. It just happens that in Visual Basic 2005 you normally have a single namespace inside a single assembly of the same name.

The MSDN Library documentation that gets installed with Visual Studio 2005 contains plenty of information about classes in the .NET Framework, so you don't often need to use the Object Browser when you're using only .NET Framework classes. It is really useful, however, when you are using a DLL from a third party that does not come with documentation. Often the method and property names can give you a clue about what's happening. Of course, this underlines why it is necessary to choose good names for your classes and their members.

On other occasions, the DLL will provide short descriptions of each of its classes and members. This is done using attributes, which is a subject outside the scope of this text.

Summary

Class libraries are an integral part of Visual Basic 2005 and, in fact, are important to all of the languages in the .NET Framework. They encompass what you use and what you need to know in terms of the common language runtime and within your development projects.

In this chapter, you have considered the nature of class libraries and how to view the properties and methods contained within them using the Object Browser. You have also seen how the .NET Framework allows developers to avoid DLL Hell through the use of keys and signatures, and looked at some of the broad issues regarding designing your own components.

In Chapter 13, you will learn how to create Windows Forms controls that are components with a user interface, as opposed to class library projects, which are purely code-based. There too, you will see the importance of reusable and stable code.

Exercise

Modify the Favorites Viewer project to use the compiled `InternetFavorites.dll` instead of the InternetFavorites project.

Creating Your Own Custom Controls

In this book, you have used many of the controls that come with the .NET Framework, from the Button and the TextBox controls to the ListBox control. You may even have tried to use some of the more advanced controls such as the DataGrid and the TreeView controls. Although at first some of them may be hard to use, they offer a lot of functionality. These controls make it easy to create a user interface in your applications. Once you get to know how to use all their features, you will find that creating user interfaces also becomes a faster experience. Another important aspect that makes controls so useful is that they are reusable. You can drag and drop a Button control onto any form in any new Windows project and it *works* as a button should. The reuse factor is an important reason why Visual Basic, in general, became one of the most popular and is presently, one of the most powerful development languages in use today. Did you know that you owe much of what you experience today in Visual Studio 2005, like Windows Forms Controls, to Visual Basic? The history of Windows Forms Controls has roots in something known as controls Visual Basic Extension (VBX). This later became more widely known as ActiveX, and today, revitalized and reborn into the .NET Framework, it is known as Windows Forms Controls.

In this chapter, you will:

- ❑ Learn what a Windows Forms Control is and how it works
- ❑ Create and use a Windows Forms Control
- ❑ Learn to add methods and events to your control
- ❑ Learn to code for design time and run time

These controls are best suited for Windows Forms rather than Web Applications. To learn about Web Server controls you should turn to Chapter 18. This chapter will concentrate on the Windows Forms version.

Windows Forms Controls

Today, there are several good reasons for wanting to create Windows Forms Controls:

❑ You can use the same control throughout an application or in lot of different applications, thus saving on code (reuse).

❑ You can keep code relating to a control within the control's class, making the code cleaner and easier to understand. For example, you could write a button that handles its own click event — meaning you don't need to handle the event in your form's code.

In terms of reusing controls between applications, there are two main ways to do this. The first is to add the control's source file to every project in which you need the control. Then, when you build the application, the control will be compiled into the main executable. This is the approach you take in this chapter, because it is simpler and will allow you to concentrate on how it works.

The second way is to build a control library. Control libraries are similar to the class libraries that you examined in the previous chapter. In fact, they *are* class libraries that happen to contain UI-driven classes. Like any other class library, a control library will compile to its own assembly, which you can use in your applications. This method is attractive, because it means you can distribute the assembly to other developers without giving away your source code. You can also make changes to the assembly, and these will be reflected in the applications that use it — even without the applications being recompiled. The techniques for building the controls are the same regardless of whether you are using a control library or using a control only within your application project.

Creating and Testing a User Control

You might find in the applications that you build, that you have a common need for a control that goes to a database to retrieve certain information, such as login information. If you want to build a robust control, you will need to make it as useful as possible to developers using it down the line, while requiring the minimum amount of labor to get it working. You will probably want to encapsulate the functionality of connecting to the database, querying the results, and populating the control with information, so that subsequent developers using your control do not have to know how to do this. This is a key principle of encapsulation — to make life easier for the next developer. In this way, you can also benefit from the more tangible advantage of reducing costs through quality application development and code reuse.

Creating a user control from scratch is not difficult. From one perspective, it is similar to building the Windows forms. In this section, you are going to create a Windows application that uses User Controls. In the first Try It Out, you are going to create a simple control that has three basic button controls inside of it.

> *When you create your own custom control that uses (hosts) existing controls inside of it, the control is known as an aggregate control.*

A different message will be displayed when each button is clicked. You will then see how this control can be used in a standard Windows Forms application.

Try It Out   Building Your First Control

1. Open Visual Studio 2005 and, on the File menu, select New ⇨ Project. In the New Project dialog box, select Visual Basic in the Project Types list and Windows Control Library in the Templates list. Enter **MyNamespaceControl** in the Name field and then click OK.

2. Now click UserControl1.vb in the Solution Explorer and then change the File Name property in the Properties Window to **MyNamespace.vb**. You will have something that looks very much like a form's designer without the title bar or borders. Usually, when building a control, you drag on other controls and define a way in which those controls interact. This extra behavior defines a control's purpose and makes it useful.

3. Drag three Button controls from the Toolbox and drop them on the form and set their Text properties using Figure 13-1 as a guide. Also resize the control so that it also looks similar to Figure 13-1.

Figure 13-1

4. Set the Name properties of the button controls to **btnApplicationCopyright**, **btnScreenBounds**, and **btnScreenWorkingArea**, respectively.

5. At the moment, this control won't do anything when the buttons are clicked — you need to wire up the event code behind the Click event for each button in order for it to work. Double-click the ApplicationCopyright button and add the highlighted code:

```
Private Sub btnApplicationCopyright_Click(ByVal sender As System.Object, _
    ByVal e As System.EventArgs) Handles btnApplicationCopyright.Click

        MessageBox.Show(My.Application.Info.Copyright)
End Sub
```

6. Now select btnScreenBounds in the Class Name combo box at the top of the Code Editor and select the Click event in the Method Name combo box. Add the following highlighted code to the Click event handler:

```
Private Sub btnScreenBounds_Click(ByVal sender As Object, _
    ByVal e As System.EventArgs) Handles btnScreenBounds.Click

        MessageBox.Show(My.Computer.Screen.Bounds.ToString)
End Sub
```

7. Finally, select btnScreenWorkingArea in the Class Name combo box and select the Click event in the Method Name combo box. Add this code to the Click event handler:

```
Private Sub btnScreenWorkingArea_Click(ByVal sender As Object, _
    ByVal e As System.EventArgs) Handles btnScreenWorkingArea.Click

        MessageBox.Show(My.Computer.Screen.WorkingArea.ToString)
End Sub
```

8. Now run your project. The user control will be displayed in a TestContainer dialog box as shown in Figure 13-2. From here, you can test your control by clicking each of the buttons and the appropriate information will be displayed in a message box. When you are done, click the Close button.

How It Works

Building the UI for the control is not at all different from building the UI for a Windows application. You simply drag the necessary controls from the Toolbox and drop them on the control designer. Then you wire up the events for the code using the same techniques that you've used all along when building Windows applications.

The code that you added for the btnApplicationCopyright button will display the copyright information for your application. This is done by using the My.Application namespace and retrieving the copyright information with the Copyright property of the Info class.

```
Private Sub btnApplicationCopyright_Click(ByVal sender As System.Object, _
    ByVal e As System.EventArgs) Handles btnApplicationCopyright.Click

    MessageBox.Show(My.Application.Info.Copyright)
End Sub
```

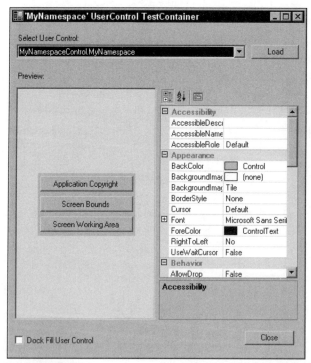

Figure 13-2

The code that you added for the btnScreenBounds button will display the current boundaries of the computer screen, which is determined from the screen resolution settings. This is done by using the `My.Computer` namespace and retrieving the screen boundary information with the `Bounds` property of the `Screen` class.

```
Private Sub btnScreenBounds_Click(ByVal sender As Object, _
    ByVal e As System.EventArgs) Handles btnScreenBounds.Click

    MessageBox.Show(My.Computer.Screen.Bounds.ToString)
End Sub
```

The code that you added for the btnScreenWorkingArea button will display the current working area of the screen. This is the area of the screen that is available to your application's forms. This is done by using the `My.Computer` namespace and retrieving the screen working area information with the `WorkingArea` property of the `Screen` class.

```
Private Sub btnScreenWorkingArea_Click(ByVal sender As Object, _
    ByVal e As System.EventArgs) Handles btnScreenWorkingArea.Click

    MessageBox.Show(My.Computer.Screen.WorkingArea.ToString)
End Sub
```

When you built the solution, the control was automatically added to the toolbox in the MyNamespace Control Components tab. This will not become evident, however, until you add a Windows application to this solution. This will allow you to use your user control in your application just as you would with any other control in the toolbox.

To test the control, you can't just run the project. Instead, you have to put the control onto a form, which will be covered in this next Try It Out.

Try It Out   **Adding Your New User Control to a Form**

1. Click the File menu and choose Add ⇨ New Project.

2. In the Add New Project dialog box, ensure that Windows Application is selected in the Templates pane, enter a project name of **Controls**, and then click OK.

3. Click the MyNamespaceControl Components tab of the Toolbox and drag the MyNamespace control onto Form1.

4. Right-click the Controls project in the Solution Explorer and choose Set as Startup Project from the context menu.

5. Now run your project. The control will appear on the form, and clicking the buttons will have the same effect as they did when you tested the control in the TestContainer dialog box.

How It Works

A custom-built control works the same as any other control that you've used up until this point. You simply drag the control from the Toolbox, drop it on your form, and run your project. You didn't need to wire up any code for the Click events of the buttons, because that functionality is part of the control itself.

Exposing Properties from User Controls

A user control is implemented as a class. Therefore, anything that you can do with a class, you can also do with a user control. This means that you can add properties, methods, and events to the user control that can be manipulated by whoever is consuming it. First, take a look at adding a new property to your control.

Your control can have two sorts of properties: those that can be manipulated from the Properties window at design time and those that have to be programmatically manipulated at run time. For example, at design time you might want to change properties pertaining to the color or the font used to draw the control. But at run time you might want to change properties that depend on the contents of a file that the user selected, and so on. Usually, if the property is a fairly simple type such as `String`, `Integer`, or `Boolean` and doesn't have parameters, it can be manipulated at design time. If the property is a complex object, such as a database or file connection, or if it has parameters, you'll have to manipulate the property at run time.

Adding Properties

In the next Try It Out, you take a look at adding a property to your control. The property you're going to add is called `ApplicationName`. This property will contain the name of your application. When this property is changed, you'll want to display the text in the title bar of the message boxes on the control.

Try it out   Adding a New Property to the MyNamespace Control

1. To add a new property you need a member variable that will store the value. Switch to the Code Editor for MyNamespace and add the following highlighted code:

```
Public Class MyNamespace
    'Private members
    Private strApplicationName As String = String.Empty
```

2. When this property is set, you'll need to set the text in the private member that you just defined. Add this code directly after the lines you added in step 1:

```
Public Property ApplicationName() As String
    Get
        Return strApplicationName
    End Get
    Set(ByVal value As String)
        strApplicationName = value
    End Set
End Property
```

3. To have the message boxes display the application name in the title bar, you need to set the `caption` parameter of the `Show` method of the `MessageBox` class. Modify the Click events for each of the buttons as shown:

```
Private Sub btnApplicationCopyright_Click(ByVal sender As System.Object, _
    ByVal e As System.EventArgs) Handles btnApplicationCopyright.Click

    MessageBox.Show(My.Application.Info.Copyright, _
        strApplicationName)
End Sub
```

```
Private Sub btnScreenBounds_Click(ByVal sender As Object, _
    ByVal e As System.EventArgs) Handles btnScreenBounds.Click

        MessageBox.Show(My.Computer.Screen.Bounds.ToString, _
            strApplicationName)
End Sub

Private Sub btnScreenWorkingArea_Click(ByVal sender As Object, _
    ByVal e As System.EventArgs) Handles btnScreenWorkingArea.Click

        MessageBox.Show(My.Computer.Screen.WorkingArea.ToString, _
            strApplicationName)
End Sub
```

4. To expose the new property for this control to Form1, you need to build the project. Right-click the MyNamespaceControl project in the Solution Explorer and select Build from the context menu. The new property will now be exposed.

5. Switch to the Form Designer for Form1 and select the MyNamespace1 control. In the Properties window the new ApplicationName property will appear under the Misc category (or in the usual place if you have the properties arranged alphabetically).

6. Set the ApplicationName property to **My Windows Application**.

7. Now run your project and click any of the buttons on the form. Each message box will display the text My Windows Application in the title bar of the message box.

How It Works

You'll notice that the default value of an empty string for the ApplicationName property has passed through to the designer. If you change the property in the Properties window, the text displayed in the title bar of the message boxes of the control will change.

When the designer needs to update the Properties window, it will call into the object and request the ApplicatioName property. Likewise, when you change the value, it will call into the object and set the property. This also happens when the form is loaded from disk when you start up the designer.

Exposing Methods from User Controls

As you've probably guessed, if you can expose new properties for your control, you can also expose new methods. All that you need to do to make this happen is to add a public function or procedure to the control, and then you'll be able to call it from the form that's hosting the control, which you do in the next Try It Out.

Try It Out   **Adding a Method to the MyNamespace Control**

1. Switch to the Code Editor for MyNamespace.vb and add this function:

```
Public Function TaskBarHeight() As Integer
    Return My.Computer.Screen.Bounds.Height - _
        My.Computer.Screen.WorkingArea.Height
End Function
```

2. Now switch to the Forms Designer for Form1. Drag a Button control from the Toolbox and drop it on your form. Set the Name property to **btnTaskbarHeight** and the Text property to **Taskbar Height**.

3. Double-click the button and add the following highlighted code to its Click event handler:

```
Private Sub btnTaskbarHeight_Click(ByVal sender As System.Object, _
    ByVal e As System.EventArgs) Handles btnTaskbarHeight.Click

        MessageBox.Show("Taskbar Height = " & _
            MyNamespace1.TaskBarHeight & " pixels", "Form1")
End Sub
```

4. Run your project and click the Taskbar Height button on Form1. You'll see a message box with the calculated height of the taskbar.

How It Works

Exposing a function or procedure from a user control is no different from exposing a function or procedure from a class. You just need to mark the function or procedure as `Public` so that it is exposed to the user of the class.

The `TaskBarHeight` function calculates the height of the taskbar by subtracting the working area height from the screen bounds height and returning the calculated value.

```
Public Function TaskBarHeight() As Integer
    Return My.Computer.Screen.Bounds.Height - _
        My.Computer.Screen.WorkingArea.Height
End Function
```

When you call the `TaskBarHeight` function from your code in Form1, you specify the control name of `MyNamespace1` and then choose the `TaskBarHeight` function from the drop-down list in IntelliSense.

```
Private Sub btnTaskbarHeight_Click(ByVal sender As System.Object, _
    ByVal e As System.EventArgs) Handles btnTaskbarHeight.Click

    MessageBox.Show("Taskbar Height = " & _
        MyNamespace1.TaskBarHeight & " pixels", "Form1")
End Sub
```

There was no need to recompile the MyNamespaceControl control to expose this new function to Form1, as it did not affect the control's user interface or properties.

Exposing Events from User Controls

Now that you've seen how to expose your own properties and methods from your control, you need to take a look at how to expose your own events from the control. When you add events to one of your own controls, people who use your control can take action in their code when the event is raised.

In the next Try It Out, you add three events that will return the data that is displayed in the message boxes that get displayed when the buttons are clicked.

Try It Out   **Defining and Raising Events**

1. Defining an event is as simple as adding an `Event` statement, the event name, and the parameters that the event will return. Add the following highlighted code to the `MyNamespace.vb` file:

```
'Private members
Private strApplicationName As String = String.Empty


'Public Events
Public Event ApplicationCopyrightChanged(ByVal text As String)
Public Event ScreenBoundsChanged(ByVal bounds As Rectangle)
Public Event ScreenWorkingAreaChanged(ByVal bounds As Rectangle)
```

2. To raise an event you need to specify the `RaiseEvent` statement, passing it the event name as well as the parameters for the event being raised. Modify the code in `MyNamespace.vb` as follows:

```
Private Sub btnApplicationCopyright_Click(ByVal sender As System.Object, _
    ByVal e As System.EventArgs) Handles btnApplicationCopyright.Click

    RaiseEvent ApplicationCopyrightChanged( _
        My.Application.Info.Copyright)
    MessageBox.Show(My.Application.AssemblyInfo.LegalCopyright, _
        strApplicationName)
End Sub

Private Sub btnScreenBounds_Click(ByVal sender As Object, _
    ByVal e As System.EventArgs) Handles btnScreenBounds.Click

    RaiseEvent ScreenBoundsChanged(My.Computer.Screen.Bounds)
    MessageBox.Show(My.Computer.Screen.Bounds.ToString, _
        strApplicationName)
End Sub

Private Sub btnScreenWorkingArea_Click(ByVal sender As Object, _
    ByVal e As System.EventArgs) Handles btnScreenWorkingArea.Click

    RaiseEvent ScreenWorkingAreaChanged(My.Computer.Screen.WorkingArea)
    MessageBox.Show(My.Computer.Screen.WorkingArea.ToString, _
        strApplicationName)
End Sub
```

3. Start your application to test your changes.

How It Works

As mentioned earlier, to define an event, you specify the `Event` statement, the event name, and the parameters that the event will return. Most events for controls are going to be Click or Changed; thus you have specified the different button names suffixed with the word `Changed`.

The Application Copyright button returns the application copyright as a string; thus, the parameter for the `ApplicationCopyrightChanged` event is specified as a `String` data type. The Screen Bounds and Screen Working Area buttons will return the screen information in a `Rectangle` structure; thus you specified the `Rectangle` structure as the data type for these events.

```
'Public Events
Public Event ApplicationCopyrightChanged(ByVal text As String)
Public Event ScreenBoundsChanged(ByVal bounds As Rectangle)
Public Event ScreenWorkingAreaChanged(ByVal bounds As Rectangle)
```

To raise an event, you have to use the `RaiseEvent` statement. This looks after the tricky aspect of actually telling the control's owner what event has been raised and passes it the appropriate parameters.

You'll have noticed that when you typed the word `RaiseEvent`, Visual Studio 2005 IntelliSense kicked in and provided a drop-down list of the events that you defined. This is just another example of how the IDE makes your life as a developer much easier.

In each instance of raising the events, you simply pass the event being raised; the data that will be displayed in the message box when the appropriate button is clicked.

```
Private Sub btnApplicationCopyright_Click(ByVal sender As System.Object, _
    ByVal e As System.EventArgs) Handles btnApplicationCopyright.Click

    RaiseEvent ApplicationCopyrightChanged( _
        My.Application.Info.Copyright)
    MessageBox.Show(My.Application.Info.Copyright, _
        strApplicationName)
End Sub

Private Sub btnScreenBounds_Click(ByVal sender As Object, _
    ByVal e As System.EventArgs) Handles btnScreenBounds.Click

    RaiseEvent ScreenBoundsChanged(My.Computer.Screen.Bounds)
    MessageBox.Show(My.Computer.Screen.Bounds.ToString, _
        strApplicationName)
End Sub

Private Sub btnScreenWorkingArea_Click(ByVal sender As Object, _
    ByVal e As System.EventArgs) Handles btnScreenWorkingArea.Click

    RaiseEvent ScreenWorkingAreaChanged(My.Computer.Screen.WorkingArea)
    MessageBox.Show(My.Computer.Screen.WorkingArea.ToString, _
        strApplicationName)
End Sub
```

All that remains now is to detect when the event has fired and do something. This is known as *consuming* an event. When a control fires an event, you can hook into the event handler. By doing this, you receive notification that the event has fired and can do something with the data that the event exposes. This is one of the core concepts of the control/event methodology that you have been using throughout this book.

Try It Out   Consuming Events

1. Switch to the Forms Designer for Form1 and add three TextBox controls as shown in Figure 13-3. Set the Name properties to **txtApplicationCopyright**, **txtScreenBounds**, and **txtScreenWorkingArea**, respectively.

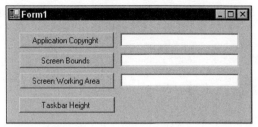

Figure 13-3

2. Now switch to the Code Editor for Form1 and select MyNamespace1 in the Class Name combo box at the top of the Code Editor. Now click in the Method Name combo box, and you'll see your ApplicationCopyrightChanged event in the Method Name combo box as shown in Figure 13-4. Remember, although you specifically defined three events for this control, you still get all of the other events that were defined on the various base classes that your control class inherits from.

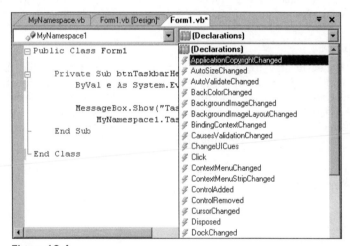

Figure 13-4

3. Of course, if you select the control and an event, you are automatically given a handler "stub" into which you can add your event-handling code, just as you have been doing with the other controls that you've used all along. Select the ApplicationCopyrightChanged event in the Method Name combo box. Now add the following highlighted code to the ApplicationCopyrightChanged event handler:

```
Private Sub MyNamespace1_ApplicationCopyrightChanged(ByVal text As String) _
    Handles MyNamespace1.ApplicationCopyrightChanged

    txtApplicationCopyright.Text = text
End Sub
```

4. Now select MyNamespace1 in the Class Name combo box and the ScreenBoundsChanged event in the Method Name combo box. Add the following highlighted code:

```
Private Sub MyNamespace1_ScreenBoundsChanged(ByVal bounds As _
    System.Drawing.Rectangle) Handles MyNamespace1.ScreenBoundsChanged

    txtScreenBounds.Text = bounds.ToString
End Sub
```

5. Finally, select MyNamespace1 in the Class Name combo box and the ScreenWorkingAreaChanged event in the Method Name combo box. Add the following highlighted code to the ScreenWorkingAreaChanged event handler:

```
Private Sub MyNamespace1_ScreenWorkingAreaChanged(ByVal bounds As _
    System.Drawing.Rectangle) Handles MyNamespace1.ScreenWorkingAreaChanged

    txtScreenWorkingArea.Text = bounds.ToString
End Sub
```

6. Now run your project. When you click each of the buttons, the corresponding text box will be populated with the data returned by the event, and then the message box will be displayed.

How It Works

Consuming control events in your application is very straightforward and something that you've been doing all along with Button and TextBox controls. You merely select the control name in the Class Name combo box in the Code Editor and the appropriate event in the Method Name combo box and then write the appropriate code to consume, or handle, the event that has been raised by the control. In the case of the MyNamespace control, you are consuming three different events; ApplicationCopyrightChanged, ScreenBoundsChanged, and ScreenWorkingAreaChanged.

For the ApplicationCopyrightChanged event, you simply take the text returned from the event and set it in the Text property of your text box.

```
Private Sub MyNamespace1_ApplicationCopyrightChanged(ByVal text As String) _
    Handles MyNamespace1.ApplicationCopyrightChanged

    txtApplicationCopyright.Text = text
End Sub
```

The ScreenBoundsChanged event is a little different. This event returns data in a Rectangle structure, which you must convert to a String data type in order to set it in the Text property of your text box. This is done using the ToString method of the Rectangle structure.

```
Private Sub MyNamespace1_ScreenBoundsChanged(ByVal bounds As _
    System.Drawing.Rectangle) Handles MyNamespace1.ScreenBoundsChanged

    txtScreenBounds.Text = bounds.ToString
End Sub
```

The ScreenWorkingAreaChanged event is like the ScreenBoundsChanged event. This event also returns data in a `Rectangle` structure, which must be converted to a `String` data type before it can be set in the `Text` property of your text box.

```
Private Sub MyNamespace1_ScreenWorkingAreaChanged(ByVal bounds As _
    System.Drawing.Rectangle) Handles MyNamespace1.ScreenWorkingAreaChanged

    txtScreenWorkingArea.Text = bounds.ToString
End Sub
```

Design Time or Run Time

In certain circumstances, it's useful to know whether your control is in design mode or run mode. The control is in design mode is when a form is being designed and the properties of the control are being set; it is in run mode when the form is being run and the control is able to expose methods and events.

As an example, imagine that you have a control that establishes a database connection when a certain property is set. It might not be appropriate for that control to establish the connection when the form is being designed, but you will want it to when the application is being run.

Usually, a control itself has a Boolean property called `DesignMode`, which returns `True` if the control is in design mode and `False` if it isn't.

In this next Try It Out, you're going to modify the MyNamespace control by adding a Label and Timer control to it. The Text property of the label will be updated with the text "Design Mode" when your MyNamespace control is in design mode and updated with the current time when the control is in run mode.

Try It Out **Creating a Control That Understands "DesignMode"**

1. Switch to the Control Designer for the MyNamespace control. Expand the height of the control so that you can place a Label control underneath the last button.

2. Drag a Label control from the Toolbox and center it underneath the last button control. Set the Name property to **lblTime**.

3. Now drag and drop a Timer control from the Toolbox onto the Control Designer. The timer will be added to the bottom of the IDE. Accept the default properties for this control and ensure that the Enabled property is set to False and that Interval is set to 100.

4. Now switch to the Code Editor for your MyNamespace control. You can detect when your control has been added to a form through the `InitLayout` method, which is defined on `System. Windows.Forms.Control`. This happens both at design time and at run time. This is the best point to determine which mode you're in and, if appropriate, to start the timer. Add this code:

```
Protected Overrides Sub InitLayout()
    'Are we in design mode?
    If DesignMode Then
        lblTime.Text = "Design Mode"
    Else
```

```
                    Timer1.Enabled = True
            End If
    End Sub
```

5. The last thing to do is to add code to the Tick event of the timer. Select Timer1 in the Class Name combo box at the top of the Code Editor and the Tick event in the Method Name combo box. Add the highlighted code to the Tick event handler:

```
Private Sub Timer1_Tick(ByVal sender As Object, _
    ByVal e As System.EventArgs) Handles Timer1.Tick

        'Display the time
        lblTime.Text = Now.ToLongTimeString
    End Sub
```

6. You'll need to build the project before the changes to the control can be picked up by your Controls application. Build the project by right-clicking the MyNamespaceControl project in the Solution Explorer and choosing Build from the context menu.

7. Open the Forms Designer for Form1 in the Controls project. Delete the current MyNamespace control from the form and drag a new one from the Toolbox and drop it on your form. You'll see the text Design Mode as shown in Figure 13-5.

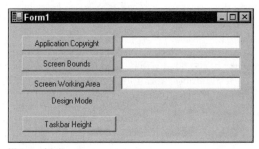

Figure 13-5

8. Now run the project. You will see that the Design Mode text is replaced by the current time.

How It Works

The InitLayout method is fired when the control is initialized, both at design time and at run time. The DesignMode property of your control returns a Boolean value of True when the control is in design mode and a value of False when the control is in run mode.

If your control is in design mode, you simply want to display the text Design Mode on your label control. When the control is in run mode, you want to enable the Timer control, and the Timer control will update the label with the current time.

```
        Protected Overrides Sub InitLayout()
            'Are we in design mode?
            If DesignMode Then
                lblTime.Text = "Design Mode"
```

```
        Else
            Timer1.Enabled = True
        End If
    End Sub
```

Of course, there are many other occasions when you might want your code to behave differently at run time than at design time. An example could be that validation rules for a property will be different. In these cases, you would check the control's `DesignMode` property in exactly the same way.

The Tick event of the Timer control gets called at the specified interval of the Timer control, which in this case is every 100 milliseconds. When the `Tick` event is fired, you want to update the `Text` property of the label control with the current time. This is done by retrieving the current long time from the `ToLongTimeString` property of the `Now` object.

```
        Private Sub Timer1_Tick(ByVal sender As Object, _
            ByVal e As System.EventArgs) Handles Timer1.Tick

            'Display the time
            lblTime.Text = Now.ToLongTimeString
        End Sub
```

Because you made changes to the actual UI of the control, you had to rebuild the control and then delete the current control from Form1 and get a new instance of it from the Toolbox. You don't have to do this when simply making code changes to the control, because those changes are automatically picked up.

Creating a Form Library

You do not always have to encapsulate this kind of functionality as a control. You could encapsulate the entire form and display it on demand. This is, in fact, what happens whenever an application wants to display the Open File or Print dialog boxes or any other standard dialog box. You may well discover a common functionality in your applications that would be useful to add to a reusable library. For example, you might want to have a "Customer Lookup" tool available to all of your applications, or a common login window like the one discussed earlier.

Luckily, building form libraries is incredibly easy in .NET. In fact, it's not different from creating the kinds of forms that you've built so far. You just need to provide some kind of interface that allows the caller to start up the form and get values back.

Building the Form Library Project Login Form

In this Try It Out, you'll build a simple login form. Don't bother adding any functionality behind it to actually authenticate the user. Instead, concentrate on getting the form to display itself to the user.

Try It Out   Creating the Form Library Project

1. Close your existing project and create a new Class Library project and call it **FormsLibrary**.

2. Right-click the project in the Solution Explorer and select Add Reference. Select `System. Windows.Forms` from the available .NET components and then click OK.

3. Now, create a new form by right-clicking the project within the Solution Explorer and selecting Add ⇨ Windows Form. Call the new form **Login.vb** and click Add.

4. To build the form, you need to change a few of the properties. Change these properties on the form:

    ❑ Set FormBorderStyle to Fixed Dialog.

    ❑ Set MaximizeBox to False.

    ❑ Set MinimizeBox to False.

    ❑ Set StartPosition to CenterScreen.

5. Now add two labels and set their `Text` properties to **User Name** and **Password**, respectively.

6. Add two text boxes called txtUserName and txtPassword. Set the `PasswordChar` property of the Password text box to *****, so that entered passwords are not displayed on the screen.

7. Now add a Button control and set the following properties:

    ❑ Set Name to **btnOk**.

    ❑ Set DialogResult to OK.

    ❑ Set Text to **OK**.

8. Add another Button control and set the following properties:

    ❑ Set Name to **btnCancel**.

    ❑ Set DialogResult to Cancel.

    ❑ Set Text to **Cancel**.

9. You completed Login form should look similar to the form shown in Figure 13-6.

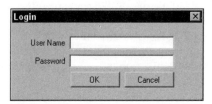

Figure 13-6

10. In the Solution Explorer, rename Class1.vb to **LoginEventArgs.vb** and then add the highlighted code to that class:

```
Public Class LoginEventArgs
    Inherits EventArgs

    'Public member
    Public UserID As Integer

    'Constructor
    Public Sub New(ByVal userIdentifier As Integer)
        UserID = userIdentifier
    End Sub
End Class
```

11. Switch to the Code Editor for the Login form and add the highlighted code:

```
Imports System.Windows.Forms

Public Class Login
    'Private members
    Private intAttemptCount As Integer = 0
    Private blnAllowClosing As Boolean = False
    Private intUserID As Integer

    'Public events
    Public Event LoginFailed(ByVal sender As Object, ByVal e As EventArgs)
    Public Event LoginSucceeded(ByVal sender As Object, _
                        ByVal e As LoginEventArgs)
    Public Event LoginCancelled(ByVal sender As Object, ByVal e As EventArgs)

End Class
```

12. You want to add a read-only property that allows the consumer of this class library to get the UserID of the user who has successfully logged on. Add the following code:

```
Public ReadOnly Property UserID() As Integer
    Get
        Return intUserID
    End Get
End Property
```

13. When the Login form is activated, you want to populate the User Name field with the domain name and user name of the user who is logged into Windows. In the Class Name combo box at the top of the Code Editor, select (Login Events) and select Activated in the Method Name combo box. Add the following highlighted code to the Activated event:

```
Private Sub Login_Activated(ByVal sender As Object, _
    ByVal e As System.EventArgs) Handles Me.Activated

    'Populate the user name text box
    txtUsername.Text = My.User.Name

    'Set focus to the password text box
    txtPassword.Focus()
End Sub
```

14. You need to control when the form closes, so you'll need to add some code to the FormClosing event. Select (Login Events) in the Class Name combo and the FormClosing event in the Method Name combo box. Add the following highlighted code:

```
Private Sub Login_FormClosing(ByVal sender As Object, _
    ByVal e As System.Windows.Forms.FormClosingEventArgs) _
    Handles Me.FormClosing

    'If we are not allowing the form to close...
    If Not blnAllowClosing Then
        'Set the Cancel flag to True
        e.Cancel = True
    End If
End Sub
```

15. When the user clicks the OK button, you'll need to validate the user's credentials. Select btnOK in the Class Name combo box and the Click event in the Method combo box. Add the following highlighted code to the Click event handler:

```
Private Sub btnOK_Click(ByVal sender As Object, _
    ByVal e As System.EventArgs) Handles btnOK.Click
```

```
        'Was a user name entered?
        If txtUserName.Text.Trim.Length > 0 Then

            'Was the password correct?
            If txtPassword.Text = "secret" Then

                'Successful login, set the User ID
                intUserID = 27

                'Raise the LoginSucceeded event
                RaiseEvent LoginSucceeded(Me, New LoginEventArgs(intUserID))

                'Turn on the allow closing flag
                blnAllowClosing = True

            Else

                'Inform the user that the password was invalid
                MessageBox.Show("The password you entered was invalid.", _
                    "Login")

                'Increment the attempt count
                intAttemptCount += 1

                'Check the attempt count
                If intAttemptCount = 3 Then

                    'Raise the LoginFailed event
                    RaiseEvent LoginFailed(Me, New EventArgs)

                    'Set the Cancel dialog result
                    Me.DialogResult = Windows.Forms.DialogResult.Cancel

                    'Turn on the allow closing flag
                    blnAllowClosing = True

                End If

            End If

        Else
            'Inform the user that they must supply a user name
            MessageBox.Show("You must supply a User Name.", "Login")
        End If
    End Sub
```

16. Finally, you need to perform some actions when the user clicks the Cancel button. Select btnCancel in the Class Name combo box and the Click event in the Method Name combo box. Add the following highlighted code to the Click event handler:

```
Private Sub btnCancel_Click(ByVal sender As Object, _
    ByVal e As System.EventArgs) Handles btnCancel.Click

        'Raise the LoginCancelled event
        RaiseEvent LoginCancelled(Me, New EventArgs)

        'Turn on the allow closing flag
        blnAllowClosing = True
End Sub
```

How It Works

The first thing that you had to do in this project was to set a reference to the `System.Windows` `.Forms.dll`. The reason for this is that a Class Library project is compiled as a DLL and does not inherently know about Windows forms.

When you added your button controls, you set the `DialogResult` property. This causes the button controls to return a dialog box result of `OK` or `Cancel` when they are clicked and will automatically close the Login form and return the dialog box result to the caller.

The `LoginEventArgs` class is derived from the `EventArgs` class and extends it by providing a constructor and a public member called `UserID`. This public member will be accessible to the consumer of the `LoginEventArgs` class, which will be the LoginSucceeded event and, eventually, the end user of the `Login` class library.

To access the MessageBox class in the Login form to display messages, you must import the `System` `.Windows.Forms` namespace. Remember that this is a Class Library project and it doesn't inherently have access to this namespace. You set a reference to the `System.Windows.Forms`, but you still need to import the name space in your form class.

```
Imports System.Windows.Forms
```

You also added some private members to the Login form that will be used by the various methods in this class. The `intAttemptCount` variable will be used to count the number of attempts a user tries to enter a user name and password. The `blnAllowClosing` variable will be used to control whether the form is allowed to close, and the `intUserID` variable will be used to hold the User ID of the user who successfully logs in.

```
'Private members
Private intAttemptCount As Integer = 0
Private blnAllowClosing As Boolean = False
Private intUserID As Integer
```

You defined three events for the form: the LoginFailed event for when a user fails to provide authentication; the LoginSucceeded event for when a user successfully logs on; and the LoginCancelled event for when a user cancels his or her logon attempt.

```
'Public events
Public Event LoginFailed(ByVal sender As Object, ByVal e As EventArgs)
Public Event LoginSucceeded(ByVal sender As Object, _
                    ByVal e As LoginEventArgs)
Public Event LoginCancelled(ByVal sender As Object, ByVal e As EventArgs)
```

The `UserID` property is a public `ReadOnly` property that will allow the consumer of this class to retrieve the User ID of the user who successfully logs on.

```
Public ReadOnly Property UserID() As Integer
    Get
        Return intUserID
    End Get
End Property
```

After the form has loaded, the Activated event will be fired, and this is where you populate the User Name field with the user name of the user who is currently logged into Windows. This is done using the `Name` property of the `Identity` property of the `User` class in the `My` namespace. Since the User Name field has been populated with the user name, you want to set focus to the Password field so that users can just start typing their passwords. This is done by calling the Focus method on the txtPassword text box control.

```
Private Sub Login_Activated(ByVal sender As Object, _
    ByVal e As System.EventArgs) Handles Me.Activated

    'Populate the user name text box
    txtUsername.Text = My.User.Name

    'Set focus to the password text box
    txtPassword.Focus()
End Sub
```

You need to control when the form closes. By default, the form will close after it processes the code in the Click event for either the OK or the Cancel button. This is because you set the `DialogResult` property for the button controls. In the FormClosing event you control whether the form can close by querying the `blnAllowClosing` variable. If this variable is `False`, you set the `Cancel` property of the `FormClosingEventArgs` class to `True`, indicating that the form should cancel the FormClosing event and stay open.

```
Private Sub Login_FormClosing(ByVal sender As Object, _
    ByVal e As System.Windows.Forms.FormClosingEventArgs) _
    Handles Me.FormClosing

    'If we are not allowing the form to close...
    If Not blnAllowClosing Then
        'Set the Cancel flag to True
        e.Cancel = True
    End If
End Sub
```

The code that you added for the OK button first ensures that some text has been entered into the txtUserName text box. You check this by first trimming any spaces from the `Text` property of the text box using the `Trim` property and then checking the length of the text in that text box using the `Length` property. Remember that the `Text` property is derived from the `String` class, so all of the usual `String` methods and properties that you're accustomed to are available in the `Text` property of the TextBox control.

If a user name has been entered, you check the password entered, if any. Here you compare the password entered against the password (here, a static value of `secret`). If the password matches, you set the `intUserID` variable (here, to a static value of `27`), raise the `LoginSucceeded` event passing it the `intUserID` variable, and set the `blnAllowClosing` flag to `True`.

This section of code is where you would typically validate the user name and password against your database or other data store where you keep your user names and passwords.

```
Private Sub btnOK_Click(ByVal sender As Object, _
    ByVal e As System.EventArgs) Handles btnOK.Click

    'Was a user name entered?
    If txtUserName.Text.Trim.Length > 0 Then

        'Was the password correct?
        If txtPassword.Text = "secret" Then

            'Successful login, set the User ID
            intUserID = 27

            'Raise the LoginSucceeded event
            RaiseEvent LoginSucceeded(Me, New LoginEventArgs(intUserID))

            'Turn on the allow closing flag
            blnAllowClosing = True
```

If the password entered does not match the correct value for this user (here, the static text `secret`), you display a message box indicating that the password is invalid. Then you increment the `intAttempt Count` variable by a value of `1`.

Next, you check the `intAttemptCount` variable and, if it is equal to a value of `3`, you raise the Login Failed event and set the `DialogResult` property of the form to a dialog box result of `Cancel`. Then you set the `blnAllowClosing` flag to `True`, which will indicate that the form can close and return a dialog box result of `Cancel`.

```
    Else

        'Inform the user that the password was invalid
        MessageBox.Show("The password you entered was invalid.", _
            "Login")

        'Increment the attempt count
        intAttemptCount += 1

        'Check the attempt count
        If intAttemptCount = 3 Then
```

```
                   'Raise the LoginFailed event
                   RaiseEvent LoginFailed(Me, New EventArgs)

                   'Set the Cancel dialog result
                   Me.DialogResult = Windows.Forms.DialogResult.Cancel

                   'Turn on the allow closing flag
                   blnAllowClosing = True

              End If

          End If
```

If no text was entered into the User Name field, you display a message box indicating that the user must enter a user name.

```
          Else
              'Inform the user that they must supply a user name
              MessageBox.Show("You must supply a User Name.", "Login")
          End If
      End Sub
```

The code that you entered for the Cancel button is really simple. If the user clicks the Cancel button, you want to raise the LoginCancelled event and set the blnAllowClosing flag to True.

```
      Private Sub btnCancel_Click(ByVal sender As Object, _
          ByVal e As System.EventArgs) Handles btnCancel.Click

          'Raise the LoginCancelled event
          RaiseEvent LoginCancelled(Me, New EventArgs)

          'Turn on the allow closing flag
          blnAllowClosing = True
      End Sub
```

Testing the FormsLibrary

To test the Login form in the FormsLibrary, you need to add a Windows Application project to your solution, just as you did when you needed to test your user controls. In this next Try It Out, you'll examine the simplest method of using the Login form.

Try It Out   Testing the Login Form in an Application

1. Click on the File menu and select Add ⇨ New Project. In the Add New Project dialog box, select Windows Application in the Templates pane and enter a project name of **Secure Login** and then click OK.

2. Next, you need to set up this new test application as the startup project, so right-click the Secure Login project in the Solution Explorer and select Set as StartUp Project from the context menu.

3. You now need to add a reference to the FormsLibrary project. Right-click the Secure Login project in the Solution Explorer and select Add Reference from the context menu. In the Add Reference dialog box, click the Projects tab. You'll see that the FormsLibrary project is already listed, so just click OK.

4. Add a Label control to Form1 and set its Name property to **lblUserID**.

5. Now switch to the Code Editor for Form1 and add the following `Imports` statement above the `Class Form1` statement:

```
Imports FormsLibrary
```

6. Select (Form1 Events) in the Class Name combo box at the top of the Code Editor and the Load event in the Method Name combo box. Add the highlighted code to the Load event for the form:

```
Private Sub Form1_Load(ByVal sender As System.Object, _
    ByVal e As System.EventArgs) Handles MyBase.Load

        Using objLogin As New Login
            If objLogin.ShowDialog(Me) = Windows.Forms.DialogResult.OK Then
                'Update the label with the User ID
                lblUserID.Text = "User ID = " & objLogin.UserID
            Else
                'Inform the user that the login failed
                MessageBox.Show("Login Failed")
                'Close this form since the login failed
                Me.Close()
            End If
        End Using
End Sub
```

7. Now run the project, and the Login form will be displayed. Your domain name and user name will be populated in the User Name field. Enter any password except `secret` and click the OK button. You'll receive a message indicating that the password is invalid. Do this two more times and you'll receive a message indicating that the login failed, and the Secure Login project will end.

8. Now run the project again, and when the Login form is displayed, click the Cancel button. Again you'll receive a message indicating that the login failed, and the Secure Login project will end.

9. Now run the project one final time. This time enter **secret** in the Password field and click the OK button. Remember that the password is case-sensitive. This time the login will be successful; Form1 will be displayed, and the user ID will appear in the Label control on the form.

How It Works

This Try It Out is a really good example of how you can provide a secure login for your application. If the user fails to log in successfully, then your application will end without even displaying the application's main form, which is typically what you want to happen.

The first thing that you have to do in this project is set a reference to the FormsLibaray project through the Add Reference dialog box. Then you imported the `FormsLibrary` namespace in your form. This is not a necessary step, but it keeps you from having to fully qualify all references to the Login form in the `FormsLibrary` class.

```
Imports FormsLibrary
```

The code that you added to the Load event of Form1 was really simple. First you enclose all of your logic in a Using . . . End Using statement block. In the Using statement, you specify the object name of objLogin followed by a new instance of the Login form.

Then, inside the Using . . . End Using block, you use an If . . . Then . . . Else statement to show the Login form and check the dialog result returned. This is done by calling the ShowDialog method, passing a value of Me to this method for the owner parameter, and checking the dialog result returned against the OK constant of the DialogResult enumeration.

If the ShowDialog method of the Login form returns a dialog result of OK, then you update the label on Form1 with the user ID returned by UserID property of the Login form.

If the Login form returns any other dialog result other than OK (it will only return OK or Cancel), then you fall through to the code in the Else block of the If . . . Then . . . Else statement. Here you display a message block indicating that the login failed and then close the application by calling the Close method on Form1 using the Me keyword as a reference to Form1.

```
Private Sub Form1_Load(ByVal sender As System.Object, _
    ByVal e As System.EventArgs) Handles MyBase.Load

    Using objLogin As New Login
        If objLogin.ShowDialog(Me) = Windows.Forms.DialogResult.OK Then
            'Update the label with the User ID
            lblUserID.Text = "User ID = " & objLogin.UserID
        Else
            'Inform the user that the login failed
            MessageBox.Show("Login Failed")
            'Close this form since the login failed
            Me.Close()
        End If
    End Using
End Sub
```

Hooking Up the Events

Now that you've seen a simple method for using the Login form, you'll want to examine a more complex method where you actually hook into the events that are exposed by the Login form. In this next Try It Out, you create an application that calls the Login form and also hooks into and handles the events that are raised by the Login form.

Try It Out Receiving Events from the Login Form

1. Using the same solution with the two projects in it, right-click the solution in the Solution Explorer and select Add ➪ New Project. In the Add New Project dialog box, select Windows Application in the Templates pane and enter a project name of **Access Control** and then click OK.

2. Next, you need to set up this new test application as the startup project, so right-click the Access Control project in the Solution Explorer and select Set as StartUp Project from the context menu.

3. You now need to add a reference to the FormsLibrary project. Right-click the Access Control project in the Solution Explorer and select Add Reference from the context menu. In the Add Reference dialog box, click the Projects tab. You'll see that the FormsLibrary and Secure Login projects are already listed. Select the FormsLibrary project and then click OK.

4. Add a Button control to Form1, and set its Name property to **btnLogin** and its Text property to **Login**.

5. Add a Label control to your form beneath the Button control, and set its Name property to **lblMessage**. You completed form should look similar to the one shown in Figure 13-7.

Figure 13-7

6. Now switch to the Code Editor for Form1 and add the following `Imports` statement above the `Class Form1` statement:

```
Imports FormsLibrary
```

7. You can tell Visual Basic 2005 that you want to automatically capture any events that an object raises by using the `WithEvents` keyword. The problem with this keyword is that it can't be used in conjunction with `New`. In other words, you need to define a member to contain an instance of `Login` and create one when you need it. Add this code:

```
Public Class Form1
    'Declare events
    Private WithEvents objLogin As Login
```

8. At this point, Visual Studio 2005 will pick up the member that raises events, and it adds that member to the Class Name and Method Name combo boxes at the top of the Code Editor. Select objLogin in the Class Name combo box and the LoginCancelled event in the Method Name combo box. Add this highlighted code to the LoginCancelled event:

```
Private Sub objLogin_LoginCancelled(ByVal sender As Object, _
    ByVal e As System.EventArgs) Handles objLogin.LoginCancelled

    lblMessage.Text = "The login was canceled."
End Sub
```

9. Now select objLogin in the Class Name combo box and the LoginFailed event in the Method Name combo box. Add this highlighted code to the LoginFailed event:

```
Private Sub objLogin_LoginFailed(ByVal sender As Object, _
    ByVal e As System.EventArgs) Handles objLogin.LoginFailed

    lblMessage.Text = "The login failed."
End Sub
```

10. Finally, select objLogin in the Class Name combo box and the LoginSucceeded event in the Method Name combo box. Add this highlighted code to the LoginSucceeded event:

```
Private Sub objLogin_LoginSucceeded(ByVal sender As Object, _
    ByVal e As FormsLibrary.LoginEventArgs) Handles objLogin.LoginSucceeded

    lblMessage.Text = "The login was successful for User ID " & e.UserID
End Sub
```

11. One final piece of code that needs to be added is the code to actually call the Login form. Select btnLogin in the Class Name combo box and the Click event in the Method Name combo box. Add this highlighted code:

```
Private Sub btnLogin_Click(ByVal sender As Object, _
    ByVal e As System.EventArgs) Handles btnLogin.Click

        'Instantiate a new instance of the Login form
        objLogin = New Login

        'Show the login form
        objLogin.ShowDialog(Me)
End Sub
```

12. Now you are ready to test this project, so start it up. Click the Login button on Form1, and when the Login form is displayed, click the Cancel button. The Label control on Form1 will be updated with text indicating that the login was canceled.

13. Now click the Login button again and enter any password other than secret in the Password field of the Login form. Keep clicking the OK button until the login fails. The Label control on Form1 will be updated with text indicating that the login failed.

14. Click the Login button one final time and then enter the password of **secret** in the Password field of the Login form. Click the OK button, and the Label control on Form1 will be updated with text indicating that the login was successful and will also display the user ID.

How It Works

This project demonstrates how an application that needs to expose restricted access to certain parts of an application could use the Login form to validate the user's credentials and handle the various events that are raised by the Login form. All users would have access to most areas of the application, but you could secure other parts of the application and prompt users for the credentials before allowing them access to the more sensitive areas of the application.

This project starts out like the last project in that you first had to set a reference to the FormsLibrary project and then import the FormsLibrary namespace in you form. The difference comes in that in this project you declare an object to receive the events from the Login form.

```
        'Declare events
        Private WithEvents objLogin As Login
```

Once this object is declared, the events exposed by the Login form are available in the Method Name combo box in the Code Editor, and you can select them to create the appropriate event handlers for the LoginCancelled, LoginFailed, and LoginSucceeded events. Once these events are raised, you display the appropriate message in a Label control on your form. Ideally, these event handlers are where you would perform some appropriate action based on the event raised.

The one event handler that needs to be pointed out is the event handler for the LoginSucceeded event. This event receives the LoginEventArgs class, which, if you recall, is a class that you created in the FormsLibrary project that exposes UserID as a public member of that class.

Here you simply access the `UserID` member of the `LoginEventArgs` to retrieve the user ID and display it in the `Text` property of the Label control.

```
Private Sub objLogin_LoginSucceeded(ByVal sender As Object, _
    ByVal e As FormsLibrary.LoginEventArgs) Handles objLogin.LoginSucceeded

    lblMessage.Text = "The login was successful for User ID " & e.UserID
End Sub
```

In the Click event for the Login button, you add the code to create a new instance of the Login form and then simply call the `ShowDialog` method of that form. In this project you actually don't care what dialog result is returned from the `ShowDialog` method, because you handle the validation of the login through the event handlers.

```
Private Sub btnLogin_Click(ByVal sender As Object, _
    ByVal e As System.EventArgs) Handles btnLogin.Click

    'Instantiate a new instance of the Login form
    objLogin = New Login

    'Show the login form
    objLogin.ShowDialog(Me)
End Sub
```

We have presented two methods for using the Login form here, and each has its own purpose, as explained in the first paragraphs of the How It Works sections. Basically, you have built a Login form that can be used in two very different scenarios. All you need to do now is to implement the actual code to validate a user's credentials in the Login form against a database or other data store that handles user names and passwords.

Summary

This chapter showed two ways of packaging a user interface together with some encapsulated functionality. You looked at building a user control that aggregated a number of existing controls usefully. You extended the new control with properties, methods, and events. This control, once compiled, was shown in the ToolBox under its own tab.

You also took a look at how to create a class library that encapsulated a form with prebuilt functionality, making it easy to provide a consistent interface in all of your applications that need to implement a login form.

To summarize, you should know:

- ❑   What a Windows Forms Control is and how it works
- ❑   How to create a control
- ❑   How to add methods and events to your control
- ❑   How to code for Design Time and Runtime
- ❑   How to create a Class Library project that exposes a Windows form

Exercise

Add a property to the MyNamespace control called `SuppressMsgBox`, which contains a `Boolean` value. Add code to the Click event handlers for each of the buttons on this control to show the message box when the `SuppressMsgBox` property is `False` and to suppress the message box when this property is `True`.

Programming Custom Graphics

So far in this book, you have built user interfaces entirely from existing controls. When you are writing programs with Visual Basic 2005, you also have the freedom to draw your own user interface. This gives you absolute freedom over the look and feel of your programs, and makes certain programming tasks possible.

In this chapter, you are going to look at the graphics and drawing functionality available in Visual Basic 2005. You will be introduced to the concepts by building a fairly complex drawing program, just to illustrate how simple drawing your own user interface actually is. Toward the end of the chapter, you will examine some of the multimedia features of Visual Basic 2005 and learn how you can display common Internet file formats such as .gif, .jpg, and .png.

In this chapter, you will:

- ❑ Learn about the `System.Drawing` namespace
- ❑ Use pens and brushes
- ❑ Learn how to select and use colors
- ❑ Size and stretch images
- ❑ Create your own Paint program

Building a Simple Paint Program

You are going to create a simple Paint program by creating a new Windows application project and build some user controls that you will wire up to provide functionality for the application.

Creating a Project with User Controls

Your motivation for building user controls for this application is simple: It's good practice to break the application down into components. By following this technique, if you want to pull your paint functionality out of this application and into another, you can do it relatively easily.

What you are doing here with your controls is taking over the responsibility for painting them. Whenever you do this, you are creating owner drawings. Therefore, the controls you build are known as owner-draw user controls.

Try It Out   **Creating the Project**

1. Create a new Visual Basic Windows Application project in the usual way. Call it **WroxPaint**.

2. In the Solution Explorer, right-click the WroxPaint project and select Add ⇨ User Control. Set the name to **PaintCanvas.vb** and click Add.

3. Make sure the Form Designer for PaintCanvas is showing. Click the background of the control, and from the Properties window, change the `BackColor` property to White. (To do this, use the `BackColor` property's drop-down list, change to the Custom tab, and click the white box in the top-left corner.)

4. Before you can use the control you need to build the project. From the menu select Build ⇨ Build WroxPaint. This will create the new PaintCanvas control and let you use it.

5. Now, go back to the Forms Designer for Form1. Click the Toolbox; then click the WroxPaint Components tab and select the new PaintCanvas control and drag it onto your form. Set the Dock property of the PaintCanvas control to Fill.

6. For the sake of neatness change the Text property of the form to **WroxPaint**.

How Drawing Programs Work

Your computer screen is made up of pixels—hundreds of thousands of them. They are very small, but when working together they make a display on the screen. Since pixels on any given display are always of a uniform size, they are the common unit of measurement used in computer graphics.

To find out how big your desktop is, minimize all your windows and right-click your Windows desktop. Select Properties and change to the Settings tab. The slider in the bottom-left corner controls the size of your desktop—or, rather, it controls the number of pixels on your display. In Figure 14-1, you can see that the screen is set to 1,024 pixels across and 768 pixels down.

There are two very common computer graphics techniques: raster and vector. It is very useful to understand the difference between the two.

Raster Graphics

Raster graphics work a little like a physical canvas: You have a space, and you fill it up with color using various tools like brushes and pens. In a raster graphics program, the space is divided up into pixels. Each pixel has a color, and it's the drawing program's responsibility to set the color of each one depending on what kind of drawing tool you're using and the position and movement of the mouse.

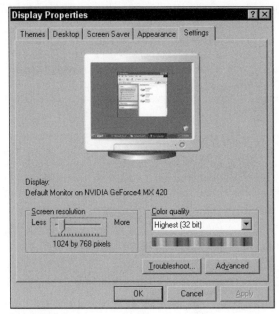

Figure 14-1

The graphics program stores the image that you've drawn as a bitmap, this being a description of the pixels that make up the image and the color of each. A bitmap is basically a two-dimensional array of pixels. Each element in the array, accessed through a pair of (x, y) coordinates, stores a color value.

The name "bitmap" comes from the days when computer displays were monochrome, so each pixel could be only black or white and therefore could be stored in a single bit.

If you draw a rectangle in a raster graphics package, that rectangle is abstracted to a set of pixels on the bitmap. After it's been drawn, you can't change the rectangle at all, other than using other tools to draw over it or draw another one.

.jpg, .gif, and .png images use a variation of the bitmap format to save images. However, they are compressed in particular ways to save space and download time when used in Web pages.

Vector Graphics

Vector graphics packages work in a different way. When you draw a rectangle onto the canvas, they physically record the fact that a rectangle exists at a given location. Vector graphics packages store a blueprint of how to draw the image, rather than storing the image that's been drawn. They do not abstract the rectangle down to a set of pixels. What this means is that you can pick it up again and move it, or change its shape or color later on, because the package has an understanding of what it is.

A number of modern graphics packages offer a hybrid approach to this, combining raster graphics with vector graphics.

Even in a vector graphics program, the screen itself works in pixels and is a raster format. Therefore, for the program to be able to display the drawing, the picture recorded by the package has to be converted into a raster format for the display. This process is known as *rendering*.

Your paint package is going to be a vector-based drawing package, for no other reason than it makes it easier to understand how drawing works in the .NET Framework. You're going to build a set of objects that represent certain shapes—namely, circles and squares—and hold them in a list.

The GraphicsItem Class

In your application, you're going to have two basic drawing types: circle and square. Each drawing type will need to have an understanding of where it appears on the canvas (and ultimately, the screen), what its color is, and whether it is filled. You'll build a base class called `GraphicsItem`, from which you'll derive `GraphicsCircle`.

Try It Out   Building GraphicsItem and GraphicsCircle

1. Create a new class by right-clicking WroxPaint in the Solution Explorer and selecting Add ➪ Class. Name the class **GraphicsItem.vb** and click Add.

2. Add this code to `GraphicsItem`. Remember to add the `MustInherit` keyword to the first line (that's why we highlighted it). The `MustInherit` keyword tells Visual Basic 2005 that you cannot create instances of `GraphicsItem` directly. Instead, you have to create classes that inherit from it.

```
Public MustInherit Class GraphicsItem
    'Public members
    Public Color As Color
    Public IsFilled As Boolean
    Public Rectangle As Rectangle

    'Public methods
    Public MustOverride Sub Draw(ByVal graphics As Graphics)

    'Add an item at the given point
    Public Sub SetPoint(ByVal x As Integer, ByVal y As Integer, _
        ByVal graphicSize As Integer, ByVal graphicColor As Color, _
        ByVal graphicIsFilled As Boolean)

        'Set the rectangle depending on the graphic and the size
        Rectangle = New Rectangle(x - (graphicSize / 2), y - (graphicSize / 2), _
            graphicSize, graphicSize)

        'Set the Color and IsFilled members
        Color = graphicColor
        IsFilled = graphicIsFilled
    End Sub
End Class
```

3. Create another class named **GraphicsCircle.vb**. Add the following highlighted code. After you type `Inherits GraphicsItem` and press Enter, an empty `Draw` procedure will be added to your class, and you can add the code shown here to it.

```
Public Class GraphicsCircle

    Inherits GraphicsItem

    Public Overrides Sub Draw(ByVal graphics As System.Drawing.Graphics)

        'Create a new pen
        Dim objSolidBrush As New SolidBrush(Me.Color)

        'Draw the circle
        graphics.FillEllipse(objSolidBrush, Me.Rectangle)
    End Sub
End Class
```

How It Works

When you created the `GraphicsItem` class, you added the `MustInherit` keyword to the `Class` declaration. This instructs Visual Basic 2005 not to let users create instances of this class but to force them to inherit this class.

When you created the `Draw` method in this class, you used the `MustOverride` keyword. This has a similar meaning to `MustInherit`—you use it to force derived classes to add their own implementation for a particular method without providing any implementation in the base class. The `MustOverride` keyword can be used only in `MustInherit` classes.

The `SetPoint` method is used to populate an object depending on the position of the mouse and the current graphic size and color. The first thing you need to do in this method is to set up the rectangle.

When you want to draw a circle, you provide the center point, whereas .NET expects the position of the top left corner of the rectangle that encloses the circle. Therefore, the top left corner of the rectangle must be adjusted up and left depending on the size provided through `graphicSize` parameter. You pass the top left corner through as the first and second parameters to the rectangle's constructor. The third parameter supplied is the width, and the fourth provides the height.

After you have the parameter, you need to store the color and also a flag that indicates whether the circle is filled.

```
Public MustInherit Class GraphicsItem
    'Public members
    Public Color As Color
    Public IsFilled As Boolean
    Public Rectangle As Rectangle

    'Public methods
    Public MustOverride Sub Draw(ByVal graphics As Graphics)

    'Add an item at the given point
    Public Sub SetPoint(ByVal x As Integer, ByVal y As Integer, _
        ByVal graphicSize As Integer, ByVal graphicColor As Color, _
        ByVal graphicIsFilled As Boolean)
```

```
                    'Set the rectangle depending on the graphic and the size
                    Rectangle = New Rectangle(x - (graphicSize / 2), y - (graphicSize / 2), _
                        graphicSize, graphicSize)

                    'Set the Color and IsFilled members
                    Color = graphicColor
                    IsFilled = graphicIsFilled
                End Sub
            End Class
```

When you created the `GraphicsCircle` class, you inherited the `GraphicsItem` class. Once you typed the `Inherits GraphicsItem` statement and pressed Enter, Visual Studio 2005 automatically added an empty `Draw` method, and all you had to do was add your own code to this method.

Painting is usually a matter of calling some simple methods on the `Graphics` object. This method draws and fills an ellipse (or circle, depending on which parameters you provide). Note that there's a similar method called `DrawEllipse`, which doesn't fill in the ellipse after it's drawn.

You'll also notice that at the top of the method you created a new `SolidBrush` object. You then pass this brush through to the `FillEllipse` method. This `SolidBrush` object, as you have probably guessed, describes the kind of brush you want to use.

```
        Public Class GraphicsCircle
            Inherits GraphicsItem

            Public Overrides Sub Draw(ByVal graphics As System.Drawing.Graphics)
                'Create a new pen
                Dim objSolidBrush As New SolidBrush(Me.Color)

                'Draw the circle
                graphics.FillEllipse(objSolidBrush, Me.Rectangle)
            End Sub
        End Class
```

Screen and Client Coordinates

When you get into the world of building your own painting code for your user interface, you usually have to work a lot with the mouse. We have already mentioned that in Windows and the .NET Framework, the base currency of drawing is the pixel. This means that when you ask the mouse for its position (for example, when verifying that the user has moved the mouse across your control or clicked one of the buttons), you get back a set of coordinates given in pixels. If the user clicks the mouse in the very top left pixel, you'll get back coordinates of (0, 0). If you're using a 1024x768 display and the user clicks in the very bottom right pixel, you'll get back coordinates of (1024, 768).

Although this seems straightforward, there is a wrinkle. When you click inside a window, the coordinates are adjusted depending on where the window itself is on the screen.

In Figure 14-2, the WroxPaint program is shown towards the bottom right corner of the screen. This display is configured at 1024 pixels across and 786 pixels down, which means that the top left corner of WroxPaint itself is at approximately (500, 300), according to the screen.

Figure 14-2

However, every window has a *client area*, which is the area the programmer can use to report the program's output. This client area is exclusive of the window border, the caption, menu, scrollbars, and the toolbar. When you are drawing onto the control or form, you are always dealing with this client area. The coordinates you use when drawing are adjusted so that the position of the window itself on the screen becomes irrelevant. These coordinates are known as *client coordinates*.

If you click the top-left corner of the WroxPaint paint area (the white part), there are actually two different coordinates that you can get:

❑   The first one will be around (510, 330), a little in and down from the top-left corner of the window. These are the *screen coordinates*, also known as the *absolute position*.

❑   The second pair will be around (0, 0), and these are the adjusted client coordinates. If you click the same graphic in the client, you will get (0, 0) irrespective of where the window is positioned on the screen. This is sometimes known as *relative position*.

Listening to the Mouse and Drawing GraphicsCircle Objects

For your graphics application to work, you'll monitor what the user is doing with the mouse, create new objects derived from `GraphicsItem`, and store them in a big list. When it is time for you to draw, you'll go through this list and ask each `GraphicsItem` in turn to render itself on the screen. You try drawing in the next Try It Out.

Try It Out   Drawing

1. In the Solution Explorer, right click the PaintCanvas control and select View Code. Add these enumerations to the class as highlighted. The first will be used to store the current graphics mode/tool, while the second stores the size of the pen used for drawing:

```
Public Class PaintCanvas

    'Public enumerations
    Public Enum GraphicTools As Integer
        CirclePen = 0
    End Enum

    Public Enum GraphicSizes As Integer
        Small = 4
        Medium = 10
        Large = 20
    End Enum
End Class
```

2. Next, add these members to this class:

```
'Public members
Public GraphicsItems As New ArrayList()
Public GraphicTool As GraphicTools = GraphicTools.CirclePen
Public GraphicSize As GraphicSizes = GraphicSizes.Medium
Public GraphicColor As Color = Color.Black
```

Here is what each member will do. Notice that you define a default value for these members to make initialization of the application easier:

- ❑ `GraphicItems` will hold a list of the `GraphicsItem` objects that make up the drawing.

- ❑ `GraphicsTool` will keep track of which graphic tool is currently being used.

- ❑ `GraphicsSize` will keep track of how big you want each graphic to be.

- ❑ `GraphicsColor` will keep track of the color of the item that you want to draw.

3. Drawing the items on the page is a two-phase process. When the user moves the mouse around on the control, you want to create new `GraphicsCircle` objects and add them to the `Graphics Items` list. At some point, Windows will ask you to paint the control, so you'll need to go through the `GraphicsItems` list and draw each one in turn. Add this method to `PaintCanvas`:

```
Private Sub DoMousePaint(ByVal e As MouseEventArgs)
    'Store the new item somewhere
    Dim objGraphicsItem As GraphicsItem
```

```
'What tool are you using?
Select Case GraphicTool

    'CirclePen
    Case GraphicTools.CirclePen

        'Create a new graphics circle
        Dim objGraphicsCircle As New GraphicsCircle()

        'Set the point for drawing
        objGraphicsCircle.SetPoint(e.X, e.Y, GraphicSize, _
            GraphicColor, True)

        'Store this for addition
        objGraphicsItem = objGraphicsCircle

End Select

'Were you given an item?
If objGraphicsItem IsNot Nothing Then

    'Add it to the list
    GraphicsItems.Add(objGraphicsItem)

    'Invalidate the control
    Me.Invalidate()

End If
End Sub
```

4. In the Class Name combo at the top of the Code Editor, select (PaintCanvas Events) and in the Method Name combo box select the MouseDown event. Add the following highlighted code to the new event handler:

```
Private Sub PaintCanvas_MouseDown(ByVal sender As Object, _
    ByVal e As System.Windows.Forms.MouseEventArgs) Handles Me.MouseDown

    'Is the left mouse button down?
    If e.Button = MouseButtons.Left Then
        DoMousePaint(e)
    End If
End Sub
```

5. Now select (PaintCanvas Events) in the Class Name combo box and the MouseMove event in the Method Name combo box. Add the following highlighted code to the MouseMove event handler:

```
Private Sub PaintCanvas_MouseMove(ByVal sender As Object, _
    ByVal e As System.Windows.Forms.MouseEventArgs) Handles Me.MouseMove

    'Is the left mouse button down?
    If e.Button = MouseButtons.Left Then
        DoMousePaint(e)
    End If
End Sub
```

435

6. Finally, select (PaintCanvas Events) in the Class Name combo box and the Paint event in the Method Name combo box. Add the following highlighted code:

```
Private Sub PaintCanvas_Paint(ByVal sender As Object, _
    ByVal e As System.Windows.Forms.PaintEventArgs) Handles Me.Paint

        'Go through the list
        For Each objGraphicsItem As GraphicsItem In GraphicsItems
            'Ask each item to draw itself
            objGraphicsItem.Draw(e.Graphics)
        Next
End Sub
```

7. Run the project and draw on the control by holding down the left mouse button and dragging the mouse over the surface.

You now have a working paint program, but you'll notice that the more you paint the more it flickers. This illustrates an important aspect of drawing, as you'll see when you fix it. For now, look at what you've done.

How It Works

When the user moves the mouse over the control, an event called `MouseMove` is fired. You have hooked into this event by adding the event handler for the `MouseMove` event. When this event handler is fired, you check to see whether the left mouse button is down, and if it is, you pass the `System.Windows.Forms.MouseEventArgs` object that you were given over to your private `DoMousePaint` method.

```
Private Sub PaintCanvas_MouseMove(ByVal sender As Object, _
    ByVal e As System.Windows.Forms.MouseEventArgs) Handles Me.MouseMove

    'Is the left mouse button down?
    If e.Button = MouseButtons.Left Then
        DoMousePaint(e)
    End If
End Sub
```

`DoMousePaint` is the method that you'll use to handle the drawing process. In this case, whenever the `MouseMove` event is received, you want to create a new `GraphicsCircle` item and add it to the list of vectors that make up your image.

As `DoMousePaint` will ultimately do more than add circles to the vector list, you need to do things in a (seemingly) counterintuitive order. The first thing you need is to declare an object to hold the new `GraphicsItem` class that will be created — so declare `objGraphicsItem`:

```
Private Sub DoMousePaint(ByVal e As MouseEventArgs)
    'Store the new item somewhere
    Dim objGraphicsItem As GraphicsItem
```

Then you look at your `GraphicTool` property to determine what you're supposed to be drawing. At this point, because you only have one tool defined, this will always be a circle:

```
'What tool are you using?
Select Case GraphicTool
```

```
'CirclePen
Case GraphicTools.CirclePen

    'Create a new graphics circle
    Dim objGraphicsCircle As New GraphicsCircle()
```

After you have the `GraphicsCircle`, you call the `SetPoint` method, which, if you recall, was defined on `GraphicsItem`. This method is responsible for determining the point on the canvas where the item should appear. You give `SetPoint` the current drawing size and color, and tell it to draw a filled shape.

```
    'Set the point for drawing
    objGraphicsCircle.SetPoint(e.X, e.Y, GraphicSize, _

        GraphicColor, True)
```

After you have called `SetPoint`, you store the `GraphicsCircle` in `objGraphicsItem` and close the `Select ... End Select` statement.

```
    'Store this for addition
    objGraphicsItem = objGraphicsCircle

End Select
```

If a new `GraphicsItem` was stored in `objGraphicsItem`, you have to add it to the list.

```
'Were you given an item?
If objGraphicsItem IsNot Nothing Then

    'Add it to the list

    GraphicsItems.Add(objGraphicsItem)
```

Finally, you have to *invalidate* the control. You have to do this to tell Windows that something about the appearance of the control has changed. The program will not tell the control to paint itself unless something has told Windows that the control needs painting. Calling `Me.Invalidate` in this way tells Windows that the appearance of the control is "invalid" and therefore needs updating.

```
    'Invalidate the control
    Me.Invalidate()

End If
```

Although you can invalidate the control with the `Invalidate` method, the control will be invalidated whenever Windows detects it needs redrawing. This may happen when the window is restored after being minimized; another window obscures an area that's been made visible, and so on.

That covers everything from the user dragging the mouse over the control to adding a new `GraphicsCircle` item to the list. Now what?

With the control marked as requiring painting, it's up to Windows to choose a time for the window to be painted. To increase the performance of the windowing subsystem, windows are drawn only when the system has enough "spare time" to do it. Painting is not considered to be a crucial task to the operating system. You cannot rely on painting being done immediately, or within a given time-span of your marking something as invalid. At some point, the control will be asked to paint itself. You may have noticed this effect when your computer is being used heavily — an image on the screen will appear to "freeze" for a period before the display is updated.

Do not try to force Windows to paint when it doesn't want to. There are thousands of lines of optimization code in the Windows operating system to make sure that things are painted at absolutely the best time. Invalidate your control when you need to flag something as needing to be redrawn, and let nature take its course.

When it is ready, the Paint event will be called. You tap into this event by adding an event handler for the Paint event. All that you have to do is loop through the entire array of `GraphicsItem` objects that you've collected in `GraphicsItems` and ask each one to draw itself.

```
Private Sub PaintCanvas_Paint(ByVal sender As Object, _
    ByVal e As System.Windows.Forms.PaintEventArgs) Handles Me.Paint

    'Go through the list
    For Each objGraphicsItem As GraphicsItem In GraphicsItems
        'Ask each item to draw itself
        objGraphicsItem.Draw(e.Graphics)
    Next
End Sub
```

The Paint event passes through its parameters as a `PaintEventArgs` object. This object, among other things, contains a property called `Graphics`. This property returns a `System.Drawing.Graphics` object.

When you have hold of a graphics object, you are able to draw to the control, the form, the printer, or whatever it is that's given you as an object. This object contains a bundle of methods and properties that are actually used for painting. To keep in line with the principle of "only painting when needed," in typical day-to-day work you shouldn't try to create or otherwise obtain one of these objects. If you're given one, then it's time to paint!

Now that you know how the painting works, let's see whether you can get rid of the flickering!

Invalidation

This example you have been working on is designed to flicker and slow down to illustrate an important consideration that you need to bear in mind when drawing controls: Do the least amount of work possible! Drawing to the screen is slow. The less you draw, the faster the performance of your application should be and the better it should look on the screen.

The control flickers because painting is a two-stage process. Before you're asked to paint, Windows automatically erases the region behind the area that needs to be painted. This means the whole control flashes white as everything is erased and then you fill in the details.

What you want to do is to invalidate only the area that contains the new `GraphicsItem`. When you invalidate the control, you don't have to invalidate the whole thing. If you want, you can just invalidate a small area, as you do in the next Try It Out.

Try It Out   Invalidating a Small Area

1.   In the `PaintCanvas` class, find the `DoMousePaint` method. Modify the `Me.Invalidate` method at the end to include this parameter to invalidate just a `Rectangle`:

```
'Invalidate the Control
Me.Invalidate(objGraphicsItem.Rectangle)
```

2.   Run the project. You'll notice now that when you paint it doesn't flicker.

How It Works

After you call `SetPoint` on the new `GraphicsCircle` object, the `Rectangle` property is updated to contain the bounding rectangle of the circle.

This time, when you call the `Me.Invalidate` method, you pass this rectangle in. In this way, only a tiny area of the control is invalidated, therefore, only that tiny area is erased. After it is erased, you get the opportunity to draw your circle.

Optimized Drawing

You'll notice that if you draw a lot on the control, after a while the edge of the line starts to become almost jagged. What you're experiencing here is that as the `GraphicsItems` list grows, more calls to `FillEllipse` are made. Because drawing on the screen is slow, the more you have to do this, the longer the drawing process takes to aggregate. This lengthened drawing process prevents all of the `MouseMove` events from being fired, and so the line appears to stutter. In the following Try It Out section you see how you can avoid this problem.

Try It Out   Optimized Drawing

1.   Find the `PaintCanvas_Paint` method on the `PaintCanvas` class. Add this code as highlighted:

```
Private Sub PaintCanvas_Paint(ByVal sender As Object, _
    ByVal e As System.Windows.Forms.PaintEventArgs) Handles Me.Paint

    'Go through the list
    For Each objGraphicsItem As GraphicsItem In GraphicsItems

        'Do we need to be drawn?
        If e.ClipRectangle.IntersectsWith(objGraphicsItem.Rectangle) Then
            'Ask each item to draw itself
            objGraphicsItem.Draw(e.Graphics)

        End If
    Next
End Sub
```

2.   Run the project. You should now find that the drawing process is smoother.

How It Works

The `PaintEventArgs` object contains another property called `ClipRectangle`. This rectangle describes the area of the control that has been invalidated and is known as the *clipping rectangle*. The `Rectangle` class contains a method called `IntersectsWith` that can tell whether two given rectangles overlap and returns a `Boolean` value indicating whether they intersect.

As you know, a rectangle describes the bounds of each of your `GraphicsItem` objects, so you can use this rectangle with `IntersectsWith`. If the `GraphicsItem` overlaps, it needs drawing; otherwise, you move on to the next control.

The two techniques you've seen here—invalidating only what changes and drawing only what falls into the invalidated region—are by far the two most important techniques you'll come across when painting. If you skip either of these, your control has a good chance of being sluggish and flickering.

Choosing Colors

Now that you can do some basic painting, you'll build a control that lets you choose the color that you're painting in. Like a lot of graphics programs, you'll build this so that you have a palette of different colors and you're able to choose two at a time—one for the left mouse button and one for the right.

There are a number of different ways to build this control, and perhaps the most logical is to create a control that contains a bundle of Button controls, each configured so that it displays the color that it represents. However, this example shows you how to build a control completely from scratch. The techniques that you'll learn here will be really useful if you want to roll your own controls that display a picture of something and have hot regions on them. *Hot regions* are regions that fire an event when you click them. What you're doing might seem a little obscure, but it's a great example!

Creating the ColorPalette Control and Sizing the Control

To create the color palette control in the next Try It Out, you're going to need two classes. One, derived from `UserControl` and named `ColorPalette`, will provide the user interface (UI) for the palette itself. The other, named `ColorPaletteButton`, will be used to display the actual color box on the palette.

Since you are handling the layout of the buttons on the control, you need to respond to the Resize event. This event is fired whenever the user changes the size of the control. You can hook into this event by adding an event handler for the Resize event.

When Resize is fired, you need to alter the position of each of the buttons, starting in the top left corner and continuing in strips across the whole width of the control. When you've filled up one row, you need to start a new row.

Try It Out   Creating the ColorPalette Control

1. In the Solution Explorer, add a new class to the WroxPaint project named **ColorPaletteButton.vb** and add the following highlighted code to it:

```
Public Class ColorPaletteButton
```

```
    'Public members
    Public Color As Color = System.Drawing.Color.Black
    Public Rectangle As Rectangle
```

```
    'Constructor
    Public Sub New(ByVal newColor As Color)
        Color = newColor
    End Sub

    'Move the button to the given position
    Public Sub SetPosition(ByVal x As Integer, ByVal y As Integer, _
                           ByVal buttonSize As Integer)

        'Update the members
        Rectangle = New Rectangle(x, y, buttonSize, buttonSize)
    End Sub

    'Draw the button
    Public Sub Draw(ByVal graphics As Graphics)
        'Draw the color block
        Dim objSolidBrush As New SolidBrush(Color)
        graphics.FillRectangle(objSolidBrush, Rectangle)

        'Draw an edge around the control
        Dim objPen As New Pen(System.Drawing.Color.Black)
        graphics.DrawRectangle(objPen, Rectangle)
    End Sub
End Class
```

2. Now add a user control to the WroxPaint project named **ColorPalette**. Right-click the control and choose View Code from the context menu. Add these members to the top of the class definition:

```
Public Class ColorPalette
```

```
    'Public members
    Public Buttons As New ArrayList()
    Public ButtonSize As Integer = 15
    Public ButtonSpacing As Integer = 5
    Public LeftColor As Color = Color.Black
    Public RightColor As Color = Color.White
```

Here is what the members will do:

- ❑ Buttons holds a list of the buttons on the palette.
- ❑ ButtonSize defines the size of each of the buttons on the palette.
- ❑ ButtonSpacing defines the gap between each button.
- ❑ LeftColor holds the current color that is assigned to the left mouse button.
- ❑ RightColor holds the current color that is assigned to the right mouse button.

3. Next, add this method to the class:

```
    'Add a new color button to the control
    Public Sub AddColor(ByVal newColor As Color)
        'Create the button
        Dim objColorPaletteButton As New ColorPaletteButton(newColor)
```

```
              'Add it to the list
              Buttons.Add(objColorPaletteButton)
        End Sub
```

4. When you create the control, you want a set of basic colors to be always available. Add this code for the constructor to the class. This will create ten basic colors. After you type **Public Sub New** and press Enter, the unhighlighted code that follows will automatically be added to the constructor. Add the following highlighted code to your constructor:

```
Public Sub New()

        ' This call is required by the Windows Form Designer.
        InitializeComponent()

        ' Add any initialization after the InitializeComponent() call.

        'Add the colors
        AddColor(Color.Black)
        AddColor(Color.White)
        AddColor(Color.Red)
        AddColor(Color.Blue)
        AddColor(Color.Green)
        AddColor(Color.Gray)
        AddColor(Color.DarkRed)
        AddColor(Color.DarkBlue)
        AddColor(Color.DarkGreen)
        AddColor(Color.DarkGray)
End Sub
```

5. In the Code Editor for the `ColorPalette` class, select (ColorPalette Events) in the Class Name combo box and the Resize event in the Method Name combo box. Add this highlighted code to the Resize event handler:

```
Private Sub ColorPalette_Resize(ByVal sender As Object, _
      ByVal e As System.EventArgs) Handles Me.Resize

          'Declare variables to hold the position
          Dim intX As Integer
          Dim intY As Integer

          'Go through the array and position the buttons
          For Each objColorPaletteButton As ColorPaletteButton In Buttons

              'Position the button
              objColorPaletteButton.SetPosition(intX, intY, ButtonSize)

              'Move to the next one
              intX += (ButtonSize + ButtonSpacing)

              'Do we need to go down to the next row
              If intX + ButtonSize > Width Then

                  'Move y
                  intY += (ButtonSize + ButtonSpacing)
```

```
                        'Reset x
                        intX = 0

                End If

        Next

        'Redraw
        Me.Invalidate()
    End Sub
```

6. You still need to paint the control. Select (ColorPalette Events) in the Class Name combo box and the `Paint` event in the Method Name combo box. Add this highlighted code:

```
Private Sub ColorPalette_Paint(ByVal sender As Object, _
    ByVal e As System.Windows.Forms.PaintEventArgs) Handles Me.Paint

        'Loop through the buttons
        For Each objColorPaletteButton As ColorPaletteButton In Buttons

            'Do we need to draw?
            If e.ClipRectangle.IntersectsWith(objColorPaletteButton.Rectangle) Then
                objColorPaletteButton.Draw(e.Graphics)
            End If

        Next
    End Sub
```

7. Before you can draw the control onto Form1, you need to build the project. Select Build ➪ Build WroxPaint from the menu.

8. After the project has been built, open the Designer for Form1. Click the PaintCanvas control on Form1 and, in the Properties window, set the Dock property to None. Now resize the form to add a little space at the bottom and make the form wider if so desired.

9. In the ToolBox under the WroxPaint Components tab, drag a ColorPalette control to the bottom of you form and set its Name property to **paletteColor**. Now set its Dock property to Bottom.

10. Now click the PaintCanvus control, resize it if necessary, and set its Anchor property to Top, Bottom, Left, Right. Your form should now look similar to Figure 14-3.

11. If you now try to rearrange the form a little, you should see that your sizing code has proven successful.

How It Works

Hopefully, the behavior of `ColorPaletteButton` shouldn't be too much of a mystery. You have members on the class that hold the color and a rectangle, and you also provide a constructor that automatically populates the color:

```
Public Class ColorPaletteButton
    'Public members
    Public Color As Color = System.Drawing.Color.Black
    Public Rectangle As Rectangle
```

```
'Constructor
Public Sub New(ByVal newColor As Color)
    Color = newColor
End Sub
```

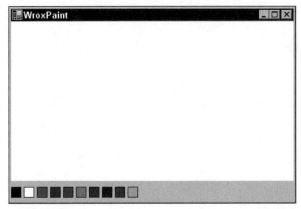

Figure 14-3

When the button is asked to paint itself, all you do is draw one filled rectangle of the color specified in the `Color` property using the `FillRectangle` method, and for neatness you surround it with a black border using the `DrawRectangle` method:

```
'Draw the button
Public Sub Draw(ByVal graphics As Graphics)
    'Draw the color block
    Dim objSolidBrush As New SolidBrush(Color)
    graphics.FillRectangle(objSolidBrush, Rectangle)

    'Draw an edge around the control
    Dim objPen As New Pen(System.Drawing.Color.Black)
    graphics.DrawRectangle(objPen, Rectangle)
End Sub
```

When you resize the form (a subject you'll deal with soon), you pass the top left corner of the button through to `SetPosition`. All this method does is update the `Rectangle` property:

```
'Move the button to the given position
Public Sub SetPosition(ByVal x As Integer, ByVal y As Integer, _
                       ByVal buttonSize As Integer)

    'Update the members
    Rectangle = New Rectangle(x, y, buttonSize, buttonSize)
End Sub
```

The `ColorPalette_Resize` method is perhaps the most interesting method here. This is a common algorithm used whenever you need to manage the position of controls or other graphic objects. You know the size of each object (in your case it's a combination of `ButtonSize` and `ButtonSpacing`) and you know the bounds of the control. All you do is start in the top left and keep moving right until you have no more space, in which case you flip down to the next row. Here is how you start—you set up a loop that iterates through all of the buttons:

```
Private Sub ColorPalette_Resize(ByVal sender As Object, _
    ByVal e As System.EventArgs) Handles Me.Resize

    'Declare variables to hold the position
    Dim intX As Integer
    Dim intY As Integer

    'Go through the array and position the buttons
    For Each objColorPaletteButton As ColorPaletteButton In Buttons
```

Throughout the loop, intX and intY hold the current coordinates of the top left corner of the control. When you start, this is (0, 0) or, rather, the very top left of the client area of the control. For each button, you call SetPosition, passing in the current coordinates together with the size of the button:

```
        'Position the button
        objColorPaletteButton.SetPosition(intX, intY, ButtonSize)
```

After each button, you move intX to the right. In addition to adjusting by the size of the button, you also add a small gap to make the control more esthetically pleasing:

```
        'Move to the next one
        intX += (ButtonSize + ButtonSpacing)
```

If you detect that you don't have enough space to fit the next control completely on the current row, you adjust intY down to the next row and reset intX back to the beginning:

```
        'Do we need to go down to the next row
        If intX + ButtonSize > Width Then

            'Move y
            intY += (ButtonSize + ButtonSpacing)

            'Reset x
            intX = 0

        End If

    Next
```

Finally, after you've moved all of the buttons, you invalidate the control so that you can see the changes.

```
    'Redraw
    Me.Invalidate()
End Sub
```

Responding to Clicks

Your control is going to fire an event whenever the left or right mouse button is clicked on a color button. To that end, in the next Try It Out you add some events to your ColorPalette control that the control will raise. The application using this control will be able to add the event handlers and take action when the event has been raised by this control.

Responding to Clicks

1. Go back to the Code Editor for `ColorPalette`. Add these events to the top of the class after your public members:

```
'Public events
Public Event LeftClick(ByVal sender As Object, ByVal e As EventArgs)
Public Event RightClick(ByVal sender As Object, ByVal e As EventArgs)
```

2. You need a general-purpose method that will return the button that's positioned directly beneath the mouse. Add this method:

```
Public Function GetButtonAt(ByVal x As Integer, ByVal y As Integer) _
    As ColorPaletteButton

    'Set the default return value
    GetButtonAt = Nothing

    'Go through each button in the collection
    For Each objColorPaletteButton As ColorPaletteButton In Buttons
        'Is this button in the rectangle?
        If objColorPaletteButton.Rectangle.Contains(x, y) Then
            Return objColorPaletteButton
        End If
    Next
End Function
```

3. Now, select (ColorPalette Events) in the Class Name combo box and then select the MouseUp event in the Method Name combo box. Your motivation for using MouseUp rather than MouseDown will become apparent soon. Add this highlighted code to the event handler:

```
Private Sub ColorPalette_MouseUp(ByVal sender As Object, _
    ByVal e As System.Windows.Forms.MouseEventArgs) Handles Me.MouseUp

    'Find the button that we clicked
    Dim objColorPaletteButton As ColorPaletteButton = GetButtonAt(e.X, e.Y)

    If Not objColorPaletteButton Is Nothing Then

        'Was the left button clicked
        If e.Button = MouseButtons.Left Then

            'Set the color
            LeftColor = objColorPaletteButton.Color

            'Raise the event
```

```
                    RaiseEvent LeftClick(Me, New EventArgs())

            ElseIf e.Button = MouseButtons.Right Then

                'Set the color
                RightColor = objColorPaletteButton.Color

                'Raise the event
                RaiseEvent RightClick(Me, New EventArgs())

            End If

        End If
    End Sub
```

4. To test the new method, open the Forms Designer for Form1. Select the PaintCanvas control and set its Name property to **Canvas**.

5. Now open up the Code Editor for Form1. Select paletteColor in the Class Name combo box, and select the LeftClick event in the Method Name combo box. Add this highlighted code to the event handler:

```
Private Sub paletteColor_LeftClick(ByVal sender As Object, _
    ByVal e As System.EventArgs) Handles paletteColor.LeftClick

        Canvas.GraphicColor = paletteColor.LeftColor
    End Sub
```

6. Now run your project. You should be able to use the color palette to change the color laid down by the left mouse button.

How It Works

Although you've called your buttons ColorPaletteButton, they don't behave in the way you're used to seeing buttons behave. Button controls, like the ones you have been using until now, have the intelligence to detect when they've been clicked and fire an event to tell you what happened. Your color palette buttons, on the other hand, have until now been areas on the control painted in a pretty color. Now you actually need to write the logic to determine when a button is clicked.

The key to this is the GetButtonAt method. This method takes a set of client coordinates and returns the ColorPaletteButton object that contains the point you asked for. In this case, you use the Contains method of the Rectangle object to see whether the coordinates are contained within the rectangle.

```
    Public Function GetButtonAt(ByVal x As Integer, ByVal y As Integer) _
        As ColorPaletteButton

        'Set the default return value
        GetButtonAt = Nothing

        'Go through each button in the collection
        For Each objColorPaletteButton As ColorPaletteButton In Buttons
            'Is this button in the rectangle?
```

```
            If objColorPaletteButton.Rectangle.Contains(x, y) Then
                Return objColorPaletteButton
            End If
        Next
    End Function
```

Of course, it could be the case that there is no button under the coordinates if the user clicks the mouse on a blank area of the control. If this is the case, GetButtonAt will return Nothing:

As you know, the Button property of MouseEventArgs tells you which button was used, or in this case, released. If it's the left button, you update LeftColor and raise the LeftClick event:

```
    Private Sub ColorPalette_MouseUp(ByVal sender As Object, _
        ByVal e As System.Windows.Forms.MouseEventArgs) Handles Me.MouseUp

        'Find the button that we clicked
        Dim objColorPaletteButton As ColorPaletteButton = GetButtonAt(e.X, e.Y)

        If Not objColorPaletteButton Is Nothing Then

            'Was the left button clicked
            If e.Button = MouseButtons.Left Then

                'Set the color
                LeftColor = objColorPaletteButton.Color

                'Raise the event
                RaiseEvent LeftClick(Me, New EventArgs())
```

Alternatively, it could be the right mouse button:

```
            ElseIf e.Button = MouseButtons.Right Then

                'Set the color
                RightColor = objColorPaletteButton.Color

                'Raise the event
                RaiseEvent RightClick(Me, New EventArgs())

            End If

        End If
    End Sub
```

At the moment, PaintCanvas can deal with only one color, which is why you've only hooked up the LeftClick event. When you receive this event, you set the appropriate property on Canvas, and this new color will be used when creating new GraphicsCircle objects:

```
    Private Sub paletteColor_LeftClick(ByVal sender As Object, _
        ByVal e As System.EventArgs) Handles paletteColor.LeftClick

        Canvas.GraphicColor = paletteColor.LeftColor
    End Sub
```

Dealing with Two Colors

In the next Try It Out you extend PaintCanvas so that it can deal with two colors. You'll do this by adding two public members that will track the color chosen for the left mouse button and the right mouse button. You'll also be modifying your existing code to determine whether the left mouse button was clicked or whether the right mouse button was clicked.

Dealing with Two Colors

1. You need an additional property in PaintCanvas that will let you store the alternative color. For the sake of clarity, you'll also change the name of the existing GraphicColor property to GraphicLeftColor. Open the Code Editor for the PaintCanvas class and make these changes:

```
'Public members
Public GraphicsItems As New ArrayList()
Public GraphicTool As GraphicTools = GraphicTools.CirclePen
Public GraphicSize As GraphicSizes = GraphicSizes.Medium

Public GraphicLeftColor As Color = Color.Black
Public GraphicRightColor As Color = Color.White
```

2. In the DoMousePaint method you need to examine the Button property of MouseEventArgs to determine which color you want to use. Make these two changes to DoMousePaint as highlighted:

```
Private Sub DoMousePaint(ByVal e As MouseEventArgs)
    'Store the new item somewhere
    Dim objGraphicsItem As GraphicsItem

    'What color do we want to use?
    Dim objColor As Color = GraphicLeftColor

    If e.Button = MouseButtons.Right Then
        objColor = GraphicRightColor
    End If

    'What tool are you using?
    Select Case GraphicTool

        'Circlepen
        Case GraphicTools.CirclePen

            'Create a new graphics circle
            Dim objGraphicsCircle As New GraphicsCircle()

            'Set the point for drawing

            objGraphicsCircle.SetPoint(e.X, e.Y, GraphicSize, _
                objColor, True)

            'Store this for addition
            objGraphicsItem = objGraphicsCircle
```

```
        End Select

        'Were you given an item?
        If objGraphicsItem IsNot Nothing Then

            'Add it to the list
            GraphicsItems.Add(objGraphicsItem)

            'Invalidate the Control
            Me.Invalidate(objGraphicsItem.Rectangle)

        End If
End Sub
```

3. At the moment, MouseDown and MouseMove events will call DoMousePaint only if the left button is pressed. You need to change this so that it will accept either the left or right button. Make these changes as highlighted:

```
Private Sub PaintCanvas_MouseDown(ByVal sender As Object, _
    ByVal e As System.Windows.Forms.MouseEventArgs) Handles Me.MouseDown

        'Is the left or right mouse button down?
        If e.Button = MouseButtons.Left Or e.Button = MouseButtons.Right Then
            DoMousePaint(e)
        End If
End Sub

Private Sub PaintCanvas_MouseMove(ByVal sender As Object, _
    ByVal e As System.Windows.Forms.MouseEventArgs) Handles Me.MouseMove

        'Is the left or right mouse button down?
        If e.Button = MouseButtons.Left Or e.Button = MouseButtons.Right Then
            DoMousePaint(e)
        End If
End Sub
```

4. Next, you need to change the event handler in Form1 to set the GraphicLeftColor property rather than the GraphicColor property. Open the Code Editor for Form1 and make this change as highlighted:

```
Private Sub paletteColor_LeftClick(ByVal sender As Object, _
    ByVal e As System.EventArgs) Handles paletteColor.LeftClick

        Canvas.GraphicLeftColor = paletteColor.LeftColor
End Sub
```

5. Finally, you need to add an event handler for the RightClick event. Select paletteColor in the Class Name combo box and the RightClick event in the Method Name combo box. Add this highlighted code:

```
Private Sub paletteColor_RightClick(ByVal sender As Object, _
    ByVal e As System.EventArgs) Handles paletteColor.RightClick

        Canvas.GraphicRightColor = paletteColor.RightColor
End Sub
```

Now, if you run the project, you should be able to assign different colors to the left and right mouse buttons and use both of the buttons to paint on the form.

Indicating the Assigned Buttons

You've no doubt noticed that, at this point, using WroxPaint is a little confusing. There's no indication as to which color is assigned to which button. You need to resolve this issue, so in the next Try It Out you'll display the letter L on the color assigned to the left button and the letter R on the color assigned to the right button.

Try It Out   Indicating the Assigned Buttons

1. First, you'll make the `ColorPaletteButton` objects aware of which button they're assigned to, if any. Open the Code Editor for the `ColorPaletteButton` class and add this enumeration to the top of the class:

```
Public Class ColorPaletteButton
```

```
    'Public enumerations
    Public Enum ButtonAssignments As Integer
        None = 0
        LeftButton = 1
        RightButton = 2
    End Enum
```

2. Next, add this new member (highlighted), which will keep track of the button's assignment:

```
    'Public members
    Public Color As Color = System.Drawing.Color.Black
    Public Rectangle As Rectangle
```

```
    Public ButtonAssignment As ButtonAssignments = ButtonAssignments.None
```

3. After the button has a way of storing what it's assigned to, you can change the `Draw` method to draw the L or R as appropriate. Add the following highlighted code to `Draw`:

```
    'Draw the button
    Public Sub Draw(ByVal graphics As Graphics)
        'Draw the color block
        Dim objSolidBrush As New SolidBrush(Color)
        graphics.FillRectangle(objSolidBrush, Rectangle)

        'Draw an edge around the control
        Dim objPen As New Pen(System.Drawing.Color.Black)
        graphics.DrawRectangle(objPen, Rectangle)
```

```
        'Are you selected?
        If ButtonAssignment <> ButtonAssignments.None Then

            'Create a font
            Dim objFont As New Font("verdana", 8, FontStyle.Bold)

            'Set the default button assignment
            Dim strButtonText As String = "L"
```

```
                'Update the button assignment if necessary
                If ButtonAssignment = ButtonAssignments.RightButton Then
                    strButtonText = "R"
                End If

                'What brush do you want?
                If Color.R < 100 Or Color.B < 100 Or Color.G < 100 Then
                    objSolidBrush = New SolidBrush(System.Drawing.Color.White)
                Else
                    objSolidBrush = New SolidBrush(System.Drawing.Color.Black)
                End If

                'Draw the text 'L' or 'R'
                graphics.DrawString(strButtonText, objFont, objSolidBrush, _
                        Rectangle.Left, Rectangle.Top)
            End If
    End Sub
```

4. To keep track of which button is selected, you need to add some private members to the
ColorPalette class. Open the Code Editor for this class and add this code:

```
'Private members
Private LeftButton As ColorPaletteButton
Private RightButton As ColorPaletteButton
```

5. The next wrinkle you have to fix is quite verbose but relatively straightforward. Basically, you
have to make sure that a button cannot be assigned to both the left and right buttons — for no
other reason than that you just don't have a way of reporting that information to the user. Also,
you have to muddle with the invalidation code. You'll detail that once you have the example
working. Make these changes to ColorPalette_MouseUp as highlighted:

```
Private Sub ColorPalette_MouseUp(ByVal sender As Object, _
    ByVal e As System.Windows.Forms.MouseEventArgs) Handles Me.MouseUp

    'Find the button that we clicked
    Dim objColorPaletteButton As ColorPaletteButton = GetButtonAt(e.X, e.Y)

    If Not objColorPaletteButton Is Nothing Then

        'Was the left button clicked
        If e.Button = MouseButtons.Left Then

            'Make sure that this button is not the current right button
            If objColorPaletteButton IsNot RightButton Then

                'Set the color
                LeftColor = objColorPaletteButton.Color

                'Clear the existing selection.
                If LeftButton IsNot Nothing Then

                    LeftButton.ButtonAssignment = _
                        ColorPaletteButton.ButtonAssignments.None
```

```vb
                    Me.Invalidate(LeftButton.Rectangle)

                End If

                'Mark the button
                objColorPaletteButton.ButtonAssignment = _
                    ColorPaletteButton.ButtonAssignments.LeftButton

                Me.Invalidate(objColorPaletteButton.Rectangle)

                LeftButton = objColorPaletteButton

                'Raise the event
                RaiseEvent LeftClick(Me, New EventArgs())

            End If

        ElseIf e.Button = MouseButtons.Right Then

            'Make sure this button is not the current left button
            If objColorPaletteButton IsNot LeftButton Then

                'Set the color
                RightColor = objColorPaletteButton.Color

                'Clear the existing selection
                If RightButton IsNot Nothing Then

                    RightButton.ButtonAssignment = _
                        ColorPaletteButton.ButtonAssignments.None

                    Me.Invalidate(RightButton.Rectangle)

                End If

                'Mark the button
                objColorPaletteButton.ButtonAssignment = _
                    ColorPaletteButton.ButtonAssignments.RightButton

                Me.Invalidate(objColorPaletteButton.Rectangle)

                RightButton = objColorPaletteButton

                'Raise the event
                RaiseEvent RightClick(Me, New EventArgs())
            End If

        End If

    End If
End Sub
```

6. Finally, you have to set up the first two colors added to the control as being the selected buttons when the control is started. This involves updating your `leftButton` and `rightButton` members as well as setting the `ButtonAssignment` property on the button itself. Add the highlighted code to `AddColor`:

```
'Add a new color button to the control
Public Sub AddColor(ByVal newColor As Color)
    'Create the button
    Dim objColorPaletteButton As New ColorPaletteButton(newColor)

    'Add it to the list
    Buttons.Add(objColorPaletteButton)

    'Do we have a button assigned to the left button yet?
    If LeftButton Is Nothing Then

        objColorPaletteButton.ButtonAssignment = _
            ColorPaletteButton.ButtonAssignments.LeftButton

        LeftButton = objColorPaletteButton

    ElseIf RightButton Is Nothing Then   'How about the right button?

        objColorPaletteButton.ButtonAssignment = _
            ColorPaletteButton.ButtonAssignments.RightButton

        RightButton = objColorPaletteButton

    End If
End Sub
```

7. Run the project now, and you should see that when you change the color selection, an L and R appear on the buttons, as shown in Figure 14-4.

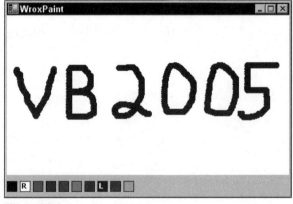

Figure 14-4

How It Works

The first thing you did was add an enumeration to the `ControlPaletteButton` class that could be used to set the state of the button:

```
'Public enumerations
Public Enum ButtonAssignments As Integer
    None = 0
    LeftButton = 1
    RightButton = 2
End Enum
```

As you can see from the enumeration, a palette button can either be assigned to no mouse buttons, the left mouse button, or the right mouse button. You also added members to the `ControlPalette` class to keep track of which button was selected. This makes your life a little easier when it comes to changing the selection. When you select a new palette button, you have to set the `ButtonAssignment` property of the old button to `ButtonAssignments.None`. Just being able to look in the `LeftButton` or `RightButton` member, as appropriate, saves you from having to look through the entire list of buttons to find the one you need to change. The `ColorPalette_MouseUp` method starts to look a little more complex when you add this new functionality. When you want to assign the left mouse button to a palette button, you have to make sure that the palette button is not already assigned to the right mouse button:

```
Private Sub ColorPalette_MouseUp(ByVal sender As Object, _
    ByVal e As System.Windows.Forms.MouseEventArgs) Handles Me.MouseUp

    'Find the button that we clicked
    Dim objColorPaletteButton As ColorPaletteButton = GetButtonAt(e.X, e.Y)

    If Not objColorPaletteButton Is Nothing Then

        'Was the left button clicked
        If e.Button = MouseButtons.Left Then

            'Make sure that this button is not the current right button
            If objColorPaletteButton IsNot RightButton Then
```

If you can set the color, you update the `LeftColor` property as you did before:

```
                'Set the color
                LeftColor = objColorPaletteButton.Color
```

If another button is already assigned to the left mouse button, you need to set its `ButtonAssignment` property back to `None`. You also have to invalidate this button so that the button is redrawn and the `L` is removed:

```
                'Clear the existing selection.
                If LeftButton IsNot Nothing Then

                    LeftButton.ButtonAssignment = _
                        ColorPaletteButton.ButtonAssignments.None

                    Me.Invalidate(LeftButton.Rectangle)

                End If
```

Next, you set the new button's `ButtonAssignment` property to `Left`. You also invalidate the button (so that you can draw the L on this one instead) and update the `LeftButton` property to point at the new button:

```
'Mark the button
objColorPaletteButton.ButtonAssignment = _
        ColorPaletteButton.ButtonAssignments.LeftButton

Me.Invalidate(objColorPaletteButton.Rectangle)

LeftButton = objColorPaletteButton
```

Finally, you fire the `LeftClick` event as you did before:

```
'Raise the event
RaiseEvent LeftClick(Me, New EventArgs())
```

The remainder of `ColorPalette_MouseUp` is the same as this but is obviously reversed to deal with the right-hand button.

When it's time to draw the button, you can check to see whether a button assignment is set. If it is, you draw some text. (You've only fleetingly covered drawing text here, but you'll deal with it in more detail later in this chapter.) To draw the text, you need to create a new `System.Drawing.Font` object. Here you're creating a new object for 8-point Verdana in bold:

```
Public Sub Draw(ByVal graphics As Graphics)
    'Draw the color block
    Dim objSolidBrush As New SolidBrush(Color)
    graphics.FillRectangle(objSolidBrush, Rectangle)

    'Draw an edge around the control
    Dim objPen As New Pen(System.Drawing.Color.Black)
    graphics.DrawRectangle(objPen, Rectangle)

    'Are you selected?
    If ButtonAssignment <> ButtonAssignments.None Then

        'Create a font
        Dim objFont As New Font("verdana", 8, FontStyle.Bold)
```

Next, you choose the text to draw:

```
'Set the default button assignment
Dim strButtonText As String = "L"

'Update the button assignment if necessary
If ButtonAssignment = ButtonAssignments.RightButton Then
    strButtonText = "R"
End If
```

Choosing the brush you want is quite tricky. You can't just choose a color, because there's a chance it won't show up on the color that you're drawing. Instead, you have to examine the color to see whether it is a light color or a dark color. If it's dark, you choose to draw the letter in white; otherwise, you draw it in black:

```
'What brush do you want?
If Color.R < 100 Or Color.B < 100 Or Color.G < 100 Then
    objSolidBrush = New SolidBrush(System.Drawing.Color.White)
Else
    objSolidBrush = New SolidBrush(System.Drawing.Color.Black)
End If
```

Finally, you actually draw the text:

```
'Draw the text 'L' or 'R'
graphics.DrawString(strButtonText, objFont, objSolidBrush, _
        Rectangle.Left, Rectangle.Top)
    End If
End Sub
```

Using Advanced Colors

So far, the only colors you've used are the ones defined by the .NET Framework, such as `Color.Black` and `Color.Blue`. The list of colors available to you on the `Color` structure is considerable, but you can define your own colors if you want to.

> *To find a list of predefined colors use the MSDN documentation to display "all members" of the "Color structure." Alternatively, you can use IntelliSense from within the code editor to display a list of possibilities.*

Windows defines a color as a 24-bit number, with the three bytes of the 24 bits representing a red value, a green value, and a blue value — this is commonly known as RGB. In effect, each component represents one of a possible 256 shades of red, green, or blue. By combining these shades you can get any color from a possible set of 16.7 million. For example, setting red to 255 and setting blue and green to 0 would result in bright red. Setting all components to 255 would give white. Setting all to 0 would give black, and so on.

> *If you're used to mixing paints, these color combinations may seem strange. This is because you are working with colored lights instead of colored paints — they combine in different ways.*

To illustrate this, in the next Try It Out section you see how you can choose a color and then manually add that color as a button to the control palette.

Try It Out   Creating Custom Colors

1. Open the Form Designer for the `ColorPalette` control. In the Properties window find the `BackColor` property.

2. Drop down the list and change to the Custom tab. Right-click in one of the 16 bottom blank squares.

3. This will bring up the Color dialog box. Use the two controls at the top to find a color you like. In the bottom-right corner, you'll see three text boxes marked Red, Green, and Blue, as shown in Figure 14-5. Note down the values in these boxes.

Figure 14-5

4. Close the Define Color dialog box.

5. Open up the Code Editor for `ColorPalette` to access the constructor. In the constructor, define a new button as in the following highlighted code, but replace the three values I've used here with three values you noted. (Do this in order — the first value is the red component, the second is green, and the third is blue.)

```
Public Sub New()

    ' This call is required by the Windows Form Designer.
    InitializeComponent()

    ' Add any initialization after the InitializeComponent() call.
    'Add the colors
    AddColor(Color.Black)
    AddColor(Color.White)
    AddColor(Color.Red)
    AddColor(Color.Blue)
    AddColor(Color.Green)
    AddColor(Color.Gray)
    AddColor(Color.DarkRed)
    AddColor(Color.DarkBlue)
    AddColor(Color.DarkGreen)
    AddColor(Color.DarkGray)

    AddColor(Color.FromArgb(208, 112, 222))
End Sub
```

6. Now run the project; the color you selected should appear in the palette.

The FromArgb method is a shared method on the Color class. You can use this to define any color that you like, so long as you follow the "red, green, blue" convention Windows itself uses.

Using the Color Dialog Box

In this Try It Out, you use the Color dialog box that's built into Windows to let the user add colors to the palette.

Try It Out   **Using the Color Dialog Box**

1. Open the Form Designer for ColorPalette. From the toolbar, select a ColorDialog control and drag it onto the form; the control will be positioned at the bottom of the IDE. Change the name of the control to **dlgColor**.

2. Now, open the Code Editor for ColorPalette. Find the ColorPalette_MouseUp method. Whenever the user clicks the background of the control (in other words, doesn't click a button), you want to display the dialog box. Go to the bottom of the method and add an Else clause along with this code. (I've omitted most of the existing code for brevity.)

```
Private Sub ColorPalette_MouseUp(ByVal sender As Object, _
    ByVal e As System.Windows.Forms.MouseEventArgs) Handles Me.MouseUp

    'Find the button that we clicked
    Dim objColorPaletteButton As ColorPaletteButton = GetButtonAt(e.X, e.Y)

    If Not objColorPaletteButton Is Nothing Then
        . . .
            RaiseEvent RightClick(Me, New EventArgs())

        End If

    End If

    Else
        'Display the color dialog
        If dlgColor.ShowDialog = DialogResult.OK Then

            'Add the new color
            AddColor(dlgColor.Color)

            'Resize the palette to show the dialog
            OnResize(New EventArgs())

        End If
    End If
End Sub
```

3. Run the project. Now if you click the background to the palette, you should have the opportunity to add your own colors (see Figure 14-6).

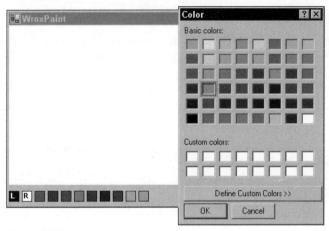

Figure 14-6

Using System Colors

Now you know that you can choose colors from a list of possibilities as well as define your own. The final thing you need to learn about colors is the idea of system colors.

When using Windows, the user has the ability to define all of the colors that are used for things like buttons, menus, captions, and so on. If you're building the UI for your own controls, it's reasonable to assume that from time to time you'll need to know what these colors are so that your controls have the same look and feel as the existing controls in the system.

System colors are exposed through the System.Drawing.SystemColors class. If you want to find a list of all the system colors, look in the MSDN documentation under System.Drawing.SystemColors class. Alternatively, use IntelliSense when in the Code Editor or the Object Browser.

In this Try It Out, you'll add a button to the control palette that is the same as the menu bar.

Try It Out   Adding System Colors

1. Open the Code Editor for ColorPalette.Designer.vb. Find the constructor and add the following highlighted code:

```
Public Sub New()

    ' This call is required by the Windows Form Designer.
    InitializeComponent()

    ' Add any initialization after the InitializeComponent() call.
    'Add the colors
    AddColor(Color.Black)
    AddColor(Color.White)
    AddColor(Color.Red)
    AddColor(Color.Blue)
    AddColor(Color.Green)
```

```
                AddColor(Color.Gray)
                AddColor(Color.DarkRed)
                AddColor(Color.DarkBlue)
                AddColor(Color.DarkGreen)
                AddColor(Color.DarkGray)
                AddColor(Color.FromArgb(208, 112, 222))

                AddColor(Drawing.SystemColors.MenuBar)
            End Sub
```

2. Run the project. You should see a new color that matches the menu bar color.

Using Different Tools

Now that you have successfully cracked the nut of drawing filled circles on the page, turn your attention to building the other tools that you can use to put your applications together. In the next Try It Out, you add a menu that lets you select the tool you want.

If you need a refresher on how to use the Visual Basic 2005 Menu Designer, refer to Chapter 8.

Try It Out   Adding a Tools Menu

1. Open the Forms Designer for Form1 and change the Anchor property for Canvas to Bottom, Right, Left.

2. Now click the title bar of the form and then resize the form so that there is enough room for a MenuStrip control at the top.

3. Drag a MenuStrip control onto the top of the form; then, at the bottom of the IDE, right-click MenuStrip1 and choose Insert Standard Items from the context menu to have the standard menus inserted.

4. Resize the form if necessary so that the Canvas control is just under the menu. Then click the Canvas control and change the `Anchor` property to Top, Bottom, Right, Left.

5. Now click the Tools menu on the MenuStrip and then click in the white Type Here box that appears at the bottom of the Tools menu and enter **&Circle**. Using the Properties window set the Checked property to True and the CheckOnClick property to True.

6. In the new Type Here box at the bottom, enter **&Hollow Circle**, and in the Properties window, set the CheckOnClick property to True. You will see the results of these steps in Figure 14-7.

Implementing Hollow Circle

Up until now, you have used a solid circle as the graphics pen to perform the drawing on your form. In this Try It Out, you'll be implementing the functionality to use the hollow circle graphics pen. You'll also be adding the necessary code that will allow you to select which pen you want to use from the Tools menu.

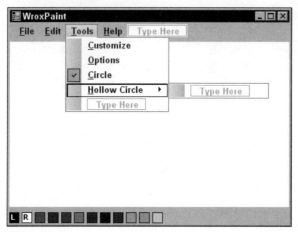

Figure 14-7

Try It Out   Implementing Hollow Circle

1. The first thing you need to do is change the `GraphicTools` enumeration defined in the `PaintCanvas` class to include the hollow circle tool. Open the Code Editor for `PaintCanvas` and add the following highlighted code to the enumeration:

```
Public Class PaintCanvas
    'Public enumerations
    Public Enum GraphicTools As Integer
        CirclePen = 0

        HollowCirclePen = 1
    End Enum
```

2. Now switch to the Code Editor for Form1. In the Class Name combo box, select CircleToolStripMenuItem, and then select the Click event in the Method Name combo box. Add the following highlighted code to the Click event handler:

```
Private Sub CircleToolStripMenuItem_Click(ByVal sender As Object, _
    ByVal e As System.EventArgs) Handles CircleToolStripMenuItem.Click

        'Set the tool
        Canvas.GraphicTool = PaintCanvas.GraphicTools.CirclePen

        'Uncheck the Hollow Circle menu item
        HollowCircleToolStripMenuItem.Checked = False
    End Sub
```

3. Now select HollowCircleToolStripMenuItem in the Class Name combo box and the Click event in the Method Name combo box. Add the following highlighted code:

```
Private Sub HollowCircleToolStripMenuItem_Click(ByVal sender As Object, _
    ByVal e As System.EventArgs) Handles HollowCircleToolStripMenuItem.Click
```

```
    'Set the tool
    Canvas.GraphicTool = PaintCanvas.GraphicTools.HollowCirclePen

    'Uncheck the Circle menu item
    CircleToolStripMenuItem.Checked = False
End Sub
```

4. It only makes sense that, since you've implemented a menu, you should add code to the Exit menu item. Select exitToolStripMenuItem in the Class Name combo box and the Click event in the Method Name combo. Then add the following highlighted code to the Click event handler:

```
Private Sub exitToolStripMenuItem_Click(ByVal sender As Object, _
    ByVal e As System.EventArgs) Handles exitToolStripMenuItem.Click

    'Close the application
    Me.Close()
End Sub
```

5. Open the Code Editor for PaintCanvas again and modify the Select Case GraphicTool statement in the DoMousePaint method as follows:

```
    'What tool are you using?
    Select Case GraphicTool

        'CirclePen
        Case GraphicTools.CirclePen

            'Create a new graphics circle
            Dim objGraphicsCircle As New GraphicsCircle()

            'Set the point for drawing
            objGraphicsCircle.SetPoint(e.X, e.Y, GraphicSize, _
                objColor, True)

            'Store this for addition
            objGraphicsItem = objGraphicsCircle

        'HollowCirclePen
        Case GraphicTools.HollowCirclePen

            'Create a new graphics circle
            Dim objGraphicsCircle As New GraphicsCircle()

            'Set the point for drawing
            objGraphicsCircle.SetPoint(e.X, e.Y, GraphicSize, _
                objColor, False)

            'Store this for addition
            objGraphicsItem = objGraphicsCircle

    End Select
```

6. Next, you need to change the GraphicsCircle class itself so that it knows when to draw a filled circle and when to draw a hollow circle. Open the Code Editor for GraphicsCircle and add the following highlighted code to the Draw method:

```
Public Overrides Sub Draw(ByVal graphics As System.Drawing.Graphics)

    If IsFilled = True Then

        'Create a new pen
        Dim objSolidBrush As New SolidBrush(Me.Color)

        'Draw the circle
        graphics.FillEllipse(objSolidBrush, Me.Rectangle)

    Else

        'Create a pen
        Dim pen As New Pen(Me.Color)

        'Use DrawEllipse instead
        Dim objRectangle As Rectangle = Me.Rectangle
        objRectangle.Inflate(-1, -1)
        graphics.DrawEllipse(pen, objRectangle)

    End If
End Sub
```

7. Finally, run the program. You should be able to select a new graphic tool from the menu and draw both filled and hollow circles, as shown in Figure 14-8.

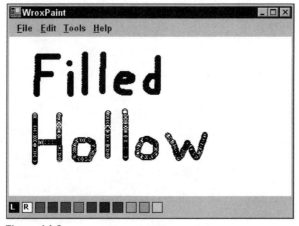

Figure 14-8

How It Works

When the menu options are selected, click events get fired. You can respond to these messages and set the GraphicsTool property on the PaintCanvas control to a new mode. When you change the mode, you also need to change the check mark on the menu. The currently selected menu item will be automatically checked, but you need to uncheck the menu item that isn't selected. You do this by setting the Checked property of the opposite menu item to False.

```
Private Sub HollowCircleToolStripMenuItem_Click(ByVal sender As Object, _
    ByVal e As System.EventArgs) Handles HollowCircleToolStripMenuItem.Click

    'Set the tool
    Canvas.GraphicTool = PaintCanvas.GraphicTools.HollowCirclePen

    'Uncheck the Circle menu item
    CircleToolStripMenuItem.Checked = False
End Sub
```

Irrespective of the mode used, PaintCanvas.DoMousePaint still gets called whenever the mouse draws on the control. However, you do need to accommodate the new tool by changing the Select Case GraphicTool statement to look for HollowCirclePen as well as CirclePen. Depending on which is selected, you pass True ("filled") or False ("not filled") through to SetPoint:

```
'What tool are you using?
Select Case GraphicTool

    'CirclePen
    Case GraphicTools.CirclePen

        'Create a new graphics circle
        Dim objGraphicsCircle As New GraphicsCircle()

        'Set the point for drawing
        objGraphicsCircle.SetPoint(e.X, e.Y, GraphicSize, _
            objColor, True)

        'Store this for addition
        objGraphicsItem = objGraphicsCircle

    'HollowCirclePen
    Case GraphicTools.HollowCirclePen

        'Create a new graphics circle
        Dim objGraphicsCircle As New GraphicsCircle()

        'Set the point for drawing
        objGraphicsCircle.SetPoint(e.X, e.Y, GraphicSize, _
            objColor, False)

        'Store this for addition
        objGraphicsItem = objGraphicsCircle

End Select
```

In GraphicsCircle itself, choosing whether to use the FillEllipse method to draw a filled circle or use the DrawEllipse method for a hollow one is a simple determination. The only wrinkle you have to contend with is DrawEllipse; the width and height of the bounding rectangle have to be one pixel smaller than those used for `FillEllipse`. This is due to an idiosyncrasy in the way the Windows graphics subsystem works. You'll often find when working with graphics features that you have to experiment a little!

```
Public Overrides Sub Draw(ByVal graphics As System.Drawing.Graphics)
    If IsFilled = True Then

        'Create a new pen
        Dim objSolidBrush As New SolidBrush(Me.Color)

        'Draw the circle
        graphics.FillEllipse(objSolidBrush, Me.Rectangle)

    Else

        'Create a pen
        Dim pen As New Pen(Me.Color)

        'Use DrawEllipse instead
        Dim objRectangle As Rectangle = Me.Rectangle
        objRectangle.Inflate(-1, -1)
        graphics.DrawEllipse(pen, objRectangle)

    End If
End Sub
```

Now that you've learned the basics of building user controls that support their own user interface, take a look at the image-handling capabilities in Visual Basic 2005.

Working with Images

The .NET Framework has very good support for loading and saving common image formats. In particular, you're able to load images of these types:

❑   `.bmp`: The standard Windows bitmap format

❑   `.gif`: The standard "lossless" common Internet file format for graphic files and small images

❑   `.jpeg` or `.jpg`: The standard "lossy" common Internet file format for photo-quality images

❑   `.png`: The competitor to `.gif` that doesn't have the tricky licensing implications

❑   `.tiff`: The standard file format for storing and manipulated scanned documents

❑   `.wmf`/`.emf`: The standard file formats for saving Windows Metafiles

❑   `.ico`: The standard file format for program icons

❑   `.exif`: The preferred file format for storage used internally with digital cameras

Prior to .NET, developers wanting to work with the most common Internet file formats (namely, `.gif` and `.jpeg`) had to buy third-party libraries. Now, support is built directly into the .NET Framework, so from day one you can start building applications that can handle these formats. What's more surprising is that the .NET Framework also supports saving these files. This allows you to load a `.gif` file and save it as, say, a `.bmp` or `.png` file. There are two ways in which you can use images with Visual Basic 2005. First, you can use the PictureBox control that you can find in the Visual Studio 2005 Toolbox. This is a control that you place on a form, set a reference to an image, either at design time or runtime and it deals with painting itself. This is a quick way of getting a fixed image on a form. The second way in which you can use images is inside your owner-draw controls. In the following exercise, you'll see how you can tweak WroxPaint so that, rather than drawing on a dull, white background, you're actually drawing on an image you load.

Drawing Images

The property on the control takes a `System.Drawing.Image` object. In addition to using the `Image` class with PictureBox and a few other controls in the .NET Framework, you can also use it with your own owner-draw controls.

In the next Try It Out, you start by providing a way for your owner-drawn controls to display an image loaded from one of the supported image formats.

Try It Out   **Setting the BackgroundImage**

1. Open the Designer for Form1. Using the Toolbox drag an OpenFileDialog control onto the form. Set the Name property of the control to **dlgFileOpenBackground**.

2. Switch to the Code Editor for Form1. You are going to wire up the Open menu item under the File menu to show the Open File dialog box. Select openToolStripMenuItem in the Class Name combo box and then select the Click event in the Method Name combo box. Add the following highlighted code to the Click event handler:

```
Private Sub openToolStripMenuItem_Click(ByVal sender As Object, _
    ByVal e As System.EventArgs) Handles openToolStripMenuItem.Click

        'Set the open file dialog properties
        With dlgFileOpenBackground
            .Filter = "Image files (*.gif,*.jpg,*.jpeg,*.bmp,*.wmf,*.png)" & _
                "|*.gif;*.jpg;*.jpeg;*.bmp;*.wmf;*.png|All files (*.*)|*.*"
            .FilterIndex = 1
            .Title = "Open Picture Files"
        End With

        'Show the dialog
        If dlgFileOpenBackground.ShowDialog() = DialogResult.OK Then

            'Create a new image that references the file
            Dim backgroundImage As Image = _
             Image.FromFile(dlgFileOpenBackground.FileName)

            'Set the background of the canvas
            Canvas.BackgroundImage = backgroundImage

        End If
    End Sub
```

3. Run the project. Select File ⇨ Open from the menu and find a `.bmp`, `.jpg`, `.jpeg`, or `.gif` file somewhere on your computer. (If you try to open a file from the network, you may get a security exception.) The image will be displayed as shown in Figure 14-9.

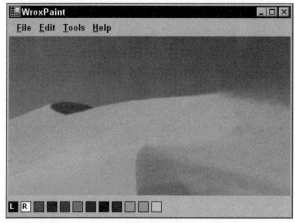

Figure 14-9

How It Works

If you said, "But I didn't do anything!" you're quite right—you didn't have to write any code to support the background image. By default, the `Control` class from which `UserControl` is ultimately derived already supports a `BackgroundImage` property, and you've set this to the image you loaded. Therefore, the base class is dealing with drawing the image.

The loading is actually done with the shared `FromFile` method on the `Image` class. This method is the easiest way of loading a file from a disk:

```
'Show the dialog
If dlgFileOpenBackground.ShowDialog() = DialogResult.OK Then

    'Create a new image that references the file
    Dim backgroundImage As Image = _
     Image.FromFile(dlgFileOpenBackground.FileName)

    'Set the background of the canvas
    Canvas.BackgroundImage = backgroundImage

End If
```

Finally, when you're actually drawing on the image, you may find the paint process sluggish. This is because the control is spending a lot of time drawing the image onto the control, and this slows everything down. Try using a smaller image, or consider this Try It Out an illustration of how to manipulate images rather than a neat paint package!

Scaling Images

If you resize the form, you'll notice that the image is actually tiled. More importantly, if you make the control too small to accommodate the whole image, the sides of the image are clipped. What you want is for the image to be scaled so that it fits the control exactly. Therefore, in the next Try It Out, you take over control of drawing the background image from the base `Control` class and provide a new implementation of the `BackgroundImage` property.

Try It Out   Drawing the Image Yourself

1. Open the Code Editor for `PaintCanvas`.

2. Rather than adding your code to draw the image to the `Paint` method, you're going to work with a different event called OnPaintBackground. This method is called before the `Paint` method. Add the following highlighted code:

```
Protected Overrides Sub OnPaintBackground( _
    ByVal e As System.Windows.Forms.PaintEventArgs)

    'Paint the invalid region with the background brush
    Dim backgroundBrush As New SolidBrush(BackColor)
    e.Graphics.FillRectangle(backgroundBrush, e.ClipRectangle)

    'Paint the image
    If Not BackgroundImage Is Nothing Then

        'Find our client rectangle
        Dim clientRectangle As New Rectangle(0, 0, Width, Height)

        'Draw the image
        e.Graphics.DrawImage(BackgroundImage, clientRectangle)

    End If
End Sub
```

3. Now select (PaintCanvas Events) in the Class Name combo box and the Resize event in the Method Name combo box. Add the following highlighted code to the Resize event handler:

```
Private Sub PaintCanvas_Resize(ByVal sender As Object, _
    ByVal e As System.EventArgs) Handles Me.Resize

        'Invalidate the control
        Me.Invalidate()
End Sub
```

4. Now run the project again. This time, when you open the image it will appear stretched or shrunken to fit the whole screen and will adjust itself as you resize the form as shown in Figure 14-10.

How It Works

All you're trying to do is take over the action of drawing the background image. As mentioned before, painting is a two-phase process: First, the background is erased (the PaintBackground event), and second, the control is given the opportunity to paint its user interface (the Paint event).

Figure 14-10

With the `BackgroundImage` property set, when the base class needs to draw the background, it will automatically draw the image. You should stop it from doing this; otherwise you'll effectively be drawing the image twice — in other words, it'll draw the image and then you'll draw your own image on top of it.

However, you do need to mimic the functionality that erases the background; otherwise things will not work properly. To do this, you create a new `SolidBrush` that uses the current background color (`BackColor`) and paint it on the area that's marked as invalid (`ClipRectangle`):

```
Protected Overrides Sub OnPaintBackground( _
    ByVal e As System.Windows.Forms.PaintEventArgs)

    'Paint the invalid region with the background brush
    Dim backgroundBrush As New SolidBrush(BackColor)
    e.Graphics.FillRectangle(backgroundBrush, e.ClipRectangle)
```

After you have painted the background, you then need to draw the image. You can do this easily by using the `DrawImage` method of the `Graphics` object. But to stretch the image you need to provide a rectangle that describes the bounds of the image. Once you have that, you give `DrawImage` both the image and the rectangle, and the image is drawn.

```
    'Paint the image
    If Not BackgroundImage Is Nothing Then

        'Find our client rectangle
        Dim clientRectangle As New Rectangle(0, 0, Width, Height)

        'Draw the image
        e.Graphics.DrawImage(BackgroundImage, clientRectangle)

    End If
End Sub
```

Preserving the Aspect Ratio

The problem you have now is that the image is stretched out of shape. Ideally, you want to make the image bigger or smaller while preserving the *aspect ratio,* which is the ratio between the width and the height, of the image. The aspect ratio describes the ratio between the width and height of the image.

The .NET Framework does not have any support for preserving the aspect ratio when it stretches an image. However, with a little work, you can do this yourself.

Try It Out   **Preserving the Aspect Ratio**

1.   Open the Code Editor for PaintCanvas again. Add the following highlighted code to OnPaintBackground.

```
Protected Overrides Sub OnPaintBackground( _
    ByVal e As System.Windows.Forms.PaintEventArgs)

    'Paint the invalid region with the background brush
    Dim backgroundBrush As New SolidBrush(BackColor)
    e.Graphics.FillRectangle(backgroundBrush, e.ClipRectangle)

    'Paint the image
    If Not BackgroundImage Is Nothing Then

        'Find our client rectangle
        Dim clientRectangle As New Rectangle(0, 0, Width, Height)

        'How big is the image?
        Dim intImageWidth As Integer = BackgroundImage.Width
        Dim intImageHeight As Integer = BackgroundImage.Height

        'What's the aspect ratio?
        Dim ratio As Double = _
            CType(intImageHeight, Double) / CType(intImageWidth, Double)

        'Scale the image
        If intImageWidth > clientRectangle.Width Then
            intImageWidth = clientRectangle.Width
            intImageHeight = _
                CType(CType(intImageWidth, Double) * ratio, Integer)
        End If

        If intImageHeight > clientRectangle.Height Then
            intImageHeight = clientRectangle.Height
            intImageWidth = _
                CType(CType(intImageHeight, Double) / ratio, Integer)
        End If

        'You need to center the image
        Dim pntImageLocation As New Point( _
            (clientRectangle.Width / 2) - (intImageWidth / 2), _
            (clientRectangle.Height / 2) - (intImageHeight / 2))
        Dim sizImageSize As New Size(intImageWidth, intImageHeight)
```

```
        Dim recImageRectangle As New Rectangle(pntImageLocation, sizImageSize)

        'Draw the image
        e.Graphics.DrawImage(BackgroundImage, recImageRectangle)

    End If
End Sub
```

2. Run the project. Now if you load an image, it will scale and preserve the aspect ratio.

How It Works

Preserving the aspect ratio is a bit of rudimentary math coupled with throwing a few rectangles together. The first thing you need to know is how big the area that you have to fit the image into actually is. You call this `clientRectangle`.

```
Protected Overrides Sub OnPaintBackground( _
    ByVal e As System.Windows.Forms.PaintEventArgs)

    'Paint the invalid region with the background brush
    Dim backgroundBrush As New SolidBrush(BackColor)
    e.Graphics.FillRectangle(backgroundBrush, e.ClipRectangle)

    'Paint the image
    If Not BackgroundImage Is Nothing Then

        'Find our client rectangle
        Dim clientRectangle As New Rectangle(0, 0, Width, Height)
```

Next, you need to look at the image itself to see how big it is. You then need to know the aspect ratio. If, for example, you had an aspect ratio of 2:1 (width:height), and you had an image that was 200 pixels wide, you would know that the height had to be 100 pixels. Alternatively, if it were 25 pixels tall, it would be 50 pixels wide.

```
        'How big is the image?
        Dim intImageWidth As Integer = BackgroundImage.Width
        Dim intImageHeight As Integer = BackgroundImage.Height

        'What's the aspect ratio?
        Dim ratio As Double = _
            CType(intImageHeight, Double) / CType(intImageWidth, Double)
```

When you calculate the aspect ratio, you want a floating-point number, so you have to convert the `Integer` width and height values to `Double`s.

Next, you look at the shape of the client area compared to the shape of the image. If the native width of the image (in other words the size before its scaled) is wider than the width of the window, you fix the width of the image as being equal to the width of the client area. Once you've done that, you use the aspect ratio to work out how tall the image should be. (Again, you've used conversions to `Double`s to make sure that the calculations work properly.)

```
        'Scale the image
        If intImageWidth > clientRectangle.Width Then
```

```
            intImageWidth = clientRectangle.Width
            intImageHeight = _
                CType(CType(intImageWidth, Double) * ratio, Integer)
        End If
```

Alternatively, if the height of the client area is taller than the height of the image, you need to do the opposite — in other words, fix the height of the image and then work out the width:

```
        If intImageHeight > clientRectangle.Height Then
            intImageHeight = clientRectangle.Height
            intImageWidth = _
                CType(CType(intImageHeight, Double) / ratio, Integer)
        End If
```

At this point you have an adjusted width and height of the image. When you have that, to start drawing, you need to work out the upper-left corner. To do this, you divide the width of the client area by two to get the exact middle and subtract half of the width of the image from it. This gives you the x coordinate at which drawing should start. Then, you do the same for the height:

```
        'You need to center the image
        Dim pntImageLocation As New Point( _
            (clientRectangle.Width / 2) - (intImageWidth / 2), _
            (clientRectangle.Height / 2) - (intImageHeight / 2))
```

Once you have the location, you build a rectangle using the adjusted width and height:

```
        Dim sizImageSize As New Size(intImageWidth, intImageHeight)
        Dim recImageRectangle As New Rectangle(pntImageLocation, sizImageSize)
```

Finally, you use DrawImage to actually draw the image on the screen:

```
        'Draw the image
        e.Graphics.DrawImage(BackgroundImage, recImageRectangle)

    End If
End Sub
```

More Graphics Methods

In this chapter, you have used a few of the graphics features available with the .NET Framework. There are some commonly used methods on the Graphics object that we haven't touched.

Whenever you have a Graphics object, either when you're building owner-draw controls or forms, try using these methods:

- ❑ DrawLine draws a single line between two points.
- ❑ DrawCurve and DrawClosedCurve draw a curve between a set of points.
- ❑ DrawArc draws a portion of a circle.

Chapter 14

- ❑   DrawBezier draws a cubic Bezier curve defined by four points.

- ❑   DrawPie draws a slice of a circle (like a pie chart).

- ❑   DrawPolygon draws regular and irregular polygons from an array of points.

- ❑   DrawIcon draws Windows icons.

All of these methods use the Brush, Pen, Point, and Rectangle objects that you've seen used throughout this chapter. Each of these methods has an associated Fill method that fills in the shape after it's drawn it.

Summary

In this chapter, you looked at how you could build your own user interface on your controls and forms. Previously, you have been able to build your user interface only by plugging other people's controls together. Here you focused on building controls derived from System.Windows.Forms.UserControl, because you're interested in building component-based software.

After discussing the difference between vector and raster graphics, you proceeded to build a simple application that allowed the user to draw dots on the screen using the mouse. You then looked at building a separate control that provided the user with a set of colors that they could choose from when drawing. You saw how to use the Color dialog box to add new colors and how to create new colors using the Windows RGB (red, green, blue) color scheme.

Finally, you took a look at the Image class and saw how this could load a variety of file formats, including Windows bitmap, .jpeg, and .gif. You also saw how to scale images and preserve their aspect ratio.

To summarize, you should know how to:

- ❑   Use the mouse events to capture the current x, y coordinates of the mouse on the screen.

- ❑   Invalidate only the rectangle that you are working in to prevent screen flicker.

- ❑   Add and use named system colors as well as custom defined colors using their RGB values.

- ❑   Use the different graphics tools such as circle and hollow circle.

- ❑   Load, resize, and preserve the aspect ratio of images.

Accessing Databases

Most applications manipulate data in some way. Visual Basic 2005 applications often manipulate data that come from relational databases. To do this, your application needs to interface with relational database software such as Microsoft Access, Microsoft SQL Server, Oracle, or Sybase.

Visual Studio 2005 provides the data access tools and wizards to connect to these databases and retrieve and update their data. In this chapter, you will look at some of these tools and wizards and use them to retrieve data from a database.

In Chapter 16, you will concentrate more on writing code directly, which gives you more flexibility and control than relying on Visual Studio 2005 to create it for you. With practice, writing code will also take less time than working through a wizard.

In this chapter, you will:

❑   Learn what a database really is

❑   Examine the SQL SELECT statement

❑   Examine data access components

❑   Examine data binding in Windows Forms

❑   Use the data access wizards in Visual Studio 2005

Note that in order to work through the exercises in this chapter, you will need Microsoft Access 2000 or higher.

What Is a Database?

Basically, a *database* consists of one or more large complex files that store data in a structured format. The database engine, in your case Microsoft Access, manages the file or files and the data within those files.

Microsoft Access Objects

A Microsoft Access database file, which has an extension of `mdb`, contains tables, queries, forms, reports, pages, macros, and modules, which are referred to as *database objects*. That's a lot of information in one large file, but Microsoft Access manages this data quite nicely. Forms, reports, pages, macros, and modules are generally concerned with letting users work with and display data. You will be writing Visual Basic 2005 applications to do this, so the only database objects you're really concerned about at the moment are tables and queries.

Tables

A *table* contains a collection of data, which is represented by one or more columns and one or more rows of data. Columns are typically referred to as *fields* in Microsoft Access, and the rows are referred to as *records*. Each field in a table represents an attribute of the data stored in that table. For example, a field named `First Name` would represent the first name of an employee or customer. This field is an attribute of an employee or customer. A record in a table contains a collection of fields that form a complete set of attributes of one instance of the data stored in that table. For example, suppose a table contains two fields: `First Name` and `Last Name`. These two fields in a single record describe the name of that one person. This is illustrated in Figure 15-1.

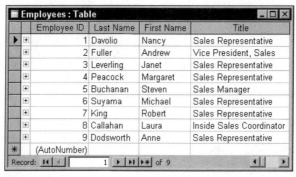

Figure 15-1

Queries

A *query* in a database is a group of Structured Query Language (SQL) statements that allow you to retrieve and update data in your tables. Queries can be used to select or update all of the data in one or more tables or to select or update specific data in one or more tables.

Query objects in Microsoft Access are a hybrid of two types of objects in SQL Server: views and stored procedures. Using database query objects can make your Visual Basic 2005 code simpler, because you have fewer complex SQL queries included in your code. They can also make your programs faster, because database engines can compile queries when you create them, whereas the SQL code in a Visual Basic 2005 program needs to be reinterpreted every time it's used.

To really understand the implications of queries, you need to learn some SQL. Fortunately, compared to *other* programming languages, SQL is really simple.

The SQL SELECT Statement

The American National Standards Institute (ANSI) defines the standards for ANSI SQL. Most database engines implement ANSI SQL to some extent and often add some features specific to the given database engine.

The benefits of ANSI SQL are that, once you learn the basic syntax for SQL, you have a solid grounding from which you can code the SQL language in almost any database. All you need to learn is a new interface for the database that you are working in. Many database vendors extended SQL to use advanced features or optimizations for their particular database. It is best to stick with ANSI standard SQL in your coding whenever possible, in case you want to change databases at some point.

The SQL SELECT statement selects data from one or more fields in one or more records and from one or more tables in your database. Note that the SELECT statement only selects data — it does not modify the data in any way.

The simplest allowable SELECT statement is like this:

```
SELECT * FROM Employees;
```

This simply means "retrieve every field for every record in the Employees table". The * indicates "every field." Employees indicates the table name. Officially, SQL statements in Microsoft Access should end in a semicolon. It usually doesn't matter if you forget it, as Access will add them automatically.

If you wanted only to retrieve first and last names, you can give a list of field names instead of a *:

```
SELECT [First Name], [Last Name] FROM Employees;
```

You need to enclose these field names in square brackets because these field names contain spaces. The square brackets indicate to the SQL interpreter that, even though there is a space in the name, it should treat "First Name" as one object name and "Last Name" as another object name. Otherwise, the interpreter would be unable to follow the syntax.

SQL is a lot like plain English — even a nonprogrammer could probably understand what it means. Now say you wanted to retrieve only the employees whose last name begins with D. To do this, you add a WHERE clause to your SELECT statement:

```
SELECT [First Name], [Last Name] FROM Employees WHERE [Last Name] LIKE 'D*';
```

A WHERE clause limits the selection of data to only those records that match the criteria in the WHERE clause. The preceding SELECT statement would cause the database to look at the Last Name column and only select those records where the employee's last name begins with the letter D.

Last, if you want to retrieve these items in a particular order, you can, for example, order the results by first name. You just need to add an ORDER BY clause to the end:

```
SELECT [First Name], [Last Name] FROM Employees
          WHERE [Last Name] LIKE 'D*' ORDER BY [First Name];
```

This means that if you have employees called Angela Dunn, Zebedee Dean, and David Dunstan, you will get the following result:

```
Angela    Dunn
David     Dunstan
Zebedee   Dean
```

You're specifying quite a specific command here, but the syntax is pretty simple — and very similar to how you would describe what you want to an English speaker. Usually, when ordering by a name, you want to order in an ascending order so that A comes first, Z comes last. If you were ordering by a number, though, you might want to have the bigger number at the top — for example, so that a product with the highest price appears first. Doing this is really simple — just add DESC (short for descending) to the ORDER BY clause, which causes the results to be ordered in descending order:

```
SELECT [First Name], [Last Name] FROM Employees
                     WHERE [Last Name] LIKE 'D*' ORDER BY [First Name] DESC;
```

The D* means "begins with a D followed by anything." If you had said *D* it would mean "anything followed by D followed by anything," basically, "contains D." This would return the following:

```
Zebedee   Dean
David     Dunstan
Angela    Dunn
```

If you want to make it very clear that you want the results in an ascending order, you can add ASC to the ORDER BY clause instead of DESC. But you don't really need to, since this is the default sort order.

You can summarize this syntax in the following way:

```
SELECT select-list
   FROM table-name
   [WHERE search-condition]
   [ORDER BY order-by-expression [ASC | DESC]]
```

This means that you must provide a list of fields to include or use a * to select them all. You must provide a *table-name*. You can choose to provide a *search-condition*. You can choose to provide an *order-by-expression*, and if you do, you can make it either ascending or descending.

SQL gets considerably more complicated when you start working with several tables in the same query. But, for various reasons, you don't need to do this all that much when working with Visual Basic 2005.

Anyway, the best way to get SQL into your head is to practice. Before moving on, please try to answer these questions in your head:

❑   How would you write a query to retrieve the Name, Description, and Price fields from a table called Product?

❑   What would you add to the query to retrieve only items with DVD in their description?

❑   How would you order the results so that the most expensive item comes first?

Queries in Access

SQL is really a basic programming language, and if you are a programmer who needs to access databases, you will need to use it. However, Microsoft Access provides wizards and visual tools that enable novice programmers to write queries without knowing SQL. Even for SQL programmers, these can sometimes prove useful. These tools, demonstrated in this section, end up producing SQL statements that you can view and modify if you wish, so they can be a good way to learn more about SQL.

Creating a Customer Query

In the next Try It Out section, you use Access to create a simple query that will select customer information from the `Customer` table in the `Northwind.mdb` database. You'll need to ensure that the sample databases were installed when you installed Microsoft Access or Microsoft Office. You'll create this query and then view the SQL `SELECT` statement that gets generated by Access.

Try It Out   **Creating aCustomer Query**

1. Open Microsoft Access and click the Open icon on the toolbar. In the Open dialog box, navigate to `C:\Program Files\Microsoft Office\Office11\Samples\` and open `Northwind.mdb`. Then click the OK button.

The path to Microsoft Office will vary depending on the version you have installed and the installation path chosen at setup.

2. When the database opens, you will see two sections in the navigation bar on the left: Objects and Groups. The Objects section lists all of your database object types, which was discussed in the section on databases. You can also use Groups to gather together related objects of any type, in any way you want (see Figure 15-2).

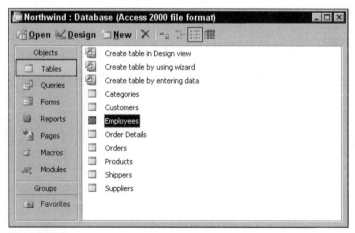

Figure 15-2

3. Since you want to take a look at how a SQL `SELECT` statement is built by Access, you need to click the Queries icon under the Objects tab.

4. You are going to build a new query, so double-click "Create query in Design view" in the results window (see Figure 15-3).

Figure 15-3

5. The Show Table dialog box appears and allows you to select one or more tables to be in your query. You only want to select one table: Customers. Click the Customers table and then click the Add button to have this table added to the Query Designer and then click the Close button to close the Show Table dialog box.

6. The Customers table is displayed with all available fields plus an asterisk. You can select the fields that you want to be added to your query, or you can select the asterisk, which will select all fields from the table. For this exercise just select a few fields for your query. Double-click CompanyName in the Customers table to add it to the first column in the grid below the table. The Field and Table cells are automatically filled in. You also want to sort the data by this field, so click in the Sort cell and choose Ascending to have the results of your query sorted by this field. Your screen should now look like Figure 15-4.

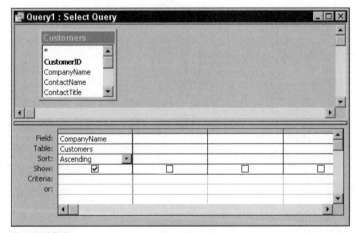

Figure 15-4

7. You now need to add the ContactName field to your grid. Double-click this field in the Customers table and it will be automatically added to the next available column in the grid. Then add ContactTitle in the same way. Your completed query should now look like the one in Figure 15-5.

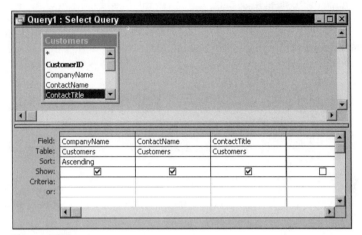

Figure 15-5

8. Click the Save icon on the toolbar, enter the name **CustomerQuery** in the Save As dialog box, and then click OK.

9. On the toolbar click the run icon, indicated by !, and you will see results similar to the ones shown in Figure 15-6. Notice that the results are sorted on the CompanyName field in ascending order, as shown in the figure.

Company Name	Contact Name	Contact Title
Alfreds Futterkiste	Maria Anders	Sales Representative
Ana Trujillo Emparedados y helados	Ana Trujillo	Owner
Antonio Moreno Taquería	Antonio Moreno	Owner
Around the Horn	Thomas Hardy	Sales Representative
Berglunds snabbköp	Christina Berglund	Order Administrator
Blauer See Delikatessen	Hanna Moos	Sales Representative
Blondel père et fils	Frédérique Citeaux	Marketing Manager
Bólido Comidas preparadas	Martín Sommer	Owner
Bon app'	Laurence Lebihan	Owner
Bottom-Dollar Markets	Elizabeth Lincoln	Accounting Manager
B's Beverages	Victoria Ashworth	Sales Representative
Cactus Comidas para llevar	Patricio Simpson	Sales Agent
Centro comercial Moctezuma	Francisco Chang	Marketing Manager
Chop-suey Chinese	Yang Wang	Owner

Record: 1 of 91

Figure 15-6

How It Works

From the choices you made, Access generates a SQL statement. To look at it, you click the View menu and select the SQL View menu item. This will display the SQL statements as shown in Figure 15-7.

Notice that you have the basic SQL SELECT statement followed by the field names. Access has prefixed each field name with the table name. Remember that brackets are required only when the field names contain spaces. The table name prefix is actually required only when selecting data from multiple tables where both tables have a field with the same name. However, to reduce the chance of errors, Access has prefixed all fields with the table name.

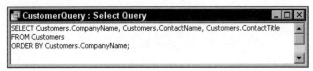

Figure 15-7

The FROM clause in your SELECT statement specifies the table that data is being selected from (in this case, the Customers table).

The ORDER BY clause specifies which fields should be used to sort the data, and in this case the CompanyName field has been specified.

So how does this SQL statement actually get built? Well, when you first started creating this query you added a table name. Before any fields were added to the grid, Access generated the following SQL statement:

```
SELECT
FROM Customers;
```

Of course, this on its own is not a valid SQL statement. Once you added the first field and set the sort order for that field, the following SQL statement was generated — which is valid:

```
SELECT Customer.CompanyName
FROM Customers
ORDER BY Customers.CompanyName;
```

As you continued to add fields, the rest of the field names were added to the SQL statement until the complete SQL statement shown in Figure 15-7 was generated.

Let's move on now and discuss the basic data access components that are needed in Windows Forms to display data. Since you have been using Microsoft Access in your examples here, I will discuss the data access components provided in Visual Studio 2005 that assists you in accessing the data in an Access database.

Data Access Components

There are three main data access components in Visual Basic 2005 that you need for retrieving and viewing data from the database: BindingSource, TableAdapter, and DataSet. The BindingSource and DataSet components are located in the Toolbox under the Data tab, as shown in Figure 15-8. The TableAdapter can be automatically generated depending on the path you take when adding data access components, as you'll soon discover. Take a brief look at each one of these components in turn.

Figure 15-8

These components are known as Data Components and are simply classes, like everything else in the .NET Framework. In this chapter, you will simply see how to use some of them in a Windows application. Data Components will be discussed as a whole in the next chapter.

DataSet

The DataSet component is a cache of data that is stored in memory. It's a lot like a mini database engine, but its data exists in memory. You can use it to store data in tables, and using the DataView component (covered in Chapter 16), you can query the data in various ways.

The DataSet is very powerful. In addition to storing data in tables, it stores a rich amount of *metadata*, or "data about the data." This includes things like table and column names, data types, and the information needed to manage and undo changes to the data. All of this data is represented in memory in Extensible Markup Language (XML). A DataSet can be saved to an XML file and then loaded back into memory very easily. It can also be passed in XML format over networks, including the Internet.

Since the DataSet component stores all of the data in memory, you can scroll through the data both forward and backward, and can also make updates to the data in memory. The DataSet component is very powerful, and you will be exploring this component in more detail in the next chapter. In this chapter, you will simply be using it to store data and bind it to a control on your form.

DataGridView

The DataGridView component is a container that allows you to bind data from your data source and have it displayed in a spreadsheet-like format, displaying the columns of data horizontally and the rows of data vertically.

The DataGridView component also provides many properties that allow you to customize the appearance of the component itself, as well as properties that allow you to customize the column headers and the display of data.

More important, though, are the quick links at the bottom of the Properties window for the DataGridView component, which allow you to customize the appearance of the DataGridView itself through several predefined format styles. You'll see this later in this chapter.

BindingSource

The BindingSource component acts like a bridge between your data source (DataSet) and your data-bound controls (that is, controls that are bound to data components). Any interaction with the data from your controls goes through the BindingSource component, which in turn communicates with your data source.

For example, your DataGridView control will be initially filled with data. When you request that a column be sorted, the DataGridView control will communicate that intention to the BindingSource, which in turn communicates that intention to the data source.

The BindingSource component is the component that you will bind to the DataSource property of your controls, as you'll see later in this chapter.

BindingNavigator

The BindingNavigator component provides a standard UI component that allows you to navigate through the records that are in your data source. It looks very similar to the record navigator shown at the bottom of Figure 15-6.

The BindingNavigator component is bound to your BindingSource component much as the DataGridView component is. When you click the Next button in the BindingNavigator component, it in turn sends a request to the BindingSource component for the next record, and the BindingSource component in turn sends the request to the data source.

TableAdapter

There's one last component that I want to talk about: the TableAdapter. This component does not reside in the ToolBox but can be automatically generated for you depending on how you add your data access components to your project.

The TableAdapter contains the query that is used to select data from your database as well as connection information for connecting to your database. It also contains methods that will fill the DataSet in your project with data from the database. You can also choose to have the TableAdapter generate insert, update, and delete statements based on the query that is used to select data.

The TableAdapter will be covered in more detail Chapter 16.

Data Binding

Data binding means taking data referenced by your BindingSource and binding it to a control. In other words, the control will receive its data from your data access components, and the data will be automatically displayed in the control for the user to see and manipulate. In Visual Basic 2005, most controls support some level of data binding. Some are specifically designed for it, such as the DataGridView and TextBox. In your next Try It Out, you will be binding data from a BindingSource component to a DataGridView control, so this is where you want to focus your attention. Later in this chapter you'll bind data to a TextBox control.

In this Try It Out, you will be using the data access wizards in Visual Studio 2005 to create the data components necessary to bind data to a DataGridView control. You will be using the Northwind.mdb sample database again as your data source.

Try It Out · Binding Data to a DataGridView Control

1. Create a new Windows Application project called **Northwind Customers DataGridView**.

2. Click the Data tab in the ToolBox and then drag a DataGridView control from the ToolBox and drop it on your form. The DataGridView control will display the Tasks dialog box as shown in Figure 15-9.

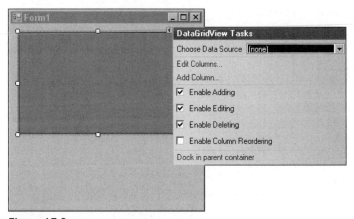

Figure 15-9

3. Click the drop-down arrow in the Choose Data Source combo box and then click the Add Project Data Source link at the bottom of the list that is displayed. This will cause the Data Source Configuration Wizard to be displayed.

4. The Choose a Data Source Type screen allows you to choose the data source for your data. As you can see from this screen, shown in Figure 15-10, you have several options for a data source.

You can click the Database icon for connecting to various databases such as SQL Server, Oracle, and Access, the Web Service icon for connecting to a Web Service, and the Object icon for connecting to your business logic components.

Click the Database icon and click the Next button.

5. In the Choose Your Data Connection screen, click the New Connection button.

6. In the Choose Data Source dialog box, select Microsoft Access Database File in the Data Source list and then click the Continue button.

7. In the Add Connection dialog box, click the Browse button and navigate to the samples folder for Microsoft office. By default, this will be in the folder `C:\Program Files\Microsoft Office\Office11\Samples\` for a default installation of Microsoft Office 2003.

    Select the `Northwind.mdb` database in the Select Microsoft Access Database File dialog box and click the Open button to have the path and file name added to the text field on the Add Connection dialog box. Click the OK button when you are done to close the Add Connection dialog box and then click the Next button on the Choose Your Data Connection screen.

    You will be prompted with a dialog box that informs you that the data file is not part of your project and asks if you want to add it. Click the Yes button in this dialog box.

8. Click the Next button on the Save the Connection String to the Application Configuration File screen.

9. The Choose Your Database Objects screen allows you to select the data that your application needs. Here you have the option to select data directly from the tables in your database, data generated from the execution of various views and stored procedures or data generated from the execution of functions.

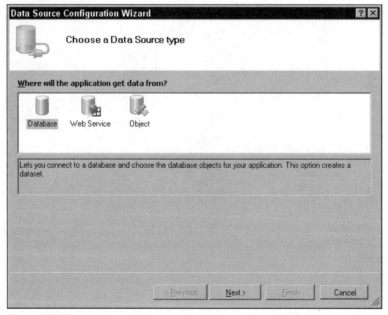

Figure 15-10

You'll be using the query that you created in the last Try It Out exercise so expand the Views node in the Database objects list and then check the check box for CustomerQuery as shown in Figure 15-11. If you expand CustomerQuery, you'll see the columns that are returned from this query. Click the Finish button when you are done.

At this point, the wizard will generate a DataSet object named `NorthwindDataSet`, a BindingSource object named `CustomerQueryBindingSource`, and a TableAdapter object named `CustomerQueryTableAdapter`.

10. Since you will not be adding, editing, or deleting records from this table, uncheck the check box next to these options in the Tasks dialog. You will, however, want to implement sorting in your DataGridView component, so check the check box next to Enable Column Reordering. When you are done, click on the title bar of the form to hide the Actions dialog.

11. Click the DataGridView control and, in the Properties window, set the Dock property to Fill.

12. At this point you can run your project to see the results. Click the Start button on the toolbar, and your form will be displayed with the DataGridView control populated with data.

You can click on the column headers to have the data in the DataGridView sorted in ascending order. Clicking the same column header again will sort the data in descending order. Each sort order will be indicated with an arrow pointing up for ascending and down for descending.

At this point you have not written a single line of code to achieve these results, which just goes to prove how powerful the data wizards in Visual Basic 2005 are.

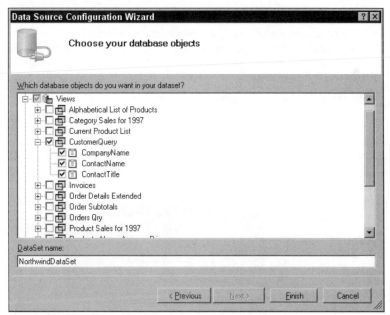

Figure 15-11

How It Works

The approach you took to creating a data-bound application in this Try It Out exercise is the most straightforward approach and the easiest. You started by adding a DataGridView control to your form, which caused you to be prompted with the Tasks dialog box for the DataGridView.

This dialog box allowed you to create a new Data Source via the Data Source Configuration Wizard, which walked you through a series of steps, the first of which was to identify the type of data source that you wanted to use. You were then allowed to specify the type of database object that you wanted to use to retrieve your data, and in this step you merely chose to use a specific table in your database and selected specific columns from that table.

Once you clicked the Finish button in the Data Source Configuration Wizard, several components were automatically generated and added to your project. These included the TableAdapter, DataSet, and BindingSource. The BindingSource was the actual component that was bound to the DataSource property of the DataGridView control.

Remember that the BindingSource's job is to communicate the data needs of the control to the data source, which in this case is the DataSet containing all of the data. The DataSet was populated with data by the TableAdapter when your form was loaded.

The most important point of this exercise was the ease with which you were able to create a data-bound application and the simple fact that you did not have to write a single line of code to achieve the end results.

In this next Try It Out exercise, you'll be using several TextBox controls on your form and will bind each text box to a certain field in your BindingSource. You'll then be using a BindingNavigator control to navigate through the records in your DataSet.

Try It Out   **Binding Data to TextBox Controls**

1. Create a new Windows Application project called **Northwind Customers BindingNavigator**.

2. Add three Label controls and three TextBox controls to your form. Arrange the controls so that your form looks similar to Figure 15-12, and set the Text properties of the Label controls as shown in the figure.

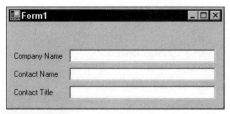

Figure 15-12

3. Click the first text box on your form and then expand the (DataBindings) property in the Properties window by clicking the plus sign next to it. Then click the Text property under the DataBindings property. Now click the drop-down arrow for the Text property

At this point you'll see the Data Source window shown in Figure 15-13. Click the Add Project Data Source link to invoke the Data Source Configuration Wizard, which you saw in the previous Try It Out exercise.

Figure 15-13

4. Select the Database icon in the Choose a Data Source Type screen and click the Next button.

5. In the Choose Your Data Connection screen, click the New Connection button.

6. In the Add Connection dialog box, click the Browse button and navigate to the samples folder for Microsoft office. By default, this will be in the folder `C:\Program Files\Microsoft Office\Office11\Samples\` for a default installation of Microsoft Office 2003.

    Select the `Northwind.mdb` database in the Select Microsoft Access Database File dialog box and click the Open button to have the path and file name added to the text field on the Add Connection dialog box. Click the OK button when you are done to close the Add Connection dialog box and then click the Next button on the Choose Your Data Connection screen.

    You will be prompted with a dialog box that informs you that the data file is not part of your project and asks if you want to add it. Click the Yes button in this dialog box.

7. Click the Next button on the Save the Connection String to the Application Configuration File screen.

8. In the Choose Your Database Objects screen expand the Tables node in the Database objects list and then expand the Customers table. Check the check box for CompanyName, ContactName, and ContactTitle. Click the Finish button when you are done.

9. Now click the drop-down arrow next to the Text property in the Properties Window. At this point, you'll see the Data Source window shown in Figure 15-14. Expand the Other Data Sources node, the Project Data Sources node, the NorthwindDataSet node, and finally the Customers node.

    Now click the CompanyName field. The window will close, and the Text field under the DataBindings property will be bound to the CompanyName field in your DataSet.

If you look at the bottom of the IDE, you'll notice that a NorthwindDataSet component, CustomersBindingSource component, and CustomersTableAdapter component have been automatically generated.

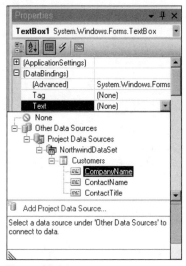

Figure 15-14

10. Click the second text box on your form, and then click the Text property under the DataBindings property in the Properties window. Now click the drop-down arrow for the Text property; then expand the CustomersBindingSource node in the Data Source window, and then click the ContactName field.

11. Click the third text box on your form, and then click the Text property under the DataBindings property in the Properties window. Click the drop-down arrow for the Text property; then expand the CustomersBindingSource node in the Data Source window, and then click the ContactTitle field.

12. Now go back to the ToolBox, drag a BindingNavigator control from the Data tab, and drop it on your form. The BindingNavigator control will be automatically docked to the top of the form.

13. In the Properties window, located the BindingSource property, and then click that field. Now click the drop-down arrow for the BindingSource property and choose CustomersBindingSource from the list.

14. Finally, click the Start button on the toolbar to run your project. Your form that is displayed should look similar to the one shown in Figure 15-15. You'll be able to navigate through the records in your data source, navigating backward and forward as well as being able to go the first and last record.

Clicking the Delete button will delete records from your DataSet but *will not* delete records from the database. Likewise, clicking the Add button will add an empty record to your DataSet but not to the database. You would need to write some code to actually have the database updated with the changes from your DataSet.

The beauty of using the DataNavigator control is that you've quickly built a form that will navigate through the records of your database without you having to write a single line of code.

Figure 15-15

How It Works

You started this Try It Out exercise by adding three Label and TextBox controls to your form. You then proceeded to set the DataBindings properties of the text boxes. When you chose to set the Text DataBinding property of the first text box, you were prompted to add a new data source, which again invoked the Data Source Configuration Wizard.

You used the Data Source Configuration Wizard in this exercise in the same manner as you did in the last exercise. When you completed the Data Source Configuration Wizard, it automatically generated a TableAdapter, DataSet, and a BindingSource component. You were then able to choose which field in the DataSet to bind to the DataBinding Text property.

Once you added the BindingNavigator control to your form, setting it up was a matter of simply choosing the BindingSource that was generated by the Data Source Configuration Wizard in the BindingSource property in the Properties window.

Again, this exercise has demonstrated the simplicity at which you can create data-bound applications without the need to write any code.

Summary

You started this chapter by exploring what a database actually is and then looked at the SQL SELECT statement. You put this knowledge to use by creating a query in the `Northwind.mdb` database to see the SQL statements that Access generated for you.

You then took a look at the basics of binding data to controls on a form, specifically the DataGridView control and TextBox controls. You have examined the necessary basic data access components required to retrieve data from an Access database and bind that data to your controls. You used the components provided in the Data tab of the Toolbox for your data access, and used the wizards to generate the necessary code to connect to the database and retrieve the data.

After working through this chapter, you should know:

- ❑ What a database is and the basic objects that make up a database
- ❑ How to use the SQL SELECT statement to select data from a database

- ❑ How to use the Data Source Configuration Wizard to create the data access components needed to perform data binding
- ❑ How to bind data to a DataGridView control
- ❑ How to bind data to TextBox controls and use the BindingNavigator control

While you have seen that the wizards provided in Visual Studio 2005 make it simple to bind data quickly to the controls on a form, you sometimes need more control on how you interact with the data in a database and how you bind the data to the controls on a form. Chapter 16 takes a different approach to data binding by programmatically binding data to controls on a form. You will also be exploring the data access components in more detail and will learn how to set their properties and to execute their methods from your code.

Exercises

Exercise 1

Create a new query in your Northwind database to select FirstName, LastName, and Title from the Employees table. Order the results by the LastName column and save your query as **EmployeeQuery**. Then create a Windows application with a DataGridView control that uses the EmployeeQuery.

Exercise 2

Using the query created in Exercise 1, create a new Windows application that uses the BindingNavigator control and bind the fields from your query to text boxes on your form.

Database Programming with SQL Server and ADO.NET

Chapter 15 introduced database programming. You obtained data from a single table in an Access database and displayed it on a grid. You managed to give the user some cool features while writing virtually no code.

You used wizards that wrote most of the code for you – including setting up the connection, configuring the data adapter, and generating a typed dataset. This works great for simple database access using one or two tables, but writing the code yourself can give you a lot more control.

This chapter dives much deeper into the topic of database access. The database access technologies you used in the previous chapter, including components for retrieving data, storing data in memory, and binding data to controls, are collectively called *ADO.NET*. You will explore how you can use the built-in capabilities of ADO.NET to retrieve and update data from databases. You will also learn to manipulate, filter, and edit data held in memory by the DataSet.

The data you extract will be bound to controls on your form, so you will also need to explore binding more thoroughly. You will see how you can use controls to view one record at a time (for example, using text boxes) and how to navigate between records, using the CurrencyManager object.

In this chapter, you will:

- ❏ Learn about ADO.NET objects
- ❏ Bind data to controls
- ❏ Search for and sort in-memory data using ADO.NET DataView objects
- ❏ Select, insert, update, and delete data in a database using ADO.NET

You will also use this chapter to see how to access SQL Server databases using the SqlClient data provider. As mentioned in the previous chapter, SqlClient is significantly faster than OleDb, but it will work only with SQL Server databases. To complete the exercises in this chapter, you need to have access to a version of MSDE, SQL Server 7, SQL Server 2000, or SQL Server 2005, as well as full access to the pubs database. As of the writing of this chapter, the pubs database was not included in the SQL Server Express version bundled with Visual Studio 2005. When this chapter uses the term *SQL Server*, the term includes SQL Server 7 and SQL Server 2000, as well as MSDE and SQL Server 2005. The database can reside in SQL Server on your local machine or in SQL Server on a network.

ADO.NET

ADO.NET is designed to provide a *disconnected architecture*. This means that applications connect to the database to retrieve a load of data and store it in memory. They then disconnect from the database and manipulate the in-memory copy of the data. If the database needs to be updated with changes made to the in-memory copy, a new connection is made and the database is updated. The main in-memory data store is the `DataSet`, which contains other in-memory data stores, such as `DataTable` objects. You can filter and sort data in a `DataSet` using `DataView` objects, as you will see later in the chapter.

Using a disconnected architecture provides many benefits, of which the most important to you is that it allows your application to *scale up*. This means that your database will perform just as well supporting hundreds of users as it does supporting ten users. This is possible because the application connects to the database only long enough to retrieve or update data, thereby freeing available database connections for other instances of your application or other applications using the same database.

ADO.NET Data Namespaces

The core ADO.NET classes exist in the `System.Data` namespace. This namespace, in turn, contains some child namespaces. The most important of these are `System.Data.SqlClient` and `System.Data.OleDb`. These provide classes for accessing SQL Server databases and OLE (Object Linking and Embedding) DB-compliant databases, respectively. You've already used classes from the `System.Data.OleDb` namespace in the previous chapter, where you used `OleDbConnection` and `OleDbDataAdapter`. In this chapter, you will be using `System.Data.SqlClient` with its equivalent classes, including `SqlConnection` and `SqlDataAdapter`.

Two other child namespaces also exist in the `System.Data` namespace: `System.Data.OracleClient` and `System.Data.Odbc`. The `System.Data.OracleClient` namespace is used exclusively for Oracle databases. Just as its `SqlClient` counterpart provides best results with SQL Server databases, the `OracleClient` namespace provides optimal performance when accessing Oracle databases. The `System.Data.Odbc` namespace provides access to older ODBC (Open Database Connectivity) data sources that do not support the `OleDb` technology.

The `System.Data.SqlClient`, `System.Data.OleDb`, `System.Data.OracleClient`, and `System.Data.Odbc` namespaces are known as *data providers* in ADO.NET. There are other data providers available; in this book, you concentrate on only the first two.

In this chapter, you will be accessing SQL Server databases using the `SqlClient` namespace. However, in ADO.NET, the different data providers work in a very similar way. So the techniques you use here can be easily transferred to the `OleDb` classes. Also, the techniques you learned in the previous chapter using `OleDb` apply to `SqlClient` classes. With ADO.NET, you use the data provider that best fits your data source — you do not need to learn a whole new interface, because all data providers work in a very similar way.

As you start working with ADO.NET, you will soon learn how the pieces fit together, and this chapter will help you in that reaching that goal.

Since the space here is limited, you focus on the specific classes that are relevant to the example programs in this chapter. The following list contains the ADO.Net classes that you will be using:

- ❑ SqlConnection
- ❑ SqlDataAdapter
- ❑ SqlCommand
- ❑ SqlParameter

Remember that these are specifically SqlClient classes, but that the OleDb namespace has very close equivalents. Whenever you want to use these classes, you must add a reference to the System.Data namespace. You can use the Imports keyword, so you do not have to fully qualify members of the SqlClient namespace in your code, as shown in the following code fragment:

```
Imports System.Data.SqlClient
```

If you want to use the core ADO.NET classes, such as DataSet and DataView without typing the full name, you must import the System.Data namespace, as shown in the next code fragment:

```
Imports System.Data
```

You should already be familiar with importing different namespaces in your project. However, to be thorough, you will also cover this when you go through our hands-on exercises. Now let's take a look at the main classes that exist in the System.Data.SqlClient namespace.

The SqlConnection Class

The SqlConnection class is at the heart of the classes that we will be discussing in this section, because it provides a connection to a SQL Server database. When you construct a SqlConnection object, you can choose to specify a *connection string* as a parameter. The connection string contains all the information required to open a connection to your database. If you don't specify one in the constructor, you can set it using the SqlConnection.ConnectionString property. In the previous chapter, Visual Studio .NET built a connection string for you from the details you specified in the Data Link Properties dialog box. However, it is often more useful or quicker to write a connection string manually — so let's take a look at how connection strings work.

Working with the Connection String Parameters

The way that the connection string is constructed will depend on what data provider you are using. When accessing SQL Server, you will usually provide a Server and a Database parameter, as shown in the following table.

Parameter	Description
Server	The name of the SQL Server that you want to access. This is usually the name of the computer that is running SQL Server. You can use (local) or localhost if SQL Server is on the same machine as the one running the application. If you are using named instances of SQL Server, then this parameter would contain the computer name followed by a backslash followed by the named instance of SQL Server.
Database	The name of the database that you want to connect to.

You also need some form of authentication information, which you can accomplish in two ways: by providing a username and password in the connection string or by connecting to SQL Server using the NT account under which the application is running. If you want to connect to the server by specifying a username and password, you need to include additional parameters in your connection string, as shown in the following table.

Parameter	Description
User ID	The username to use to connect to the database. An account with this user ID will need to exist in SQL Server and have permission to access the specified database.
Password	The password for the specified user.

However, SQL Server can be set up to use the Windows NT account of the user who is running the program to open the connection. In this case, you don't need to specify a username and password. You just need to specify that you are using *integrated security*. (The method is called integrated security because SQL Server is integrating with Windows NT's security system and provides the most secure connection because the User ID and Password parameters need not be specified in the code.) You do this using the Integrated Security parameter, which you set to True when you want the application to connect to SQL Server using the current user's NT account.

Of course, for this to work, the user of the application must have permission to use the SQL Server database. This is granted using the SQL Server Enterprise Manager.

To see how these parameters function in a connection string to initialize a connection object, look at the following code fragment. It uses the SqlConnection class to initialize a connection object that uses a specific user ID and password in the connection string:

```
Dim objConnection As SqlConnection = New _
    SqlConnection("Server=localhost;Database=pubs;" & _
    "User ID=sa;Password=vbdotnet;")
```

This connection string connects to a SQL Server database. The Server parameter specifies that the database resides on the local machine. The Database parameter specifies the database that you want to access — in this case it is the pubs database. Finally, the User ID and Password parameters specify the User ID and password of the user defined in the database. As you can see, each parameter has a value assigned to it using =, and each parameter-value pair is separated by a semicolon.

Opening and Closing the Connection

After you initialize a connection object with a connection string, as shown previously, you can invoke the methods of the `SqlConnection` object such as `Open` and `Close`, which actually open and close a connection to the database specified in the connection string. An example of this is shown in the following code fragment:

```
' Open the database connection...
objConnection.Open()
' ... Use the connection
' Close the database connection...
objConnection.Close()
```

Although many more properties and methods are available in the `SqlConnection` class, the ones mentioned so far are all you are really interested in to complete the hands-on exercises, and they should be enough to get you started.

SqlCommand

The `SqlCommand` class represents a SQL command to execute against a data store. The command will usually be a select, insert, update, or delete query, and can be a SQL string or a call to a stored procedure. The query being executed may contain parameters or it may not.

In the example in Chapter 15, the Data Adapter Configuration Wizard generated a command object for you (although in that case it was an `OleDbCommand`). In that case, a data adapter was using the command to fill a dataset. You look at how to write code to do this later in the chapter. For the moment, look at command objects alone. You learn how they relate to data adapters in the next section.

The constructor for the `SqlCommand` class has several variations, but the simplest method is to initialize a `SqlCommand` object with no parameters. Then, after the object has been initialized, you can set the properties you need to perform the task at hand. The following code fragment shows how to initialize a `SqlCommand` object:

```
Dim objCommand As SqlCommand = New SqlCommand()
```

When using data adapters and datasets, there isn't much call for using command objects on their own. They will mainly be used for executing a particular select, delete, insert, or update, so that is what you will cover in this chapter. You can also use command objects with a data reader. A *data reader* is an alternative to a `DataSet` that uses fewer system resources but provides far less flexibility. In this book, you will concentrate on using the `DataSet`, because it is the more common and useful of the two.

The Connection Property

Certain properties must be set on the `SqlCommand` object before you can execute the query. The first of these properties is the `Connection` property. This property is set to a `SqlConnection` object, as shown in the next code fragment.

```
objCommand.Connection = objConnection
```

For the command to execute successfully, the connection must be open at the time of execution.

The CommandText Property

The next property that must be set is the `CommandText` property. This property specifies the SQL string or stored procedure to be executed. Most databases require that you place all *string* values in single quote marks, as shown here:

```
Dim objConnection As SqlConnection = New _
               SqlConnection("server=(local);database=pubs;user id=sa;password=")
Dim objCommand As SqlCommand = New SqlCommand()
objCommand.Connection = objConnection
objCommand.CommandText = "INSERT INTO authors " & _
                    "(au_id, au_lname, au_fname, contract) " & _
                    "VALUES('123-45-6789', 'Barnes', 'David', 1)"
```

The `INSERT` statement is a very simple one that means "Insert a new row into the `authors` table. In the `au_id` column put `'123-45-6789'`, in the `au_lname` column put `'Barnes'`, in the `au_fname` column put `'David'`, and in the contract column put `'1'`."

This is the basic way that `INSERT` statements work in SQL. You have `INSERT INTO` followed by a table name. You then have a series of column names, in parentheses. You then have the `VALUES` keyword followed by a set of values, to be inserted into the columns that you've just named and in the same order.

This assumes that you know the values to insert when you are writing the program, which is unlikely in most cases. Fortunately, you can create commands with parameters and then set the values of these parameters separately. Let's have a look at how to use parameters.

The Parameters Collection

Placeholders are variables prefixed with an at (@) sign in the SQL statement; they get filled in by parameters. So if you want to update the authors table as discussed in the previous section, but didn't know the values at design time, you would do this:

```
Dim objConnection As SqlConnection = New _
               SqlConnection("server=(local);database=pubs;user id=sa;password=")
Dim objCommand As SqlCommand = New SqlCommand()
objCommand.Connection = objConnection
objCommand.CommandText = "INSERT INTO authors " & _
                    "(au_id, au_lname, au_fname, contract) " & _
                    "VALUES(@au_id,@au_lname,@au_fname,@au_contract)"
```

Here, instead of providing values, you provided placeholders. Placeholders, as mentioned, always start with an @ symbol. They do not need to be named after the database column that they represent, but it is often easier if they are, and it helps to self-document your code.

Next, you need to create parameters that will be used to insert the values into the placeholders when the SQL statement is executed. You need to create and add parameters to the `Parameters` collection of the `SqlCommand` object. The term *parameters* here refers to the parameters required to provide data to your SQL statement or stored procedure, *not* to the parameters that are required to be passed to a Visual Basic 2005 method.

You can access the `Parameters` collection of the `SqlCommand` object by specifying the `Parameters` property. After you access the `Parameters` collection, you can use its properties and methods to create one or more parameters in the collection. The easiest way to add a parameter to a command is demonstrated in the following example:

```
Dim objConnection As SqlConnection = New _
                SqlConnection("server=(local);database=pubs;user id=sa;password=")
Dim objCommand As SqlCommand = New SqlCommand()
objCommand.Connection = objConnection
objCommand.CommandText = "INSERT INTO authors " & _
                "(au_id, au_lname, au_fname, contract) " & _
                "VALUES(@au_id,@au_lname,@au_fname,@au_contract)"
objCommand.Parameters.AddWithValue ("@au_id", txtAuId.Text)
objCommand.Parameters.AddWithValue ("@au_lname", txtLastName.Text)
objCommand.Parameters.AddWithValue ("@au_fname", txtFirstName.Text)
objCommand.Parameters.AddWithValue ("@au_contract", chkContract.Checked)
```

The `AddWithValue` method here accepts the name of the parameter and the object that you want to add. In this case, you are using the `Text` property of various Text box objects on a (fictitious) form for most of the columns. For the Contract column you use the `Checked` property of a check box on the same form. In previous versions of ADO.NET, you could use the add method to add a parameter with a value. That overload is now obsolete.

The ExecuteNonQuery Method

Finally, you can execute the command. To do this, the connection needs to be opened. You can invoke the ExecuteNonQuery method of the `SqlCommand` object. This method executes the SQL statement and causes the data to be inserted into the database. It then returns the number of rows that were affected by the query, which can be a useful way to check that the command worked as expected. To complete your code fragment, you need to open the connection, execute the query, and close the connection again:

```
Dim objConnection As SqlConnection = New _
                SqlConnection("server=(local);database=pubs;user
id=sa;password=")
Dim objCommand As SqlCommand = New SqlCommand()
objCommand.Connection = objConnection
objCommand.CommandText = "INSERT INTO authors " & _
                "(au_id, au_lname, au_fname, contract) " & _
                "VALUES(@au_id,@au_lname,@au_fname,@au_contract)"
objCommand.Parameters.AddWithValue("@au_id", txtAuId.Text)
objCommand.Parameters.AddWithValue("@au_lname", txtLastName.Text)
objCommand.Parameters.AddWithValue("@au_fname", txtFirstName.Text)
objCommand.Parameters.AddWithValue("@au_contract ", chkContract.Checked)
objConnection.Open()
objCommand.ExecuteNonQuery()
objConnection.Close()
```

SqlDataAdapter

The `SqlDataAdapter` class is similar to the `OleDbDataAdapter` that you configured with wizards in the previous chapter. The main difference is that the `OleDbDataAdapter` can access any data source that supports OLE DB, while the `SqlDataAdapter` supports only SQL Server databases. You can use them in a similar way though; you can configure a SqlDataAdapter using wizards, just as you configured an OleDbDataAdapter in the previous chapter (provided you are accessing an SQL Server data source). In this chapter, you look at how to configure and use an SqlDataAdapter in code, but these guidelines also apply to the OleDbDataAdapter.

Data adapters act as bridges between your data source and in-memory data objects such as the DataSet. To access the data source, they use the command objects you've just looked at. These command objects are associated with connections, so the data adapter relies on command and connection objects to access and manipulate the data source.

The SqlDataAdapter class's SelectCommand property is used to hold a SqlCommand that retrieves data from the data source. The data adapter then places the result of the query into a DataSet or DataTable. The SqlDataAdapter also has UpdateCommand, DeleteCommand, and InsertCommand properties. These are also SqlCommand objects, used to write changes made to a DataSet or DataTable back to the data source. This may all seem complicated, but in fact the tools are really easy to use. You learned enough SQL in the previous chapter to write a SelectCommand, and there are tools called *command builders* that you can use to automatically create the other commands based on this.

Take a look at the SelectCommand property, and then look at how you can create commands for updating, deleting, and inserting records.

The SelectCommand Property

The SqlDataAdapter class's SelectCommand property is used to fill a DataSet with data from a SQL Server database, as shown in Figure 16-1.

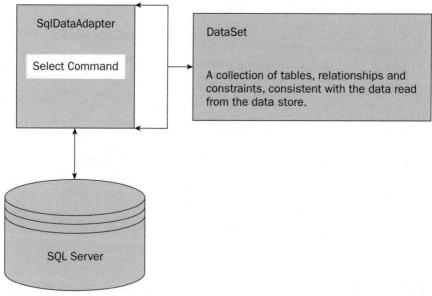

Figure 16-1

When you want to read data from the data store, you must set the `SelectCommand` property of the `SqlDataAdapter` class first. This property is a `SqlCommand` object and is used to specify what data to select and how to select that data. Therefore the `SelectCommand` property has properties of its own, and you need to set them just as you would set properties on a normal command. You've already seen the following properties of the `SqlCommand` object:

❑   `Connection`: Sets the `SqlConnection` object to be used to access the data store.

❑   `CommandText`: Sets the SQL statements or stored procedure name to be used to select the data.

In the previous examples of `SqlCommand` objects, you used straight SQL statements. If you want to use stored procedures, you need to be aware of an additional property, `CommandType`, which sets a value that determines how the `CommandText` property is interpreted.

In this chapter, you are going to concentrate on SQL statements, but stored procedures are often useful too, particularly if they already exist in the database. If you want to use one, set the `CommandText` property to the name of the stored procedure (remember to enclose it in quote marks because the compiler treats this as a string), and set the `CommandType` property to `CommandType.StoredProcedure`.

Setting SelectCommand to a SQL String

Take a look at how you set these properties in code. The code fragment that follows shows the typical settings for these properties when executing a SQL string:

```
' Declare a SqlDataAdapter object...
Dim objDataAdapter As New SqlDataAdapter()

' Assign a new SqlCommand to the SelectCommand property
objDataAdapter.SelectCommand = New SqlCommand()

' Set the SelectCommand properties...
objDataAdapter.SelectCommand.Connection = objConnection
objDataAdapter.SelectCommand.CommandText = _
    "SELECT au_lname, au_fname FROM authors " & _
    "ORDER BY au_lname, au_fname"
```

The first thing that this code fragment does is declare a `SqlDataAdapter` object. This object has a `SelectCommand` property set to a `SqlCommand`; you just need to set that command's properties. You set the properties by first setting the `Connection` property to a valid connection object, one that will already have been created before the code that you see here. Next, you set the `CommandText` property to your SQL `SELECT` statement.

Setting SelectCommand to a Stored Procedure

This next code fragment shows how you could set these properties when you want to execute a *stored procedure*. A stored procedure is a group of SQL statements that are stored in the database under a unique name and are executed as a unit. The stored procedure in this example (`usp_select_author_titles`) uses the same SQL statement that you used in the previous code fragment:

```
' Declare a SqlDataAdapter object...
Dim objDataAdapter As New SqlDataAdapter()

' Assign a new SqlCommand to the SelectCommand property
```

```
objDataAdapter.SelectCommand = New SqlCommand()

' Set the SelectCommand properties...
objDataAdapter.SelectCommand.Connection = objConnection
objDataAdapter.SelectCommand.CommandText = "usp_select_author_titles"
objDataAdapter.SelectCommand.CommandType = CommandType.StoredProcedure
```

The `CommandText` property now specifies the name of the stored procedure that you want to execute instead of the SQL string that was specified in the last example. Also notice the `CommandType` property. In the first example, you did not change this property, because its default value is `CommandType.Text`, which is what you need to execute SQL statements. In this example, it is set to a value of `CommandType.StoredProcedure`, which indicates that the `CommandText` property contains the name of a stored procedure to be executed.

Using Command Builders to Create the Other Commands

The `SelectCommand` is all you need to transfer data from the database into your `DataSet`. After you let your users make changes to the `DataSet`, though, you will want to write the changes back to the database. You can do this by setting up command objects with the SQL for inserting, deleting, and updating. Alternatively, you can use stored procedures. Both of these solutions require knowledge of SQL outside the scope of this book. Fortunately, there is an easier way; you can use *command builders* to create these commands. It takes only one more line:

```
' Declare a SqlDataAdapter object...
Dim objDataAdapter As New SqlDataAdapter()

' Assign a new SqlCommand to the SelectCommand property
objDataAdapter.SelectCommand = New SqlCommand()

' Set the SelectCommand properties...
objDataAdapter.SelectCommand.Connection = objConnection
objDataAdapter.SelectCommand.CommandText = "usp_select_author_titles"
objDataAdapter.SelectCommand.CommandType = CommandType.StoredProcedure
' automatically create update/delete/insert commands
Dim objCommandBuilder As SqlCommandBuilder = New SqlCommandBuilder(objDataAdapter)
```

Now you can use this `SqlDataAdapter` to write changes back to a database. You will look more at this later in the chapter. For know, look at the method that gets data from the database to the `DataSet` in the first place: the `Fill` method.

The Fill Method

You use the `Fill` method to populate a `DataSet` object with the data that the `SqlDataAdapter` object retrieves from the data store using its `SelectCommand`. However, before you do this you must first initialize a `DataSet` object. To use the `DataSet` object in your project, you must add a reference to `System.Xml`.

```
' Declare a SqlDataAdapter object...
Dim objDataAdapter As New SqlDataAdapter()

' Assign a new SqlCommand to the SelectCommand property
objDataAdapter.SelectCommand = New SqlCommand()
```

```
' Set the SelectCommand properties...
objDataAdapter.SelectCommand.Connection = objConnection
objDataAdapter.SelectCommand.CommandText = "usp_select_author_titles"
objDataAdapter.SelectCommand.CommandType = CommandType.StoredProcedure
Dim objDataSet as DataSet = New DataSet()
```

Now that you have a `DataSet` and a `SqlDataAdapter`, you can fill your `DataSet` with data. The `Fill` method has several overloaded versions, but you will be discussing the one most commonly used. The syntax for the `Fill` method is shown here:

```
SqlDataAdapter.Fill(DataSet, string)
```

The *DataSet* argument specifies a valid `DataSet` object that will be populated with data. The *string* argument gives the name you want the table to have in the `DataSet`. Remember that one `DataSet` can contain many tables. You can use any name you like, but usually it's best to use the name of the table from which the data in the database has come. This helps you self-document your code and makes the code easier to maintain.

The following code fragment shows how you invoke the `Fill` method. The string `"authors"` is specified as the *string* argument. This is the name you want to use when manipulating the in-memory version of the table; it is also the name of the table in the data source.

```
' Declare a SqlDataAdapter object...
Dim objDataAdapter As New SqlDataAdapter()

'Create an instance of a new select command object
objDataAdapter.SelectCommand = New SqlCommand

' Set the SelectCommand properties...
objDataAdapter.SelectCommand.Connection = objConnection
objDataAdapter.SelectCommand.CommandText = "usp_select_author_titles"
objDataAdapter.SelectCommand.CommandType = CommandType.StoredProcedure
Dim objDataSet as DataSet = New DataSet()
' Fill the DataSet object with data...
objDataAdapter.Fill(objDataSet, "authors")
```

The `Fill` method uses the `SelectCommand.Connection` property to connect to the database. If the connection is already open, the data adapter will use it to execute the `SelectCommand` and leave it open after it's finished. If the connection is closed, then the data adapter will open it, execute the `SelectCommand`, and then close it again.

You now have data in memory and can start manipulating it independently of the data source. Notice that the `DataSet` class does not have `Sql` at the start of its class name. This is because `DataSet` is not in the `System.Data.SqlClient` namespace, it is in the parent `System.Data` namespace. The classes in this namespace are primarily concerned with manipulating data in memory, rather than obtaining data from any particular data source. Once you have the data loaded into a `DataSet`, it no longer matters what data source it came from (unless you need to write it back). Let's have a look at two of the classes in this namespace: the `DataSet` and the `DataView`.

The DataSet Class

The DataSet class is used to store data retrieved from a data store and stores that data in memory on the client. The DataSet object contains a collection of tables, relationships, and constraints that are consistent with the data read from the data store. It acts as a lightweight database engine all by itself, enabling you to store tables, edit data, and run queries against it using a DataView object.

The data in a DataSet is disconnected from the data store, and you can operate on the data independently from the data store. You can manipulate the data in a DataSet object by adding, updating, and deleting the records. You can apply these changes back to the original data store afterwards using a data adapter.

The data in a DataSet object is maintained in Extensible Markup Language (XML, which is discussed in detail in Chapter 18), meaning that you can save a DataSet as a file or easily pass it over a network. The XML is shielded from you as a developer, and you should never need to edit the XML directly. All editing of the XML is done through the properties and methods of the DataSet class. Many developers like using XML and will sometimes choose to manipulate the XML representation of a DataSet directly, but this is not essential.

Like any XML document, a DataSet can have a *schema* (a file that describes the structure of the data in one or more XML files). When you generated a typed dataset in the previous chapter, an XML Schema Definition (XSD) file was added to the Solution Explorer, as shown in Figure 16-2.

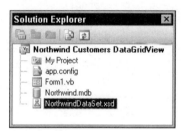

Figure 16-2

This file is an XML schema for the data that the CustomerDataSet would hold. From this, Visual Studio .NET was able to create a class that inherited from the DataSet and that used this particular schema. A DataSet schema contains information about the tables, relationships, and constraints stored in the DataSet. Again, this is shielded from you, and you do not need to know XML to work with a DataSet.

Since the DataSet contains the actual data retrieved from a data store, you can bind the DataSet to a control or controls to have them display (and allow editing of) the data in the DataSet. You did this a bit in Chapter 15, and you will see more later in this chapter.

DataView

The DataView class is typically used for sorting, filtering, searching, editing, and navigating the data from a DataSet. A DataView is *bindable*, meaning that it can be bound to controls in the same way that the DataSet can be bound to controls. Again, you learn more about data binding in code later in this chapter.

A `DataSet` can contain a number of `DataTable` objects; when you use the `SqlDataAdapter` class's `Fill` method to add data to a `DataSet`, you are actually creating a `DataTable` object inside the `DataSet`. The `DataView` provides a custom view of a `DataTable`; you can sort or filter the rows, for example, as you can in a SQL query.

You can create a `DataView` from the data contained in a `DataTable` that contains only the data that you want to display. For example, if the data in a `DataTable` contains all authors sorted by last name and first name, you can create a `DataView` that contains all authors sorted by first name and then last name. Or, if you wanted, you could create a `DataView` that contained only last names or certain names.

Although you can view the data in a `DataView` in ways different from the underlying `DataTable`, it is still the same data. Changes made to a `DataView` affect the underlying `DataTable` automatically, and changes made to the underlying `DataTable` automatically affect any `DataView` objects that are viewing that `DataTable`.

The constructor for the `DataView` class initializes a new instance of the `DataView` class and accepts the `DataTable` as an argument. The following code fragment declares a `DataView` object and initializes it using the `authors` table from the `DataSet` named `objDataSet`. Notice that the code accesses the `Tables` collection of the `DataSet` object, by specifying the `Tables` property and the table name:

```
' Set the DataView object to the DataSet object...
Dim objDataView = New DataView(objDataSet.Tables("authors"))
```

The Sort Property

Once a `DataView` has been initialized and is displaying data, you can alter the view of that data. For example, suppose you want to sort the data in a different order than in the `DataSet`. To sort the data in a `DataView`, you set the `Sort` property and specify the column or columns that you want sorted. The following code fragment sorts the data in a `DataView` by author's first name and then last name:

```
objDataView.Sort = "au_fname, au_lname"
```

Notice that this is the same syntax as the ORDER BY clause in a SQL SELECT statement. As in the SQL ORDER BY clause, sorting operations on a `DataView` are always performed in an ascending order by default. If you wanted to perform the sort in descending order, you would need to specify the DESC keyword, as shown in the next code fragment:

```
objDataView.Sort = "au_fname, au_lname DESC"
```

The RowFilter Property

When you have an initialized `DataView`, you can filter the rows of data that it will contain. This is similar to specifying a WHERE clause in an SQL SELECT statement; only rows that match the criteria will remain in the view. The underlying data is not affected, though. The `RowFilter` property specifies the criteria that should be applied on the `DataView`. The syntax is similar to the SQL WHERE clause. It contains at least a column name followed by an operator and the value. If the value is a string, it must be enclosed in single quote marks as shown in the following code fragment, which retrieves only the authors whose last names are `Green`:

```
' Set the DataView object to the DataSet object...
objDataView = New DataView(objDataSet.Tables("authors"))
objDataView.RowFilter = "au_lname = 'Green'"
```

If you want to retrieve all rows of authors except those with the last name of Green, you would specify the "not equal to" operator as shown in this example:

```
' Set the DataView object to the DataSet object...
objDataView = New DataView(objDataSet.Tables("authors"))
objDataView.RowFilter = "au_lname <> 'Green'"
```

You can also specify more complex filters, as you could in SQL. For example, you can combine several criteria using an AND operator:

```
objDataView.RowFilter = "au_lname <> 'Green' AND au_fname LIKE 'D*'"
```

This returns authors whose last names are not Green and whose first names begin with D.

The Find Method

If you want to search for a specific row of data in a DataView, you invoke the Find method. The Find method searches for data in the sort key column of the DataView. Therefore, before invoking the Find method, you first need to sort the DataView on the column that contains the data that you want to find. The column that the DataView is sorted on becomes the sort key column in a DataView object.

For example, suppose you want to find the author who has a first name of Ann. You would need to sort the DataView by first name to set this column as the sort key column in the DataView, and then invoke the Find method, as shown in the following code fragment:

```
Dim intPosition as Integer
objDataView.Sort = "au_fname"
intPosition = objDataView.Find("Ann")
```

If it finds a match, the Find method returns the position of the record within the DataView. Otherwise, the DataView returns a null value, indicating that no match was found. If the Find method finds a match, it stops looking and returns only the position of the first match. If you know there is more than one match in your data store, you could filter the data in the DataView, which is a subject that is covered shortly.

The Find method is not case sensitive, meaning that to find the author who has a first name of Ann, you could enter either the text Ann or the text ann.

The Find method looks for an exact case-insensitive match, so this means that you must enter the whole word or words of the text that you are looking for. For example, suppose you are looking for the author who has the last name of Del Castillo. You cannot enter Del and expect to find a match; you must enter all the words that make up the author's name. Notice that the following example specifies all lowercase letters, which is perfectly fine:

```
objDataView.Sort = "au_lname"
intPosition = objDataView.Find("del castillo")
```

You have seen that a DataView can be sorted on more than one column at a time. If you want to sort on more than one column, you need to supply an array of values to the Find method instead of just a single value. For example, you may want to find where Simon Watts appears in the DataView, if at all:

```
Dim intPosition As Integer
Dim arrValues(1) As Object
objDataView.Sort = "au_fname, au_lname"

' Find the author named "Simon Watts".
arrValues(0) = "Simon"
arrValues(1) = "Watts"
intPosition = objDataView.Find(arrValues)
```

The ADO.NET Classes in Action

You've now looked at the basics of the ADO.NET classes and how they allow you to retrieve and insert data into SQL Server. No doubt your head is spinning from information overload at this point, so the best way to ensure that you understand how to use all of the objects, methods, and properties that you have been looking at is to actually use them. In the next two Try It Outs, you'll see how to exploit the power of the DataSet object to expose data to your users. You may find that you'll want to come back and reread the previous section after you've completed the Try It Outs; this will help to clarify ADO.NET in your mind.

The first Try It Out will implement the SqlConnection, SqlDataAdapter, and DataSet classes. You will see firsthand how to use these classes in a simple example in which you need to retrieve read-only data and display that data in a data grid. In fact, what you do here will be very similar to the example in the previous chapter, but you will be doing it in code instead of using wizards.

> When writing your programs, you may often use a combination of wizards and coding to create powerful programs quickly and easily. The components created in the previous chapter by drag and drop can be manipulated in code in exactly the same way as objects created in code. In the previous chapter, you used wizards almost all the time. In this chapter you will concentrate on code.

Examining a DataSet Example

Before you dive into the details of creating the program, take a look at the data and the relationships of the data that you want to display. The data that you want comes from the pubs database in SQL Server 2000. However, if you are using SQL Server 7.0, SQL Server 2005 or MSDE you should be seeing the exact same data. Some versions SQL Server 2005 may not come with the pubs database.

You want to display a list of authors, their book titles, and the price of their books. Figure 16-3 shows the tables that this data resides in and also the relationship of the tables:

You want to display the author's first and last names, which reside in the authors table, and the title and price of the book, which reside in the titles table. Because an author can have one or more books and a book can have one or more authors, the titles table is joined to the authors table via a *relationship table* called titleauthor. This table contains the many-to-many relationship of authors to books.

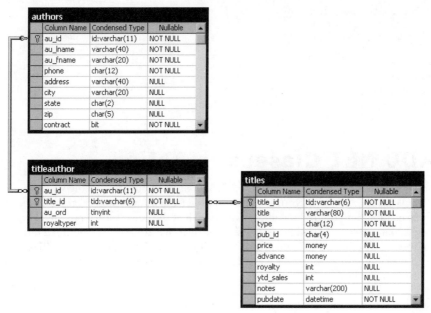

Figure 16-3

Having looked at the relationship of the tables and knowing what data you want, take a look at the SQL SELECT statement that you need to create to get this data:

```
SELECT au_lname, au_fname, title, price
FROM authors
JOIN titleauthor ON authors.au_id = titleauthor.au_id
JOIN titles ON titleauthor.title_id = titles.title_id
ORDER BY au_lname, au_fname
```

The first line of the SELECT statement shows the columns that you want to select. The second line shows the main table that you are selecting data from, which is authors.

The third line *joins* the titleauthor table to the authors table using the au_id column. Therefore, when you select a row of data from the authors table, you will also get every row in the titleauthor table that matches the au_id in the selected row of the authors table. This join returns only authors who have a record in the titleauthor table.

The fourth line joins the titles table to the titleauthor table using the title_id column. Hence, for every row of data that is selected from the titleauthor table, you will select the corresponding row of data (having the same title_id value) from the titles table. The last line of the SELECT statement sorts the data by the author's last name and first name using the ORDER BY clause. Now, create the project in the next Try It Out.

Try It Out   **DataSet Example**

1. Create a new Windows Application called **DatasetExample**.

2. Set the following properties of the form:

     ❑   Set Size to **600, 230**.

     ❑   Set StartPosition to **CenterScreen**.

     ❑   Set Text to **Bound DataSet**.

3.   From the Toolbox, locate the DataGridView control under the Windows Forms tab and drag it onto your form. Set the properties of the DataGridView as follows:

     ❑   Set Name to **grdAuthorTitles**.

     ❑   Set Anchor to Top, Bottom, Left, Right.

     ❑   Set Location to **0, 0**.

     ❑   Set Size to **592, 203**.

4.   First, add references to the `System.Data` and `System.Xml` namespaces. Next, you will add the `Imports` statements for the namespaces you will use. Open the code window for your form and add these namespaces as highlighted at the very top of your code:

```
' Import Data and SqlClient namespaces...
Imports System.Data
Imports System.Data.SqlClient


Public Class Form1

End Class
```

5.   Next, you need to declare the objects necessary to retrieve the data from the database, so add the following highlighted code. Ensure that you use a user ID and password that have been defined in your installation of SQL Server:

```
Public Class Form1
    Dim objConnection As New SqlConnection _
        ("server=bnewsome;database=pubs;user id=sa;password=!p@ssw0rd!")

    Dim objDataAdapter As New SqlDataAdapter()
    Dim objDataSet As New DataSet()
End Class
```

Notice your connection string in the constructor for this object. You will need to change the server *parameter to point to the machine where SQL Server is running if it is not running on your local machine. You will also need to change the* user id *and* password *parameters to use a valid login that has been provided or that you set up yourself. If the* user id *that you use has no password assigned, then specify the* password *argument but do not enter anything for the actual password. For example,* password=;.

6.   To add a handler for the form's Load event, select (Form1 Events) in the Class Name combo box and then select Load in the Method Name combo box. Insert the following highlighted code:

```
Private Sub Form1_Load(ByVal sender As Object, ByVal e As System.EventArgs) _
        Handles Me.Load
    ' Set the SelectCommand properties...
    objDataAdapter.SelectCommand = New SqlCommand()
    objDataAdapter.SelectCommand.Connection = objConnection
    objDataAdapter.SelectCommand.CommandText = _
```

```
            "SELECT au_lname, au_fname, title, price " & _
            "FROM authors " & _
            "JOIN titleauthor ON authors.au_id = titleauthor.au_id " & _
            "JOIN titles ON titleauthor.title_id = titles.title_id " & _
            "ORDER BY au_lname, au_fname"
        objDataAdapter.SelectCommand.CommandType = CommandType.Text

        ' Open the database connection...
        objConnection.Open()

        ' Fill the DataSet object with data...
        objDataAdapter.Fill(objDataSet, "authors")

        ' Close the database connection...
        objConnection.Close()

        ' Set the DataGridView properties to bind it to our data...
        grdAuthorTitles.AutoGenerateColumns = True
        grdAuthorTitles.DataSource = objDataSet
        grdAuthorTitles.DataMember = "authors"

            ' Clean up
            objDataAdapter = Nothing
            objConnection = Nothing
    End Sub
```

7. Run the project to see what you get. You should see results similar to Figure 16-4.

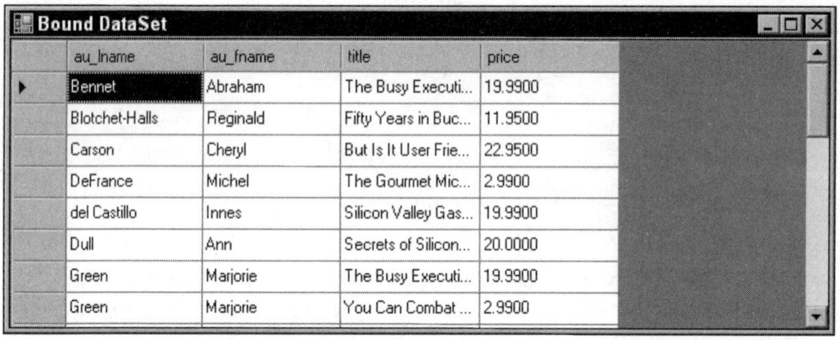

au_lname	au_fname	title	price
Bennet	Abraham	The Busy Executi...	19.9900
Blotchet-Halls	Reginald	Fifty Years in Buc...	11.9500
Carson	Cheryl	But Is It User Frie...	22.9500
DeFrance	Michel	The Gourmet Mic...	2.9900
del Castillo	Innes	Silicon Valley Gas...	19.9900
Dull	Ann	Secrets of Silicon...	20.0000
Green	Marjorie	The Busy Executi...	19.9900
Green	Marjorie	You Can Combat ...	2.9900

Figure 16-4

8. Note that the DataGridView control has built-in sorting capabilities. If you click a column header, the data in the grid will be sorted by that column in ascending order. If you click the same column again, the data will be sorted in descending order.

Note that error handling has been omitted from the exercise, to preserve space. You should always add the appropriate error handling to your code. Review Chapter 9 for error-handling techniques.

How It Works

To begin with, you imported the following namespaces:

```
' Import Data and SqlClient namespaces...
Imports System.Data
Imports System.Data.SqlClient
```

Remember that the System.Data namespace is required for the DataSet and DataView classes, and that the System.Data.SqlClient namespace is required for the SqlConnection, SqlDataAdapter, SqlCommand, and SqlParameter classes. You will be using only a subset of the classes just mentioned in this example, but you do require both namespaces.

Then you declared the objects that were necessary to retrieve the data from the database. These objects were declared with class-level scope, so you placed those declarations just inside the class:

```
Public Class Form1
    Inherits System.Windows.Forms.Form

    Dim objConnection As New SqlConnection _
        ("server=bnewsome;database=pubs;user id=sa;password=!p@ssw0rd!")

    Dim objDataAdapter As New SqlDataAdapter()
    Dim objDataSet As DataSet = New DataSet()
```

The first object that you declared was a SqlConnection object. Remember that this object establishes a connection to your data store, which in this case is SQL Server.

The next object that you declared was a SqlDataAdapter object. This object is used to read data from the database and populate the DataSet object.

The last object in your declarations was the DataSet object, which serves as the container for your data. Remember that this object stores all data in memory and is not connected to the data store.

In this particular example, there was no need to give these objects class-level scope. You use them in only one method, and they could have been declared there. However, if your application enabled users to write changes back to the database, you would want to use the same connection and data adapter objects for reading and writing to the database. In that case, having class-level scope would be really useful.

With your objects defined, you placed some code to populate the DataSet object in the initialization section of the form. Your SqlDataAdapter object is responsible for retrieving the data from the database. Therefore, you set the SelectCommand property of this object. This property is a SqlCommand object, so the SelectCommand has all the properties of an independent SqlCommand object:

```
    ' Set the SelectCommand properties...
    objDataAdapter.SelectCommand = New SqlCommand()
    objDataAdapter.SelectCommand.Connection = objConnection
    objDataAdapter.SelectCommand.CommandText = _
        "SELECT au_lname, au_fname, title, price " & _
        "FROM authors " & _
        "JOIN titleauthor ON authors.au_id = titleauthor.au_id " & _
        "JOIN titles ON titleauthor.title_id = titles.title_id " & _
        "ORDER BY au_lname, au_fname"
```

511

First, you initialize the `SelectCommand` by initializing an instance of the `SqlCommand` class and assigning it to the `SelectCommand` property.

Then you set the `Connection` property to your connection object. This property sets the connection to be used to communicate with your data store.

The `CommandText` property is then set to the SQL string that you wanted to execute. This property contains the SQL string or stored procedure to be executed to retrieve your data. In this case you used an SQL string, which was explained in detail in the `SQLDataAdapter` section earlier.

After all of the properties are set, you open your connection, fill the dataset, and then close the connection again. You open the connection by executing the `Open` method of your `SqlConnection` object:

```
' Open the database connection...
objConnection.Open()
```

You then invoke the `Fill` method of the `SqlDataAdapter` object to retrieve the data and fill your `DataSet` object. In the parameters for the `Fill` method, you specify the `DataSet` object to use and the table name. You set the table name to `authors`, even though you are actually retrieving data from several tables in the data store:

```
' Fill the DataSet object with data...
objDataAdapter.Fill(objDataSet, "authors")
```

After you fill your `DataSet` object with data, you need to close the database connection. You do that by invoking the `Close` method of the `SqlConnection` object:

```
' Close the database connection...
objConnection.Close()
```

As you learned earlier, you do not have to open and close the connection explicitly. The `Fill` method of the `SqlDataAdapter` executes the `SelectCommand` and leaves the connection in the same state as when the method was invoked. In this case, the `Fill` method left the connection open. If you did not explicitly write code to open and close the connection, the `SqlDataAdapter.Fill` method would open and close the connection for you.

Then you set some properties of the DataGridView to bind your data to it. The first of these properties is the `AutoGenerateColumns` property. Here you let the control create all of the columns you needed by setting the `AutoGenerateColumns` property to `True`. The next property is the `DataSource` property, which tells the DataGridView where to get its data:

```
' Set the DataGridView properties to bind it to our data...
grdAuthorTitles.AutoGenerateColumns = True
grdAuthorTitles.DataSource = objDataSet
grdAuthorTitles.DataMember = "authors"
```

The `DataMember` property selects the table in the data source, and here you set it to `authors`, which is the table used in your `DataSet` object.

Then, to free memory, you clean up the objects that are no longer being used.

```
' Clean up
objDataAdapter = Nothing
objConnection = Nothing
```

When you ran the example, the DataGridView control read the schema information from the `DataSet` object (which the `DataSet` object created when it was filled) and created the correct number of columns for your data in the DataGridView control. It has also used the column names in the schema as the column names for the grid, and each column had the same default width. The DataGridView also read the entire `DataSet` object and placed the contents into the grid.

In the next Try It Out, you take a look at some of the DataGridView properties that you can use to make this a more user-friendly display of data.

Try It Out   Changing the DataGridView Properties

1. Here are some changes you can make to make your DataGridView more user-friendly:

❑   Add your own column header names

❑   Adjust the width of the column that contains the book titles so that you can easily see the full title

❑   Change the color of every other row so that the data in each one stands out

❑   Make the last column in the grid (which contains the price of the books) right-aligned

You can do all this by making the following highlighted modifications to your code in the `Form1_Load` method:

```
' Set the DataGridView properties to bind it to our data...
grdAuthorTitles.DataSource = objDataSet
grdAuthorTitles.DataMember = "authors"

' Declare and set the currency header alignment property...
Dim objAlignRightCellStyle As New DataGridViewCellStyle
objAlignRightCellStyle.Alignment = DataGridViewContentAlignment.MiddleRight

' Declare and set the alternating rows style...
Dim objAlternatingCellStyle As New DataGridViewCellStyle()
objAlternatingCellStyle.BackColor = Color.WhiteSmoke
grdAuthorTitles.AlternatingRowsDefaultCellStyle = objAlternatingCellStyle

' Declare and set the style for currency cells ...
Dim objCurrencyCellStyle As New DataGridViewCellStyle()
objCurrencyCellStyle.Format = "c"
objCurrencyCellStyle.Alignment = DataGridViewContentAlignment.MiddleRight

' Change column names and styles using the column index
grdAuthorTitles.Columns(0).HeaderText = "Last Name"
grdAuthorTitles.Columns(1).HeaderText = "First Name"
grdAuthorTitles.Columns(2).HeaderText = "Book Title"
grdAuthorTitles.Columns(2).Width = 225
```

```
    ' Change column names and styles using the column name
    grdAuthorTitles.Columns("price").HeaderCell.Value = "Retail Price"
    grdAuthorTitles.Columns("price").HeaderCell.Style = objAlignRightCellStyle
    grdAuthorTitles.Columns("price").DefaultCellStyle = objCurrencyCellStyle


    ' Clean up
    objDataAdapter = Nothing
    objConnection = Nothing
    objCurrencyCellStyle = Nothing
    objAlternatingCellStyle = Nothing
    objAlignRightCellStyle = Nothing

End Sub
```

2. Run your project again. You should now see results similar to Figure 16-5. You can compare this figure to Figure 16-4 and see a world of difference. It's amazing what setting a few properties will do and how it makes this a more user-friendly display:

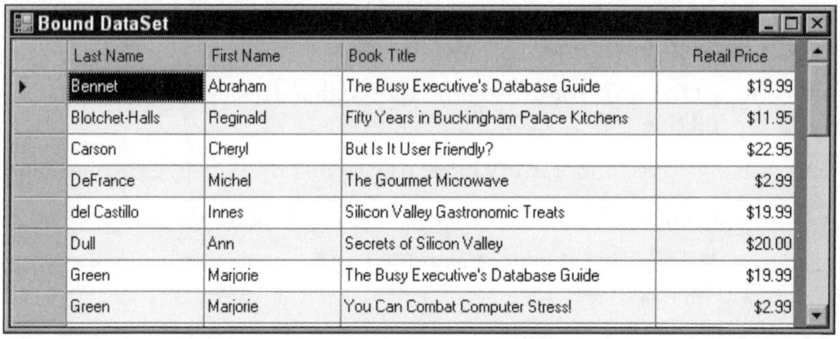

Bound DataSet				_ □ ×
Last Name	First Name	Book Title	Retail Price	
Bennet	Abraham	The Busy Executive's Database Guide	$19.99	
Blotchet-Halls	Reginald	Fifty Years in Buckingham Palace Kitchens	$11.95	
Carson	Cheryl	But Is It User Friendly?	$22.95	
DeFrance	Michel	The Gourmet Microwave	$2.99	
del Castillo	Innes	Silicon Valley Gastronomic Treats	$19.99	
Dull	Ann	Secrets of Silicon Valley	$20.00	
Green	Marjorie	The Busy Executive's Database Guide	$19.99	
Green	Marjorie	You Can Combat Computer Stress!	$2.99	

Figure 16-5

How It Works

The DataGridView uses inherited styles to format the output table the users see. Style inheritance allows you to apply default styles that cascade to all cells, rows, columns, or headers under the parent style. Then, you can change only individual items that do not match the default styles. The architecture of styles is very powerful. You can set individual style properties or create your own DataGridView CellStyle objects to set multiple style properties and reuse them.

To start, you declare a DataGridViewCellStyle object. Then you change the alignment to middle right. (This allows you to align the price column later.)

```
    ' Declare and set the currency header alignment property...
    Dim objAlignRightCellStyle As New DataGridViewCellStyle
    objAlignRightCellStyle.Alignment = DataGridViewContentAlignment.MiddleRight
```

The first thing that you do here is alternate the background color of each row of data. This helps each row of data stand out and makes it easier to see the data in each column for a single row. The Color structure provides a large list of color constants, as well as a few methods that can be called to generate colors:

```
' Declare and set the alternating rows style...
Dim objAlternatingCellStyle As New DataGridViewCellStyle()
objAlternatingCellStyle.BackColor = Color.WhiteSmoke
grdAuthorTitles.AlternatingRowsDefaultCellStyle = objAlternatingCellStyle
```

Next, changes to the currency cells for Retail Price are set up. You change the format to currency and right-align the column.

```
' Declare and set the style for currency cells ...
Dim objCurrencyCellStyle As New DataGridViewCellStyle()
objCurrencyCellStyle.Format = "c"
objCurrencyCellStyle.Alignment = DataGridViewContentAlignment.MiddleRight
```

Some changes to the format of the DataGridView are easy to make at the property level. Column titles can simply be changed by accessing the column and setting `HeaderText` or `HeaderCell.Value` properties. You set both properties in the code that follows.

You changed the book title column width to 225 to display the title in a more readable format. Next, you set the styles on the price column based on the style objects above. What is great about using style objects is you can apply the same styles to multiple objects. For example, if you have three columns that hold dollar amounts, you would set up one style object and reuse this style on all three columns.

```
' Change column names and styles using the column index
grdAuthorTitles.Columns(0).HeaderText = "Last Name"
grdAuthorTitles.Columns(1).HeaderText = "First Name"
grdAuthorTitles.Columns(2).HeaderText = "Book Title"
grdAuthorTitles.Columns(2).Width = 225

' Change column names and styles using the column name
grdAuthorTitles.Columns("price").HeaderCell.Value = "Retail Price"
grdAuthorTitles.Columns("price").HeaderCell.Style = objAlignRightCellStyle
grdAuthorTitles.Columns("price").DefaultCellStyle = objCurrencyCellStyle
```

You have now seen how to bind the `DataSet` object to a control, in this case a DataGridView control. In the next Try It Out, you expand on this knowledge by binding several controls to a `DataView` object and using the `CurrencyManager` object to navigate the data in the `DataView` object. However, before you get to that point, read about data binding and how you can bind data to simple controls, such as the TextBox control, and how to navigate the records.

Data Binding

The DataGridView control is a great tool for displaying all your data at one time. You can also use it for editing, deleting, and inserting rows, provided you have the logic to write changes back to the data source. However, you often want to use a control to display a single column value from one record at a time. In cases like these, you need to bind individual pieces of data to simple controls, such as a TextBox, and display only a single row of data at a time. This type of data binding gives you more control over the data, but it also increases the complexities of your programs, because you must write the code to bind the data to the controls and also write the code to navigate between records. This section takes a look at what is involved in binding data to simple controls and also how to manage the data bindings.

In this discussion, the term *simple controls* refers to controls that can display only one item of data at a time, such as TextBox, a Button, a CheckBox, or a RadioCheck. Controls such as ComboBox, ListBox, and DataGridView can contain more than one item of data and are not considered simple controls when it comes to data binding. Generally speaking, nonsimple controls have particular properties intended for binding to a data object such as a `DataTable` or `Array`. When binding to simple controls, you are actually binding a particular item of data to a particular property. This is usually the Text property, but it does not need to be.

BindingContext and CurrencyManager

Each form has a built-in `BindingContext` object that, which manages the bindings of the controls on the form. Since the `BindingContext` object is already built into each form, you don't need to do anything to set it up.

The `BindingContext` object manages a collection of `CurrencyManager` objects. The `CurrencyManager` is responsible for keeping the data-bound controls in sync with its data source and with other data-bound controls that use the same data source. This ensures that all controls on the form are showing data from the same record. The `CurrencyManager` manages data from a variety of objects such as `DataSet`, `DataView`, `DataTable`, and `DataSetView`. Whenever you add a data source to a form, a new `CurrencyManager` is automatically created. This makes working with data-bound controls very convenient and simple.

> The `CurrencyManager` gets its name because it keeps the controls current with respect to the data in the data source. The controls do not have to represent currency (money) amounts.

If you have multiple data sources in your form, you can declare a `CurrencyManager` variable and set it to refer to the appropriate `CurrencyManager` object for a given data source in the collection managed by the `BindingContext` object. You then have the capability to manage the data in the data-bound controls explicitly.

The following code fragment, using the `DataSet` object that you have been using in the previous example, defines and sets a reference to the `CurrencyManager` that manages the data source that contains the local `authors` table. First, the code declares a variable using the `CurrencyManager` class. Then it sets this `CurrencyManager` variable to the currency manager for the `DataSet` object (`objDataSet`) contained in the `BindingContext` object. The `CType` function is used to return an object that is explicitly converted. The `CType` function accepts two arguments: the expression to be converted and the type to which the expression is to be converted. Since the expression is to evaluate to a `CurrencyManager` object, `CurrencyManager` is specified for the type argument:

```
Dim objCurrencyManager As CurrencyManager
objCurrencyManager = _
    CType(Me.BindingContext(objDataSet), CurrencyManager)
```

After you have a reference to the data source object, you can manage the position of the records using the `Position` property, as shown in the following example. This example advances the current record position in the `objDataSet` object by one record:

```
objCurrencyManager.Position += 1
```

If you wanted to move backward one record, you would use the following code:

```
objCurrencyManager.Position -= 1
```

To move to the first record contained in the `DataSet` object, you would use the following code:

```
objCurrencyManager.Position = 0
```

The `Count` property of the `CurrencyManager` contains the number of records in the `DataSet` object managed by the `CurrencyManager`. Therefore, to move to the very last record, you would use the following code:

```
objCurrencyManager.Position = objCurrencyManager.Count - 1
```

Notice that this code specified the `Count` value minus one. Since the `Count` property contains the actual number of records and the `DataSet` object has a base index of zero, you must subtract one from the `Count` value to get the index to the last record.

Binding Controls

When you want to bind a data source to a control, you set the `DataBindings` property for that control. This property accesses the `ControlBindingsCollection` class. This class manages the bindings for each control, and it has many properties and methods. The method of interest here is `Add`.

The `Add` method creates a binding for the control and adds it to the `ControlBindingsCollection`. The `Add` method has three arguments, and its syntax is shown here:

```
object.DataBindings.Add(propertyname, datasource, datamember)
```

In this syntax, note the following:

- ❑ *object* represents a valid control on your form.
- ❑ The *propertyname* argument represents the property of the control to be bound.
- ❑ The *datasource* argument represents the data source to be bound and can be any valid object, such as a `DataSet`, `DataView`, or `DataTable`, that contains data.
- ❑ The *datamember* argument represents the data field in the data source to be bound to this control.

An example of how the `Add` method works is shown in the following code. This example binds the column name au_fname in the `objDataView` object to the `Text` property of a text box named txt FirstName:

```
txtFirstName.DataBindings.Add("Text", objDataView, "au_fname")
```

Sometimes, after a control has been bound, you may want to change the bindings for that control. To do this, you can use the `Clear` method of the `ControlBindingsCollection`. The `Clear` method clears the collection of all bindings for this control. Then you can make the change you need. An example of this method is shown in the following code fragment:

```
txtFirstName.DataBindings.Clear()
```

Now that you have had a look at the `BindingContext`, `CurrencyManager`, and `ControlBindingsCollection` objects, learn how all of these pieces fit and work together in a practical hands-on exercise.

Binding Example

The following Try It Out will demonstrate not only how to use the `BindingContext`, `Currency Manager` and `ControlBindingsCollection` objects but also how to use the `DataView`, `SqlCommand`, and `SqlParameter` classes.

> *You will be using the query from the previous example as the base for your new query and will display all authors' first and last names, as well as their book titles and the prices of their books. However, this example differs from the last one in that this will display only one record at a time.*

You will use the `CurrencyManager` object to navigate the records in the `DataView` object and provide the functionality to move forward and backward as well as to the first and last records.

Try It Out   Binding Simple Controls

1. Create a new Windows Application project called **BindingExample**.

2. Drag a ToolTip control from the toolbox and drop it on your form to add it to the designer. Set the various form properties as follows:

   ❑ Set FormBorderStyle to **FixedDialog**.

   ❑ Set MaximizeBox to **False**.

   ❑ Set MinimizeBox to **False**.

   ❑ Set Size to **430, 360**.

   ❑ Set StartPosition to **CenterScreen**.

   ❑ Set Text to **Binding Controls**.

3. You are going to add objects to the form, so that the form ends up looking like Figure 16-6.

   The steps that follow provide property settings to produce an exact replica of this form. However, the "cosmetic" properties are not as important; if you wish, you can approximate the layout visually. It is crucial, however, to use the same control names as those used here in your own application.

4. Add a GroupBox control to the form. Set the GroupBox1 properties according to the following list:

   ❑ Set Location to **8, 8**.

   ❑ Set Size to **408, 128**.

   ❑ Set Text to **Authors && Titles**.

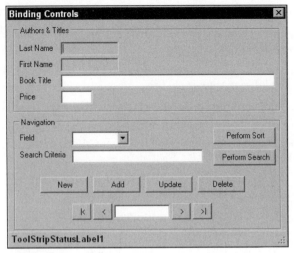

Figure 16-6

Note that to have an ampersand (&) displayed in the GroupBox *title you have to write* && *because a single & causes the character following it to be underlined.*

5. Using this list, add the required controls to GroupBox1 and set their properties:

❏ Add a Label control. Name it **Label1** and set its Location to **8, 26**; Size to **64, 16**; Text to **Last Name**; AutoSize to **False**.

❏ Add a Label control. Name it **Label2** and set Location to **8, 50**; Size to **64, 16**; Text to **First Name**; AutoSize to **False**.

❏ Add a Label contol. Name it **Label3** and set Location to **8, 74**; Size to **56, 16**; Text to **Book Title**; AutoSize to **False**.

❏ Add a Label control. Name it **Label4** and set Location to **8, 98**; Size to **64, 16**; Text to **Price**; AutoSize to **False**.

❏ Add a TextBox control. Name it **txtLastName** and set Location to **72, 24**; Size to **88, 20**; ReadOnly to **True**.

❏ Add a TextBox control. Name it **txtFirstName** and set Location to **72, 48**; Size to **88, 20**; ReadOnly to **True**.

❏ Add a TextBox control. Name it **txtBookTitle** and set Location to **72, 72**; Size to **328, 20**.

❏ Add a TextBox control. Name it **txtPrice** and set Location to **72, 96**; Size to **48, 20**.

6. Now add a second GroupBox and set its properties according to this list:

❏ Set Location to **8, 144**.

❏ Set Size to **408, 168**.

❏ Set Text to **Navigation**.

7. In GroupBox2, add the following controls:

- ❑ Add a Label control. Name it **Label5** and set Location to **8, 23**; Size to **64, 16**; Text to **Field**; AutoSize to False.

- ❑ Add a Label control. Name it **Label6** and set Location to **8, 48**; Size to **80, 16**; Text to **Search Criteria**; AutoSize to False.

- ❑ Add a ComboBox control. Name it **cboField** and set Location to **88, 21**; Size to **88, 21**; DropDownStyle to **DropDownList**.

- ❑ Add a TextBox control. Name it **txtSearchCriteria** and set Location to **88, 48**; Size to **200, 20**.

- ❑ Add a TextBox control. Name it **txtRecordPosition** and set Location to **152, 130**; Size to **85, 20**; TabStop to **False**; TextAlign to **Center**.

- ❑ Add a Button control. Name it **btnPerformSort** and set Location to **304, 16**; Size to **96, 24**; Text to **Perform Sort**.

- ❑ Add a Button control. Name it **btnPerformSearch** and set Location to **304, 48**; Size to **96, 24**; Text to **Perform Search**.

- ❑ Add a Button control. Name it **btnNew** and set Location to **40, 88**; Size to **72, 24**; Text to **New**.

- ❑ Add a Button control. Name it **btnAdd** and set Location to **120, 88**; Size to **72, 24**; Text to **Add**.

- ❑ Add a Button control. Name it **btnUpdate** and set Location to **200, 88**; Size to **72, 24**; Text to **Update**.

- ❑ Add a Button control. Name it **btnDelete** and set Location to **280, 88**; Size to **72, 24**; Text to **Delete**.

- ❑ Add a Button control. Name it **btnMoveFirst** and set Location to **88, 128**; Size to **29, 24**; Text to **|<**; ToolTip on ToolTip1 to **Move First**.

- ❑ Add a Button control. Name it **btnMovePrevious** and set Location to **120, 128**; Size to **29, 24**; Text to **<**; ToolTip on ToolTip1 to **Move Previous**.

- ❑ Add a Button control. Name it **btnMoveNext** and set Location to **240, 128**; Size to **29, 24**; Text to **>**; ToolTip on ToolTip1 to **Move Next**.

- ❑ Add a Button control. Name it **btnMoveLast** and set Location to **272, 128**; Size to **29, 24**; Text to **>|**; ToolTip on ToolTip1 to **Move Last**.

8. Finally, add a StatusStrip control. Leave its name as the default StatusStrip1, and its default location and size. Click the new StatusStrip1, and you will have an option to add a StatusLabel control in the menu. Select StatusLabel from the menu and leave the default settings.

9. When you are done, your completed form should look like the one shown in Figure 16-6.

10. Again, you need to add imports to the namespaces needed. First, remember to add references to System.Data and System.Xml. To do this, switch to Code Editor view and then insert the following lines of code at the very top:

```
' Import Data and SqlClient namespaces...
Imports System.Data
Imports System.Data.SqlClient
```

11. Next you need to declare the objects that are global in scope to this form, so add the following highlighted code:

```
Public Class Form1
    ' Declare objects...
    Dim objConnection As New SqlConnection _
        ("server=bnewsome;database=pubs;user id=sa;password=!p@ssw0rd!;")
    Dim objDataAdapter As New SqlDataAdapter( _
        "SELECT authors.au_id, au_lname, au_fname, " & _
        "titles.title_id, title, price " & _
        "FROM authors " & _
        "JOIN titleauthor ON authors.au_id = titleauthor.au_id " & _
        "JOIN titles ON titleauthor.title_id = titles.title_id " & _
        "ORDER BY au_lname, au_fname", objConnection)
    Dim objDataSet As DataSet
    Dim objDataView As DataView
    Dim objCurrencyManager As CurrencyManager
```

Be sure to update the connection string to match your settings for the user id and password, and also set the Server to the machine where SQL Server is running if it is not your local machine.

12. The first procedure you need to create is the `FillDataSetAndView` procedure. This procedure, along with the following ones, will be called in your initialization code. Add the following code to the form's class, just below your object declarations:

```
Private Sub FillDataSetAndView()
    ' Initialize a new instance of the DataSet object...
    objDataSet = New DataSet()

    ' Fill the DataSet object with data...
    objDataAdapter.Fill(objDataSet, "authors")

    ' Set the DataView object to the DataSet object...
    objDataView = New DataView(objDataSet.Tables("authors"))

    ' Set our CurrencyManager object to the DataView object...
    objCurrencyManager = CType(Me.BindingContext(objDataView), CurrencyManager)
End Sub
```

13. The next procedure you need to create will actually bind the controls on your form to your `DataView` object:

```
Private Sub BindFields()
    ' Clear any previous bindings...
    txtLastName.DataBindings.Clear()
    txtFirstName.DataBindings.Clear()
    txtBookTitle.DataBindings.Clear()
    txtPrice.DataBindings.Clear()

    ' Add new bindings to the DataView object...
    txtLastName.DataBindings.Add("Text", objDataView, "au_lname")
    txtFirstName.DataBindings.Add("Text", objDataView, "au_fname")
    txtBookTitle.DataBindings.Add("Text", objDataView, "title")
    txtPrice.DataBindings.Add("Text", objDataView, "price")

    ' Display a ready status...
```

```
    ToolStripStatusLabel1.Text = "Ready"
End Sub
```

14. Now you need a procedure that will display the current record position on your form:

```
Private Sub ShowPosition()
    'Always format the number in the txtPrice field to include cents
    Try
        txtPrice.Text = Format(CType(txtPrice.Text, Decimal), "##0.00")
        Catch e As System.Exception
            txtPrice.Text = "0"
        txtPrice.Text = Format(CType(txtPrice.Text, Decimal), "##0.00")
    End Try
    ' Display the current position and the number of records
    txtRecordPosition.Text = objCurrencyManager.Position + 1 & _
    " of " & objCurrencyManager.Count()
End Sub
```

15. You've added some powerful procedures to your form. But at the moment, there is no code to call them. You want these procedures, as well as some other code, to execute every time the form loads. So return to the Form Designer, double-click the Form Designer, and add the following highlighted code to the `Form_Load` method. (Note that you must click an area outside of the GroupBox controls.)

```
Private Sub Form1_Load(ByVal sender As System.Object, _
                        ByVal e As System.EventArgs) Handles MyBase.Load
    ' Add items to the combo box...
    cboField.Items.Add("Last Name")
    cboField.Items.Add("First Name")
    cboField.Items.Add("Book Title")
    cboField.Items.Add("Price")

    ' Make the first item selected...
    cboField.SelectedIndex = 0

    ' Fill the DataSet and bind the fields...
    FillDataSetAndView()
    BindFields()

    ' Show the current record position...
    ShowPosition()
End Sub
```

16. Next, you add the code for your navigation buttons. You need to switch back and forth between the design and code views, double-clicking each button and then adding the code, or you can select the buttons in the Class Name combo box and then select the Click event in the Method Name combo box. Add the code as highlighted to the procedure for the btnMoveFirst button first:

```
Private Sub btnMoveFirst_Click(ByVal sender As Object, _
            ByVal e As System.EventArgs) Handles btnMoveFirst.Click
    ' Set the record position to the first record...
    objCurrencyManager.Position = 0
```

```
      ' Show the current record position...
      ShowPosition()
   End Sub
```

17. Add code as highlighted to the btnMovePrevious button next:

```
Private Sub btnMovePrevious_Click(ByVal sender As Object, _
         ByVal e As System.EventArgs) Handles btnMovePrevious.Click
      ' Move to the previous record...
      objCurrencyManager.Position -= 1

      ' Show the current record position...
      ShowPosition()
   End Sub
```

18. The next procedure you want to add code to is the btnMoveNext procedure:

```
Private Sub btnMoveNext_Click(ByVal sender As Object, _
         ByVal e As System.EventArgs) Handles btnMoveNext.Click
      ' Move to the next record...
      objCurrencyManager.Position += 1

      ' Show the current record position...
      ShowPosition()
   End Sub
```

19. The final navigation procedure that you need to code is the btnMoveLast procedure:

```
Private Sub btnMoveLast_Click(ByVal sender As Object, _
         ByVal e As System.EventArgs) Handles btnMoveLast.Click
      ' Set the record position to the last record...
      objCurrencyManager.Position = objCurrencyManager.Count - 1

      ' Show the current record position...
      ShowPosition()
   End Sub
```

20. At this point, you have entered a lot of code and are probably anxious to see the results of your work. Run the project to see how your `DataView` object gets bound to the controls on the form and to see the `CurrencyManager` object at work as you navigate through the records.

After your form displays, you should see results similar to Figure 16-7. The only buttons that work are the navigation buttons, which change the current record position. Test your form by navigating to the next and previous records and by moving to the last record and the first record. Each time you move to a new record, the text box between the navigation buttons will be updated to display the current record.

While you are on the first record, you can try to move to the previous record, but nothing will happen, because you are already on the first record. Likewise, you can move to the last record and try to navigate to the next record, and nothing will happen, because you are already on the last record.

If you hover your mouse pointer over the navigation buttons, you will see a ToolTip indicating what each button is for. This just provides a nicer interface for your users.

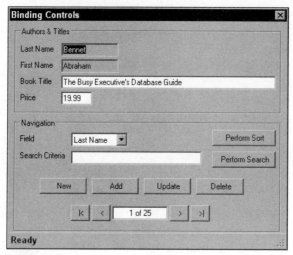

Figure 16-7

Note that error handling has been omitted from the exercise to preserve space. You should always add the appropriate error handling to your code. Please review Chapter 9 for error-handling techniques.

How It Works: Namespaces and Object Declaration

As usual, you import the `System.Data` and `System.Data.SqlClient` namespaces. Next, you declare the objects on your form. The first three objects should be familiar to you, because you used them in your last project.

Take a closer look at the initialization of the `SqlDataAdapter` object. You use a constructor that initializes this object with a string value for the `SelectCommand` property and an object that represents a connection to the database. This constructor saves you from writing code to manipulate the `SqlData Adapter` properties; it's already set up.

The `SELECT` statement that you use here is basically the same as in the previous project, except that you add a couple more columns in the *select list* (the list of columns directly following the word `SELECT`).

The `au_id` column in the select list is prefixed with the table name `authors`, because this column also exists in the `titleauthor` table. Therefore, you must tell the database which table to get the data from for this column. This is the same for the `title_id` column, except that this column exists in the `titles` and `titleauthor` tables:

```
Dim objConnection As New SqlConnection _
    ("server=bnewsome;database=pubs;user id=sa;password=!p@ssw0rd!;")
Dim objDataAdapter As New SqlDataAdapter( _
    "SELECT authors.au_id, au_lname, au_fname, " & _
    "titles.title_id, title, price " & _
    "FROM authors " & _
    "JOIN titleauthor ON authors.au_id = titleauthor.au_id " & _
    "JOIN titles ON titleauthor.title_id = titles.title_id " & _
    "ORDER BY au_lname, au_fname", objConnection)
```

```
Dim objDataSet As DataSet
Dim objDataView As DataView
Dim objCurrencyManager As CurrencyManager
```

The last two objects are new but were discussed in the section on binding. You use the `DataView` to customize your view of the records returned from the database, and stored in the dataset. The `Currency Manager` object controls the movement of your bound data, as you saw in the previous section.

How It Works: FillDataSetAndView

The first procedure you create is the `FillDataSetAndView` procedure. This procedure will be called several times throughout your code and will get the latest data from the database and populate your `DataView` object.

The first thing you need to do is initialize a new instance of the `DataSet` object. You do this here because this procedure might be called more than once during the lifetime of the form. If it is, you do not want to add new records to the records already in the dataset; you always want to start afresh:

```
Private Sub FillDataSetAndView()
    ' Initialize a new instance of the DataSet object...
    objDataSet = New DataSet()
```

Next, you invoke the `Fill` method on `objDataAdapter` to populate the `objDataSet` object. Then you specify that your `DataView` object will be viewing data from the `authors` table in the `DataSet` object. Remember that the `DataView` object allows you to sort, search, and navigate through the records in the dataset:

```
    ' Fill the DataSet object with data...
    objDataAdapter.Fill(objDataSet, "authors")

    ' Set the DataView object to the DataSet object...
    objDataView = New DataView(objDataSet.Tables("authors"))
```

After you initialize your `DataView` object, you want to initialize the `CurrencyManager` object. Remember that the `BindingContext` object is built into every Windows form and contains a collection of `CurrencyManagers`. The collection contains the available data sources, and you choose the `DataView` object:

```
    ' Set our CurrencyManager object to the DataView object...
    objCurrencyManager = _
        CType(Me.BindingContext(objDataView), CurrencyManager)
```

How It Works: BindFields

The next procedure that you create (`BindFields`) actually binds the controls on your form to your `DataView` object. This procedure first clears any previous bindings for the controls and then sets them to your `DataView` object.

> It is important to clear the bindings first because, after you modify the `DataView` object by adding, updating, or deleting a row of data, the `DataView` object will show only the changed data. Therefore, after you update the database with your changes, you must repopulate our `DataView` object and rebind your controls. If you didn't do this, the data that would actually be in the database and the data in the `DataView` may not be the same.

Using the `DataBindings` property of the controls on you form, you execute the `Clear` method of the `ControlBindingsCollection` class to remove the bindings from them. Notice that the controls that you bound are all the text boxes on your form that will contain data from the `DataView` object:

```
Private Sub BindFields()
    ' Clear any previous bindings to the DataView object...
    txtLastName.DataBindings.Clear()
    txtFirstName.DataBindings.Clear()
    txtBookTitle.DataBindings.Clear()
    txtPrice.DataBindings.Clear()
```

After you clear the previous bindings, you can set the new bindings back to the same data source, our `DataView` object. You do this by executing the `Add` method of the `ControlBindingsCollection` object returned by the `DataBindings` property. As described earlier, the `Add` method has three arguments, which are shown in the code that follows:

❑ The first argument is *propertyname* and specifies the property of the control to be bound. Since you want to bind your data to the `Text` property of the text boxes, you have specified `"Text"` for this argument.

❑ The next argument is the *datasource* argument and specifies the data source to be bound. Remember that this can be any valid object, such as a `DataSet`, `DataView`, or `DataTable`, that contains data. In this case, you are using a `DataView` object.

❑ The last argument specifies the *datamember*. This is the data field in the data source that contains the data to be bound to this control. Notice that you have specified the various column names from your `SELECT` statement that you executed in the previous procedure.

```
    ' Add new bindings to the DataView object...
    txtLastName.DataBindings.Add("Text", objDataView, "au_lname")
    txtFirstName.DataBindings.Add("Text", objDataView, "au_fname")
    txtBookTitle.DataBindings.Add("Text", objDataView, "title")
    txtPrice.DataBindings.Add("Text", objDataView, "price")
```

The last thing you did in this procedure was set a message in the status bar using the `Text` property of `ToolStripStatusLabel1`:

```
    ' Display a ready status...
    ToolStripStatusLabel1.Text = "Ready"
End Sub
```

How It Works: ShowPosition

The `CurrencyManager` object keeps track of the current record position within the `DataView` object.

The price column in the titles table in pubs is defined as a `Currency` data type. Therefore, if a book is priced at 40.00 dollars, the number that you get is 40; the decimal portion is dropped. The `ShowPosition` procedure seems like a good place to format the data in the `txtPrice` text box, because this procedure is called whenever you move to a new record:

```
Private Sub ShowPosition()
'Always format the number in the txtPrice field to include cents
    Try
```

```
        txtPrice.Text = Format(CType(txtPrice.Text, Decimal), "##0.00")
    Catch e As System.Exception
        txtPrice.Text = "0"
        txtPrice.Text = Format(CType(txtPrice.Text, Decimal), "##0.00")
    End Try

    ' Display the current position and the number of records
    txtRecordPosition.Text = objCurrencyManager.Position + 1 & _
                                " of " & objCurrencyManager.Count()
End Sub
```

This part of the function is enclosed in a `Try` ... `Catch` block in case the `txtPrice` is empty. If `txt Price` is empty, the `Format` function throws a handled exception, and the exception handler defaults the price to 0. The second line of code in this procedure uses the `Format` function to format the price in the `txtPrice` text box. This function accepts the numeric data to be formatted as the first argument and a format string as the second argument. For the format function to work correctly, you need to convert the string value in the `txtPrice` field to a decimal value using the `CType` function.

The last line of code displays the current record position and the total number of records that you have. Using the `Position` property of the `CurrencyManager` object, you can determine which record you are on. The `Position` property uses a zero-based index, so the first record is always 0. Therefore, you specified the `Position` property plus 1 to display the true number.

The `CurrencyManager` class's `Count` property returns the actual number of items in the list, and you are using this property to display the total number of records in the `DataView` object.

How It Works: Form_Load

Now that you've looked at the code for the main procedures, you need to go back and look at your initialization code.

You have a combo box on your form that will be used when sorting or searching for data. This combo box needs be populated with data representing the columns in the `DataView` object. You specify the `Add` method of the `Items` property of the combo box to add items to it. Here you are specifying text that represents the columns in the `DataView` object in the same order that they appear in the `DataView` object:

```
'Add any initialization after the InitializeComponent() call

' Add items to the combo box...
cboField.Items.Add("Last Name")
cboField.Items.Add("First Name")
cboField.Items.Add("Book Title")
cboField.Items.Add("Price")
```

After you have loaded all of the items into your combo box, you want to select the first item. You do this by setting the `SelectedIndex` property to 0. The `SelectedIndex` property is zero-based, so the first item in the list is item 0.

```
' Make the first item selected...
cboField.SelectedIndex = 0
```

Next, you call the `FillDataSetAndView` procedure to retrieve the data, and then call the `BindFields` procedure to bind the controls on your form to your `DataView` object. Finally, you call the `ShowPosition` procedure to display the current record position and the total number of records contained in your `DataView` object:

```
' Fill the DataSet and bind the fields...
FillDataSetAndView()
BindFields()

' Show the current record position...
ShowPosition()
```

How It Works: Navigation Buttons

The procedure for the btnMoveFirst button causes the first record in the `DataView` object to be displayed. This is accomplished using the `Position` property of the `CurrencyManager` object. Here you set the `Position` property to 0, indicating that the `CurrencyManager` should move to the first record:

```
' Set the record position to the first record...
objCurrencyManager.Position = 0
```

Because your controls are bound to the `DataView` object, they will always stay in sync with the current record in the `DataView` object and display the appropriate data.

After you reposition the current record, you need to call the `ShowPosition` procedure to update the display of the current record on your form:

```
' Show the current record position...
ShowPosition()
```

Next, you add the code for the btnMovePrevious button. You move to the prior record by subtracting 1 from the `Position` property. The `CurrencyManager` object will automatically detect and handle the beginning position of the `DataView` object. It will not let you move to a position prior to the first record; it will just quietly keep its position at 0:

```
' Move to the previous record...
objCurrencyManager.Position -= 1
```

Again, after you have repositioned the current record being displayed, you need to call the `ShowPosition` procedure to display the current position on the form.

In the btnMoveNext procedure, you want to increment the `Position` property by 1. Again, the `Currency Manager` will automatically detect the last record in the `DataView` object and will not let you move past it:

```
' Move to the next record...
objCurrencyManager.Position += 1
```

You call the `ShowPosition` procedure to display the current record position.

When the btnMoveLast procedure is called, you want to move to the last record in the `DataView` object. You do accomplish this by setting the `Position` property equal to the `Count` property minus one. Then you call the `ShowPosition` procedure to display the current record:

```
' Set the record position to the last record...
objCurrencyManager.Position = objCurrencyManager.Count - 1

' Show the current record position...
ShowPosition()
```

Now that you have built the navigation, you move on to add sorting functionality to this project in the next Try It Out.

Try It Out   Including Sorting Functionality

1.   Double-click the Perform Sort button on the form in design mode to have the empty procedure added to the form class, or select the button in the Class Name combo box and then select the Click event in the Method Name combo box. Insert the following highlighted code in the btnPerformSort_Click event procedure:

```
Private Sub btnPerformSort_Click(ByVal sender As Object, _
        ByVal e As System.EventArgs) Handles btnPerformSort.Click
    ' Determine the appropriate item selected and set the
    ' Sort property of the DataView object...
    Select Case cboField.SelectedIndex
        Case 0  'Last Name
            objDataView.Sort = "au_lname"
        Case 1  'First Name
            objDataView.Sort = "au_fname"
        Case 2  'Book Title
            objDataView.Sort = "title"
        Case 3  'Price
            objDataView.Sort = "price"
    End Select

    ' Call the click event for the MoveFirst button...
    btnMoveFirst_Click(Nothing, Nothing)

    ' Display a message that the records have been sorted...
    ToolStripStatusLabel1.Text = "Records Sorted"
End Sub
```

2.   Test out this newest functionality that you have added to your project by running it; click the Start button to compile and run it. Select a column to sort and then click the Perform Sort button. You should see the data sorted by the column that you have chosen. Figure 16-8 shows the data sorted by book price:

How It Works

The first thing you do in this procedure is determine which field you should sort on. This information is contained in the cboField combo box.

```
    ' Determine the appropriate item selected and set the
    ' Sort property of the DataView object...
    Select Case cboField.SelectedIndex
        Case 0  'Last Name
            objDataView.Sort = "au_lname"
        Case 1  'First Name
```

```
            objDataView.Sort = "au_fname"
        Case 2  'Book Title
            objDataView.Sort = "title"
        Case 3  'Price
            objDataView.Sort = "price"
    End Select
```

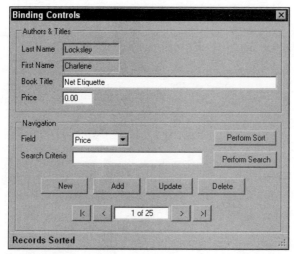

Figure 16-8

Using a `Select Case` statement to examine the `SelectedIndex` property of the combo box, you can determine which field the user has chosen. After you have determined the correct entry in the combo box, you can set the `Sort` property of the `DataView` object using the column name of the column that you want sorted. After the `Sort` property has been set, the data will be sorted.

After the data has been sorted, you want to move to the first record, and there are a couple of ways you can do this. You could set the `Position` property of the `CurrencyManager` object and then call the `ShowPosition` procedure, or you can simply call the `btnMoveFirst_Click` procedure, passing it `Nothing` for both arguments. This is the procedure that would be executed had you actually clicked the Move First button on the form.

The `btnMoveFirst_Click` procedure has two arguments: `ByVal sender As Object` and `ByVal e As System.EventArgs`. Since these arguments are required (even though they're not actually used in the procedure), you need to pass something to them, so you pass the `Nothing` keyword. The `Nothing` keyword is used to disassociate an object variable from an object. Thus by using the `Nothing` keyword, you satisfy the requirement of passing an argument to the procedure, but have not passed any actual value:

```
' Call the click event for the MoveFirst button...
btnMoveFirst_Click(Nothing, Nothing)
```

After the first record has been displayed, you want to display a message in the status bar indicating that the records have been sorted. You did this by setting the `Text` property of the status bar as you have done before.

Note that another way would have been to have had a procedure called MoveFirst, and to have called that from here *and* from the btnMoveFirst_Click procedure. Some developers would opt for this instead of having to pass Nothing to a procedure.

In the next Try It Out, you take a look at what's involved in searching for a record.

Including Searching Functionality

1. Double-click the Perform Search button or select the button in the Class Name combo box and then select the Click event in the Method Name combo box, and add the following highlighted code to the btnPerformSearch_Click event procedure:

```
Private Sub btnPerformSearch_Click(ByVal sender As Object, _
    ByVal e As System.EventArgs) Handles btnPerformSearch.Click
    ' Declare local variables...
    Dim intPosition As Integer

    ' Determine the appropriate item selected and set the
    ' Sort property of the DataView object...
    Select Case cboField.SelectedIndex
        Case 0   'Last Name
            objDataView.Sort = "au_lname"
        Case 1   'First Name
            objDataView.Sort = "au_fname"
        Case 2   'Book Title
            objDataView.Sort = "title"
        Case 3   'Price
            objDataView.Sort = "price"
    End Select

    ' If the search field is not price then...
    If cboField.SelectedIndex < 3 Then
        ' Find the last name, first name, or title...
        intPosition = objDataView.Find(txtSearchCriteria.Text)
    Else
        ' otherwise find the price...
        intPosition = objDataView.Find(CType(txtSearchCriteria.Text, Decimal))
    End If
    If intPosition = -1 Then
        ' Display a message that the record was not found...
        ToolStripStatusLabel1.Text = "Record Not Found"
    Else
        ' Otherwise display a message that the record was
        ' found and reposition the CurrencyManager to that
        ' record...
        ToolStripStatusLabel1.Text = "Record Found"
        objCurrencyManager.Position = intPosition
    End If

    ' Show the current record position...
    ShowPosition()
End Sub
```

2. Test the searching functionality that you added. Run the project and select a field in the Field combo box that you want to search on, and then enter the search criteria in the Search Criteria textbox. Finally, click the Perform Search button.

If a match is found, you see the first matched record displayed, along with a message in the status bar indicating that the record was found, as shown in Figure 16-9. If no record was found, you see a message in the status bar indicating the record was not found.

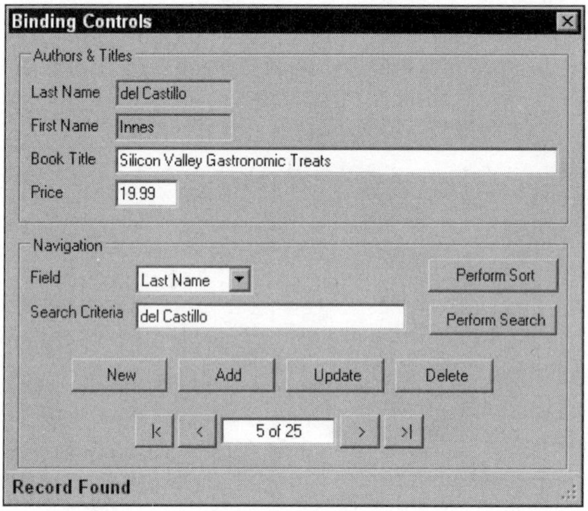

Figure 16-9

How It Works

This is a little more involved than previous Try It Outs, because there are multiple conditions that you must test for and handle, such as a record that was not found. The first thing that you do in this procedure is to declare a variable that will receive the record position of the record that has been found or not found.

```
' Declare local variables...
Dim intPosition As Integer
```

Next, you sort the data based on the column used in the search. The Find method will search for data in the sort key. Therefore, by setting the Sort property, the column that is sorted on becomes the sort key in the DataView object. You use a Select Case statement, just as you did in the previous procedure:

```
' Determine the appropriate item selected and set the
' Sort property of the DataView object...
Select Case cboField.SelectedIndex
    Case 0  'Last Name
        objDataView.Sort = "au_lname"
    Case 1  'First Name
        objDataView.Sort = "au_fname"
    Case 2  'Book Title
        objDataView.Sort = "title"
    Case 3  'Price
        objDataView.Sort = "price"
End Select
```

The columns for the authors' first and last names, as well as the column for the book titles, all contain text data. However, the column for the book price contains data that is in a currency format. Therefore, you need to determine which column you are searching on, and if that column is the price column, you need to format the data in the `txtSearchCriteria` text box to a decimal value.

Again, you use the `SelectedIndex` property of the `cboField` combo box to determine which item has been selected. If the `SelectedIndex` property is less than 3, you know that you want to search on a column that contains text data.

You then set the `intPosition` variable to the results returned by the `Find` method of the `DataView` object. The `Find` method accepts the data to search for as the only argument. Here you pass it the data contained in the `Text` property of the `txtSearchCriteria` text box.

If the `SelectedIndex` equals 3, you are searching for a book with a specific price, and this requires you to convert the value contained in the `txtSearchCriteria` text box to a decimal value. The `CType` function accepts an expression and the data type that you want to convert that expression to and returns a value, in this case a decimal value. This value is then used as the search criterion by the `Find` method.

```
' If the search field is not price then...
If cboField.SelectedIndex < 3 Then
    ' Find the last name, first name or title...
    intPosition = objDataView.Find(txtSearchCriteria.Text)
Else
    ' otherwise find the price...
    intPosition = objDataView.Find(CType(txtSearchCriteria.Text, Decimal))
End If
```

After you have executed the `Find` method of the `DataView` object, you need to check the value contained in the `intPosition` variable. If this variable contains a value of –1, no match was found. Any value other than –1 points to the record position of the record that contains the data. So, if the value in this variable is –1, you want to display a message in the status bar that says that no record was found. If the value is greater than –1, you want to display a message that the record was found and position the `DataView` object to that record using the `Position` property of the `CurrencyManager` object:

```
ToolStripStatusLabel1.Text = "Record Found"
objCurrencyManager.Position = intPosition
```

It is worth noting that the `Find` method of the `DataView` object performs a search looking for an exact match of characters. There is no "wildcard" search method here, so you must enter the entire text string that you want to search for. The case, however, does not matter, so the name `Ann` is the same as `ann`, and you do not need to be concerned with entering proper case when you enter your search criteria.

The last thing that you want to do in this procedure is to show the current record position, which you do by calling the `ShowPosition` procedure.

Now all that is left is to add the functionality to add, update, and delete records. Take a look at what is required to add a record first.

Try It Out   **Adding Records**

1.   First, you need to add just two lines of code to the `btnNew_Click` procedure:

```
Private Sub btnNew_Click(ByVal sender As Object, _
            ByVal e As System.EventArgs) Handles btnNew.Click
    ' Clear the book title and price fields...
    txtBookTitle.Text = ""
    txtPrice.Text = ""
End Sub
```

2.   The next procedure that you want to add code to is the `btnAdd_Click` procedure. This procedure is responsible for adding a new record. This procedure has the largest amount of code by
far of any of the procedures you have coded or will code in this project. The reason for this is
the relationship of book titles to authors and the primary key used for book titles:

```
Private Sub btnAdd_Click(ByVal sender As Object, _
            ByVal e As System.EventArgs) Handles btnAdd.Click
    ' Declare local variables and objects...
    Dim intPosition As Integer, intMaxID As Integer
    Dim strID As String
    Dim objCommand As SqlCommand = New SqlCommand()

    ' Save the current record position...
    intPosition = objCurrencyManager.Position
    ' Create a new SqlCommand object...
    Dim maxIdCommand As SqlCommand = New SqlCommand _
        ("SELECT MAX(title_id) AS MaxID " & _
         "FROM titles WHERE title_id LIKE 'DM%'", objConnection)

    ' Open the connection, execute the command
    objConnection.Open()
    Dim maxId As Object = maxIdCommand.ExecuteScalar()

    ' If the MaxID column is null...
    If maxId Is DBNull.Value Then
        ' Set a default value of 1000...
        intMaxID = 1000
    Else
        ' otherwise set the strID variable to the value in MaxID...
        strID = CType(maxId, String)
        ' Get the integer part of the string...
        intMaxID = CType(strID.Remove(0, 2), Integer)
        ' Increment the value...
        intMaxID += 1
    End If

    ' Finally, set the new ID...
    strID = "DM" & intMaxID.ToString

    ' Set the SqlCommand object properties...
    objCommand.Connection = objConnection
    objCommand.CommandText = "INSERT INTO titles " & _
        "(title_id, title, type, price, pubdate) " & _
```

```
                "VALUES(@title_id,@title,@type,@price,@pubdate);" & _
                "INSERT INTO titleauthor (au_id, title_id) VALUES(@au_id,@title_id)"

        ' Add parameters for the placeholders in the SQL in the
        ' CommandText property...

        ' Parameter for the title_id column...
        objCommand.Parameters.AddWithValue ("@title_id", strID)

        ' Parameter for the title column...
        objCommand.Parameters.AddWithValue ("@title", txtBookTitle.Text)

        ' Parameter for the type column
        objCommand.Parameters.AddWithValue ("@type", "Demo")
        ' Parameter for the price column...
        objCommand.Parameters.AddWithValue ("@price", txtPrice.Text).DbType _
                                = DbType.Currency

        ' Parameter for the pubdate column
        objCommand.Parameters.AddWithValue ("@pubdate", Date.Now)

        ' Parameter for the au_id column...
        objCommand.Parameters.AddWithValue _
                    ("@au_id", BindingContext(objDataView).Current("au_id"))

        ' Execute the SqlCommand object to insert the new data...
        Try
            objCommand.ExecuteNonQuery()
        Catch SqlExceptionErr As SqlException
            MessageBox.Show(SqlExceptionErr.Message)
        End Try

        ' Close the connection...
        objConnection.Close()

        ' Fill the dataset and bind the fields...
        FillDataSetAndView()
        BindFields()

        ' Set the record position to the one that you saved...
        objCurrencyManager.Position = intPosition

        ' Show the current record position...
        ShowPosition()

        ' Display a message that the record was added...
        ToolStripStatusLabel1.Text = "Record Added"
    End Sub
```

3. Run your project. Find an author that you want to add a new title for and then click the New button. The Book Title and Price fields will be cleared, and you are ready to enter new data to be added as shown in Figure 16-10. Take note of the number of records in the DataView (26 in Figure 16-10).

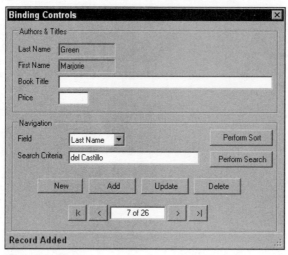

Figure 16-10

4. Now enter a title and price for the new book and click the Add button. You will see a message in the status bar indicating that the record has been added, and you will also see that the number of records has changed (to 27) as shown in Figure 16-11.

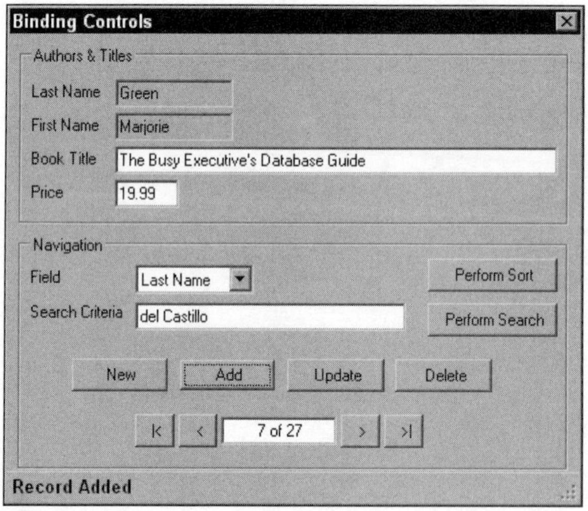

Figure 16-11

Now that you have added a record, examine what you actually did.

How It Works

Remember that the only data that you can add is a new book title and its price. So instead of selecting the data in each of these fields, deleting it, and then entering the new data, you want to be able to simply click the New button. The job of the New button is to clear the book title and price fields for you. All you need to do is set the Text properties of these text boxes to an empty string as shown here:

```
' Clear the book title and price fields...
txtBookTitle.Text = ""
txtPrice.Text = ""
```

When you click the New button, the fields are cleared. If you are updating or editing a record, those changes are lost. You would normally put logic into your application to prevent that problem, but for this example that type of validation was left out.

The primary key used in the titles table is not the database's Identity column. Identity columns use a sequential number and automatically increments the number for you when a new row is inserted. Instead of an Identity column, the primary key is made up of a category prefix and a sequential number. This means that you must first determine the maximum number used in a category and then increment that number by 1 and use the new number and category prefix for the new key.

The first thing that you want to do in the btnAdd_Click event procedure is declare your local variables and objects that will be used here. The intPosition variable will be used to save the current record position, and the intMaxID variable will be used to set and increment the maximum sequential number for a category. The strID will be used to store the primary key from the authors table and to set the new key for the authors table. Finally, the objCommand object will be used to build a query to insert a new record into the titleauthor and titles tables.

Before you do anything, you want to save the position of the current record that you are on. This enables you to go back to this record once you reload the DataView object, which will contain the new record that you will add in this procedure:

```
intPosition = objCurrencyManager.Position
```

You need to execute a command on the database to work out what ID to give your new title. You us a SqlCommand object to do this. You pass in an SQL string and the connection that you use throughout your program. This SQL string will select the maximum value in the title_id column, where the title_id value begins with the prefix of DM.

> There is no category for demo, so you add all of the test records under this category and use the category prefix of DM, enabling you to identify quickly the records that you have inserted just in case you want to get rid of them manually later.

Because the MAX function you use is an *aggregate function* (meaning that it is a function that works on groups of data), the data is returned without a column name. Therefore, you use the AS keyword in the SELECT statement and tell SQL Server to assign a column name to the value, in this case MaxID. You use a LIKE clause in the SELECT statement to tell SQL Server to search for all values that begin with DM:

```
Dim maxIdCommand As SqlCommand = New SqlCommand( _
    "SELECT MAX(title_id) AS MaxID " & _
    "FROM titles WHERE title_id LIKE 'DM%'", objConnection)
```

This sets up your command object but doesn't execute it. To execute it, you need to open the connection and then call one of the `SqlCommand` execute methods. In this case you use `ExecuteScalar`:

```
' Open the connection, execute the command
objConnection.Open()
Dim maxId As Object = maxIdCommand.ExecuteScalar()
```

`ExecuteScalar` is a useful method when you have a database command that returns a single value. Other commands you've used so far have returned a whole table of values (you have used these as the `SelectCommand` of a data adapter), or no values at all (you have executed these with `ExecuteNonQuery`). In this case, you are interested only in only one number, so you can use `ExecuteScalar`. This returns the first column of the first row in the result set. In this case, there is only one column and one row, so that is what you get.

You want to check for a `Null` value returned from the command, so you compare the resulting `Object` against the `Value` property of the `DBNull` class:

```
' If the MaxID column is null...
If maxId Is DBNull.Value Then
```

If the expression evaluates to `True`, you have no primary key in the titles table that begins with `DM`, so you set the initial value of the `intMaxID` variable to a value of `1000`. You choose 1000 because all of the other primary keys contain a numeric value of less than 1000:

```
' Set a default value of 1000...
intMaxID = 1000
```

If the column value evaluates to `False`, then you have at least one primary key in the titles table that begins with `DM`. In this case, you need to obtain the integer portion of this ID to work out which integer to use for your ID. To do this, you must convert your `maxId` object to a `String`:

```
Else
    ' otherwise set the strID variable to the value in MaxID...
    strID = CType(maxId, String)
```

Then you can extract the integer portion of the key by using the `Remove` method of the string variable, `strID`. The `Remove` method removes the specified number of characters from a string. You specify the offset at which to begin removing characters and the number of characters to be removed. This method returns a new string with the removed characters. In this line of code, you are removing the prefix of `DM` from the string so that all you end up with is the integer portion of the string. You then use the `CType` function to convert the string value, which contains a number, to an `Integer` value, which you place in the `intMaxID` variable. Finally, you increment it by one to get the integer portion of the ID that you will use:

```
    ' Get the integer part of the string...
    intMaxID = CType(strID.Remove(0, 2), Integer)
    ' Increment the value...
    intMaxID += 1
End If
```

After you get the integer part, you build a new primary key in the `strID` variable by concatenating the numeric value contained in the `intMaxID` variable with the prefix `DM`:

```
' Finally, set the new ID...
strID = "DM" & intMaxID.ToString
```

Next, you build the SQL statements to insert a new row of data into the `titles` and `titleauthor` tables. If you look closely, there are two separate `INSERT` statements in the `CommandText` property of your `objCommand` object. The two separate `INSERT` statements are separated by a semicolon, which enables you to concatenate multiple SQL statements. The SQL statements that you build use placeholders that will get filled in by the `SqlParameter` objects.

> *Note that because of the relationship between the* `titles` *table and the* `authors` *table, you must first insert a new title for an author into the* `titles` *table and then insert the relationship between the title and the author in the* `titleauthor` *table. You'll notice that your* `INSERT` *statements are specifying the columns that you want to insert data into and then the values that are to be inserted, some of which are represented by placeholders.*

You have seen the properties of the `SqlCommand` object before. This time, however, you are using properties rather than the constructor. You set the `Connection` property to a `SqlConnection` object and then set the `CommandText` property to the SQL string that you want executed, in this case, the two separate `INSERT` statements:

```
objCommand.Connection = objConnection
objCommand.CommandText = "INSERT INTO titles " & _
    "(title_id, title, type, price, pubdate) " & _
    "VALUES(@title_id,@title,@type,@price,@pubdate);" & _
    "INSERT INTO titleauthor (au_id, title_id) VALUES(@au_id,@title_id)"
```

You then add entries to the `Parameters` collection property for each of your placeholders in the preceding SQL statements. Where the same parameter name is used twice in the `CommandText` property — as `title_id` is here — you need only one `SqlParameter` object:

```
' Add parameters for the placeholders in the SQL in the
' CommandText property...

' Parameter for the title_id column...
objCommand.Parameters.AddWithValue ("@title_id", strID)

' Parameter for the title column...
objCommand.Parameters.AddWithValue ("@title", txtBookTitle.Text)

' Parameter for the type column
objCommand.Parameters.AddWithValue ("@type", "Demo")

' Parameter for the price column...
objCommand.Parameters.AddWithValue _
                    ("@price", txtPrice.Text).DbType = DbType.Currency

' Parameter for the pubdate column
objCommand.Parameters.AddWithValue ("@pubdate", Date.Now)

' Parameter for the au_id column...
objCommand.Parameters.AddWithValue ("@au_id", BindingContext _
    (objDataView).Current("au_id"))
```

For the @title_id parameter, you use the strID variable that you created and set earlier in this method. For the @title parameter, you use the text in the Book Title text box entered by the user. For the @price parameter, you use the text in the Price text box. However, the Text property is a String. SQL Server cannot automatically convert between a String and a Currency data type, so you specify that the parameter is of the DbType.Currency data type.

For @au_id you need to use the ID of the currently selected author. There are no bound controls for the au_id column, so you need to use some code to obtain the value. Take a close look at that particular statement:

```
BindingContext(objDataView).Current("au_id")
```

Here you are getting the form's BindingContext for the objDataView data source, which is the one you're using for all of your bound controls. When you're accessing a DataView through Binding Context, the Current property returns a DataRowView object. This object represents the view of the particular row that the user is currently looking at. You are then able to select a particular column from that row, thus giving you a specific value. Here, of course, you are obtaining the au_id column.

The remaining parameters mark that the new record is a Demo record and timestamp the record with the current date and time:

```
' Parameter for the type column
objCommand.Parameters.AddWithValue ("@type", "Demo")

' Parameter for the pubdate column
objCommand.Parameters.AddWithValue ("@pubdate", Date.Now)
```

After you add all your parameters, you execute the command using the ExecuteNonQuery method. This causes your SQL statements to be executed and the data inserted. After your new data is inserted, you close the database connection.

This is the one spot in your code that is really subject to failure, so very basic error handling is included here. You execute your INSERT statement inside the Try block of your error handler, and if an error is encountered, the code in the Catch block will be executed. The code there simply displays a message box that shows the error encountered:

```
' Execute the SqlCommand object to insert the new data...
Try
    objCommand.ExecuteNonQuery()
Catch SqlExceptionErr As SqlException
    MessageBox.Show(SqlExceptionErr.Message)
Finally
    ' Close the connection...
    objConnection.Close()
End Try
```

Then the FillDataSetAndView and BindFields procedures are called to reload the DataView object and to clear and rebind your controls. This ensures that you get all new data added, updated, or deleted in the tables in SQL Server.

You then reposition the DataView object back to the record that was being displayed by setting the Position property of the CurrencyManager using the intPosition variable. This variable was set using the current record position at the beginning of this procedure.

The position that you set here is only approximate. It does not take into account any records that have been inserted or deleted by someone else or you. It is possible that the title you just inserted for a specific author could be returned prior to the title that was displayed before. If you need more detailed control over the actual record position, you need to add more code to handle finding and displaying the exact record that was displayed; however, this is beyond the scope of this book.

After you reposition the record that is being displayed, you call the ShowPosition procedure to show the current record position.

Finally, you display a message in the status bar indicating that the record has been added.

In the next Try It Out, you code the btnUpdate_Click procedure. This procedure is a little simpler because all you need to do is update existing records in the titles table. You do not have to add any new records, so you do not have to select any data to build a primary key.

Try It Out   Updating Records

1. To the btnUpdate_Click event procedure, add the following highlighted code:

```
Private Sub btnUpdate_Click(ByVal sender As Object, _
        ByVal e As System.EventArgs) Handles btnUpdate.Click
    ' Declare local variables and objects...
    Dim intPosition As Integer
    Dim objCommand As SqlCommand = New SqlCommand()

    ' Save the current record position...
    intPosition = objCurrencyManager.Position

    ' Set the SqlCommand object properties...
    objCommand.Connection = objConnection
    objCommand.CommandText = "UPDATE titles " & _
            "SET title = @title, price = @price WHERE title_id = @title_id"
    objCommand.CommandType = CommandType.Text

    ' Add parameters for the placeholders in the SQL in the
    ' CommandText property...

    ' Parameter for the title field...
    objCommand.Parameters.AddWithValue ("@title", txtBookTitle.Text)

    ' Parameter for the price field...
    objCommand.Parameters.AddWithValue ("@price", txtPrice.Text).DbType _
                                = DbType.Currency

    ' Parameter for the title_id field...
```

```
objCommand.Parameters.AddWithValue _
            ("@title_id", BindingContext(objDataView).Current("title_id"))

' Open the connection...
objConnection.Open()

' Execute the SqlCommand object to update the data...
objCommand.ExecuteNonQuery()

' Close the connection...
objConnection.Close()

' Fill the DataSet and bind the fields...
FillDataSetAndView()
BindFields()
' Set the record position to the one that you saved...
objCurrencyManager.Position = intPosition

' Show the current record position...
ShowPosition()

' Display a message that the record was updated...
ToolStripStatusLabel1.Text = "Record Updated"
End Sub
```

2. Run your project. You can update the price of the book that you have just added, or you can update the price of another book. Choose a book, change the price in the Price field, and then click the Update button.

Once the record has been updated, you will see the appropriate message in the status bar and the record will still be the current record, as shown in Figure 16-12.

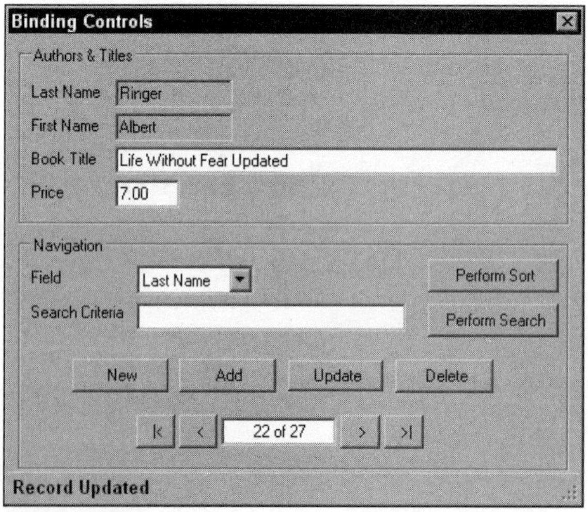

Figure 16-12

How It Works

As always, the first thing that you want to do is declare your variables and objects. You need one variable to save the current record position and one object for the `SqlCommand` object. Next, you save the current record position just as you did in the last procedure.

By adding the following code, you set the `Connection` property of the `SqlCommand` object using your `objConnection` object. Then you set the `CommandText` property using a SQL string. The SQL string here contains an UPDATE statement to update the title and price columns in the `titles` table. Notice that there are three placeholders in this UPDATE statement. Two placeholders are for the `title` and `price`, and one is for the `title_id` in the WHERE clause:

```
' Set the SqlCommand object properties...
objCommand.Connection = objConnection
    objCommand.CommandText = "UPDATE titles " & _
            "SET title = @title, price = @price WHERE title_id = @title_id"
objCommand.CommandType = CommandType.Text
```

Again, after you set the `CommandText` property, you set the `CommandType` property to indicate that this is a SQL string.

You need to add the appropriate parameters to the `Parameters` collection. The first parameter that you add is for the title column in your UPDATE statement. The title of the book is coming from the `Text` property of the `txtBookTitle` text box on your form.

The second parameter is for the price in your UPDATE statement. This parameter will be used to update the price of a book, and the data is coming from the txtPrice text box on your form. Once again, you need to set the `DbType` explicitly for this parameter.

This last parameter was for your WHERE clause in the UPDATE statement. The data for the `Value` property comes directly from the form's `BindingContext`, as the `au_id` did in the Adding Records example.

The rest of the procedure is similar to the `btnAdd_Click` event procedure.

You code the final procedure, `btnDelete_Click`, in the next Try It Out.

Try It Out   **Deleting Records**

1. To include delete functionality in your project, add the following highlighted code to the `btnDelete_Click` event procedure:

```
Private Sub btnDelete_Click(ByVal sender As Object, _
        ByVal e As System.EventArgs) Handles btnDelete.Click
    ' Declare local variables and objects...
    Dim intPosition As Integer
    Dim objCommand As SqlCommand = New SqlCommand()

    ' Save the current record position - 1 for the one to be
    ' deleted...
    intPosition = Me.BindingContext(objDataView).Position - 1

    ' If the position is less than 0 set it to 0...
```

```
      If intPosition < 0 Then
          intPosition = 0
      End If

      ' Set the Command object properties...
      objCommand.Connection = objConnection
      objCommand.CommandText = "DELETE FROM titleauthor " & _
              "WHERE title_id = @title_id;" & _
              "DELETE FROM titles WHERE title_id = @title_id"
      ' Parameter for the title_id field...
      objCommand.Parameters.AddWithValue _
                  ("@title_id", BindingContext(objDataView).Current("title_id"))

      ' Open the database connection...
      objConnection.Open()

      ' Execute the SqlCommand object to update the data...
      objCommand.ExecuteNonQuery()

      ' Close the connection...
      objConnection.Close()

      ' Fill the DataSet and bind the fields...
      FillDataSetAndView()
      BindFields()

      ' Set the record position to the one that you saved...
      Me.BindingContext(objDataView).Position = intPosition

      ' Show the current record position...
      ShowPosition()

      ' Display a message that the record was deleted...
      ToolStripStatusLabel1.Text = "Record Deleted"
  End Sub
```

2. That's it for this project, so test this newest functionality. Run your project, choose any book that you want to delete, and then click the Delete button. Keep in mind, though, that the pubs database is a sample database for everyone to use, and it's probably a good idea to delete a book that you have added. Before you delete a book, however, take note of the record count that is displayed on the form. (See Figure 6-13.) You may see an error because of a constraint in the database. This is because there is sales data for this book. Find the book you added and it will not have sales data associated with it.

After the delete has been performed, you will see one less record in the record count on the form.

How It Works

This procedure is a little more involved than the btnUpdate_Click procedure, because of the relationship of titles to authors. Remember that there is a relationship table to join authors and titles. You must delete the row in the titleauthor relationship table before you can delete the row of data in the titles table. Therefore, you need two DELETE statements in your SQL string.

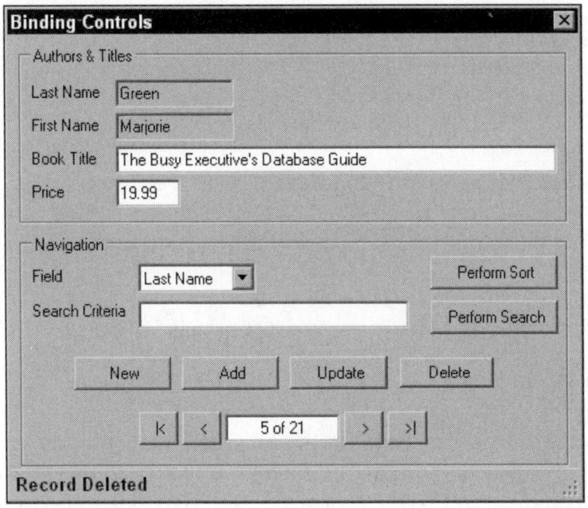

Figure 16-13

Notice that this time after you declare your variables, you specify the `Position` property minus 1. This will allow for the user being on the last record and deleting it. You have also allowed for the user being on the first record as you check the value of the `intPosition` variable. If it is less than 0, you know that the user was on the first record, so you set it to 0; this means that when you restore the record position later, it will once again be on the first record.

Notice also that you have not used the `CurrencyManager` object this time. Instead, you used the `Binding Context` object and specified the `objDataView` object as the object to be manipulated. Remember that the `BindingContext` object is automatically part of the form, and there is nothing you need to do to have it added. The reason for using the `BindingContext` object here is to demonstrate how to use it and so that you know that you do not have to use the `CurrencyManager` object to navigate the records contained in the `objDataView`:

```
' Declare local variables and objects...
Dim intPosition As Integer
Dim objCommand As SqlCommand = New SqlCommand()

' Save the current record position - 1 for the one to be
' deleted...
intPosition = Me.BindingContext(objDataView).Position - 1

' If the position is less than 0 set it to 0...
If intPosition < 0 Then
    intPosition = 0
End If
```

When you set the properties of your `SqlCommand` object, the SQL string specified in the `CommandText` property contained two `DELETE` statements separated by a semicolon. The first `DELETE` statement deletes the relationship between the `titles` and `authors` tables for the book being deleted. The second `DELETE` statement deletes the book from the `titles` table:

```
        ' Set the Command object properties...
        objCommand.Connection = objConnection
        objCommand.CommandText = "DELETE FROM titleauthor " & _
            "WHERE title_id = @title_id;" & _
            "DELETE FROM titles WHERE title_id = @title_id"
```

Again, you used placeholders for the primary keys in WHERE clauses of your DELETE statements.

This statement uses only one parameter. The next line sets it up in the normal way:

```
        ' Parameter for the title_id field...
        objCommand.Parameters.AddWithValue ("@title_id", _

    BindingContext(objDataView).Current("title_id"))
```

The rest of the code is the same as the code for the previous two methods, and should be familiar by now. That wraps up this project and this chapter. Hopefully you will walk away with some valuable knowledge about data binding and how to perform inserts, updates, and deletes using SQL to access a database.

Before you leave, remember that error handling is a major part of any project. Except for one place in your code, it was omitted to conserve space. You also omitted data validation, so trying to insert a new record with no values could cause unexpected results and errors.

Summary

This chapter has taken a look at a few very important ADO.NET classes, particularly the `SqlConnection`, `SqlDataAdapter`, `SqlCommand`, and `SqlParameter` classes. You saw firsthand how valuable these classes can be when selecting, inserting, updating, and deleting data. These particular classes are specifically for accessing SQL Server, but similar principles apply to the OLE DB counterparts.

You also saw the `DataSet` and `DataView` classes from the `System.Data` namespace put to use, and you used both of these classes to create objects that were bound to the controls on your forms. Of particular interest to this discussion is the `DataView` object, as it provides the functionality to perform sorting and searching of data. The `DataView` class provides the most flexibility between the two classes, because you can also present a subset of data from the `DataSet` in the `DataView`.

You saw how easy it is to bind the controls on your form to the data contained in either the `DataSet` or the `DataView`. You also saw how to manage the navigation of the data in these objects with the `CurrencyManager` class. This class provides quick and easy control over the navigation.

This chapter has demonstrated using manual control over the navigation of data on the form and manual control over the insertion, update, and deletion of data in a data store. You should use the techniques that you learned in this chapter when you need finer control of the data, especially when dealing with complex table relationships such as you have dealt with here.

To summarize, after reading this chapter you should:

- ❑ Feel comfortable using the ADO.NET classes discussed in this chapter
- ❑ Know when to use the `DataSet` class and when to use the `DataView` class
- ❑ Know how to bind controls on your form manually to either a `DataSet` or a `DataView` object
- ❑ Know how to use the `CurrencyManager` class to navigate the data in a `DataSet` or `DataView` object
- ❑ Know how to sort and search for data in a `DataView` object

Exercises

Exercise 1

Create a Windows application that will display data to the user from the Authors table in the Pubs database. Use a DataGridView object to display the data. Use the simple select statement here to get the data:

```
Select * From Authors
```

Exercise 2

Looking at the DataGridView, it is not very user-friendly. Update the column headings to make more sense. If you know SQL, you can give each column an alias. The current column header names are `au_id`, `au_lname`, `au_fname`, `phone`, `address`, `city`, `state`, `zip`, and `contract`. The solution to this exercise will give each column an alias in SQL.

Web Forms

The Internet is a vital part of many of our business and personal lives. Over the last few years, online banking and shopping have saved almost everyone time and money by their no longer having to drive to brick-and-mortar locations to do business. Today, the Internet is mostly a secure marketplace for commerce. With most, if not all, credit cards offering zero liability, the security risk of a Web site transaction is basically eliminated. The growth of the Internet is not going to slow down as consumers embrace the ease of use and businesses save millions of dollars with self-service Web sites for customers. With Visual Studio 2005, you will be building data-driven sites in no time.

As we look to the future, the Internet is sure to have its place in business. Developers need to gain knowledge of building robust, dynamic Web sites. In this chapter, you will learn about building Web Forms applications. You will focus on the basics for Web site development and move to database-driven applications. Before you get your first look at the code, you will have a short lesson on the building blocks developers use to create Web applications.

In this chapter, you will:

- ❑ Look at a basic overview of Web applications (thin-client applications)
- ❑ See the advantages of Web Forms versus Windows Forms
- ❑ Understand the control toolbox
- ❑ Explore client and server processing
- ❑ Learn about data validation controls
- ❑ Discover themes, site navigation controls, forms authentication, and master pages
- ❑ Use the GridView control to build a data driven ASP.NET Web Form
- ❑ Assess the possible locations for Web sites in VS 2005

Error handling has been omitted from all of the Try It Outs in this chapter to save space. You should always add the appropriate error handling to your code. Review Chapter 9 for error-handling techniques.

Thin-Client Architecture

In previous chapters, you have seen thick-client applications in the type of Windows Forms applications. Most of the processing is completed by the client application you built earlier, and many of the applications stood on their own and needed no other applications or servers. In Web development, on the other hand, most of the processing is completed on the server and then the result is sent to the browser.

When you develop Web Forms applications, you do not have to distribute anything to the user. Any user who can access your Web server and has a Web browser can be a user. You must be careful with the amount of processing you place on the client. When you design a thin-client system, you must be aware that your users or customers will use different clients to access your application. If you try to use too much processing on the client, it may cause problems for some users. This is one of the major differences between Windows and Web Forms applications. Next, you will learn about the major difference between these two types of Visual Studio 2005 applications.

When dealing with a Windows Forms application, you have a compiled program that must be distributed to the user's desktop before they can use it. Depending upon the application, there may also be one or more supporting DLLs or other executables that also need to be distributed along with the application.

In thin-client architecture, there is typically no program or DLL to be distributed. Users merely need to start their browsers and enter the URL of the application Web site. The server hosting the Web site is responsible for allocating all resources the Web application requires. The client is a navigation tool that displays the results the server returns.

All code required in a thin-client application stays in one central location: the server hosting the Web site. Any updates to the code are immediately available the next time a user requests a Web page.

Thin-client architecture provides several key benefits. First and foremost is the cost of initial distribution of the application — there is none. In traditional client/server architecture, the program would have to be distributed to every client who wanted to use it, which could be quite a time-consuming task if the application is used in offices throughout the world.

Another major benefit is the cost of distributing updates to the application: again, there are none. All updates to the Web site and its components are distributed to the Web server. Once an update is made, it is immediately available to all users the next time they access the updated Web page. In traditional client/server architecture, the updated program would have to be distributed to every client, and the updates could take days or weeks to roll out. This allows a new version of an application to be distributed instantly to all the users without having to touch a single desktop.

Another major benefit is that you can make changes to the back-end architecture and not have to worry about the client. Suppose, for example, that you want to change the location of the database from a low-end server to a new high-end server. The new server would typically have a new machine name. In a traditional client/server application, the machine name of the database server is stored in the code or Registry setting. You would need to modify either the code or the Registry setting for every person who uses the application. In thin-client architecture, you simply need to update the setting of the Web server to point to the new database server and you are in business, and so are all of the clients.

You can see that in a thin-client architecture model, any client with a browser can access your Web site and immediately have access to updates. In fact, if your changes were transparent to the user, the client wouldn't even know that changes had been made.

Now that you have a basic understanding of thin-client architecture, look at how Web Forms work.

Web Forms versus Windows Forms

In this section, you will get an overview of the advantages of both Windows Forms and Web Forms. This will give you an idea of when you build each type of application to solve a customer's problem. You will almost always have to choose between these two types of architecture when building solutions. It is important to understand some of the advantages of both.

Windows Forms Advantages

Windows Forms applications have advantages in some types of systems. Typically, applications that require a responsive interface, such as a point-of-sale system at a retail store, are Windows Forms applications. Also, in most cases, processor-intensive applications such as games or graphics programs are better suited to a Windows Forms program.

A major advantage for Windows Forms is trust. When a user installs the application, it is given trust in the current zone. With this high enough level of trust, you can store data and state about the current session on the local computer. The user can run the application and it can interact with the local file system or Registry seamlessly. Trust is very limited, however, for an Internet application.

Another advantage is having control over the client application. This allows you to build a very powerful, rich user interface. You will see that there are numerous controls not available to a Web Form (although this is becoming less of a difference) that permit the developer to create user-friendly applications. Windows Forms allow for a more ample user interface.

Also, application responsiveness is an advantage with Windows Forms. With most or all of the processing being done on the client, the need to send data over the wire can be reduced. Any amount of data sent to servers can cause latency. For an application running locally on a computer, the normal events are handled more quickly. Also, the speed of data transmission over a local network is much faster than the typical Internet connection. This speed will allow data to move across the wire faster and create less of a bottleneck for the user.

Web Forms Advantages

The advantages of Web Forms may seem to be greater than the advantages of Windows Forms. Do not permit this to transform you into a full-time Web developer for every project. There will always be times when Windows Forms are a better solution.

The greatest advantage for a Web application is distribution. To distribute a Web Forms application, just install it on the Web server. That is it. No need to create an installation for every version of Windows and ship CDs. When you make a change, just publish the change to the Web server, and the next time a customer comes to the site, he or she will use the latest application.

Version control, or change control, is another advantage. With all of your application code at the same location, making changes is a breeze. You never have to worry about one user on version 8 and another on version 10; all users access the same application. As soon as you publish the change, all users see the update with no user intervention necessary.

Have you heard the term *platform independence*? Web applications have it. It doesn't matter what type of computer the user has — as long as there is a browser and a connection to your Web server, the user can access your application. There is no need to build application versions for different operating systems.

These advantages can add up to millions of dollars of savings over a Windows application. Being able to make quick changes and maintain one code base are great advantages. Still, there are times when a Web application will not provide an adequate user experience. Make sure you evaluate both options for every project. Now, let's look more closely at Web Forms development.

Web Applications: The Basic Pieces

In its simplest form, a Web application is just a number of Web pages. For the user to access the Web pages, there needs to be a Web server and browser. A request is made by the browser for the page on the server. The server then processes the Web page and returns the output to the browser. The user sees the page inside the browser window. The pages that the users see may contain HyperText Markup Language (HTML), Cascading Style Sheets (CSS), and client-side script. Finally, the page displays in the browser for the user.

In this section, you will receive a basic overview of each piece of the system.

Web Servers

There are many Web servers on the market today. The most well known Web servers in use today are Microsoft Internet Information Services (IIS) and Apache. For this book, you will focus exclusively on IIS.

Browsers

Every user of a Web Forms application must have a browser. The four most popular browsers are Microsoft Internet Explorer (IE), Mozilla Firefox, Netscape, and Opera. When you develop public Web sites, you must be aware that the site may render differently in each browser. You will find the IE is the most lenient when it comes to valid HTML. We will focus on IE 6 for this book.

HyperText Markup Language

Also known as HTML, this is the presentation or design layout of the Web page. HTML is a tag-based language that allows you to change the presentation of information. For example, to make text bold in HTML, just place the <b> tag around the text. The following text is an example of HTML.

```
This is <b>bold</b> in HTML.
```

If the previous text was rendered by a browser, it would be displayed like this:

```
This is bold in HTML.
```

Browsers will interpret HTML and should conform to the standards from the World Wide Web Consortium (W3C). The W3C was created to develop common protocols for the Web in the 1990s. You can read more about the W3C at their website, at www.w3.org/.

Although VS 2005 allows you to design Web sites without firsthand knowledge of HTML, you will have hands-on exercises creating Web pages with HTML later in the chapter.

VBScript and JavaScript

A major part of Web development is client-side script. If you are creating an application for the public that uses client-side script, you will need to use JavaScript for support in all browsers. VBScript is a Microsoft-centric language that is more like Visual Basic syntax, so when developing an intranet site where you can control which version of IE the user uses, you can use VBScript.

Client-side scripting is typically used for data validation and dynamic HTML (DHTML). Validation scripts enforce rules that may require the user to complete a field on the screen before continuing. DHTML scripts allow the page to change programmatically after it is in memory on the browser. Expanding menus is an example of DHTML. Currently, IE supports more DHTML than is required by the W3C. This may cause you to have to create DHTML for each target browser.

One of the great features of Visual Studio 2005 is the validation and navigation controls. You can drag these controls onto your Web page without writing any client-side script. In most instances, these controls will manage, but for others, you will need to be self-sufficient in the creation of client-side script. For this reason, you will write some of your own scripts later in this chapter.

Cascading Style Sheets

Cascading Style Sheets (CSS) allows for the separation of layout and style from the content of a Web page. You can use CSS to change fonts, colors, alignment, and many other aspects of Web page presentation. The best part of CSS is it can be applied to entire site. By using a master CSS page, you can easily maintain and quickly change the look and feel of the entire Web site by changing one page. You will learn more about CSS in this chapter.

Active Server Pages

With Visual Studio 2005, a new version of Active Server Pages (ASP.NET 2.0) is here. This new version makes it even easier to create dynamic, data-driven Web sites. This section will explain the concept of ASPX or Web Forms.

Benefits

When you create Web applications, you could use many solutions. The most common types of pages are Active Server Pages (.asp and .aspx), JavaServer Pages (.jsp), Cold Fusion Pages (.cfm) and basic HTML (.htm or .html). In this book, you will mainly focus on ASPX, but you will see some HTML also.

Execution time is one benefit in which ASP.NET 2.0 stands out above the rest. When an ASP.NET 2.0 page is requested the first time, a compiled copy is placed into memory on the server for the next request. This provides for great performance gains over interpreted languages.

Using Visual Studio 2005 to design your applications also makes a big difference in productivity. The .NET Framework supplies thousands of namespaces, objects, and controls for use developing Web Forms applications. Also, ASP.NET 2.0 also supports all .NET-compatible languages. By default, Visual Basic.2005, C#, and JScript.NET are all available in Visual Studio 2005.

Special Web Site Files

When you work with ASP.NET 2.0, you will see many special files. These files are very important and each could have an entire chapter written about it. The two files you will learn about next are files that you can change to make sitewide changes from one location. There is much more to learn about these, and you can do research at `http://msdn2.microsoft.com/`.

Global.asax

This file allows you to add code to certain application-level events. The most common events are `Application_Start`, `Application_End`, `Session_Start`, `Session_End`, and `Application_Error`. Application start and end events fire when the actual Web application inside of IIS changes state. This event will fire with the first request to a Web site after the server or IIS is restarted. The session events fire on a per user/browser session on the Web server. When you save data to the user's session, you must be careful. This data will be saved for every user/browser that is browsing the application. This can create an extra load on the server. The final event is `Application_Error`. You can use this to log all unhandled events in one common place. Make sure to redirect users to a friendly error page after logging the error.

Web.config

`Web.config` is exactly what it appears to be—a configuration file for the Web application; it is an XML document. You can update many application settings for security, errors and much, much more. For this chapter, you will store your connection string to the database here.

Development

As you build Web Forms applications in Visual Studio 2005, you will work in the IDE you are familiar with from Windows Forms applications. As you work with Web pages, you will have the option of using what is known as a *code-behind* page. This will allow you to keep your application logic separate from the presentation code. You will have three views to work from: Design, Source, and Code view, the common ways to build applications. Design and Source view are for the `.aspx` page that contains the user interface and data validation. The Code view is the `.vb` file that is the code-behind page. Visual Studio 2005 makes creating Web applications an easy task.

Controls: The Toolbox

The default controls you will use to build Web applications are all in the Toolbox. If you do not see the Toolbox, press Ctrl+Alt+X to view it. The controls are organized by category. The categories along with some controls are shown in Figure 17-1. At left, the Toolbox is shown with just the categories; at center, the Standard controls tab is expanded to show the list of controls; at right, the Data tab has been expanded.

Figure 17-1

The Toolbox is fully customizable. You can add, remove, or rearrange any tab or control by right-clicking the Toolbox and using the context menu options. Also, you can copy common code snippets to the Toolbox as a shortcut. To copy code to the Toolbox, highlight the text and drag it onto the tab where you want to add the shortcut. Next, right-click the shortcut and rename it so that it makes sense. To insert code onto a page, just drag the shortcut to the location where you want the code. In this chapter, you will gain hands on experience working with controls on every tab except Login, Web Parts, and Crystal Reports.

Building Web Applications

In this section, you will create small Web applications demonstrating different aspects of Web development. To accomplish this, you will see how the basics of Web Forms applications work.

Creating a Web Form for Client- and Server-Side Processing

The Web form in this Try It Out will contain HTML and server controls. The HTML controls will have client-side processing, and the server controls will process the code on the server.

Try it out   **Server and Client-Side Processing**

1.   Start this project by choosing File ⇨ New Web Site. Make sure Visual Basic is the language, and
select ASP.NET Web Site on the Templates pane. For the Location, change the drop-down box to
File System and enter **C:\WebSites\Client_ServerProcessing**. You may need to change the
drive letter based on your computer configuration. Click OK, and this will create a file system
site that will use the built-in development Web server for testing. The New Web Site dialog will
look like Figure 17-2.

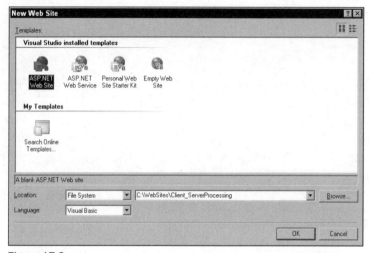

Figure 17-2

2.   Visual Studio will create the default folders and files for the Web site. Take a look at the Solution
Explorer window. It will look like Figure 17-3. The `Default.aspx` page will be open in the IDE.

Figure 17-3

3.   Now you will add the controls. Add the following standard controls to `Default.aspx` while in
Design mode. (To get to Design mode, while viewing the `.aspx` page click the Design option on
the lower left of the pane, or simply press Shift+F7.) Do not worry about the position of the controls for now, but make sure you use controls from the Standard and HTML tabs on the toolbox.

The area at the bottom of the Default.aspx *page that has Design, Source, and other HTML tags to the right is known as the tag navigator.*

First, add the controls to the form. You can arrange them in any order for now.

❑ From the Standard controls tab, add one Button and two Label controls.

❑ From the HTML controls tab, add one Input (Button) control.

4. Now, change the properties of the controls. Use Figure 17-4 as a guide.

❑ Set the ID of the Standard:Button to **btnServer** and the Text to **Server**.

❑ Set the ID of the HTML:Input (Button) to **btnClient** and the Value to **Client**.

❑ Set the ID of the upper Standard:Label to **lblServer** and the Text to **Server**.

❑ Set the ID of the lower Standard:Label to **lblClient** and the Text to **Client**.

5. Now, hold down the Ctrl key and select all four controls. Use the menus of VS 2005 and choose Layout ⇨ Position ⇨ Absolute. This will set the controls to function like the grid layout you are familiar with from Windows Forms development. You are able to move the controls anywhere on the form now. Arrange the control so they resemble Figure 17-4. When you finish, press Ctrl+F5 to run the project without debugging and see the page in the browser.

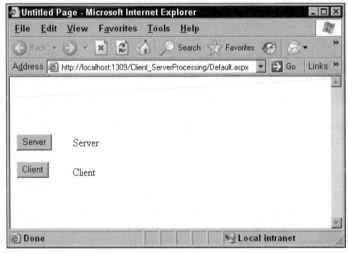

Figure 17-4

6. Close the browser and go back to VS 2005. Double-click the btnServer to jump to the btnServer_Click event handler. Depending on your settings, you will be either on the code-behind page or working in the source of the .aspx page. Add the following highlighted code to the event.

```
Sub btnServer_Click(ByVal sender As Object, ByVal e As System.EventArgs)

    lblServer.Text = "Changed"
End Sub
```

Run the program again by pressing Ctrl+F5 and test the button click event code. The label will display Changed after you click the Server button.

7. Now, you will create an event handler for the HTML Input (Button) and add a title to the page. (Make sure you have the Default.aspx page open in the IDE.) First, you need to change the default language to VBScript. To do this, view the Properties Explorer and select DOCUMENT from the combo box. Find the DefaultClientScript property and set it to **VBScript**. VBScript is very similar to all of the code you have learned so far in this book. To avoid confusion from new syntax, and because you can control the browser that you will use, you will write all client-side code using VBScript in this example. To add a title, find the Title property and set it to **My First Page**. On the tag navigator, click Source to change to HTML view. In the Client Object & Events combo box, choose btnClient. Next, select onclick in the event combo box and add this high-lighted code to the event VS 2005 creates.

```
Sub btnClient_onclick

    document.getElementById("lblclient").innerText = "Changed"
    document.getElementById("lblServer").innerText = "Server"
End Sub
```

8. Run the project again by pressing Ctrl+F5. Test both buttons.

How It Works

So, now you can see that Web Forms development is very similar to Windows Forms development. This is one of the benefits of .NET development and Visual Studio 2005. The ability for any developer to switch from device to Web to Windows development with a small learning curve is a goal of Microsoft, and they did it.

Let's get start by looking at the HTML source. The first line of code is the Page directive:

```
<%@ Page Language="VB" AutoEventWireup="false" CodeFile="Default.aspx.vb"
Inherits="_Default" %>
```

Depending on the mode you develop in, you will see different default attributes set by VS 2005. If you work with code in the .aspx page, only the Language attribute is set by VS 2005.

The Page directive has over 30 attributes that can be set. I will discuss only the default attributes. If you want to explore the rest, search for @Page in the help files for VS 2005 or on http://msdn2.microsoft.com/.

Take a look at the default attributes in the Default.aspx page. First, you see the Language attribute. This is set to the language that all server code will compile into. AutoEventWireup is the second attribute. VS 2005 sets this attribute to false. If you leave this attribute out of the Page directive, the default value is true, and certain events can be executed twice. Microsoft recommends always setting the AutoEventWireup attribute to false. Next, you have the CodeFile attribute. This is the page that contains the code when using a separate code file or the code-behind page. Finally, there is the Inherits attribute. This is simply the class name the page will inherit from.

The next line in the source code is the !DOCTYPE element. This tells IE 6 and later that the document conforms to the XHTML 1.1 Document Type Definition (DTD) specified by the W3C for English.

```
<!DOCTYPE html PUBLIC "-//W3C//DTD XHTML 1.1//EN"
"http://www.w3.org/TR/xhtml11/DTD/xhtml11.dtd">
```

The actual HTML root element is next. You will see this element with no attributes set in many instances. Here VS has specified that the namespace for custom tags will be http://www.w3.org/1999/xhtml. If you browse to this site, you will see that this is the XHTML namespace defined by the W3C.

```
<html xmlns="http://www.w3.org/1999/xhtml" >
```

After the root HTML element is the HEAD element. Children of this element are items that are not rendered, but may affect how the page displays. You will place SCRIPT, META, TITLE, LINK, STYLE, and other elements here to define the page's look and feel. LINK and STYLE elements are both used for Cascading Style Sheets (CSS). You will learn about CSS later in this chapter.

The first element is TITLE. This is the title the browser displays for the page. Next, there is a META object that defines the client scripting language as VBScript. After the META object is the client script you created.

The root script tags define the section of the page that is available to add procedures. The only event is the onclick event of the btnClient control. When you click the client button, this procedure executes. The first line of the subroutine uses the getElementById function to find the object in the document that has an ID of lblclient. Once it is found, the innerText is set to Changed. The same function is used to find the lblServer object on the next line. The innerText is then changed to Server. This is added to reset the Server button's label.

```
<head runat="server">
    <title>My First Page</title>
    <meta http-equiv="content-script-type" content="text/VBScript" />
<script language="vbscript" type="text/vbscript">

Sub btnClient_onclick
  document.getElementById("lblclient").innerText = "Changed"
  document.getElementById("lblServer").innerText = "Server"
End Sub

</script>
</head>
```

What you may not notice is the difference between the way the two buttons perform event handling. It is hard to notice running locally, but go back to the Web page and watch the status bar of the browser while you click each button. When you click the Server button, the page actually calls the Web server to process the event. The Client button did not call back to the server; the browser handled the event itself. Over a slow dial-up connection, you can see the difference right away. Keep this in mind as you develop with the runat="server" model.

Now, you are at the BODY tag. This is where Visual Studio adds the controls. All objects inside the FORM tag are sent back to the server for processing.

```
<body>
    <form id="form1" runat="server">
```

When you click the Server button, the form is actually submitted to the server. Here are two lines of HTML that are sent to the browser from the ASP.NET DLL.

```
<form method="post" action="Default.aspx" id="form1">
<input type="submit" name="btnServer" value="Server" id="btnServer" style="z-index:
20; left: 40px; position: absolute; top: 72px" />
```

You can look at the HTML source set to the browser by choosing View ➪ Source from the IE menu.

So the browser knows that btnServer is a submit button. The function of a submit button is to pass form data back to a Web server. In this case, the action is set to Default.aspx. The form uses the post method to send data to Default.aspx. If you looked at the code IE uses for the page, you notice the style attribute on btnServer. This is how ASP.NET 2.0 handles positioning when you set a control's position attribute to absolute. As you build more Web pages, you will realize that Visual Studio extracts the need to know HTML syntax to design Web applications. For most pages you will create, you can stay in design mode and never look at the HTML if you are not comfortable with it.

The final portion of the code displayed on the Default.aspx page was the markup for the controls. These are the controls you placed onto the design area of the form.

```
<div>
    <asp:Button ID="btnServer" Runat="server" Text="Server" style="z-index: 20;
        left: 40px; position: absolute; top: 72px" OnClick="btnServer_Click" />
    <asp:Label ID="lblServer" Style="z-index: 19; left: 104px; position:
        absolute; top: 80px" Runat="server" Text="Server"></asp:Label>
    <asp:Label ID="lblClient" Style="z-index: 17; left: 104px; position:
        absolute; top: 120px" Runat="server" Text="Client"></asp:Label>
    <input id="btnClient" style="z-index: 21; left: 40px; position:
        absolute; top: 112px" type="button" value="Client" />
</div>
</form>
</body>
</html>
```

In the code for the OnClick event of the btnServer control, you set the text of the label to Changed.

```
Partial Class Default_aspx
    Sub btnServer_Click(ByVal sender As Object, ByVal e As System.EventArgs)
        lblServer.Text = "Changed"
    End Sub
End Class
```

You have completed your first ASP.NET 2.0 page. In this exercise, you saw a few basic controls and learned that client and server code was handled differently. In the next section, you will learn data entry and validation skills.

Performing Data Entry and Validation

One of the basic functions of almost every Web site is to gather some kind of information from the user. You probably have seen screens to "contact us" or "create an account". Any place you see a text box on a webpage, data entry and validation are probably taking place. In this Try It Out, you will learn the basics of using built in validation controls and accessing the data the user enters into the Web page.

Try It Out   Data Entry and Validation

1. Create a new Web site and name it **DataEntry**. Do this by choosing File ⇨ New Web Site from the menu.

2. Add four labels, three text boxes, and one button to the `Default.aspx` page. Make sure you use server controls from the Standard tab of the Toolbox. Using the layout menu, set each control's positioning to absolute. Finally, align the controls to resemble Figure 17-5.

Figure 17-5

3. Now, set the properties of the eight controls and the document.

    ❑ Set the Title of the Document to **Data Entry and Validation**.

    ❑ Set the ID of the Button to **btnComplete** and the Text to **Complete**.

    ❑ Set the ID of the upper left TextBox to **txtFirstName**.

❑ Set the ID of the upper right TextBox to **txtLastName**.

❑ Set the ID of the lower TextBox to **txtEmail**.

❑ Set the ID of the upper left Label to **lblFirstName** and the Text to **First Name**.

❑ Set the ID of the upper right Label to **lblLastName** and the Text to **Last Name**.

❑ Set the ID of the middle Label to **lblEmail** and the Text to **Email**.

❑ Set the ID of the lower Label to **lblWelcome** and Text to **Welcome**.

4. Test the page by pressing Ctrl+F5. When the page opens, you will test three items. First, enter your name and e-mail and then click the Complete button. The page will post back to the server, and the HTML returned will still have your data in the textboxes. This is default behavior known as *view state*. Second, type the text **<SCRIPT>alert "Hi"</SCRIPT>** into the First Name box and click Complete. You will see the error message shown in Figure 17-6. ASP.NET 2.0 has a feature called *request validation* that will check for any dangerous input from the user unless you explicitly turn it off. Finally, test the tab order. You can control the tab order by the order the controls appear in the HTML source or by the TabIndex property on each control. Change the tab order if it is not correct.

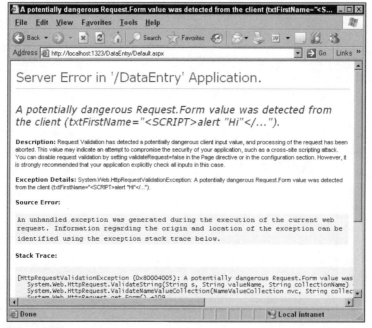

Figure 17-6

5. It is time to do something with the data the user enters. First, you need to open the code-behind page. The easiest way to do this is press F7. Next, add an event handler for page load. To do this, select Page Events from the Objects combo box on the left and Load from the Events combo box. Add the following highlighted code to update lblWelcome with the data input.

```
Private Sub Page_Load(ByVal sender As Object, ByVal e As System.EventArgs) _
Handles Me.Load
```

```
    If Page.IsPostBack Then
        'If this is a postback and not the initial page load
        'Display the data to the user
        Me.lblWelcome.Text = "Hello " + Me.txtFirstName.Text + " " + _
        Me.txtLastName.Text + "<BR>" + "Your email address is " + _
        Me.txtEmail.Text
    End If
End Sub
```

6. Now, you need to add validation to the input. Visual Studio has built in controls just for this. To see the controls, you will need to switch to Design mode by clicking the View Designer icon on the Solution Explorer. Go to the Toolbox and find the Validation tab, which includes prebuilt controls to assist with data validation. Add two RequiredFieldValidator controls and one Validation Summary control to the form. Use the layout menu to set each control's positioning to absolute.

Set the following properties for RequiredFieldValidator:

❑ Set ID to **rfvFirstName**.

❑ Set Display to None.

❑ Set ControlToValidate to txtFirstName.

❑ Set ErrorMessage to **First name is required.**

Set the following properties for RequiredFieldValidator:

❑ Set ID to **rfvEmail**.

❑ Set Display to None.

❑ Set ControlToValidate to txtEmail.

❑ Set ErrorMessage to **Email is required.**

Set ValidationSummary's ID to **ValidationSummary**. Your page will look like Figure 17-7 when you finish.

7. Run your project and try to submit blank entries for first name and e-mail. You will see two error messages similar to Figure 17-8.

This quick example explains how easy data validation is in ASP 2.0. Other controls are available for enforcing data validation. The CompareValidator *control tests a control to make sure it matches a value. This value can be a constant, another control, or even a value from a data store.* RangeValidator *tests that a value is within a specified range. For example, you can test to make sure a person is between 18 and 35 years old.*

How It Works

Without writing any code, you were able to require that data entry fields were completed on a Web page. You took advantage of controls already created for quick and hearty data validation.

You use the RequiredFieldValidator control to make sure the user entered data. You set a couple of properties on the control, and it was done. You set the ErrorMessage to a string that displayed in the ValidationSummary control. Setting Display="None" caused the error message not to be shown inside of the RequiredFieldValidator control. The required property, ControlToValidate, was set to the ID of the control that was required.

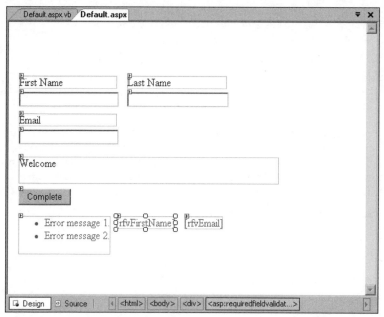

Figure 17-7

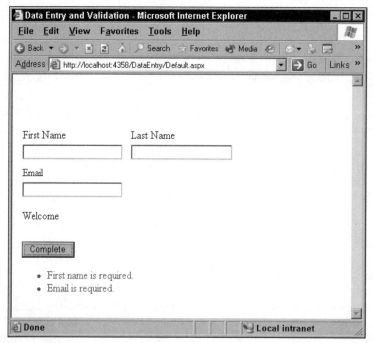

Figure 17-8

```
<asp:RequiredFieldValidator ID="rfvFirstName" Style="z-index: 35; left: 168px;
position: absolute; top: 288px" Runat="server" ErrorMessage="First name is
required." Display="None" ControlToValidate="txtFirstName">
</asp:RequiredFieldValidator>
```

You used the `ValidationSummary` control as a central location for displaying all error messages. If you decide not to use a summary object, you could set the `display` property of the individual validation controls to `true`. Then, the error messages is displayed within the validation control. No property changes are needed to use the `ValidationSummary` control. You just add it to the form at the location you wanted to display validation messages.

```
<asp:ValidationSummary ID="ValidationSummary1" Style="z-index: 37; left: 16px;
position: absolute; top: 288px" Runat="server" />
```

The only code you wrote was added to the `Page_Load` event. Here, you tested for a postback using the `IsPostBack` property of the `Page` object. If it was a postback, you displayed the name and e-mail entered by the user.

```
If Page.IsPostBack Then
    'If this is a post back and not the initial page load
    'Display the data to the user
    Me.lblWelcome.Text = "Hello " + Me.txtFirstName.Text + " " + _
    Me.txtLastName.Text + "<BR>" + "Your email address is " + Me.txtEmail.Text
End If
```

Designing the Site's Look and Feel

In the past, a major drawback of Web development was maintaining a consistent look and feel across an entire site in a manageable way. Developers created user controls and inserted server-side includes in every page to try and accomplish this. For the most part, this worked. The hard part was making sure the opening tags that were in certain include files were closed in the pages that included them. Another cause of frustration for the designer was making sure all user controls or include files displayed in the same location. This took time, and with every page changed, someone had to make sure the entire site looked OK. Today, VS 2005 has the tools that can be used to maintain a consistent look and feel.

Themes, navigation controls, and master pages are the tools to accomplish a consistent look and feel. You will learn about all three in the next *Try It Out*.

Try It Out   Building Your First Web Site

1. Create a new site and name the project SiteLookAndFeel.

2. To start the project, you add many files and folders. First, add a master page by right-clicking the project name in Solution Explorer and selecting Add New Item from the context menu. In the dialog box that opens, choose Master Page and click Add.

3. Change the page directive on the `Default.aspx` page to reference the new master page:

```
<%@ Master Language="VB" CodeFile="MasterPage.master.vb" Inherits="MasterPage" %>
```

4. Add the following new files and folders.

❑ Add a new Theme Folder under the root and name it Red. To do this, right-click the solution in Solution Explorer and choose Add Folder ➪ Theme Folder. This will create a main folder named App_Themes and a subfolder named Red. Under App_Themes, add another folder named **Brown**. Next, add a new text file (Brown.skin) to the Brown subfolder. Also, add a new style sheet to the Brown folder and name it **Brown.css**. To the Red subfolder, add three new text files. Name them **Button.Skin**, **TextBox.Skin**, and **Red.Skin**.

❑ Under the root directory for the site, add five new Web Forms: **News.aspx**, **News Yesterday.aspx**, **NewsToday.aspx**, **Events.aspx**, and **Contact.aspx**. Make sure you check the box to select a master page for each new Web Form and check the box. Place code in separate file. After you click Add, you will see a dialog box for choosing a master page with one option; MasterPage.master. Select MasterPage.master and continue for each new page.

❑ Finally, add a new site map. Right-click the project in Server Explorer and add a new item. In the dialog box, select Site Map and click Add. You can leave the default name of Web.sitemap. When you finish, the Solution Explorer window will look like Figure 17-9.

Figure 17-9

5. Open the Web.sitemap file and update the code to match this code as highlighted:

```
<?xml version="1.0" encoding="utf-8" ?>
<siteMap xmlns="http://schemas.microsoft.com/AspNet/SiteMap-File-1.0" >

    <siteMapNode url="Default.aspx" title="Home"
    description="Back to the main page" roles="" >
```

```
        <siteMapNode url="News.aspx" title="News"
        description="Your front page news." roles="">
            <siteMapNode url="NewsToday.aspx" title="Today's News"
            description="Today's top stories" roles="" />
            <siteMapNode url="NewsYesterday.aspx" title="Yesterday's News"
            description="Yesterday's top stories" roles="" />
        </siteMapNode>
        <siteMapNode url="Events.aspx" title="Upcoming Events"
        description="Today's top stories" roles="" />
        <siteMapNode url="Contact.aspx" title="Contact Us"
        description="Today's top stories" roles="" />
    </siteMapNode>
</siteMap>
```

6.   Double-click the `Brown.css` style sheet in Solution Explorer to open the file. By default, it has a blank definition for the BODY element in the file. To add a definition, you can hand-code it after you learn the syntax, but for now use the built-in designer. Right-click anywhere on the page and select Add Style Rule from the context menu. The Add Style Rule dialog opens as shown in Figure 17-10. Select the HR element and add it to the style rule hierarchy by clicking the right arrow button. When you click OK, an empty element with no style definitions is added to the page.

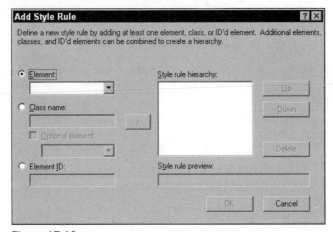

Figure 17-10

To add the style definitions you want to modify, you can use the Designer again or IntelliSense. To use the Designer, right click inside of the element definition start and end tags and select Build Style from the context menu. Go ahead and open the Designer. The designer looks like Figure 17-11. To use IntelliSense, start typing inside any element and you will see all styles for that element. Now, close the designer and add the following highlighted code to the HR definition by typing the code, and you will see the IntelliSense feature.

```
HR
{
    color:#cc0000;
    height:12px;
}
```

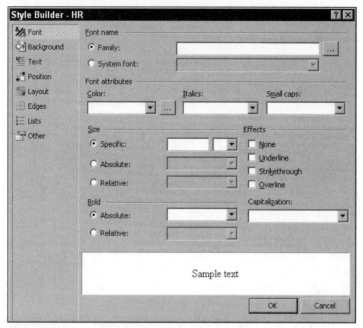

Figure 17-11

7. Now, you define the master page layout. Double-click the `MasterPage.master` file in the root directory to open the file. While in Source view, update the HTML code for the master page as highlighted:

```
<%@ Master Language="VB" CodeFile="MasterPage.master.vb" Inherits="MasterPage" %>

<!DOCTYPE html PUBLIC "-//W3C//DTD XHTML 1.1//EN"
"http://www.w3.org/TR/xhtml11/DTD/xhtml11.dtd">

<html xmlns="http://www.w3.org/1999/xhtml" >
<head runat="server">
    <title>Untitled Page</title>

    <Style>
    .TableLayout {width: 700px; background-color:#ffcc66;}
    .border{border-style:solid; border-color:black; border-width:thin;}
    </Style>
</head>

<body bgcolor="#cc0000">

    <form id="form1" runat="server">
    <div>

        <table id="tblMasterLayoutHeader" class="TableLayout" cellpadding="0"
            cellspacing="0" align="center" height="450">
        <tr>
```

```
        <td style="width: 100px" rowspan=2 class="border">
        <!-- Add the menu to the page -->
            <asp:Menu ID="Menu1" Runat="server" >
                <Items>
                    <asp:MenuItem Value="Home" Text="Home"
                        NavigateUrl="Default.aspx"></asp:MenuItem>
                    <asp:MenuItem Value="News" Text="News"
                        NavigateUrl="News.aspx">
                            <asp:MenuItem Value="Today" Text="Today"
                                NavigateUrl="NewsToday.aspx"></asp:MenuItem>
                            <asp:MenuItem Value="Yesterday" Text =
                                "Yesterday" NavigateUrl=
                                "NewsYesterday.aspx"></asp:MenuItem>
                    </asp:MenuItem>
                    <asp:MenuItem Value="Events" Text="Events"
                        NavigateUrl="Events.aspx"></asp:MenuItem>
                    <asp:MenuItem Value="Contact Us" Text="Contact Us"
                        NavigateUrl="Contact.aspx"></asp:MenuItem>
                </Items>
            </asp:Menu>
        </td>
        <td bgcolor="#000000" class="border" >
            <!-- Main title -->
            <asp:Label ID="Label1" Runat="server" Text="Beginning Visual
                Basic 2005" Font-Names="Arial" Font-Bold="true"
                ForeColor="#ffcc33" Font-Size="28pt" />
        </td>
    </tr>
    <tr>
        <td class="border">
            <!-- Site map path under Title -->
            <asp:SiteMapPath ID="smpMain" Runat="server"></asp:SiteMapPath>
        </td>
    </tr>
    <tr>
        <td class="border" colspan="2" height="100%" valign="top"
            align="center">
            <!-- All site content will go here -->
            <asp:contentplaceholder id="cphPageContent" runat="server">
            </asp:contentplaceholder><br />
        </td>
    </tr>
    <tr>
        <td class="border" align="center" colspan="2">
            <!-- Footer -->
            <asp:Label ID="Label2" Runat="server" Text="(c)2004, All rights
                reserved." Font-Names="Arial" Font-Bold="true"
                ForeColor="black" Font-Size="10pt" ></asp:Label>
        </td>
    </tr>
    </table>
    </div>
    </form>
</body>
</html>
```

569

8. Open the `Default.aspx` page. Make sure the Page declarations match these and add the following.

```
<%@ Page Language="VB" MasterPageFile="~/MasterPage.master" AutoEventWireup="false"
ClassName="Default_aspx" title="Untitled Page" Theme="Red"%>
<asp:Content ContentPlaceHolderID=cphPageContent Runat=Server>
    <asp:TextBox ID="txtTest" Runat="server">Just some text</asp:TextBox>
    <hr /><br />
    <asp:Button ID="btnTest" Runat="server" Text="Button" /></asp:Content>
```

9. Next, change the `News.aspx` page to match the code here.

```
<%@ Page Language="VB" MasterPageFile="~/MasterPage.master" AutoEventWireup="false"
ClassName="News_aspx" title="Untitled Page" theme="Brown"%>
<asp:Content ID="Content1" ContentPlaceHolderID=cphPageContent Runat=Server>
    <asp:TextBox ID="txtTest" Runat="server">Just some text</asp:TextBox>
    <asp:Button ID="btnTest" Runat="server" Text="Button" /></asp:Content>
```

10. Here is the code listing for the `Button.Skin` page under the Red theme. Open this page and add the code listed here.

```
<asp:Button runat="server" ForeColor="Red" Font-Name="Arial" Font-Size="28px" Font-
Weight="Bold" />
```

11. Open `TextBox.Skin` under the Red theme folder and add the code listed here.

```
<asp:TextBox runat="server" ForeColor="Red" Font-Name="Arial" Font-Size="28px"
Font-Weight="Bold" />
```

12. Open `Brown.Skin` under the Brown theme folder and add the code listed here.

```
<asp:Button runat="server" ForeColor="Brown" Font-Name="Arial" Font-Size="28px"
Font-Weight="Bold" />
<asp:TextBox runat="server" ForeColor="Brown" Font-Name="Arial" Font-Size="28px"
Font-Weight="Bold" />
```

13. On the other Web forms, you must change the ContentPlaceHolderID to cphPageContent. This is because you changed the master page after adding these forms. So the second line of code for Contact.aspx, Events.aspx, NewToday.aspx, and NewsYesterday will be changed to the listing here:

```
<asp:Content ID="Content1" ContentPlaceHolderID="cphPageContent" Runat="Server">
```

14. Run the application and test the navigation and layout. Play around; the site has a lot of functionality. Pay close attention to the navigation controls. Your site will resemble Figure 17-12.

Server controls render HTML based on the calling browser. If you have Netscape 7.2, you can see this in action. If not, you can download Netscape at `http://channels.netscape.com/ns/browsers/`
`default.jsp.`

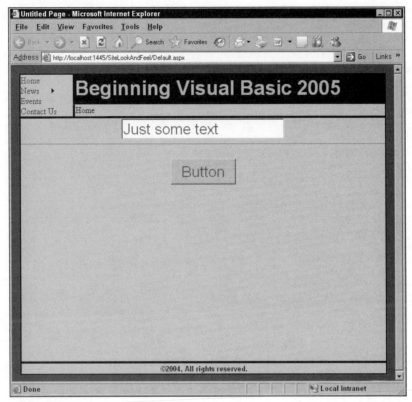

Figure 17-12

Open Netscape and browse to the Default.aspx *page for your site. Look at the main menu. The mouse-over action for* News *is not supported by Netscape in the same format. The ASPX engine renders the markup for the* Menu *control specifically for Netscape 7.2. To see the* News *submenu, click the* News *menu item. You will see the* News *submenu with an option to move up one level to the root menu. Before server controls, you had to write logic for many browsers. That is not necessary in ASP.NET 2.0 when you use server controls.*

How It Works

You were able to take advantage of some of the newest controls to ASP.NET 2.0 in this Try It Out. The combination of these controls allowed you to create a simple, yet powerful example of proper site design and layout. The master page maintains the same page layout across the entire site. You added the HTML used to lay out the look and feel of the site. All of the navigation for the entire site is located in this one page. If you ever need to change the menu or site map, you could change one page and that change would cascade across the entire site.

ContentPlaceHolder offers a mistake-free way to add logic to each additional page. If you work in a team, a designer would create the site layout and the master page.

Another element you added was the reusable styles. You used styles to apply a class name to objects that you wanted to modify. Styles are very powerful and play a huge role in Web site design.

The final item used for the layout of the master page was the Menu control. You used XML format to build a hierarchy of parent/child menu items that rendered the site navigation main menu. Here is the full code listing for MasterPage.master.

```
<!DOCTYPE html PUBLIC "-//W3C//DTD XHTML 1.1//EN"
"http://www.w3.org/TR/xhtml11/DTD/xhtml11.dtd">


<html xmlns="http://www.w3.org/1999/xhtml" >
<head runat="server">
    <title>Untitled Page</title>
    <Style>
    .TableLayout {width: 700px; background-color:#ffcc66;}
    .border{border-style:solid; border-color:black; border-width:thin;}
    </Style>
</head>
<body bgcolor="#cc0000">
    <form id="form1" runat="server">
    <div>
        <table id="tblMasterLayoutHeader" class="TableLayout" cellpadding="0"
            cellspacing="0" align="center" height="450">
            <tr>
                <td style="width: 100px" rowspan=2 class="border">
                <!-- Add the menu to the page -->
                    <asp:Menu ID="Menu1" Runat="server" >
                        <Items>
                            <asp:MenuItem Value="Home" Text="Home"
                                NavigateUrl="Default.aspx"></asp:MenuItem>
                            <asp:MenuItem Value="News" Text="News"
                                NavigateUrl="News.aspx">
                                    <asp:MenuItem Value="Today" Text="Today"
                                        NavigateUrl="NewsToday.aspx"></asp:MenuItem>
                                    <asp:MenuItem Value="Yesterday" Text =
                                        "Yesterday" NavigateUrl=
                                        "NewsYesterday.aspx"></asp:MenuItem>
                            </asp:MenuItem>
                            <asp:MenuItem Value="Events" Text="Events"
                                NavigateUrl="Events.aspx"></asp:MenuItem>
                            <asp:MenuItem Value="Contact Us" Text="Contact Us"
                                NavigateUrl="Contact.aspx"></asp:MenuItem>
                        </Items>
                    </asp:Menu>
                </td>
                <td bgcolor="#000000" class="border" >
                    <!-- Main title -->
                    <asp:Label ID="Label1" Runat="server" Text="Beginning Visual
                        Basic 2005" Font-Names="Arial" Font-Bold="true"
                        ForeColor="#ffcc33" Font-Size="28pt" />
                </td>
            </tr>
            <tr>
                <td class="border">
```

```
                            <!-- Site map path under Title -->
                            <asp:SiteMapPath ID="smpMain" Runat="server"></asp:SiteMapPath>
                        </td>
                    </tr>
                    <tr>
                        <td class="border" colspan="2" height="100%" valign="top"
                            align="center">
                            <!-- All site content will go here -->
                            <asp:contentplaceholder id="cphPageContent" runat="server">
                            </asp:contentplaceholder><br />
                        </td>
                    </tr>
                    <tr>
                        <td class="border" align="center" colspan="2">
                            <!-- Footer -->
                            <asp:Label ID="Label2" Runat="server" Text="(c)2004, All rights
                                reserved." Font-Names="Arial" Font-Bold="true"
                                ForeColor="black" Font-Size="10pt" ></asp:Label>
                        </td>
                    </tr>
                </table>
            </div>
            </form>
    </body>
    </html>
```

Although you kept it simple, the Menu control is very customizable. Instead of hard-coding the menu, you could bind the menu to a dataset. You could also change the orientation. The menu displayed vertically for the site, but you could use a horizontal format by changing the Orientation property. The other items you could have changed were the styles of the menu items. You could have changed the look of the menu using styles or themes.

You left the Red.Skin page blank. You will change this later in the chapter.

The Button.Skin page defined the styles for a Button control when the Red theme was applied.

```
<asp:Button runat="server" ForeColor="Red" Font-Name="Arial" Font-Size="28px" Font-
Weight="Bold" />
```

This TextBox.skin page defined the styles for a TextBox control when the Red theme was applied.

```
<asp:TextBox runat="server" ForeColor="Red" Font-Name="Arial" Font-Size="28px"
Font-Weight="Bold" />
```

For the Default.aspx page, you added a reference to the master page and set the theme to Red in the Page directive. Then, inside the Content control, you added a text box, horizontal rule, line break, and button. When you saw the page, the text was red, bold, and large just as the theme defined. (See Figure 17-12.)

```
<%@ Page Language="VB" MasterPageFile="~/MasterPage.master" AutoEventWireup="false"
ClassName="Default_aspx" title="Untitled Page" Theme="Red"%>
<asp:Content ContentPlaceHolderID=cphPageContent Runat=Server>
```

```
    <asp:TextBox ID="txtTest" Runat="server">Just some text</asp:TextBox>
    <hr /><br />
    <asp:Button ID="btnTest" Runat="server" Text="Button" />
</asp:Content>
```

You applied the `Brown.css` style sheet to the theme. The only element you modified in the style sheet was the horizontal rule. You changed the color (red) and height. You can update any object using the style sheet. Your output should have displayed the updated styles as in Figure 17-13.

```
body {}
HR
{
    color:#cc0000;
    height:12px;
}
```

The `Brown.skin` page defined the styles for Button and TextBox controls when the Brown theme was applied.

```
<asp:Button runat="server" ForeColor="Brown" Font-Name="Arial" Font-Size="28px"
Font-Weight="Bold" />
<asp:TextBox runat="server" ForeColor="Brown" Font-Name="Arial" Font-Size="28px"
Font-Weight="Bold" />
```

On `News.aspx` you added a reference to the master page and set the theme to `Brown` in the `Page` directive. Then, inside the Content control, you added a textbox, horizontal rule, line break, and button. When you saw the page, the text was red, bold, and large just as the theme defined. You should have seen a page like Figure 17-13 in your browser.

```
<%@ Page Language="VB" MasterPageFile="~/MasterPage.master" AutoEventWireup="false"
ClassName="News_aspx" title="Untitled Page" theme="Brown"%>
<asp:Content ID="Content1" ContentPlaceHolderID=cphPageContent Runat=Server>
    <asp:TextBox ID="txtTest" Runat="server">Just some text</asp:TextBox>
    <hr /><br />
    <asp:Button ID="btnTest" Runat="server" Text="Button" /></asp:Content>
```

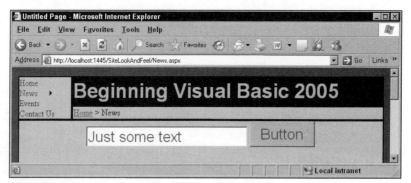

Figure 17-13

The sitemap file is used by the SiteMap control. This control allows you to see what level you are on at the site. You could easily navigate up one level at a time or all the way to the home page. The control gives you an easy interface for navigating through the site. The outer most level of the SiteMap control is displayed on the Today's News page as shown in Figure 17-14.

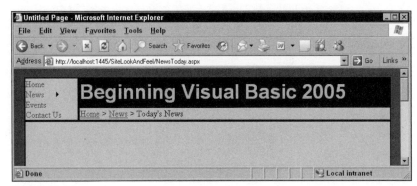

Figure 17-14

Using the GridView to Build a Data-Driven Web Form

The new data controls in ASP.NET 2.0 add the ability to program *declaratively*. This new "no code" architecture allows you to look at the source of the Web Form and see your layout and design along with attributes that allow for data access and data manipulation. If you have any experience with HTML or ASP.NET 1.1, you will find this new method of data access compact and astoundingly simple.

In this Try It Out, you will see two of the best controls in ASP.NET 2.0. The first is the SqlDataSource control, and the second is the GridView control. You will set properties and attributes of these controls and also the child elements of them. Without writing any server-side or client-side code, you will create a Web application to display data in the pubs database and update it.

Try It Out   No-Code Data Viewing and Updating

1. Create a new Web Site and name it **DataGridView**.

2. Use the Source view and add the changes highlighted here to the Default.aspx page. Make sure to change the values of the ConnectionString to your development environment.

```
<%@ Page Language="VB" AutoEventWireup="false" CodeFile="Default.aspx.vb"
        Inherits="_Default" %>

<!DOCTYPE html PUBLIC "-//W3C//DTD XHTML 1.1//EN"
        "http://www.w3.org/TR/xhtml11/DTD/xhtml11.dtd">

<html xmlns="http://www.w3.org/1999/xhtml" >
<head runat="server">

    <title>Grid View</title>
</head>
<body>
```

```
<form id="form1" runat="server">
<div>

    <asp:SqlDataSource ID="sdsAuthors" Runat="server"
                       ProviderName = "System.Data.SqlClient"
                       ConnectionString = "Server=bnewsome; User ID=sa;
                       Password=!p@ssw0rd!;Database=pubs; "
                       SelectCommand = "SELECT au_id, au_lname, au_fname, phone,
                       address, city, state, zip FROM authors"
                       UpdateCommand = "UPDATE authors SET au_lname = @au_lname,
                       au_fname = @au_fname, phone = @phone, address = @address,
                       city = @city, state = @state, zip = @zip
                       WHERE au_id = @original_au_id" >
        <UpdateParameters>
            <asp:Parameter Type="String" Name="au_lname"></asp:Parameter>
            <asp:Parameter Type="String" Name="au_fname"></asp:Parameter>
            <asp:Parameter Type="String" Name="phone"></asp:Parameter>
            <asp:Parameter Type="String" Name="address"></asp:Parameter>
            <asp:Parameter Type="String" Name="city"></asp:Parameter>
            <asp:Parameter Type="String" Name="state"></asp:Parameter>
            <asp:Parameter Type="String" Name="zip"></asp:Parameter>
            <asp:Parameter Type="String" Name="au_id"></asp:Parameter>
        </UpdateParameters>
    </asp:SqlDataSource>

    <asp:GridView ID="gdvAuthors" Runat="server" DataSourceID="sdsAuthors"
                  AllowPaging="True" AllowSorting="True" AutoGenerateColumns=False
                  DataKeyNames="au_id" >
        <PagerStyle BackColor="Gray" ForeColor="White" HorizontalAlign="Center" />
        <HeaderStyle BackColor="Black" ForeColor="White" />
        <AlternatingRowStyle BackColor="LightGray" />
        <Columns>
            <asp:CommandField ButtonType="Button" ShowEditButton="true" />
            <asp:BoundField Visible="false" HeaderText="au_id" DataField="au_id"
                        SortExpression="au_id"></asp:BoundField>
            <asp:BoundField HeaderText="Last Name" DataField="au_lname"
                        SortExpression="au_lname"></asp:BoundField>
            <asp:BoundField HeaderText="First Name" DataField="au_fname"
                        SortExpression="au_fname"></asp:BoundField>
            <asp:BoundField HeaderText="Phone" DataField="phone"
                        SortExpression="phone"></asp:BoundField>
            <asp:BoundField HeaderText="Address" DataField="address"
                        SortExpression="address"></asp:BoundField>
            <asp:BoundField HeaderText="City" DataField="city"
                        SortExpression="city"></asp:BoundField>
            <asp:BoundField HeaderText="State" DataField="state"
                        SortExpression="state"></asp:BoundField>
            <asp:BoundField HeaderText="Zip Code" DataField="zip"
                        SortExpression="zip"></asp:BoundField>
        </Columns>
    </asp:GridView>
</div>
</form>
</body>
</html>
```

3. Run the application without debugging by pressing Ctrl+F5. You will see the data grid display similar to Figure 17-15.

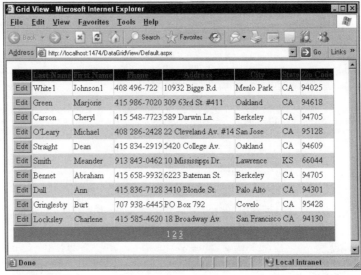

Figure 17-15

Test the functions of the grid. At the bottom, you can move to any page of the data. Also, sorting is available by clicking any of the column headers. After trying both of these, update a row. To edit an author's data, click the Edit button on the left of the author's row. The screen will refresh, and you will see a new grid that looks like Figure 17-16.

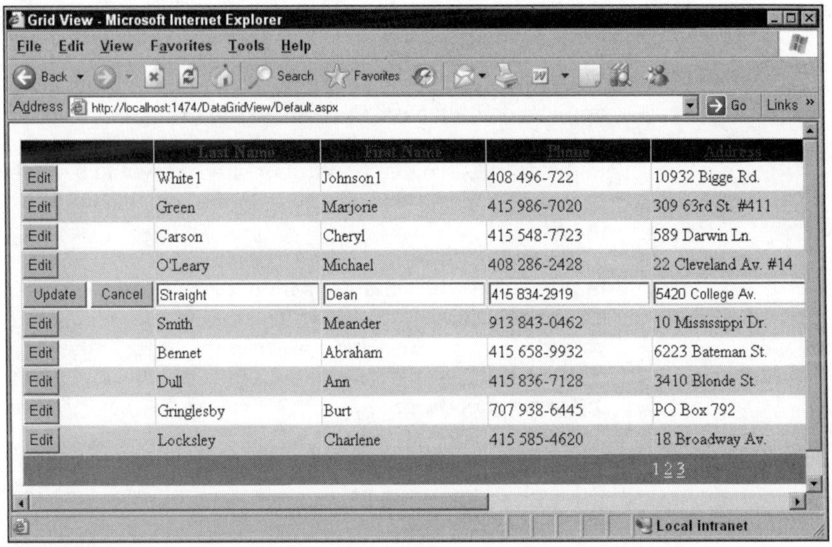

Figure 17-16

Change any field and click the update button to make the change permanent. You can cancel a change by clicking any link or button other than the Update button.

How It Works

Now that was easy. By adding two controls, you created a fairly robust data access page. Let's explain how this happened.

First, you created a `SqlDataSource` control. The following table will explain each attribute you added or changed for the `SqlDataSource` control. The code follows.

Attribute or Element	Description
ID	The control's identifier.
Runat	Defined that the code for the control was run at the server before the page was sent to the browser.
ProviderName	Used to set the provider to access the data store. In this case, it was SQLClient, the managed provider for SQL Server.
ConnectionString	This string value was used to gain access to the database resource, pubs, requested. (In the exercises at the end of this chapter, you will investigate a more secure and manageable method of storing the connection string in the web.config file.)
SelectCommand	The SQL statement passed to the database to retrieve the data that was displayed in the grid. This could have been a stored procedure name.
UpdateCommand	The SQL statement that was used to update the data. You could have used a stored procedure name in place of the SQL statement in this case.
UpdateParameters and Parameter objects	The update parameters object is a collection of parameters the application used to fill in the blanks in the update statement. For example, the parameter @city in the update statement passed a value to the database so that the Author's record would be updated. This parameter, @city, was replaced with the actual value you entered into the city text box. In the future, when you use parameters, the database will determine the syntax. Some databases will just use a question mark for each parameter name. Also, in some cases the order of the parameter object matters. For this application, the names are the only part that makes a difference, not the order. Another common property not used here is DefaultValue. The Default-Value property would have replaced a null value with the value set in the property itself.

Parameter: Type	This was string for every parameter. This value was determined based on the data type on each column in the database.
Parameter: Name	The name property was the actual name used by the UpdateCommand for each parameter.

```
<asp:SqlDataSource ID="sdsAuthors" Runat="server"
                   ProviderName = "System.Data.SqlClient"
                   ConnectionString = "Server=bnewsome; User ID=sa;
                   Password=!p@ssw0rd!;Database=pubs; "
                   SelectCommand = "SELECT au_id, au_lname, au_fname, phone,
                   address, city, state, zip FROM authors"
                   UpdateCommand = "UPDATE authors SET au_lname = @au_lname,
                   au_fname = @au_fname, phone = @phone, address = @address,
                   city = @city, state = @state, zip = @zip
                   WHERE au_id = @original_au_id" >
    <UpdateParameters>
        <asp:Parameter Type="String" Name="au_lname"></asp:Parameter>
        <asp:Parameter Type="String" Name="au_fname"></asp:Parameter>
        <asp:Parameter Type="String" Name="phone"></asp:Parameter>
        <asp:Parameter Type="String" Name="address"></asp:Parameter>
        <asp:Parameter Type="String" Name="city"></asp:Parameter>
        <asp:Parameter Type="String" Name="state"></asp:Parameter>
        <asp:Parameter Type="String" Name="zip"></asp:Parameter>
        <asp:Parameter Type="String" Name="au_id"></asp:Parameter>
    </UpdateParameters>
</asp:SqlDataSource>
```

The second control you added to the form was the GridView. Its attributes are described in the following table.

Attribute or Element	Description
ID	The control's identifier.
Runat	Defines that the code for the control was run at the server before the page was sent to the browser.
DataSourceID	The ID of the SqlDataSource object was used here.
AllowPaging	Can be set to TRUE or FALSE. Turns on sorting features of the grid.
AllowSorting	Can be set to TRUE or FALSE. Turns on sorting features of the grid.
AutoGenerateColumns	Can be set to TRUE or FALSE. Turns on sorting features of the grid.
DataKeyNames	The primary key used by the database table.
PagerStyle	This element defines the style of the paging area of the grid.
HeaderStyle	This element defines the style of the header row area of the grid.
AlternatingRowStyle	This element defines the style of the every other row of the grid.
Columns	A collection of column objects.

Attribute or Element	Description
CommandField	Two properties of this object were used. The first was ButtonType. This was set to a type of button. You can insert a button, image, or link as a value. If left blank, the default is link.
BoundField	This element allows for the binding of the data to the grid. For a better user interface, you used the Visible property to hide the primary key column. Also, you set the SortExpression of each column. This converts every column header to a link. When clicked, the data is sorted by that column. Next, you changed the column headers with the HeaderText property. If this is blank, the column names are used as headers. Finally, the field to bind to was set using the DataField property.

```
<asp:GridView ID="gdvAuthors" Runat="server" DataSourceID="sdsAuthors"
            AllowPaging="True" AllowSorting="True" AutoGenerateColumns=False
            DataKeyNames="au_id" >
  <PagerStyle BackColor="Gray" ForeColor="White" HorizontalAlign="Center" />
  <HeaderStyle BackColor="Black" ForeColor="White" />
  <AlternatingRowStyle BackColor="LightGray" />
  <Columns>
     <asp:CommandField ButtonType="Button" ShowEditButton="true" />
     <asp:BoundField Visible="false" HeaderText="au_id" DataField="au_id"
                 SortExpression="au_id"></asp:BoundField>
     <asp:BoundField HeaderText="Last Name" DataField="au_lname"
                 SortExpression="au_lname"></asp:BoundField>
     <asp:BoundField HeaderText="First Name" DataField="au_fname"
                 SortExpression="au_fname"></asp:BoundField>
     <asp:BoundField HeaderText="Phone" DataField="phone"
                 SortExpression="phone"></asp:BoundField>
     <asp:BoundField HeaderText="Address" DataField="address"
                 SortExpression="address"></asp:BoundField>
     <asp:BoundField HeaderText="City" DataField="city"
                 SortExpression="city"></asp:BoundField>
     <asp:BoundField HeaderText="State" DataField="state"
                 SortExpression="state"></asp:BoundField>
     <asp:BoundField HeaderText="Zip Code" DataField="zip"
                 SortExpression="zip"></asp:BoundField>
  </Columns>
</asp:GridView>
```

Web Site Locations with VS 2005

All of the examples in this chapter use the file system location for all of the Web sites as shown in Figure 17-17. One advantage of this location is that the Web server is not accessible to external users. Always make sure you test your site on the actual version of IIS running on the production server before going live.

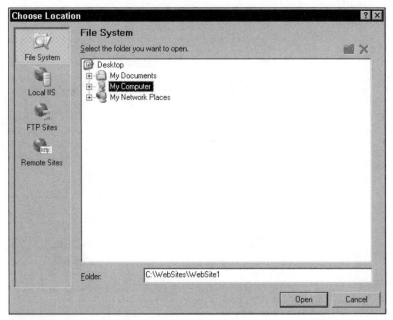

Figure 17-17

There are three other ways to work with Web site projects. To see the other options, just click the Browse button on the New Web Site dialog box. The first is using local IIS. (See Figure 17-18.)

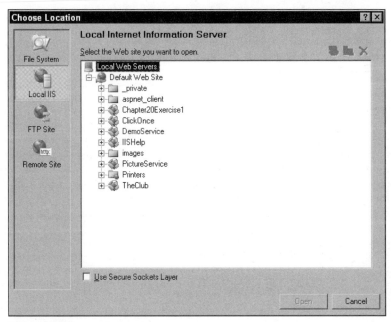

Figure 17-18

If you have a local Web server, you can host your application there. This allows others to see the site and test it. The second option is to use an FTP site. In this case, you are most likely using a hosting company. All you have to do is add the location and authentication information, and you can code your application on the production server. You can see the setup screen for an FTP site in Figure 17-19.

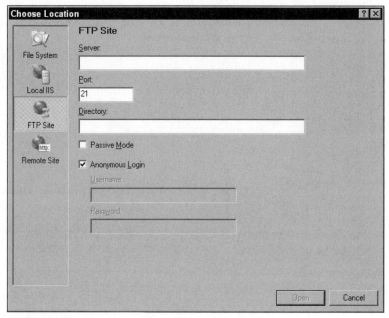

Figure 17-19

The final option is a Remote Site. Again, this also may be used when you use a hosting company. If your hosting company supports FrontPage Extensions, you can use this option as shown in Figure 17-20.

Summary

In this chapter, you learned what thin-client development is. You saw the advantages of Web Forms and Windows Forms and why you would choose one type of application over the other. Maybe the low distribution cost of Web applications is a major factor in your decision to create a Web application over a Windows application. Also, you read about the basic pieces that constitute a typical Web application. From layout and formatting to database integration, you gained knowledge on the best features of ASP.NET 2.0 and how they were implemented. Finally, you designed a code-free page that updated data in a database.

If you like Web development, there is much more than can be explained in this chapter. To continue learning, I suggest you find a book that is entirely based on ASP.NET 2.0. You can learn much more that way. The best title from WROX to complete next would either be *Beginning ASP.NET 2.0* or *Professional ASP.NET 2.0*. Either one would take you to the next level for Web development.

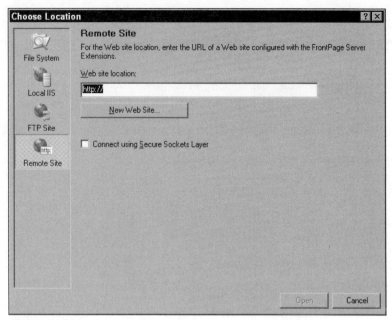

Figure 17-20

To summarize, you should know how to:

❑ Choose between Web Forms versus Windows Forms applications

❑ Use the toolbox for ASP.NET 2.0

❑ Create a Web site project in Visual Studio 2005

❑ Validate data for a Web application

❑ Manage site layout using themes, navigation controls, and master pages

❑ Use the GridView control to build a data driven ASP.NET Web Form

❑ Choose between the possible locations for Web sites in VS 2005

Exercise

Open up your DataGridView project. A better way to store the connection string would be to store it in the `web.config` file. For the exercise, you should store the connection string in the `web.config` file and retrieve it when setting the property of the SqlDataSource control.

First, you will add a `web.config` file to the project. Then add this code as a child of the `<appSettings>` element.

```
<add key="ConnectionString" value="Server=bnewsome; User ID=sa; Password=!p@ssw0rd!;
Database=pubs;" />
```

Make sure to change the values to match your development environment.

Next, remove the `ConnectionString` property from the `sdsAuthors` declaration.

Finally, you need to add a server event on the `Default.aspx`. Use the Objects and Events combo boxes to add a subroutine to fire for the `sdsAuthors_Init` event. Inside of this, set the `ConnectionString` property of `sdsAuthors` equal to the `web.config` value.

To get the value, this function returns the value from the config file:

```
ConfigurationManager.AppSettings("ConnectionString")
```

Forms Authentication

In Chapter 17, you learned how to implement many pieces of the puzzle that is Web development. Now, you will put it all together to build the foundation for a secure public Web site. You will create a skeleton Web site in this chapter, with security, that is ready for content. While writing no Visual Basic code, you will end up with a consistent look and feel and role-based forms authentication. You will be amazed at the ease of creation and the flexibility built into ASP.NET 2.0.

In this chapter, you will:

❑   Have an overview of the two most popular methods of Web site security

❑   Learn about the Web Site Administration Tool

❑   Implement Web site security using forms authentication

❑   Add rules and roles to a security scheme

❑   Create a secure Web site with little or no code written

Web Site Authentication

As you design Web applications, you need to consider security at an early point in the project. Always understand who will need access to your site and who will not have access. In many cases, parts of the site will be open to the public and parts will be secure and for members only. This may require multiple methods of security. There are two standard types of Web authentication strategies: windows and forms authentication.

Windows Authentication

The simplest type of authentication is windows authentication. This type of authentication is perfect for intranet sites. It is actually implemented by IIS and keeps the authentication mechanisms separate from the tasks of developing the actual intranet site. What happens is that IIS requires the user either to be logged into the server's domain to log in with a valid domain account. If the user is already authenticated with a valid domain account, access to the site is seamless with no interruption to the user experience. When the user is not logged into the server's domain, a valid login is required. This method of authentication is set up via the IIS Management Console.

Forms Authentication

For a public Web site, forms authentication is an easy solution to implement. Users that visit the site must provide credentials to gain authorization to the site. When an unauthorized user requests a Web page, the user is redirected to the login page. From here, a current user can log in, or new users can click a link to create an account. Without a valid user name or password, the visitor cannot browse secured areas of the site. With ASP .NET 2.0, built-in controls make forms authentication quick and easy to implement as a security model.

Web Site Administration Tool (WAT)

ASP .NET 2.0 is driven by `web.config` files. In the past, developers had to hand-code the XML configuration files to set up functionality such as debugging, security, or tracing. Now, there is an interface to set up these configuration files for Web applications: the Web Site Administration Tool (WAT).

When you use the WAT, you will see five tabs (Home, Security, Profile, Application, and Provider). You will set site security using the Security tab in this chapter, and we will give you a brief summary of the others. The first tab is Home. Home is the main tab and displays info on your other options. Next is the Profile tab. You use this tab to collect and store data on your site's visitors. Application is another tab, enabling application configuration. Here you can set up site attributes such as counters, tracing, and Simple Mail Transfer Protocol (SMTP). The final tab is Provider. Use this tab to change the default data provider for the site. The default provider is AspNetAccessProvider for Microsoft Access. You will use the WAT to set up the Web site in the next Try It Out.

In this Try It Out, you will set up the files for a new Web site and use the WAT to implement forms authentication.

Try It Out ___ Forms Authentication Configuration

In this exercise, you will start the Web site that you will work on during this chapter. First, you will add the file structure to the new site. Then you will set up the forms authentication security model.

1. Create a new Web site project named **TheClub**. Be sure to use the file system for the site location.

2. Make the following changes to the site using Solution Explorer. To add items to a site using Solution Explorer, right-click the root folder or project and choose Add new item. In the dialog box, select the type of item (Web form, text file, etc) and supply the name. When you finish with step 2, your site will look like Figure 18-1. For all of the pages you add, uncheck the box to place code in a separate file.

Add a master page and name it **Main.master**. Set all Web Forms you add to use this master page. You will have an option to select a master page when you add the forms by checking a box to Select Master Page.

Add the following regular folders to the site:

❑ Admin

❑ Members

Add the following theme folder to the site: You should right click the project name in Solution Explorer and then choose Add Folder ➪ Theme Folder. The folder you add will be placed under a new App_Themes directory.

❑ MainTheme

Add the following Web Forms to the site's root folder (and remember to check the box to select a master page):

❑ Login.aspx

❑ ChangePassword.aspx

❑ CreateNewUser.aspx

Set the Login.aspx page to the start page.

Right-click the page in Solution Explorer and choose Set As Start Page.

Add the following Web Forms to the Admin folder (and remember to check the box to select a master page):

❑ Default.aspx

❑ ViewUsers.aspx

Add the following Web Forms to the Members folder (and remember to check the box to select a master page):

❑ Default.aspx

❑ ViewAuthors.aspx

❑ ViewTitles.aspx

Add the following text file to the MainTheme folder:

❑ Main.skin

3. Next, choose Website ➪ ASP.NET Configuration under the Main menu to use the WAT. The menu is shown in Figure 18-2.

Figure 18-1

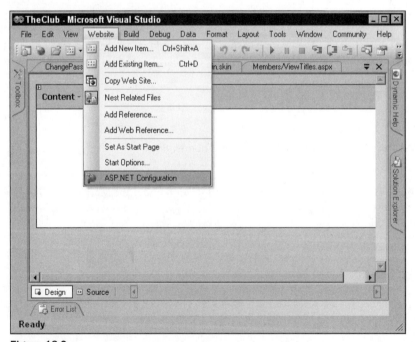

Figure 18-2

4. The Visual Web Developer Web Server will start and open the Web Site Administration Tool. Figure 18-3 shows the default page for the tool. You will use this tool to set up security for the site.

5. Now, click the Security link to set up the site security.

6. We will walk you through the wizard. Know that you can make any changes using the wizard from the main security page. Click the link on the security home page to use the Security Setup Wizard.

7. The Security Setup Wizard has seven steps. The first is the welcome screen, which gives you an overview of the entire process. At the lower right of each step, you will see options to navigate through the wizard. On the Welcome screen, move to step 2 by clicking Next.

8. Step 2 allows you to select the access method. You have two options here, as shown in Figure 18-4. The first option is "From the internet." If you choose this option, the wizard will set the site up for forms authentication. This method will use a data source to store user account information and allow the public to access the site. The second option is "From a local area network" and will set the site to use windows authentication. You can use this option for an intranet application within a private network. For TheClub Web site, choose "From the internet" and click Next to move to step 3.

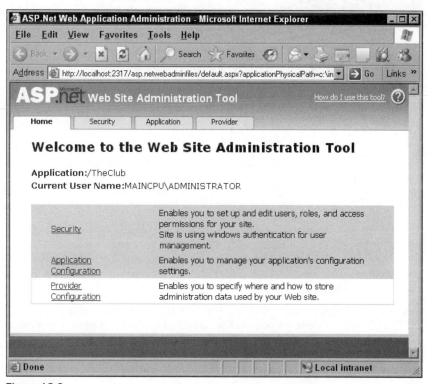

Figure 18-3

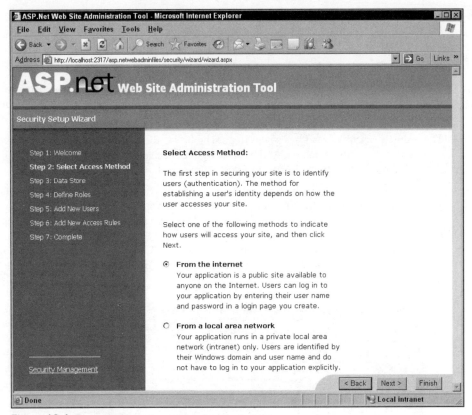

Figure 18-4

9. The third step is for data store information. You will see the default data provider for the site. To change this, you have to quit the wizard and make the change on the Provider tab. Just click Next to keep the default and move to step 4. The default data store uses Microsoft Access behind the scenes.

10. You can enable roles-based security on step 4. With roles-based security, you can manage site access for many users in a role quickly. Check the box to enable roles, and then click Next to add a new role. Figure 18-5 shows the Create New Role screen. Type the role name **Admin** into the text box and click Add Role. On the next screen, you can edit or add roles. For this site, you will have just one role, Admin. To move to step 5, click Next.

11. Step 5 allows you to create new users. You do not have to create users here, but it is an easy interface if you have a few to create. For this project, add the Admin user as shown in Figure 18-6. Set the User Name to **Admin**. You can set the rest of the fields to any values you can remember. When you finish, click the Create User button. You will see a successful creation note on the next screen. Since you are only adding one user, click Next to go to step 6.

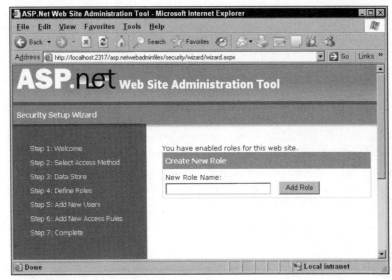

Figure 18-5

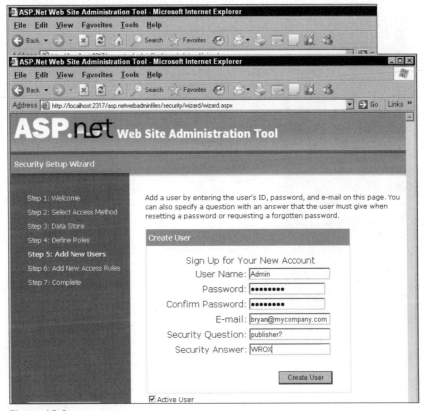

Figure 18-6

12. The last step prior to completing the wizard is step 6, Add New Access Rules. This is where you will set up the users who will have access to areas of the site. You will add three rules. You need to remember that rules are applied to Web folders. Always make sure the correct folder is highlighted when you add a rule.

As shown in Figure 18-7, the default rule is to allow anonymous users to access the site. Now, add a new rule. Make sure the Admin directory is highlighted, and click the radio button beside Role. Select the Admin role and then, under the Permission heading, turn on the radio button for Allow and click Add This Rule. You will add the two other rules after completing the wizard. To finish the wizard, click Next to move to the final confirmation and then click Finish. You will be taken back to the main security page, where you will complete the rest of the rules.

13. From the main security page, click the Manage Access Rules link. On the next screen, click the Admin folder to see the new rule. Now click the Add New Access Rule link. You will add a rule to deny all-user access to this folder. Move the rules up or down so that they match Figure 18-8.

14. Next, click the Members directory and add a rule to deny anonymous users. The rules for the Members folder will look like Figure 18-9.

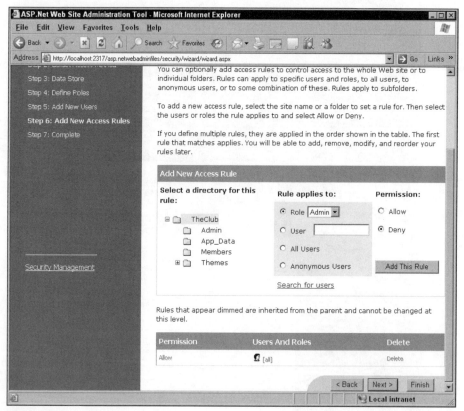

Figure 18-7

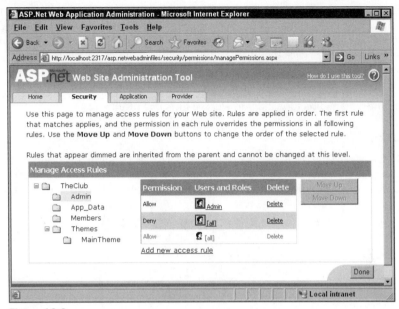

Figure 18-8

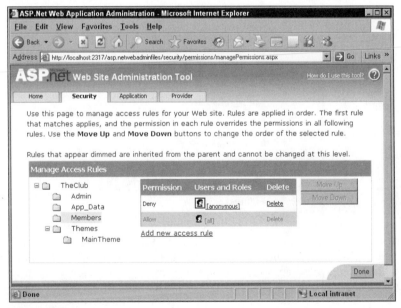

Figure 18-9

15. Now, you will test the security settings. Do not worry that the Web forms are blank. This test is just for the security settings.

Run the Web site and you will be taken to the home page of the root directory. Our URL is `http://localhost/TheClub/Login.aspx`. You will be prompted to enable debugging. Select Add a New Web.Config File with Debugging Enabled and then click OK to run the site. Once the browser opens, click the View Authors submenu under Members. The security should return you to the `Login.asp` page. The URL should look like `http://localhost/TheClub/login.aspx?ReturnUrl=%2fTheClub%2fmembers%2fdefault.aspx`.

16. Test the Admin directory and you will see the same result.

How It Works

So what did the wizard do? Well, first take a look at the project's Solution Explorer. Make sure you refresh the view. It will resemble Figure 18-10. Look closely and you will see new `web.config` files and an Access database. These new additions will manage the security options you set using the wizard.

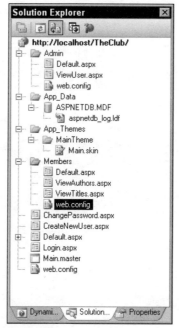

Figure 18-10

A site can be changed with settings in a `web.config` file. When you went through the wizard, settings were configured in `web.config` files per folder. If you opened one of the config files, you would see the settings that were added. Also, an Access database was created to manage the users and roles. That was it. To manage the security of the site, you do not need to know how to manipulate the `web.config` files manually.

Take a closer look at this URL, which sent you to the login page while testing (`http://localhost:11278/TheClub/login.aspx?ReturnUrl=%2fTheClub%2fmembers%2fdefault.aspx`) and you will see a question mark. The question mark represents the beginning of the query string. The query string is one way to pass data between the browser and server to maintain state. In this case, a variable (`ReturnUrl`) has a value from the Web server. The value has some encoded characters that may seem confusing. The forward slash is encoded in the query string and represented by `%2f`. So if you replace the characters `%2f` with a forward slash, then the value of `ReturnUrl` is `/TheClub/members/default.aspx`. When your login is successful, the sever will use the `ReturnUrl` to send you back to the place you were trying to visit — in this case, the Members folder.

Okay, so now you have a secure site. Next, you will take a look at the built-in login controls available in ASP.NET 2.0.

Login Controls

The Microsoft ASP team has encapsulated the most common functionality for authentication into a group of login controls that make your job as a developer easier. You can take the default behavior of these controls or customize almost every aspect of the controls functionality and design. The following table lists the login controls available. You are not required to use these controls. If you prefer, you can hand-code your own logic to use the same membership APIs to enforce forms authentication.

Control Name	Description
Login	Contains all of the elements necessary to provide a login area for a Website.
LoginView	Allows for templates to display the correct information to a user based on authentication and roles.
LoginStatus	Displays a link to log in or log out based on the users status.
LoginName	Displays the current user's name.
ChangePassword	Allows users change their password.
CreateUserWizard	Creates an area for new users to create a new account on the web site.
PasswordRecovery	Sends a user's forgotten or new password via email. *Note:* Email is not a secure means of data transmission. The security risks of this control should be considered before it is implemented on your Web site.

In the next Try It Out, you will use most of the login controls to implement a membership strategy.

Try It Out   Layout and Login Controls

Now that you have security set up, you need to add the layout and functionality to allow visitors to log in. In this Try It Out, you refresh your layout skills from Chapter 17 and gain knowledge about most of the Login controls in ASP.NET 2.0.

To complete this exercise, make the following changes to the pages of the site. As you make these changes, type the HTML markup into the pages as highlighted. You will get firsthand experience working with the IntelliSense for ASP.NET 2.0. As you type, you will be able to set properties and attributes quickly. You may find it faster than dragging controls from the Toolbox onto the form.

1. Main.master:

```
<%@ Master Language="VB" %>

<!DOCTYPE html PUBLIC "-//W3C//DTD XHTML 1.1//EN"
"http://www.w3.org/TR/xhtml11/DTD/xhtml11.dtd">

<script runat="server">
</script>

<html xmlns="http://www.w3.org/1999/xhtml" >
<head runat="server">
    <title>Untitled Page</title>
</head>

<body bgcolor="black">
    <form id="form1" runat="server">
    <div>
    <table cellpadding="5" cellspacing="0" width="600" height="400" bgcolor="white"
border="1" bordercolor="black">
        <tr>
          <td width="150" valign="top">
          <!-- Menu Column -->
            <asp:Menu ID="Menu1" Runat="server">
              <Items>
                <asp:MenuItem NavigateUrl="~/Default.aspx"
Text="Home"></asp:MenuItem>
                <asp:MenuItem Text="Members">
                  <asp:MenuItem NavigateUrl="Members/ViewAuthors.aspx"
Text="View Authors"></asp:MenuItem>
                  <asp:MenuItem NavigateUrl="Members/ViewTitles.aspx" Text="View
Titles"></asp:MenuItem>
                </asp:MenuItem>
                <asp:MenuItem Text="Admin">
                  <asp:MenuItem NavigateUrl="Admin/ViewUser.aspx" Text="View
Users"></asp:MenuItem>
                </asp:MenuItem>
              </Items>
            </asp:Menu>
            <br /><br /><br />
            <asp:LoginView ID="LoginView1" Runat="server">
              <AnonymousTemplate>
                <asp:Menu ID="Menu2" Runat="server">
                  <Items>
                    <asp:MenuItem NavigateUrl="~/CreateNewUser.aspx"
Text="Create Account"></asp:MenuItem>
```

```
                        </Items>
                    </asp:Menu>
                </AnonymousTemplate>
                <LoggedInTemplate>
                    <asp:Menu ID="Menu3" Runat="server">
                        <Items>
                            <asp:MenuItem NavigateUrl="~/ChangePassword.aspx"
Text="Change Password"></asp:MenuItem>
                        </Items>
                    </asp:Menu>
                </LoggedInTemplate>
            </asp:LoginView>
        </td>
        <td valign="top">
            <table cellpadding="0" cellspacing="0" width="100%" border="0">
                <tr>
                    <td width="85%">
                        <asp:Label ID="Label1" Runat="server" Text="My First Company
Site" Font-Bold="true" Font-Size="24px"></asp:Label>
                    </td>
                    <td width="15%">
                        <!-- Login Status Area -->
                        <asp:LoginStatus ID="LoginStatus1" Runat="server" />
                    </td>
                </tr>
                <tr>
                    <td colspan="2">
                        <hr color="black" size="2" />
                    </td>
                </tr>
                <tr>
                    <td colspan="2">
                        User:
                        <asp:LoginView ID="LoginView2" Runat="server">
                            <AnonymousTemplate>Guest, Please log in</AnonymousTemplate>
                            <LoggedInTemplate><asp:LoginName ID="LoginName1"
Runat="server" /></LoggedInTemplate>
                        </asp:LoginView>
                    </td>
                </tr>
                <tr>
                    <td colspan="2">
                        <hr color="black" size="2" />
                    </td>
                </tr>
                <tr>
                    <td colspan="2" valign="top" height="100%">
                        <asp:contentplaceholder id="cphMain" runat="server">
                        </asp:contentplaceholder>
                    </td>
                </tr>
            </table>
```

```
          </td>
        </tr>
      </table>
    </div>
  </form>
 </body>
 </html>
```

2. In `Default.aspx` (under root folder), delete the default code and insert the following code (see Figure 18-11):

```
<%@ Page Language="VB" MasterPageFile="~/Main.master" Title="Home" %>
```

3. In `Login.aspx` (see Figure 18-12), delete the default code and add the following code:

```
<%@ Page Language="VB" MasterPageFile="~/Main.master" Title="Login" %>
<asp:content ContentPlaceHolderID="cphMain" Runat="server">
   <asp:Login ID="Login1" runat="server">
   </asp:Login>
</asp:content>
```

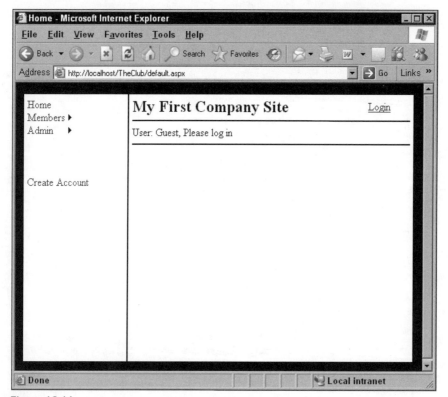

Figure 18-11

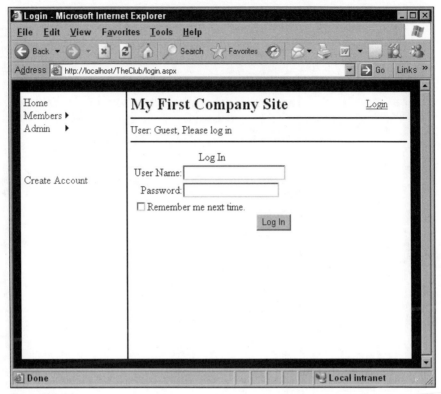

Figure 18-12

4. In `ChangePassword.aspx` (see Figure 18-13), delete the default code and add the following code:

```
<%@ Page Language="VB" MasterPageFile="~/Main.master" Title="Change Password" %>
<asp:Content ContentPlaceHolderID="cphMain" Runat="server">
   <asp:ChangePassword ID="ChangePassword1" Runat="server">
   </asp:ChangePassword>
</asp:Content>
```

5. In `CreateNewUser.aspx` (see Figure 18-14), delete the default code and add the following code:

```
<%@ Page Language="VB" MasterPageFile="~/Main.master" Title="Create New Account" %>
<asp:Content ContentPlaceHolderID="cphMain" Runat="server">
   <asp:CreateUserWizard ID="CreateUserWizard1" Runat="server">
   </asp:CreateUserWizard>
</asp:Content>
```

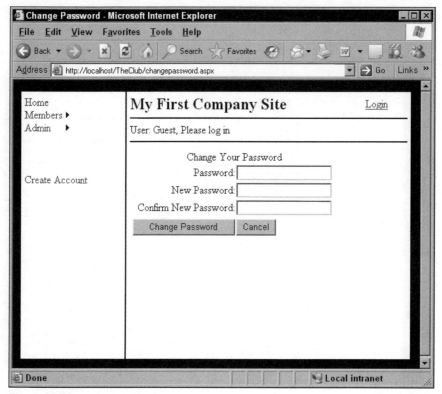

Figure 18-13

6. In `ViewAuthors.aspx`, delete the default code and add the following:

```
<%@ Page Language="VB" MasterPageFile="~/Main.master" Title="View Authors" %>
<asp:Content ID="Content1" ContentPlaceHolderID="cphMain" Runat="server">
   <asp:Label ID="Label1" Runat="server" Text="Add Code to View Author Info
Later"></asp:Label>
</asp:Content>
```

7. In `ViewTitles.aspx`, delete the default code and add the following:

```
<%@ Page Language="VB" MasterPageFile="~/Main.master" Title="View Titles" %>
<asp:Content ID="Content1" ContentPlaceHolderID="cphMain" Runat="server">
   <asp:Label ID="Label1" Runat="server" Text="Add Code to View Title Info
Later"></asp:Label>
</asp:Content>
```

8. In `ViewUsers.aspx`, delete the default code and add the following:

```
<%@ Page Language="VB" MasterPageFile="~/Main.master" Title="View Users" %>
<asp:Content ContentPlaceHolderID="cphMain" Runat="server">
   <asp:Label ID="Label1" Runat="server" Text="Add Code to View User Info
Later"></asp:Label>
</asp:Content>
```

Figure 18-14

9.   Now test the site. You can add a new account and then log in. Test the new pages to make sure they all work correctly. All of the authentication functionality will work. As you test the site using IIS and work with the configuration tool, you may see errors where the Access database is locked by another process. You can shut down the Web servers to free the lock.

How It Works

As you played with the new site, you should have been amazed. In older technologies, that level of functionality would have taken days to complete.

All you did for the site layout was on the master page. Let me explain these changes.

The first change sets the background color for the page to black:

```
<body bgcolor="black">
```

The next change involved the table layout for the page. Tables are a common layout tool in Web development. To set up the table layout, you added rows and cells and, in some cases, nested tables inside of cells. Table layout is an art you will learn with experience. First, take a look at the HTML tags used to format a table in the following table.

Tag	Description
<table>	The root tag for a table.
<tr>	A row in a table.
<td>	A cell in a row in a table.

When you set up the table layout, the cells by default were spaced apart. Setting the `cellpadding` and `cellspacing` properties made it easier to lay out the page the way you wanted it. The `colspan` attribute of the cell tag allowed the cell to span 2 columns. Basically, both columns were merged into one in that row.

The main table was set to a size of 600 by 400 with a white background. This allowed for the table to maintain a standard size even when no content was present. The main table contained one row and two columns. The first column was used for the menu. The second column had a nested table with 5 rows that contained one or two columns each. This table was set to a width of `100%` to force the table to fill up the second column. This allowed the HR controls to span the entire length of the parent column. The second table was for the site title, user name, and content place holder.

```
<table cellpadding="5" cellspacing="0" width="600" height="400" bgcolor="white"
border="1" bordercolor="black">
  <tr>
    <td width="150" valign="top">
    </td>
    <td valign="top">
      <table cellpadding="0" cellspacing="0" width="100%" border="0">
        <tr>
          <td width="85%">
          </td>
          <td width="15%">
          </td>
        </tr>
        <tr>
          <td colspan="2">
            <hr color="black" size="2" />
          </td>
        </tr>
        <tr>
          <td colspan="2">
          </td>
        </tr>
        <tr>
          <td colspan="2">
            <hr color="black" size="2" />
          </td>
        </tr>
        <tr>
          <td colspan="2" valign="top" height="100%">
          </td>
```

```
                </tr>
             </table>
          </td>
      </tr>
   </table>
```

The next part of the master page is the menu. Just as in Chapter 17, you add the menu control for site navigation. The difference is that you add multiple menu controls based on the login status. The `LoginView` control templates you worked with allows the user to see a validate menu based on the authentication status of the user.

```
<asp:Menu ID="Menu1" Runat="server">
  <Items>
    <asp:MenuItem NavigateUrl="~/Default.aspx" Text="Home"></asp:MenuItem>
    <asp:MenuItem Text="Members">
      <asp:MenuItem NavigateUrl="Members/ViewAuthors.aspx" Text="View Authors" />
      <asp:MenuItem NavigateUrl="Members/ViewTitles.aspx" Text="View Titles">
    </asp:MenuItem>
    <asp:MenuItem Text="Admin">
      <asp:MenuItem NavigateUrl="Admin/ViewUser.aspx" Text="View Users" />
    </asp:MenuItem>
  </Items>
</asp:Menu>
<br /><br /><br />
<asp:LoginView ID="LoginView1" Runat="server">
  <AnonymousTemplate>
    <asp:Menu ID="Menu2" Runat="server">
      <Items>
        <asp:MenuItem NavigateUrl="~/CreateNewUser.aspx" Text="Create Account" />
      </Items>
    </asp:Menu>
  </AnonymousTemplate>
  <LoggedInTemplate>
    <asp:Menu ID="Menu3" Runat="server">
      <Items>
        <asp:MenuItem NavigateUrl="~/ChangePassword.aspx" Text="Change Password" />
      </Items>
    </asp:Menu>
  </LoggedInTemplate>
</asp:LoginView>
```

The Web site title was added with a `Label` control:

```
<asp:Label ID="Label1" Runat="server" Text="My First Company Site" Font-Bold="true"
Font-Size="24px"></asp:Label>
```

Under the title, you added a section to display the user name. Again, you used the `LoginView` control and displayed the name when the user was logged in. For anonymous users, you displayed "Guest, Please log in."

```
<!-- Login Status Area -->
<asp:LoginStatus ID="LoginStatus1" Runat="server" />
User:
```

```
<asp:LoginView ID="LoginView2" Runat="server">
  <AnonymousTemplate>Guest, Please log in</AnonymousTemplate>
  <LoggedInTemplate>
    <asp:LoginName ID="LoginName1" Runat="server" />
  </LoggedInTemplate>
</asp:LoginView>
```

Finally, to validate the site layout, you added a contentplaceholder control. This control is where the actual content will appear on other pages.

```
<asp:contentplaceholder id="cphMain" runat="server"></asp:contentplaceholder>
```

The change you made to the default page was to add the hookup to the master page and change the title to Home.

```
<%@ Page Language="VB" MasterPageFile="~/Main.master" Title="Home" %>
```

For the Login page, you changed the title, added the Content control, and hooked it up with the contentplaceholder you added on the master page. This is where you allow content to be added throughout the site.

Inside the Content control, you placed a Login control, and it was displayed in the appropriate location on the page. The Login control has all of the logic you need built in.

```
<%@ Page Language="VB" MasterPageFile="~/Main.master" Title="Login" %>
<asp:content ContentPlaceHolderID="cphMain" Runat="server">
   <asp:Login ID="Login1" runat="server">
   </asp:Login>
</asp:content>
```

For the Change Password page, you changed the title, added the Content control, and hooked it up with the contentplaceholder you added on the master page.

Inside the Content control, you placed the ChangePassword control, and it was displayed in the appropriate location on the page. The ChangePassword control has all of the logic you need built in.

```
<%@ Page Language="VB" MasterPageFile="~/Main.master" Title="Change Password" %>
<asp:Content ContentPlaceHolderID="cphMain" Runat="server">
   <asp:ChangePassword ID="ChangePassword1" Runat="server">
   </asp:ChangePassword>
</asp:Content>
```

For the Create New User page, you changed the title, added the Content control, and hooked it up with the contentplaceholder you added on the master page.

Inside the Content control, you placed the CreateUserWizard control, and it was displayed in the appropriate location on the page. The CreateUserWizard control has all of the logic you need built in.

```
<%@ Page Language="VB" MasterPageFile="~/Main.master" Title="Create New Account" %>
<asp:Content ContentPlaceHolderID="cphMain" Runat="server">
   <asp:CreateUserWizard ID="CreateUserWizard1" Runat="server">
```

```
    </asp:CreateUserWizard>
  </asp:Content>
```

For the View Authors page, you changed the title, added the `Content` control, and hooked it up with the `contentplaceholder` you added on the master page.

Inside the `Content` control you placed the `Label` control, and it was displayed in the appropriate location on the page. This page was left without functionality for this project.

```
<%@ Page Language="VB" MasterPageFile="~/Main.master" Title="View Authors" %>
<asp:Content ID="Content1" ContentPlaceHolderID="cphMain" Runat="server">
    <asp:Label ID="Label1" Runat="server" Text="Add Code to View Author Info
Later"></asp:Label>
</asp:Content>
```

For the View Titles page, you changed the title, added the `Content` control, and hooked it up with the `contentplaceholder` you added on the master page.

You placed the `Label` control inside of the `Content` control, and it was displayed in the appropriate location on the page. This page was left without functionality for this project.

```
<%@ Page Language="VB" MasterPageFile="~/Main.master" Title="View Titles" %>
<asp:Content ID="Content1" ContentPlaceHolderID="cphMain" Runat="server">
    <asp:Label ID="Label1" Runat="server" Text="Add Code to View Title Info
Later"></asp:Label>
</asp:Content>
```

For the View Users page, you changed the title, added the `Content` control, and hooked it up with the `contentplaceholder` you added on the master page.

Inside the `Content` control, you placed the `Label` control, and it was displayed in the appropriate location on the page. This page was left without functionality for this project.

```
<%@ Page Language="VB" MasterPageFile="~/Main.master" Title="View Users" %>
<asp:Content ContentPlaceHolderID="cphMain" Runat="server">
    <asp:Label ID="Label1" Runat="server" Text="Add Code to View User Info
Later"></asp:Label>
</asp:Content>
```

You cannot access the View Users page yet. When you try, you will be sent to the `Login.aspx` page, because you are not a member of the Admin role. You will add the Admin user to the Admin role in the next Try It Out.

Try It Out   **Managing Roles**

The Web Site Administration Tool has an interface to mange roles.

1.   To open the tool, click Website ⇨ ASP.NET Configuration. From the home page, choose the Security tab. On the bottom half of the screen, you will see a table of options for Roles. Click the link to Create or Manage Roles. (See Figure 18-15.)

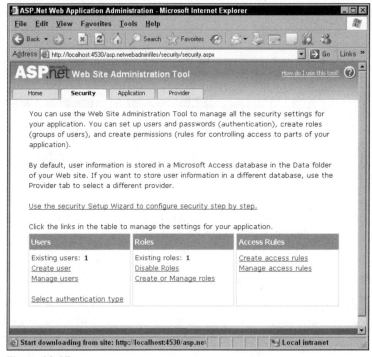

Figure 18-15

2. On the next screen, you will see a list of roles for the Web site. The only role will be Admin. Click Manage for the Admin role, as shown in Figure 18-16.

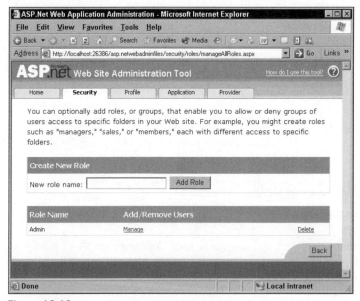

Figure 18-16

3. Click the link for user names starting with the letter *A*. All of the users that match your criteria will be available to add to the Admin role. Check the box User Is In Role to add the Admin user to the role, as shown in Figure 18-17. Clicking the box adds the user to the role. After you click the check box, close the browser and see whether you can access the View Users page. You should be able to access the page now.

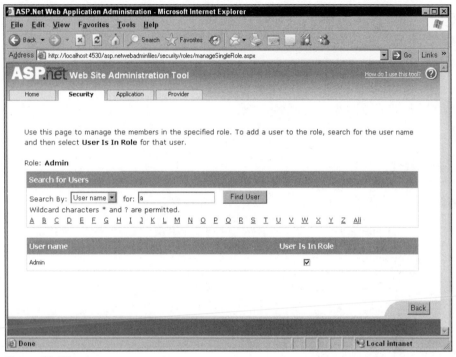

Figure 18-17

How It Works

When you made the change to the Admin folder, which contains the View Users page, only users that were part of the Admin role were allowed access. The tool allowed you to add the Admin user to the Admin role. Once this was done, the Admin user could access the Admin folder and therefore the View Users page.

Summary

In this chapter, you built the skeleton for a functional Web site with security. You used built-in controls and what you learned in Chapter 17 to complete a site with no Visual Basic code. The controls were self-contained, and the default values worked well.

You were able to set up security using the WAT. You saw how easy it was to enforce forms authentication in ASP.NET 2.0. After you completed the work in this chapter, you should have been flabbergasted. The amount of code required to implement flexible these features in ASP .NET 2.0 was reduced to almost 100 nothing. You saw the future of Web development in this chapter.

To summarize, you should know how to:

❑ Use the Web Site Administration Tool

❑ Define site layout using master pages

❑ Implement site security using forms authentication

❑ Apply role management to site security

❑ Work with the built-in Login controls

Exercises

Exercise 1

Change the font to appear red for an `asp:label` control using the `Main.skin` page (created in TheClub site already) for every page under the Members directory. To do this, you can change the theme attribute on every page or change the `web.config` file for the directory. For this exercise, change the `web.config` file. You have not seen the `web.config` file syntax for this, so I will show it to you. Add the change to the `web.config` file that will apply the theme to the Web forms under the Members folder. Use the code snippet here as a guide:

```
<?xml version="1.0" encoding="utf-8"?>
<configuration xmlns="http://schemas.microsoft.com/.NetConfiguration/v2.0">
    <system.web>
        <pages theme="MainTheme" />
        <authorization>
            <deny users="?" />
        </authorization>
    </system.web>
</configuration>
```

The page will look like Figure 18-18.

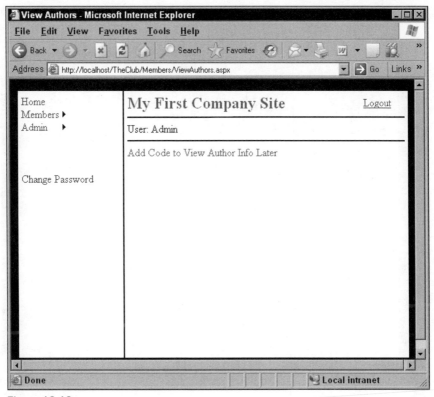

Figure 18-18

Exercise 2

The Login controls you used in this chapter are fully customizable. In this exercise, you will make some a change to the look of the login control on the Login.aspx page. Change the font color of the Login control to **Red** by adding the tag and font color properties to the Main.skin file. Point the web.config file under the root folder to use the MainTheme. (You did this in Exercise 1 under a different directory.)

The login.aspx page should look like Figure 18-19 when you are finished.

Figure 18-19

Visual Basic 2005 and XML

Put simply, Extensible Markup Language (or XML, as it is known) is used for exchanging data between applications. Although it has been around for some time, XML has established itself as the de facto data exchange standard for Internet applications. Today, XML is used not only on the Internet but to exchange data between many different platforms and applications.

In this chapter, you are not going to get bogged down in the details regarding XML, for example, its validation and "well-formedness." Instead, XML is going to be introduced generally, and then you will look at its role with Visual Basic 2005. After that, you will focus on using XML inside an application.

In this chapter, you will:

- ❑ Gain a deeper understanding of XML and what it looks like
- ❑ Learn how to read and write XML files
- ❑ Learn how to serialize and deserialize XML data
- ❑ Learn how to navigate through an XML document
- ❑ Learn how to change existing XML data and add new data to an XML document

Understanding XML

The need for XML is simple: In commercial environments, applications need to exchange information in order to integrate. This integration is more applicable to the line-of-business software that a company may have rather than desktop productivity applications like Microsoft Office. For example, a company may have invested in a piece of software that allows it to track the stock in its warehouse — that piece of software would be an example of line-of-business software.

Integration has traditionally been very difficult to do, and XML, together with Web Services (which are discussed in Chapter 20) are technologies designed to reduce the difficulty and cost involved in software integration. In reducing the difficulty of software integration, there is a knock-on benefit in terms of the ease with which more general data/information exchange can occur.

For example, imagine you are a coffee retailer who wants to place an order with a supplier. The old-school technique of doing this is to phone or fax your order. However, this introduces a human element into the equation. It is likely that your own line-of-business applications (telling you what products you have sold) are suggesting that you buy more of a certain machine or certain blend of coffee. From that suggestion, you formulate an order and transmit it to your supplier. In the case of phone or fax orders, a human being at the supplier then has to transcribe the order into his or her own line-of-business system for processing.

An alternative way of carrying out this order would be to get the "suggestion" that has been raised by your line-of-business system to create an order automatically in the remote system of your supplier. This makes life easier and more efficient for both you and the management of your chosen supplier. However, getting to a point where the two systems are integrated in this way requires a lot of negotiation, coordination, and cost. Thus, it is relevant only for people doing a lot of business with each other.

Before the Internet, for two companies to integrate in this way, specific negotiations had to be undertaken to set up some sort of proprietary connection between the two companies. With the connection in place, data is exchanged not only in order to place the order with the supplier, but also for the supplier to report the status of the order back to the customer. With the Internet, this proprietary connection is no longer required. As long as both parties are on the Internet, data exchange can take place.

However, without a common language for this data exchange to be based on, the problem is only half solved. XML is this common language. As the customer, you can create an XML document that contains the details of the order. You can use the Internet to transmit that order written in XML to the supplier, either over the Web, through e-mail, or by using Web Services. The supplier receives the XML document, decodes it, and raises the order in their system. Likewise, if the supplier needs to report anything back to the customer, they can construct a different document (again using XML), and use the Internet to transmit it back again.

The actual structure of the data contained within the XML document is up to the customer and supplier to decide. (Usually it's for the supplier to decide upon and the customer to adhere to.) This is where the "eXtensible" in XML comes in. Any two parties who wish to exchange data using XML are completely free to decide exactly what the documents should look like.

This does not sound amazing, because companies in the past and even today still use comma-separated files. These files had a format and worked within the same "philosophy." So what does XML have that the previous formats did not?

XML is a lot more descriptive, and it can be validated against a schema. A schema defines what the XML document or fragment should look like. Even without a schema, XML can potentially describe itself well enough for others to ascertain what the data is. In line with the benefits of previous file formats, XML is also a text-based format. This means that XML can be moved between platforms using Internet technologies such as e-mail, the Web, FTP, and other file copy techniques. Traditional software integration was difficult when binary data had to be moved between platforms such as Windows, UNIX, Macintosh, AS/400, or OS/390, so the fact that XML is text-based adds to making it easier to send these across platforms.

What Does XML Look Like?

If you have any experience with HTML, XML is going to look familiar to you. In fact, both have a common ancestor in Standard Generalized Markup Language (SGML). In many ways, XML is not a language, as the name suggests, but is rather a set of rules for *defining your own* markup languages that allow the exchange of data. XML is not a stand-alone technology, either; in fact, a whole lot of different related specifications form what you can and cannot do with XML. Such specifications include the following (not the best late-night reading, at least if you wish to be an alert and attentive reader):

❑   URI (Uniform Resource Identifiers): `www.ietf.org/rfc/rfc2396.txt`

❑   UTF-8 (Unicode Transformation Format): `www.utf-8.com/`

❑   XML (Extensible Markup Language): `www.w3.org/TR/REC-xml`

❑   XML Schema: `www.w3.org/XML/Schema`

❑   XML Information Set: `www.w3.org/TR/xml-infoset/`

Although the specifications may not beat a book such as this in terms of format, layout, and ease of understanding, they have a whole lot to offer the XML fan. If you feel up to it, you can read more about XML after this introduction.

XML is tag based, meaning that the document is made up of *tags* that contain data. Here is how you might choose to describe this book in XML:

```
<Book>
    <Title>Beginning VB 2005</Title>
    <ISBN>xxxx574019</ISBN>
    <Publisher>Wrox</Publisher>
</Book>
```

In XML, you delimit tags using the < and > symbols. There are two sorts of tags: start tags such as `<Title>` and end tags such as `</Title>`. Together, the tags and the content between them are known as an *element*. In the previous example, the Title element is written like this:

```
<Title>Beginning VB 2005 </Title>
```

The ISBN element looks like this:

```
<ISBN>xxxx574019</ISBN>
```

And the Publisher element looks like this:

```
<Publisher>Wrox</Publisher>
```

Note that elements can contain other elements. In this case, for example, the Book element contains three subelements:

```
<Book>
    <Title>Beginning VB 2005</Title>
    <ISBN>xxxx574019</ISBN>
    <Publisher>Wrox</Publisher>
</Book>
```

The structure formed by elements nested inside other elements can also be represented as a tree with, for example, Title, ISBN, and Publisher as branches from the root Book. Therefore, many use terms such as node, parent, and child instead of element.

If you were given this XML document, you would need to have an understanding of its structure. Usually, the company that designed the structure of the document will tell you what it looks like. In this case, someone might tell you that if you first look for the Book element and then the Title element, you will determine the title of the book. The value between the `<Title>` start tag and the `</Title>` end tag is the title (in this case, `Beginning VB 2005`.)

As in HTML, XML can also use what are known as *attributes*. An attribute is a named piece of information descriptive to the node (element) wherein it is located. When you use attributes, you must enclose them in quotes. Here is the same XML fragment as the previous one, but this time using attributes:

```
<Book>
    <Title ISBN="xxxx574019">Beginning VB 2005</Title>
    <Publisher>Wrox</Publisher>
</Book>
```

XML is largely common sense, which is one of the things that make it so simple. For example, you can probably guess what this document represents, even though you may have only just started thinking about XML:

```
<Books>
    <Book>
        <Title>Beginning VB 2005 </Title>
        <ISBN>xxxx574019</ISBN>
        <Publisher>Wrox</Publisher>
    </Book>
    <Book>
        <Title>Professional Visual Basic.Net</Title>
        <ISBN>1861005555</ISBN>
        <Publisher>Wrox</Publisher>
    </Book>
</Books>
```

XML for Visual Basic Newcomers

As a newcomer to programming and Visual Basic, it is unlikely that you will be undertaking projects that involve complex integration work. If XML is so popular because it makes systems integration so much easier, how is it relevant to a newcomer?

The answer to this question is that, as well as being a great tool for integration, XML is also a great tool for storage and general data organization. Before XML, the two ways that an application could store its data were by using a separate database or by having its own proprietary file format with code that could save into and read from it.

In many cases, a database is absolutely the right tool for the job, because you need the fast access, shared storage, and advanced searching facilities that a database such as Access or SQL Server gives you. In other cases, such as with a graphics package or word processor, building your own proprietary format is the right way to go. The reasons for this may be you want the application to be light and do not want to have the hassle of showing the user how to set up and maintain a database, or simply do not want to deal with the licensing implications of needing a separate application to support yours.

XML gives you a new way of storing application data, though it is still based on the concept of defining your own proprietary application storage format. The key difference, in contrast to formats such as .doc files for Word documents, however, is that the XML storage format is a universal standard.

The Address Book Project

You're going to build a demonstration application that allows you to create an XML file format for an address book. You'll be able to create a list of new addresses and save the whole lot as an XML file on your local disk. You'll also be able to load the XML file and walk through the addresses one by one.

Creating the Project

As always, the first thing you have to do is create a new project.

Try It Out   **Creating the Project**

1.   Open Visual Studio 2005 and select File ➪ New Project from the menu. Create a new Visual Basic .NET Windows Application project and call it **Address Book**.

2.   The Form Designer for Form1 will open. Change its Text property to **Address Book**. Now add ten text boxes, twelve labels, and a button to the form so that it looks like Figure 19-1. Notice that you have grid alignment bars to help align the controls on the form. Another option to align controls is the Format menu options.

Figure 19-1

3.   The text boxes should be named as follows, in the order given:

1.   **txtFirstName**

2.   **txtLastName**

   3.   **txtCompanyName**

   4.   **txtAddress1**

   5.   **txtAddress2**

   6.   **txtCity**

   7.   **txtRegion**

   8.   **txtPostalCode**

   9.   **txtCountry**

   10. **txtEmail**

4. Set the text propeties of the labels and button to match Figure 19-1.

5. The button should be named **btnSave**. Finally, the Label control marked (number) should be called **lblAddressNumber**.

That's all you need to do with respect to form design. Let's move on and write some code to save the data as an XML file.

The SerializableData Class

Your application is going to have two classes: `Address` and `AddressBook`. `Address` will be used to store a single instance of a contact in the address book. `AddressBook` will store your entire list of addresses and provide ways for you to navigate through the book.

Both of these classes will be inherited from another class called `SerializableData`. This base class will contain the logic needed for saving the addresses to disk and loading them back again. In XML parlance, the saving process is known as *serialization* and the loading process is known as *deserialization*. In this next Try It Out, you're going to build the `SerializableData` and `Address` classes so that you can demonstrate saving a new address record to disk.

Try It Out   **Building SerializableData**

   1. The first class you need to build is the base `SerializableData` class. Using the Solution Explorer, right-click the Address Book project and select Add ➪ Class. Call the new class **SerializableData** and click Add.

   2. Right click on the project in Project Explorer and choose Add Reference. Click the .NET tab and then select `System.XML.dll`. Next, add these namespace import directives at the top of the class definition:

```
Imports System.IO
Imports System.Xml.Serialization
Public Class SerializableData
End Class
```

3. Next, add these two methods to the class:

```
' Save - serialize the object to disk...
Public Sub Save(ByVal filename As String)
    ' make a temporary filename...
    Dim tempFilename As String
    tempFilename = filename & ".tmp"
    ' does the file exist?
    Dim tempFileInfo As New FileInfo(tempFilename)
    If tempFileInfo.Exists = True Then tempFileInfo.Delete()
    ' open the file...
    Dim stream As New FileStream(tempFilename, FileMode.Create)
    ' save the object...
    Save(stream)
    ' close the file...
    stream.Close()
    ' remove the existing data file and
    ' rename the temp file...
    tempFileInfo.CopyTo(filename, True)
    tempFileInfo.Delete()
End Sub
' Save - actually perform the serialization...
Public Sub Save(ByVal stream As Stream)
    ' create a serializer...
    Dim serializer As New XmlSerializer(Me.GetType)
    ' save the file...
    serializer.Serialize(stream, Me)
End Sub
```

4. Add a new class called `Address`. Set the class to derive from `SerializableData`, like this:

```
Public Class Address
    Inherits SerializableData
End Class
```

5. Next, add the members to the class that will be used to store the address details:

```
Public Class Address
    Inherits SerializableData
    ' members...
    Public FirstName As String
    Public LastName As String
    Public CompanyName As String
    Public Address1 As String
    Public Address2 As String
    Public City As String
    Public Region As String
    Public PostalCode As String
    Public Country As String
    Public Email As String
End Class
```

6. Go back to the Form Designer for Form1 and double-click the Save button to have the Click event handler created. Add this highlighted code to it:

```
Private Sub btnSave_Click(ByVal sender As System.Object, _
    ByVal e As System.EventArgs) Handles btnSave.Click
    ' create a new address object...
    Dim address As New Address()
    ' copy the values from the form into the address...
    PopulateAddressFromForm(address)
    ' save the address...
    Dim filename As String = DataFilename
    address.Save(filename)
' tell the user...
    MsgBox("The address was saved to " & filename)
End Sub
```

7. Visual Studio will highlight the fact that you haven't defined the DataFilename property or the PopulateAddressFromForm method by underlining these respective names. To remove these underlines, first add the DataFileName property to the Form1 code:

```
' DataFilename - where should we store our data?
Public ReadOnly Property DataFilename() As String
    Get
        ' get our working folder...
        Dim folder As String
        folder = Environment.CurrentDirectory
        ' return the folder with the name "Addressbook.xml"...
        Return folder & "\AddressBook.xml"
    End Get
End Property
```

8. Now you need to add the PopulateAddressFromForm method to your Form1 code:

```
' PopulateAddressFromForm - populates Address from the form fields...
Public Sub PopulateAddressFromForm(ByVal address As Address)
    ' copy the values...
    address.FirstName = txtFirstName.Text
    address.LastName = txtLastName.Text
    address.CompanyName = txtCompanyName.Text
    address.Address1 = txtAddress1.Text
    address.Address2 = txtAddress2.Text
    address.City = txtCity.Text
    address.Region = txtRegion.Text
    address.PostalCode = txtPostalCode.Text
    address.Country = txtCountry.Text
    address.Email = txtEmail.Text
End Sub
```

9. Run the project and fill in an address.

10. Click the Save button. You will see a message dialog box that lets you know where the file has been saved.

11. Use Windows Explorer to navigate to the folder that this XML file has been saved into. Double-click it, and Internet Explorer should open and list the contents. What you see should be similar to the contents listed here:

```
<?xml version="1.0" encoding="utf-8"?>
<Address xmlns:xsi="http://www.w3.org/2001/XMLSchema-instance"
xmlns:xsd="http://www.w3.org/2001/XMLSchema">
  <FirstName>Bryan</FirstName>
  <LastName>Newsome</LastName>
  <CompanyName>Wiley Publishing</CompanyName>
  <Address1>11 First Avenue</Address1>
  <Address2 />
  <City>No where</City>
  <Region>South East</Region>
  <PostalCode>28222</PostalCode>
  <Country>USA</Country>
  <Email>Bryan@email.com</Email>
</Address>
```

How It Works

First of all, look at the XML that's been returned. For this discussion, you can ignore the first line, starting `<?xml`, because all that's doing is saying, "Here is an XML version 1.0 document." You can also ignore the `xmlns` attributes on the first and second lines, because all they are doing is providing some extra information about the file, which at this level is something that you can let .NET worry about and don't need to get involved with. With those two parts removed, this is what you get:

```
<Address>
  <FirstName>Bryan</FirstName>
  <LastName>Newsome</LastName>
  <CompanyName>Wiley Publishing</CompanyName>
  <Address1>11 First Avenue</Address1>
  <Address2 />
  <City>No where</City>
  <Region>South East</Region>
  <PostalCode>28222</PostalCode>
  <Country>USA</Country>
  <Email>Bryan@email.com</Email>
</Address>
```

You can see how this is pretty similar to the code described previously in this chapter — you have start tags and end tags, and when taken together these tags form an element. Each element contains data, and it's pretty obvious to see that, for example, the `CompanyName` element contains Bryan's company name.

You'll notice as well that there are `Address` start and end tags at the top and at the bottom of the document. All of the other elements are enclosed by these tags, and this means that each of the elements in the middle belongs to the `Address` element. The `Address` element is the first element in the document and is therefore known as the *top-level element* or *root element*.

> *It's worth noting that an XML document can only have one root element; all other elements in the document are child elements of this root.*

Look at the `<Address2 />` line. By placing the slash at the end of the tag, what you're saying is that the element is empty. You could have written this as `<Address2></Address2>`, but this would have used more storage space in the file. The `XmlSerializer` class itself chooses the naming of the tags, which is discussed later in this chapter.

So now you know what was created; but how did you get there? Follow the path of the application from the clicking of the Save button.

The first thing this method did was create a new `Address` object and call the `PopulateAddressFromForm` method. (This method just reads the `Text` property for every text box on the form and populates the matching property on the `Address` object.)

```
Private Sub btnSave_Click(ByVal sender As System.Object, _
    ByVal e As System.EventArgs) Handles btnSave.Click
    ' create a new address object...
    Dim address As New Address()
    ' copy the values from the form into the address...
    PopulateAddressFromForm(address)
```

Then, you ask the `DataFilename` property (which you wrote in step 7 of this Try It Out) to give you the name of a file that you can save the data to. You do this by using the `Environment.CurrentDirectory` property to return the folder that the address book is executing in and then tacking `"\AddressBook.xml"` to the end of this directory pathway. This is going to be the convention you use when saving and loading files with your application — you won't bother with giving the user the opportunity to save a specific file. Rather, you'll just assume that the file you want always has the same name and is always in the same place:

```
    ' save the address...
    Dim filename As String = DataFilename
```

You then call the `Save` method on the `Address` object. This method is inherited from `SerializableData`, and in a moment you'll take a look at what this method actually does. After you've saved the file, you tell the user where it is:

```
    address.Save(filename)
    ' tell the user...
    MsgBox ("The address was saved to " & filename)
End Sub
```

It's the two `Save` methods on `SerializableData` that are the really interesting part of this project. The first version of the method takes a filename and opens the file. The second version of the method actually saves the data using the `System.Xml.Serialization.XmlSerializer` class, as you'll soon see.

When you save the file, you want to be quite careful. You have to save over the top of an existing file, but you also want to make sure that, if the file save fails for any reason, you don't end up trashing the only good copy of the data the user has. This is a fairly common problem with a fairly common solution: You save the file to a different file, wait until you know that everything has been saved properly, and then replace the existing file with the new one.

To get the name of the new file, you just tack `.tmp` onto the end. So, if you had the filename given as `C:\MyPrograms\AddressBook\AddressBook.xml`, you'd actually try and save to `C:\MyPrograms\AddressBook\AddressBook.xml.tmp`. If this file exists, you delete it by calling the `Delete` method:

```
    ' Save - serialize the object to disk...
    Public Sub Save(ByVal filename As String)
        ' make a temporary filename...
        Dim tempFilename As String
```

```
    tempFilename = filename & ".tmp"
    ' does the file exist?
    Dim tempFileInfo As New FileInfo(tempFilename)
    If tempFileInfo.Exists = True Then tempFileInfo.Delete()
```

Once the existing `.tmp` file is gone, you can create a new file. This will return a `System.IO.FileStream` object:

```
    ' open the file...
    Dim stream As New FileStream(tempFilename, FileMode.Create)
```

You then pass this stream to another overloaded `Save` method. You'll go through this method in a moment, but for now all you need to know is that this method will do the actual serialization of the data.

Then, you close the file:

```
    ' close the file...
    stream.Close()
```

Finally, you replace the existing file with the new file. You have to do this with `CopyTo` (the `True` parameter you pass to this method means "overwrite any existing file") and finally delete the temporary file:

```
    ' remove the existing data file and
    ' rename the temp file...
    tempFileInfo.CopyTo(filename, True)
    tempFileInfo.Delete()
End Sub
```

The other version of `Save` takes a `Stream` argument instead of a `String` and looks like this:

```
' Save - actually perform the serialization...
Public Sub Save(ByVal stream As Stream)
    ' create a serializer...
    Dim serializer As New XmlSerializer(Me.GetType)
    ' save the file...
    serializer.Serialize(stream, Me)
End Sub
```

The `System.Xml.Serialization.XmlSerializer` class is what you use to actually serialize the object to the stream that you specify. In this case, you're using a stream that points to a file, but later in this chapter you'll use a different kind of file.

`XmlSerializer` needs to know ahead of time what type of object it's saving. You use the `GetType` method to return a `System.Type` object that references the class that you actually are saving, which in this case is `Address`. The reason `XmlSerializer` needs to know the type is because it works by iterating through all of the properties on the object, looking for ones that are both readable and writable (in other words, ones that are not flagged as read-only or write-only). Every time it finds such a property, `XmlSerializer` writes the property to the stream, which in this case means that the property subsequently gets written to the `AddressBook.xml` file.

`XmlSerializer` bases the name of the element in the XML document on the name of the matching property. For example, the `FirstName` element in the document matches the `FirstName` property on `Address`. In addition, the top-level element of `Address` matches the name of the `Address` class; in other words, the root element name matches the class name.

`XmlSerializer` is a great way of using XML in your programs because you don't need to mess around creating and manually reading XML documents — it does all the work for you.

Loading the XML File

Now you can load the address back from the XML file on the disk. In this next Try It Out, you'll be adding the methods necessary to deserialize the XML back into data that you can work with in your application.

Try It Out   Loading the XML File

1. Using the Solution Explorer, open the code editor for `SerializableData`. Add these two methods:

```
' Load - deserialize from disk...
Public Shared Function Load(ByVal filename As String, _
                ByVal newType As Type) As Object
    ' does the file exist?
    Dim fileInfo As New FileInfo(filename)
    If fileInfo.Exists = False Then
        ' create a blank version of the object and return that...
        Return System.Activator.CreateInstance(newType)
    End If
    ' open the file...
    Dim stream As New FileStream(filename, FileMode.Open)
    ' load the object from the stream...
    Dim newObject As Object = Load(stream, newType)
    ' close the stream...
    stream.Close()
    ' return the object...
    Return newObject
End Function
Public Shared Function Load(ByVal stream As Stream, _
                ByVal newType As Type) As Object
    ' create a serializer and load the object....
    Dim serializer As New XmlSerializer(newType)
    Dim newObject As Object = serializer.Deserialize(stream)
    ' return the new object...
    Return newobject
End Function
```

2. Go back to the Form Designer for Form1. Add a new button. Set the Text property of the new button to **&Load** and the Name to **btnLoad**.

3. Double-click the Load button and add the following highlighted code to the event handler:

```
Private Sub btnLoad_Click(ByVal sender As System.Object, _
      ByVal e As System.EventArgs) Handles btnLoad.Click
```

```
    ' load the address using a shared method on SerializableData...
    Dim newAddress As Address = _
     SerializableData.Load(DataFilename, GetType(Address))
    ' update the display...
    PopulateFormFromAddress(newAddress)
End Sub
```

4. You'll also need to add this method to Form1:

```
' PopulateFormFromAddress - populates the form from an
' address object...
Public Sub PopulateFormFromAddress(ByVal address As Address)
    ' copy the values...
    txtFirstName.Text = address.FirstName
    txtLastName.Text = address.LastName
    txtCompanyName.Text = address.CompanyName
    txtAddress1.Text = address.Address1
    txtAddress2.Text = address.Address2
    txtCity.Text = address.City
    txtRegion.Text = address.Region
    txtPostalCode.Text = address.PostalCode
    txtCountry.Text = address.Country
    txtEmail.Text = address.Email
End Sub
```

5. Run the project and click the Load button or press Alt + L. The address should be loaded from the XML file and displayed on the screen. After clicking the Load button, you should see what you typed and saved previously as shown in Figure 19-2.

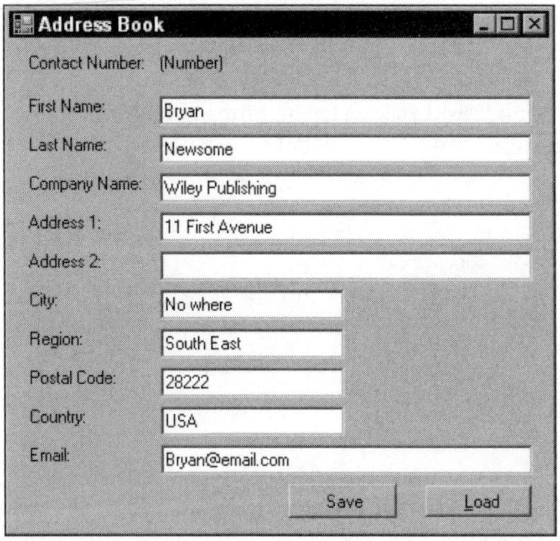

Figure 19-2

How It Works

Deserialization is the opposite of serialization. It can be used to load the XML data from the file, whereas before you saved the XML data to the file. (Note that here I'm using the word file for simplification. In fact, you can serialize to and deserialize from any kind of stream.)

Whenever you ask `XmlSerializer` to deserialize an object for you, it will create a new object. You can use this functionality to get `XmlSerializer` to create a new object for you rather than having to create one yourself. This is a good candidate for an overloaded method on the `SerializableData` object. You create an overloaded method called `Load`, the first version of which takes a filename and also a `System.Type` object. This `Type` object represents the type of object you ultimately want to end up with. Specifically, you'll need to pass in a `Type` object that tells `XmlSerializer` where to find a list of properties that exist on your `Address` object.

Since `XmlSerializer` doesn't save .NET class namespaces or assembly information into the XML file, it relies on an explicit statement saying what class the file contains; otherwise things get ambiguous. (Imagine you had a hundred assemblies on your machine, each containing a class called `Address`. How could `XmlSerializer` know which one you mean?)

Obviously, when the method is called, the first thing you do is check to see whether the file exists. If it doesn't, you'll return a blank version of the object that you asked for.

```
' Load - deserialize from disk...
Public Shared Function Load(ByVal filename As String, _
                ByVal newType As Type) As Object
    ' does the file exist?
    Dim fileInfo As New FileInfo(filename)
    If fileInfo.Exists = False Then
        ' create a blank version of the object and return that...
        Return System.Activator.CreateInstance(newType)
    End If
```

If the file does exist, you open it and pass it to the other version of `Load`, which you'll see in a moment. You then close the file and return the new object to the caller:

```
    ' open the file...
    Dim stream As New FileStream(filename, FileMode.Open)
    ' load the object from the stream...
    Dim newObject As Object = Load(stream, newType)
    ' close the stream...
    stream.Close()
    ' return the object...
    Return newObject
End Function
```

The other version of `Load` uses the `XmlSerializer` again and, as you can see, it's no more complicated than when you used it last time. Except, of course, that the `Deserialize` method returns a new object to you:

```
Public Shared Function Load(ByVal stream As Stream, _
                ByVal newType As Type) As Object
    ' create a serializer and load the object....
    Dim serializer As New XmlSerializer(newType)
    Dim newObject As Object = serializer.Deserialize(stream)
```

```
        ' return the new object...
        Return newobject
    End Function
```

When it's deserializing, `XmlSerializer` goes through each of the properties on the new object that it has created, again looking for ones that are both readable and writable. When it finds one, it takes the value stored against it in the XML document and sets the property. The result: You are given a new object, fully populated with the data from the XML document.

Once you've called `Load` and have gotten a new `Address` object back, you pass the new object to `PopulateFormFromAddress`:

```
    Private Sub btnLoad_Click(ByVal sender As System.Object, _
            ByVal e As System.EventArgs) Handles btnLoad.Click
        ' load the address using a shared method on SerializableData...
        Dim newAddress As Address = _
         SerializableData.Load(DataFilename, GetType(Address))
        ' update the display...
        PopulateFormFromAddress(newAddress)
    End Sub
```

Changing the Data

To prove that nothing funny is going on, in the next Try It Out you'll change the XML file using Notepad and try clicking the Load button again.

Try It Out   Changing the Data

1. Open up Windows Notepad and load the XML file into it. Inside the `FirstName` element, change the name that you entered to something else. Then save the file and exit Notepad.

2. Go back to the Address Book program. Click the Load button again. The new name that you entered will be loaded.

How It Works

What you've done here is proven that `XmlSerializer` does indeed use the `AddressBook.xml` file as the source of its data. You changed the data, and when you loaded the `Address` object again, the `FirstName` property had indeed been changed to the new name that you entered.

Sending E-mail

For this next Try It Out, you'll see how you can integrate this application with an e-mail client such as Outlook or Outlook Express using the e-mail data from your addresses. You'll be using the Process class to start the e-mail client associated with the `mailto` protocol, as you see in a few moments.

Try It Out   Sending E-mail from the Client

1. Go back to the Form1 designer and, using the Toolbox, draw a LinkLabel control underneath the Email label. Set its Text property to **Send Email** and change its Name property to **lnkSendEmail** as shown in Figure 19-3.

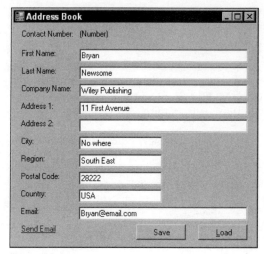

Figure 19-3

Note that this will work with a normal Button control, too.

2. Double-click the LinkLabel control. This will create an event handler for the `LinkClicked` event. Add this code:

```
Private Sub lnkSendEmail_LinkClicked(ByVal sender As System.Object, _
   ByVal e As System.Windows.Forms.LinkLabelLinkClickedEventArgs) _
   Handles lnkSendEmail.LinkClicked
      ' start the e-mail client...
      System.Diagnostics.Process.Start("mailto:" & txtEmail.Text)
End Sub
```

3. Run the project and click the Load button. Ensure you have an e-mail address entered in the Email field and then click the Send Email link. Your e-mail client should display a new mail message with the To: field filled in with your e-mail address.

How It Works

Windows has a built-in capability to decode Internet addresses and fire up the programs that are associated with them.

When an e-mail client such as Outlook or Outlook Express is installed, it registers a protocol called `mailto` with Windows, just as, when a Web browser such as Internet Explorer is installed, it registers the protocol HTTP, familiar to anyone who browses the Web.

If you were to close the mail message, click the Start button from the Windows task bar, select Run, enter **mailto:** followed by the e-mail address from your program, and then click OK, the same mail message would appear.

In your code, you take the current value of the txtEmail field and put `mailto:` at the beginning. This turns the e-mail address into a URL. You then call the shared `Start` method on the `System.Diagnostics.Process` class, passing it this URL:

```
Private Sub lnkSendEmail_LinkClicked(ByVal sender As System.Object, _
    ByVal e As System.Windows.Forms.LinkLabelLinkClickedEventArgs) _
    Handles lnkSendEmail.LinkClicked
        ' start the e-mail client...
        System.Diagnostics.Process.Start("mailto:" & txtEmail.Text)
End Sub
```

The `Start` method behaves in exactly the same way as the Run dialog box does. Both tap into Windows' built-in URL-decoding functionality. In this case, you've used this functionality to integrate your application with Outlook. However, if you'd specified a protocol of `http:` rather than `mailto:`, your application could have opened a Web page. Likewise, if you had supplied a path to a Word document, or Excel spreadsheet, the application could open those too. Note that when you're working with a file, you don't need to supply a protocol — for example, you only need to do this:

```
c:\My Files\My Budget.xls
```

Creating a List of Addresses

The purpose of this Try It Out is to build an application that allows you to store a list of addresses in XML. At the moment you can successfully load just one address, so now you have to turn your attention to managing a list of addresses.

The class you're going to build to do this is called `AddressBook`. This class will inherit from `SerializableData` because ultimately you want to get to a point where you can tell the `AddressBook` object to load and save itself to the XML file without you having to do anything.

Try It Out   Creating AddressBook

1. Using Solution Explorer, create a new class called `AddressBook`.

2. First, add this namespace declaration:

```
Imports System.Xml.Serialization
Public Class AddressBook
End Class
```

3. Second, set the class to inherit from `SerializableData`:

```
Imports System.Xml.Serialization
Public Class AddressBook
    Inherits SerializableData
End Class
```

4. To store the addresses, you're going to use a `System.Collections.ArrayList` object. You also need a method that you can use to create new addresses in the list. Add the following highlighted member and method to the class:

```
Imports System.Xml.Serialization
Public Class AddressBook
    Inherits SerializableData
    ' members...
    Public Items As New ArrayList()
    ' AddAddress - add a new address to the book...
```

```
        Public Function AddAddress() As Address
            ' create one...
            Dim newAddress As New Address()
            ' add it to the list...
            Items.Add(newAddress)
            ' return the address...
            Return newAddress
        End Function
    End Class
```

5.   Open the code editor for Form1. Add these members to the top of the class:

```
Public Class Form1
    ' members...
    Public AddressBook As AddressBook
    Private _currentAddressIndex As Integer
```

6.   Next, add this property to Form1:

```
' CurrentAddress - property for the current address...
ReadOnly Property CurrentAddress() As Address
    Get
        Return AddressBook.Items(CurrentAddressIndex - 1)
    End Get
End Property
```

7.   Then add this property to Form1:

```
' CurrentAddressIndex - property for the current address...
Property CurrentAddressIndex() As Integer
    Get
        Return _currentAddressIndex
    End Get
    Set(ByVal Value As Integer)
        ' set the address...
        _currentAddressIndex = Value
        ' update the display...
        PopulateFormFromAddress(CurrentAddress)
        ' set the label...
        lblAddressNumber.Text = _
        _currentAddressIndex & " of " & AddressBook.Items.Count
    End Set
End Property
```

8.   Double-click the form to create the Load event for Form1 and add this highlighted code to the handler:

```
Private Sub Form1_Load(ByVal sender As System.Object, _
        ByVal e As System.EventArgs) Handles MyBase.Load
    ' load the address book...
    AddressBook = _
      SerializableData.Load(DataFilename, GetType(AddressBook))
    ' if the address book only contains one item, add a new one...
    If AddressBook.Items.Count = 0 Then AddressBook.AddAddress()
    ' select the first item in the list...
    CurrentAddressIndex = 1
End Sub
```

9. Now that you can load the address book, you need to be able to save the changes. From the left drop-down list, select (Form1 Events). From the right list, select FormClosed. Add the highlighted code to the event handler, and also add the SaveChanges and UpdateCurrentAddress methods:

```
Private Sub Form1_FormClosed(ByVal sender As Object, ByVal e As
System.Windows.Forms.FormClosedEventArgs) Handles Me.FormClosed
    ' save the changes...
    UpdateCurrentAddress()
    SaveChanges()
End Sub

' SaveChanges - save the address book to an XML file...
Public Sub SaveChanges()
    ' tell the address book to save itself...
    AddressBook.Save(DataFilename)
End Sub
' UpdateCurrentAddress - make sure the book has the current
' values currently entered into the form...
Private Sub UpdateCurrentAddress()
    PopulateAddressFromForm(CurrentAddress)
End Sub
```

Before you run the project, it's very important that you delete the existing AddressBook.xml *file. If you don't,* XmlSerializer *will try to load an* AddressBook *object from a file containing an* Address *object, and an exception will be thrown.*

10. Run the project. Don't bother entering any information into the form, because the save routine won't work — we've deliberately introduced a bug to illustrate an issue with XmlSerializer. Close the form, and you should see the exception thrown as shown in Figure 19-4.

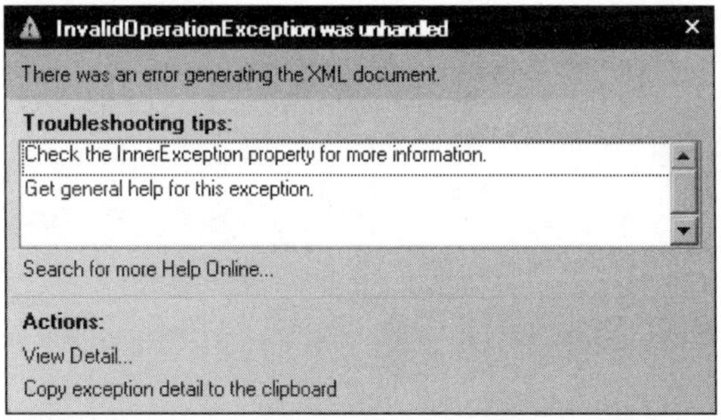

Figure 19-4

How It Works (or Why It Doesn't!)

When the form is loaded, the first thing you do is ask SerializableData to create a new AddressBook object from the AddressBook.xml file. Because you deleted this before you ran the project, this file won't exist, and, as you recall, you rigged the Load method so that if the file didn't exist it would just create an instance of whatever class you asked for. In this case, you get an AddressBook:

```
Private Sub Form1_Load(ByVal sender As System.Object, _
        ByVal e As System.EventArgs) Handles MyBase.Load
    ' load the address book...
    AddressBook = _
        SerializableData.Load(DataFilename, GetType(AddressBook))
```

However, the new address book won't have any addresses in it. You ask `AddressBook` to create a new address if the list is empty:

```
    ' if the address book only contains one item, add a new one...
    If AddressBook.Items.Count = 0 Then AddressBook.AddAddress()
```

At this point, either you'll have an `AddressBook` object that's been loaded from the file and therefore contains a set of `Address` objects, or you'll have a new `AddressBook` object that contains one, blank address. You set the `CurrentAddressIndex` property to 1, meaning the first item in the list:

```
    ' select the first item in the list...
    CurrentAddressIndex = 1
End Sub
```

The setter for the `CurrentAddressIndex` property does a number of things. First, it updates the private `_currentAddressIndex` member:

```
' CurrentAddressIndex - property for the current address...
Property CurrentAddressIndex() As Integer
    Get
        Return _currentAddressIndex
    End Get
    Set(ByVal Value As Integer)
        ' set the address...
        _currentAddressIndex = Value
```

Then the setter uses the `CurrentAddress` property to get the `Address` object that corresponds to whatever `_currentAddressIndex` is set to. This `Address` object is passed to `PopulateFormFromAddress`, whose job it is to update the display:

```
        ' update the display...
        PopulateFormFromAddress(CurrentAddress)
```

Finally, it changes the `lblAddressNumber` control so that it displays the current record number:

```
        ' set the label...
        lblAddressNumber.Text = _
            _currentAddressIndex & " of " & AddressBook.Items.Count
    End Set
End Property
```

You'll just quickly look at `CurrentAddress`. This property's job is to turn an integer index into the corresponding `Address` object stored in `AddressBook`. However, because `AddressBook` works on the basis of an `ArrayList` object that numbers items from 0, and your application starts numbering items at 1, you have to decrement your index value by 1 to get the matching value from `AddressBook`:

```
' CurrentAddress - property for the current address...
ReadOnly Property CurrentAddress() As Address
    Get
        Return AddressBook.Items(CurrentAddressIndex - 1)
    End Get
End Property
```

All good so far, but why is XmlSerializer throwing an exception? Well the problems occur when you close the application. This fires the FormClosed method, which ultimately calls the Save method of AddressBook.

As you know, to save an object to disk, XmlSerializer walks through each of the properties looking for ones that are readable and writable. So far, you've used XmlSerializer only with System.String, but when the object comes across a property that uses a complex type, such as Address, it uses the same principle — in other words, it looks through all of the properties that the complex type has. If properties on that that object return complex types, it will drill down again. What it's doing is looking for simple types that it knows how to turn into text and write to the XML document.

However, some types cannot be turned into text, and at this point XmlSerializer chokes. The ArrayList object that you're using to store a list of addresses had some properties that cannot be converted to text, which is the reason the exception is being thrown. What you need to do is provide an alternative property that XmlSerializer can hook into in order to get a list of addresses and tell it not to bother trying to serialize the ArrayList.

Ignoring Members

Although XmlSerializer cannot cope with certain data types, it has no problems with arrays. You've also seen that XmlSerializer has no problems with your Address class, simply because this object doesn't have any properties of a type that XmlSerializer cannot support. In the next Try It Out, you'll provide an alternative property that returns an array of Address objects and tells XmlSerializer to keep away from the Items property because XmlSerializer cannot deal with ArrayList objects.

Try It Out   Ignoring Members

1. Open the code editor for AddressBook. Find the Items property and prefix it with the System.Xml.Serialization.XmlIgnore attribute:

```
Public Class AddressBook
    Inherits SerializableData
    ' members...
    <XmlIgnore()>Public Items As New ArrayList
```

2. Now, add this new property to the AddressBook class:

```
' Addresses - property that works with the items
' collection as an array...
Public Property Addresses() As Address()
    Get
        ' create a new array...
        Dim addressArray(Items.Count - 1) As Address
        Items.CopyTo(addressArray)
```

```
            Return addressArray
        End Get
        Set(ByVal Value As Address())
            ' reset the arraylist...
            Items.Clear()
            ' did you get anything?
            If Not Value Is Nothing Then
                ' go through the array and populate items...
                Dim address As Address
                For Each address In Value
                    Items.Add(address)
                Next
            End If
        End Set
    End Property
End Property
```

3. Run the project and then close the application; this time everything functions correctly. Run the project again, and this time around, enter some data into the address fields. Close the application and you should now find that `AddressBook.xml` does contain data. (We've removed the `xmlns` and `?xml` values for clarity here.)

```
<AddressBook>
  <Addresses>
    <Address>
      <FirstName>Bryan</FirstName>
      <LastName>Newsome</LastName>
      <CompanyName>Wiley</CompanyName>
      <Address1>123 Main St</Address1>
      <Address2 />
      <City>Big City</City>
      <Region>SE</Region>
      <PostalCode>28222</PostalCode>
      <Country>USA</Country>
      <Email>Bryan@email.com</Email>
    </Address>
  </Addresses>
</AddressBook>
```

How It Works

The XML that got saved into your file proves that your approach works, but why?

At this point, your `AddressBook` object has two properties: `Items` and `Addresses`. Both are read/write properties, so both are going to be examined as candidates for serialization by `XmlSerializer`. As you know, `Items` returns an `ArrayList` object, and `Addresses` returns an array of `Address` objects.

However, you have now marked `Items` with the `XmlIgnore` attribute. This means, not surprisingly, that `XmlSerializer` will ignore the property, despite the fact that it is readable and writable. Instead, the serializer will move on to the `Addresses` property.

The Get portion of the Addresses property is what interests you. All you do is create a new array of Address objects and use the CopyTo method on the ArrayList to populate it:

```
' Addresses - property that works with the items
' collection as an array...
Public Property Addresses() As Address()
    Get
        ' create a new array...
        Dim addressArray(Items.Count - 1) As Address
        Items.CopyTo(addressArray)
        Return addressArray
    End Get
    Set(ByVal Value As Address())
        ...
    End Set
End Property
```

When XmlSerializer gets an array of objects that it can deal with, all it does is iterate through the array, serializing each of these contained objects in turn. You can see this in the XML that you received: The structure of the XML contained within the Addresses element exactly matches the structure of the XML you saw when you tested the process and wrote a single Address object to the file:

```
<AddressBook>
  <Addresses>
    <Address>
      <FirstName>Bryan</FirstName>
      <LastName>Newsome</LastName>
      <CompanyName>Wiley</CompanyName>
      <Address1>123 Main St</Address1>
      <Address2 />
      <City>Big City</City>
      <Region>SE</Region>
      <PostalCode>28222</PostalCode>
      <Country>USA</Country>
      <Email>Bryan@email.com</Email>
    </Address>
  </Addresses>
</AddressBook>
```

Loading Addresses

If you're lucky, loading addresses should just work! Close the program and run the project again. You will see a record as shown in Figure 19-5.

You already set up the project to load the address book the first time you ran the project after creating the AddressBook class itself. This time, however, AddressBook.Load can find a file on the disk, and so, rather than creating a blank object, it's getting XmlSerializer to deserialize the lot. As XmlSerializer has no problems writing arrays, you can assume that it has no problem reading them.

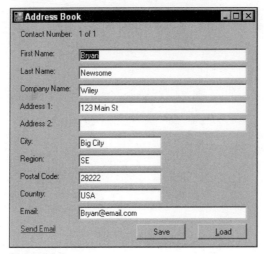

Figure 19-5

It's the Set portion of the Addresses property that does the magic this time. One thing you have to be careful of with this property is that, if you are passed a blank array (in other words. Nothing), you want to prevent exceptions being thrown:

```
' Addresses - property that works with the items
' collection as an array...
Public Property Addresses() As Address()
    Get
        ...
    End Get
    Set(ByVal Value As Address())
        ' reset the arraylist...
        Items.Clear()
        ' did you get anything?
        If Not Value Is Nothing Then
            ' go through the array and populate items...
            Dim address As Address
            For Each address In Value
                Items.Add(address)
            Next
        End If
    End Set
End Property
```

For each of the values in the array, all you have to do is take each one in turn and add it to the list.

Adding New Addresses

Next, you'll look at how you can add new addresses to the list. In this Try It Out, you'll be adding four new buttons to your form. Two buttons will allow you to navigate through the list of addresses, and two buttons will allow you to add and delete addresses.

Try It Out   Adding New Addresses

1. Open the Form Designer for Form1 and disable the Load and Save buttons before adding the four new buttons shown in Figure 19-6.

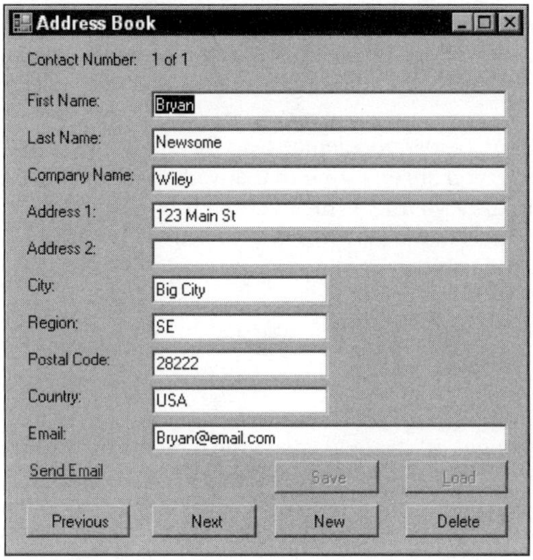

Figure 19-6

2. Name the buttons in turn **btnPrevious**, **btnNext**, **btnNew**, and **btnDelete** and set their Text properties to **Previous**, **Next**, **New**, and **Delete**, respectively.

3. Double-click the New button to create a Click handler. Add the highlighted line to the event handler, and also add the AddNewAddress method:

```
Private Sub btnNew_Click(ByVal sender As System.Object, _
        ByVal e As System.EventArgs) Handles btnNew.Click
    AddNewAddress()
End Sub
Public Function AddNewAddress() As Address
    ' save the current address...
    UpdateCurrentAddress()

    ' create a new address...
    Dim newAddress As Address = AddressBook.AddAddress
    ' update the display...
    CurrentAddressIndex = AddressBook.Items.Count
    ' return the new address...
    Return newAddress
End Function
```

4. Run the project. Click New and a new address record will be created. Enter a new address:

5. Close the program and the changes will be saved. Open up AddressBook.xml, and you should see the new address.

How It Works

This time you have a new `Address` object added to the XML document. It is contained within the `Addresses` element, so you know that it is part of the same array.

The implementation was very simple—all you had to do was ask `AddressBook` to create a new address, and then you updated the `CurrentAddressIndex` property so that it equaled the number of items in the `AddressBook`. This had the effect of changing the display so that it went to record 2 of 2, ready for editing.

However, it is important that, before you actually do this, you save any changes that the user might have made. With this application, you are ensuring that any changes the user makes will always find themselves being persisted into the XML file. Whenever the user closes the application, creates a new record, or moves backward or forward in the list, you want to call `UpdateCurrentAddress` so that any changes will be saved:

```
Public Function AddNewAddress() As Address
    ' save the current address...
    UpdateCurrentAddress()
```

After you've saved any changes, it is safe to create the new record and show the new record to the user:

```
    ' create a new address...
    Dim newAddress As Address = AddressBook.AddAddress
    ' update the display...
    CurrentAddressIndex = AddressBook.Items.Count
    ' return the new address...
    Return newAddress
End Function
```

Navigating Addresses

Now that you can add new addresses to the address book, you need to wire up the Next and Previous buttons so that you can move through the list. In this Try It Out, you'll be adding the code that will read the next or previous address from the array of addresses maintained by the `AddressBook` class. Before reading the next or previous address, however, you'll also want to ensure that any updates made to the current address are updated, and you'll be calling the appropriate procedures to update the current address before navigating to a new address.

Try It Out   Navigating Addresses

1.   Open the Form Designer for Form1. Double-click the Next button to create a new Click handler. Add this code and the associated `MoveNext` method:

```
Private Sub btnNext_Click(ByVal sender As System.Object, _
    ByVal e As System.EventArgs) Handles btnNext.Click
    MoveNext()
End Sub
Public Sub MoveNext()
    ' get the next index...
    Dim newIndex As Integer = CurrentAddressIndex + 1
    If newIndex > AddressBook.Items.Count Then
        newIndex = 1
```

```
        End If
        ' save any changes...
        UpdateCurrentAddress()
        ' move the record...
        CurrentAddressIndex = newIndex
    End Sub
```

2. Next, flip back to the Form Designer and double-click the Previous button. Add the highlighted code:

```
Private Sub btnPrevious_Click(ByVal sender As System.Object, _
    ByVal e As System.EventArgs) Handles btnPrevious.Click
    MovePrevious()
End Sub
Public Sub MovePrevious()
    ' get the previous index...
    Dim newIndex As Integer = CurrentAddressIndex - 1
    If newIndex = 0 Then
        newIndex = AddressBook.Items.Count
    End If
    ' save changes...
    UpdateCurrentAddress()
    ' move the record...
    CurrentAddressIndex = newIndex
End Sub
```

3. Run the project. You should now be able to move between addresses.

How It Works

All you've done here is wire up the buttons so that each one changes the current index. By incrementing the current index, you move forward in the list. By decrementing it, you move backward.

However, it's very important that you don't move outside the bounds of the list (in other words, try to move to a position before the first record or to a position after the last record), which is why you check the value and adjust it as appropriate. When you move forward (MoveNext), you flip to the beginning of the list if you go off the end. When you move backward (MovePrevious), you flip to the end if you go off the start.

In both cases, you make sure that before you actually change the CurrentAddressIndex property, you call UpdateCurrentAddress to save any changes:

```
    Public Sub MoveNext()
        ' get the next index...
        Dim newIndex As Integer = CurrentAddressIndex + 1
        If newIndex > AddressBook.Items.Count Then
            newIndex = 1
        End If
        ' save any changes...
        UpdateCurrentAddress()
        ' move the record...
        CurrentAddressIndex = newIndex
    End Sub
```

Deleting Addresses

To finish the functionality of your address book, you'll deal with deleting items. When deleting items, you must take into account that the item you are deleting is the last remaining item. In this case, you'll have to provide the appropriate code to add a new blank address. This Try It Out will provide this and all necessary functionality to delete an address properly.

Deleting Addresses

1. Go back to the Form Designer for Form1 and double-click the Delete button. Add this code to the event handler, and also add the `DeleteAddress` method:

```
Private Sub btnDelete_Click(ByVal sender As System.Object, _
        ByVal e As System.EventArgs) Handles btnDelete.Click
    ' ask the user if they are ok with this?
    If MsgBox ("Are you sure you want to delete this address?", _
        MsgBoxStyle.Question Or MsgBoxStyle.YesNo) = _
        MsgBoxResult.Yes Then
        DeleteAddress(CurrentAddressIndex)
    End If
End Sub
' DeleteAddress - delete an address from the list...
Public Sub DeleteAddress(ByVal index As Integer)
    ' delete the item from the list...
    AddressBook.Items.RemoveAt(index - 1)
    ' was that the last address?
    If AddressBook.Items.Count = 0 Then
        ' add a new address?
        AddressBook.AddAddress()
    Else
        ' make sure you have something to show...
        If index > AddressBook.Items.Count Then
            index = AddressBook.Items.Count
        End If
    End If
    ' display the record...
    CurrentAddressIndex = index
End Sub
```

2. Run the project. You should be able to delete records from the address book. Note that if you delete the last record, a new record will automatically be created.

How It Works

The algorithm you've used here to delete the records is an example of how to solve another classic programming problem.

Your application is set up so that it always has to display a record. That's why, when the program is first run and there is no `AddressBook.xml`, you automatically create a new record. Likewise, when an item is deleted from the address book, you have to find something to present to the user.

To physically delete an address from the disk, you use the `RemoveAt` method on the `ArrayList` that holds the `Address` objects.

```
' DeleteAddress - delete an address from the list...
Public Sub DeleteAddress(ByVal index As Integer)
    ' delete the item from the list...
    AddressBook.Items.RemoveAt(index - 1)
```

Again, notice here that, because you're working with a zero-based array, when you ask to delete the address with an index of 3, you actually have to delete the address at position 2 in the array.

The problems start after you've done that. It could be that you've deleted the one remaining address in the book. In this case, because you always have to display an address, you create a new one:

```
' was that the last address?
If AddressBook.Items.Count = 0 Then
    ' add a new address?
    AddressBook.AddAddress()
```

Alternatively, if there are items in the address book, you have to change the display. In some cases, the value that's currently stored in `CurrentAddressIndex` will be valid. For example, if you had five records and are looking at the third one, `_currentAddressIndex` will be 3. If you delete that record, you have four records, but the third one as reported by `_currentAddressIndex` will still be 3 and will still be valid. However, as 4 has now shuffled into 3's place, you need to update the display.

It could be the case that you've deleted the last item in the list. When this happens, the index isn't valid, because the index would be positioned over the end of the list. (Suppose you have four items in the list; delete the fourth one, and you only have three, but `_currentAddressIndex` would be 4, which isn't valid.) So, when the last item is deleted, the index will be over the end of the list, so you set it to be the last item in the list:

```
Else
    ' make sure you have something to show...
    If index > AddressBook.Items.Count Then
        index = AddressBook.Items.Count
    End If
End If
```

Whatever actually happens, you still need to update the display. As you know, the `CurrentAddressIndex` property can do this for you:

```
    ' display the record...
    CurrentAddressIndex = index
End Sub
```

Testing at the Edges

This brings us on to a programming technique that can greatly help you test your applications. When writing software, things usually go wrong at the "edge". For example, you have a function that takes an integer value, but in order for the method to work properly, the value supplied must lie between 0 and 99.

Once you're satisfied that your algorithm works properly when you give it a valid value, test some values at the "edge" of the problem (in other words, at the boundaries of the valid data). For example: _1, 0, 99, and 100. In most cases, if your method works properly for one or two of the possible valid values, it will work properly for the entire set of valid values. Testing a few values at the edge will show you where potential problems with the method lie.

A classic example of this is with your `MoveNext` and `MovePrevious` methods. If you had a hundred addresses in your address book and only tested that `MoveNext` and `MovePrevious` worked between numbers 10 and 20, it most likely would have worked between 1 and 100. However, the moment you move past 100 (in other words "go over the edge"), problems can occur. If you hadn't handled this case properly by flipping back to 1, your program would have crashed.

Integrating with the Address Book Application

So far, you've built an application that is able to save and load its data as an XML document. You've also taken a look at the document as it's been changing over the course of the chapter, so by now you should have a pretty good idea of what an XML document looks like and how it works.

The beginning of this chapter pitched XML as a technology for integrating software applications. It then went on to say that for newcomers to Visual Basic, using XML for integration is unlikely to be something that you would do on a day-to-day basis, and so you've been using XML to store data. In the rest of this chapter, we're going to demonstrate why XML is such a good technology for integration. What you'll do is build a separate application that, with very little work, is able to read in and understand the proprietary data format that you've used in `AddressBook.xml`.

Using XML is an advanced topic, so, if you would like to learn more about the technology and its application, try the following books:

❑   *Beginning XML, 2nd Edition* (ISBN 1-86100-559-8)

❑   *Visual Basic .NET and XML: Harness the Power of XML in VB.NET Applications* (ISBN 0-471-26509-8)

Demonstrating the Principle of Integration

Before you build the application that can integrate with your address book application, you should try to understand the principles involved. Basically, XML documents are good for integration because they can be easily read, understood, and changed by other people. Old-school file formats require detailed documentation to understand and often don't "evolve" well — that is, when new versions of the format are released, software that worked with the old formats often breaks.

XML documents are typically easily understood. Imagine you'd never seen or heard of your address book before, and look at this XML document:

```
<Addresses>
    <Address>
      <FirstName>Bryan</FirstName>
      <LastName>Newsome</LastName>
      <CompanyName>Wiley</CompanyName>
      <Address1>123 Main St</Address1>
```

```
        <Address2 />
        <City>Big City</City>
        <Region>SE</Region>
        <PostalCode>28222</PostalCode>
        <Country>USA</Country>
        <Email>Bryan@email.com</Email>
      </Address>
    </Addresses>
```

Common sense tells you what this document represents. You can also perceive how the program that generated it uses it. In addition, you can use the various tools in .NET to load, manipulate, and work with this document. To an extent, you still need to work with the people that designed the structure of the document, especially when more esoteric elements come into play, but you can use this document to some meaningful effect without too much stress.

Providing you know what structure the document takes, you can build your own document or add new things to it. For example, if you know that the Addresses element contains a list of Address elements, and that each Address element contains a bunch of elements that describe the address, you can add your own Address element using your own application.

To see this happening, you can open the AddressBook.xml file in Notepad. You need to copy the last Address element (complete with the contents) to the bottom of the document, but make sure it remains inside the Addresses element. Change the address data to something else. Here's mine:

```
<?xml version="1.0" encoding="utf-8"?>
<AddressBook xmlns:xsi="http://www.w3.org/2001/XMLSchema-instance"
xmlns:xsd="http://www.w3.org/2001/XMLSchema">
  <Addresses>
    <Address>
      <FirstName>Bryan</FirstName>
      <LastName>Newsome</LastName>
      <CompanyName>Wiley</CompanyName>
      <Address1>123 Main St</Address1>
      <Address2 />
      <City>Big City</City>
      <Region>SE</Region>
      <PostalCode>28222</PostalCode>
      <Country>USA</Country>
      <Email>Bryan@email.com</Email>
    </Address>
    <Address>
      <FirstName>Jennifer</FirstName>
      <LastName>Newsome</LastName>
      <CompanyName />
      <Address1>123 Main St</Address1>
      <Address2 />
      <City>Big City</City>
      <Region>SE</Region>
      <PostalCode>28222</PostalCode>
      <Country>USA</Country>
      <Email />
    </Address>
  </Addresses>
</AddressBook>
```

Finally, if you save the file and run the address book application, you should find that you have two addresses and that the last one is the new one that you added. What this shows is that, providing you understand the format of the XML that the application uses, you can manipulate the document and gain some level of integration.

Reading the Address Book from Another Application

To further the illustration, what you'll do in the next Try It Out is build a completely separate application from Address Book that's able to load in the XML file that Address Book uses and do something useful with it. Specifically, you'll extract all of the addresses in the file and display a list of names together with their matching e-mail addresses.

Try It Out   Reading Address Book Data

1. Create a new Visual Basic .NET Windows Application project. Call it **Address List**.

2. On Form1, draw a ListBox control. Change its IntegralHeight property to False, its Dock property to Fill, and its Name to **lstEmails**, as shown in Figure 19-7.

Figure 19-7

3. Double-click the form's title bar. Add this code to the Load event handler. Remember to add a reference to `System.Xml.dll` this namespace declaration:

```
Imports System.Xml
Public Class Form1
Private Sub Form1_Load(ByVal sender As System.Object, _
        ByVal e As System.EventArgs) Handles MyBase.Load
    ' where do we want to get the XML from...
    Dim filename As String = _
        " C:\Documents and Settings\Administrator\My Documents\Visual Studio
2005\Projects\Address Book\Address Book\bin\Debug\AddressBook.xml"
    ' open the document...
    Dim reader As New XmlTextReader(filename)
    ' move to the start of the document...
```

```
        reader.MoveToContent()
        ' start working through the document...

        Dim addressData As Collection = Nothing
        Dim elementName As String = Nothing
        Do While reader.Read
            ' what kind of node to we have?
            Select Case reader.NodeType
                ' is it the start of an element?
                Case XmlNodeType.Element
                    ' if it's an element start, is it "Address"?
                    If reader.Name = "Address" Then
                        ' if so, create a new collection...
                        addressData = New Collection()
                    Else
                        ' if not, record the name of the element...
                        elementName = reader.Name
                    End If
                ' if we have some text, try storing it in the
                ' collection...
                Case XmlNodeType.Text
                    ' do we have an address?
                    If Not addressData Is Nothing Then
                        addressData.Add(reader.Value, elementName)
                    End If
                ' is it the end of an element?
                Case XmlNodeType.EndElement
                    ' if it is, we should have an entire address stored...
                    If reader.Name = "Address" Then
                        ' try to create a new listview item...
                        Dim item As String = Nothing
                        Try
                            item = addressData("firstname") & _
                                " " & addressData("lastname")
                            item &= " (" & addressData("email") & ")"
                        Catch
                        End Try
                        ' add the item to the list...
                        lstEmails.Items.Add(item)
                        ' reset...
                        addressData = Nothing
                    End If
            End Select
        Loop
End Sub
```

We've assumed in this code listing that your AddressBook.xml *will be in C:\Documents and Settings\Administrator\My Documents\Visual Studio 2005\Projects\Address Book\Address Book\bin\Debug. If yours isn't, change the filename value specified at the top of the code.*

4. Run the project; you should see something like what is shown in Figure 19-8. Notice that addresses that don't have an e-mail address display without problems, as the Email element in your XML file contains an empty string value instead of a null value as is typically found in databases.

Figure 19-8

How It Works

To fully appreciate the benefit of this exercise (and therefore the benefit of XML), imagine that before writing the application you'd never seen the XML format used by the Address Book application. Since XML is a text-based format, you're able to open it in a normal text editor, read it, and make assumptions about how it works. You know that you want to get a list of names and e-mail addresses, and you understand that you have an array of `Address` elements, each one containing the three elements you need: `FirstName`, `LastName`, and `Email`. All that remains is to extract and present the information.

Since announcing .NET, Microsoft has a made a big play about how it is built on XML. This shows in the .NET Framework support for XML — there is a dazzling array of classes for reading and writing XML documents. The `XmlSerializer` object that you've been using up until now is by far the easiest one to use, but it relies on your having classes that match the document structure exactly. Therefore, if you are given a document from a business partner, you won't have a set of classes that matches the document. As a result, you need some other way to read the document and fit it into whatever classes you do have.

In your Address List project, you don't have applicable `AddressBook` or `Address` classes, so you had to use some classes to "walk" through a file. The one you're using is `System.Xml.XmlTextReader`. This class provides a "pointer" that starts at the top of the document and, on command, moves to the next part of the document. (Each of these parts is called a *node*.) The pointer will stop at anything, and this includes start tags, end tags, data values, and white space.

So, when you start walking, the first thing `XmlTextReader` will tell you about is this node:

```
<?xml version="1.0" encoding="utf-8"?>
```

When you ask it to move on, it will tell you about this node:

```
<AddressBook xmlns:xsi="http://www.w3.org/2001/XMLSchema-instance"
xmlns:xsd="http://www.w3.org/2001/XMLSchema">
```

Then, when you ask it to move on again, it will tell you about this node:

```
<Addresses>
```

Then it will tell you about `<Address>`, `<FirstName>`, Bryan, `</FirstName>`, and `<LastName>`, and so on until it gets to the end of the document. In between each one of these, you may or may not get told about white space nodes. By and large, you can ignore these.

What your algorithm has to do, then, is get hold of an `XmlTextReader` and start moving through the document one piece at a time. When you first start, the pointer will be set ahead of the first node in the document. Each call to `Read` moves the pointer along one node, so the first call to `Read` that you see at the start of the `Do . . . While` loop actually sets the pointer to the first node:

```
Private Sub Form1_Load(ByVal sender As System.Object, _
        ByVal e As System.EventArgs) Handles MyBase.Load
    ' where do you want to get the XML from...
    Dim filename As String = _
"C:\Documents and Settings\Administrator\My Documents\" & _
"Visual Studio\Projects\Address Book\Address Book\bin\Debug\" & _
"AddressBook.xml"

    ' open the document...
    Dim reader As New XmlTextReader(filename)
    ' move to the start of the document...
    reader.MoveToContent()
    ' start working through the document...
    Dim addressData As Collection, elementName As String
    Do While reader.Read
```

You can use the `NodeType` property of `XmlTextReader` to find out what kind of node you're looking at. If you have an `Element` node, this maps directly onto a start tag in the document. You can use the `Name` property to get the name of the tag. When you find the `<Address>` start tag, you create a new collection called `addressData`. If the start tag that you're looking at isn't the `<Address>` tag, you store the name in `elementName` for later use:

```
' what kind of node to we have?
Select Case reader.NodeType
    ' is it the start of an element?
    Case XmlNodeType.Element
        ' if it's an element start, is it "Address"?
        If reader.Name = "Address" Then
            ' if so, create a new collection...
            addressData = New Collection()
        Else
            ' if not, record the name of the element...
            elementName = reader.Name
        End If
```

Alternatively, the node you get might be a lump of text. If this is the case, you check to see whether `addressData` points to a `Collection` object. If it does, you know that you are inside an `Address` element. Remember, you've also stored the name of the element that you are looking at inside `elementName`. This means that if `elementName` is set to `FirstName`, you know you're in the `FirstName` element, and therefore the text element you're looking at must be the first name in the address. You then add this element name and the value into the collection for later use:

```
' if we have some text, try storing it in the
' collection...
```

```
Case XmlNodeType.Text
    ' do we have an address?
    If Not addressData Is Nothing Then
        addressData.Add(reader.Value, elementName)
    End If
```

As you work through the file, you'll get to this point for each of the elements stored in the `Address` element. Effectively, by the time you reach `</Address>`, `addressData` will contain entries for each value stored against the address in the document.

To detect when you get to the `</Address>` tag, you need to look for `EndElement` nodes:

```
' is it the end of an element?
Case XmlNodeType.EndElement
```

When you get one of these, if `Name` is equal to `Address`, you know that you have reached `</Address>`, and this means that `addressData` should be fully populated. You form a string and add it to the list:

```
' if it is, you should have an entire address stored...
If reader.Name = "Address" Then
    ' try to create a new listview item...
    Dim item As String
    Try
        item = addressData("firstname") & _
            " " & addressData("lastname")
        item &= " (" & addressData("email") & ")"
    Catch
    End Try
    ' add the item to the list...
    lstEmails.Items.Add(item)
    ' reset...
    addressData = Nothing
End If
```

You'll notice that in your `Try` . . . `Catch` you won't do anything if an exception does occur. To keep this example simple, you're going to ignore any problems that do occur. Specifically, you'll run into problems if the `Address` element you're looking through has subelements missing—for example, you might not always have an e-mail address for each address, as was shown in Figure 19-8.

You then continue the loop. On each iteration of the loop, `XmlTextReader.Read` will be called, which advances the pointer to the next node. If there are no more nodes in the document, `Read` returns `False`, and the loop stops:

```
        End Select
    Loop
End Sub
```

I hope that this example has illustrated the power of XML from a software integration perspective. With very little work, you've managed to integrate the Address Book and Address List applications together.

If you want to experiment with this a little, try adding and deleting addresses from the Address Book. You'll need to close the program to save the changes to `AddressBook.xml`, but each time you start Address List, you should see the changes you made.

Summary

This chapter introduced the concept of XML. XML is a language based on open standards that can be used as a tool for software integration. Within a single organization, XML can be used to transport data across platforms easily. It also allows two organizations to define a common format for data exchange and, because XML is text-based, it can easily be moved around using Internet technologies such as e-mail, the Web, and FTP. XML is based on building up a document constructed of tags and data.

XML is primarily used for integration work to make the tasks of data transportation and exchange easier, and you, as a newcomer to Visual Basic and programming in general, are unlikely to do integration work (as it's typically done by developers with lots of experience). Nevertheless, this chapter has "dipped your toes in" so to speak, by focusing on using the System.Xml.Serialization.XmlSerializer class to save entire objects to disk (known as serialization). This same object was used to load objects from disk (known as deserialization). You built a fully functional address book application that was able to use an XML file stored on the local computer as its primary source of data.

To round off the chapter and to demonstrate that XML is great for software integration work, you wrote a separate application that was able to load and make sense of the XML document used by the Address Book application.

To summarize, you should:

❏ Have a better understanding of XML and know what it looks like

❏ How to serialize and deserialize XML data into objects

❏ How to manipulate XML data in your applications

❏ How to use the XMLTextReader class to walk through an XML document

Exercises

Exercise 1

Create an XML document that describes a table lamp. You can describe the lamp using a number of different alternatives. You should describe items such as shade, bulbs and base. You can validate your XML at a site such as www.w3schools.com/dom/dom_validate.asp that offers a free validator.

Exercise 2

For exercise 2, you will expand on what you learned in the chapter by investigating how to place comments in an XML file. As a beginner, one of the most important tasks you can learn is how to research and find answers to questions. For this exercise, search the Web using your favorite search engine and try to find the syntax for inserting comments in XML Once you find the answer, test the comment in the same XML validator you used to test Exercise 1.

Web Services and .NET Remoting

Industry watchers have been predicting for some time that Web Services are going to be the "next big thing" in Internet development. This chapter introduces the concept of Web Services and shows you how to build your own. This chapter also looks at .NET Remoting and offers some guidance for choosing between .NET Remoting and XML Web Services.

In this chapter, you will:

- ❏ Get an overview of SOAP, the method used to exchange data with Web Services
- ❏ Build multiple Web Services
- ❏ Learn how to test the Web Services using the built-in test harness
- ❏ Build front-end applications that consume Web services
- ❏ Get an overview and hands-on experience with .NET Remoting

What Is a Web Service?

When you use the Internet, the two things you most likely use it for are sending (and receiving) e-mail and surfing the Web. These two applications are, by far, the most popular uses of the Internet.

However, from time to time as Internet usage grows, new technologies and applications that have the potential to change forever the way you use the Internet are released. In recent times, Napster was a commercial product that grew from nothing to "ridiculously huge" in a very short space of time. (In fact, the rate of growth of Napster, until the various court decisions that clipped its wings took hold, was far in excess of the rate of growth of the Web itself!) Naturally, its fall from grace was just as fast!

Building upon the success of the World Wide Web as you know it today, Web Services have the potential to be "the next big thing."

The Web is a great way to share information. However, the problem with the Web as it is today is that to use it you have to be a human. Web sites are built to be read with human eyes and interpreted with the human mind. Web Services, on the other hand, are built to be read and interpreted by computer programs, not by humans. Web services are, in effect, Web sites for computers to use. These Web sites tend to be dynamic in nature, so they don't contain static unchanging content but can react and adapt to choices and selections. For example, I might want to use a Web Service that accepts a quantity in U.S. dollars and returns the number of equivalent euros.

Why is this a good thing? Well, when building computer systems in a commercial information technology environment, the most costly factor always involved is integrating disparate computer systems. Imagine you have two pieces of software: one used to keep track of stock in your warehouse, the other used to capture customer orders. These two pieces of software were developed by different companies and bought at different times. However, when an order is placed using the second piece of software, that software should be able to tell the warehousing software that a quantity of a particular product has been sold. This may trigger some autonomous action in the warehousing software, such as placing an order to replenish the stock or asking someone to go and pick it off the shelf.

When two pieces of software work together, you call it *integration*. Integration is rarely easy, and on large installations it often involves hiring teams of consultants and spending thousands of dollars on custom-written integration software.

Without going into too much detail, Web Services make integration far, far easier. By making something that much easier, you inevitably make it far, far cheaper, and that's why it's predicted to be the next big thing. Not only will companies who are already integrating have a more cost-effective option than before, but companies will also be able to integrate their computer systems in previously unseen ways. Web Services will also provide opportunities for new businesses wanting to introduce specialized services with relative ease.

The commercial pros and cons of Web Services, together with a discussion of the movers and shakers in this particular space, are beyond the scope of this book. However, if you would like to learn more, take a look at `http://msdn.microsoft.com/webservices`.

How Does a Web Service Work?

First of all, Web Services are based upon completely open standards that are not tied to any particular platform or any particular company. Part of their attraction is that it doesn't matter whether you deploy your Web Service on Solaris, Unix, Macintosh, or Windows; anyone will be able to connect to and use your Web Service. This is the same with normal Web sites; you do not care what platform the Web sites you visit every day actually run on, as long as they work.

Second, the .NET implementation of Web Services is entirely based around a programming paradigm with which developers have been falling in love for years: object orientation. If you're used to using objects (and by Chapter 20 of this book, you should be!), you'll have absolutely no problems with Web Services.

The principle behind a Web Service is that you build a class that has methods. However, the traditional method of deployment and instantiation does not apply. Here is what happens traditionally:

- ❑ A developer builds a class.
- ❑ That class is installed (copied onto a computer).
- ❑ A piece of software running on that *same* computer creates an instance of the class (the "object").
- ❑ The piece of software calls a method on the object.
- ❑ The object does something and returns a value.
- ❑ The piece of software receives the value and does something with it.

But here is what happens with a Web Service:

- ❑ A developer builds a class.
- ❑ That class is copied onto a server computer running a Web server such as Microsoft IIS.
- ❑ A piece of software running on a *different, remote* computer (usually located somewhere on the Internet) asks the Web server to run a particular method on the class.
- ❑ The server creates an instance of the class and calls the method.
- ❑ The server returns the results of the method to the calling computer.
- ❑ The piece of software on the remote computer receives the value and does something with it.

You can see that the technique is very similar, but there's a disconnection between the server that the object is actually installed on and the computer that wants to use the object. In fact, with a Web Service, there is a huge process gulf (namely, the Internet) between the client of the object and the object itself. A solution to handle this disconnection is provided by the standards used by and specifically developed for Web Services.

SOAP

As Web services are, in effect, "Web sites for computers to use," they've been built on the same technology that's made the World Wide Web so popular — specifically, the Hypertext Transfer Protocol (HTTP) standard that powers all Web servers.

When you're dealing with "Web sites for people to read," the client (browser) and server usually exchange a mixture of documents. Hypertext Markup Language (HTML) documents, and their extension technologies like Dynamic HTML and JavaScript, describe the page layout and text on the page, and common image formats like GIF and JPEG are used to exchange images.

However, when you're dealing with "Web sites for computers to use," you exchange only one kind of document. These are known as SOAP documents.

> SOAP was originally an acronym for Simple Object Access Protocol, but the current standard at W3C has removed this terminology.

When a client application wants to ask the Web Service for some information, such as the current stock level for a product or the status of an order or to get the computer at the end of the connection to do something such as converting currencies or placing an order, the application constructs a SOAP request document. Using HTTP, this document is sent over the Internet to the Web server that powers the Web Service. This document contains all the information that the Web Service needs to determine what has been asked for. As Web Services work on the common object/method paradigm, the request document includes such things the name of the method and any data that should be passed through to the method as parameters.

At the server end, the Web Service receives the SOAP request, deserializes it, and runs the appropriate piece of software. (You're going to build some of these appropriate pieces of software in this chapter.) During the call, the method generates a SOAP response document that contains the information to be passed back to the caller. Like the request document, this new document is transferred using HTTP through the Web server.

SOAP documents are constructed with XML. This means that if you read a SOAP document, it'll look very similar to the sort of document that you saw in Chapter 19. However, at the level of Visual Basic, you don't need to look too hard at the SOAP documents. As you work through the chapter, you'll see some of the SOAP response documents that come back from the server, but you won't be seeing any of the request documents.

You know that Web Service technology is not tied to a specific platform, so from a developer's perspective the value of choosing one platform over another is determined by how transparent this SOAP document construction and transfer work actually is or what is available at the site where development will take place. .NET is very good for both building and using Web Services; you don't have to go within a hundred yards of a SOAP document. (This is why in this chapter you're not going to dwell on SOAP too much, even though without SOAP you wouldn't be able to do anything you can do in this chapter.) On some other platforms that are equally good for building Web Services, you need to jump through a few more hoops to create powerful Web Services.

Obviously, this chapter is concerned with how Web Services work with .NET. But first, have a close look at Figure 20-1, as it provides a simple form of the architecture behind Web Services.

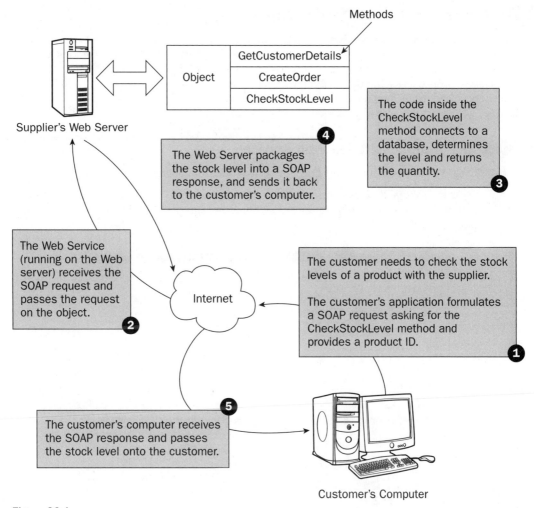

Methods

Object	GetCustomerDetails
	CreateOrder
	CheckStockLevel

Supplier's Web Server

4 The Web Server packages the stock level into a SOAP response, and sends it back to the customer's computer.

3 The code inside the CheckStockLevel method connects to a database, determines the level and returns the quantity.

2 The Web Service (running on the Web server) receives the SOAP request and passes the request on the object.

Internet

1 The customer needs to check the stock levels of a product with the supplier.

The customer's application formulates a SOAP request asking for the CheckStockLevel method and provides a product ID.

5 The customer's computer receives the SOAP response and passes the stock level onto the customer.

Customer's Computer

Figure 20-1

Building a Web Service

Building Web Services with Visual Studio 2005 is a breeze! In this section, you'll build a simple Web Service and will be introduced to some of the concepts involved. Specifically, you'll see how to include the appropriate attributes to expose a method as a Web Service method. You'll also learn how to test your Web methods using the test harness built into Web Services.

A Web Services Demonstration

A Web Service is basically a class that sits on the server. Some of the methods on that class are marked in a special way, and it's by looking for these special marks that .NET knows which methods to publish on the service. You'll see how this works as you go through the first Try It Out in this chapter. Anyone wishing to use the Web Service can then call these methods on the remote Web Service, as if the method existed in a class installed on their local computer. You'll also see a method that allows us to test the Web Service from within Internet Explorer.

A Demonstration Web Service

1. Open Visual Studio and select File ⇨ New Web Site from the menu.

2. Make sure Visual Basic is selected in the language box and HTTP in the location box and select ASP.NET Web Service from the upper list. Enter the name as **http://DemoService** and click OK (see Figure 20-2).

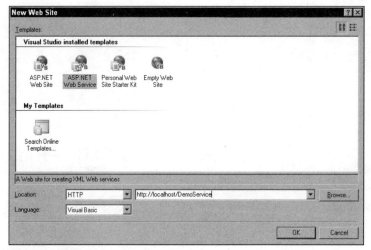

Figure 20-2

Web Services are based on ASP.NET technology, so the project will be created in the same way as the Web applications you worked with in Chapter 17. If you have problems creating the project, look back at that chapter for troubleshooting information.

Visual Studio 2005 will create a new virtual directory and create a new page called `Service` `.asmx`, where `.asmx` stands for Active Server Methods. (The extra `x` comes from the original name of ASP.NET: ASP+. The `x` is the plus sign turned through 45 degrees.) This page represents one service, and a Web Service project (or site) can contain many different services.

3. If the `service.vb` code-behind page is not open, use the Solution Explorer to open it. Just right-click `Service.asmx` and select View Code. When Visual Studio 2005 created the page, it put an example method on the service called `HelloWorld`. The code looks like the code shown here:

```
<WebMethod()> _
Public Function HelloWorld() As String
    Return "Hello World"
End Function
```

Run the project by selecting Debug ➪ Start Debugging from the menu. You will be asked to either run the project without debugging or add a config file to enable debugging. Choose to create a config file with debugging enabled, and continue. For security reasons, you would turn off debugging before releasing an application into production. The project will be compiled and Internet Explorer will open and display the `Service.asmx` page. This is the test interface. On this initial page, all of the methods supported by the service appear in a bulleted list at the top of the page.

You will use the `web.config` *file to make numerous changes to your site configuration in the real world. For the purposes of this example, we will not go into detail on this file, but know that you can make sitewide changes to security, caching, custom settings and more. You can learn more about using the* `web.config` *file by searching for* `web.config` *at* `http://msdn2.microsoft.com`.

4. Click the HelloWorld link. This will open another page that lets you run the method. This page contains the Web method name, a button to invoke the Web method for testing, and the protocols supported for this Web method. Notice that two protocols are listed: SOAP and HTTP POST.

5. Click the Invoke button. This will open another browser window. This window contains the SOAP response from the server, as shown in the following code:

```
<?xml version="1.0" encoding="utf-8" ?>
<string xmlns="http://tempuri.org/">Hello World</string>
```

How It Works

Just as in Web forms you have a class behind the `.aspx` page, you also have a class behind each `.asmx` page with Web Services. This class is the one that you enabled the `HelloWorld` method on. If you look at the definition for the class, you'll see that it's inherited from `System.Web.Services.WebService`:

```
Public Class Service
    Inherits System.Web.Services.WebService
```

The `WebService` class is responsible for presenting the pages that you clicked through in Internet Explorer to invoke the `HelloWorld` method. (You can use another browser to test the service, but Visual Studio 2005 chooses Internet Explorer by default.) These pages are known as the *test interface*. Methods on the class that you want exposed to the Web Service must be marked with the `WebMethod` attribute. You can see this attribute defined at the beginning of the method (note that it must be encased in a similar fashion to HTML tags):

```
<WebMethod()> __
Public Function HelloWorld() As String
    Return "Hello World"
End Function
```

Before the test page opens, you are asked to add a config file to enable debugging or continue without debugging. If you plan to test the web service, choose to add a config file. A new file, named `web. config`, is added to the project. Remember always to disable debugging before releasing your Web

Service to a production environment. When the test interface starts, it displays the methods flagged to be exposed on the server. When you click through to the page tied to a specific method, the test interface presents a form that you can use to invoke it.

When the method is invoked, to the method it "feels" just like a normal call — in other words, there's nothing special about writing Web Services, and everything that you've learned so far still applies.

You already know that Web Services are powered by SOAP. When you click the Invoke button, the SOAP message that's returned to the caller (in this case, your Internet Explorer) contains the response. You can see that this is indeed the value you returned from the method buried within a block of XML:

```
<?xml version="1.0" encoding="utf-8" ?>
<string xmlns="http://tempuri.org/">Hello World</string>
```

The structure of the XML that makes up the SOAP message, by and large, is not important. However, when you're working through more examples, we'll point out where the actual results can be found.

Adding More Methods

Let us build some methods that illustrate your Web Service actually doing something. In this next Try It Out exercise, you'll be adding a Web method that will calculate the square root of the number that you pass into it. You'll be adding the Web method and writing the code to calculate the square root, as well as testing this new Web method.

Try It Out   Adding a SquareRoot Method

1.   Open the Code Editor for `Service.asmx`. Add this new method to the `Service` class below the existing `HelloWorld` method:

```
Public Function GetSquareRoot(ByVal number As Double) As Double
    Return Math.Sqrt(number)
End Function
```

If you can't type into the code window, it means that the instance of Internet Explorer that Visual Studio 2005 opened is still running. Close down the test interface windows and any extra windows displaying the SOAP responses, and the project should stop running. Alternatively, select Debug ⇨ Stop Debugging from the menu.

2.   Run the project. You'll notice that the new method does not appear in the list at the top of the page. In fact, you will see the same screen that was shown previously. This is due to the fact that you didn't mark the method with the `WebMethod` attribute. I did this to show you that a class can contain methods that, although public, are not exposed on the Web Service. Close the browser and add the `WebMethod` attribute:

```
<WebMethod()> _
Public Function GetSquareRoot(ByVal number As Double) As Double
    Return Math.Sqrt(number)
End Function
```

3. Run the project again and you should see the new method at the top of the page.

4. To see the correct error message for this example, you may have to change a setting in your browser. Make sure you uncheck "Show friendly HTTP error messages" under the Advanced tab from the Tools ⇨ Internet Options menu in Internet Explorer.

5. Click the GetSquareRoot link. This time, the Invoke form should offer a way to enter a number because of the WebMethod parameter. Without entering a number, click Invoke.

6. When the new browser appears, you won't see a SOAP response; instead you'll see something that looks like this:

```
System.ArgumentException: Cannot convert  to System.Double.
Parameter name: type ---> System.FormatException: Input string was not in a correct
format.
```

You'll see this kind of message whenever you enter invalid information into the Invoke form. In this case, it's telling us that it cannot convert to System.Double, which should be a big giveaway that it can't convert an empty string to a floating-point value.

7. Close the browser window and enter 2 into the number field. Click Invoke and you'll get this response:

```
<?xml version="1.0" encoding="utf-8" ?>
<double xmlns="http://tempuri.org/">1.4142135623730952</double>
```

How It Works

If you look in the SOAP message that was returned, you'll find a double value that's as close as you can get to the square root of 2.

```
<?xml version="1.0" encoding="utf-8" ?>
<double xmlns="http://tempuri.org/">1.4142135623730952</double>
```

So you know that the method works. You should have also seen by now that building simple Web Services is not hard. This was Microsoft's intent with the Web Services support in .NET — the plumbing to build a service is remarkably easy. Everything you've learned about creating classes, building methods with parameters, and returning values is paying dividends here, because there's virtually no learning curve to climb. You can concentrate on building the logic behind the Web Service, which, after all, is the bit you get paid to do!

The Picture Server Service

Because building simple Web Services is so straightforward, you'll move on relatively quickly to building a proper application that does something practical with a Web Service. You'll also look at building a desktop client application that uses the Web Service, because up to now all you've used is the test interface provided by the WebService class. The specific example you'll use will be to build a Web Service that allows an application to view pictures placed on a remote server.

Creating the Project

In this section, you will:

❏ Set up a folder on your Web Service server (this could be your local machine or a remote machine where the Web Service will run) that contains pictures downloaded from a digital camera. You'll divide this folder into subfolders for different events, for example, "Deborah's Graduation," "Trip to Boston," and so on.

❏ Build a Web Service that can interrogate the folder to return a list of subfolders. You'll also be able to return a list of the files in each subfolder.

❏ When you do return a file, also return details on the file, such as graphic format, width, height, and so on.

❏ Set up the Web site so that you can view the pictures you find using a Web browser.

That doesn't sound like anything you can't do using an ASP.NET Web site. However, what you can do with the Web Service that you cannot do with a standard Web site is build your own custom front-end Windows Forms application. With a Web site, you are tied to using HTML and a Web browser to present the information on the server to the user.

Try It Out   Creating the Project

1. Select File ➪ New Web Site from the menu to create a new ASP.NET Web Service project and call it PictureService. You can place the Web Service anywhere you want on your hard drive. Using the built in Web server with Visual Studio 2005 you do not have to worry about IIS integration during development.

2. When the project loads, you don't want to use the default `Service.asmx` or `Service.vb` files. As extra practice, you will delete the default Web Service files and add them back. Using the Solution Explorer right-click both `Service.asmx` and `Service.vb` and select Delete. Click OK when asked.

3. Using the Solution Explorer again, right-click the PictureService project. Select Add New Item. In the Add New Item dialog box, choose the Web Service template. Enter the name of the service as **Service** and click Add. The Solution Explorer should now contain `Service.asmx`.

4. Now that you've created this new `.asmx` page, when you run the project, you want this to be the one that gets loaded into Internet Explorer. In the Solution Explorer, right-click the `Service.asmx` entry and select Set as Start Page.

5. To make the pictures available over the Web site, you need to create a folder called `Pictures`, directly within the folder out of which the Web Service itself runs. Right click the project in Solution Explorer and choose Add Folder ➪ Regular Folder. Name the folder **Pictures**.

6. Now, right-click `Service.asmx` in the Solution Explorer and select the View Code menu item. Find the `HelloWorld` method again and alter the code so that it looks like this:

```
Public Class Service
    Inherits System.Web.Services.WebService

    Public Sub Service
```

```
                     End Sub

                     <WebMethod()> _
                     Public Function HelloWorld() As String

                         Return Server.MapPath(Context.Request.ServerVariables.Item("script_name"))
                     End Function
                 End Class
```

7.   Run the project. As usual, when Internet Explorer starts, click the HelloWorld method link. Click the Invoke button when the page loads. TheWeb Service should now tell you the full path of `Service.asmx`:

```
<?xml version="1.0" encoding="utf-8" ?>
<string xmlns="http://tempuri.org/">c:\inetpub\wwwroot\PictureService\Service.asmx
</string>
```

8.   You can see that, on the computer on which this exercise was run, the folder containing `Service.asmx` is c:\inetpub\wwwroot\PictureService\. You'll refer to this folder as the *service root folder* from this point on. Now, open a copy of Windows Explorer (the local file explorer, not Internet Explorer). Go to the service root folder, and you will see the new subfolder you created called Pictures, as shown in Figure 20-3.

Figure 20-3

9.   Now you'll need to find some pictures to use with the service. You can use any picture you like as long as they are in either GIF or JPEG format.

10. Divide the pictures into a set of three subfolders under the Pictures folder. Use any folder name that you like for your three subfolders. In this example, the folders are Beach, Mountains, and Remodel.

How It Works

At this point, you should have both a Web Service and a load of pictures that you can use with the service. In a moment, you'll start building methods on the service that are able to return the folders to the user.

The only piece of code you wrote in this section was the code that returned the complete path of `Service.asmx`:

```
<WebMethod()> _
Public Function HelloWorld() As String
    Return Server.MapPath(Context.Request.ServerVariables.Item("script_name"))
End Function
```

This is quite an advanced ASP.NET trick (Web Services are, after all, based on ASP.NET technology) and is beyond the scope of the book. However, what we can tell you is that all pages running on ASP.NET are able to make many determinations about their environment, including the physical path in which the server is located.

For more information on building Web sites with ASP.NET 2.0, check out ASP.NET 2.0 Beta Preview (ISBN: 0-7645-7286-5).

Returning Arrays

In the first part of this chapter, you looked at a Web Service that returned single values from each method call, such as a string or a number.

In some cases, you want to return arrays of information. This is particularly true when you ask the Web Service for a list of the picture subfolders. In the next Try It Out, you return an array of string values, each one containing the name of a folder.

Try It Out   Returning a List of Picture Subfolders

1. Open the code editor for `Service.asmx` again. Delete the `HelloWorld` method.

2. You need a reference to the `System.IO` namespace for this exercise, so go to the top of the code listing and add this new namespace reference:

```
Imports System.Web
Imports System.Web.Services
Imports System.Web.Services.Protocols

Imports System.IO
```

When you're building methods, you're going to need a way to get the full path to your `Pictures` folder. This uses the work you did before to find the service root folder, but with an extra bit of code to actually get the full path to the `Pictures` folder. Add this property to `Service`:

```
' PictureFolderPath - read-only property to return the picture
' folder...
Public ReadOnly Property PictureFolderPath() As String
```

```
    Get
        ' get the full path of this asmx page...
        Dim strAsmxPath As String, strPicturePath As String
        strAsmxPath = My.Request.PhysicalPath.ToString()
        ' get the service path - everything up to and including
        ' the "\"
        Dim strServicePath As String = _
            strAsmxPath.Substring(0, strAsmxPath.LastIndexOf("\") + 1)
        ' append the word "Pictures" to the end of the path...
        strPicturePath = strServicePath & "Pictures"     ' return the path...
        Return strPicturePath
    End Get
End Property
```

3. Having the name of the folder is just half the battle. In order to do anything useful, you need an object that lets you search through the folder looking for subfolders. `System.IO.DirectoryInfo` is the class for such an object, so add this property to `Service`:

```
' PictureFolder - property to the DirectoryInfo containing
' the pictures...
Public ReadOnly Property PictureFolder() As DirectoryInfo
    Get
        Return New DirectoryInfo(PictureFolderPath)
    End Get
End Property
```

4. Now you can actually build the `GetPictureFolders` Web method:

```
' GetPictureFolders - return an array of the picture folders...
<WebMethod(Description:="Return an array of the picture folders")> _
Public Function GetPictureFolders() As String()
    ' get hold of the picture folder...
    Dim pictureFolder As DirectoryInfo = Me.PictureFolder
    ' get the array of subfolders...
    Dim objPictureSubFolder() As DirectoryInfo = _
        pictureFolder.GetDirectories()
    ' create a string array to accommodate the names...
    Dim arrFolderNames(objPictureSubFolder.Length - 1) As String
    ' now, loop through the folders...
    Dim pictureSubFolder As DirectoryInfo, intIndex As Integer
    For Each pictureSubFolder In objPictureSubFolder
        ' add the name...
        arrFolderNames(intIndex) = pictureSubFolder.Name
        ' next...
        intIndex += 1
    Next
    ' finally, return the list of names...
    Return arrFolderNames
End Function
```

5. Run the project. When Internet Explorer appears, click the GetPictureFolders link. When prompted, click Invoke, and you should see something similar to the following. Of course, the folders returned will be the folders that you created:

```
<?xml version="1.0" encoding="utf-8" ?>
<ArrayOfString xmlns:xsi="http://www.w3.org/2001/XMLSchema-instance"
xmlns:xsd="http://www.w3.org/2001/XMLSchema" xmlns="http://tempuri.org/">
    <string>Beach</string>
    <string>Mountains</string>
    <string>Remodel</string>
</ArrayOfString>
```

How It Works

You can see by the results that you do, indeed, have an array of strings returned. You know this because first, you have the `ArrayOfString` tag appearing in the string, and second, you actually have the three strings for your three folders.

```
<?xml version="1.0" encoding="utf-8" ?>
<ArrayOfString xmlns:xsi="http://www.w3.org/2001/XMLSchema-instance"
xmlns:xsd="http://www.w3.org/2001/XMLSchema" xmlns="http://tempuri.org/">
    <string>Beach</string>
    <string>Mountains</string>
    <string>Remodel</string>
</ArrayOfString>
```

The `PictureFolderPath` property is quite important, because you'll frequently use this in your methods. The first thing you do is to get hold of the complete path to the `Service.asmx` file that's powering the service:

```
' PictureFolderPath - read-only property to return the picture
' folder...
Public ReadOnly Property PictureFolderPath() As String
    Get
        ' get the full path of this asmx page...
        Dim strStrAsmxPath As String, strPicturePath As String
        strStrAsmxPath = My.Request.PhysicalPath.ToString()
```

However, this string will return something like this:

```
C:\WebSites\PictureService\Service.asmx
```

And what you ultimately want is this:

```
C:\WebSites\PictureService\Pictures
```

Therefore, you have to clip off the `Service.asmx` at the end and replace it with `Pictures`. To do this, you use the `Substring` method of the `String` class to extract just the portion of the path that you need and return it in the `strServicePath` variable. The substring that you want to extract starts at position 0 of the string and ends with the last backslash in the path. Using the `LastIntIndexOf` method of the `String` class you can easily find the position of the last backslash in the path. You then add 1 to that position to ensure that the last backslash is included in the string returned:

```
' get the service path - everything up to and including
' the "\"
Dim strServicePath As String = _
    strStrAsmxPath.Substring(0, strStrAsmxPath.LastIntIndexOf("\") + 1)
```

Next, you want to append the `Pictures` folder to the `strServicePath` variable and return the complete path from the property:

```
        ' append the word "Pictures" to the end of the path...
        strPicturePath = strServicePath & "Pictures"
        ' return the path...
        Return strPicturePath
    End Get
End Property
```

`System.IO.DirectoryInfo` is a class that can help you learn more about a folder on the computer or the network. You create a new property called `PictureFolder` that returns a `DirectoryInfo` object based on the value returned by the `PictureFolderPath` property:

```
' PictureFolder - property to the DirectoryInfo containing
' the pictures...
Public ReadOnly Property PictureFolder() As DirectoryInfo
    Get
        Return New DirectoryInfo(PictureFolderPath)
    End Get
End Property
```

Once you have that, you can create your `GetPictureFolders` method. Notice that you have included a description for your `WebMethod` attribute. This description is displayed on your Service page under the GetPictureFolders link, and it helps to document the Web methods available to be consumed. The first thing this Web method does is use the `PictureFolder` property to get hold of the `DirectoryInfo` object that points to `C:\WebSites\PictureService\Pictures`. You have to use the `Me` keyword, because you have a local variable with the same name. This removes the ambiguity of the call and makes sure that when you ask for `PictureFolder`, you actually go off to find the value of the property, rather than returning the current value of `pictureFolder`, which would be an empty string:

```
' GetPictureFolders - return an array of the picture folders...
<WebMethod(Description:="Return an array of the picture folders")> _
Public Function GetPictureFolders() As String()
    ' get hold of the picture folder...
    Dim pictureFolder As DirectoryInfo = Me.PictureFolder
```

The `GetDirectories` method will return an array of `DirectoryInfo` objects, one for each of the subfolders:

```
' get the array of subfolders...
Dim objPictureSubFolder() As DirectoryInfo = _
    pictureFolder.GetDirectories()
```

Once you have this array, you can use its `Length` property to determine how many subfolders the `Pictures` folder actually has. You can then use this folder to create an empty array of the correct length:

```
' create a string array to accommodate the names...
Dim arrFolderNames(objPictureSubFolder.Length - 1) As String
```

With the array in place, you can loop through the `objPictureSubFolder` array and copy the name of each folder into the `arrFolderNames` array:

```
' now, loop through the folders...
Dim objPictureSubFolder As DirectoryInfo, intIndex As Integer
For Each objPictureSubFolder In pictureSubFolders
    ' add the name...
    arrFolderNames(intIndex) = objPictureSubFolder.Name
    ' next...
    intIndex += 1
Next
```

Finally, you can return the array back to the caller:

```
    ' finally, return the list of names...
    Return arrFolderNames
End Function
```

You might have noticed the inconsistency in naming between "directories" and "folders." With the introduction of Windows 95, Microsoft decided that directories, as they had been called for over a decade, should now be called folders. The group in charge of the DirectoryInfo *class in the .NET team, however, apparently believed that "directory" was a better name than "folder." If you noticed, you've always called folders "folders" and the .NET Framework has always called folders "directories." Providing that each party sticks to its own convention, things shouldn't get confusing.*

Returning Complex Information

So far, whenever you've returned anything from a Web Service, you've returned only simple values, although you now know how to return arrays of simple values. With a little work, however, you can return complex structures of information from the Web Service.

In this section, you want to return a list of the pictures that are contained within each folder. With the picture subfolders you needed only to know the name, but now for each picture you would like to return the following information:

- ❑ The filename of the picture (for example, PIC00001.jpg)

- ❑ The complete URL that points to the picture (for example, C:\WebSites PictureService/Pictures/Beach/PIC00001.jpg)

- ❑ The name of the folder that contains the picture (for example, Beach)

- ❑ The size of the image (for example 26,775 bytes)

- ❑ The date the image was created (for example, 6/26/2002)

- ❑ The format of the image (for example, JPG)

<hr>

Try It Out   **Returning Complex Information**

1.   To return a set of information, you need to create a structure that you can populate with the information you want. To do this, add a new class to the project by right-clicking on the App_Code directory in the Solution Explorer and selecting Add New Item and then selecting Class. You must add the class to the App_Code directory. Call it PictureInfo. You want to create a structure rather than a class (although in this particular case either will do), so change Class and End Class to Structure and End Structure and add these members:

```
Public Structure PictureInfo
    ' members...
    Public Name As String
    Public Url As String
    Public FolderName As String
    Public FileSize As Long
    Public FileDate As Date
    Public ImageFormat As String
End Structure
```

2. To get the pictures contained within a folder, you'll create a new Web method that takes the name of the folder as a parameter. Open the code editor for `Service.asmx` and add this code:

```
' GetPicturesInFolder - return an array of pictures from the folder...
<WebMethod(Description:="Return an array of pictures from the folder")> _
Public Function GetPicturesInFolder(ByVal folderName _
    As String) As PictureInfo()
    ' get hold of the folder that we want...
    Dim pictureSubFolder As DirectoryInfo
    pictureSubFolder = _
            New DirectoryInfo(PictureFolderPath & "\" & folderName)
    ' we need to get the URL of the picture folder...
    Dim pictureFolderUrl As String
    pictureFolderUrl = My.Request.ServerVariables("URL")
    ' manipulate the URL to return an absolute URL to the Pictures folder
    pictureFolderUrl = "http://" & _
        My.Request.ServerVariables("SERVER_NAME") & ":" & _
        My.Request.ServerVariables("SERVER_PORT") & "/" & _
        pictureFolderUrl.Substring(0, pictureFolderUrl.LastIndexOf("/") + 1) & _
        "Pictures"
    ' get the list of files in the subfolder...
    Dim pictureFiles() As FileInfo = pictureSubFolder.GetFiles
    ' create somewhere to put the picture infos...
    Dim pictureList(pictureFiles.Length - 1) As PictureInfo
    ' loop through each picture...
    Dim pictureFile As FileInfo, intIndex As Integer
    For Each pictureFile In pictureFiles
        ' create a new pictureinfo object...
        Dim pictureInfo As New PictureInfo()
        pictureInfo.Name = pictureFile.Name
        pictureInfo.FolderName = folderName
        pictureInfo.Url = pictureFolderUrl & "/" & _
        folderName & "/" & pictureFile.Name
        pictureInfo.FileSize = pictureFile.Length
        pictureInfo.FileDate = pictureFile.LastWriteTime
        pictureInfo.ImageFormat = _
        pictureFile.Extension.Substring(1).ToUpper
        ' add it to the array...
        pictureList(intIndex) = pictureInfo
        intIndex += 1
    Next
    ' return the list of pictures...
    Return pictureList
End Function
```

3.   Run the service. When Internet Explorer loads, click the GetPicturesInFolder link. When prompted, enter the name of the folder whose images you want to return, such as Beach.

4.   When you click Invoke, you'll get a list of files back. The Beach folder has nine images, for example, so the document that comes back is relative to this. Here is an abbreviated version of the document containing information regarding two of the files:

```xml
<?xml version="1.0" encoding="utf-8" ?>
<ArrayOfPictureInfo xmlns:xsi="http://www.w3.org/2001/XMLSchema-instance"
xmlns:xsd="http://www.w3.org/2001/XMLSchema" xmlns="http://tempuri.org/">
<PictureInfo>
  <Name>BeachAddedBirds.jpg</Name>
  <Url>http://localhost:11780/PictureService/Pictures/beach/BeachAddedBirds.jpg
  </Url>
  <FolderName>beach</FolderName>
  <FileSize>472134</FileSize>
  <FileDate>2002-02-10T19:19:03.8437500-05:00</FileDate>
  <ImageFormat>JPG</ImageFormat>
</PictureInfo>
<PictureInfo>
  <Name>DSC00042 copy.jpg</Name>
  <Url> http://localhost:11780/PictureService/Pictures/beach/DSC00042 copy.jpg
  </Url>
  <FolderName>beach</FolderName>
  <FileSize>2073882</FileSize>
  <FileDate>2002-07-28T11:05:40.3437500-04:00</FileDate>
  <ImageFormat>JPG</ImageFormat>
</PictureInfo>
</ArrayOfPictureInfo>
```

How It Works

Once you have a folder name, you can get a `DirectoryInfo` object from it and use a method called `GetFiles` to return an array of `System.IO.FileInfo` objects that describe each file. However, you have to mate the folder name with the value returned by `PictureFolderPath`. This way, if you ask for Beach, you'll get a folder name of `c:\inetpub\wwwroot\PictureService\Pictures\Beach`:

```vbnet
' GetPicturesInFolder - return an array of pictures from the folder...
<WebMethod(Description:="Return an array of pictures from the folder")> _
Public Function GetPicturesInFolder(ByVal folderName_As String)
    As PictureInfo()
    ' get hold of the folder that we want...
    Dim pictureSubFolder As DirectoryInfo
    pictureSubFolder = New DirectoryInfo(PictureFolderPath & "\" & folderName)
```

When the user has used the service to learn what pictures are available on the server, you'll expect the user to use a Web browser to download them. The user can use IIS later to share the folders and files without you having to do any extra configuration work.

However, the URL that you need on the client has to be an absolute name that includes the name of the server and the `http://` part. If you ask the Web Service to return the name of its own `.asmx` file, you get a relative URL like this: `/PictureService/Service.asmx`.

```
' we need to get the URL of the picture folder...
Dim pictureFolderUrl As String
pictureFolderUrl = My.Request.ServerVariables("URL")
```

Now you want to build the absolute URL to the Picture folder in the `pictureFolderUrl` variable. To do this, start by adding a text string of `"http://"` followed by the server name where the Web Service is running. Next, use the `SubString` method of the `String` class to extract just the virtual directory name of the Web Service and then append the text string of `Pictures` to end up finally with a string like `"http://localhost/PictureService/Pictures"`:

```
' manipulate the URL to return an absolute URL to the Pictures folder
pictureFolderUrl = "http://" & _
    My.Request.ServerVariables("SERVER_NAME") & ":" & _
    My.Request.ServerVariables("SERVER_PORT") & "/" & _
    pictureFolderUrl.Substring(0, pictureFolderUrl.LastIndexOf("/") + 1) & _
    "Pictures"
```

The next thing you need is a list of the files that the folder contains:

```
' get the list of files in the subfolder...
Dim pictureFiles() As FileInfo = pictureSubFolder.GetFiles
```

For each file in the folder, you're going to create and populate a new `PictureInfo` structure. You'll be returning these in an array, so next you create that array:

```
' create somewhere to put the picture infos...
Dim pictureList(pictureFiles.Length - 1) As PictureInfo
```

Now you can start looping through the files. For each one, you create a new `PictureInfo` and populate it. When you come to populate the `ImageFormat` member, you want to chop off the initial period (hence the need for `Substring`) and then convert the remaining characters to uppercase (hence `ToUpper`):

```
' loop through each picture...
Dim pictureFile As FileInfo, intIndex As Integer
For Each pictureFile In pictureFiles
    ' create a new pictureinfo object...
    Dim pictureInfo As New PictureInfo()
    pictureInfo.Name = pictureFile.Name
    pictureInfo.FolderName = folderName
    pictureInfo.Url = pictureFolderUrl & "/" & _
    folderName & "/" & pictureFile.Name
    pictureInfo.FileSize = pictureFile.Length
    pictureInfo.FileDate = pictureFile.LastWriteTime
    pictureInfo.ImageFormat = _
    pictureFile.Extension.Substring(1).ToUpper
```

Once you have the image information, you can put it into its position in the array:

```
    ' add it to the array...
    pictureList(intIndex) = pictureInfo
    intIndex += 1
Next
```

Finally, you return the results to the caller:

```
    ' return the list of pictures...
    Return pictureList
End Function
```

That's it! Your service needs only those two methods. So now let's look at how you can use this Web Service with your applications.

The Picture Server Client

So far in this chapter you've seen how to create Web Services and how to manipulate them using the browser interface that the .NET Framework creates for you. This browser interface is actually a test interface — it's not what you would expect people using your Web Service to use.

The principle behind Web Services is that they enable software to integrate; therefore, when you actually want to use a Web Service, you effectively build the functionality that the service offers into your own applications.

In this section, you're going to build a desktop Windows application that can display a list of the picture subfolders on the remote server. The user can select one of these folders and see the list of files contained within. Clicking on one of the images will show the image in Internet Explorer.

(As a special treat, you're going to host Internet Explorer inside your own application!)

> Using a Web Service is often known as consuming the Web Service.

Web Services Description Language

To consume a Web Service, you can use something called a Web Services Description Language (WSDL) document. This is an XML document that contains a list of all of the methods available on the Web Service. It details the parameters for each method and what each method is expected to return.

Your WebService class automatically creates a WSDL document for you, but because WSDL is an accepted industry standard, it is good practice for each Web Service on any platform to expose a WSDL document. If you have the WSDL document for a Web Service running on .NET or on another platform, you'll be able to build a Visual Basic 2005 application that can use the Web Service it belongs to.

Creating the Client

In the next Try It Out, you'll create the client. Because you're going to use Internet Explorer inside your application, you'll also customize the Toolbox to include the Microsoft Web Browser control.

Try It Out   Creating the Client

1. In Visual Studio 2005, create a new Windows Application project called **PictureClient**.
2. On the Toolbox, expand the Windows Forms controls.

3. Near the bottom of the Toolbox, you'll find a WebBrowser control, as shown in Figure 20-4. This control is a managed wrapper of the WebBrowser ActiveX control.

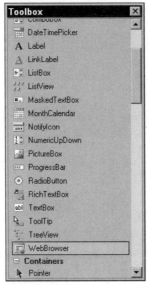

Figure 20-4

4. Select the WebBrowser control from the ToolBox and draw the control onto the form, as shown in Figure 20-5. You may need to change the Dock property to None.

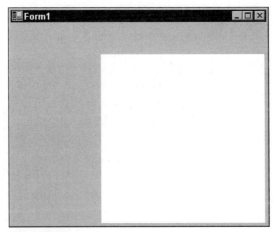

Figure 20-5

5. Using the Properties window, change the name of the control to **iePicture**. Also, set its Anchor property to Top, Bottom, Left, Right.

6. You're going to use the browser to display the pictures, but it seems a shame not to verify that it actually works as a fully functioning Web browser. So add some code to show how the full-blown features of Internet Explorer can be utilized within Windows Forms in .Visual Studio 2005. Double-click on the background of the form and add this code to the Load event handler:

```
Private Sub Form1_Load(ByVal sender As System.Object, ByVal e As _
    System.EventArgs) Handles MyBase.Load
    ' set the browser to a default page...
    Me.iePicture.Navigate("http://www.google.com/")
End Sub
```

7. Run the project and you should see Google's home page. Try entering some search terms, and you'll notice that this browser behaves in exactly the same way as the full Internet Explorer does.

If you try using the browser, you'll notice you don't have a toolbar, so if you want to go back a page, right-click the page and select Back.

Adding a Web Reference

To use a Web Service you need to add a Web reference to the project, which you do in the next Try It Out. This will prompt Visual Studio 2005 to go away and create some classes for you that will let you call methods on the Web Service. The two classes that are created are PictureInfo and Service.

Try It Out   **Adding a Web Reference**

1. Right-click the PictureClient project in the Solution Explorer and select Add Web Reference. This will open the Add Web Reference dialog box shown in Figure 20-6. In the drop-down box indicated by the URL label, type the full name of your Web Service location, **http://localhost/PictureService/Service.asmx**, where *localhost* is replaced with the name of your computer or Web server, and then click the Go button. You need to make sure your Visual Web Developer Web Server is running the Web Service if you are not using IIS.

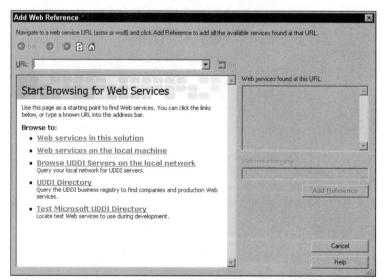

Figure 20-6

2. When it finds the service, you will see the Service page listing the available Web methods that you saw in your previous exercises. If you have typed the URL incorrectly, you will get a "The resource cannot be found" message. When you have located the correct URL, click the Add Reference button.

3. A new Web reference will be added to the Solution Explorer, and this will match the name of the server (your computer name). Right-click the new reference and select Rename. Change the name to **PictureService**, as shown in Figure 20-7.

Figure 20-7

How It Works

At this point, Visual Studio 2005 has successfully added a reference to the remote (or local) server. It has also created a new class for you called PictureService.Service. By creating instances of this object (as you're about to see), you can call methods on the Web Service.

The name that you choose when you renamed the Web Service in Solution Explorer acts as the namespace for the new class.

In this case, you've used PictureService, *but if you hadn't renamed it from, say,* localhost, *the new class that exposes the Web Service methods would be called* localhost.Service.

Displaying the Folder List

You can now call methods on the Web Service. In the next Try It Out, start by adding a drop-down list to the project that will display a list of the remote picture subfolders by calling the GetPictureFolders method.

Try It Out   Displaying the Folder List

1. Open the Designer for Form1. Draw on a ComboBox control at the top of the form, as shown in Figure 20-8.

2. Using the Properties window, change the Name property to **cboFolders**. Change the DropDownStyle to **DropDownList** and the Anchor property to Top, Left, Right.

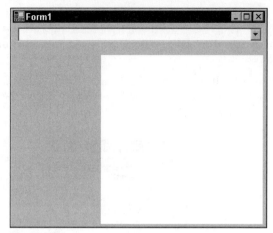

Figure 20-8

3. Double-click the form background to open the Load event handler for the form. When you start the application, you'll want to run the remote `GetPictureFolders` method. Add the following highlighted code, replacing the previous code that you added:

```
Private Sub Form1_Load(ByVal sender As System.Object, _
        ByVal e As System.EventArgs) Handles MyBase.Load

    ' get the pictures...
    Try
        ' create a connection to the service...
        Dim service As New PictureService.Service()
        ' get a list of the folders...
        Dim arrFolderNames() As String
        arrFolderNames = service.GetPictureFolders
        ' go through the list and add each name...
        Dim strFolderName As String
        For Each strFolderName In arrFolderNames
            cboFolders.Items.Add(strFolderName)
        Next
    Catch ex As Exception
        HandleException(ex)
    End Try
End Sub
```

4. You'll notice a blue wavy line appear under `HandleException`. This is to indicate an error: You haven't built this method yet. Add it now:

```
' HandleException - handle a Web service exception...
Private Sub HandleException(ByVal e As Exception)
    ' loop through the inner exceptions...
    Do While Not e.InnerException Is Nothing
        e = e.InnerException
    Loop
    ' report the problem...
    MessageBox.Show("An exception occurred." & e.Message)
End Sub
```

Remember, if you need a refresher on how exceptions work, take a look at Chapter 9.

5. Run the project. You'll notice that the form takes a while to appear (the first connection to a Web Service is often slower than the rest because .NET takes a little time to get its "house in order" before establishing the connection), but when it does, the folder names will be available if you drop-down the list.

How It Works

That was not complicated! .NET abstracts away a lot of the complexity involved in consuming a Web Service.

You start with a `Try . . . Catch` block:

```
Private Sub Form1_Load(ByVal sender As System.Object,_
        ByVal e As System.EventArgs) Handles MyBase.Load
    ' get the pictures...
    Try
```

It is very important that, when consuming a Web Service, you use exception handling around any code that could cause an exception. A lot of things can go wrong in connecting to a Web Service and passing data between service and client, and if anything does go wrong, you'll get an exception.

Next, you create an instance of the `PictureService.Service` class that Visual Studio created for you. At this point you have not connected to the Web Service — you have just prepared things for when you do:

```
    ' create a connection to the service...
    Dim service As New PictureService.Service()
```

The beauty of Web Services in Visual Studio 2005 is that calling methods on a remote object is no different from calling methods on an object installed on your local machine. Here, you call `GetPictureFolders` and get back an array of strings:

```
    ' get a list of the folders...
    Dim arrFolderNames() As String
    arrFolderNames = service.GetPictureFolders
```

Once you have the array, you loop through each of the strings and add the folder name to the ComboBox list:

```
    ' go through the list and add each name...
    Dim strFolderName As String
    For Each strFolderName In arrFolderNames
        cboFolders.Items.Add(strFolderName)
    Next
```

If an exception is thrown, you call `HandleException`:

```
    Catch ex As Exception
        HandleException(ex)
    End Try
End Sub
```

That is all you have to do to call the Web Service. But, before you go on, look at `HandleException`.

The SOAP standard dictates that whenever the service detects a problem, it must use an exception-handling model to tell the client about the problem.

Notice the word model. Web Services can be deployed on any platform, and that platform may well not have the great exception-handling functionality that .NET has. But the principle is the same—shout about the problem and hope someone hears it.

When .NET detects that an exception has been thrown on the server, it will wrap that exception in its own "problem on the server" exception. The actual exception that occurred on the server will be buried within the `InnerException` property, so `HandleException` has the logic to keep stepping down through the buried exceptions until it gets the one that the server actually threw:

```
' HandleException - handle a Web service exception...
Private Function HandleException(ByVal e As Exception)
    ' loop through the inner exceptions...
    Do While Not e.InnerException Is Nothing
        e = e.InnerException
    Loop
    ' report the problem...
    MessageBox.Show("An exception occurred." & e.Message)
End Function
```

You can test out the exception handling by stopping the Web server. To do this in IIS, click the Start button at the bottom of your screen, select Run, and enter this command:

```
net stop iisadmin
```

You'll see a list of services that depend on the IIS Admin Service, and you'll be prompted as to whether or not you want to continue with the process of stopping IIS. Enter **Y** and press Return. If you are using the developer Web server instead of IIS, right-click the icon in the task bar and select Stop. If you now run the project, you will see an exception like the one shown in Figure 20-9.

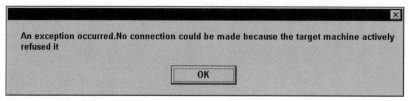

Figure 20-9

This exception can also occur if your URL cannot be located due to its nonexistence and/or network connection problems in general.

To start IIS once again, you type the following in the text box in the Start ⇨ Run dialog:

```
net start iisadmin
```

If you would like to restart IIS for any reason, though, the following command is more useful:

```
iisreset
```

Displaying the File List and Choosing Files

When you change the selected folder, you want to connect to the Web Service once more and get a list of the files in the folder you requested. You'll do this in the next Try It Out by extracting the folder name from the ComboBox and calling the GetPicturesInFolder Web method. You'll then take that list of pictures returned from the Web method and populate a list box.

Try It Out   **Displaying the File List**

1. To display the file list, you need to create a new class that encapsulates the PictureInfo structures you're going to get back from the server. Create a new class using the Solution Explorer by right-clicking on the PictureClient project and selecting Add ➪ New Item and then select Class. Call it **PictureItem**.

   Add the following highlighted code to PictureItem:

```
Public Class PictureItem

    Public PictureInfo As PictureService.PictureInfo
    ' Constructor...
    Public Sub New(ByVal info As PictureService.PictureInfo)
        PictureInfo = info
    End Sub
    ' ToString - provide a better representation of the object...
    Public Overrides Function ToString() As String
        Return PictureInfo.Name
    End Function
End Class
```

2. Go back to the Designer for Form1. Add a ListBox control to the form. Change its Name property to **lstFiles**. Set its IntegralHeight property to **False** and its Anchor property to Top, Bottom, Left. Your form should look like Figure 20-10.

3. Double-click the cboFolders drop-down list. This will create a new SelectedIndexChanged handler. Add the following highlighted code:

```
Private Sub cboFolders_SelectedIndexChanged(ByVal sender As System.Object, _
    ByVal e As System.EventArgs) Handles cboFolders.SelectedIndexChanged

    ' what folder did we select?
    Dim folderName As String =_cboFolders.Items(cboFolders.SelectedIndex)
    ' clear the files list...
    lstFiles.Items.Clear()
    ' connect to the service again and get the files back...
    Try
        ' connect...
        Dim service As New PictureService.Service()
        ' get the files back...
        Dim pictureList() As PictureService.PictureInfo
```

```
        pictureList = service.GetPicturesInFolder(folderName)
        ' add the pictures to the list...
        Dim pictureInfo As PictureService.PictureInfo
        For Each pictureInfo In pictureList
            ' just add the name...
            lstFiles.Items.Add(New PictureItem(pictureInfo))
        Next
    Catch ex As Exception
        HandleException(ex)
    End Try
End Sub
```

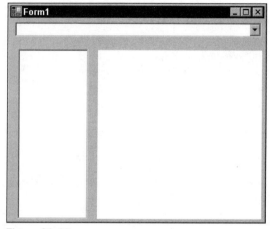

Figure 20-10

4.   After you've done that, go back to the Designer for Form1 and double-click the lstFiles list. Add
     the following highlighted code to the new event handler:

```
Private Sub lstFiles_SelectedIndexChanged(ByVal sender As System.Object, _
    ByVal e As System.EventArgs) Handles lstFiles.SelectedIndexChanged

    ' get the pictureitem...
    Dim item As PictureItem = lstFiles.Items(lstFiles.SelectedIndex)
    If Not item Is Nothing Then
        ' tell ie to show the picture...
        iePicture.Navigate(item.PictureInfo.Url)
    End If
End Sub
```

5.   Try running the project and selecting a picture from the list on the left. Internet Explorer should
     load the image.

How It Works

The ListBox control in Windows Forms works best if you can supply a custom-built object for each item.
In this case, you build a separate object that contains an instance of a PictureInfo object and overload
the ToString method available on all objects in .NET to return the Name property of PictureInfo:

```
Public Class PictureItem
    Public PictureInfo As PictureService.PictureInfo
    ' Constructor...
    Public Sub New(ByVal info As PictureService.PictureInfo)
        PictureInfo = info
    End Sub
    ' ToString - provide a better representation of the object...
    Public Overrides Function ToString() As String
        Return PictureInfo.Name
    End Function
End Class
```

When the item gets added to the list, the ListBox will call ToString on the object to get the value that should be displayed in the list. If you wanted, rather than returning Name, you could return the URL, in which case the list would appear as a list of URLs rather than a list of names.

One thing that's worth noting is that the PictureInfo you have on the client is not the same object that you had on the server. Visual Studio 2005 has also automatically created the PictureInfo class just as it did for the Service class. (This is why on the client PictureInfo is a class, whereas on the server it's actually a structure.)

When the drop-down list selection changes, you find the currently selected item, which is the folder name, and clear the file list:

```
Private Sub cboFolders_SelectedIndexChanged(ByVal sender As
        System.Object, ByVal e As System.EventArgs)
        Handles cboFolders.SelectedIndexChanged
    ' what folder did we select?
    Dim folderName As String = _cboFolders.Items(cboFolders.SelectedIndex)
    ' clear the files list...
    lstFiles.Items.Clear()
```

You then open up a Try . . . Catch so that you can manage any problem that occurs:

```
' connect to the service again and get the files back...
Try
```

Connecting the service is just a matter of creating a Service object again:

```
' connect...
Dim service As New PictureService.Service()
```

Calling GetPicturesInFolder and providing the folder name retrieves the list of files contained in the folder as an array of PictureInfo objects. If the folder doesn't exist on the server, the service itself will throw an exception, and this will find its way back and be perceived as an exception in your own code, where HandleException can deal with it:

```
' get the files back...
Dim pictureList() As PictureService.PictureInfo
pictureList = service.GetPicturesInFolder(folderName)
```

When you have the array, you create new `PictureItem` objects and add them to the file list:

```
        ' add the pictures to the list...
        Dim pictureInfo As PictureService.PictureInfo
        For Each pictureInfo In pictureList
            ' just add the name...
            lstFiles.Items.Add(New PictureItem(pictureInfo))
        Next
    Catch ex As Exception
        HandleException(ex)
    End Try
End Sub
```

When the selection on the file list itself changes, the currently selected item will be a `PictureItem` object. You can use the `PictureInfo` property of this object to get hold of the `PictureInfo` that was returned by the server, and then use the `Url` property of `PictureInfo` to find the URL that relates to the selected file and tell Internet Explorer to display that URL. You also check to make sure that item is not `Nothing`, because if it is, it would cause an exception if the user clicked on the `lstFiles` control when no files were displayed:

```
Private Sub lstFiles_SelectedIndexChanged(ByVal sender As System.Object, _
        ByVal e As System.EventArgs) Handles lstFiles.SelectedIndexChanged
    ' get the pictureitem...
    Dim item As PictureItem = lstFiles.Items(lstFiles.SelectedIndex)
    If Not item Is Nothing Then
        ' tell ie to show the picture...
        iePicture.Navigate(item.PictureInfo.Url)
    End If
End Sub
```

.NET Remoting

As is Web Services, .NET Remoting is used to connect to a service located elsewhere (on the same or different computer). IIS can also expose an assembly for .NET Remoting as it can for XML Web Services. .NET Remoting can also use SOAP, the standard protocol of Web Services. In these few aspects .NET Remoting is extremely similar to Web Services.

.NET Remoting is distinctive in that it can also communicate via the Transmission Control Protocol (TCP) Channel and allows you to customize what is transported and how. The data that is transported can also be sent in binary form, which you cannot do with Web Services. .NET Remoting is lot more flexible, but does not replace the need for Web Services, which is regarded as the extensible, open standards-based means of communicating between different programming environments and operating systems. Remoting is more specific to .NET but offers much more flexibility.

Since this is a beginner's guide, we will not go deep into any .NET Remoting details, but you do need to know a few things.

One necessary concept is *marshaling*. In simple terms, an object or value is transported (*marshaled*) from one process to another. It can also be marshaled from a process on one machine to a process on another machine. Marshaling is such a vital part of .NET Remoting that anything that travels across boundaries (such as the process boundary) must inherit from `MarshByRefObject` (MBRO).

Another aspect to understand is the difference between a server and a client. A *server* is typically the application that registers a type on a channel and a port. The *client*, on the other hand, sends a request to a channel and a port. The request is to create a type. The server, having registered the type, creates an instance of it when the client requests it. The server passes the instance back to the client. You can see by this explanation that it is important that the server and client communicate on the same channel and the same port. The way in which .NET Remoting does this is by using a Uniform Resource Identifier (URI) in the form of:

```
<transport>://<machine>:<portnumber>/<name>
```

In your examples, you will see the following URI being used, where `maincpu` is the name of your computer.

```
tcp://maincpu:8000/MyPongEngine
```

If you chose to use HTTP as the transport, the URI could have been:

```
http://localhost:8000/MyPongEngine
```

The port number used here could be anything, as long as the server and client know the same number.

You will soon see this in action. Without further explanation for now, you will create your small .NET Remoting example in the next Try It Out. As the architecture described in Figure 20-11 suggests, .NET Remoting requires a server and a client. You will first create the server application.

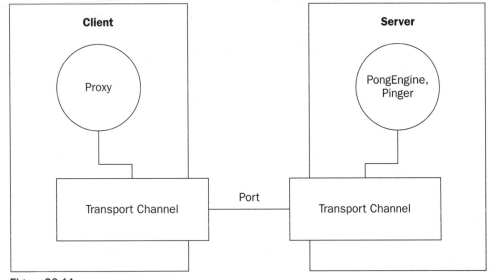

Figure 20-11

Try It Out   Creating the Pong Server and PongEngine project

1. Create a new ClassLibrary project named **PongEngine**.

2. Rename the `Class1.vb` file created by default in the PongEngine project to **Pinger.vb**.

3. Save the solution and add a Console Application project to the solution, named **PongServer**.

4. Next, add two references to the PongServer project. (See the diagram in Figure 20-12.) To add a reference, right-click the project in Solution Explorer and choose Add Reference.

    ❑   Add a reference to the PongEngine project inside the solution.

    ❑   Add a reference to `System.Runtime.Remoting`, found as one of the standard References in the References Dialog box.

5. Your references should look like Figure 20-12. To see yours, right-click PongServer in Soultion Explorer and select .Properties from the context menu. Now, choose References on the left tab.

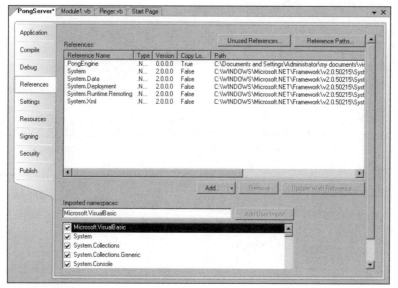

Figure 20-12

6. Now open the class named `Pinger.vb` in the PongEngine ClassLibrary project and change the code as highlighted here:

```
Public Class Pinger

    Inherits MarshalByRefObject

    Public ReadOnly Property Name() As String
        Get
            Return My.Computer.Name
        End Get
    End Property
End Class
```

7. Now add the following code to `Module1.vb` in the PongServer project:

```vb
Imports System.Runtime.Remoting
Imports System.Runtime.Remoting.Channels
Imports System.Runtime.Remoting.Channels.Tcp

Module Module1
    Sub Main()

        Dim channel As TcpChannel = New TcpChannel(8000)
        ChannelServices.RegisterChannel(channel, False)

RemotingConfiguration.RegisterWellKnownServiceType(GetType(PongEngine.Pinger), _
        "MyPongEngine", WellKnownObjectMode.SingleCall)
        Console.Write("PongEngine Registered." + Environment.NewLine)
        Console.Write("Server Active . . .")
        Console.Read()
    End Sub
End Module
```

8. Now right-click the PongServer project and choose Set as Startup Project from the context menu.

9. Run the project, and you should see the console application as shown in Figure 20-13. If you have a firewall or any type of security software, it may block this kind of server. You should allow this if your software asks you to block it.

Figure 20-13

How It Works

At this point, all you have really done is create a Class Library and a Console application. The strange code using the `Remoting` namespace does not seem to do much. If you see the Console window as in Figure 20-13, it is working. But what has it done?

The server has created and registered a channel on port 8000. It uses this channel and port number for communications. You are specifying that you require a channel and a port. This port number could be any number as long as the server and client (which you will create next) use the same number.

```vb
Dim channel As TcpChannel = New TcpChannel(8000)
ChannelServices.RegisterChannel(channel, False)
```

Next, the code registered your Pinger type on this port. This provides .NET Remoting with the schema or interfaces so that it knows what it should create when a client makes the request. This effectively exposes it to the outside world via TCP and, of course, through port 8000. Your code has also given it a friendly name MyPongEngine.

```
RemotingConfiguration.RegisterWellKnownServiceType(GetType(PongEngine.Pinger),_
        "MyPongEngine", WellKnownObjectMode.SingleCall)
```

The WellKnownObjectMode.SingleCall enumeration used in the previous code specifies that it will be destroyed after a call is made to the object. This means that a new object would be created for every call you make on it. A term often used for this kind of behavior is *stateless*.

Next, you will create a client to talk to PongServer. But before that, you need to create a proxy.

Generating the Proxy

A *proxy* is required for your client because you need to provide the client something that defines the PongEngine interface. You could use the actual PongEngine.dll and make a reference to it within your client application, but since the client will never create the PongEngine on the machine it is located on, you do not need all the code that is inside it. All you need is the interface. A proxy is the interfaces for a real assembly. It looks like the real assembly but it is not. It does not contain the code. It is made up of the interface definitions and the code to make it a proxy. A client references the proxy instead of the real assembly. The actual object is always created on the server (which is where the channel is registered). In the next Try It Out, you generate the proxy.

Try It Out   Generating the Proxy

1. To generate a proxy for PongEngine.dll, open Visual Studio .NET command prompt. You do this by navigating to All Programs on the Start menu, finding where Visual Studio 2005 is installed, and then clicking Visual Studio Tools followed by clicking the Visual Studio 2005 Command Prompt icon. The Visual Studio .NET Command Prompt icon executes a batch file that sets up your environment to include the appropriate paths to execute the command line tools installed with Visual Studio 2005.

2. Next, change your current working directory to the path where the PongEngine.dll was compiled. An example is shown in Figure 20-14.

3. Then type the following command line:

```
soapsuds -ia:PongEngine -oa:PongEngine_proxy.dll
```

soapsuds.exe comes with the .NET Framework and can be found in the SDK directory:

```
<installdir>\Microsoft Visual Studio 8\SDK\<version>\Bin
```

Running the command creates a new Assembly named PongEngine_proxy.dll.

4. To see that there is indeed a difference between the new Assembly and the original, you can view the two assemblies in .NET's Intermediate Language Disassembler (ILDASM). While still in the Visual Studio .NET command prompt, type **ildasm**. This will open the ILDASM application.

Figure 20-14

5. Drag and drop the `PongEngine_proxy.dll` onto ILDASM. You will see the entries as shown in Figure 20-15.

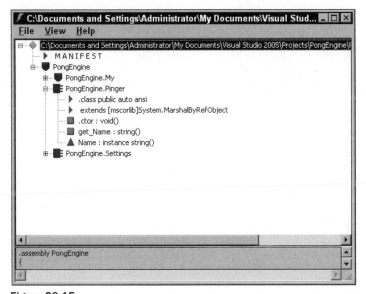

Figure 20-15

You can open another instance by opening another ILDASM window and dragging the original Assembly onto the second copy. You should now have two instances open showing the two different assemblies. You will immediately realize that they are different.

You can think of the proxy as the "dumb" representative of the original Assembly. It deploys with the client so that it can reference the correct Object, but not the actual one. In the next Try It Out, you create the Remoting client.

Try It Out	Creating a Remoting Client

1. Create a new Console Application project named **PongClient** in a new solution.

2. Add a reference to `System.Runtime.Remoting`, found in the References dialog box by right-clicking the Project and selecting Add Reference.

3. Next, you need to add a reference to the proxy of the PongEngine that you created previously. Open the Add References dialog box again and click the Browse tab. Locate and select the PongEngine_proxy.dll file that you created.

4. Your project and its references should now look like the one shown in Figure 20-16.

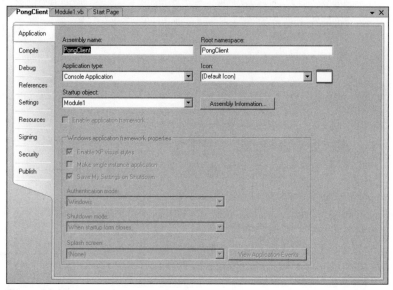

Figure 20-16

5. Next, you need to add the code that creates the PongEngine.Pinger type. Add the following code to Module1.vb in the PongClient project. Don't forget to change the machine name Maincpu to your machine name.

```
Imports System.Runtime.Remoting.Services.RemotingClientProxy
Module Module1
    Sub Main()

        Dim client As PongEngine.Pinger

        Console.Write("Trying to obtain Type from Server . . ." + _
        Environment.NewLine)
        client = CType(Activator.GetObject(GetType(PongEngine.Pinger), _
        "tcp://Maincpu:8000/MyPongEngine"), PongEngine.Pinger)
        Console.Write("Type Created and returned" + Environment.NewLine)
        Console.Write("The object returned:" + client.Name + _
        Environment.NewLine)
        Console.Read()
    End Sub
End Module
```

6. You'll need to start the PongServer application by navigating to the bin folder where the executable was compiled and double clicking on PongServer.exe. Your security software may try to block this type of program.

7. Next, run the PongClient project, and the client should connect to the server and provide the name of the server machine (see Figure 20-17).

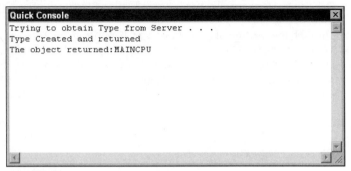

Figure 20-17

How It Works

If you copy `PongClient.exe` and `PongEngine_proxy.dll` to another machine on the network that has the .NET Framework installed and run it from there, it will still return the name of the machine the server is running on. This is due to .NET Remoting, which marshals the object and its values through the network. Have a look at the code:

```
Dim client As PongEngine.Pinger
client = CType(Activator.GetObject(GetType(PongEngine.Pinger),
"tcp://Maincpu:8000/MyPongEngine"), PongEngine.Pinger)
```

The code here first defines a variable of type `PongEngine.Pinger` and then creates the object by using the `Activator` class. There are two parameters used from `Activator.GetObject` call: the type that should be created and the URI pointing to where the object resides.

You will then see this wrapped by the `CType` function. This is because `Activator.GetObject` call returns a `System.Object` and you have to cast it to the type you want.

If you did not cast `System.Object` to your `Pinger` class, you would not see the `ReadOnly Property Name`, as it does not exist on `System.Object`. This is why you need the proxy: so that the client can know what the object looks like. You say that the client *knows* the interface.

Summary

In this chapter, you were introduced to Web Services and .NET Remoting. Web Services work by allowing a developer to expose an object that is accessible through a Web server. Web Services are based on open standards such as SOAP and WSDL and are underpinned by tried and tested technologies such as HTTP and XML.

You started off this chapter by building a basic Web Service that could return some information and also do something useful—namely, return the square root of a number that you gave it. As a more practical example, you then built a Web Service that allowed the consumer to download a list of pictures from the service. With the service in place, you built a simple client application that connected to the Web Service and called methods on the remote object. This also briefly demonstrated how to utilize the COM interoperability layer on .NET in order to actually put Internet Explorer inside your application.

Finally, you went through the creation of a Server and a Client using .NET Remoting. You created a class library and used it from another machine. .NET Remoting is a powerful way of creating machine communications and more. You could use .NET Remoting for networking support in your next game (did you wonder why it was named PongEngine?) or any other machine-to-machine communication that requires quick interoperation.

To summarize, you should know:

- ❑ What a Web Service is and how it works
- ❑ How to create Web methods in a Web Service and test them with the test harness built into a Web Service
- ❑ How to create a client application that accesses a Web Service
- ❑ What .NET Remoting is and generally how it works
- ❑ The different protocols used by Web Services and .NET Remoting

Exercises

Exercise 1

Create a Web Service that returns information about the Web server. Add three methods that return the Web server date, Web server time, and Web server name, respectively. Run the project to test the three methods.

Exercise 2

Create a Remoting server and client that act like the Web Service in Exercise 1. The server will have two methods. One will return the server date, and the other will return the server time. The client should test both methods functionality. Since you are running the application locally, there is no need to create a proxy.

Deploying Your Application

Deploying an application can be a complicated process, especially when dealing with large, complex applications. A wealth of knowledge is required on nearly every aspect of a development. A large software installation for Windows requires you to have knowledge ranging from Registry settings, MIME types, and configuration files to database creation and manipulation. Companies tend to rely on dedicated deployment software for these large installations, together with key people who understand the processes involved. However, Visual Studio 2005 does provide some basic deployment functionality, which is tremendously helpful for the standard developer and smaller installations.

Under the Visual Studio .2005 banner, you can create many different types of applications, from desktop to Web applications and services. All of these have varying degrees of complexity or peculiarities when it comes to installation time.

Since this is a beginner's guide, this chapter will not go into depth on specifics regarding the deployment of the different applications; rather, it provides an overview of deployment.

In this chapter, you will:

❑   Learn concepts and terminology

❑   Deploy a ClickOnce Application with Visual Studio 2005

❑   Create a setup program with Visual Studio 2005

❑   Edit the installer user interface

What Is Deployment?

Deployment is the activity of delivering copies of an application to other machines so that the application runs in the new environment. It is the larger, architectural view for what you may know as an installation or a setup. There is a subtle difference between deployment and installation.

Deployment is the art of distribution. It is concerned with how something is distributed. In other words, deployment is the way in which software is delivered.

The installation or setup is a process, where you load, configure, and install the software. So an *installation* is what you do to configure the software, and *deployment* is how you get it where you want it.

With this terminology, a CD is a deployment mechanism, as is the Internet. The two deployment mechanisms may have different installation requirements. As an example, if an installation is on a CD, you may have all the additional dependent software on that CD. This would be fine for a CD, but perhaps not for delivery via the Internet. Another example that may affect the installation option is where you may have written an installation in JavaScript. This may work fine when executed on a machine by the user having the correct Windows User Rights, but would not work through Internet Explorer. These kinds of considerations are important to consider when deciding what your best deployment option is. The type of installations you require could also be different per application.

Now that you have an understanding of the terminology, let me show you how to deploy applications using Visual Studio 2005.

ClickOnce Deployment

ClickOnce deployment is the concept of sending an application or its referenced assemblies to the client in a way that allows self-updating applications. You have three distribution options for a ClickOnce application: file share, Web page, or external media (CD, DVD, and so on). ClickOnce deployment has benefits with limitations. It is a useful deployment option for small- to medium-sized applications.

The benefits of ClickOnce deployment include three major factors. First, using this deployment option allows for self-updating Windows applications. You can post the latest version of the application at the original location, and the next time the user runs the application, it will install the latest version and run it. Next, any user can install most ClickOnce applications with only basic user security. With other technologies, administrator privileges are required. Finally, the installation has little impact on the user's computer. The application is run from a secure per-user cache and adds entries only to the Start menu and the Add/Remove Programs list. For programs that can run in the Internet or intranet zones that do not need to access the Global Assembly Cache (GAC), this is a terrific deployment solution for distribution via the Web or a file share. If you distribute the ClickOnce application through external media, the application will be run with full trust.

In the following Try It Out, you learn how to deploy a ClickOnce application from the Web.

Try It Out   Deploying a ClickOnce Application from the Web

1. Create a new Windows Application named **ClickOnce**.

2. On Form1, add a button and label. Change the button's Name property to **btnVersion** and Text to **Version**. Change the label Name to **lblVersion** and set Text to **""**.

3. Add the following highlighted code to the Click event for `btnVersion`:

```
Private Sub btnVersion_Click(ByVal sender As System.Object, ByVal e As _
    System.EventArgs) Handles btnVersion.Click
    lblVersion.Text = "Version 1.0"
End Sub
```

4. Test the form. When the user clicks the button, the label should display "Version 1.0." Your form should look like Figure 21-1. Next, build the project. To build the project, click the Build menu and choose Build ClickOnce in the submenu.

Figure 21-1

5. Now, publish the assembly to the Web. If you do not have IIS installed, you can publish the file to a local or network drive. Just remember how you chose to publish the assembly.

6. Right click the ClickOnce project in the Solution Explorer and choose Publish from the context menu. The Publish Wizard will open. (See Figure 21-2.) Choose a location to publish the file. In this example, we choose the default location for IIS.

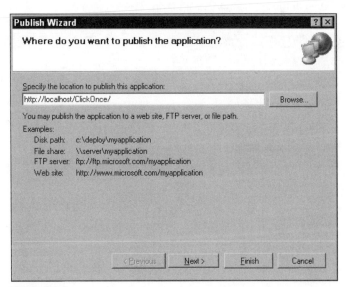

Figure 21-2

7. Click Next to go to step 2 of the wizard. Here you can choose whether to install a shortcut on the Start menu and add a listing in Add/Remove Programs. Select Yes as shown in Figure 21-3.

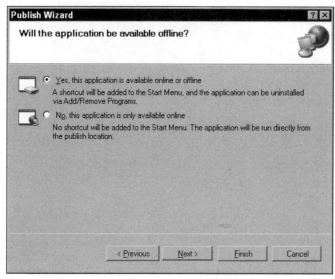

Figure 21-3

8. Now, you will see the summary of your choices. Click Finish to complete the wizard. This wizard will complete and open the default Web page users will use to install the application. Click the link to install the application. (See Figure 21-4.)

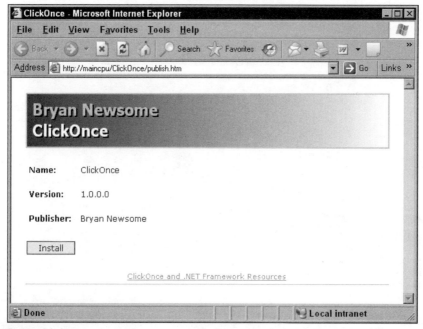

Figure 21-4

9. When you run the install from the Web, you may see a security warning (see Figure 21-5). If you see this, just click Install to continue. The form you created will open. Click the Version button and you will see Version 1.0. You can close the form.

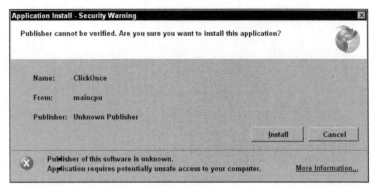

Figure 21-5

10. Check the Program Files directory, and you will see firsthand that no files were added. A new shortcut has been added to the Start menu.

   Now, you will update the application and see the self-updating capabilities in action.

11. Go back to the ClickOnce Windows application in Visual Studio and change the button Click event to update the label to **Version 1.1**. Your Click event handler should look like this:

```
Private Sub btnVersion_Click(ByVal sender As System.Object, ByVal e As _
    System.EventArgs) Handles btnVersion.Click
    lblVersion.Text = "Version 1.1"
End Sub
```

12. Test and build the application.

13. Right-click the project in Solution Explorer and choose Properties from the context menu. This time you will not use the wizard to publish the assembly. Click the Publish tab on the left side of the main window.

14. Take a look at the options. You can see all the choices you made using the wizard. All you have to do is scroll down to the bottom right of the Publish window and click Publish Now.

15. The Install page will be displayed, but do not click Install. Just close the window.

16. Now, run the application using the shortcut on the Start menu. You will be prompted to update the application, and you should click OK (see Figure 21-6). After the form opens, click the Version button, and you will see by the text of the label that the application is updated.

How It Works

That was easy, but what happened? After a few clicks, you deployed a Windows Forms application that was self-updating. Behind the scenes, Visual Studio completed many tasks that make this deployment strategy easy to implement.

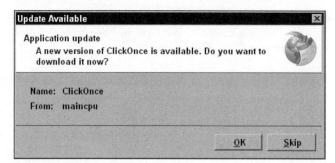

Figure 21-6

First, you chose the location to publish the assembly. `http://localhost/ClickOnce` was created as a virtual directory to host the deployment files for you. If you open the IIS MMC to investigate the virtual directory, you will see what was published. Your console will look like Figure 21-7. Notice that each version of the assembly has its own directory. By default, the .NET Framework would be installed if the user does not have version 2.0 of the Framework. The installer would download it from Microsoft. Feel free to browse around the Web directory. We will discuss the other files later.

The next step of the wizard allows you to specify whether offline access is allowed. A shortcut is added to Add/Remove Program files and the Start menu based on your choice to allow offline access. The application also installed to a secure cache on your computer. If you decide not to allow offline access, the user must return to the publishing location to launch the application on each use. In this case, the user would be required to have access to the Web site to launch the application.

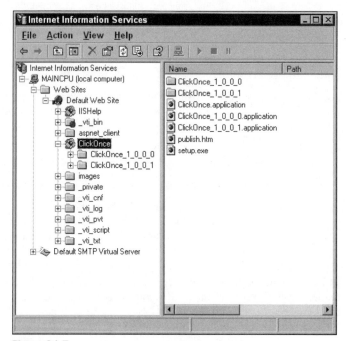

Figure 21-7

That's it. When you click Finish, Visual Studio 2005 goes to work. What happens behind the scenes is not magic. Actually, you could manually complete everything without Visual Studio if you ever needed to do so.

Now, take a look at IIS (Figure 21-7), and I will explain what made this happen. First, a virtual directory was added to IIS. This is where the application was deployed. A subdirectory was then created for the current version's files. Also, required manifest files were generated and placed under the root and version subdirectory.

Other files were part of the deployment. A Web page (`publish.htm`) was created for the user interface. Finally, a `setup.exe` file for deployment was created. Both the `setup.exe` and `publish.htm` files were added to the root virtual directory.

To install the application, you navigated to the `publish.htm` Web page. Each time you launched the installed application, a check was made to see whether a newer version was available. When a new version was available, you were notified and presented with the option to install the update. ClickOnce deployment has an almost unlimited number of deployment options. You just scratched the surface in this exercise.

XCOPY Deployment

XCOPY deployment gets its name from the MS DOS `XCOPY` command. XCOPY is a copy procedure that copies a directory and all files including subfolders. This is commonly associated with Web applications, but with Visual Studio 2005 it can also apply to a desktop application. Since a standard .NET assembly does not need any form of registration, it fully supports this option. XCOPY does not work with shared assemblies because they require installation (if they are used from the Global Assembly Cache). You learn more about shared assemblies later in this chapter.

Creating a Visual Studio 2005 Setup Application

Visual Studio 2005 supports the Windows Installer. But what is it? The Windows Installer service is a general platform for installing applications in Windows and gets installed with Visual Studio 2005. It provides a lot of functionality, such as uninstall capabilities and transactional installation options (the ability to roll back if something fails) as well as other general features. Many of these features either are built in (so that you do not have to do anything) or are configurable and/or extensible.

The Visual Studio 2005 Windows Installer support has made it easier to create a simple installation. Visual Studio has provided templates in the New Project dialog box for this purpose.

Visual Studio 2005 exposes four main templates for creating Windows installer projects:

❑ Setup Project for desktop or general setup

❑ Web Setup Project for Web applications or Web Services

❑ Merge Module, a package that can only be merged into another setup

❑ Cab Project creates a package that can be used as a type of install

Finally, Visual Studio 2005 also has a Setup Wizard Project, which aids you in creating one of the Windows Installer templates listed here.

Creating a Setup application

When you are creating setup applications, always be aware of the user. All of the applications you will create with Visual Studio 2005 require version 2.0 of the .NET Framework on the installation system. For internal applications, you will know what prerequisites are installed on each computer, but in many cases you will deliver your application to users with no idea of the target system configuration. When you are not sure of the user's configuration, it is up to you to make all required components available.

Visual Studio 2005 makes the process of including prerequisites easy. Most common requirements can be included (bootstrapping) by just checking a box. By default, the .NET Framework is automatically boot-strapped. Any setup application that is created with the default settings will prompt the end user to install the Version 2.0 of the Framework if it is not installed prior to setup.

In the following Try It Out, you create a setup application.

Try It Out   Creating a Setup application

1.   Open Visual Studio and create a New Windows Application named **Prerequisite**. You will not make any changes to the form design or code.

2.   Save All and then build the project.

3.   Add a setup project to the solution, named **Installer** as shown in Figure 21-8. To add a new project, choose File ➪ Add ➪ New Project from the main menu bar.

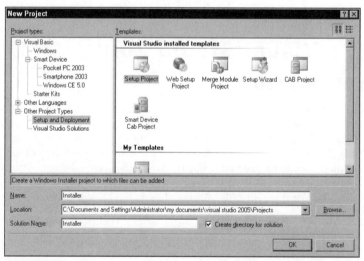

Figure 21-8

When Visual Studio creates the project, it adds a Designer. There are three main folders in the left pane of the Designer: Application Folder, User's Desktop, and User's Program Menu. (See Figure 21-9.)

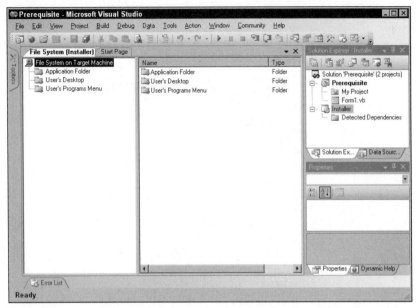

Figure 21-9

4. In the Solution Explorer, right-click the Installer project and choose Properties.

5. Find the Settings button at the right and click it. You will see the Prerequisite form as shown in Figure 21-10. Notice that, by default, the .NET Framework 2.0 is selected.

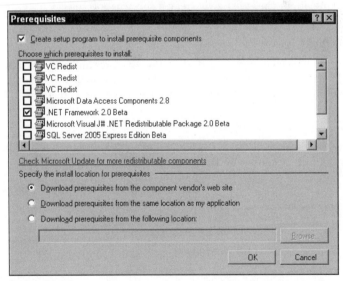

Figure 21-10

6. Check the box beside Microsoft Data Access Components 2.8 and click OK twice to both dialogs. Notice that by default, the components are set to download from the vendor's Web site.

695

7. Right-click the Application Folder node in the Designer (left pane) and select Add ⇨ Project Output. The form will look like Figure 21-11.

8. Next, select "Primary output" from the Add Project Output Group form and click OK.

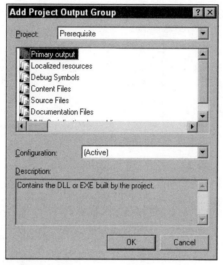

Figure 21-11

9. Now, right-click Primary output from Prerequisite, which you just added. From the context menu, select Create a Shortcut to Primary Output from Prerequisite. Rename the shortcut **Prerequisite**. Right-click the newly created shortcut and select Cut from the context menu. On the left pane, right-click User's Program Menu and click Paste.

10. Save and build the Installer project.

11. Right-click the Installer project in the Solution Explorer and select Install. A Windows Installer will be loaded. This is the Setup project you have just created. Remember the shortcut you added to the user's program menu. Take a peek at your menu, and you will see the shortcut.

How It Works

When you created the setup application, Visual Studio created a Windows Installer application. Changes you made, such as adding the ClickOnce program to the project, were included in the Installer database file.

In this example, you added one executable. It is also possible to add many other types of files including text files, help files, and other assemblies.

When you built the project, two files were created:

❑ The msi file

❑ An installation loader named setup.exe

When you looked, you saw these files in your <solution directory>\Installer\Release folder. You can find the path by selecting the Solution and looking at the Path property in the Properties window of Visual Studio. If the user did not have MDAC 2.8 or the correct version of the .NET Framework 2.0, it would have been downloaded from the vendor. You can change that under the settings where you added the dependency for MDAC 2.8.

User Interface Editor

Installations can be configured to meet almost any need with Visual Studio 2005. One of the easiest ways to make your installation look professional is to customize the interface the user sees during installation. A tool, User Interface Editor, is available to do just this.

With the User Interface Editor, you can configure the installation to do just about anything you want. You can add prebuilt dialog boxes such as a license agreement. Also, a number of customizable dialog boxes are available. You can even add a custom dialog box to ensure that a valid serial number is entered during installation.

In the next Try It Out, you will customize the installation of a setup application. We will show you some of the options, but know that almost every aspect of the installation is customizable.

Try It Out   **Customizing the User Interface**

1.   Open Visual Studio and create a New Setup Project. Name the project **UserInterface**.

2.   Now, select View ⇨ Editor ⇨ User Interface from the menu.

3.   The editor will open as shown in Figure 21-12.

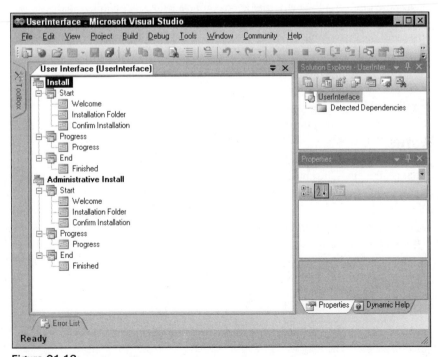

Figure 21-12

4. You will see two main items. Install and Administrative Install both have customizable interfaces. The administrative install is for a special type of installation that we will not explain in detail; it is used when an administrator installs an application image to a network share.

5. Under the Install node at the top, right-click Start and choose Add Dialog from the context menu. (See Figure 21-13.)

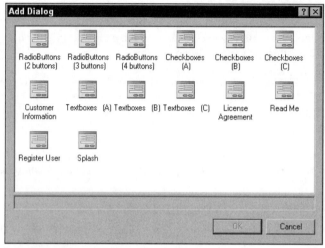

Figure 21-13

6. Select the License Agreement dialog box and click OK. By default, the dialog box will be added as the last dialog box under the Start node. You will make the dialog the second window the user will see by moving it up the tree node. Right-click the License Agreement dialog and choose Move Up until it is the second dialog box. Your project will look similar to Figure 21-14.

7. This is where you would normally add a license agreement file using the LicenseFile property. The only requirement is that is it must be in Rich Text Format (RTF). For this example, you will leave this property blank.

8. Next, add a Customer Information dialog box and make it the third step under the Start process. Change the SerialNumberTemplate property to %%-###-%%% and the ShowSerialNumber to True.

9. That is all it takes. Just build the application and install. You will see the license agreement dialog box as the second screen of the installation. The third step is the customer information screen.

10. The third step is the customer information screen. Enter **77-000-777** for the serial number. See Figure 21-15.

11. Now, complete the installation by clicking Next through the rest of the steps.

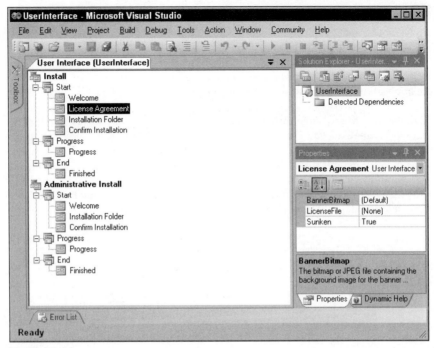

Figure 21-14

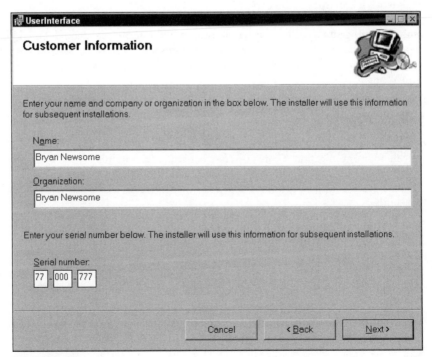

Figure 21-15

How It Works

Wow. How easy was that? You customized the installation package with just a few clicks of the mouse. Visual Studio made this easy. As you saw, you can control the installation interface.

The second step of the installation was the license agreement you added. You were forced to agree to install the application. Visual Studio added the dialog boxes in the order you chose.

The third dialog was the customer information screen. Without a valid serial number, the installation would cancel. We created a valid serial number based on the `SerialNumberTemplate` property you changed to `%%-###-%%%`. The `%` character signifies that a required digit is included in the algorithm, and the `#` character is entered for digits that are not included. The serial number algorithm summed all required digits and then divided by 7. If the remainder was 0, the serial number entered passed validation. So, the first two and the last three digits were added together for a total of 35. Then 35 was divided by 7 for a remainder of 0, and you were allowed to install the application.

Deploying Different Solutions

Deploying applications is actually a large and complex task, made easier by various tools. But if you consider, for a moment, a large suite of applications, something like Microsoft Office, you will notice that there can be a vast number of files. All these files require explicit locations or Registry entries. They all tie together to make the application work. As well as being a large installation, there can also be many other complexities, such as database creation: What happens if the database exists? What happens with the data that is already there? This kind of activity, commonly referred to as *migration*, could potentially mean a lot of work for an installation expert.

Having multiple application types can also make an installation complex, and detailed knowledge of the different applications is required for a successful installation. The following section discusses some items regarding the different deployment scenarios surrounding the different types of applications that can be created with Visual Studio 2005.

Private Assemblies

Private assemblies are installed in a directory named `bin` located under the application directory. These files are private to the application. There are a few benefits in doing this:

❑ No versioning is required, as long as it is the same version as the one with which the application was built.

❑ The private assembly is not a shared assembly, and therefore it cannot be updated by another application (at least it is not meant to be).

❑ You can manually replace the assembly as long as it is the same version.

❑ It enables XCOPY deployment (the ability simply to copy and paste files to a location and have it work).

❑ You can make changes to the assembly, and if two different applications use it, you could update one independently from the other.

- ❑   There is no configuration or signing (see next section) to do. It just works.

- ❑   It is great for small utility Assemblies and/or application-specific code.

Private assemblies have the following negatives:

- ❑   When you have multiple applications using one assembly, you have to deploy the assembly to the `bin` directory of each application.

- ❑   You would normally have to include the assembly in each setup project where it is used.

- ❑   Versioning is not enforced as it is in a shared assembly.

- ❑   It is not strongly named, which means someone could spoof your assembly.

Spoofing an assembly is when someone creates an assembly that looks identical to yours and replaces yours with the spoof copy. This spoof copy could do malicious things.

Shared Assemblies

Shared assemblies are actually more stable than private assemblies are, and they have a thorough approach to assembly deployment. A shared assembly can also behave like a private assembly, so all the benefits of that approach apply here too. The traditional shared assembly is different because of the extra work you need to do and the extra capabilities it then gains.

A shared assembly is like going back in time. In Windows 3.1, the main deployment location for these kinds of DLLs was the `Windows\System` directory. Then you were advised to have these files in the local application path, because it made for easier installation and uninstallation. Today, the System directory concept returns in a new guise named the Global Assembly Cache (GAC). However, the strong naming of assemblies is a definite step up.

To install a shared assembly, you have to add the file to a new folder named `Global Assembly Cache`. By default, this folder is not visible in the three default folders that are listed. To add the GAC folder you must right-click the node named File System on Target Machine and select Add Special Folder ➪ Global Assembly Cache.

Note that any project type can use a shared assembly, including a Web application.

Following is a list of the main benefits of a shared assembly:

- ❑   It is signed and cannot be spoofed.

- ❑   It has strong versioning support and configuration options.

- ❑   It is stored in one central location and does not need to be copied to the `bin` directory of every application that uses it.

- ❑   You can have many different versions running side by side.

Shared assemblies have the following negatives:

❑ You have to sign the assembly.

❑ You have to be careful not to break compatibility with existing applications, or else you have to configure the different versions.

❑ Configuration can be a nightmare depending on the requirements.

Deploying Desktop Applications

In the second project, you created a setup for a desktop application. All that you installed was the one executable. It had no dependencies other than the .NET Framework, which is always required. In a more complete application, you may have various assemblies, WinForm controls, or other files that you created for the application. Installing a private assembly with the Setup project means that you include the file by adding it to the setup application.

Deploying Web Applications

A Web application, when using private assemblies, can be simple to deploy. You can use the Visual Studio 2005 Web Application setup project to create a simple Web setup. The setup creates a virtual directory and copies the files you specify to the physical directory location.

> You do not need to deploy the Visual Basic code files. These are compiled into an assembly in the `bin` directory. Only `aspx`, `ascx`, `js`, `css`, and other HTML files or scripting files are required.

Deploying XML Web Services

A Web Service is deployed in much the same way as a Web application is deployed. It also has a virtual directory. The files that it requires are somewhat different, though. You need to deploy the `asmx` and `discovery` files together with the assembly.

Useful Tools

There are a few tools that either come with .NET or are in Windows already for you to use. This section briefly points to these tools. When creating an installation, you also need to test it by installing it on various machines. Sometimes, when things do not go according to plan, you may need to do some or all of the activities by hand to see which one was the cause of the problem. As an example, perhaps you suspect that the `ASPNET_WP.dll` process has become unstable or broken in some fashion and it has affected the installation. In this scenario, you may wish to restart IIS before you run the install. In a similar vein, perhaps an assembly that was supposed to be registered in the GAC as a shared assembly cannot be found by the client, and then you may want to register it manually to check whether there was a problem with the registration. The following list briefly describes the tools you may need to use:

❑ **ASPNET_RegIIS:** The `aspnet_regiis.exe` command line tool can be found in the `<sysdir>\Microsoft.NET\ Framework\<version>` directory. This tool makes it an easy task to reinstall various aspects of the ASP.NET runtime.

❑ **IISReset:** IISReset simply restarts IIS without requiring you to open the IIS management console. Simply open a DOS prompt and type `IISReset`, and it will immediately restart IIS.

❑ **ILDasm:** If you wish to inspect the metadata of an assembly, ILDASM is the tool for the job. With the tool, you can inspect everything from the Namespaces to the version. Start ILDasm by typing `ILDasm` at a Visual Studio command prompt.

❑ **GACUtil:** This is a Visual Studio command line tool for registering/unregistering assemblies from the Global Assembly Cache. The `/I` option is for registering the assembly, and the `/u` option is for unregistering.

❑ **RegAsm:** This Visual Studio command line utility is used for creating the necessary Component Object Model (COM) information from an assembly. This is used when you need to expose an assembly for COM Interop. The `regasm` tool includes switches for registering/unregistering type libraries.

❑ **InstallUtil:** This is a Visual Studio command line tool for executing the Installer classes within an assembly. This can execute the InstallerHelper sample you did earlier in this chapter.

❑ **MageUI (Manifest Generation and Editing Tool):** This is a graphical tool for generating, editing, and signing the application and deployment manifest for ClickOnce applications. Run MageUI from a Visual Studio command prompt to start the tool. A command line tool is available if you prefer to not have the user interface. `Mage.exe` is the command line version of the tool.

Summary

Well, we hope you enjoyed looking at some general aspects of deployment. In the first section of this chapter, you were introduced to some terminology, and then you saw how to create a ClickOnce Application and a simple Setup application inside Visual Studio. You also learned the positives and negatives of private versus shared assemblies. Ultimately, we hope you learned that there is potentially a lot to learn in this area, from getting to know more about the features of the Windows Installer templates to learning how to do more with ClickOnce deployment.

Now that you have finished this chapter, you should know how to:

❑   Create a ClickOnce deployment application

❑   Create a Visual Studio 2005 setup application

❑   Use general deployment terms such as XCOPY, shared versus private assemblies

❑   Edit the installer user interface

Exercises

Exercise 1

Create a setup project for Notepad and install the program. You should be able to find the `notepad.exe` file in your Windows System directory. *Hint:* You will need to add the file to a setup project. Have the setup application add a shortcut to the Start menu. Deploy the `notepad.exe` file to the Program Files directory. For extra credit, change the Manufacturer property of the project and change it from Default Company Name to **Wrox**. Also, change the Author property to your name.

Exercise 2

Using the setup application created in Exercise 1, add a splash screen dialog box that is displayed first during the installation. We have included a bitmap in the code for the book named `Wrox_Logo.bmp`. This bitmap is the correct size, 480 _ 320, and you can use this image for the dialog box. *Hint:* You have to add the image you use to the setup application before you can add it to the splash dialog box.

Building Mobile Applications

Mobile devices — more specifically, personal digital assistants (PDAs) — are being shipped to more and more people around the world. A market once owned by Palm's Operating System is now a market full of devices running Microsoft Windows CE. According to a report published November 12, 2004, by the Associated Press, Windows CE first took the top place over Palm in number of PDAs shipped in the third quarter 2004. Of the 2.8 million PDAs shipped worldwide, Windows CE was the operating system on 48.1 percent. The demand for applications to make PDAs and other smart devices valuable to companies is growing with the number of PDAs in use by corporations. As you build skills in Visual Studio 2005, know that building applications for smart devices is definitely a skill many employers are and will be looking for in their developers.

Designing mobile applications for Windows CE, Pocket PC 2003, and Smartphone 2003 devices is simplified using Visual Studio 2005. This chapter will focus on applications built for PDAs running Microsoft Windows Pocket PC operating system.

Understanding the Environment

If you have never used a PDA, it is a small version of a stripped-down PC. A typical Pocket PC from 2002 has 64 MB of internal memory and a 206-MHz processor. It weighs less than a pound and has a 3.5 inch screen that supports 240x320 pixels and 65K colors. Now, compare that to a desktop computer. A normal PC may have a spec sheet like this: 3 GHz processor, 120 GB hard drive, 512 MB RAM and a 19-inch monitor that supports 1600x1200 pixels and 32-bit color (over 4 billion colors). Another important difference is that the screen on a Pocket PC is tall, whereas a desktop monitor is wide. One more issue to consider is that when the battery dies, you lose all data and applications stored in memory. The user must add a storage device, such as a compact Flash card, to avoid having to reinstall applications when the battery loses power. Keep these differences in mind as you build applications for mobile devices.

Now that you know the basics of a PDA, I will try to outline what Visual Studio 2005 has for you to work with when you create mobile applications. To start, you have the .NET Compact Framework (CF). The best part of the CF is that it is a subset of the .NET Framework you know about from earlier chapters. Most of what you know is part of the CF, and this knowledge will allow you to start creating mobile applications with a small learning curve. Just like the parent Framework, the CF is based on the Common Language Runtime (CLR) and executes Microsoft Intermediate Language (MSIL) to maintain platform independence. The greatest difference you will see is the number of controls that are missing and the number of overloaded methods, properties, and constructors that are not present for controls. Application deployment is different also. Deploying applications to a PDA is not going to be done via CD or floppy disk. You will use Microsoft ActiveSync to facilitate deploying applications to a Pocket PC. Next, we will elaborate on what you need to know before you create your first mobile application.

Common Language Runtime

One goal of the CLR, also known as the *execution engine*, is to allow multiple languages to run side by side. The CLR manages the following items:

❑ Memory management or garbage collection

❑ Platform independence via Microsoft Intermediate Language

❑ Common type system

❑ Exception handling

❑ Just-In-Time compilation

ActiveSync

To connect your mobile device to your desktop, you will most likely use ActiveSync. This software will quickly get you connected to your PC, your network resources, and even a shared Internet connection. You can use the ActiveSync connection to synchronize your application data, access Web Services, or even replicate data to a SQL Server machine on your network. All you need is to download the software and connect your device to your desktop. When you are connected using ActiveSync, you will have options such as those shown in Figure 22-1 and Figure 22-2. The first figure is the interface for the ActiveSync program. Figure 22-2 shows the use of Windows Explorer on the desktop to browse a Pocket PC.

Figure 22-1

Figure 22-2

Since most of you do not have Pocket PCs, I will briefly explain the ease of deploying a smart device application to a Pocket PC. To deploy a smart device application, Visual Studio 2005 includes a smart device .cab file template under setup and deployment projects. For deploying, add the .cab file project to your device application project. When you build the project, just copy the output to the device using ActiveSync. Next, double click on the .cab file using the device, and it will install the application. That is all it takes to deploy your applications.

You can download the latest version of Microsoft ActiveSync from Microsoft. The .exe for ActiveSync version 3.7.1, used here, was a 3.77MB download. Use the Search for **ActiveSync** at the Microsoft download site. http://www.microsoft.com/downloads/.

Common in the Compact Framework

The type system available in the Compact Framework should look familiar to you when you start to program mobile applications. Table 22-1 lists the types available in the CF. As you allocate memory with variables in your applications, remember this chapter and the fact that you are working with very limited resources. Refer here for a quick reference to make sure you use the smallest data type possible to store data.

Table 22-1: Common Types

VB type	CLR type	Size	Value range
Boolean	Boolean	Depends	True or False
Byte	Byte	1 byte	0 through 255 (unsigned)
Char	Char	2 bytes	Single unicode character
Date	DateTime	8 bytes	0:00:00 (midnight) on January 1, 0001, through 11:59:59 PM on December 31, 9999

Table continued on following page

Table 22-1: Common Types *(continued)*

VB type	CLR type	Size	Value range
Decimal	Decimal	16 bytes	0 through +/- 79,228,162,514,264,337,593,543,950,335 (+/- 7.9...E+28) with no decimal point; 0 through +/-7.9228162514264337593543950335 with 28 places to the right of the decimal; smallest nonzero number is +/-0.0000000000000000000000000001 (+/-1E-28)
Double	Double	8 bytes	-1.79769313486231570E+308 through -4.94065645841246544E-324 for negative values; 4.94065645841246544E-324 through 1.79769313486231570E+308 for positive values
Integer	Int32	4 bytes	-2,147,483,648 through 2,147,483,647 (signed)
Long	Int64	8 bytes	-9,223,372,036,854,775,808 through 9,223,372,036,854,775,807 (9.2...E+18) (signed)
Object	Object	4 bytes	Any type can be stored in a variable of type `Object`
SByte	SByte	1 byte	-128 through 127 (signed)
Short	Int16	2 bytes	-32,768 through 32,767 (signed)
Single	Single	4 bytes	-3.4028235E+38 through -1.401298E-45 for negative values; 1.401298E-45 through 3.4028235E+38 for positive values
String	String	Depends	0 to approximately 2 billion Unicode characters
UInteger	UInt32	4 bytes	0 through 4,294,967,295 (unsigned)
ULong	UInt64	8 bytes	0 through 18,446,744,073,709,551,615 (1.8...E+19) (unsigned)
UShort	UInt16	2 bytes	0 through 65,535 (unsigned)

The Compact Framework Classes

The .NET Compact Framework classes are a subset of the .NET Framework classes plus a few inclusions that you do not need for desktop applications. Overall, you will not be surprised by the controls you find in the CF.

The .NET Compact Framework is approximately 12 percent of the size of the full framework. That makes it easy to see that, although many of the common controls and namespaces are included, the functionality has been greatly reduced. You will notice quickly that controls like the Label control are missing properties. Take a look at Figure 22-3 to see the differences between label properties available in both frameworks.

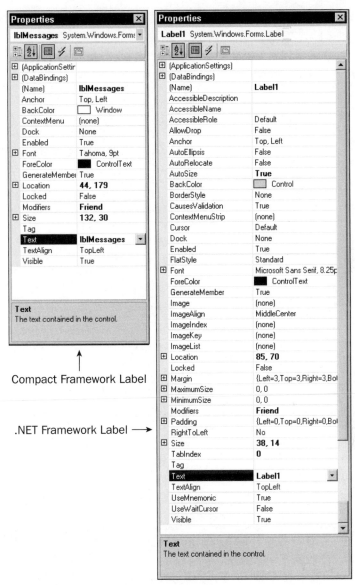

Figure 22-3

Two other missing pieces are method overrides and events. Figure 22-4 compares the events of the Button control in both frameworks. The events listed from the full framework on the right of Figure 22-4 are just a partial list and represent about half of the available events.

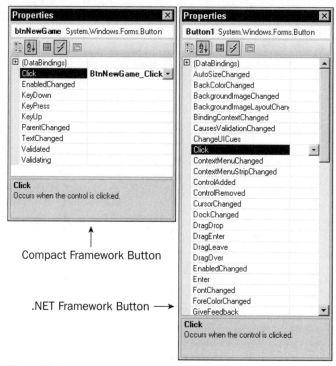

Figure 22-4

How many overloaded methods have been removed? Based on the size of the CF, you can estimate that more than 75 percent are missing. When you look at the `System.IO.FileStream` constructors, you will see that the full Framework boasts 14 overloaded constructors, while the CF has been whittled down to only five. When you write applications that will be used on smart devices and desktops, you will have to adjust certain parts of your code to address these differences.

A partial list of the default controls available to a Pocket PC application is shown in Table 22-2.

Table 22-2: Default Controls in the .NET Compact Framework

Name	Name
Button	NumericUpDown
CheckBox	OpenFileDialog
ComboBox	Panel
ContextMenu	PictureBox
DataConnector	ProgressBar
DataGrid	RadioButton
DateTimePicker	RichInk

Name	Name
DocumentList	SaveFileDialog
DocumentList	SaveFileDialog
DomainUpDown	Splitter
HScrollBar	StatusBar
ImageList	TabControl
InputPanel	TextBox
Label	Timer
LinkLabel	ToolBar
ListBox	TrackBar
ListView	TreeView
MainMenu	VScrollBar
MonthCalendar	WebBrowser
Notification	

Building a Pocket PC Game

For your first mobile application, you will build a simple game of tic-tac-toe. You will see how different the screen is and design a user interface that is simple for the user.

Try It Out: Tic Tac Toe

1. In Visual Studio 2005, select the File ➪ New Project menu. This will display the New Project dialog box.

2. Select Visual Basic from the Project Types pane on the left. Next, expand the Smart Device label and then select Pocket PC 2003. In the templates pane on the right, choose Pocket PC 2003 Application. Change the project name to **PocketPC_TicTacToe** and click the OK button. The dialog is shown in Figure 22-5.

3. The project opens to a view of a Pocket PC, as shown in Figure 22-6. This is the design environment. As you build the application, you will see the screen and be able to design the graphical interface on a replica of the actual device screen. You will know exactly how the application will look when the user installs it.

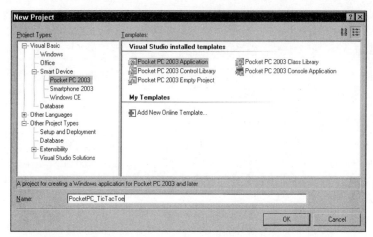

Figure 22-5

Figure 22-6

4. Now, you will build the user interface. Add ten buttons to the form as shown in Figure 22-7. The three rows of three buttons represent the tic-tac-toe board. Set the Size to **40, 40** for the 9 buttons that make up the board. Starting with the button in the upper left of the board, move left to right, down a row, left to right, down a row, and then left to right again, and name the buttons on the board **btn00**, **btn01**, **btn02**, **btn10**, **btn11**, **btn12**, **btn20**, **btn21**, **btn22**. The name begins with *btn* followed by the row (0, 1 or 2) and column (0, 1 or 2) of the button. So btn02 is on the first row (Row 0) and the third column (Column 2). When you use these names in code, you will know the location on the board. Next, set the Font for all of the board buttons to Tahoma, 24pt, Bold. Finally, set the Text property to **X** and the Anchor property to None for the board buttons. The final button is the New Game button. Set the Name to **btnNewGame** and the Text to **&New Game**. Below the board, add a label named **lblMessages**. Make the label tall enough to display two lines of text. Now, change the Text property of Form1 to **TicTacToe**, and the user interface is complete.

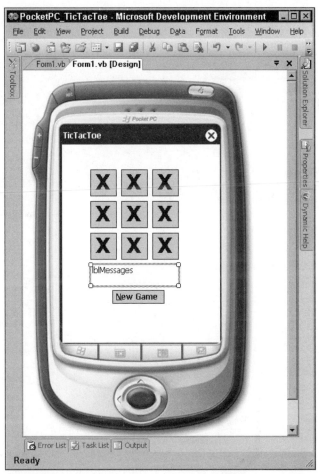

Figure 22-7

5. Switch to the code behind view and add the following highlighted code to the `Form1` class:

```
Public Class Form1


'Get the game ready to start again
Sub ResetGame()
    Dim ctrl As Control
    'Loop through the board controls and set them to ""
    For Each ctrl In Me.Controls
        If TypeOf (ctrl) Is Button And ctrl.Name <> "btnNewGame" Then
            ctrl.Text = String.Empty
        End If
    Next
    lblMessages.Text = ""
    'Enable the board buttons
    CorrectEnabledState(True)
End Sub

Private Sub CorrectEnabledState(ByVal ButtonEnabledState As Boolean)
    Dim ctrl As Control
    For Each ctrl In Me.Controls
        If TypeOf (ctrl) Is Button And ctrl.Name <> "btnNewGame" Then
            ctrl.Enabled = ButtonEnabledState
        End If
    Next
End Sub

Private Sub CorrectEnabledState()
    Dim ctrl As Control
    For Each ctrl In Me.Controls
        If TypeOf (ctrl) Is Button And ctrl.Name <> "btnNewGame" Then
            If ctrl.Text = String.Empty Then
                ctrl.Enabled = True
            Else
                ctrl.Enabled = False
            End If
        End If
    Next
End Sub

Sub ComputerPlay()
    Dim RandomGenerator As New Random()
    Dim intRandom As Integer
    Dim intCount As Integer = 0
    Dim ctrl As Control
    intRandom = RandomGenerator.Next(20, 100)
    While intCount < intRandom
        For Each ctrl In Me.Controls
            If TypeOf (ctrl) Is Button And ctrl.Name <> "btnNewGame" Then
                If ctrl.Text = String.Empty Then
                    intCount += 1
                    If intCount = intRandom Then
                        ctrl.Text = "O"
```

```
                ctrl.Enabled = False
            Exit For
        End If
      End If
      End If
   Next
   End While
End Sub

Private Sub TicTacToe_Click(ByVal sender As Object, ByVal e As _
System.EventArgs)   Handles btn00.Click, btn20.Click, btn10.Click, _
btn01.Click, btn21.Click, btn11.Click, btn02.Click, btn22.Click, btn12.Click
   CorrectEnabledState(False)
   Application.DoEvents() 'Allows the screen to refresh
   CType(sender, Button).Text = "X"
   If IsGameOver() Then
      MsgBox("Game Over")
   Else
      lblMessages.Text = "Computer selecting ..."
      Application.DoEvents() 'Allows the screen to refresh
      ComputerPlay()
      If IsGameOver() Then
         MsgBox("Game Over")
      Else
         lblMessages.Text = "Select your next position ..."
         CorrectEnabledState()
      End If
   End If
End Sub

Sub Winner(ByVal strWinner As String)
   Dim strMessage As String
   If strWinner = "X" Then
      strMessage = "You win!!"
   ElseIf strWinner = "O" Then
      strMessage = "Computer wins!!"
   Else
      strMessage = strWinner
   End If
   lblMessages.Text = strMessage
End Sub

Function IsGameOver() As Boolean
   If btn00.Text = btn01.Text And btn01.Text = btn02.Text And _
   btn02.Text <> String.Empty Then
      'Winner on top Row
      Call Winner(btn00.Text)
         Return True
   End If

   If btn10.Text = btn11.Text And btn11.Text = btn12.Text And _
   btn12.Text <> String.Empty Then
      'Winner on middle Row
      Call Winner(btn10.Text)
```

```
        Return True
    End If

    If btn20.Text = btn21.Text And btn21.Text = btn22.Text And _
    btn22.Text <> String.Empty Then
        'Winner on bottom Row
        Call Winner(btn20.Text)
        Return True
    End If

    If btn00.Text = btn10.Text And btn10.Text = btn20.Text And _
    btn20.Text <> String.Empty Then
        'Winner on first column
        Call Winner(btn00.Text)
        Return True
    End If

    If btn01.Text = btn11.Text And btn11.Text = btn21.Text And _
    btn21.Text <> String.Empty Then
        'Winner on second column
        Call Winner(btn01.Text)
        Return True
    End If

    If btn02.Text = btn12.Text And btn12.Text = btn22.Text And _
    btn22.Text <> String.Empty Then
        'Winner on third column
        Call Winner(btn02.Text)
        Return True
    End If

    If btn00.Text = btn11.Text And btn11.Text = btn22.Text And _
    btn22.Text <> String.Empty Then
        'Winner on diagonal top left to bottom right
        Call Winner(btn00.Text)
        Return True
    End If

    If btn20.Text = btn11.Text And btn11.Text = btn02.Text And _
    btn02.Text <> String.Empty Then
        'Winner on diagonal bottom left to top right
        Call Winner(btn20.Text)
        Return True
    End If

    'Test for a tie, all square full
    Dim ctrl As Control
    Dim intOpenings As Integer = 0
    For Each ctrl In Me.Controls
        If TypeOf (ctrl) Is Button And ctrl.Name <> "btnNewGame" Then
            If ctrl.Text = String.Empty Then
                intOpenings = intOpenings + 1
            End If
        End If
```

```
      Next
      If intOpenings = 0 Then
         Call Winner("It's a tie.")
         Return True
      End If
      Return False
   End Function
End Class
```

6. Add this highlighted code to the `Form1_Load` event handler.

```
Private Sub Form1_Load(ByVal sender As Object, ByVal e As System.EventArgs) Handles
Me.Load

   CorrectEnabledState(False)
   lblMessages.Text = "Click new game to begin."
End Sub
```

7. Add this code to the `btnNewGame_Click` event handler.

```
Private Sub btnNewGame_Click(ByVal sender As System.Object, ByVal e As
System.EventArgs) Handles btnNewGame.Click

   ResetGame()
End Sub
```

8. Run the program mode in debug mode to see how it works. You will be asked how to deploy the application. Choose Pocket PC 2003 SE Emulator and click the Deploy button shown in Figure 22-8. Be patient, because it will take some time to start the entire process.

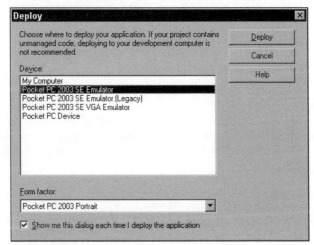

Figure 22-8

9. When the application starts, you will see the Pocket PC emulator, and the TicTacToe program will be running. Wait for the application to start. The emulator will look like Figure 22-9. You may be prompted with an Establishing Connection dialog box. Choose Internet to continue.

Figure 22-9

10. Click New Game and play against the computer. The computer player chooses a random play and is easy to defeat.

How It Works

This game gave you a basic understanding of smart device development. It is relatively the same as the work you completed in earlier chapters. The first thing you may have noticed is the screen size. You had limited real estate to design the user interface. The screen was the perfect size for a simple game of tic tac toe.

To start, you created the user interface. When you added the buttons and labels, it was just like building a desktop application. The controls had many of the same properties you were familiar with from previous chapters. You should have had no problem with the user interface.

Most of the work you did for the game was with code. Again, everything you learned earlier in the book applies to smart device applications. You saw the functions and subroutines created to run the game, and you should have remembered most of this logic from previous chapters. We will go through the code one routine at a time to explain what happened.

After a game ends, you needed a standard way to get the board and screen ready for a new game. This was accomplished with the ResetGame procedure. This procedure used the collection of controls on the form and iterated through each control that was a button. If the button was a part of the board, the text property was reset to an empty string. After all buttons had been reset, the message label text was set to blank and all board buttons were enabled.

```
'Get the game ready to start again
Sub ResetGame()
    Dim ctrl As Control
    'Loop through the board controls and set them to ""
    For Each ctrl In Me.Controls
        If TypeOf (ctrl) Is Button And ctrl.Name <> "btnNewGame" Then
            ctrl.Text = String.Empty
        End If
    Next
    lblMessages.Text = ""
    'Enable the board buttons
    CorrectEnabledState(True)
End Sub
```

The CorrectEnabledState subroutine had two signatures. This was an example of overloaded methods. When you called CorrectEnabledState with one Boolean argument, the procedure set the Enabled property of all buttons on the board to the value of the parameter you passed. The other method signature expected no parameters. So when it was called, that procedure tested every button on the board. If a button was blank, it was enabled. Otherwise, the button was disabled.

```
Private Sub CorrectEnabledState(ByVal ButtonEnabledState As Boolean)
    Dim ctrl As Control
    For Each ctrl In Me.Controls
        If TypeOf (ctrl) Is Button And ctrl.Name <> "btnNewGame" Then
            ctrl.Enabled = ButtonEnabledState
        End If
    Next
End Sub

Private Sub CorrectEnabledState()
    Dim ctrl As Control
    For Each ctrl In Me.Controls
        If TypeOf (ctrl) Is Button And ctrl.Name <> "btnNewGame" Then
            If ctrl.Text = String.Empty Then
                ctrl.Enabled = True
            Else
                ctrl.Enabled = False
            End If
        End If
    Next
End Sub
```

Another procedure created was ComputerPlay. This procedure made the play for the computer. At the top of the code, declarations were made for local variables. The meat of the logic started before the while loop. The Next method of the Random class generated a random number between 20 and 100. The program looped through every open square on the board, counting each one, until the lucky random number square was found and it was marked with an O.

```
Sub ComputerPlay()
    Dim RandomGenerator As New Random()
    Dim intRandom As Integer
    Dim intCount As Integer = 0
    Dim ctrl As Control
    intRandom = RandomGenerator.Next(20, 100)
    While intCount < intRandom
        For Each ctrl In Me.Controls
            If TypeOf (ctrl) Is Button And ctrl.Name <> "btnNewGame" Then
                If ctrl.Text = String.Empty Then
                    intCount += 1
                    If intCount = intRandom Then
                        ctrl.Text = "O"
                        ctrl.Enabled = False
                    Exit For
                End If
            End If
            End If
        Next
    End While
End Sub
```

When you clicked any square, the `TicTacToe_Click` procedure was called. Take a look at the `Handles` keyword in the declaration of the subroutine. The `Click` event from every button on the board has been added to the comma-delimited list. So when you clicked any square, this procedure handled the event. The first step of the procedure disabled all squares, followed by a call to `Application.DoEvents`. The `DoEvents` method allowed all waiting events in the queue to complete. This was placed here to avoid the problems associated with clicking more than one button in a turn. If you removed these two lines of code, you could quickly click three squares in a row before the computer made one pick. Next, the button that was clicked, the `sender`, is marked with an `X`. After the square is marked, the board is checked for a winner. If no winner is found, the computer makes the next move. Again, the board is checked for a winner. If no winner is found, the player is asked to select again.

```
Private Sub TicTacToe_Click(ByVal sender As Object, ByVal e As _
System.EventArgs)    Handles btn00.Click, btn20.Click, btn10.Click, _
btn01.Click, btn21.Click, btn11.Click, btn02.Click, btn22.Click, btn12.Click
    CorrectEnabledState(False)
    Application.DoEvents() 'Allows the screen to refresh
    CType(sender, Button).Text = "X"
    If IsGameOver() Then
        MsgBox("Game Over")
    Else
        lblMessages.Text = "Computer selecting ..."
        Application.DoEvents() 'Allows the screen to refresh
        ComputerPlay()
        If IsGameOver() Then
            MsgBox("Game Over")
        Else
            lblMessages.Text = "Select your next position ..."
            CorrectEnabledState()
        End If
    End If
End Sub
```

The `Winner` procedure is called when a winner is found. The outcome of the game is displayed on the message label.

```
Sub Winner(ByVal strWinner As String)
    Dim strMessage As String
    If strWinner = "X" Then
        strMessage = "You win!!"
    ElseIf strWinner = "O" Then
        strMessage = "Computer wins!!"
    Else
        strMessage = strWinner
    End If
    lblMessages.Text = strMessage
End Sub
```

After every move, `IsGameOver` is called to look for a winner. Every possible combination of squares is tested. If three squares in a row are marked by the same player, the `Winner` procedure is called and `True` is returned from the function. If no winner is found, the board is tested to see whether all squares are marked. When all squares are marked, the game is a tie.

```
Function IsGameOver() As Boolean
    If btn00.Text = btn01.Text And btn01.Text = btn02.Text And _
    btn02.Text <> String.Empty Then
        'Winner on top Row
        Call Winner(btn00.Text)
            Return True
    End If

    If btn10.Text = btn11.Text And btn11.Text = btn12.Text And _
    btn12.Text <> String.Empty Then
        'Winner on middle Row
        Call Winner(btn10.Text)
        Return True
    End If

    If btn20.Text = btn21.Text And btn21.Text = btn22.Text And _
    btn22.Text <> String.Empty Then
        'Winner on bottom Row
        Call Winner(btn20.Text)
        Return True
    End If

    If btn00.Text = btn10.Text And btn10.Text = btn20.Text And _
    btn20.Text <> String.Empty Then
        'Winner on first column
        Call Winner(btn00.Text)
        Return True
    End If

    If btn01.Text = btn11.Text And btn11.Text = btn21.Text And _
    btn21.Text <> String.Empty Then
        'Winner on second column
        Call Winner(btn01.Text)
        Return True
    End If
```

```
    If btn02.Text = btn12.Text And btn12.Text = btn22.Text And _
    btn22.Text <> String.Empty Then
        'Winner on third column
        Call Winner(btn02.Text)
        Return True
    End If

    If btn00.Text = btn11.Text And btn11.Text = btn22.Text And _
    btn22.Text <> String.Empty Then
        'Winner on diagonal top left to bottom right
        Call Winner(btn00.Text)
        Return True
    End If

    If btn20.Text = btn11.Text And btn11.Text = btn02.Text And _
    btn02.Text <> String.Empty Then
        'Winner on diagonal bottom left to top right
        Call Winner(btn20.Text)
        Return True
    End If

    'Test for a tie, all square full
    Dim ctrl As Control
    Dim intOpenings As Integer = 0
    For Each ctrl In Me.Controls
        If TypeOf (ctrl) Is Button And ctrl.Name <> "btnNewGame" Then
            If ctrl.Text = String.Empty Then
                intOpenings = intOpenings + 1
            End If
        End If
    Next
    If intOpenings = 0 Then
        Call Winner("It's a tie.")
        Return True
    End If
    Return False
End Function
```

The remaining code is part of the handlers for the form's Load event and the New Game button Click
event. On form load, the overloaded method `CorrectEnabledState` is called and all buttons are disabled.
When you click the New Game button, `ResetGame` is called to set up the board to start a new game.

```
    Private Sub Form1_Load(ByVal sender As Object, ByVal e As System.EventArgs) _
    Handles Me.Load
        CorrectEnabledState(False)
        lblMessages.Text = "Click new game to begin."
    End Sub

    Private Sub btnNewGame_Click(ByVal sender As System.Object, ByVal e As _
    System.EventArgs) Handles btnNewGame.Click
        ResetGame()
    End Sub
```

Summary

Visual Studio 2005 and the Compact Framework make developing mobile applications very similar to desktop application development. This small learning curve for .NET developers is one of the reasons more PDAs are shipping with a Windows operating system than with any other competitor. The trend has been growing, and companies are starting to value the developer with mobile application skills. Take advantage of your knowledge and leverage it to start developing mobile applications.

In this chapter, you learned the basics of mobile development. You saw what is similar and what is different between the full version of the .NET Framework and the Compact Framework. You were shown examples of the missing pieces that explain how the CF has been shrunk by over 80 percent. Finally, you built your first application, tic-tac-toe.

To summarize, you should know how to:

❑ Find differences between the full .NET framework and the Compact Framework

❑ Use ActiveSync to connect to smart devices

❑ Create mobile applications

❑ Use the built in emulator to test mobile applications

Exercise

The computer player is a random picker. Give the computer player some brains. Add at least one function named `ComputerPlayToWin` to the application. When the computer moves, call `ComputerPlayToWin` and check for a spot on the board that will create a win for the computer. If it exists, the computer should play that move rather than a random move. You can add other procedures if needed.

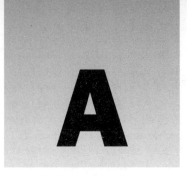

Where To Now?

Now that you have come to the end of this book, you should have a relatively good idea of how to write code using Visual Basic 2005. The topics and example code covered in this book have been designed to provide you with a firm foundation, but it is just the beginning of your journey. In fact, this book is just one of the many steps you are going to take on your road to becoming a full fledged Visual Basic 2005 programmer. Although you have come a long way, there is still a lot farther to go, and you will certainly have many more questions on the way.

The problem now is, where do you get these questions answered, and, of course, "What next?"

This appendix offers you some advice on what your possible next step(s) could be. As you can imagine, a number of different routes are open to any one person. The path you choose will probably depend on what your goal is or what you are being asked to do by your employer. Some of you will want to continue at a more general level with some knowledge about all aspects of Visual Basic 2005, while others may want to drill down into more specific areas.

Well, it is extremely important not to take a long break before carrying on with Visual Basic 2005. If you do so, you will find that you will quickly forget what you have learned. The trick is to practice. You can do this in a number of ways.

- ❑ Continue with the examples from this book. Try to add more features and more code to it. Try to merge and blend different samples together.

- ❑ You may have an idea for a new program. Go on and write it.

- ❑ Try to get a firm understanding of the terminology.

- ❑ Read as many articles as you can. Even if you do not understand them at first, bits and pieces will come together.

- ❑ Make sure you communicate your knowledge. If you know other programmers, get talking and ask questions.

- ❑ Consult our online and offline resources for more information.

The rest of this appendix lists available resources, both online and offline, to help you decide where to go next.

Online Resources

Basically, there are thousands of places you can go online for help with any problems you may have. The good news is that many of them are free. Whenever you come across a problem — and, unfortunately, you will — there are always loads of people out there willing to help. These unknown souls include others who were at the same stage as you and may have had a similar problem, or experts with a great deal of knowledge. The key is not to be intimidated and to use these resources as much as you like. Remember, everyone was a complete beginner at some point and has had many of the same experiences as you.

In this section, we are going to begin by examining the P2P site provided by Wrox and then follow on with some of the more general sites around. If you can't find what you want through any of the sites listed here or if you have some time and want to explore, just search for Visual Basic 2005 and you will be on your way!

P2P.Wrox.com

P2P provides programmer-to-programmer support on mailing lists, forums, and newsgroups in addition to a one-to-one e-mail system. You can join any of the mailing lists for author and peer support in Visual Basic 2005 (plus any others you may be interested in).

You can choose to join the mailing lists, and you can receive a weekly digest of the list. If you don't have the time or facilities to receive mailing lists, you can search the online archives using subject areas or keywords.

Should you wish to use P2P for online support, go to `http://p2p.wrox.com`. On P2P, you can view the groups without becoming a member. These lists are moderated, so you can be confident of the information presented. Also, junk mail and spam are deleted, and your e-mail is protected by the unique Lyris system from Web-bots, which can automatically cover up newsgroup mailing list addresses.

Microsoft Resources

Probably one of the first sites you'll intuitively turn to is the Microsoft site (`www.microsoft.com`). That makes sense, because it is full of information, including support, tips, hints, downloads, and newsgroups (`news://msnews.microsoft.com/microsoft.public.dotnet.languages.vb`). To see more newsgroups, navigate to `http://communities2.microsoft.com/communities/newsgroups/en-us/default.aspx`.

There are also a number of sites on MSDN that you may find to be very helpful, including the following:

❑ **Visual Studio 2005 site:** `http://lab.msdn.microsoft.com/vs2005/`.

❑ **Visual Studio 2005 documentation:** `http://lab.msdn.microsoft.com/library/`.

❑ **MSDN Library:** `http://msdn.microsoft.com/library/`.

❑ **Microsoft Developer Network site:** `http://msdn.microsoft.com`.

❑ **Microsoft Visual Basic site:** `http://msdn.microsoft.com/vbasic/`.

❑ **.NET download site:** `http://msdn.microsoft.com/netframework/downloads/`.

❑ **GotDotNet:** `www.gotdotnet.com`.

Other Resources

As said earlier, there are hundreds of sites online that discuss both Visual Basic .NET and Visual Basic 2005. These sites give everything from news on moving from Visual Basic .NET to Visual Basic 2005, to listings of up and coming conferences worldwide. Although you can do a search for Visual Basic 2005, the number of sites returned can be extremely overwhelming. Let's look quickly at two of these possible sites: one for the United Kingdom and another for the United States.

In the United Kingdom, `www.vbug.co.uk` offers a wealth of information on Visual Basic. This is the Web site for the Visual Basic Users Group (VBUG), which you can join. Besides the Web site, this group holds meetings and an annual conference, plus provides a magazine. There is a listing of further links on the Web site, and you may want to use this to start your search over the Internet.

In the United States you can get a journal, *The Visual Studio Magazine*, from a similar user group. Again, this journal is backed by meetings and four yearly conferences along with a Web site, `http://www.devx.com/vb/`, which can give e-mail updates. On the Web site, you have access to a number of different areas both in Visual Basic and other related and nonrelated Visual Studio areas.

Of course, these are just two among the many out there to try to get you started. Some of you may decide to use these two, and many of you may choose others as your favored sites, it's all up to you! What you need to remember, though, is that the Internet is not the only place to find information, so we will go on to look at some resources not found on the Web.

Offline Resources (Books)

Wrox Press is committed to providing books that will help you develop your programming skills in the direction that you want. We have a selection of tutorial-style books that build on the Visual Basic 2005 knowledge gained here. These will help you to specialize in particular areas. Here are the details of a few key titles.

Professional VB .NET, 2nd Edition

(Wrox Press, ISBN 0-7645-7536-8)

This book takes a deeper look at all aspects of Visual Basic 2005 and is probably the most logical of "next steps." It provides the next level from this book; however, it will be worth practicing your programming skills beforehand.

Topics include the following:

- ❏   Common Language Runtime
- ❏   Variables and Data Types
- ❏   Object Syntax Introduction
- ❏   Inheritance and Interfaces
- ❏   Applying Objects and Components

- ❏ Namespaces
- ❏ Error Handling and Debugging
- ❏ ADO.NET
- ❏ XML with VB.NET
- ❏ Forms
- ❏ Security
- ❏ ASP.NET 2.0 Advanced Features and much more!

ASP.NET 2.0 Beta Preview

(Wrox Press, 0-7645-7286-5)

ASP.NET 2 Beta Preview is timed to coincide with the first widespread beta release of ASP.NET, "Whidbey" — the new version of Microsoft's popular technology for creating dynamic Web sites that pull unique information for each visitor rather than showing everyone the same static HTML pages. The book gets developers up to speed with the new features and capabilities that ASP.NET 2.0 provides. Developers will learn how to build ASP.NET 2.0 applications for themselves from the examples that the book provides.

This book is for ASP.NET developers making the transition to this new version of the technology. The changes are many, and in some cases they're quite dramatic. The book spends a good deal of time alerting you to all that has changed and explaining what you need to know to make the transition to ASP.NET 2.0.

Finally, the book focuses on both the Visual Basic 2005 and C# developer. Examples throughout the book do not favor one developer over another. Instead, every example is provided in both languages.

This book covers the following:

- ❏ Introduction to ASP.NET 2.0
- ❏ Visual Studio 2005
- ❏ Application and Page Frameworks
- ❏ New Ways to Handle Data
- ❏ Site Navigation
- ❏ Working with Master Pages
- ❏ Themes and Skins
- ❏ Membership and Role Management
- ❏ Personalization

- ❑ Portal Frameworks and Web Parts
- ❑ SQL Cache Invalidation
- ❑ Additional New Controls
- ❑ Changes to ASP.NET 1.0 Controls
- ❑ Administration and Management
- ❑ Visual Basic 8.0 and C# 2.0 Language Enhancements

Implementing the Microsoft Solutions Framework

So here you are, ready to go out into the world and build applications with Visual Basic 2005. Congratulate yourself; your accomplishment of finishing the chapters of the book should excite you. Soon, creating applications will become second nature to you. As you work in IT, you will play many roles on teams. In some cases, your manager will only ask you to write code. By finishing this book, you have a strong understanding of what you will need to do in that situation. Other times, management will ask you to wear many hats on a project and be responsible for delivering an entire solution. This appendix shows you how to create a successful solution.

Let's start with a basic question. How is a solution different from an application? A solution is the entire process of creating a system for a customer. The solution includes planning, documenting, testing, releasing, training, and supporting the application. The application is just one part of the solution.

Microsoft has a set of processes and models that to some is the standard for solution delivery in the IT industry. Known as MSF (Microsoft Solutions Framework), software developers around the globe apply this framework to internal strategies to ensure best practices when building software. The MSF is a recent interpretation of the classic software development life cycle.

In this appendix, you will do the following:

- ❑ Learn about the software development life cycle.
- ❑ Get an overview of the MSF and how it relates to the software development life cycle.
- ❑ See how to manage trade-offs.
- ❑ Learn how to define success for a project.

A detailed explanation of the Framework would take two or three hundred pages. This appendix is just a concise summary to wet your whistle, so to speak. Keep this in mind as you begin to explore this tool.

Software Development Life Cycle

The software development life cycle (SDLC) is a set of building blocks for software design. Microsoft and others in the industry continue to develop methodologies to interpret the SDLC into a set of steps or milestones. Depending on whom you ask, you may get five steps or even seven steps in an SDLC implementation. Here is one interpretation of the SDLC steps:

❑ Defining the problem

❑ Gathering requirements

❑ Analysis and design

❑ Development

❑ Testing

❑ Installation

❑ Maintenance

Theoretically, the work progresses in a linear fashion from each of these steps to the next. In practice, it is often the case that the need for further design work, more specific requirements, or a clearer definition of the problem is discovered during development or testing, and the process loops back to the earlier stage.

Microsoft Solutions Framework

The Microsoft Framework Solution (MSF) is built for the implementation of large software projects. Two distinct models (Team Model and Process Model) define the entire framework. To set up a large project team, you will need to use the Team Model. As you begin your career, you will most likely work on smaller projects. Because of this, I will not go into detail about the Team Model. The Process Model defines how to complete the solution. In this appendix, I will show you how to use the principles of the Process Model in smaller projects.

In the Team Model, a developer is only one role in a large project and is recommended to work on only one task: develop the application code. As you work on small solutions, be aware that you will take on many roles. One day you may be gathering requirements, and the next week you may be developing code for the application. Think back and realize that it is difficult to write the code and take on other project roles. As a developer, it will be easy to focus your efforts on the code writing and put the analysis, testing, and documentation on the back burner. This will almost always result in an unsuccessful project. Although the code may work, the documentation may not be good enough to maintain or change the application. You may not understand this concept yet, but in my opinion writing the code is easy part of the solution. When your manager asks you to play many roles on a project, remember that in most cases you will need to spend more time designing, testing, and documenting code than writing it.

The Process Model, consisting of five phases, is the portion of the MSF that puts the SDLC into practice. It describes the order in which you should complete each phase of the SDLC. Also, this model involves iterations of all phases, known as *versions*. If you are familiar with MS software, you know that Microsoft updates software via new versions. The Process Model is a continuous loop of milestones that incorporates deploying multiple versions of software. Each version of the software will go through all phases of the Framework. Next, I will explain the five phases of the process model listed here.

- ❑ Envisioning

- ❑ Planning

- ❑ Developing

- ❑ Stabilizing

- ❑ Deploying

The Envisioning Phase

To start the MSF, you begin in the envisioning phase. The success of the project starts here. Make sure you take the time to nail down all loose ends before moving forward with the project. Your customers expect and deserve to understand how the project is going to proceed and the scope document at the end of this phase will do that. After completing the envisioning phase, everyone with a stake in the project will be on the same page. There are five goals of the envisioning phase that you need to accomplish before moving on to the planning phase.

Problem Statement

Why is the customer willing to spend $80,000 on a new system? This seems like an easy question. Don't take this lightly, because all of your decisions will be driven by the problem statement. Here is an example of a problem definition:

> *As government regulations change, the current system cannot meet the time requirements to implement changes and stay in compliance. To compete in our industry, we must have a system that is flexible enough to make changes easily so as to maintain governmental compliance.*

Goals

You need to agree on measurable goals with the customer. These will be used to help define the success of the project. The key word is *measurable*. Here is the difference. The following are the same goals, but the latter is measurable.

- ❑ The system should improve customer service by being able to complete a phone order quickly.

- ❑ The system will improve customer service by allowing a phone order to be completed in less than 60 seconds.

The first goal is vague and is not measurable. If you base the system on goals like the first one, it is easy for the customer to believe the system is not fast enough when you feel the system is much faster than it had been. You may think the system is a success, but the customer thinks it is a failure. Remember to make sure that you can measure system goals.

Define Roles

Here is an easy one. On smaller projects, only a few people will be working on the project. You will need to determine who is responsible for planning, development, testing, documentation, and releasing the system. This is where you will use the Team Model for large projects.

Create a Scope Document

This document will be a blueprint of the solution. All stakeholders in the project should sign off on the final version of the scope document. Sections of the scope document include the following.

- ❏ A vague set of user requirements
- ❏ The problem statement
- ❏ Definition of team roles
- ❏ A set of measurable goals
- ❏ A brief statement defining the planning process upcoming

Risk Analysis

Your customer will need to know any risks that may cause problems for the project. These risks may be that you are working with new technologies that are unproven or that system bandwidth requirements may exceed available network resources.

The Planning Phase

During the planning stage, you will create documents to validate that the project can succeed. The documents you create will be transformed through feedback from the customer and project stakeholders. Make sure that all project stakeholders have time to review and validate each document. Even for a small project, this process can take many rounds of changes to gain sign-off from all parties. Finally, you will create a project schedule and cost estimate before moving to the developing stage. Listed here are the documents you need to create.

- ❏ Conceptual, logical, and physical design documents
- ❏ Use cases and usage scenarios
- ❏ System specification
- ❏ Project schedule
- ❏ Cost estimate

The Developing Phase

This is the stage you are most familiar with. The MSF encapsulates everything from actually building the development environment to completing documentation into the development stage. The milestone for this phase is a complete application ready for testing.

Setup: Building Staging Areas for Development and Testing

For any project, you need a development and test environment that matches the production environment. Take precautions to build the staging areas so that they are the same as the production environment. Something as simple as different printer drivers between test staging and production areas can cause unanticipated results on release of the application.

Completing the Prototype

You must allow the customer to approve a prototype. Do not underestimate the value of this. Imagine you were building a car. Without proper models, how hard is it to determine the proper location of the steering wheel or how to add six inches of leg room for rear passengers? Take this time to let the customer make changes to the design. You will find that it is easy to change a prototype. Once you have three months of coding under way, changes to the user interface can be costly.

Completing the Code

The application is ready for testing. Validate modules through unit testing.

Supply Application Documentation

The documentation from prior phases is compiled with a user manual and system documentation. The test team will rely on this data for testing.

The Testing Phase

As a beginner, you may not understand the importance of this phase. There is no better way to make a small project over budget and late than to find 500 bugs while testing. Make sure you have adequate time in your schedule to test and make test plans. Like basically everything else in the MSF, testing is an iterative process. You will need test plans that you can repeat and validate after bug fixes. After each round of testing, complete your test plans. Remember to document your result. When bugs arise in the application after release, you will want to see why the test plan did not uncover the bug and then adjust the test plan. After the customer has signed off on the test results, complete any documentation changes and package all files for deployment.

You should plan for the following subphases during the testing process:

- ❑ Application tier testing
- ❑ Security testing
- ❑ Performance testing
- ❑ User acceptance testing
- ❑ System integration testing

The Deployment Phase

Now, you are ready for production. If you are on time and within budget, your customer will be happy with the project. With all of the planning and customer interaction, there will be few surprises at this point. You will put the solution into production and have a small team available to train and support the users. After the agreed-upon amount of time, the application will be turned over to the support staff. You will need to train them and turn over system documentation. That is it. You have managed a successful implementation of a project.

There is one item left: how to handle changes using tradeoffs. To have any chance of getting to the end of a project successfully, you must be able to manage tradeoffs. The next section explains this in more detail next.

Managing Tradeoffs

To complete a successful project, you must be able to manage tradeoffs. You will find very quickly that your customer will ask you questions of the form "... Can you do that?" And your answer should be in almost every instance, "Yes, we can." You will find that you *can* do just about anything. The problem is that it takes a certain amount of time and money for every project or change request. What your customer means to say is; "Can you do that for $50,000 by the end of this year?" So when you answer the "can it be done" question, make sure the customer knows that you can do it for the right price with enough time.

When you work with clients, internal or external, you have to make them aware of project tradeoffs. There are three tradeoffs (budget, deadlines, and functionality). A fourth tradeoff could be quality. You should never consider reducing quality to lower price, finish sooner, or add features to make a project successful. While you define the project scope, make sure that the project team and customers understand the priorities of tradeoffs. As you make changes to any one tradeoff, you will have to adjust at least one of the others.

For example, suppose you are working with the marketing department on a small application. You are the only resource available to work on the solution for the next two weeks during planning. While you are gathering the system requirements, you speak to the marketing vice-president, Tina, about the priorities of the solution. Very quickly she makes it clear that she needs the application by the end of the year and for a cost of under $50,000. As you pry more, you find that Tina cannot spend more than $50,000 this year. She wants the system to be live in three months with at least the core functionality in the first version. Next year, she may be able free up more money in her budget to finish the lower-priority features.

You quickly write down the tradeoffs to consider and the priorities. In order of priority, you write budget, deadline, and features. Take a look at the project priorities listed in Table B-1. You and Tina sign off on the tradeoff priorities, and now you know how to make the solution a success. Meeting the budget and deadline are required for success. For example, functionality will be moved to the next version if the project gets behind schedule.

Table B-1: Project priorities

Tradeoff	Priority
Under Budget	First
Deliver Functionality	Third
Meet Deadline	Second

Halfway through the project, Tina wants to add more core functionality to the system. You look at the budget and see that if you add more functionality to this release, you will need more resources to make the deadline. Adding another developer to meet the deadline will cost an extra $10,000. Looking back at the project priorities, you see that Tina cannot spend more than $50,000. You have set aside the entire $50,000 budget, and $10,000 more is too much. It is time to call Tina and explain the situation.

While talking to Tina, you explain the top priority for the project is budget. Adding the extra functionality will cost an additional $10,000, bringing the budget estimate to $60,000. During the discussion, you mention that the only way to add more functionality without increasing the deadline or budget is to drop some of the functionality already planned. After 30 minutes, she agrees that $50,000 is all she can spend, and the additional functionality can be part of a later version.

By understanding and agreeing on tradeoff priorities, you are able to work with customers to manage change. If a customer wants to change any of the tradeoff priorities, you will have to adjust one or both of the others.

Defining Success with the MSF

A successful project is hard to achieve. If you follow the framework, success can be achieved more easily. It all comes down to customer satisfaction and one simple question: Did you make the customer happy? This simple question can be hard to answer. Let me clarify how to find the answer to this question. To make the customer happy, you must succeed in most of these four areas; achieve system goals, meet release date, stay under budget, and manage trade offs.

With the Framework implementation, you will find defining success possible. The two milestones that are straightforward are meeting the budget and release date. Take a look at the project plan and make sure these milestones were met. System goals are also straightforward if you defined measurable goals. Test the system against the project goals to verify the system meets the standards agreed upon. The final milestone is change or tradeoff management. Pull out the final tradeoff chart and review it. For the project to be successful, you must have met the top priority of your customer. Changes may have caused you to miss the other milestones, but if you managed tradeoffs with the customer, the project will still be successful. Success can be that simple if you follow the game plan.

Summary

As you grow in the information technology field, you will work on larger projects and have more responsibility. Use this appendix as a basis for further study. Always keep in mind how many steps you have to take to be successful managing a project. When you do get into a position to lead a project, take the time to plan and test, and always work toward making the customer happy. You will not always be successful by following the framework, so take misfortunes in stride and learn from them. As you complete projects, you will come up with your own interpretation of the SDLC or the MSF, and you will be a success.

An Introduction to Security

In today's electronic world, consumers are bombarded with scams via the Internet and e-mail. If you plan to write applications that take advantage of these technologies, you must be aware of fraudulent activity of others. The most rampant activity today is a tactic known as *phishing*. Here a fraudulent e-mail or pop-up message lures a user to a fake site on the pretext that a breach in bank security or unwanted account activity has made it necessary to "verify" the user's account information. Tricked users will see a site that looks like their bank's site but is actually being hosted by criminals in an attempt to bait them into entering their personal and financial information. In these schemes, it is easy for concerned customers to be tricked and enter their card number, social security number, or PIN into the Web forms to avoid their accounts being frozen. Little do they know they are giving away their private information to thieves.

Phishing is not the only scam consumers must deal with; it is one of the most prevalent. As a developer, it is your job to make applications safe. In some cases, features of your application can make it easier for criminals to impersonate your application. Simple things like never asking for personal information that you do not need over e-mail or the Web can make users aware of a scam. For e-mail, you can never assume that e-mail will not be intercepted over the Internet. Make sure you never treat e-mail as a secure means of data transmission.

You must also be aware of security for your Windows applications and assemblies. It seems as though a new hole is found every week in some browser or operating system that allows a hacker to run code on a user's machine. One way in which this type of attack is commonly accomplished is by a *buffer overflow*. To give you a simple explanation, hackers discover that a program has memory allocated to store data only up to a certain size. The attacker sends a larger object than the memory allocated. The extra data is not discarded, but rather it gets written to adjacent areas of memory that are intended to store code or the addresses of code. This may corrupt valid allocations of memory, but more important, it installs the attacker's the malicious code in memory. The victim program runs the attacker's code as if it were its own, and the damage is done. The root cause of this problem is not one most Visual Basic 2005 developers will encounter, but it should make you aware that people may use your functions in ways you did not intend them to be used.

Take a look at another example of a software bug that might be a security risk. Say you wrote an assembly or Web Service that would upload files to your company's Web site. This application is for salespeople to upload comma-separated files of current sales data each night. The code allows the path and file name to be passed as parameters, and it can be used by numerous departments because of this flexibility. The problem is the flexibility allows a hacker to upload a Web page, place it into the root Web directory, and do almost anything to the server or network. You should change this Web Service to store files in a locked-down directory and modify the file name so that an attacker would not be able to access the file by name. Functions like this one are prevalent in many companies' code libraries and create most of the security holes these companies will face.

In this appendix you will learn about security issues and how to handle them within the following topics:

❑   Understanding Code Access Security

❑   Secure Sockets Layer (SSL)

❑   Where to look for security answers

Code Access Security (CAS)

The goal for Code Access Security is simple: Stop unwanted code from running or accessing resources. This is accomplished by the runtime's security system. When an assembly needs access to a resource, all assemblies on the call stack should have permission to access that resource. Take a look at the following example.

An assembly is run from the Internet. By default, it is granted access to a *permission set* (explained in the next subsection) based on the Internet zone. The application has no access to the local file system. If that assembly were to call a public method on an assembly that did have access to the file system, the runtime would throw a security exception. When the permissions of each assembly on the stack were tested, the assembly that was run from the Internet would fail the permission check.

On the other hand, an administrator could grant a signed assembly more permissions. So, if this assembly had the correct digital signature, it could be granted access to a larger set of permissions.

CAS allows the system administrator to apply permissions to code rather than to users. Before CAS, if a hacker could get a user to run code or an attachment that contained a virus, it was granted security based on the *user's* security level. If that user was an administrator on the machine, the virus had full access to do its dirty work. Now, a virus may be stopped by the Common Language Runtime and not have access to corrupt the file system, even if the user has permissions.

The way this works is through permissions, security policy, and evidence. When an assembly requests a file, for example, the runtime makes sure that file is available from a security aspect by checking permissions, security levels, and evidence. Let's start with permissions.

Permissions

Permissions are granted to resources based on trust and origination. Administrators can grant higher or lower levels of access to individual assemblies or zones. Here is a list of six common permissions used by the runtime.

- ❏ `EnvironmentPermission`: Access control for system and user environment variables
- ❏ `EventLogPermission`: Event logging control for code access permissions
- ❏ `FileDialogPermission`: File system access control for file dialogs
- ❏ `FileIOPermission`: File system access control
- ❏ `PrintingPermission`: Controls access to printers
- ❏ `RegistryPermission`: Controls access to the Registry

It would be hard to manage a large group of permissions without a way of grouping them. Grouping permissions is accomplished by using *permission sets*. The .NET Framework has of six predefined permission sets. You can use any of these sets listed here in your code.

- ❏ `Nothing`: This named permission set will not allow code to run.
- ❏ `Execution`: The Execution set allows the code to run, but no access is granted to protected resources.
- ❏ `FullTrust`: The most forgiving permission set. Access to all resources is granted.
- ❏ `Internet`: You can think of this as the access you would permit when browsing. This would be used when running code from the Internet or any nontrusted source.
- ❏ `LocalIntranet`: This is for trusted code running on a trusted network.
- ❏ `Everything`: This is a set of all standard permissions. The permission to skip verification is not granted to this set.

Your code can request any level of permission, and the runtime will verify before running the code that these permissions will be granted.

Security Policy

The runtime enforces policy based on the identity or evidence of the assembly. When loading an assembly, the assembly is inspected for evidence of its origin. Based on the origin, the runtime determines what permissions to grant the assembly.

Evidence

To determine the origin of an assembly, the CLR looks at many attributes of the assembly. This is known as the *evidence*. Table C-1 has a complete list of evidence types. The runtime may use any or all of these to determine the permissions to grant the assembly.

Table C-1: Types of Evidence	
Evidence Type	**Description**
Application directory	Installation directory
Hash	Assembly hash
Publisher	The Authenticode signature
Site	Web site — for example, `wrox.com`.
Strong name	Assembly's Strong name
URL	URL of the assembly
Zone	Origination zone

When permissions are tested, an intersection of zones and permissions is evaluated to verify that all permissions for every zone and assembly on the stack are met. If permission is not granted to the code, the zone, or the user, an exception is thrown and access is denied.

Secure Sockets Layer

Secure Sockets Laye (SSL) was a protocol developed to secure communication between a Web server and a browser. Today, 128-bit SSL encryption is the standard for secure data transmission over the Internet. If you need to secure parts of a Web site, your customers will expect this type of encryption. To promote the level security to the end user, Internet Explorer and Netscape display a locked lock similar to Figure C-1 at the bottom of the browser window.

Figure C-1

Another way users know a site is secure is by the URL. Looking at the URL of a SSL site shows `https://` versus the standard `http://`. The user can also look at details of the certificate by double clicking the lock icon or viewing the page's properties or info. Figure C-2 is an actual certificate info screen from a large Web site. We have removed the company's name from the image.

Two of the largest companies that issue SSL certificates are Thawte and VeriSign. They are both well respected in the industry and offer free trial certificates for you to test with.

Trial certificates can be found at the following site.

❑ `verisign.com/products-services/security-services/ssl/index.html`: Click the Try link for the certificate type you wish to try.

❑ `thawte.com/`: Click the link for a 21 day trial.

You should keep in mind that encryption slows down the experience for the user and creates more load for the server. Keep marketing and nonessential areas of your site unencrypted. Only encrypt pages that communicate data that would be considered private.

Figure C-2

Finding Answers

I will list some Web sites that can be helpful to do more research and find answers.

- ❑ microsoft.com/security/: Microsoft's security home page. Read the latest is security notes about Microsoft products.

- ❑ microsoft.com/security/guidance/checklists/: Microsoft's security checklists. Here you can print checklists to make sure your applications consider the appropriate security risks.

- ❑ ftc.gov: The Federal Trade Commission Web site. Here you can see what types of scams are being reported.

- ❑ owasp.org: Open Web Application Security Project (OWASP). This site has free tools, documentation, and standards available.

- ❑ sans.org/rr/: The SANS Institute Information Security Reading Room. Read thousands of white papers on security issues.

- ❑ webappsec.org: The Web Application Security Consortium. Read white papers on the latest news about Web site security.

Summary

Security is the hottest topic in the information technology industry. Making applications 100 percent secure is not possible with the openness of the Internet, but minimizing risks to vital data should be a top priority in application design. As you build applications with VS 2005, know that you have the best tool available to create secure Windows applications, but it is your responsibility to maintain the security of the applications you write.

Administrators will be able to use CAS to stop many types of attacks. Being able to apply permissions to assemblies and validate the origination of the code makes implementing a secure network easier. The widespread use of certificates and code signing will make spoofing applications more difficult and keep users' computers safer.

The world of application security is by no means perfect. You will probably have to design your applications around security risks forever. But you can win by keeping security at the top of the priority list in your application design. Soon you will begin to develop applications for wireless access, and more security implications will need to be understood. Keeping applications secure in a world where information access is expanding will continue to be a challenge.

Just make sure you keep your head up and pay attention. Security holes are announced throughout the media, and as a developer, you should pay attention and learn from the mistakes of the past. One of your applications may one day be under attack.

Solutions

Chapter 1 Solution

Exercise 1

To display the text from a text box on a form when the user clicks the button, you add code as highlighted here to the button's Click event handler:

```
Private Sub Button1_Click(ByVal sender As System.Object, _
    ByVal e As System.EventArgs) Handles Button1.Click

    MessageBox.Show(TextBox1.Text, "Exercise 1")
End Sub
```

Chapter 3 Solutions

Exercise 1

The first part of this exercise requires you to declare two `Integer` variables and set their values and then to perform a math operation on these variables and display the results in a message box. The variables can be declared and set as:

```
'Declare variables and set their values
Dim intX As Integer = 5
Dim intY As Integer = 10
```

A math operation can be performed and the results displayed as:

```
'Multiply the numbers and display the results
MessageBox.Show("The sum of " & intX & " * " & intY & " = " & _
    intX * intY, "Exercise 1")
```

The second part of this exercise requires you to declare two `String` variables, set their values, and concatenate the variables and display the results in a message box. The `String` variables can be declared and set as:

```
'Declare variables and set their values
Dim strOne As String = "Visual Basic "
Dim strTwo As String = "2005"
```

To concatenate the variables and display the results, you could write code such as:

```
'Concatenate the strings and display the results
MessageBox.Show(strOne & strTwo, "Exercise 1")
```

Exercise 2

This exercise requires you to display the length of the string entered into a text box and then to display the first half of the string and the last half of the string. To display the length of the string, you can use the `Length` property of the `Text` property of the text box as shown here:

```
'Display the length of the string from the TextBox
MessageBox.Show("The length of the string in the TextBox is " & _
    TextBox1.Text.Length, "Exercise 2")
```

To display the first half of the string, you need to use the `Substring` method with a starting index of 0, and for the length you use the length of the string divided by 2, as shown here:

```
'Display the first half of the string from the TextBox
MessageBox.Show(TextBox1.Text.Substring(0, TextBox1.Text.Length / 2), _
    "Exercise 2")
```

To display the last half of the string, you again use the `Substring` method, but this time you simply give it a starting index of the length of the string divided by 2, as shown here:

```
'Display the last half of the string from the TextBox
MessageBox.Show(TextBox1.Text.Substring(TextBox1.Text.Length / 2), _
    "Exercise 2")
```

Chapter 4 Solutions

Exercise 1

This exercise required you to create a Select Case statement to select and display the numbers 1 through 5 from the text box on the form. The code to do this is shown here:

```
'Determine which number was entered
Select Case TextBox1.Text
    Case 1
        MessageBox.Show("The number 1 was entered", "Exercise 1")
    Case 2
```

```
                    MessageBox.Show("The number 2 was entered", "Exercise 1")
                Case 3
                    MessageBox.Show("The number 3 was entered", "Exercise 1")
                Case 4
                    MessageBox.Show("The number 4 was entered", "Exercise 1")
                Case 5
                    MessageBox.Show("The number 5 was entered", "Exercise 1")
```

To handle numbers other than 1 through 5, you need to provide a `Case Else` statement as shown here:

```
                Case Else
                    MessageBox.Show("A number other that 1 - 5 was entered", _
                        "Exercise 1")
            End Select
```

Exercise 2

In this exercise, you were tasked with creating two `For . . . . . . Next` loops. The first loop is supposed to count from 1 to 10 and display the numbers in a list box. The code to execute this loop is shown here:

```
            'Count from 1 to 10
            For intCount As Integer = 1 To 10
                ListBox1.Items.Add(intCount)
            Next
```

The second `For . . . Next` loop should count backward from 10 to 1 and display those numbers in a list box. The code to execute this loop is shown here:

```
            'Count backwards from 10 to 1
            For intCount As Integer = 10 To 1 Step -1
                ListBox1.Items.Add(intCount)
            Next
```

Chapter 5 Solutions

Exercise 1

This exercise required you to create an enumeration of three names and to display the member string value as well as the numeric value when a button was clicked. To create an enumeration of names, you would use code similar to this:

```
Public Class Form1

    Private Enum Names As Integer
        Norman = 1
        Mike = 2
        Reece = 3
    End Enum
```

To display the member names and values from the enumeration, you would use code like this:

```
        Private Sub Button1_Click(ByVal sender As System.Object, _
            ByVal e As System.EventArgs) Handles Button1.Click

            MessageBox.Show(Names.Norman.ToString & " = " & Names.Norman, _
                "Exercise 1")
        End Sub

        Private Sub Button2_Click(ByVal sender As System.Object, _
            ByVal e As System.EventArgs) Handles Button2.Click

            MessageBox.Show(Names.Mike.ToString & " = " & Names.Mike, _
                "Exercise 1")
        End Sub

        Private Sub Button3_Click(ByVal sender As System.Object, _
            ByVal e As System.EventArgs) Handles Button3.Click

            MessageBox.Show(Names.Reece.ToString & " = " & Names.Reece, _
                "Exercise 1")
        End Sub
```

Exercise 2

You were tasked with creating an application that would redimension an array, preserving its current elements and adding a new element to the array, and display the new element in a message box. To create and initialize an array at the form level with just one name, you would code like this:

```
    Public Class Form1

        Private strNames() As String = {"Norman"}
```

To redimension the array, preserving the existing data, you would use code like this. Notice that you use the GetUpperBound(0) method to get the upper boundary of the array and then add 1 to it to enlarge the array by one element:

```
            ReDim Preserve strNames(strNames.GetUpperBound(0) + 1)
```

To add the new name from the text box, you would use code like this. Again you are using GetUpperBound(0) to determine the upper boundary of the array:

```
            strNames(strNames.GetUpperBound(0)) = TextBox1.Text
```

Finally, to display the last name added to the array in a message box, you would use code like this:

```
            MessageBox.Show(strNames(strNames.GetUpperBound(0)), "Exercise 2")
```

Chapter 6 Solutions

Exercise 1

For this exercise, you were required to create a Windows application with two button controls. You were to wire up the MouseUp and LostFocus events for the first button. The code for the MouseUp event should look similar to this:

```
Private Sub Button1_MouseUp(ByVal sender As Object, _
    ByVal e As System.Windows.Forms.MouseEventArgs) Handles Button1.MouseUp

    'Display a MessageBox
    MessageBox.Show("The MouseUp event has been fired.", "Exercise 1")
End Sub
```

And the code for the LostFocus event should look similar to this:

```
Private Sub Button1_LostFocus(ByVal sender As Object, _
    ByVal e As System.EventArgs) Handles Button1.LostFocus

    'Display a MessageBox
    MessageBox.Show("Button1 has lost focus.", "Exercise 1")
End Sub
```

When you ran this application, you may have noticed some unexpected behavior when you clicked the first button. As soon as you let the mouse button up, you saw the message box indicating that the button had lost focus, and then immediately after that, you saw the message box indicating that the MouseUp event had been fired.

What has actually happened here is that the code in the MouseUp event was fired, but the code in that event causes a message box to be displayed. In the course of seeing that code, Visual Basic 2005 has determined that the Button control will lose focus and has fired the LostFocus event, which displays the message box in that event handler first.

Exercise 2

This exercise tasked you with creating an application that has a toolbar and status bar. You were to insert the standard buttons for the toolbar, create event handlers for the Click event of each button, and to display a message in the status bar when any of the buttons was clicked. The code for the event handlers is listed here:

```
Private Sub newToolStripButton_Click(ByVal sender As System.Object, _
    ByVal e As System.EventArgs) Handles newToolStripButton.Click

    'Update the status bar
    sspStatus.Text = "The New button was clicked."
End Sub

Private Sub openToolStripButton_Click(ByVal sender As System.Object, _
    ByVal e As System.EventArgs) Handles openToolStripButton.Click
```

```
        'Update the status bar
        sspStatus.Text = "The Open button was clicked."
    End Sub

    Private Sub saveToolStripButton_Click(ByVal sender As System.Object, _
        ByVal e As System.EventArgs) Handles saveToolStripButton.Click

        'Update the status bar
        sspStatus.Text = "The Save button was clicked."
    End Sub

    Private Sub printToolStripButton_Click(ByVal sender As System.Object, _
        ByVal e As System.EventArgs) Handles printToolStripButton.Click

        'Update the status bar
        sspStatus.Text = "The Print button was clicked."
    End Sub

    Private Sub cutToolStripButton_Click(ByVal sender As System.Object, _
        ByVal e As System.EventArgs) Handles cutToolStripButton.Click

        'Update the status bar
        sspStatus.Text = "The Cut button was clicked."
    End Sub

    Private Sub copyToolStripButton_Click(ByVal sender As System.Object, _
        ByVal e As System.EventArgs) Handles copyToolStripButton.Click

        'Update the status bar
        sspStatus.Text = "The Copy button was clicked."
    End Sub

    Private Sub pasteToolStripButton_Click(ByVal sender As System.Object, _
        ByVal e As System.EventArgs) Handles pasteToolStripButton.Click

        'Update the status bar
        sspStatus.Text = "The Paste button was clicked."
    End Sub
```

Chapter 7 Solutions

Exercise 1

The exercise required you to create a simple application that uses the `OpenFileDialog` and `SaveFileDialog` classes.

The code for the Open button starts by declaring an object using the `OpenFileDialog` class:

```
Private Sub btnOpen_Click(ByVal sender As System.Object, _
    ByVal e As System.EventArgs) Handles btnOpen.Click

    'Declare a OpenFileDialog object
    Dim objOpenFileDialog As New OpenFileDialog
```

The bulk of the code to display the contents of the file in your text box remains the same as the code in the Dialogs project but uses the objOpenFileDialog object versus the OpenFileDialog control:

```
    'Set the Open dialog properties
    With objOpenFileDialog
        .Filter = "Text files (*.txt)|*.txt|All files (*.*)|*.*"
        .FilterIndex = 1
        .Title = "Demo Open File Dialog"
    End With

    'Show the Open dialog and if the user clicks the Open button,
    'load the file
    If objOpenFileDialog.ShowDialog = Windows.Forms.DialogResult.OK Then
        Dim allText As String
        Try
            'Read the contents of the file
            allText = My.Computer.FileSystem.ReadAllText( _
                objOpenFileDialog.FileName)
            'Display the file contents in the TextBox
            txtFile.Text = allText
        Catch fileException As Exception
            Throw fileException
        End Try
    End If
```

Since you are using an object, you need to perform the necessary cleanup to have the object you created release its resources. You do this by calling the Dispose method on your object, and then you release your reference to the object by setting it to Nothing:

```
    'Clean up
    objOpenFileDialog.Dispose()
    objOpenFileDialog = Nothing
End Sub
```

The code for the Save button starts by declaring an object using the SaveFileDialog class, and the rest of the code is pretty much the same as the code in the Dialogs project. The code at the end of this procedure also performs the necessary cleanup of your object:

```
Private Sub btnSave_Click(ByVal sender As System.Object, _
    ByVal e As System.EventArgs) Handles btnSave.Click

    'Declare a SaveFileDialog object
    Dim objSaveFileDialog As New SaveFileDialog

    'Set the Save dialog properties
    With objSaveFileDialog
        .DefaultExt = "txt"
```

```
            .FileName = "Test Document"
            .Filter = "Text files (*.txt)|*.txt|All files (*.*)|*.*"
            .FilterIndex = 1
            .OverwritePrompt = True
            .Title = "Demo Save File Dialog"
        End With

        'Show the Save dialog and if the user clicks the Save button,
        'save the file
        If objSaveFileDialog.ShowDialog = Windows.Forms.DialogResult.OK Then
            Try
                Dim filePath As String
                'Open or Create the file
                filePath = System.IO.Path.Combine( _
                    My.Computer.FileSystem.SpecialDirectories.MyDocuments, _
                    objSaveFileDialog.FileName)
                'Replace the contents of the file
                My.Computer.FileSystem.WriteAllText(filePath, txtFile.Text, False)
            Catch fileException As Exception
                Throw fileException
            End Try
        End If

        'Clean up
        objSaveFileDialog.Dispose()
        objSaveFileDialog = Nothing
    End Sub
```

Exercise 2

This exercise requires you to display the Browse For Folder dialog box with the Make New Folder button displayed and to set My Documents as the root folder for the browse operation. You start your procedure off by declaring an object using the FolderBrowserDialog class:

```
    Private Sub btnBrowse_Click(ByVal sender As System.Object, _
        ByVal e As System.EventArgs) Handles btnBrowse.Click

        'Declare a FolderBrowserDialog object
        Dim objFolderBrowserDialog As New FolderBrowserDialog
```

Next, you set the various properties of your objFolderBrowserDialog object to customize the Browse For Folder dialog box. Notice that you need to use the Personal constant to have the dialog start browsing at the My Documents root folder:

```
        'Set the FolderBrowserDialog control properties
        objFolderBrowserDialog.Description = "Select your favorite folder:"
        objFolderBrowserDialog.RootFolder = Environment.SpecialFolder.Personal
        objFolderBrowserDialog.ShowNewFolderButton = True
```

You then display the dialog box, and if the user selected the OK button in the dialog box, you display the folder chosen in the label control on your form:

```
                 'Show the Browse For Folder dialog
                 If objFolderBrowserDialog.ShowDialog = Windows.Forms.DialogResult.OK Then
                     'Display the selected folder
                     Label1.Text = objFolderBrowserDialog.SelectedPath
                 End If
```

You end this procedure by performing the necessary cleanup of your object:

```
                 'Clean up
                 objFolderBrowserDialog.Dispose()
                 objFolderBrowserDialog = Nothing
             End Sub
```

Chapter 8 Solution

This exercise asked you to complete your Menus application by adding a StatusStrip control and writing the necessary code to display a message when text was cut, copied, and pasted in your text boxes. If you followed the same basic procedures to add a StatusStrip control as you did in the Text Editor project in Chapter 6, you will have added the control and added one panel named sspStatus.

All that is required at this point is to add code to the procedures that actually perform the cut, copy, and paste operations. Starting with the cutToolStripMenuItem_Click procedure, you should have added a single line of code similar to the following:

```
             Private Sub cutToolStripMenuItem_Click(ByVal sender As Object, _
                 ByVal e As System.EventArgs) Handles cutToolStripMenuItem.Click

                 'Declare a TextBox object and set it to the ActiveControl
                 Dim objTextBox As TextBox = Me.ActiveControl
                 'Copy the text to the clipboard and clear the field
                 objTextBox.Cut()

                 'Display a message in the status bar
                 sspStatus.Text = "Text Cut"
             End Sub
```

And the code for the copyToolStripMenuItem_Click procedure should be similar to this:

```
             Private Sub copyToolStripMenuItem_Click(ByVal sender As Object, _
                 ByVal e As System.EventArgs) Handles copyToolStripMenuItem.Click

                 'Declare a TextBox object and set it to the ActiveControl
                 Dim objTextBox As TextBox = Me.ActiveControl
                 'Copy the text to the clipboard
                 objTextBox.Copy()

                 'Display a message in the status bar
                 sspStatus.Text = "Text Copied"
             End Sub
```

And finally, the code for the `pasteToolStripMenuItem_Click` procedure should be similar to this:

```
Private Sub pasteToolStripMenuItem_Click(ByVal sender As Object, _
    ByVal e As System.EventArgs) Handles pasteToolStripMenuItem.Click

    'Declare a TextBox object and set it to the ActiveControl
    Dim objTextBox As TextBox = Me.ActiveControl
    'Copy the data from the clipboard to the textbox
    objTextBox.Paste()

    'Display a message in the status bar
    sspStatus.Text = "Text Pasted"
End Sub
```

Chapter 9 Solutions

Exercise 1

The `Try...Catch` block that you add is very simple, as shown here:

```
Private Sub ListCustomer(ByVal customerToList As Customer)
    Try
        lstData.Items.Add(customerToList.CustomerID & _
            " - " & customerToList.CustomerName)
    Catch ExceptionErr As Exception
        MessageBox.Show(ExceptionErr.Message, "Debugging", _
            MessageBoxButtons.OK, MessageBoxIcon.Error)
    End Try
End Sub
```

Exercise 2

Your modified `Try` block should look similar to the following code. When you run your project and click the Start button, you should see a message box with the message that you added to your `Throw` statement.

```
Try
    Throw New Exception("Customer object not initialized.")
    lstData.Items.Add(customerToList.CustomerID & _
        " - " & customerToList.CustomerName)
Catch ExceptionErr As Exception
    MessageBox.Show(ExceptionErr.Message, "Debugging", _
        MessageBoxButtons.OK, MessageBoxIcon.Error)
End Try
```

Chapter 10 Solutions

Exercise 1

Once you add the Implements statement highlighted as follows and press Enter, the rest of the code shown below it is automatically inserted by Visual Studio 2005 to handle disposing of your class.

```
Namespace CarPerformance
    Public Class Car
        Implements IDisposable

        Private disposed As Boolean = False

        ' IDisposable
        Private Overloads Sub Dispose(ByVal disposing As Boolean)
            If Not Me.disposed Then
                If disposing Then
                    ' TODO: put code to dispose managed resources
                End If

                ' TODO: put code to free unmanaged resources here
            End If
            Me.disposed = True
        End Sub

#Region " IDisposable Support "
        ' This code added by Visual Basic to correctly implement the disposable
pattern.
        Public Overloads Sub Dispose() Implements IDisposable.Dispose
            ' Do not change this code.  Put cleanup code in Dispose(ByVal disposing
As Boolean) above.
            Dispose(True)
            GC.SuppressFinalize(Me)
        End Sub

        Protected Overrides Sub Finalize()
            ' Do not change this code.  Put cleanup code in Dispose(ByVal disposing
As Boolean) above.
            Dispose(False)
            MyBase.Finalize()
        End Sub
#End Region
```

The code modifications needed in the Main procedure in Module1 are shown in the highlighted section that follows. Even though you did not implement the IDisposable interface in the SportsCar class, it is available to this class through inheritance. Remember that the SportsCar class inherits from the Car class; thus, all of the methods available in the Car class are available to the SportsCar class.

```
'Display the details of the car
DisplayCarDetails(objCar)
DisplaySportsCarDetails(objCar)
```

```
        'Dispose of the object
        objCar.Dispose()
        objCar = Nothing

    'Wait for input from the user
    Console.ReadLine()
```

Exercise 2

This exercise required you to encapsulate the declaration and usage of the SportsCar class in a Using . . . End Using statement. Keeping in mind that the Using . . . End Using statement automatically handles disposal of objects that implement the IDisposable interface; the code can be implemented as highlighted here.

```
Sub Main()
    Using objCar As New SportsCar
        'Set the horsepower and weight(kg)
        objCar.HorsePower = 240
        objCar.Weight = 1085

        'Display the details of the car
        DisplayCarDetails(objCar)
        DisplaySportsCarDetails(objCar)
    End Using

    'Wait for input from the user
    Console.ReadLine()
End Sub
```

Chapter 11 Solution

You should have added code similar to this at the end of the Form1_Load event. First you use the Count property of the Items property to ensure that one or more items exist in the list view control before proceeding. Then you select the first item in the list view control by setting the Selected property to True for the first item in the Items collection. Finally, you call the Click event of the list view control, passing it a value of Nothing for the Object and System.EventArgs parameters.

```
        'If one or more items exist...
        If lstFavorites.Items.Count > 1 Then
            'Select the first item
            lstFavorites.Items(0).Selected = True
            lstFavorites_Click(Nothing, Nothing)
        End If
```

Chapter 12 Solution

Modifying the Favorites Viewer project requires two steps. First, you right-click the InternetFavorites project in the Solution Explorer and choose Remove from the context menu. Then you right-click the Favorites Viewer project in the Solution Explorer and choose Add Reference from the context menu. You scroll down the list of components in the .NET tab, select InternetFavorites, and then click OK. Then you run your project as normal with no code changes required.

Chapter 13 Solution

You start by adding a `Private Boolean` variable to hold the value that determines whether a message box is shown. Since this is a `Boolean` variable, you also provide a default value of `True` so that when the control is dragged onto a form, the `SuppressMsgBox` property will have a default value set.

```
Public Class MyNamespace
    'Private members
    Private strApplicationName As String = String.Empty
    Private blnSuppressMsgBox As Boolean = True
```

Next, you add a `Public` property to get and set the private variable `blnSuppressMsgBox`. This property will be exposed by the MyNamespace control in the Properties Window.

```
    Public Property SuppressMsgBox() As Boolean
        Get
            Return blnSuppressMsgBox
        End Get
        Set(ByVal value As Boolean)
            blnSuppressMsgBox = value
        End Set
    End Property
```

Now you add code to each of the button to show the message box if the property is not set to True.

```
    Private Sub btnApplicationCopyright_Click(ByVal sender As System.Object, _
        ByVal e As System.EventArgs) Handles btnApplicationCopyright.Click

        RaiseEvent ApplicationCopyrightChanged( _
            My.Application.Info.Copyright)

        If Not blnSuppressMsgBox Then
            MessageBox.Show(My.Application.Info.Copyright, _
                strApplicationName)
        End If
    End Sub

    Private Sub btnScreenBounds_Click(ByVal sender As Object, _
        ByVal e As System.EventArgs) Handles btnScreenBounds.Click

        RaiseEvent ScreenBoundsChanged(My.Computer.Screen.Bounds)

        If Not blnSuppressMsgBox Then
            MessageBox.Show(My.Computer.Screen.Bounds.ToString, _
                strApplicationName)
        End If
    End Sub

    Private Sub btnScreenWorkingArea_Click(ByVal sender As Object, _
```

```
        ByVal e As System.EventArgs) Handles btnScreenWorkingArea.Click

        RaiseEvent ScreenWorkingAreaChanged(My.Computer.Screen.WorkingArea)

        If Not blnSuppressMsgBox Then
            MessageBox.Show(My.Computer.Screen.WorkingArea.ToString, _
                strApplicationName)
        End If
    End Sub
```

Next, you need to rebuild the control so that it can pick up the code changes in order to display the `SuppressMsgBox` property in the Properties Window. After that, you switch to the Controls project and can select a `True/False` value for the `SuppressMsgBox` property in the Properties Window.

Chapter 15 Solutions

Exercise 1

The SQL statements for your EmployeeQuery should look like this:

```
SELECT Employees.FirstName, Employees.LastName, Employees.Title
FROM Employees
ORDER BY Employees.LastName;
```

You should have followed most of the steps in the "Binding Data to a DataGridView Control" Try It Out exercise and used the EmployeeQuery above in the Choose Your Database Objects screen of the Data Source Configuration Wizard. Your results should look similar to those shown in Figure D-1.

FirstName	LastName	Title
Steven	Buchanan	Sales Manager
Laura	Callahan	Inside Sales Coordinator
Nancy	Davolio	Sales Representative
Anne	Dodsworth	Sales Representative
Andrew	Fuller	Vice President, Sales
Robert	King	Sales Representative
Janet	Leverling	Sales Representative
Margaret	Peacock	Sales Representative
Michael	Suyama	Sales Representative

Figure D-1

Exercise 2

To create this application, you should have followed most of the steps in the "Binding Data to TextBox Controls" Try It Out exercise. Your completed form should look similar to the one shown in Figure D-2, and you should be able to navigate through the records in the database.

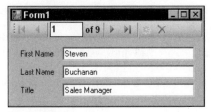

Figure D-2

Chapter 16 Solutions

Exercise 1

To complete this exercise, you were to use a DataGridView object to display the data from the pubs database. First, you should have created a Windows Application and added two references, one to the System.Data namespace and one to the System.XML namespace. Next, you needed to add a datagrid-view control to your form. That was all you needed to do before adding the code listed here.

```
Imports System.Data
Imports System.Data.SqlClient
Public Class Form1
    Dim strConnectionString As String = "server=bnewsome;" & _
        "database=pubs;uid=sa;pwd=!p@ssw0rd!"
    Dim cnnAuthors As New SqlConnection(strConnectionString)
    Dim daAuthors As New SqlDataAdapter
    Dim dsAuthors As New DataSet

    Private Sub Form1_Load(ByVal sender As Object, _
            ByVal e As System.EventArgs) Handles Me.Load
        daAuthors.SelectCommand = New SqlCommand
        daAuthors.SelectCommand.Connection = cnnAuthors
        daAuthors.SelectCommand.CommandText = "Select * From Authors"
        daAuthors.SelectCommand.CommandType = CommandType.Text

        cnnAuthors.Open()

        daAuthors.Fill(dsAuthors, "authors")

        cnnAuthors.Close()

        dgvAuthors.AutoGencrateColumns = True
        dgvAuthors.DataSource = dsAuthors
        dgvAuthors.DataMember = "authors"

        daAuthors = Nothing
        cnnAuthors = Nothing
    End Sub
End Class
```

Exercise 2

To complete this exercise, you were to use a DataGridView object to display the data from the pubs database. First, you should have created a Windows Application and added two references, one to the System.Data namespace and one to the System.XML namespace. Next, you needed to add a datagrid-view control to your form. That was all you needed to do before adding the code listed here. You will notice the difference from the first solution is just the SQL.

```
Imports System.Data
Imports System.Data.SqlClient
Public Class Form1
    Dim strConnectionString As String = "server=bnewsome;" & _
        "database=pubs;uid=sa;pwd=!p@ssw0rd!"
    Dim cnnAuthors As New SqlConnection(strConnectionString)
    Dim daAuthors As New SqlDataAdapter
    Dim dsAuthors As New DataSet

    Private Sub Form1_Load(ByVal sender As Object, _
            ByVal e As System.EventArgs) Handles Me.Load
        Dim strSQL As String
        strSQL = "Select au_id as ID, au_lname as [Last Name], " & _
            "au_fname as [First Name], Phone, Address, City, State, " & _
            "Zip, Contract From Authors"
        daAuthors.SelectCommand = New SqlCommand
        daAuthors.SelectCommand.Connection = cnnAuthors
        daAuthors.SelectCommand.CommandText = strSQL
        daAuthors.SelectCommand.CommandType = CommandType.Text

        cnnAuthors.Open()

        daAuthors.Fill(dsAuthors, "authors")

        cnnAuthors.Close()

        dgvAuthors.AutoGenerateColumns = True
        dgvAuthors.DataSource = dsAuthors
        dgvAuthors.DataMember = "authors"

        daAuthors = Nothing
        cnnAuthors = Nothing
    End Sub
End Class
```

Chapter 17 Solution

The entire code listings follow the answer.

You should have made the following additions.

❑   To web.config:

```
<configuration>
   <appSettings>
      <add key="ConnectionString" value="Server=bnewsome; User ID=sa;
         Password=!p@ssw0rd!; Database=pubs;" />
   </appSettings>
</configuration>
```

❑ To `Default.aspx`, add script for the `<Head>` element:

```
<script runat="server" language=vbscript>
   Sub sdsAuthors_Init(ByVal sender As Object, ByVal e As System.EventArgs)
      sdsAuthors.ConnectionString = _
      ConfigurationManager.AppSettings("ConnectionString")
   End Sub
</script>
```

You should have made the following changes to Default.aspx.

❑ Removed the attribute `ConnectionString` from `sdsAuthors` on `Default.aspx`

The complete code starting with the `<HTML>` element for `Default.aspx` should look like this.

```
<html xmlns="http://www.w3.org/1999/xhtml" >
<head id="Head1" runat="server">
   <title>Grid View</title>
   <script runat="server" language=vbscript>
      Sub sdsAuthors_Init(ByVal sender As Object, ByVal e As System.EventArgs)
         sdsAuthors.ConnectionString = _
         ConfigurationManager.AppSettings("ConnectionString")
      End Sub
   </script>
</head>
<body>
<form id="form1" runat="server">
<div>
   <asp:SqlDataSource ID="sdsAuthors" Runat="server"
                      ProviderName = "System.Data.SqlClient"
                      SelectCommand = "SELECT au_id, au_lname, au_fname, phone,
                      address, city, state, zip FROM authors"
                      UpdateCommand = "UPDATE authors SET au_lname = @au_lname,
                      au_fname = @au_fname, phone = @phone, address = @address,
                      city = @city, state = @state, zip = @zip
                      WHERE au_id = @original_au_id" OnInit="sdsAuthors_Init">
      <UpdateParameters>
         <asp:Parameter Type="String" Name="au_lname"></asp:Parameter>
         <asp:Parameter Type="String" Name="au_fname"></asp:Parameter>
         <asp:Parameter Type="String" Name="phone"></asp:Parameter>
         <asp:Parameter Type="String" Name="address"></asp:Parameter>
         <asp:Parameter Type="String" Name="city"></asp:Parameter>
         <asp:Parameter Type="String" Name="state"></asp:Parameter>
         <asp:Parameter Type="String" Name="zip"></asp:Parameter>
         <asp:Parameter Type="String" Name="au_id"></asp:Parameter>
      </UpdateParameters>
```

```
            </asp:SqlDataSource>

            <asp:GridView ID="gdvAuthors" Runat="server" DataSourceID="sdsAuthors"
                       AllowPaging="True" AllowSorting="True" AutoGenerateColumns=False
                       DataKeyNames="au_id" >
            <PagerStyle BackColor="Gray" ForeColor="White" HorizontalAlign="Center" />
            <HeaderStyle BackColor="Black" ForeColor="White" />
            <AlternatingRowStyle BackColor="LightGray" />
            <Columns>
                <asp:CommandField ButtonType="Button" ShowEditButton="true" />
                <asp:BoundField Visible="false" HeaderText="au_id" DataField="au_id"
                            SortExpression="au_id"></asp:BoundField>
                <asp:BoundField HeaderText="Last Name" DataField="au_lname"
                            SortExpression="au_lname"></asp:BoundField>
                <asp:BoundField HeaderText="First Name" DataField="au_fname"
                            SortExpression="au_fname"></asp:BoundField>
                <asp:BoundField HeaderText="Phone" DataField="phone"
                            SortExpression="phone"></asp:BoundField>
                <asp:BoundField HeaderText="Address" DataField="address"
                            SortExpression="address"></asp:BoundField>
                <asp:BoundField HeaderText="City" DataField="city"
                            SortExpression="city"></asp:BoundField>
                <asp:BoundField HeaderText="State" DataField="state"
                            SortExpression="state"></asp:BoundField>
                <asp:BoundField HeaderText="Zip Code" DataField="zip"
                            SortExpression="zip"></asp:BoundField>
            </Columns>
        </asp:GridView>
    </div>
    </form>
    </body>
    </html>
```

The complete code for web.config should look like this.

```
<?xml version="1.0" ?>

<!-- Note: As an alternative to hand editing this file you can use the web admin
tool to configure settings for your application. Use the Website->Asp.Net
Configuration option in Visual Studio.  A full list of settings and comments can be
found in machine.config.comments usually located in
\Windows\Microsft.Net\Frameworks\v2.x\Config -->

<configuration xmlns="http://schemas.microsoft.com/.NetConfiguration/v2.0">
    <appSettings>
        <add key="ConnectionString" value="Server=bnewsome; User ID=sa;
Password=!p@ssw0rd!;Database=pubs;" />
    </appSettings>


    <connectionStrings />

    <system.web>
```

```
<!-- Set compilation debug="true" to insert debugging symbols into the compiled
page.  Because this affects performance, set this value to true only during
development.  -->
        <compilation debug="false" />

<!-- The <authentication> section enables configuration of the security
authentication mode used by ASP.NET to identify an incoming user.  -->
        <authentication mode="Windows" />


<!-- The <customErrors> section enables configuration of what to do if/when an
unhandled error occurs during the execution of a request.  Specifically, it enables
developers to configure html error pages to be displayed in place of a error stack
trace.
        <customErrors mode="RemoteOnly" defaultRedirect="GenericErrorPage.htm">
            <error statusCode="403" redirect="NoAccess.htm"/>
            <error statusCode="404" redirect="FileNotFound.htm"/>
        </customErrors>
        -->

    </system.web>
</configuration>
```

Chapter 18 Solutions

Exercise 1

Your web.config file in the Members folder should look like this:

```
<?xml version="1.0" encoding="utf-8"?>
<configuration>
    <system.web>
        <pages theme="MainTheme" />
        <authorization>
            <deny users="?" />
        </authorization>
    </system.web>
</configuration>
```

The Main.skin file should look like this (only one line of code in file):

```
<asp:Label runat="server" ForeColor="Red" />
```

Exercise 2

Your web.config file in the Root folder should look like this (although you will find some additional items and comments):

```
<?xml version="1.0" encoding="utf-8"?>
<configuration>
    <system.web>
        <pages theme="MainTheme" />
        <roleManager enabled="true" />
        <authentication mode="Forms" />
    </system.web>
</configuration>
```

The `Main.skin` file should look like this:

```
<asp:Label runat="server" ForeColor="Red" />
<asp:Login runat="server" ForeColor="Red" />
```

Chapter 19 Solutions

Exercise 1

For this exercise, you were required you to create an XML document that described a table lamp. There are a number of ways to correctly describe a lamp. You could have used child elements and no attributes. Also, you could have used different language to describe a lamp. Either way, you should have used the same case and closed your elements.

You can validate your XML at a site like www.w3schools.com/dom/dom_validate.asp that offers a free validator. The code for the document should look similar to this:

```
<?xml version="1.0" encoding="utf-8"?>
<lamps xmlns:xsi="http://www.w3.org/2001/XMLSchema-instance"
xmlns:xsd="http://www.w3.org/2001/XMLSchema">
 <lamp type="table" desing="modern" price="269">
        <base shape="square" color="black" height_inches="24"></base>
        <bulbs max_watts="60" number_of_bulbs="3" type="soft white"></bulbs>
        <shade color="white" shape="oval" size_inches="18 X 8"></shade>
 </lamp>
</lamps>
```

Exercise 2

For this exercise, you were to find the syntax for a valid XML comment. The comment is like a HTML comment and starts with <!-- and ends with -->. Your comment should look similar to this:

```
<!-- This is a valid XML comment -->
```

Chapter 20 Solutions

Exercise 1

For this exercise, you were required to create a Web Service with three methods. The three methods should have individually returned the server date, time, and name. First, you had to create a new Web site project and then add the Web Service methods. The code for the methods should look similar to these:

```
Imports System.Web
Imports System.Web.Services
Imports System.Web.Services.Protocols

<WebService(Namespace := "http://tempuri.org/")> _
<WebServiceBinding(ConformsTo:=WsiProfiles.BasicProfile1_1)> _
Public Class WebService
    Inherits System.Web.Services.WebService

    Public Sub WebService

    End Sub

    <WebMethod()> _
    Public Function ServerName() As String
        Return My.Computer.Name
    End Function

    <WebMethod()> _
    Public Function ServerDate() As Date
        Return Now().Date
    End Function

    <WebMethod()> _
    Public Function ServerTime() As String
        Return Now().ToShortTimeString
    End Function

End Class
```

When you ran the Web Service, you may have been asked to add a `web.config` file for debugging. You could have chosen either to add the file or to continue without debugging. When you tested each method, you should have seen the date, time, and name of your server.

Exercise 2

In Exercise 2, you needed to create a Remoting server that would return the date and time on the server. You had to create a class that inherits from `MarshalByRefObject`. Next, you needed to create an application (we used a console application) that registered the object on a known channel and port. Finally, you were to create a client that could consume the object and test the methods that returned the date and time. Here is an example of the Remoting server code:

```
Public Class Server
    Inherits MarshalByRefObject

    Public ReadOnly Property ServerTime() As String
        Get
            Return Now().ToShortTimeString
        End Get
    End Property

    Public ReadOnly Property ServerDate() As Date
        Get
            Return Now().Date
        End Get
    End Property

End Class
```

Here is an example of the server code used to register the channel and port for the Remoting engine:

```
Imports System.Runtime.Remoting
Imports System.Runtime.Remoting.Channels
Imports System.Runtime.Remoting.Channels.Tcp
Module Module1

    Sub Main()
        Dim channel As TcpChannel = New TcpChannel(8500)
        ChannelServices.RegisterChannel(channel)

        RemotingConfiguration.RegisterWellKnownServiceType( _
            GetType(Chapter20Exercise2.Server), "Engine", _
            WellKnownObjectMode.SingleCall)
        Console.Write("Engine Registered." + Environment.NewLine)
        Console.Write("Server Active . . .")
        Console.Read()

    End Sub
End Module
```

Remember that for the server and client you also have to add a reference to `System.Runtime.Remoting` and to the server class you created. The final part of the exercise was to create the client. Your code will look similar to this:

```
Sub Main()
    Dim client As Chapter20Exercise2.Server

    Console.Write("Trying to obtain Type from Server . . ." + Environment.NewLine)
    client = CType(Activator.GetObject(GetType(Chapter20Exercise2.Server), _
        "tcp://Maincpu:8500/Engine"), Chapter20Exercise2.Server)
    Console.Write("Type Created and returned" + Environment.NewLine)
    Console.Write("Server date: " + client.ServerDate + Environment.NewLine)
    Console.Write("Server time: " + client.ServerTime + Environment.NewLine)
    Console.Read()
End Sub
```

After creating the client, make sure that you start the project that registers and starts the server. If you used a console application to test your server, you saw a command window with the return values from the remoting object. Congratulations, you have just created a Remoting system.

Chapter 21 Exercise Solutions

Exercise 1

For this example, you created a setup project for Notepad. We created a new setup project named `Chapter21Exercise1`. Under the Application folder, we browsed for and added the `notepad.exe` file. After adding the file, we created a shortcut to the executable and moved the shortcut to User's Program. Menu. Next, we selected the project in Solution Explorer and then found and changed the author and manufacturer properties in the Properties window. Finally, we built and then ran the `setup.exe` file.

You may be asking why we changed the author and manufacturer properties. The manufacturer is used to determine the default location for the installed application. When we installed the application, `C:\Program Files\Wrox\Chapter21Exercise1\` was the default installation directory. Without updating the manufacturer, the default directory would have been `C:\Program Files\Default Company Name\Chapter21Exercise1\`. The second reason to change the manufacturer was the support info screen under Add/Remove Programs. When you look at your application's support info screen, you'll see that the publisher is Wrox.

Exercise 2

In the completed exercise, you would have added a bitmap image to the application. You should have added the image to the application folder or a subfolder of the application folder. Next, you would have added a splash screen via the user interface editor. The `SplashBitmap` property of the Splash dialog box was changed to the bitmap you added, and the dialog box was moved up to the first screen shown. When you ran the installation, you saw the splash screen as the first dialog box.

Chapter 22 Solution

This exercise has numerous correct answers. If you ask 10 programmers to complete it, you will get 10 different answers. So, if your changes work, you have a valid answer. The following is what we came up with to solve the problem.

You need to add a call to the new function, `ComputerPlayToWin`, from `ComputerPlay`. It should be the first call in the procedure. If you find a win here and make a move, you can exit the subroutine without allocating any of the local variables in `ComputerPlay`.

```
Sub ComputerPlay()
    If ComputerPlayToWin() Then Exit Sub
```

Your solution will look different from ours. Compare your solution to ours and see which you think is better. The first function, `CheckForWin`, allows you to check an entire row or column of buttons for a chance to win. If two squares are marked and the third is empty, the computer will make this move by changing the text for all buttons. This is done by passing the buttons `ByRef` to the function. `ComputerPlayToWin` calls this function for every row, column, or diagonal win possibility on the board.

```
Private Function CheckForWin(ByRef btnFirst As Windows.Forms.Button, _
ByRef btnSecond As Windows.Forms.Button, ByRef btnThird As _
Windows.Forms.Button, ByVal stringToFind As String, _
ByVal strOpponentsMark As String) As Boolean
    Dim intSum As Int16 = 0S

    'Check to see if we can win on this row
    'We can we if we have two marks and no opponent marks on the row
    'If there is an opponents mark we are blocked so return false

    If btnFirst.Text = stringToFind Then
        intSum += 1S
    ElseIf btnFirst.Text = strOpponentsMark Then
        Return False
    End If

    If btnSecond.Text = stringToFind Then
        intSum += 1S
    ElseIf btnSecond.Text = strOpponentsMark Then
        Return False
    End If

    If btnThird.Text = stringToFind Then
        intSum += 1S
    ElseIf btnThird.Text = strOpponentsMark Then
        Return False
    End If

    'We will win on this turn
    'so just mark the entire row to save some resources

    If intSum = 2 Then
        btnFirst.Text = stringToFind
        btnSecond.Text = stringToFind
        btnThird.Text = stringToFind
        Return True
    Else
        Return False
    End If
End Function
```

All that the `ComputerPlayToWin` function does is pass the buttons and strings to check `CheckForWin` for each possible win. If a win is found, the game is over. The computer will not make a random play if it can win.

```
Private Function ComputerPlayToWin() As Boolean
    If CheckForWin(btn00, btn01, btn02, "O", "X") Then
        'Winner on top Row
        Call Winner("0")
```

```
            Return True
        End If
        If CheckForWin(btn10, btn11, btn12, "O", "X") Then
            'Winner on middle Row
            Call Winner("O")
            Return True
        End If
        If CheckForWin(btn20, btn21, btn22, "O", "X") Then
            'Winner on third Row
            Call Winner("O")
            Return True
        End If
        If CheckForWin(btn00, btn10, btn20, "O", "X") Then
            'Winner on first column
            Call Winner("O")
            Return True
        End If
        If CheckForWin(btn01, btn11, btn21, "O", "X") Then
            'Winner on second column
            Call Winner("O")
            Return True
        End If
        If CheckForWin(btn02, btn12, btn22, "O", "X") Then
            'Winner on third column
            Call Winner("O")
            Return True
        End If

        If CheckForWin(btn00, btn11, btn22, "O", "X") Then
            'Winner on diagonal top left to bottom right
            Call Winner("O")
            Return True
        End If
        If CheckForWin(btn20, btn11, btn02, "O", "X") Then
            'Winner on diagonal bottom left to top right
            Call Winner("O")
            Return True
        End If
    End Function
```

Index

Index